SAYING NO TO POWER

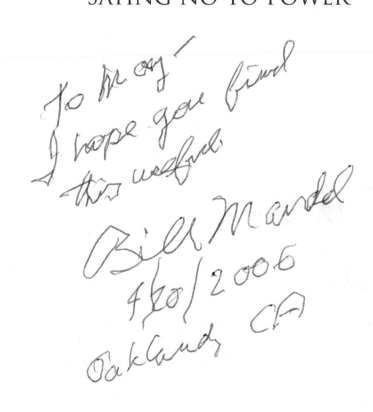

To Mary —
I hope you find
this useful.

Bill Mandel
4/20/2006
Oakland, CA

SAYING NO TO POWER

AUTOBIOGRAPHY OF A 20TH CENTURY
ACTIVIST AND THINKER

WILLIAM MANDEL

CREATIVE ARTS BOOK COMPANY
BERKELEY · CALIFORNIA · 1999

Saying No to Power is published by Donald S. Ellis and distributed by Creative Arts Book Company

For Information contact:
Creative Arts Book Company
833 Bancroft Way
Berkeley, California 94710

For ordering information call:
1-800-848-7789
Fax: 1-510-848-4844

Cover Design by David Bullen
Graphics and Book Design by Pope Graphic Arts Center

ISBN 0-88739-286-5
Library of Congress Catalog Number 99-63842

Printed in the United States of America

To Tanya, for 63 years
companion, comrade, collaborator, critic

Acknowledgments

The first to suggest that I write an autobiography were my colleagues of the late 1960s on the editorial board of *The Movement*, organ of the Student Nonviolent Coordinating Committee (SNCC), who were struck by my activities in the South before the civil rights movement. In 1969 the same suggestion was made by pioneering second-wave feminist Laura X, because of what she had learned of my life as I provided her with information about female activists of the Great Depression and World War II years. The idea also arose out of listening to my radio broadcasts, from which she found out about the existence of International Women's Day, then unknown to her generation. In 1970 my late friend Stephen P. Dunn, who acquired a Ph.D. and professional respect as a scholar despite severe motor and speech difficulties due to cerebral palsy, elicited an oral history from me with an eye to doing a piece for the *New Yorker*. They weren't interested, but his 70-page single-spaced transcript provided the skeleton for my writing about the first two-thirds of my life. In the 1990s he did a careful critique of several chapters of the present manuscript.

I am grateful to Erik Bauersfeld, long-term Drama and Literature Director of KPFA (Pacifica) Radio in Berkeley, for having provided me a full year of half-hour slots in 1984-5 on which I broadcast an early version of what became this book.

For reading and critique of the entire manuscript in one draft or another, my deepest thanks to playwright Jeff Goldsmith and Kris Cardall who did so as a team, to film director-writer Steph Lady, to sound designer John Whiting, to workingman activist George Winter, and individually to each of my children Phyllis, Bob, and David, whose other identities emerge in the book.

For reading and critique of a synopsis equivalent in length to a small book, my appreciation to literary magazine editor Linda Ferguson and distinguished book editor Luther Nichols. Chapters were read and suggestions offered by journalist George Kauffman and Prof. Harry Shaffer, economist.

I circulated a draft of a preface in which I let my hair way down to a list of people deliberately chosen for their diversity in many respects and the fact that they would have one thing in common—that I could expect absolutely candid replies. I got them. For which I wish to acknowledge Allan Affeldt, Zaphrirah Bauman, Lincoln Bergman, William Blum, Bob Cirese, the late George David, Clara Felix, Esther Franklin, Ray

Gatchalian, Barbara Hazard, Fred Hirsch, Liza Hirsch, Leon Lefson, Tom Luddy, Malcolm Margolin, Rosemary Matson, Prof. Tom Mayer, Adam David Miller, Henry Noyes, Norman Roth, Dr. Shura Saul, Pete Seeger, Veronica Selver, and Peter White.

The Mahler Foundation of the Gray Panthers gave me a grant specifically for this book. A Hammett-Hellman grant from Human Rights Watch in recognition of the difficulties caused me as a writer by McCarthyism was made with the knowledge that I would use it for doing this autobiography. A grant from the Rabinowitz Foundation helped with travel contributing to the accumulation of knowledge of the Soviet Union that has been a large part of my life.

The support of Ethel Dunn and Alice Hamburg is deeply appreciated.

My most profound thanks are to my wife, Tanya, who knows me better than anyone else, who has shared most of the experiences that comprise my story, has argued out with me the various intellectual conclusions that readers will encounter—whether she ultimately agreed or not, and who did some research for and edited at least three complete drafts of this manuscript, as she has all my previous books.

Finally, I wish to express my appreciation to my editor, Sienna Craig, for her fine sense of what does not belong and what does, where it belongs, and, highly important, for bringing to bear the point of view of a person of my grandchildren's generation.

Table of Contents

Introduction

by Howard Zinn

There are countless autobiographies and biographies of powerful and "important" personages, whose stories are designed to encourage young people to become powerful and influential in just the same way—that is, in a way that will perpetuate the existing hierarchies of society. But we are in serious need of the stories of those who challenged authority, those dissenters whose words and actions kept alive the hopes and dreams that we might build a just society, a peaceful world. Bill Mandel's autobiography arrives to help us fulfill that need.

His extraordinary life virtually spans the century. He missed its first seventeen years, else he would have been on the platform when Big Bill Haywood pounded the table to open the founding convention of the Industrial Workers of the World. He might well have marched with Mother Jones when she led a children's march to Washington to confront President Theodore Roosevelt with the demand to end the brutality of child labor. And he almost certainly would have joined those socialists and anarchists who opposed our entrance into the first World War in 1917. That was the year he was born and it is possible, knowing his lifelong refusal to keep still in the face of horrors, that his infant cries were protests against the war.

But it did not take long for him to catch up. While the Twenties were, and still are, portrayed as "The Jazz Age," a time of prosperity for all, ten-year old Bill Mandel knew different, and collected money in the New York subway for the starving children of miners on strike. Part of his youth was spent in the Soviet Union where his father had taken a job as an engineer, and his knowledge of Russia and the Russian language enabled him later to become an expert on Russia and its history.

The traditional accounts of the Thirties are dominated by the Depression and the efforts of Roosevelt's New Deal to stabilize the nation. What is neglected is the drama of labor unrest and radical agitation during that period.

There was the battle of Communists and other Americans to save the lives of "the Scottsboro Boys," young black men falsely accused of rape in the lynch-atmosphere of rural Alabama. There were the momentous labor struggles of that era: the general strikes in San Francisco and Minneapolis, the great textile strikes in the South, the newly-formed

CIO's organization of workers in the mass industries of auto, steel, rubber. There were the creation of unemployed councils and tenants' organizations all over the country. A general atmosphere of rebellion and turmoil persuaded the national government that it had better enact reforms that would stabilize the capitalist system, and head off a possible revolution.

The second World War halted both the depression and the domestic turmoil, but when it ended, and the cold war with the Soviet Union began, the campaign against domestic radicals became intense. The FBI and the House Committee on Un-American Activities, with the collaboration of the Truman Administration, and the sensational accusations of Senator Joseph McCarthy, created an atmosphere of fear. Communists were put on trial, millions of Americans were entered into F.B.I. files, blacklists were created, men and women went to prison for refusing to testify about their political beliefs.

Julius and Ethel Rosenberg were convicted of giving atomic secrets to the Soviet Union, in a trial permeated with hysteria, and were executed in an anti-radical atmosphere heated up by the victory of Communists in China, the Korean War, and the first explosion of nuclear weapons by the Soviet Union. In that atmosphere the U.S. government expanded its power across the globe, with thousands of military bases around the world, with U.S. corporations spreading their influence on all continents. More and more of the national resources were now devoted to the military, and government contracts brought great wealth to a handful of corporations.

The first breakthrough from the closed society, the first demands for change, came in the sudden and dramatic rise of black people in the South, determined to bring to a close the century of racial segregation and racial violence that followed soon after the end of the Civil War. The Montgomery Bus Boycott of 1955, the sit-ins at lunch counters in 1960, the Freedom Rides of 1961, the mass demonstrations in Birmingham, Alabama, and all over the south, the organization of black people in Mississippi, galvanized the nation and finally brought about the end of legal segregation, and the enforcement of voting rights for blacks.

The resentment against the Establishment—not just in the South but the national Government—for maintaining racism, helped fuel the suspicion, as the United States invaded Vietnam, that the government was not to be trusted in its pretensions to stand for liberty and democracy. The movement against the war in Vietnam, in a few years, became a national phenomenon, causing the government to draw back from further escalation of the war.

Perhaps more important, the civil rights and anti-war movements, and revelations about the FBI and the CIA—that is, about crimes committed by the U.S. against its own citizens and against people abroad—created a general distrust of the Establishment. Women began to organize and a new feminist movement began to change the national consciousness about sexual equality.

The decades that followed—the late Seventies, the Eighties, the Nineties—found the United States trying to re-establish its hold on the American people, and regain influence in other parts of the world. Brief military forays under the Reagan and Bush administrations—in Grenada, Panama, Iraq—were intended to put aside "the Vietnam syndrome," that is, the reluctance of the American people to support the American military machine as it waged war abroad.

Through all of this, with racism, anti-immigration laws, and a deepening gap between rich and poor, there was resistance throughout the country. Local groups everywhere in the nation struggled against militarism, the power of corporations, the discrimination against blacks, women, Latinos, immigrants. Against the overwhelming power of media giants, community newspapers and radio stations, a persistent radical press, struggled to get information to the public.

As always in the history of the United States, its greatness rested not in its wealth or power, but in the courage of those people who continued to insist that the principles of the Declaration of Independence be fulfilled—the equal right of all people to life, liberty, and the pursuit of happiness.

In that long struggle, the ideas and actions of people like Bill Mandel have played an important part. His life story is not only dramatic, but instructive and inspiring.

SAYING NO TO POWER

CHAPTER 1

Stickball and Belly-Whopping

My paternal grandfather, Abraham Mandelman, was a tailor in that portion of Poland which was part of the Russian Empire. His was the smallest of private enterprises. Essentially he was a self-employed craftsman. I assume he set his own prices, because I never heard talk of a guild or any other association.

Particularly in such tiny businesses, employees, if any, were of the same ethnic origin. The language spoken was Yiddish, which is rooted in 10th century German, and therefore very different from Hebrew, the language of Israel. My grandfather once did employ a worker, in the small city, Radom, where my father was born. This apprentice tailor walked the many miles from his home village, slept in the tailor shop, and went home occasionally. He ate with the family, which, with many children, lived in the room or— when they were more prosperous— rooms behind the store. In early childhood I experienced that myself in New York whenever my father, a young engineer finding his feet in his profession, was unemployed. We moved into the room behind those converted from the "front room" and dining room of a once-elegant apartment, in which my maternal grandmother had the eight-table restaurant which supported all of us.

Usually my grandfather's only helpers were his sons, of whom the eldest was killed as a drafted soldier in the Russo-Japanese War of 1904. That war was the major reason for the family's emigration to the United States before World War I, as avoidance of military service was for a great many emigrants of diverse backgrounds throughout this country's history, starting with the English Quakers and the French Huguenots. In our case, my grandparents reasoned: Why should we die for a country that would not let us, Jews, live east of a fixed geographic line, and imposed about a hundred other laws specifically directed against us? First a military-age older brother of my father was smuggled out, and then the family followed.

It was that Russo-Japanese War of 1904 which set the flames of revolution ablaze in the Russian Empire. 1905 witnessed a genuine mass revolution that failed, partly because of concessions by the tsar. These events, starting with the purposeless death of his eldest brother, turned my father toward socialism. He was never satisfied, neither there nor here, with a system that could not overcome war, the chasm between rich and poor, and ethnic hostility. At eleven, he linked arms with older students and still older workingmen to stop a charge by mounted Cossacks against a large demonstration during that revolution. He distributed and sold socialist publications in Yiddish and explained points of principle to workers on street corners. He also became an atheist at age ten.

My father's mother was a traditional housewife, with many children. She was devoutly religious and could read Hebrew when few women in that patriarchal culture could. She was also literate in Polish. When my father was more than a hundred, he said he was sorry he had become an atheist because it hurt his mother so deeply—but that did not change his convictions. I knew her only as the kindly grandmother at whose home we would occasionally have dinner. I was never close with that side of the family, except for one quite beautiful and vivacious aunt and her daughter. Relationships in Jewish families and, in my experience, within the unpropertied classes of all origins, are usually closer with one's mother's relatives, and we were no exception.

Grandfather Mandel's life consisted of his work, the strong cigars he enjoyed, and the nip of *slivovitz*—plum brandy—that was kept in a huge demijohn behind the door, in the Prohibition years as otherwise. He never discussed politics or even whether life was better here than in Europe. The latter was probably taken for granted. He and his wife now had an apartment for themselves alone, and so did each of the many sons and daughters when they married.

I keep on my study wall a foot-high blow-up of a photograph of a three-inch woodcarving by an artist I knew, of a tailor bringing all his weight to bear on the massive steam-iron used in the old days. That is my chief memory of grandfather Mandel, a very short but sturdy man, sweating away endless hours, the merciless midsummer sun of New York baking through the glass storefront of his shop and up from the concrete sidewalks of the Bronx. He lived to an advanced age, as did nearly everyone on that side of the family.

Grandfather Schachter, my mother's father, though also a small businessman, was a very different person from grandfather Mandel. He was what was known as a *Dyech-yoodeh*. This word, literally meaning "German Jew", was applied to those who affected Western dress, rather than the then traditional appearance of the Jewish male: full beard, long black gown fitted at the waist, and distinctive skull-fitting hat with broad fur-trimmed brim. My maternal grandfather's departure from tradition was not surprising, because the Schachters lived in an area where the official language was German. This region, known to Jews as Galicia, is a traditional province of the western portion of the Ukraine. The peasants speak Ukrainian, a language closely related to Russian, and call the territory Halych. The landowners spoke Polish, because Poland had conquered the region many centuries earlier. Their princely prerogatives remained. But when Poland itself was conquered and divided up at about the same time as the American Revolution, this province came under the rule of the Austro-Hungarian Empire. It was ruled by the German Habsburg family. So Mother grew up knowing Polish, German, Ukrainian, and Yiddish.

Grandfather Schachter ran two businesses. He was a master builder of the old-fashioned European type. He also ran a tavern. Mother saw him cheat the illiterate Ukrainian peasants who patronized it. Because she witnessed such behavior by neighboring Jewish businessmen as well, and didn't hesitate to express her distaste for it, some thought of her as anti-Semitic. I remember mother, a perfect lady, responding in the sharpest terms when she heard total strangers speaking to each other and using anti-Semitic language.

I never knew grandfather Schachter. The family maintained absolute unanimity until I was past fifty—decades after his death, my maternal grandmother's death, my mother's death, and the passing of two of her three brothers and sisters—in pretending to my brother, me, and everyone outside the family that he had separated from grandma Schachter in New York, gone back to Europe, and died there.

The truth, as my father told me when he was already an old man, was that when still in Europe, when my mother was twelve, her father tried to rape her. My grandmother stayed with him until they could come to this country—there were four children to feed—and she could begin to operate the minuscule restaurants that would enable her to care for them independently. Then she ordered him out. He lived out his life in that same neighborhood, but if we ever passed him on the street, no one pointed him out.

My parents met through my mother's older brother, Simon. By coincidence he was born on the same day of the same year as my father, although in a different country. These immigrant boys all worked while they pursued their educations, but unlike his brothers my father did not work in his father's tailor shop. Instead, at age fifteen he had insisted that he would go to America only if he could pursue his education, and not become a tailor.

Dad worked whatever kind of sweatshop job was available and studied civil engineering at night at Cooper Union, the free private college just a block from grandma's. At college he was active in the Intercollegiate Socialist Society. Those were the years when Eugene

Victor Debs ran repeatedly for president, and the socialist vote was, both in numbers and in proportion of the electorate, incomparably higher than any socialist or communist vote in any later period. In those years immediately before American entry into World War I there was a bloc of five Socialist Party members in the New York State Assembly,and one congressman. The word "congress*man*" is totally in place for that period. Women could vote in only a handful of states. New York was not one of them.

At that time, my parents-to-be, my uncle-to-be, two then teenage women who were to be mother's lifelong friends, and some others, had a discussion club. At Dad's proposal, they named it for Henrik Ibsen, the Norwegian dramatist. It is interesting that the name was not that of a socialist, but of one who most masterfully exposed the evils of existing society, particularly the oppression of women, in "*A Doll's House.*"

When it came to naming children, Dad was most partisan, and Mother had no objection. I am deeply indebted to an uncle of mine who died just before my birth, for whom I was given the name William. The tittering was bad enough when in the 1950s, during his bookburning hearings, Senator Joe McCarthy's nasty little counsel, Roy Cohn, asked me to state my full name, and I responded: "William Marx Mandel." The giggles stopped in shock when I added in the next phrase, "and I *am* a Jew." A later chapter explains the reasons for that. Imagine what the reaction would have been had I had to respond: "Karl Marx Mandel". That's what it was supposed to be, since my parents were both atheists. Normally, they would have rejected on principle the Jewish religious rule of naming a boy after the most recently deceased close male relative; but this particular brother of my father, who had suffered a crippling intestinal problem of some sort, made the desperate choice of having an operation that, with the level of medicine of that day, would cure him or kill him. Shortly before I was scheduled to come into this world it killed him. Dad loved that brother of his deeply, and admired him for the courage of choosing to be operated upon rather than live disabled. His name had been Velvil, which is rendered in English as William, and that is what I became.

I was born on June 4th, 1917. June 5th was Registration Day for the draft of World War I. President Wilson had taken the country into it just a couple of months earlier. (This was after he had been re-elected on the slogan, "he kept us out of war.") Dad opposed the war as imperialist, which was the position of the Socialist Party of the United States. It regarded the countries on both sides as equally guilty of wanting control over the rest of the world. The difference was that one group, consisting chiefly of the British and French empires, with which the U.S. allied itself, already had it. The other, primarily Germany and the Austro-

Hungarian Empire, wanted to replace them. All other Socialist parties, except those of Russia and Bulgaria, found justification for being on whatever side the government of their particular country was allied with.

When the draft registrar came to the door—that's how it was done then—and asked Dad if he had any children, my one day of existence enabled him to answer yes. That exempted him from the draft.

I was born in a hospital in Brooklyn. I'm told that my parents moved from the apartment they then had because the landlord was so stingy with steam heat that my diapers froze. Dad had threatened to kill him if I fell victim to the deadly flu epidemic then raging, and died. My brother, three years younger than I—my only sibling—had worse luck when it came to being named. In the first place, he was supposed to have been a she. My parents didn't particularly care about the gender of their first-born, but they did want one of each. They had even chosen a name. It's interesting that, in the case of a girl, the one they chose was not that of a revolutionary, but simply a pretty name out of literature: Leonore. But, finding themselves with another boy, he became Eugene Victor Mandel. Eugene Victor were the given names of the American Socialist Party leader, Debs. Fortunately for my brother's comfort in public situations, although unfortunately from the standpoint of American political awareness, Debs, and particularly his given names, quickly faded from public consciousness. Karl Marx' did not.

My earliest memory is from before my brother's birth. I must have been two. It was of a large model airplane—the work of my uncle Dave, who was about eight years older than I. It stood on his dresser in his dingy little room in Grandma's slum apartment near Grand Street in New York's Lower East Side. This was the first of several times that my parents moved us in with her when Dad was out of work.

I don't remember Grandma's first restaurant. Dad tells me it was in a room behind a saloon in the heart of the Lower East Side, on or near Hester Street in what was the pushcart district. The old elevated trains of the subway system, the EL, ran within four or five feet of tenement windows one story up, and noise and darkness were incessant.

During World War I, my father had been among the first Jewish engineers and other technical personnel to be hired by private industry. It was a result of labor shortage, just as the labor shortage in World War II gave African-Americans their first chance at jobs from which they had previously been barred. In 1920, after the war, when I was three, he took a job with Bethlehem Steel in Bethlehem, Pennsylvania—Pennsylvania Dutch country, where my brother was born. The old air-cooled Franklin car was made there, and our landlord was a mechanic on Franklins. I loved watching him work.

The cultural ambience in Bethlehem was the same as in New York, for my parents' only friends there were a Jewish couple, Noah and Helen Kahn. The relationship between Noah and Dad must have had some effect on me, for then and all the years later until Noah's death in New York, their time together was one of constant debate. Noah was a metallurgist, and rose over many years to be Chief Metallurgist at the Brooklyn Navy Yard. He had a marvelous, sardonic sense of humor and a very pronounced accent different from any in our family. I believe he was from Rumania. He was darkly handsome. Rumanian Jews are known to be swarthier than those from elsewhere in Europe. The friendship was remarkable in that Noah was a staunch Zionist and Dad an equally staunch sympathizer of the Communist Party. Considering that Dad's overriding passion was always political discussion, and that he was both persistent and exceedingly stubborn in upholding his views, I find it remarkable that they got along. Noah, too, was an unusually stubborn man. Perhaps his sense of humor saved the friendship.

The years of my early childhood, the beginning of the 1920s, marked the transition from horses and gaslight to electricity and the internal combustion engine. We had gaslight in the hallways and bathrooms, but electricity in main rooms. Stoves on New York's Lower East Side were fed by coal. During an early period of unemployment for Dad, perhaps just after the time in Bethlehem, we slept in the room with the huge cook-stove between Grandma's restaurant rooms up front and the pantry behind. One night I was awakened by thumping noises. Big rats had taken refuge behind the stove and Dad and Uncle Dave were shagging fist-size lumps of coal at them. Mother was shuddering with disgust.

Uncle Dave was the daredevil in the family. He had a bike and would ride it in the very narrow space between street cars as they passed in opposite directions on Second Avenue. Tiny Grandma would be driven to distraction by such escapades, and, with no time to spare for child-rearing—he was her youngest—would deal with him the only way she knew how. I remember her ordering him to stand over a sink—why there I don't know, unless she thought perhaps he might bleed—and then delivering blow after blow on his back with her rolling-pin. Small she was, but there had to be plenty of muscle from the daily hour of rolling out thin sheets of dough after first vigorously kneading it, endlessly it seemed to me. And there was the scrubbing of clothes on a washboard, stirring their heavy mass in a huge laundry tub in which they were boiled. I think Dave took this as a normal and legitimate exercise of his mother's authority. I don't remember blood from the beatings, or injury. Neither did Dave reform. There was talk of mysterious places called pool-halls, where he would hang out. They were clearly bad. I think he did some boxing. He certainly skipped rope a lot—part of a boxer's training. And he told me with admiration about Benny Leonard, the lightweight champ. Imagine, a Jewish champion in boxing!

Life on the Lower East Side had its sensory pleasures. Many older boys and young men kept pigeons in cages on the tenement roofs. Watching them fly in circles but always come home to roost was fun. Keeping pigeons, too, was bad for some reason, probably because it was neither work nor study. Dave kept pigeons of course.

Fire engines were the most wonderful sight of all. The most magnificent was the pump wagon, more splendid even than the hook-and-ladder. The pump was steam-powered, and the steam boiler was a glorious vertical carafe of shining brass, narrowing sharply to a chimney on top. It was pulled by two sleek white horses, always driven at a gallop.

Milk and ice-wagons were also horse-drawn. One horse was enough, and it didn't have to be nearly as powerful as those that pulled the pump engine. I marveled at the delivery-wagon horses' knowledge of the stops on their routes. The milkman or iceman would come out of a tenement after each delivery and walk to the next one. The horse, with no guidance, walked to the next building entrance, or even skipped one or two if that was the sequence, and stopped of its own accord. Rarely did one wander. In such cases a heavy flat-bottomed stone drag, attached by a leather thong to the bridle, would pull its head to one side if it tried to move on.

There was no problem of parking, much less double-parking. In our Manhattan neighborhoods private cars were non-existent and not even thought of. Trucks, large two-cylinder chug-chugs with tires of solid rubber, did rumble down the streets. They were indestructible. I saw them into the 1970s in the most crowded parts of lower Manhattan. There, no vehicle can make speed of any kind, and the only consideration is whether the truck can move its load from one point to another nearby.

When I was old enough to be allowed to cross streets by myself, I acquired my father's passion for walking. The nearest point of interest didn't require crossing at all, but merely walking around the block to Seventh Street. There, I could hurry with a mixture of fear and curiosity past McSorley's Saloon. This was a famous place that did its business, with police cooperation, through the years of Prohibition and nearly half a century thereafter. Whether because its business was illegal, or because it bore an Irish name, or because no one in grandma Schachter's family touched alcohol (except perhaps for Uncle Simon who didn't live with us) it was on the list of "bad" places, and therefore attractive.

But when street-crossing did become permitted, a genuinely wonderful world awaited me. Just a block away, across Third Avenue, was Cooper Union. Rising at the south of its triangle was the first statue I recall, a giant representation of Peter Cooper. The remarkable son of an officer in our Revolutionary War, he built the Tom Thumb locomotive in 1830, rolled the first structural-iron beams for buildings, invented a washing-machine, and advocated free education. That's why he founded Cooper Union.

South of the Cooper statue, and beneath the gloomy El train structure, ran the Bowery, with flop-houses and eateries for the poorest of the poor. The Bowery was forbidden to me, and I think I obeyed because I was taught to be afraid of kidnapping. The ragged, often drunken, stubble-faced men frightened me. But north of Cooper Union, and probably prompted by its existence, was block after block of some of the very finest second-hand bookstores anywhere on earth. I don't remember being in them too much, but I browsed their outside stands endlessly, looking at their peculiar window displays. I particularly remember a drawing—probably a print— of the head of Christ, whose eyes followed you no matter at what angle you looked at it.

Across the wide avenue—Fourth, I believe—was that awesome place, John Wanamaker's department store. Once it had been the favorite of the rich, and perhaps it still was. To people who did most of their buying at the cheap immigrant-owned stores a block or two away, or even from pushcarts, cheaper still, anything purchased at John Wanamaker's was worth bragging about. My mother would take me there occasionally.

Much more interesting to me was the walk due west: Greenwich Village proper. Imagine a family having an entire house to itself, even though they touched wall to wall! And a patch of green in front. Many homes had truly splendid wrought-iron balconies draped with wistaria or other vines. Then, at the limit of the walk, past the arch marking the bottom of Fifth Avenue, was the Mews with its cobblestoned paving right up to the building fronts, and an occasional whiff of manure to indicate that some still kept horses there. Work horses were kept in livery stables, of course. There would be one every few blocks. Their dark interiors and rich smells of hay, leather, horse-sweat, and manure provided a counterpoint to the streets, essentially sterile but for automotive exhaust.

Half a block to the east of us, on the corner diagonally across Second Avenue, was the source of an entirely different kind of intriguing smell, the pharmacy. In those days prescriptions were compounded on the spot, out of the contents of vials and jars with Latin words and abbreviations in large Gothic lettering. In the windows hung the inevitable identifications of a pharmacist: huge suspended blownglass vase-like containers of colored liquids. They were purely decorative but an absolute requirement like the striped poles outside barber shops or the life-size wooden Indians at cigar stores. The pharmacy was presided over by an immense man of enormous dignity and girth. His handlebar moustache dipped and swept upward again in a manner that left me with the life-long impression that he was Polish, until Dad told me he was a German Jew.

The confusion was understandable. Prior to the coming of the refugees from Hitler at the close of the '30s, contact between German and East European Jews was virtually non-existent. The former had come to America in the middle of the 19th century, the latter not until its end and the early years of this one. The former were deliberately assimilated, universally English-speaking, and some had actually become rich. Their politics were mainstream. Even their Judaism had been reformed. The latter were mainly Yiddish-speaking, overwhelmingly wage-workers, very largely socialist or even communist. Their children, like my father and elder maternal uncle, sought to enter the professions. Generally that was simply a dream, a goal toward which, as in my family, they were just working.

When they did earn more than workers' wages, they tried to get out of the Lower East Side. In our case, the first move after Bethlehem was to Brooklyn—Bensonhurst to be exact. We had the second floor of a white frame house. A tremendous richly-producing cherry tree touched one of our windows, and one could reach out and eat them, just like that! My mother made the most scrumptious cherry preserves, just right, with the fruits still whole, thick as molasses. She made the richest orange cake, with a top layer of grated orange peel an eighth of an inch thick, and we had lambchops on the table.

We had no car, ever, and no radio until I was in my teens—although Uncle Dave had built himself a crystal set at the very beginning of the '20s. We had a standing hand-cranked phonograph with a collection of two hundred 78s, almost all classical and predominantly operatic — Caruso, Galli-Curci, Ponselle, Tetrazzini, Chaliapin, John McCormack. My father would swear that I knew all two hundred by heart, both the music, the composers, and performers. I loved to stand and conduct the symphonic records—all the old war-horses, "Semiramide Overture" and "Marche Slave," and "Turkish March." Beethoven, Brahms, and Chaikovsky was about the range.

Uncle Dave, a red-head, who earned his living in the garment district as a cutter on ladies' underwear, sang Italian opera. To this day I measure the most famous baritones against the color and particularly the drama of his voice—he's long dead—and few survive the comparison. He put his money into teachers and marvelous records—Stracciare, Tito Ruffo—and taught me how to listen. He had the necessary single-mindedness, the long-term discipline, and the sheer, raw vocal power. Did he fail to make it because a poor East Side immigrant Jewish kid didn't have a chance in the 1920s, as he believed? Or was it because, moving as his voice was, he never could master enough roles to quality for an audition at the only place there was—the Metropolitan? But when he transformed himself into Rigoletto singing "Cortigiani, vil' razza dannata"—courtiers, vile race—with the bitterness of the poor father whose daughter had been betrayed by those he was powerless to act against, my spine tingled as it always has to truly great performances.

Mother sang all day long, operetta chiefly, although I can name only "Chocolate Soldier," a 1908 hit musical based on George Bernard Shaw's pacifist play, *Arms and the Man.* She also sang arias from *Carmen* , in Polish. She was the only person I have ever known who could make that language sound good to my ears. Her younger sister, my aunt Fannie, merry and red-headed like her brother, also sang, frequently in harmony with mom.

I have always sung. "Parlami d'amore, Mariu" is knocking 'em dead at a Communist summer camp when I was seventeen for the sheer mischievous pleasure of seeing the results it produced in the girls. "I've Got You Under My Skin" was me at nineteen, hormones raging, in the first year of a marriage that is now in its seventh decade.

I had a reputation for absent-mindedness in childhood that apparently was well-deserved. There was the time I was sent to the store with a dollar in my hand (a single then was worth a twenty of today's) became entranced with the store-fronts I passed, and tumbled down the steps of an open street-front cellar. A doctor had to be called to the house to stitch me up. Someone opened my clenched fist to clean it, and there was the dollar. Mother had said to be sure not to lose it.

It was when we lived in Brooklyn that I saw my first movie. Count me lucky: Charlie Chaplin in *The Kid,* with Jackie Coogan. It was released in 1921, so I must have been four.

There is a bit of the legendary about that house in Brooklyn. It belonged to the mother of "Legs" Diamond, who lived in it and was our landlady. "Legs" was one of the most murderous and perhaps the first of the major Jewish gangsters. Anything in that house was quite safe against burglars or thieves. Knowing my parents, I am positive that they had no knowledge of the landlady's family when they rented the place. Mother, certainly, would have been repelled even by indirect contact with a professional criminal.

The move back from Brooklyn to my grandmother's was because another of my father's jobs came to an end. In the absence of unemployment insurance, and with the banking system not yet willing to offer signature loans to wage or salary earners, periods without work meant recourse either to the pawn shop or to relatives. With us, it was always the latter, perhaps because at that stage in their lives my parents had nothing of value to pawn.

Dad's next job brought another effort to get out of the Lower East Side, this time by moving a few blocks uptown. East 14th Street was the northern border of the ghetto. We made it to 15th, just seven blocks north of grandma's. Here, beneath the El, were the saloons, eating places, and small shops of the old ethnic-German workingclass of New York. These places left so strong an impression on me that, twenty years later, I dreamed a short story set in them, and, waking up, tried to set it down on paper. But by that date I'm afraid I'd suppressed whatever creative imagination I had in favor of logic and disciplined thought. (I never tried using my imagination creatively again but for occasional poems in the 1950s, when deeply moved by the assaults on liberty of that period.) Half a block eastward from our apartment on 15th Street was, and is, a pleasant park, perhaps three blocks long. Just as St. Mark's Church at 10th Street and Second Avenue gave its immediate surroundings a special, rather gracious character—a number of single-family brownstones still remained—so the Quaker Meeting House at the edge of the park gave our new neighborhood a touch of class.

Synagogues were totally out of my experience. I don't even remember their locations accurately. This is probably because they had no architectural distinction, for they were flush with adjoining buildings, wall to wall. An atheist family represented conscious rebellion in its own generation, and would not set foot in a synagogue for any occasion . My grandmother would quietly go to *shul* (synagogue) on Saturday, but the matter was simply not discussed. That evasion was the manner in which the Orthodox immigrant generation and their less observant or even outright secular children co-existed. However, my grandmother resented that I had been circumcised by a physician, not a *moil*, the Jewish religious specialist at this operation. She insisted it hadn't been done right—I can't quite agree. My guess is that my parents had it done because they thought there was some health benefit, cleanliness or whatever. I'm told that on one occasion, when I had wet my diaper in or near her restaurant kitchen, she yelled at my mother: "Get that *shayget-zl* out of here." The word means "baby Christian", and in that world of mutual religious bigotry it was no compliment.

Churches were something else. The simplest of them were architecturally distinctive, on the East Side, for the mere fact that they did not touch adjacent buildings. Furthermore, they almost always had a few trees and some grass around them. I don't remember flowers. But if, according to my upbringing, a synagogue simply represented the stupidity and superstition of religion, churches had a far more complex symbolism. They represented Christians, and Christians were *Americans*. We wanted desperately to be Americans —all Jews did: religious and agnostic and atheist; Democrats and Socialists and Communists, workers and bosses. (You never said "employer" and not even "capitalist," except in speech or political argument.) The only Catholic Church nearby was Polish, and Poles were immigrants or the young children of immigrants, just like the Jews.

But Protestant St. Mark's and the Quakers were "real" Christians, and therefore real Americans. We had no notion that many Friends don't consider themselves Christians. I would walk past a church or Friends meeting house with the strangest combination of awe and respect, curiosity and fear. Though American-born, I apparently had absorbed too much of what Christians had done to Jews in the old country, and of Jews as the eternal outsiders, to be free of fear. I don't remember ever hearing a description of a pogrom, but I was a favorite of the customers in grandma's restaurant. These workingmen had had the full range of Jewish experience, which I had evidently absorbed by listening.

My attitude toward WASP churches as distinct from synagogues had a counterpart on the purely personal level. Later, in public school, I developed a best friend, Sidney Horowitz. The name is unmistakeably Jewish, but the family had come from England, not the continent. Although I was blond he was truly straw-blond and very fair-skinned. I visited their home, and his father bore no resemblance in manner, cast of features, or speech, to the European Jews with whom I was familiar. And I found that I envied the Horowitzes' Anglo-Saxonness.

When Dad's next job ended, he tried to keep us in that apartment on 15th St. by, for the only time ever, trying to make a living as a salesman. He had a route placing and servicing penny gum ball and other machines. It didn't work out, and we moved back to grandma's. However, Dad did work at his profession almost all the time, and our total stays at grandma's represent only a small part of my childhood. Yet memories of life in our own apartments are much less vivid. This is probably, in part, because of the more intriguing surroundings at grandma's—the customers coming and going, talking and paying attention to me. I had more freedom there, since mother had to help out in the restaurant. In the movies I saw the cowboy films of William S. Hart, imagined myself Bill Hart, and spun yarns of my adventures to the customers. They did more than tolerate me. I imagine that a lot of them were lonely single men eating out by themselves each night.

Grandma Schachter was very, very beautiful. When I was a grown man, elderly gentlemen would come to look up the famous Hinda Schachter, the prize catch that swashbuckling grandfather of mine had gotten. I remember appreciating her beauty when I was a very small child. She would stand at a mirror, combing hair that can only be described in the old-fashioned phrase "auburn tresses", which cascaded to her waist. She would then braid and coil them on top of her head. It

was the only pleasure, sensual or otherwise, the only sign of self-awareness that she ever had time for—that is, until arthritis crippled her
hands. Then she retired, watched the new wonder, television, and from
it learned the English that her never-ending tasks had kept her from
mastering in her working years.

The restaurant she had longest was on St. Mark's Place, which today
is called the East Village. That's funny to those of us who knew it them.
It was simply the Lower East Side, different from Hester or Delancy or
Grand or Cannon streets only in that it was not exclusively Jewish.
Across the street was the Polish National Home. There was no love lost
between Polish and Jewish immigrants. But there may have been few
Poles living on the block: I recall no street fights between gangs of Polish
and Jewish boys, as there were when Jewish kids wandered into Irish or
Italian turf.

The Irish were definitely enemies. The cops were Irish, and cops
were enemies by definition. Religious bigotry was extreme, and to
devout Catholics, Jews were Christ-killers. That is the only reason I can
think of for hostility with Italians, except for the very simple matter of
turf. Italian workers were the other major ethnic component, with Jews,
in the garment industry. Workers of one of these nationalities would not
scab against the other during strikes. They belonged to the same unions,
although to different locals, because of language problems which reinforced the tendency of employers to hire members of their own ethnic
group. Meetings were conducted in the language of the particular group
of immigrants, although the top leaderships of both the International
Ladies Garment Workers and the Amalgamated Clothing Workers were
predominantly Jewish—a consequence of the militancy brought from
Russia in a time of revolution.

To grandma Schachter that was an unknown world, although her son
Dave became a union member as a matter of course. Her other son,
Simon, initially a Zionist, was converted to communism by my father,
and her daughter Dora married my father. I distinctly remember from
very early childhood that political arguments raged endlessly in grandma's kosher restaurants. For some reason, the arguments were usually
in English.

Grandma was busy literally every waking minute, shopping, cleaning
food, cooking. The serving was usually done by her younger daughter,
my aunt Fannie. One never tipped a member of the owner's family. That
was a universal rule. Grandma would occasionally take me on her daily
shopping in the very early mornings. She bought from wonderful old-
fashioned stores under the First-Avenue El train structure. Beans and
peas and rice and coffee sat in huge, open, aromatic sacks. The meat and
chickens came, of course, from a kosher butcher.

She wanted to serve her fish absolutely fresh, so she would buy it live and dump it into the bathtub, which was kept filled with water on weekdays for that purpose.This makes me wonder how the family kept clean. It certainly did. My mother was the most fastidious person I have ever met. In the restaurant, the tablecloths were linen and spotless. If a customer soiled one, a fresh linen napkin would be spread carefully over the spot for the rest of that evening. Grandma made no profit in any real sense. At best, she was able to save money to move to a larger place, which failed because she refused to add to her dinners the vegetables that even her immigrant customers had learned were good for health.

When I was six and about to enter school, we moved to the Bronx, where we remained for the next eight years. I believe my parents chose the particular apartment building because a new public school was being erected right across the street, which I was to attend. It wasn't finished on time, and so my education began in an old-fashioned wooden schoolhouse with a peaked roof. It was no bigger than a comfortable home.

The Bronx was not what it is today. There was a working farm about six blocks away, and its lovely row of poplars still stands as part of the grounds of Cedars of Lebanon Hospital now occupying the site. The Grand Concourse, a raised boulevard that was quite an engineering project for the pre-bulldozer age, towered three blocks away. Atop it were the Lewis Morris Apartments, populated by people we kids on the streets beneath regarded as plutocrats. A constant war raged between the Lewis Morris boys and us. We would charge up the twenty-foot-high boulder embankment raised to carry the Grand Concourse, and they would charge down. There was stone-throwing and, I think, slingshots. But I don't recall anyone ever hurt enough to require more than a mother's patching. Even though the weapons weren't that deadly, I was quite afraid.

On the far side of the Grand Concourse, directly adjacent to the Lewis Morris, was genuine suburban wilderness—at 174th Street. Never mind the ugly and smelly sumach trees, there were real rabbits, lizards, snakes, and many flowers. Behind our apartment house was an empty lot which people used as a dump.

The great event of our first year in the Bronx was the total eclipse of 1923. It must have occurred in winter, because there was snow on the roof of our building, from which we watched it through exposed snapshot film. My most vivid impression, not predicted by the press, possibly because there was no previous record of a total eclipse being observed over snow, was of the running shadows on the snow caused by the corona. The temporary darkness was complete but for the halo of light around the disk of the moon.

Politics, in any form, did not yet play any significant role in my life. I was aware that there was a president named Harding in my early child-hood, and that he followed Wilson. However, the first time a political personality made an impact upon me was when Lenin died in January 1924. I was six-and-a-half. The Russian Revolution, which he had led, split every Socialist Party in the world. Those who supported that revolution became Communist. Since the U.S. Socialist Party had been one of the very few to oppose World War I, the Bolshevik Revolution in Russia won majority support. Debs, no theorist but workingman and organizer of the railwaymen, declared in the face of federal martial law and the U.S. Army, "I am a Bolshevik from the crown of my head to the soles of my feet."

But the anti-revolutionary minority in the Socialist Party managed to gain control of its machinery by electoral shenanigans and with the aid of the courts. Warren Beatty's film of the 1980s,"Reds", depicted this with historical accuracy. In consequence, the majority of the party, which saw in Russia the socialist revolution Marx had called for in 1848, organized itself into what ultimately was called the Communist Party. Mother opposed Dad's joining, so he belonged for just a few weeks. But he contributed the equivalent of what his dues would have been, plus whatever more he could afford during special-issue fund drives.

The death of Lenin was as much a historical event as his life had been. It may even have been as important, when one considers that he had restored considerable scope for private business (which Stalin subsequently nationalized, ultimately condemning Soviet socialism to collapse). Enormous memorial meetings were held in every industrial country on earth and even in some of the semi-colonies and colonies that comprised a very large part of the world at that time. In New York City, the meeting was at old Madison Square Garden, within easy reach of workingclass neighborhoods. Dad took me. I remember the Lenin memorial because of its dance pageantry. I recall chiefly a mass of young women, in flowing red, sweeping diagonally across the stage, carrying stupendous red banners. It was choreographed and led by Edith Segal, then about twenty. (Nearly forty years later she and I danced, ad lib, before the Havana Ballet company in its quarters. We both happened to be in Cuba on the second anniversary of Castro's revolution, just before the U.S. invasion at the Bay of Pigs. She died in 1997.) The innovative dance style of San Franciscan Isadora Duncan was at the height of its popularity at this time. She had gone to red Russia, founded a school of dance there, married the poet Yesenin, and brought him to this country. Here, anti-Communist crowds booed her off the stage.

A few years earlier, in a rally to raise money for striking textile workers, top journalist John Reed, the hero of Beatty's film and an actual historical figure, had introduced the pageant as part of major

Left gatherings.

Lenin's death occurred in January, almost exactly at the beginning of the new school term. The block-square, brick public school we had moved to the Bronx for me to attend was now ready, and I was transferred to it from the wooden schoolhouse where my education had begun. Up to this point I had never encountered anti-Semitism that I can recall. I'm not sure that I had even heard the word. But this new P.S. 70 had a Polish janitor who was sodden drunk a very large part of the time. He would invite children—only boys I imagine, but don't remember—to sit on the school steps as he told stories of World War I in which he had been a soldier. He would show us—one couldn't help seeing it anyhow—the awful, livid red gash on one of his wrists where he had been stuck by a bayonet five years earlier. This display would be accompanied by the most awful curses and accusations against Jews.

I don't remember his specific words. Hitler had then only just conducted his abortive beer-hall rebellion in Munich, was a decade from power, and was not taken seriously by anyone inside Germany or out. In retrospect, that poor, drunken, wounded janitor focusing all his frustrations upon the Jews was pure Nazism in microcosm.

Another event that brought me into contact with the broader world was a guest speaker at a school assembly. My world up to then had been totally white. I knew that there were Chinese in the world not only from reading but also because there were Chinese restaurants, universally referred to as "let's go eat Chinks'." I knew that there were African-Americans—Negroes was the polite word at the time—and must have seen a few, but have no recollection of that. I learned a decade later that my future wife's family employed a Black woman to help out after the third child was born, when Tanya was already nine. Such regular help could be hired only in homes that were relatively well-to-do. The father of my wife-to-be was a dentist. I do remember that Blacks were referred to in conversation. Among Jews the Yiddish word, *Shvartseh*, was universally used to refer to them. It simply means "Black," but it was not complimentary.

The very notion of a Black Jew simply did not exist among Jews of European or Near Eastern origin. One day an Ethiopian Jew came to speak at our school. I reported to my parents on the man and what he said, and they were as astounded as I. So there was a world outside my immediate family and friends and school and neighborhood! But my life was still centered there. I didn't lack for things to do.

Games came in seasons. I would play marbles in marble season, fly kites at that time of year, and so forth. I'm told that I would read the entire term's public school class assignments in two weeks, and would then spend endless hours playing stoopball.

Stoopball is a game played with a rubber ball the size of a tennis ball without its cloth cover. The preferred ball, with the best bounce, was made by the Spalding Company. You stood in the roadway ("gutter" in New Yorkese) just off the sidewalk, and threw it in an effort to hit the edge of a house stoop. If you succeeded, the ball would fly back through the air, sometimes almost horizontally, sometimes up high. To catch it before it hit the ground was the equivalent of a home run. If it bounced once before you caught it, that was a smaller score, one point I believe. But if it bounced more than once, you were out, and the opposing boy got his inning. I don't recall girls playing it, or playing with girls in general.

Our top game was stickball. This was simply baseball using a broom-stick for a bat, a Spalding ball, and no gloves. In games among little boys, rules called for the pitcher to cause the ball to bounce once before reaching the batter, the equivalent of slow-pitch softball. But for bigger boys the ball was thrown exactly as in baseball. The easy way to play was without a strike zone. You could pick the pitches you wanted to swing at, but three swinging strikes put you out all the same. Called strikes didn't exist. The hard game, truly skilled, was one that used a strike zone and umpire, usually a kid who arrived late for that game. A good pitcher could make that tennis-size rubber ball curve in or out, drop or rise, to a degree impossible with a baseball. One with a good arm could throw it extremely fast. If hit by a pitched ball, it really stung, but you were not injured. Fielding was difficult, too. The ball would almost always curve in the air, and, when throwing to an infielder, you had to avoid twisting your wrist, which would give the ball a spin and produce a curve.

We played either in the concrete schoolyard, which was best, or, if that were occupied, on a city street. Even if in a schoolyard, a power hitter could propel the ball its full length, meaning the narrow side of a New York City gridiron block—two hundred feet—and over the standard 15-foot-high wire-mesh fence that surrounded the yard. My school's yard had been levelled from a hillside, so the outfield wall on the uphill side had a good ten feet of concrete retaining wall below the wire mesh. And, still, home-run hitters would clear it. We smaller or less able boys would worship them. The best was a boy, I imagine in his early teens, quite literally with a limp wrist. I think he carried it that way in imitation of one of our heroes on the New York Yankees. In that respect, we Bronx kids were the luckiest in America. Baseball was unarguably the national pastime then. Football was followed and played only during the short season when a mysterious group of rich kids' colleges called the Ivy League was in action. Basketball was a game to play, like handball, not one in which you were a fan of some team.

We in the Bronx rooted for perhaps the greatest baseball team ever fielded. In right field was Babe Ruth himself. In center there was Earle

Combs of the marvelous shoe-string catches who would then flip the ball underhand to ex-pitcher Ruth, from whose mighty arm it would reach any base faster and on a straighter line than most fielders could get it in even without the delay of the relay. I saw that with my own eyes. There was Lou Gehrig on first, second in homers only to Ruth. Among the pitchers was Herb Pennock, with perhaps the most graceful wind-up the big leagues knew—neither Satchel Paige nor any other African-American was allowed in them then. (The fight led by the Communist *Daily Worker's* unsurpassed all-sports-writer, Lester Rodney, that brought Jackie Robinson onto the Dodgers was not won until twenty years later.)

Baseball was beneath my father. My mother was not interested and besides, she was legally blind.

If you couldn't get to see a big league game—a very rare treat—and you couldn't get into a team stickball game, there was a very good substitute, stickball against the wall. You could play another boy singly, or pairs, as in tennis doubles. We played this game against walls marked off for handball. More often than not, others would be playing the same game against the adjacent section of wall. One day I dashed to the right to field the ball just hit by my opponent. At that very moment a boy playing in the court to my right—batting position was at the left-hand line—took a mighty swing. The end of his broomstick caught me square across the eye. It knocked me to the ground, and I found myself, before getting up, supporting myself on my palms and letting out a string of curses I didn't realize I knew. It really relieved the soul.

I was wearing glasses, as I did from the age of eight, horn-rimmed at this point. Shatterproof glass did not exist. The human body has remarkable built-in protective devices. Although I was not conscious of seeing the oncoming bat, the eye reflex worked, and it was closed at the moment of impact. So a piece of the frame was driven into the heavy bone shielding the eye from above, and the glass fragments cut my lid to shreds, but my eye was not injured at all.

One winter day I went belly-whopping with friends on the hill in Clarement Park. Belly-whopping means starting with a run, carrying your Flexible Flyer in front of you—no self-respecting boy would leave his parents alone until they bought him that make of sled—and then throwing it down and flop yourself belly-first onto it to start downhill at maximum speed. Even a big sled was not over four feet long, so your head would hang over it in front and your feet behind. There was a steering bar up front that twisted the frame to turn it in the direction you wished. Running on snow, there was of course a skid factor in the turn, which depended upon your speed, how icy the surface was, and the momentum determined by the weight being carried.

That day I was double belly-whopping with a friend. This meant that when the boy with the sled hit the ground, the other would jump on top of him in the same position, stomach down and head forward. His arms would reach around the boy beneath and grip the slats of the sled. This was in a city park, and the hill, which in summer was grassland marked with "Keep Off" signs, was separated from the paved asphalt paths by a low fence of two round iron bars, an inch in diameter, one above the other, the higher perhaps eighteen inches off the ground. If one came dangerously close to such a fence, the boy on top was supposed to let go the body of the sled and roll off, so the boy beneath could do likewise. I was beneath on one trip, the momentum was too great for the sled to turn away from the fence, and my buddy failed to roll off. I smashed head on into the bar fence, just above my hairline.

Packs of paper tissue didn't exist then, so mother always provided me with a large white linen handkerchief. I put it to my head—I was bleeding profusely—and got myself to the nearest dispensary, as out-patient clinics were then called. An intern who proved not to know his business stitched me up. I hailed a cab for the first time in my life. When I arrived at 203 E. 174th St., I walked up the three flights of stairs—a building with an elevator was beyond our purse—rang the bell, and when Mother came to the door, said with deliberate calm, "Mother, there's a cab downstairs. Please pay him."

In the few seconds it took me to get that out, her eyes adjusted to the background light. She saw the blood-stained head-bandage and the steady trickle still coming down my face and, for the only time ever, my mother—normally self-possessed to the point of iciness—threw her arms in the air and screamed. An Anglo-Saxon friend believes his mother would have remained calm, if he had come home under his own power. Maybe that's a difference between Yankees and Jews. Now that my hairline has receded, the two parallel scars are clearly visible.

Of course my glasses were smashed. They were always being smashed. The only sport I was forbidden to play because of that was basketball. One basketball game, one pair of glasses. That was too much.

In those years most parents didn't get their children glasses unless poor vision was a serious handicap. So boys with glasses were called "four-eyes," and girls avoided glasses for fear of spoiling their looks. How early do girls become looks-conscious, anyway? My parents apparently realized that I needed glasses when I was eight. Mother was a person of exceptional pride. For her to ask for a favor of any kind was virtually unthinkable. But she also felt that we must get the very best medical care. That was, by definition in our society, the most costly. There were no HMOs, no Medicare, no employer-administered system. You paid for what you got or you went to the hospitals for the poor. In New

York, that hospital was Bellevue, and poor people believed it was a slaughterhouse.

The best ophthalmologist of the day, in New York in any case, was Dr. Charles May, a German Jew, with an office on Park Avenue. As I write, instruments and procedures still bear his name. Mother seems to have persuaded him to accept me as a patient at some reduced rate. That was not at all unknown, but for her to demean herself—I'm putting it in the terms in which she would see it—to make any such request was a measure of her motherly love.

Dr. May examined me, found that I was extremely near-sighted as well as astigmatic, and also had a chronic inflammation of the underside of the lids that he treated with a really painful caustic. I don't recall crying, but doubtless shrank and otherwise manifested my discomfort, to which he responded with imperious commands to "take it like a man."

Wearing glasses didn't bother me except that they were part of a complex of things that for years gave me a sense of physical inferiority. The underlying cause was not physical at all. Both my father and a friend of my mother who survived until I was elderly described the following incident to me, in essentially identical terms. My teacher sent a note home with me when I was in the fifth grade, asking mother to come in to see her. That was not unusual, and had happened frequently since the first grade. I was the bad boy in school because I talked all the time. Generally Mother's response was to laugh and say, "We all talk, in our family."

This time the teacher said, "What am I doing up *here*, and William down *there*?" So they sent me to the Educational Clinic at CCNY for the new-fangled procedure called intelligence-quotient testing. My IQ turned out to be high. Some of the specific findings in the clinic director's report, of which Dad, as always, saved the initial typescript, are interesting for where they proved right and wrong. He found my arithmetical reasoning to be lower than my general mental age, which was given as 50 percent higher than my age in years. About math he was right. I have never had much interest—and therefore much ability—in abstract reasoning. Numbers *of* something can interest me greatly. Numbers as such, and manipulations of mathematical formulas, leave me utterly cold. If I am a theorist of any kind, it is as a practical one. Call it applied social science.

But there was one thing in the good doctor's finding about me when I was ten that really annoys me. He wrote: "His auditory rote memory is very good, being equal to that of superior adults." Now, I admit that I have an excellent memory for things that interest me. I have superb visual memory for works of art, scenery, my poor unaided eyesight notwithstanding. But, specifically at that age, I was notorious for absent-mindedness. I simply could not remember what did not interest me. I remember things that, associated with others, make sense. I remember things that do not make sense if I understand or think I understand why they don't make sense. I can remember what one has to remember, like the multiplication table. But I do not remember isolated facts. And that's what I think rote memory is. My Webster's New International Dictionary supports me. It defines "rote" as "use of the memory with little intelligence."

That same report found that I was 4 1/2" above median height for my age, and fifteen pounds heavier than median, or about three pounds per extra inch. So I was a big, well-built kid. Then what caused my sense of physical inferiority in the years that followed? The bottom line—literally the last line in the report—was, "it is advisable to place him in a grade in which the work is more nearly commensurate with his mentality."

Oh, dear. From that point on I was promoted from grade to grade during the term, sent from elementary school to junior high, and from there to the city-wide rapid-advancement academic high school for boys, Townsend Harris. The best description of that place was a jingle learned by my wife-to-be—I didn't meet her until years afterward—at Hunter High, the equivalent school for girls. It goes:

> Ta-root, ta-root, ta-root, ta-root,
> We are the boys of the Institute.
> We aren't rough, we aren't tough,
> But oh are we determined!

Townsend Harris lopped one year off the usual four years for high school, and gave you one hell of a fine academic education. When McCarthyism hit me a quarter century after graduation, I was able to make a living translating from German and French—there was no work from Russian as yet—on the basis of what I was taught in that remarkable high school. But I graduated four years younger than the norm for high school completion. This meant that then, later in college, and above all during my undergraduate semester at Moscow University in 1932, I was very much younger than the young men around me. I didn't have their physical strength; I didn't have their coordination. For a boy entering puberty and adolescence, that's very difficult.

My beliefs were quite serious and settled early on. The Communist *Daily Worker*, which Dad read, serialized the French novelist Henri Barbusse's Under Fire, about World War I. The *Encyclopaedia Britannica* describes it thus: "The horror of bloodshed and destruction led Barbusse to an indictment of society as a whole. He became a pacifist, then a militant Communist." Thus I began to know what war meant. I believed I knew who was responsible for it. I knew it could happen again, and that if it did, it would be the same interests who would bring it about. I hated it, and I hated them.

The *Worker* also carried another series that made Barbusse pale into insignificance. It was from the international Communist organization to help political prisoners. It described the tortures to which the ruling class—no quotation marks needed, then or now—subjects its victims. The one that burned itself into my memory for life was an incident in Brazil, in which a Communist couple, just married, were roped tight to each other, nude, face to face, and kept that way day and night until they went mad.

In that year, 1927, the U.S. Marines had intervened in Nicaragua, and Augusto Sandino had begun his guerrilla warfare in the hills. To radicals of my generation, no one had to explain the origin of the word, "Sandinista," when it appeared fifty years later.

On August 23, 1927, my father sent me down to the corner candy store, as usual, to buy the Sunday *New York Times*. Lying next to it, on the stand, was the *Daily News*, a tabloid. Its front page consisted entirely of photographs of the heads of two men. I knew who they were and what had happened before I read the headline: "Sacco, Vanzetti Dead." That was the first great anti-workingclass frame-up of my lifetime. The two men, immigrants, a shoemaker and a fish peddler, philosophical anarchists, had been arrested for murder in connection with a robbery in 1920, and convicted the next year.

In 1925, a condemned criminal gave evidence that the double murder had been committed by ordinary criminals. But the Sacco-Vanzetti Case had by then become a test of the strength of worldwide protest against the determination of the capitalist state to demonstrate its power against radicals. The case is described in the *Britannica* and an endless number of books. Vanzetti's last letter is taught as a classic of literature. In paraphrase, he said: we, a good shoemaker and a poor fish peddler, do more good in our dying than we could ever have done in life.

Finally, 1927 saw the triumphant entry into Shanghai of the united Communist and Kuomintang nationalist armies. I had followed their march north from Canton with a map on my wall on which I moved pins to mark their advances.

I fell in love then, at age ten. Her name was Vera Babad. She asked me to join the Young Pioneers, the Communist children's organization. I did. It was love all right. It lasted five years, including the final year when I was in Moscow and she wasn't even around to be looked at. That's all I ever did, anyhow. To *tell* a girl you loved her? What if she said she didn't love you? You'd fall through the floor and never be able to crawl out of the hole. You wouldn't want to, you'd be so embarrassed.

So I would walk clear across the park every chance I got and stand across the street from her apartment house, out of sight I hoped, and wait to see her at the window or going in or out of the building. I never did, but I saw her a good deal at meetings.

The Young Pioneers then existed in sixty-three cities. They sought free hot lunches in schools, more playgrounds, opposed militarism in education, and supported striking workers by collecting money, while advocating socialism as the basic solution to the problems of society. It was not only the reading that brought me to join but also the fact that my father had been away for most of a year, in Siberia, helping, in his belief, to build socialism. The fact that Marxist socialism ultimately suffocated in the burocracy it had to create to replace the market it illegalized is another matter.

In 1926 Dad had joined a group of American, Dutch, and English politically radical engineers and skilled workers who understood that for the Russian experiment to be successful, industry was needed to provide a modern living standard. They were organized as the Autonomous Industrial Colony, formally headed at the outset by Big Bill Haywood, a major figure in the Industrial Workers of the World—"Wobblies"—who had turned Communist. The first on-the-ground manager was a Native American. This was probably the first time that an Indian headed an industrial enterprise anywhere.

I corresponded with my daddy, of course. He kept the letters permanently. As I read those letters I find that when Dad was in the Soviet Union I was a normal, ordinary kid. There were absolutely no insights, unless you can regard as a discovery finding that animals in the zoo would stand stock still when I made unusual types of sounds. I had nothing at all to say about the human condition, but was most fascinated by a circus act in which a woman on a horse was carried upward by a balloon that proved to be half filled with fireworks when it got near the ceiling. In response to questions Dad asked me in his letters—I remember a pressed forget-me-not in one of them as proof that spring in Siberia was glorious—I dutifully listed my grades in school, reported that I would be skipped a class, and proudly informed him that I had been chosen for a play, as a member of the chorus.

The books I read those days were the endless Tom Swift series. I wrote my father: "These books tell about new inventions and the inventor is 'Tom Swift'. They have impressed me very much and have added to my knowledge of machines used these days." In another letter I wrote that I had read the last book of the *Iliad*, but all I could find to say about it was that "I like it much."

Mother, I reported, had taken me to some very good movies (silents, of course) as well as some that were not. There was Flaherty's *Moana of the South Seas, The Merry Widow,* and *The Vanishing American.* There were also *The Flaming Frontier, Hands Up,* and *Don Q.* To which I added: "and others, the names of which I don't remember." That at least showed some discrimination.

I wrote about my stamp collection, about swimming in the school pool, and about coasting on my sled in the snow "when I remembered." One sentence indicated that I was aware of the need for political caution where anything pertaining to the Soviet Union is concerned. It reads: "My teacher knew you're over 'there' since you left." Another confirms that I had no particular psychological problems about being an atheist. About Easter-time (Passover for Jews), I wrote: "We're having a 13-day vacation. Other kids, religious ones, having 18 days, [I] went to school the first week and read *Robin Hood.*"

Schools were kept open during religious holidays. Most kids did not attend, however. Consequently, teachers did not attempt to proceed with their curricula. So I read. But I do remember one piece of original thought from that period, albeit an idea that had occurred to many others before me. I was having an argument over the existence of god with some other kids while we were lined up for something. I was about nine. I said: "If god made us, who made god?" I'm certain that that was not a repetition of what I'd heard at home, or at least not a conscious one, because I remember it as a flash of perception.

Dad returned from Siberia after less than a year. Sixty years later he wrote me this explanation of why he didn't take us with him: "Couldn't see how I could have the family, accustomed to West Bronx living conditions, live in this primitive 'town'. No roads or running water, questionable housing, etc., etc. Didn't know much about the schools."

My letters to Dad indicate no sign of a belief system other than atheism. But the following year, when I turned ten, brought a rush awareness of—and physical, emotional and mental commitment to—opposing injustice and to changing the world for the better.

CHAPTER 2

Kid Power in the New York Schools

Joining the Communist children's organization, the Young Pioneers, soon faced me with the first important psychological decision of my life, the first involving courage. The position of organized labor in the prosperity years of the 1920s was extraordinarily similar to that in the 1990s. The coal-mine owners demanded that the union agree to a reduction in the work force. The union president, John L. Lewis, was a dozen years later to play a major role in establishing unionism in the auto, steel, and other mass-production industries during the New Deal period. However, in the '20s he accepted the employers' position, and himself put forth the slogan, "200,000 miners must go." His cooperation in downsizing mine employment brought into being a tremendous pool of men who, to eat, had to work at whatever wages and under whatever conditions were offered. By 1927 the unionized mines accounted for only 40 percent of coal production, as against 60 percent in 1924. Finally, there was no alternative but to strike in an effort to protect existing conditions. The employers hung tough. The strike lasted a full year, and the workers and their families literally starved before finally giving in. A British film of 1997, "Brassed Off," tells an amazingly similar true story. Some things do not change.

The Communists, at all age levels—the Party, the Young Communist League, and the Young Pioneers—went all-out collecting food, clothing, and money for the miners. A permit was obtained from New York City for collection of funds in public places one weekend. I don't know whether my fear of participating had anything to do with possible physical danger: being roughed up by police or whoever. They were more probably the fears of an intellectual kid whose life had been spent going to school, roller-skating and playing ball games, reading and listening to his father talk. Now I had to go out and put my body where my heart was.

I do know that nothing that I have done since took as much guts as forcing myself, at age ten, to take one of the collection cans, go into the subway on a Saturday morning, and spend that full day and all the next day going from car to car calling out, "Help the starving miners' children!"

As the weekend progressed, it seemed that my arm would fall off. No one on the miners' side could afford to give paper money —$25 a week was the average wage—so the can, like an oversize beer can with cardboard sides, got fuller and fuller with coins. I could have burst with pride when it was broken open to count the contents when I brought it in. $18.03. That number has stayed with me for a lifetime. It is equivalent to hundreds of dollars in purchasing power today.

Our Young Pioneer troop put out a little local paper, mimeographed. A very pretty girl informed me that one should use a *nom de plume* for protection against possible persecution by the authorities. This was not paranoia. On July 15, 1930, an early red-hunting committee of the House of Representatives heard New York school principals and city government personnel at an executive session devoted to the Young Pioneers. Its transcript came to seventy-two pages. One witness, a Mr. Doty, principal of DeWitt Clinton High School in the Bronx, testified that he had been investigating Communist activities for ten years. He presented, as material evidence, a Young Pioneer membership card and a copy of our distinctive pledge of allegiance, which was to the cause of liberation of the working class. So I chose a pseudonym. As my mother was constantly insiting that my handwriting was terrible, my *nom de plume* was Splotch. Nice to know that I could joke at my own expense.

In the Young Pioneers we did a lot of very enjoyable, useful, commendable things. The first clubs of that organization had come into being in Chicago in 1923. Kids learned revolutionary songs, were taught the history of workers' movements, and engaged in sports and games. It came of age in 1926, when sixteen thousand textile workers in Passaic, New Jersey, went on strike after Botany Mills cut pay 10 percent and fired the entire committee of forty-five workers who had presented the demand that the cut be rescinded. The workers, who had been making $20 a week, joined a Communist-led union and walked out. Those who gave on-the-spot support included the famous and boundlessly courageous orator Elizabeth Gurley Flynn, then not yet a Communist. The strike lasted thirteen months, and actually won. The wage cut was cancelled, the right to organize into the American Federation of Labor was agreed to, and some recognition was granted to union grievance committees.

For such a strike to win, tremendous efforts were required to feed the workers. In Passaic, late teenage leaders of the Young Pioneers coming from New York City organized strike kitchens, clubs for strikers' children as well as child laborers, and set up playgrounds. The Pioneers advanced a simple slogan: "Children must not starve and freeze," and went door to door asking for donations of canned goods or whatever people could give.

The high point, related by the most militant of the New York Young Pioneers, Harry Eisman, then eleven years old and subsequently a buddy of mine in New York and the Soviet Union, came when the kids persuaded a worker who owned a tiny Ford truck to take them to Passaic for a day. They draped it with sympathetic slogans. After the bustle of teeming New York, these slum children were astonished by the quiet of the old New Jersey milltown. They were thrilled to meet the children their efforts had fed and clothed, and who were as determined to win as their parents.

I have other memories of that time. There were rides on the New York Central Railroad, for which Dad worked and on which he was therefore entitled to free or reduced-fare tickets. We would picnic at magnificent Kensico Reservoir, north of White Plains, about an hour from the city. I recall the masonry face of the dam, impressive even today, and at that time a wonder. I had learned to read, once I was past the alphabet, from Dad's copies of the *Engineering News-Record*, so dams were more meaningful to me than to others my age. I remember the marvel of the Hetch-Hetchy Aqueduct, and the professional pride with which Dad explained the achievement of carrying water to San Francisco over such a vast distance. All this was in the magazine. In real life there was no land west of the Hudson for me.

Someone we knew must have had an automobile, for at least once we were taken for a ride on the charming Bronx River Parkway that extends from New York clear to Kensico. In those days it was two lanes. There was nothing wider anywhere, outside cities. It really meandered, crossing that gentle stream on low stone-arch bridges again and again.

Like our family, the Jewish Communist sweatshop workers in New York sought a place to get out into fresh air. In 1925, they got together enough money to open a tent summer camp at a spectacular location on the east side of the Hudson River almost opposite West Point. The camp was called "Nitgedaiget," which is Yiddish for "Don't Worry."

It was decided that Camp Nitgedaiget would house children not only with their parents, but would also set aside a camp area for the Young Pioneers. This was truly exciting. We went out with fund-collection sheets to labor union meetings, Left political rallies, and picnics. Picnics run by workers' organizations were a favorite form of recreation in those years when the private car was an unimaginable luxury for most laboring people living in apartment-house cities. Buses were chartered to get to the picnic sites, which were often at or near the end of streetcar or subway lines. By the summer of 1926, the Young Pioneers had their first very own camp. A measure of Communist influence in this country in those years is that by the spring of 1930 there were fifteen such camps from coast to coast.

After elementary school—I attended P.S. 70—I went on to junior high schools 55 and 61, also in the Bronx. So did Eisman, a tough orphan whose parents had died back in Bessarabia, today Moldova. He came to America at age four, accompanied only by his ten-year-old sister. Here, they met the two older sisters—the eldest seventeen—and two older brothers. P.S. 61 boasted the most active, militant, and effective Young Pioneer troop in the country. It was one of the first to be established and reflected the largely Left-wing and predominantly poor Jewish workingclass neighborhood it drew its pupils from. Even those who came from the somewhat better-off outskirts of its district, like myself, were either of or very close to that social origin.

One of the first and most pressing issues at this junior-high school, which ran through the ninth grade, was overcrowding. It had three thousand five hundred pupils. The first issue of the monthly paper put out by the Pioneer troop, entitled *Young Spark,* carried a cover cartoon showing the school with kids popping out of the windows, from under the roof, and even from the chimney. There were morning and afternoon shifts, plus another starting at noon for first and second graders. Although the building was six stories high and a block long, no room was found for a buffet or cafeteria. Kids usually brought lunches from home and ate seated on the floor of the gymnasium, taking in their food along with the smell of sweat.

Either there or at Jr. High 55, which I attended before or after 61 (had we moved?) there was a nearby candy store where one could buy hot dogs. The store also served those marvelous New York malted milks, which cost a dime. I would crowd in with the other kids, order a malted, drink it, and sneak out without paying. I was broke because I spent my allowance— a quarter a week—on halvah, the Near Eastern sweet of which we Jews are very fond.

The Pioneers began issuing leaflets demanding that a new school be built nearby to relieve the overcrowding, and also that a cafeteria be opened at P.S. 61. The principal, Mr. McGuire, regarded himself as very democratic and established a student government modeled on that of New York City, with a mayor, a district attorney, a judge, and a city council, plus, of course, two political parties, called Independent and Tempo. Young Pioneers' meetings were often devoted to a serious discussion of what student self-government should be like. It was decided to demand the right to vote for seventh-graders—in addition to eighth and ninth-graders, to launch a third party with a platform (the others didn't have any), and to nominate candidates. A founding convention was held in the school auditorium, and the new party was given the name, Progressive. It put forth a three-plank platform: 1) open a cafeteria, 2) reduce overcrowding, and 3) bring that about by building an annex. A coalition was formed with the Tempo Party, which gladly endorsed the platform. Of the seven candidates on the joint slate, five won.

The first issue of our paper, *The Young Spark*, which I wrote for, was four pages long, the second eight. We produced the paper at the Young Pioneers' local headquarters on Boston Road, and funded it by collecting donations from adults and those kids who could afford it, for paper, ink, and stencils. I was never good at any of the technical work except turning the handle of the mimeograph. I wrote in longhand. We were totally thrilled when the more than a thousand copies of the first issue ran out in an hour or so. I think we charged a penny for it.

Mr. McGuire's devotion to democracy lasted exactly two issues. He then began to hunt out the Pioneers involved with the paper and tried to determine who did the distributing or selling. He gave speeches at school assemblies denouncing the Pioneers and the paper. The Pioneers responded to each of McGuire's speeches either in our paper or with special leaflets or speeches given by our representatives in the pupil legislature.

Principal McGuire realized that the legislature had changed from a body designed perhaps to give pupils a taste for politics, into one acting effectively in the interests of workers' children, so he dissolved it and set up an appointive honor society instead. When that coal miners' strike occurred, we tried to organize a collection program in school. McGuire urged that the collection be for the Red Cross instead of the coal miners' children. The Red Cross, however, would never come to the aid of workers on strike. The Pioneers' collection at school was successful.

May Day in those years was a holiday rigorously observed by working people of our persuasion. The holiday arose out of the 1886 execution of leaders of a Chicago demonstration for the eight-hour day. The United States was closer to its origins then and a genuine symbolism still reigned over holidays like July 4th and Memorial Day. For us, the workers' celebration on May Day remained the most important.

Through 1929, the May Day celebration was held indoors. That year it was in Madison Square Garden, on a weekday afternoon. The fact that a hall seating nearly twenty thousand was needed for those who would stay away from work or school speaks for the importance of this day. After the Great Depression began in October 1929, no hall could hold the crowds that wished to attend, and the thrilling May Day parades that climaxed with stupendous rallies at Union Square began in 1930. It was that year, I believe, that I heard Lucy Parsons speak.

Lucy came from a time nearly as far removed from then as the events

I am describing are from today's America. She seemed as totally archaic to us then as I found I did in 1989 to the actor in a professional Los Angeles theater company who was portraying me in a play, *McCarthy*. Lucy was the widow of Albert Parsons, one of the Haymarket Martyrs. In 1886 a demonstration demanding a reduction of the hours worked per day to eight was held at Haymarket Square in Chicago. McCormick Reaper Works employees had gone on strike for this. The demonstrations continued on May 1st, and the police killed six on May 3rd. At a meeting on the 4th, which also served to protest the previous day's events, a bomb was thrown and seven policemen died. The police then opened fire into the crowd. Although no one ever discovered or even pretended to know who had thrown the bomb, the eight leaders of the movement were tried on grounds of conspiracy to murder. The conspiracy law was used because it permits involvement to be shown by *circumstantial* evidence of association, and does not require proof that any of the individuals charged committed the deed. (During the McCarthy era, that, not espionage, was the law under which Ethel and Julius Rosenberg were executed.)

Four of the leaders of the eight-hour-day movement at Haymarket Square were executed, including Lucy's husband. Albert Parsons was white. It is a reflection of the depth of racism extending well into my time that Lucy always described herself as an American Indian. It is now known that she was part Black—but to have admitted that would have been to close most doors in her lifelong fight to vindicate and perpetuate the memories of her husband and his fellows. People belonging to a race the U.S. sought to exterminate were more acceptable than those whose enslavement was justified by the claim that they were mentally inferior to whites.

Starting in 1928 the Young Pioneers conducted school strikes on May Day. The number of pupils involved must have been pretty large, for fourteen gathering points all over New York were specified where kids were to assemble before proceeding to Madison Square Garden. The authorities tried to counter May Day by proclaiming May first Child Health Day. The Pioneers responded with a leaflet reminding its readers that, by official count, there were 3.5 million child laborers in the country. The U.S. Supreme Court had recently thrown out as unconstitutional two federal child labor laws that had made it through Congress.

Principal McGuire sought to prevent absenteeism on May Day by announcing general examinations. Anyone who missed them would not be promoted to the next higher grade at the end of the term. The Pioneers consulted with their advisors of the Young Communist League, who said that he could leave back ten or a dozen Pioneers, but could not do this if mass absenteeism occurred. So a picket line was set up and vigorous discussions took place as children decided whether or not to go to school.

Suddenly police emerged from the building. Police assigned to school-buildings were simply unheard-of in those pre-drug, pre-weapons days. Five children were arrested, including my friend Harry Eisman. They were taken before a judge who ordered them taken back to school to attend class. Harry protested vocally, and was taken to juvenile hall. That night a demonstration was held outside the detention center to demand his freedom. Freed on bail, he was called before Mr. McGuire and asked to guarantee that the Young Pioneers' school paper would fold. Harry said he would promise not to engage personally in its distribution, but could not speak for others. He was expelled.

Perhaps the temper of the times among workingpeople is indicated best by the Young Pioneers' move in 1929, *before* the stock-market crash and great depression, to send a children's delegation to observe the life of children in the Soviet Union. It consisted of a white Appalachian boy, Elmar MacDonald, who was from the textile town of Gastonia, North Carolina, where Communists were leading a strike; Delia Morelli, daughter of a Pennsylvania coal-miner; Jessie Taft, a Jewish girl from the Bronx; an auto worker's son named Marion; and Shelley Strickland, an African-American from Philadelphia who had left the Boy Scouts, which we opposed as militarist. Labor unions were approached to fund the delegation. One union that supported the delegation said, "The Hotel, Restaurant, and Cafeteria Workers' Union warmly approves your campaign to send the first delegation of children of American workers to the Soviet Union. Our union recently conducted a major struggle with the bosses, and workers' children belonging to the Young Pioneers often helped our fight for better working conditions for food workers. It was impossible to cow these children with threats of arrests and beatings. They continued to walk the picket lines even though truant officers were sent after them. This proves that the workers' children are loyal fighters for the cause of the working class."

That group's trip to the USSR was voluntary. Harry Eisman's was not. A Young Pioneer demonstration against the Boy Scouts was dispersed by mounted police. Harry used an established technique in dealing with that kind of interference. He stuck a cop's horse with an open safety pin. Since he was not a citizen, he was deported. The federal authorities were going to send him to Rumania, a semi-fascist country. We mounted a national campaign to permit his emigration to the Soviet Union, which was willing to accept him. We won.

At age ten, I was both an activist and a little boy. My father would come home by subway, first on the elevated IRT West Bronx train, and then on the "A" train under the Grand Concourse. I remember the very clean smell through its air grates when the concrete was still fresh and the trains rushed by. Dad could snap his fingers very loudly indeed. My head out the window of our third-floor apartment, I could hear the snaps when he was a full block away, and would run down to meet him.

I also had a special fantasy world, distinctly a boy's. In his autobiography, the 20th-century writer Alexei Tolstoy describes how in his childhood he was the hero of great imaginary events, on horseback. I had read *The Three Musketeers* and Jules Verne, of course. I too fantasized about a group I called the "59"—I don't know why I chose that particular number. We rode on horseback, naturally, and I was the leader. We were out serving the interests of the Revolution.

Between my father's interest in social change and my mother's in culture (I inherited my quite decent singing voice from her), I chose to follow my father. Nonetheless, Mother was my rescuer in certain situations. When Dad would pressure me too much to stop day-dreaming and do my homework, Mother would intervene with a Polish phrase, "Dai mu spokoj"—leave him alone. The reason she used Polish, and would occasionally converse with Dad in that language, was that I quickly learned to understand Yiddish since they used it to prevent me from knowing what was being said. English was the language at home except for saying things the children were not to hear.

My youngest uncle, Dave, was eight years older than I and had a serious interest in girls when I was not yet a teenager. Dad was always trying to convert everyone to communism. Naturally, I believed what my father wanted me to believe, particularly as my mother supported the same ideas, albeit always secondary to the immediate welfare of her family. But Dave would taunt me endlessly with the question, What would communism do about the eternal triangle? And inasmuch as I had fallen in love with Vera Babad, and was quite aware that she might choose to love some boy other than myself, I didn't know how to answer. I still don't.

Memories of Grandma's lima-bean soup and the rich, fat roast chicken that East-European Jewish people loved, the gravy-laden mashed potatoes and the homemade applesauce that, to me, is still the best of all desserts when made right, evoke images of her tiny Lower East Side restaurant. We lived over eight miles north, in the Bronx. Somewhere between the ages of ten and fourteen I took it upon myself, doubtless with permission, to walk down to her place while the family went by subway. It is quite possible that the first walk was with my father. Long walks were his one exercise, throughout life, and they also became one of mine. I got to know the bridges across the Harlem River, Morningside Heights with its stunning view westward across the Hudson, and the fine view eastward over Harlem and the East River to Queens and Brooklyn. Then came the dip to the valley of 125th St., and, most wonderful of all, Central Park from 110th down to 59th.

I looked with curiosity and with disdain for all things luxurious and aristocratic, at the marvelous painted Easter eggs from the treasures of the Russian tsar in the Armand Hammer store window on 5th Avenue. Half a century later, Hammer was the oil tycoon who made money by his willingness to do business with the USSR under Brezhnev. I did not know then that those eggs, the oil paintings that hung above them, and the golden dinnerware and jewelry glittering behind the glass were the manner in which Lenin had paid him for building the first factory to make pencils in the Soviet Union so common people could enjoy the tools of literacy.

Farther down 5th was the awesome Public Library, meaningful to me because I had known from very early childhood the treasures the local branches held. From 5th I would swing a block west to 6th Avenue, later renamed Avenue of the Americas. Then, as today, it was the teeming garment district. Neither the art nouveau Chrysler Building, nor the Empire State, with its tower designed as a mooring for dirigibles, yet existed. Within a couple of years, I would watch the Chrysler Building be erected from my classroom in Townsend Harris High School at 23rd St. at Lexington Avenue. But at this time the skyscrapers huddled around Wall Street near the 60-story neo-Gothic Woolworth Building—the world's tallest for probably a full generation.

In those early years of kid power and independence, we roasted mickeys in a can over a coal fire in an empty lot on Boston Road near my junior high school in the East Bronx. This was a boyhood ritual of autumn and winter. Mickeys, if you don't know, are potatoes, and the word doubtless has to do with the Irish, who were potato eaters. (Or, rather, they ate more potato than the other poor, but Russians sure eat them a lot).

I have no idea where we got the potatoes. We could have snatched them from stores or from our mothers' pantries, or possibly bought them from pushcart peddlers. I do know where we got the coal. The steam heat that warmed the apartment houses and tenements, more or less—depending on whether the landlord was sufficiently afraid of the law, or unsuccessful in bribing it, to give heat the number of hours and at the temperature a city ordinance required—came from coal-fired boilers. Every day, somewhere in the neighborhood, a house would be getting its load of coal delivered down a chute. In my earliest memories, the coal wagons were horse-drawn, but they were just about the first to be replaced by trucks. Coal that bounced out of the chute and onto the street was ours to take, by some unwritten rule. Strangely, it was harder to find wood to start fires. We would scout around fruit and vegetable stores for broken crates to get the coal burning.

The mickeys were always over-roasted, their skins hard enough for only children's teeth to bite through. Spots were charred to carbon. Generally we were not successful in getting them out without burning our fingers, but I don't remember burns bad enough to blister.

The movies provided more cheap thrills. Chaplin's *The Gold Rush*, was released when I was eight. Douglas Fairbanks, who I first saw at three in *The Mark of Zorro*, remains etched in my mind, leaping from bannister to cabinet top and always successfully scratching his "Z" with his sword-tip on the bad guys. I remember Harold Lloyd, when I was six, hanging from the hands of a clock several stories above a street, in *Safety Last*. In later years I learned it was not photographic trickery, but a stunt as dangerous as it looked, which he performed himself. This was in an ethnically-charged time. The fact that Fairbanks and Chaplin were Jewish was not public knowledge. I should add, for young generations, that there simply was no such thing as a Black in films then, outside some made by and for Harlem, except as caricatured targets of comedy. African-Americans were not to be taken seriously, not even as villains.

Some films were no fun at all. Fritz Lang's *Metropolis*, which I saw when I was nine, scared me to death. His notion of human beings later in the 20th century as empty robots assaulted my sense of humanity, my gut attitude toward life. The film that really shook me was Conrad Veidt in *The Man Who Laughs*. It is essentially a Pagliacci story about a child of the times when human beings were physically made into grotesques for entertainment. That great actor portrayed movingly the sufferings of a complete human being reduced outwardly to a two-dimensional cartoon.

The first great Soviet films were made at this very stage of my life. I saw them as soon as they were brought to this country, within about a year of their release. *Potemkin* was made when I was eight, and Pudovkin's *Mother* was released when I was nine. The former is the true story of a mutiny on a Russian warship during that revolution of 1905 in which my father participated as an eleven-year-old. The latter, based on the novel by Maxim Gorky, tells of a strike in that same period. The mother of a young worker, who initially opposes his militant and revolutionary activity, learns from the treachery and faithlessness of the police and other authorities which side she should be on.

The USSR was the only country whose films, virtually without exception, left one with a feeling of hope for the future even when they ended tragically. Downbeat films were suppressed. But why were many optimistic ones successful as movies? The answer would seem to be faith. Just as the great cathedrals represent not reality but the ideals of their builders, so these films embodied the ideals and hopes of human brotherhood that underlay the Communist experiment. That it failed does not invalidate these movies any more than the failure of Christianity to bring peace on earth negates the genius of those who built or painted or sculpted with inspired piety.

I suppose some people become courageous all at once, or are born with tremendous courage. That was not my experience. For me, courage had more to do with how deeply an issue or event moved me personally, and also with matters in which I was personally challenged either to defend my dignity or slink away with my tail between my legs.

In January, 1930, the New York City police murdered a striking bakery worker, Steve Katovis.Two other striking workers were killed elsewhere in the nation that year, and six were slain in a single volley the previous year in a North Carolina textile strike. However, such events had never previously occurred in New York. The sense of horror, revulsion, and protest among working people and their supporters at the Katovis murder was intense. Fifty thousand turned out for the funeral procession, including me. I was twelve.

The parade started somewhere on the middle East Side of New York, proceeded up to one of the bridges across the East River, then over it to the cemetery in Queens— several miles in all. I don't know how many mounted police New York City kept as its private cavalry, or whether those who reached the cemetery first galloped or were trucked back to the rest of the parade. However, I know that, marching a dozen or more abreast, we were hemmed in by so many mounted cops that my memory is of horses muzzle to crupper as far as the eye could see.

Though I had the guts to attend that event, I shrank, knowing the danger, from attending the first nationwide mass demonstrations two months later for what is now called welfare—then it was called "relief". This movement was conducted under Communist leadership. Although that organization had no more than ten thousand members at the time nationwide, most of them foreign-born, the attendance at the rallies on March 6, 1930 was stupendous: 110,000 in New York, 100,000 in Detroit, 50,000 each in Chicago and Pittsburgh, 40,000 in Milwaukee, 30,000 in Philadelphia, 25,000 in Cleveland, 20,000 in Youngstown, and others in Los Angeles, Boston, San Francisco, Seattle, Denver, and elsewhere.

These unemployed were not Communists. They were hungry. With no unemployment insurance or welfare system, the Salvation Army and other private charities could not begin to feed the millions suddenly thrown out of work after the Great Crash of October 1929. The Communists were alone in saying that the government had the responsibility to do something, and people followed them. William Schneiderman, leader of the Communist Party in California later in the decade, tells in his autobiography of a line stretching around the block to join the Communist Party in San Francisco after one such demonstration. It included bankrupt businessmen, jobless engineers, even an ex-cop.

I decided not to go because the New York City authorities stated in advance that the demonstration would not be allowed to march to City Hall to present its demands to the playboy mayor, Jimmy Walker, the very personification of the movie version of the Roaring '20s. Twenty-five thousand police and firemen were mobilized to attack demonstrators. They did, with great brutality. Five leaders of the demonstration were sent to jail for three years. They included Robert Minor, who, a dozen years earlier, was America's most famous cartoonist, working at Pulitzer's *St. Louis Post-Dispatch* and New York *World,* but who was now editor of the Communist *Daily Worker.* The son of a Texas judge, Minor was a broad-shouldered giant with a glorious, kindly smile and a voice that could be heard throughout Madison Square Garden in the years before amplification. He had been in Russia right after the Revolution. (I always regretted that Minor had abandoned his crayons for direct politics. One of his cartoons showing Black sharecroppers fleeing North in the early 1920s, and another depicting mounted police herding striking miners into a stockade remain in my mind's eye to this day.) Later he was one of those responsible for instilling leader-worship into the American Communist movement. I remember him introducing Earl Browder, the Kansas accountant who later led the Party, as "the greatest living American." If John Reed deserved a movie, so unquestionably does Bob Minor.

So, too, does another of the men sent to jail for organizing the demonstration of March 6, 1929, William Zebulon Foster, Irish-English from the poorest slums of Philadelphia, and at that time the head of the Communist Party. Foster began as a laborer in a stinking factory where horses were melted down for glue and maggots carpeted the floor. Later he became a railroad worker and then, before the Party existed, he was an American Federation of Labor organizer who led the first nationwide strikes *ever* in the supposedly unorganizable meat-packing and steel industries. When a heart attack during his campaign for the presidency in 1932 made him a semi-invalid, he turned to writing books, both political histories and personal reminiscences. One of them, *Pages From a Worker's Life,* contains enough true adventure to make a TV series that would go on for years.

My political convictions had already been firmly established by the execution of Sacco and Vanzetti in 1927, the semi-permanent U.S. military occupation of Nicaragua turned that year against Augusto Sandino, the beheadings of Communists by Nationalists in China reported in our general press, by Harry Eisman's deportation, by the shootings of the North Carolina strikers, by hearing Lucy Parsons and others, by the readings I have described, and by discussions with my father, who had spent most of a year in the Soviet Union, 1925-26, and believed socialism was being built there. It is also a matter of historical record that Joseph Stalin had predicted the Great Depression a year or two before its onset. I knew of that and found his reasoning sound. To me, therefore, the conduct of the authorities, whether in killing Steve Katovis or in clubbing down and jailing the March 6th demonstrators, was simply to be expected. I was convinced that a socialist revolution was the only solution. I never dreamed, nor did my father, that it could eat its own children. The only thing unusual about all this is that it occurred in the mind of a child between the ages of eight and ten. We recognize precocity in art, music, mathematics. Perhaps it can also exist in civic thought and activity.

An event in March 1931 made me think about the status of Blacks in this country for the first time. Nine young African-Americans, aged thirteen to twenty, riding the rails in search of work, were pulled off a train in Scottsboro, Alabama, and charged with raping two young white women on the same train. The nine were very quickly convicted, and *The Daily Worker* carried a banner headline calling it a frame-up. My reaction was to wonder how the *Daily Worker* knew that the defendants were not guilty? I did not yet know that allegations of rape had been the historical excuse for lynching or legally framing African-Americans, thereby terrorizing them into accepting whatever pay or conditions plantation owners would offer subsequent to the abolition of slavery, and for generally preventing Blacks from raising their heads.

One of the alleged victims in this case, Ruby Bates, had the extraordinary courage to walk into an Alabama courtroom in1933, at age nineteen, and deny the testimony she had given two years earlier. This reopened the case. On the earlier occasion she had been jailed, feared being tried for vagrancy, and cooperated with the prosecution.

The fight for the lives of the Scottsboro Boys, as they were universally known, lasted seven years, and was successful. It resulted in one of several extensions of American democracy for which the Communist Party deserves credit, in this case a U.S. Supreme Court ruling that systematic exclusion of Blacks from jury service constitutes a violation of Federal law. There were no Blacks on juries when I was a kid, and of course no Black judges. Black female judges were beyond anyone's imagining.

There were some African-American lawyers, and one of them led that fight, more in public demonstrations and the press than in the courts. San Francisco-born William L. Patterson had a thriving practice in Harlem in the '20s, and was a friend of Paul Robeson's. Convinced that Sacco and Vanzetti were innocent, he was chased around Boston Commons as the only Black in a demonstration in that case. He became a Communist and abandoned his law practice, devoting the rest of his life to organizing the defense of victims of political, labor, and racial persecution.

CHAPTER 3

Affirmative-Action University: Moscow

My memories of high school are sporadic and a bit fickle. The "Hygiene" teacher in New York's public high school for bright boys, Townsend Harris, scared a crowd of kids entering puberty, including me, by telling us we could get syphilis from dirty toilet seats. I hated gym classes. I have always loved athletics, but not the monotonous motions of calisthenics or indoor conditioning machines. I see the faces of two French teachers, one a young woman, very pretty and very good; the other, a veteran of World War I, interested us in the language by teaching us the dirty songs learned by Americans who fought in France. I still remember the tunes, but few of the words. The German teacher was excellent, a Prussian if ever there was one. His favorite story, told to each successive class, was how his father made him eat lentil soup which he couldn't stand, and he got even by vomiting it into father's boot. My senior-year math teacher was a walking cartoon of someone who lived by numbers. Never mind his stiff starched collar, held on by a collar-pin. Naturally, all male teachers wore ties and suits. And of course the suits were three-piece, complete with vest, no matter how hot the New York weather in May or September.

My math teacher had his grading system down to what he thought was a numerical science. We were graded three times per semester. In the second third of my final term I flunked four subjects out of six. The rules required that such a student drop one or more courses, on the assumption that he would be able to concentrate on the others enough to pass. That wasn't my problem. I was bored to tears. At math, however, I was really bad. I love applied statistics, and for years calculated Soviet economic growth rates or educational progress, or comparisons between the rate of advance of Soviet Central Asia and neighboring non-Soviet countries, using simple arithmetic and algebra. But abstract math for its own sake, even things as simple as the rules of geometry, is not for me.

At this time Dad had signed a contract with the Soviet railroad system to work there as a civil engineer. The whole family was to go: mother, kid brother, and myself. My father had scheduled departure for immediately after my graduation from high school. With dropped courses, I would not get a diploma. Dad sat me down and asked, "Don't you want to go to Moscow University?" Sure I did. In the first place, what else would I do over there? I was fourteen, entirely too young to work, and a little frightened of the idea. Secondly, here was my chance to become a geneticist and follow in the footsteps of my childhood hero, Luther Burbank, the developer of extraordinary hybrid flowers in far-off Santa Rosa, California. Theoretical genetics didn't interest me. It was still all Mendelian, involving breeding quick generations of fruit flies. Molecular genetics didn't yet exist. Dad had sold me on communism. We would help build the brave new world—the Soviet Union was just as old as I was then, in 1931—and live there happily forever after. We took all our belongings, the complete furnishings of a four-room apartment. Dad knew of the shortages of consumer goods from his job in Siberia in 1926. We shipped an upright piano for me, and a standing phonograph with our two hundred breakable records.

I promised Dad that I would drop my handball playing for that final month and buckle down to study. My father also went to my school and persuaded the principal to bend the rules and give me the chance to try to graduate, because many plans depended upon it. I kept my end of the promise and all went well, except that the math teacher calculated that my term's work was worth a sixty-four, one point below the passing grade. Dad traipsed back to school and somehow persuaded him to let the Moscow authorities jack up my knowledge of his precious discipline. So I graduated.

The evening before our departure for the Soviet Union I was quite excited. I guess we had previously moved out of our apartment in the Bronx, because the walk I took that evening was from Grandma's little restaurant on East 7th St. in Manhattan to the bottom of Central Park at 59th. By the time I got there it was dark. On the way back I walked eastward on 56th Street. A man approached me, and invited me into a doorway to say he'd show me something interesting. I realized it was a sexual approach, and walked away as fast as I could. I didn't run. Dignity has always apparently been important to me. I run for fun, or toward someone who has been hurt in an accident. Otherwise I walk. I don't remember ever having run away from cops attacking a demonstration. I walk. Strangely, my slow pace probably saved me from getting clubbed or run down by their motorbikes or horses. Cops generally assume that if you run, you're one of the people they're supposed to teach a lesson to.

I gave no conscious thought to that man's approach. I imagine that, combined with the universal rejection of "deviant" behavior in that day and for decades later, it led to my unthinking acceptance of stereotypical attitudes toward homosexuals until the rebellion of gays and, subsequently, lesbians, in the 1960s and '70s, compelled me to re-examine my views.

The next morning we left for the USSR. Trans-Atlantic air travel was then only dreamed of by writers for *Fantastic Stories*, the magazine that gave birth to sci-fi . We crossed the Atlantic on the S.S. Majestic, the biggest ship of its day, a war trophy gained from Germany. I remember the distinctive, not unpleasant smell of ship's cabins and corridors, the solid meals, the turns around deck, and particularly the shuffleboard games. That was serious political business. I quickly learned that one of the regular players was an American Socialist on his way to a convention of the Socialist International. Since I was a Communist, he was, of course, the enemy—a betrayer of the workingclass. That was not my invention, but the Party line, based on its view of the behavior of Socialist parties in Germany and elsewhere immediately following World War I. At that time they had refused to conduct, and in some cases smashed, revolutions of the workingclass designed to bring that class to power. I don't remember whether I won the shuffleboard competition or not, but I sure tried.

My most vivid memory of that trip is of an incident as I stood high on the deck of the *Majestic* when we put in to the Irish port of Cobh. When it came to rest, a tiny raft clung to its bow, bearing a young man and woman. Did they have an instrument, a harp? I don't recall. But I will never forget the gauntness of his face, the cap extended for coins, and the excruciating sadness of that high tenor. It was music I had never heard before, but the mark of poverty, and a misery that was not material, was in it. I knew of Ireland's Easter Rebellion from the reading matter to which I had been guided by my father. It is no accident that, thirty-five years later, my daughter named one of her boys for Kevin Barry, executed martyr of that struggle, although her son is Jewish on both sides. She had grown up to the strains of:

> Shoot me like an Irish soldier,
> Do not hang me like a dog,
> For I fought for Ireland's freedom
> On that dark September morn.

My hymns were of all nations: German—"Auf, auf, zum Kampf, zum Kampf"—Arise to the Struggle, to the Communist martyrs Karl Liebknecht and Rosa Luxembourg; Polish—"Czerwoni Sztandar"—The Red Flag, from my father; the marvelously satirical anthem of the American Industrial Workers of the World: "Long-haired preachers come out every night, Just to tell us what's wrong and what's right" and their equally sardonic jibes at employer-owned police and judges. And, of course, the stupendous sweep of the Polish-into-Russian and then worldwide revolutionary anthem, "Whirlwinds of danger are raging around us." As the years went by, the chorus of Beethoven's Ninth— "Alle Menschen werden Brüder", all humans will be brothers—became more and more important to me.

Of London I remember coal soot. It was so deep on the columns of neo-classical buildings that I could sink my finger in it up to the joint. I loved those great old square black taxis, their bodies then still shaped to imitate the horse-drawn carriages they had replaced, their roofs high enough so gentlemen didn't need to doff their top hats. Coming from New York, where tidal changes are so small that dwellers near the Hudson and East rivers are unaware of them, I was amazed, when we went to the Soviet ship that was to take us to Leningrad, to see that vessel sitting high and dry on the bottom of the Thames.

I have only one memory of the remaining days of our journey to Moscow: the extraordinary platters of smoked salmon and sturgeon that graced the tables. Those luxuries attracted foreign passengers who would pay their fares in hard currency. There was also the aroma of a porridge, *pshenau*, that was one of the hallmarks of Moscow in that hungry year. The diet was limited to that, cabbage, and bread. Surviving Russians of my generation simply will not touch *pshenau*.

Leningrad remains in memory as a gloomy turn-of-the-century hotel with rooms immensely large, immensely over-furnished, and immensely high. Today the train to Moscow is an overnight ride. Then it was considerably longer, but I have no memory of it. Dramatic terrain would have caught my eye, but this is virtually flat, wooded country. When I was seventy, I made that trip on foot in a Soviet-American Peace Walk, and became aware of every rise and dip and landscape, but at fourteen I probably had my head buried in a book.

Dad's contract provided for a private apartment, but it wasn't ready for many weeks after we arrived. In those days Russians had no sense of time. It is no accident that one of the first factories Stalin had built made watches. Their "seechahss", meaning "right now", was the equivalent of the Spanish "mañana"—any time down the road. We were put up in the Balchug Hotel, right at the end of the Moscow River bridge leading to the Kremlin. Under Yeltsin, some foreign firm rebuilt it for the ultra-luxury trade, because of its location, and its casino became a hangout for the Al Caponeskis of the period. In our day it was one step above a flophouse, no sign of elegance. There was a cafeteria beneath us, which stank, and open garbage cans on the sidewalk. Flies throve on this, entered our windows innocent of screens, and drove my mother wild. They were huge blue-bottles, with plenty of manure to vary their diet, for the one-horse peasant wagon, with no sides, was the prevalent vehicle, except for streetcars.

I remember the streetcars' control-boxes, with the cast-iron imprimatur of the major German firm that supplied them before the Revolution. They had open platforms, which were fearsome in the freezing winter, when the bottom step was plain ice. For that matter, there was danger in the summer too, because the city was bursting at the seams with the industrialization of the First Five-Year Plan. People would stand on the steps, forced to lean outward by the tremendous press of bodies when the last passenger leapt on. To leap on when the car was moving as fast as one could run was common. It was not uncommon to fail to make it, and suffer a fracture or loss of limb or life either from the wheels of the car or from being brushed by a passing truck. Construction of the metro had only just begun.

For the great holidays, May Day and November 7th, anniversary of the Communist revolution, all streetcar lines were re-routed so a million or so people could assemble, parade through Red Square, and drift out the other end. On those days the lines that ran were fairly empty. On May Day I remember standing on a streetcar platform in my plus-fours, the knickers boys in the U.S. wore at that time. I also had on vivid blue knee-socks and a bulky jacket, topped by a beret worn at a rakish angle. A month short of fifteen, I had shot up three inches without gaining a pound during my, by then, nearly full year in Moscow, and could best be described as willowy. A bearded peasant in homespun jacket, standard hand-plaited birchbark sandals atop rag leggings, and a huge gunny-sack over his shoulder, looked up at me from the street. He was totally confused by the holiday re-routing. He peered at my outfit, which was unlike anything he had ever seen before, could not decide on my gender, and asked: "Does this car go to the Square of the Revolution?" Long pause: "Citizeness?"

The streets were fascinating. I imagine there was a barracks not far away from our hotel, past which soldiers marched to and from the Kremlin. The truly wonderful Russian marching songs designed to eat up the dozens or hundreds of miles as one trudged from the nearest railway station could be heard day and night. All my life, on long hikes, I have paced myself by singing those songs. They have a long swing that is as distinctly Russian as military precision identifies their German counterpart. One man would carry the tune, and the whole platoon would take up the chorus, devising harmonies.

The songs were revolutionary, not only in their words but also in their music. I have heard the soldiers' songs of prerevolutionary times. They reflected the sadness of being drafted for unwanted service, and the hopeless expectation of dying far from home. There was a diametrically opposite spirit in the songs that came out of, or were written for, the Red Army during the Civil War of 1918-20 and that were still sung most wholeheartedly when I was there that year of 1931-32. I still heard them once in a while half a century later from Sunday workingclass crowds on the Moscow River taxis going to and from picnics in Gorky Park or Lenin Hills.

Across the street from our hotel was the first huge residential development of the post-revolutionary period. It housed government and party personnel and staff of the Communist International. After Khrushchev denounced Stalin's mass murders in 1956, the walls sprouted an endless series of handsome plaques to its distinguished— executed— one-time residents. This massive high-rise block also contained an architecturally splendid movie theater, erected just in time for the fine film-making of the early '30s. Downriver, between that housing project on our side and the Kremlin on the other, were the golden domes of a stupendous cathedral built by public subscription in the late 19th century to commemorate Napoleon's retreat from Moscow in 1812. It was torn down while I was in Moscow, one of the very few major religious structures to be physically destroyed under communism. It was rebuilt by Moscow's mayor under Yeltsin.

I knew no Russian when we arrived in Moscow, so my parents hired a tutor. She was what was then called "*bivshaya*," a woman of the past. Not at all a woman *with* a past. The term meant a member of the classes ousted from wealth and power by the Revolution.

In addition to learning Russian, I spent the first months exploring the city and doing sports in Gorky Park. There were a bunch of American kids in Moscow and some in Leningrad. A very few, like my brother and me, were the children of professionals, mostly engineers. Most were the children of skilled workers. The parents in both categories were chiefly emigrants from the Russian Empire like my father, and nearly all had come because of a desire to help build a new kind of human society. Not only those of my generation, but also our immigrant parents had been thoroughly Americanized in their fifteen or twenty years in the U.S., despite foreign accents and retention of their mother tongues. They had generally come to America in their teens, and now found it impossible to accept Russian inefficiency, sloppiness, and primitive work methods, particularly the distinctively Russian combination of loafing or dawdling followed by a stupendous outburst of energy and endless hours of work to get something finished. I'm inclined to think this habit originates from Russia's climatic conditions, with six months of snowed-in winter hibernation during which there really wasn't much a peasant could do outdoors, followed by a brief growing season during which he had to labor like a Titan to get the plowing, seeding, and harvesting done before snow and cold shut everything down again.

My brother and all the other kids attended the Anglo-American School. As a university student I was in a category of my own, even thought I didn't enter until I acquired a working knowledge of Russian. In the meanwhile I went to the Central Park of Culture and Recreation named in honor of the writer Maxim Gorky. The park's unique and pioneering staff of recreation leaders served whoever chose to come. They would teach round dances, old and new, lecture on the evils of alcoholism and the wonders of farm machinery or aviation, or on world affairs. There were farm machines on exhibit, as awesome to the Russian countryfolk as to us city kids from the States. There were great papier-mache cartoon sculptures of drunks, and really fine models of the aircraft of the day, including one called the Maxim Gorky, with six or eight engines, the largest dry-land aircraft anywhere. The Germans had a flying boat that was bigger.

The government was then busily deciding what sports to popularize. There hadn't been any in old Russia, except wrestling, a primitive kind of weightlifting that didn't use barbells, and indigenous folk games, plus fencing and riding among the rich . But within weeks of arriving in the Soviet Union I saw women rowing eight-oar shells in the Moscow River, a sport to which they were not admitted in the West till decades later.

There were two huge Vassar canoes on the river, real U.S. Indian design, holding sixteen persons. A young adult Soviet steersman always went along, but that didn't prevent a wonderful accident one day. We Americans filled one of the canoes: fifteen of us plus the Russian. We headed away from the city, then with a quarter of its present population. Soon we came to a bathing beach. In those days, nude bathing was the rule rather than the exception. There was a long, not particularly solid fence separating the women's and men's beaches—something new to these American adolescents. I think we were all boys in the boat. One yelled: "Hey, do you see what I see?" and stood up to see better. Everyone else followed suit. I was in the bow of the boat, and next thing I knew I was diving to the bottom for dear life as the immense parrot-beak prow of the capsized canoe bore down on me through the water. Fortunately, there were numerous kayaks on the river—a type of boat unknown in the U.S. at that time, but popular in Germany—and they quickly rescued us all.

The softballs we played with were much harder than the pillow-like ball used at that time back home. We knew how to catch a hard-hit softball barehanded by pulling our hands back at impact to cushion the shock. The Russians who joined us in pick-up games didn't, and caught in the style of a soccer goalie: arms extended in front of the head directly in the path of the ball, heels of palms together and fingers spread out stiffly. When they'd go for a real high fly or a line drive that way, I always winced in anticipation of a broken nose or finger. It never happened.

I once played softball before a World-Series size crowd, although I doubt that the crowd appreciated it. As part of the attempt to popularize unfamiliar sports, we were asked to play an exhibition game between halves of a major-league soccer game that filled the 50,000-seat Dynamo Stadium. I'm sure the spectators were totally mystified. I had a raging fever that day, but concealed it from my mother until I got home. However, I was so sick that I spent most of the game lying on my back. That had its reward. That biggest-plane-in-the-world, the Maxim Gorky, swooped over very low en route to a landing at the then Moscow airport, a mile from the stadium, and gave me a great thrill.

During winter vacation, the kids attending the Anglo-American School were taken for a week to a camp outside Moscow that was normally a rest, recreation, and high-nutrition facility for pre-tubercular Soviet children. I was asked to come along as a liaison between the American kids and the Soviet staff, since I was the age of the former, but a university student. There were a couple dozen pair of skis behind the doors and on the porch of the main building. None of us had ever seen skis before. Skiing didn't exist in America, but for some Scandinavians in the Midwest, a few descendants of mountain men in California, and a handful of rich kids who had been to Europe.

The biggest or toughest kids grabbed what they thought were the best skis, carved their initials in them and told the littler ones they'd knock them silly if they dared to use the skis. The Soviet teachers were horrified. They came to our teachers and asked what they were going to do about this. Meetings were held, with both staffs present, to explain the collectivist approach to property. For the first few days the kids supported the toughs because they were the gang leaders. Gradually the staff won them over. I helped, but don't remember details. Finally, the children ostracized those who had hogged the skis, as the Soviet staff proposed they do. The skis were not taken from the "outlaws" by force. Nor were these kids ousted from the camp, although there was some talk of sending them home. What impressed me was the real shock of the Soviet staff at the very notion that kids would be proprietary. I was left with the thought that the less than fifteen years since the Revolution had been sufficient to give Russian children a collectivist outlook, and therefore when they encountered individualism they were appalled. In retrospect, knowing Soviet psychology in the last decades of that system, when the notion was widespread that something that belonged to no-one individually had no owner, and therefore could be taken by anyone, I wonder whether the Soviet camp staff and children both came from devoted Communist families rather than representing the general public attitude.

The camp had its Russian faults. The outhouses were so filthy that I preferred to freeze my behind in that ferocious cold rather than use them. One night in our bunks in converted peasant log cottages, I woke to a peculiar low sound and unpleasant odor. When I opened my eyes the wall seemed diagonally striped. As my vision became sharper, I realized it was an army, or perhaps all the world's armies, of cockroaches. Yet we not only survived but had a wonderful time despite things like this. I was a skiier for over sixty years thereafter, thanks to learning how to ride those wide boards with nothing but toe-straps down the rolling hills of that camp outside Moscow, and shuffle them cross country.

While at the camp I also got to meet Mikhail Borodin. Four years earlier, the name Mikhail Borodin would appear almost daily in the American press. In 1923 the father of Chinese independence, Dr. Sun Yat-sen, turned to the USSR for assistance. It sent him, says the *Britannica,* "an extraordinarily capable agent, Mikhail Borodin." In my eyes he was a hero. After Dr. Sun's death, Chiang Kai-shek won out over the Communists for what was to be more than twenty years, and sent Borodin home.

The probable reason for his visiting our camp was that Borodin's wife was the head of the Institute of Foreign Languages. They were both Jewish. He had the type of walrus moustache that sweeps down into the mouth, and I watched in fascination as he wiped it with his napkin after each spoonful of the thick borshch or *shchi* that we were served at camp. After the meal, he pulled out a small pistol from the pocket of his bulky winter coat, and gave us the first display of target shooting I had ever seen. He was good.

In Moscow I also met Americans who fleshed out my knowledge of my own country. There were two clubs for foreigners, the Engineers' Club, to which my father belonged, and the Anglo-American Workers' Club, which is where I hung out. One night I ran into four Americans, sandy-haired, blue-eyed, speaking an obviously native English that at first I simply could not understand. In 1929 there had been a textile strike in Gastonia, North Carolina, against conditions that make those in a feature film of the 1980s, "Norma Rae," look Utopian. Communists from the North had offered support in the strike, and it had been accepted. They included a young woman of nineteen from the Bronx, Sophie Gerson, very much alive at this writing. Ella May Wiggins, a local Appalachian mother of five children, strike leader, writer and singer of workers' folk-songs, was shot dead on her way to a strike meeting. From then on there was no stopping the mountain people from carrying and loading the guns they normally used for hunting. When the chief of police led a raid on the strikers' tent colony—they had been evicted from the company-owned houses—he was shot and killed. He had been hit in the balls, incidentally. Mountain men usually hit where they aim. Seven strike leaders were sentenced to terms of from five to twenty years. They appealed, were out on bail, and several skipped and went to Moscow.

Their presence, and the conditions they sought to combat, led to my meeting another American, and also unexpectedly earning my first money ever. The *Moscow News,* an English-language paper, had just been established. I read the American press. I was struck by a story about kids in Appalachia who were, at the time, reduced to living off dandelions. I wrote a little piece based on that fact, probably sentimental and emotional, and submitted it to the *Moscow News.* Next time I came to its office—was it to submit another story?—the editor came out and gave me a bunch of rubles. I asked, "What's this for?" She said, "Here they pay for everything they print." Her name was Anna Louise Strong.

She held a Ph.D. and was one of the greatest journalists this country ever produced. Originally a Seattle social worker, she unknowingly prepared herself for the physical rigors of her later career by back-packing around Mt. Rainier. Anna Louise had been an elected member of that city's school board for one term fifteen years before we met, and had published good poetry, some of it feminist in a manner that is totally valid today although written before women had the vote. Shortly afterward she became feature editor of the *Seattle Union Record,* then the country's only general-circulation daily owned and operated by organized labor. During her tenure the city witnessed one of the very few general strikes in American history. Her editorial on how the workers would feed and care for the city as long as the strike lasted won enduring nationwide fame in labor circles. Going to Russia less than four years after the revolution changed her life. Leon Trotsky, second only to Lenin among the Communist leaders, wrote the introduction to her first book. She covered every revolutionary event in the world during the next thirty years, on the spot—the Chinese Red Army's Long March, the Civil War in Spain, Indo-China, the Soviet take-over of Lithuania, post-World War II events in Poland—and produced books on them. She was jailed by Stalin as a spy because he didn't want her to find out how badly relations with Mao Tse-tung had deteriorated immediately after World War II. She had wanted to ride the Trans-Siberian railroad to China. Strong's remains are buried in Tienanmen Square in Beijing.

But in Moscow in the early '30s she was that awesome editor, a tall and exceptionally bulky woman who had difficulty extricating herself from the arms of a chair when she visited our home. She was also the figure with top-level access who presented the problems foreign engineers, including my father, were having with bureaucracy, to a meeting of the Political Bureau of the Communist Party, chaired by Stalin. Strong was not a party member, but the issue was regarded as of sufficient importance for her to be invited to make a presentation.

Her personality was not simple. She would risk her life for the oppressed en masse. She would undergo the physical torture of weeks on horseback to bring back the story of what was happening in Central Asia's mountains near Afghanistan in the late 1920s. She thrilled and excited a thousand or more people who came to hear her lecture in Cleveland in 1935, but badgered to tears the very young woman, my wife, then eighteen, who had organized the event.

Anna Louise's greatness grew out of the fact that, although an archtypical WASP who never tried to act or speak like anything else— her accent in Russian was atrocious—she absorbed and understood the psychology of the post-revolutionary Russian like no one else who sought to understand and write about the Soviet Union. The post-Stalin leadership would not let the Soviet people know that this great friend of their country had ever lived, because she moved to China after the Sino-Soviet dispute began. I was happy to learn that before her death Anna Louise realized the damage Mao Tse-tung's so-called Cultural Revolution was doing, and supported what she perceived as Chou En-lai's moderating efforts.

Not that Americans can look down their noses at the Soviets for treating her as an un-person. Strong would be unknown in this country but for the fact that a collateral descendant and his wife published a volume of her letters and then a biography. A feminist movie-maker began a film on her. Anna Louise would regard that as incredible, although she would not oppose it. She knew her worth. But to her the idea that her life would be of interest because she was a *woman* who had made it, rather than as a publicizer and advocate of socialism, would have made her a little bit sad.

At Moscow University, everyone with the same major took took all their courses together. I was in biochemistry, having failed to gain admission to genetics, which was my goal. There were thirty-two in our group. I was the only foreigner. Everyone except one Soviet student and myself belonged to the Young Communist League. I sought to join, but was not admitted, without explanation. Possibly it was because I was not a Soviet citizen, or because the other guy and I were not working-class or peasant by social origin. All the others were. None of them had gone straight through the earlier levels of school as I had.

The leader of the Young Communist League group in my class was typical. Physically he had the appearance of a lightweight body-builder: muscles on top of muscles, but not an ounce of fat. Even his face seemed muscled; when he frowned or was puzzled, he looked like a Hokusai picture of a samurai. He was Armenian, Pohosian by name, and from that country. He had been a shepherd boy, and under the Russian monarchy would have been extremely lucky to have gotten four years of schooling. Later a foundry had been built in his very small ethnic republic, launching industry there. He had been very active in building that foundry. It was not only a job, but rather something important to his own previously agricultural nationality and to the USSR. Pohosian was also active in his trade union, which under those conditions did not mean fighting management but helping to instill a collectivist attitude in workers.

This led his fellow-workers to nominate him to go to Moscow University. To qualify to take its courses he—and this was true of every one of my classmates but that intellectual's son and me—attended a special prep school called a Workers' Faculty. His future was secure. Never mind the absence of unemployment: in those years of the Great Depression working people in the United States generally knew that the one country on earth where there was no unemployment was the Soviet Union. The First Five-Year Plan then in progress called for the founding of a new higher educational institution in Armenia, and this young man was guaranteed a teaching job there if he successfully completed his studies in Moscow .

In American terms, one would say that my fellow-students simply took it for granted that they should repay the country for the unprecedented opportunities they were being offered. In actuality, they didn't even think of it as repayment, but simply as normal participation in a joint undertaking. Moscow University did not have a campus at that time. The classroom buildings were across from the Kremlin, but students lived in dorms far away. They were four, six, eight to a room: as many cots as possible were crowded in, with only enough space between to squeeze by. Students would ride to campus by streetcar in the morning and put in a very long day of classes and lab work. Then they would pile into open trucks and go out to some industrial construction site to teach workers how to read and write. They would be trucked home, and study until one or two in the morning. That's how the 80 percent illiteracy rate inherited from the tsarist empire was done away with in one decade.

Food standards were absolutely minimal. Stalin was exporting whatever he could to buy the equipment needed to modernize Russia. That meant grain and lumber, chiefly. Even we, the family of a foreign engineer being paid partly in scarce dollars and with access to a special food store, had no sugar in any form, including candy, for months. There was no coffee, for its importation required convertible currency, which was reserved for buying machinery and hiring technical services. Russians were tea drinkers. Since the country then grew no tea (the Soviets subsequently developed large plantations in Georgia) they made a tea-colored drink of shredded carrots. It probably was healthful, but was the puckeriest stuff that ever crossed my lips, worse than unripe persimmons. And there was nothing to sweeten it with.

Once, during biology lab, I absent-mindedly put my elbow in a vial of hydrochloric acid while peering through a microscope. The elbow repaired itself, but the large hole in the sweater was serious business. Even materials for patching were hard to find. When I cut through my shoe with a shovel while planting a tree in a volunteer work project at the university, that was a major tragedy. Shoes were simply not to be had.

Because lunch at the university was an unsweetened thick spaghetti cake, day after day, my mother scoured our privileged store for something with which to make me sandwiches. She found only one thing regularly available—black caviar. I ate my lifetime quota of caviar at Moscow University. Within Russia it was not expensive. When she first told me that was what I'd be getting, I rebelled. The only caviar I'd ever previously had was the red variety, up at a Left children's summer camp in New York. It was a great place for learning to row—I was the champ—and to swim, and to learn labor history and songs from a one-time Wobbly (member of the IWW: Industrial Workers of the World), Jim Larkin. But when served red caviar there as a great treat, I dubbed it rat poison. Fortunately, the black stuff has a very different taste, still very much to my liking even after that daily diet in Moscow.

But my kid brother, who is not as catholic an eater, grew anemic during our year there. My fellow students, husky young workingmen and women at the beginning of the term, grew visibly drawn, worn, and thin near its end. Aside from their poor diet and volunteer work after class, they were exhausted from the long hours of an activity unfamiliar to them: study. It was easier for me, despite the problem of an unfamiliar language, because I was a professional student, as it were.

When I knew we were returning to the States, I wanted to make sure that I understood my fellow students properly. I got Young Communist League leader Pohosian in a corner of the quad one day, and said, "At the rate you're going you'll get TB and die by the time you're 40. What's the point?" He looked at me in a manner that said, What a ridiculous question!

He responded: "We're building socialism." To him that was not theory, although we studied theory. It was the previously unthinkable opportunities that he, his fellow Armenians, and Soviet workingpeople as a whole were obtaining. It was this personal experience that convinced me, a decade later when Hitler attacked the USSR, and the American and West European military were sure he would win, that the Soviets could never be defeated, although Germany had licked Russia in World War I.

I wonder how many people barely into their teens have met or at least heard as many very prominent people engaged in changing the world as I did while in then still-revolutionary Russia.

On International Women's Day, 1932, my parents took me to the celebration of that event by the Foreign Engineers' Club. I don't think that even one of them was female, but Communist sympathizers and Party members were numerous, and this was a holiday in the Soviet Union. The event took place in the Hall of Columns, in pre-revolutionary days the grand ballroom of the club of the Moscow nobility. The speaker was Nadezhda Krupskaya, Lenin's widow, a fellow revolutionary and in Soviet times revered for her contributions to education. She looked exactly like her pictures: a round-faced, gray-haired grandmotherly person, then sixty-two, with small round eyeglasses.

There were two other things I recall from that evening. The first was the performance by a small baritone with a large mouth and a stupendous voice of the song, "Comintern," meaning Communist International—a truly stirring anthem. It was destined to be known for many fewer years than its fine music deserved. The lyrics were a forthright call to world revolution. Only three years later, thanks to the rise of Hitler, the Communist International changed its basic policy to the defense of democracy against the danger of fascism, and the song became a no-no.

After the meeting, we walked home, perhaps two miles. It was a wonderful crisp late-winter night. The moon reflected against fresh snow on sidewalks and roads. At that time horse-drawn sleighs were still very common in the city itself. The night was silent but for the soft clip-clopping of the hooves.

Our route took us past the Museum of the History of the Revolution. (I wonder what it is today?) Like all converted palaces, it had carriageways where the curb was cut away and sloped. The streets were not kept as clear then as in later Soviet times, and the slope had iced. Dad, a proper gentleman, was walking closest to the street, and as he stopped on the cutaway curb he slipped and fell. He was not hurt, but mother let out a peal of laughter, in which brother Gene and I both joined. Dad, you see, although kind, intelligent, and in many ways most admirable, was however one of those people who was quite sure that he never made a misstep—in any sense of the word.

Another speaker I heard in Moscow that year was one whose name most Japanese still recognize, although he died in 1933, only a year after speaking at the Anglo-American Workers' Club. Peasant-born in Japan, Sen Katayama graduated from Yale University in 1895—he addressed us in English—and immediately returned to Japan, where he founded that country's first labor union before the turn of the century. Four years later he was among the founders of its Social-Democratic Party. He was elected to the Socialist International in 1900, opposed the Russo-Japanese War of 1904, was the translator into Japanese of Lenin's *State and Revolution,* and had been a leader of the Communist International for ten years before I heard him. Japanese, whatever their political views, acknowledge him as the founder of their country's labor movement.

Naturally the foreigners I met in Moscow who stand out most in memory were Americans. One day I wandered into the Library of Foreign Languages, then occupying a closed church on the square in front of city hall—the Moscow Soviet—with the severe modern Marx-Engels-Lenin Institute opposite it. In those years a shaft erected to commemorate the Revolution stood at its center. A light brownskin man was seated reading. I thought I recognized him from Soviet newspaper photographs. I approached him and asked, "Pardon me, sir, but aren't you Langston Hughes?" He was. Twenty years later that great African-American poet wrote me kind words about a poem I had written about the Martinsville Seven, young Black men in Virginia executed after an unsuccessful struggle to save them in which I had participated a decade before the so-called freedom rides.

In 1932 we left the Soviet Union to return home. Dad was frustrated with the bureaucrats who wouldn't let him do the very engineering work that they had carefully selected him for and for which they paid him in their hard-earned foreign currency. Our sea voyage back from Leningrad to London included a one-day stop in Hamburg, Germany. The Soviet Union, during that period of weaning the people away from religion, had substituted a week of five days, four workdays and one for rest, for the traditional seven-day week with Sunday as holiday. Consequently, when we arrived in Hamburg, I didn't know what day of the week it was. I had come from a country that was booming, the port of Leningrad included. Now I was in a port city sunk in the greatest depression ever in the capitalist world. Even though Hamburg's port is one of the world's largest, immense ocean liners were anchored in midstream, bow to stern, rank upon rank, like the Liberty ships after World War II upriver in the Hudson's Tappan Zee in New York and in Suisun Bay, California.

Hamburg's docks were just as dead. The enormous crane that was to take part of the cargo out of our combined freight-and-passenger ship was pushed into place by a gang of sweating men, who were cheaper to hire at the bottom of the depression than a donkey-engine or a tractor.

I was able to converse in German then as I had kept up my high school German to get by in Moscow until I gained proficiency in

Russian. English was virtually unknown in the Soviet Union in those years. I left the ship for a stroll through the city. Apparently my parents took it for granted that I'd be all right. Perhaps they'd gotten used to that notion in the USSR, where streets were safe, as they were in New York in those years.

At the head of the pier was a very small shack, utterly neat, with a lightning-wire fence around it and flowers growing in the tiny patch of earth behind. Standing there, with his bicycle leaning against the fence, was a German workingman. He wore a cap and a tweed jacket with a lapel pin showing two fists.

I recognized the symbol, having seen it in the Soviet press. It represented the *Antifaschistische Einheitsfront*, the Anti-Fascist United Front, a Communist-influenced organization. I asked the man what day of the week it was. He said: "Wednesday." Then I told him that I recognized the pin, had just come from the Soviet Union, and asked what things were like in Germany. At one point in the conversation, he said, in a tone of hatred: *"Und die Faschisten!"*— "And the fascists!"— and turned around to show me the back of that good-looking jacket. It had been cut to shreds and stitched back together again, inch by inch, with extraordinary German neatness. The Nazi Storm-Troopers had taken him out and horsewhipped him.

I followed his directions for getting to the center of the city. I don't recall which way I walked, going or coming, but I do recall taking the S-Bahn, the subway, which at one point is above ground on steel columns, like New York's old EL. At the station overlooking the port, I gazed out at that sea of dead ships. It was so quiet that when one of them blew its whistle, I nearly fell onto the tracks.

Near the city center, on a huge artificial lagoon, I went aboard the world's biggest plane of that day, the D-OX, a flying boat with twelve engines in six pairs, one pulling and one pushing. In the center of town there was a Woolworth store. Down the street was the Braun Haus, the local Nazi headquarters. They came to power just a few months later, in early 1933. From the Braun Haus hung an immense red flag, with a small white circle in its center and, within the circle, a thin black swastika. For the first time, I appeciated the social demagogy of the Nazis. The red flag was that of the workingclass, Socialist or Communist, and the full name of Hitler's party was Nationalist *Socialist* German *Workers'* Party.

Seated on the entry stoop of the Woolworth's, with a rack of magazines and newspapers for sale, was a hunchbacked man in his 20s. I recognized the publications he was selling as Communist, the daily *Rote Fahne* (Red Flag), and *AIZ,* a marvelous illustrated weekly whose concept was borrowed shortly afterward when *Life* magazine, our first glossy picture news weekly, appeared in the United States. *AIZ,* short for Workers' Illustrated Paper, employed an artist, John Heartfield, a German who had anglicized his name from Herzfeld. Heartfield would use photographic paste-ups and collages to devastating effect as political satire. It was only when his politics were effectively dead, in the 1990s, that the American museum-going public was permitted to see his work, in a traveling exhibition.

I said to the news vendor, pointing to the Nazi flag, "Isn't it danger-ous to sell these here?" He shrugged and said: "It has to be done. This is where the people are."

Hamburg was being patrolled by squads of *Schutzpolizei*, a milita-rized police, who rode bicycles in comic-opera uniforms and patent-leather hats. There was nothing funny about the rifles slung on their backs. Cops with rifles were a new experience. The Soviet cops I had grown accustomed to didn't even carry clubs, and their attitude then was typified by the arrest of milk black-marketeers I had seen a couple of months earlier. When this occurred, a crowd argued the pros and cons. Then, when a cop asked one of the detainees to drive his horse-and-wagon to the station house, the suspect said, "Go fuck your mother. Do it yourself." The cop reddened, but picked up the reins. No violence, no handcuffs.

As I got back to the port area of Hamburg to re-board our ship, the neat brick fences around the docks were covered with painted appeals to vote for one or another party in the upcoming elections. In that work-ingclass area, Communist signs far outnumbered all others. I left Hamburg with the distinct feeling that an explosion was imminent. When we arrived in London, I read that there had been a massive attack in Hamburg by police on anti-fascist demonstrators, with numerous casualties.

New York City, midsummer 1932. The Great Depression that had begun in 1929 was now at its worst. An election campaign in progress that Franklin Delano Roosevelt, running against President Hoover, would win that fall. When in trouble, Americans vote out the incumbent.

I was unhappy, for good reason. The atmosphere at home, with Dad unemployed, could hardly be upbeat. Who needed construction engi-neers when there was no market for the output of existing plants? Eventually, city and then federal public works projects enabled him to use his skills at survival wages. Until then, we could buy food and pay rent thanks to the fact that his contract in Moscow provided that he could convert up to 30 percent of his year's pay into dollars upon leav-ing. To accumulate those rubles, we had sold what we could before leav-ing the USSR. The students on our floor who bought our standing hand-cranked phonograph were either Azerbaijanis or Iranians, and were utterly determined to master Western culture as completely as possible. The week before our departure the building rang day and night with Caruso.

During my one year at the City College of New York (CCNY), we lived in Washington Heights, so I could walk to the campus. Alexander Hamilton's home was across the street from CCNY, and an orphanage, Jewish I believe, bordered the campus in another direction. Whether *Oliver Twist* was sharp in my memory, or my parents had said things to me, I was horrified at the notion of an orphanage. I remember my pleasant surprise, a generation later, when a fellow activist turned out to have been raised in that place, and proved to be a totally balanced individual despite his institutional upbringing.

I also recall an electric car, jet black and highly polished, truly corresponding in design to a horseless carriage. There was always a fresh flower in the slender cut-glass vase where front and side window met. The vehicle had to be thirty years old. That matched the history of its owner, an elegant, trim, elderly Black man who had been the last African-American member of Congress to be forced out at the turn of the century by disenfranchisement in the South through special legislation, Ku Klux Klan terror, and the firing of those who sought to vote. I hope he survived to the election of Adam Clayton Powell a few years later, re-establishing a voice for the Negro in Congress.

The ex-congressman was a mysterious presence. But I had direct contact with Blacks in a very different way. There were always rent parties in Harlem apartments downhill from us. I probably learned about them from fellow radical students or from the "What's On?" column in the *Daily Worker*. I have no recollection of there having been any African-American students at all in day session, which I attended. Rent parties meant dancing, real close, one-step, to the jazz records of the day. I recall no drunkenness or rowdy behavior, and no problems as a white teenager in Harlem at night. I came and went alone—I had no girl friend yet— so I must have danced with Black young women. No sex. What if a girl got pregnant? The notion of abandoning her never crossed my mind. What if I got a disease? My main fear was of being shamed by either in the eyes of my parents.

After I was expelled from college—which is another story— and the need to pay the higher Manhattan rents no longer existed, we moved back to the West Bronx. The building was relatively new, but our apartment windows faced the elevated subway tracks a block away. The noise of frequent trains probably brought the rent down. Here Mother tried to contribute to family income with her one skill, cooking. She opened a restaurant in a ground-floor apartment for that, as her mother had on the East Side. Unfortunately for the success of the business, Mother was incapable of using anything but the very finest and freshest ingredients. That required charging a price higher than the neighborhood traffic could bear, and the restaurant failed.

Having no friends in this new neighborhood, I spent a lot of time dreaming about the vivid life I had left behind in the USSR. Here I read actual baseball scores, about a sport I loved but knew was no more than a game. In Moscow I had eagerly turned to the back of *Pravda*'s single-sheet four pages each morning to read what I had dubbed the ball scores. This was the daily report of how much coal had been mined nationwide the previous day in the Soviet Union, how much pig iron smelted, how much steel made, how many tractors built. Business news? Not in the slightest. Those four figures, laid out in visual graphs, were the measure of the country's unaided advancement into the 20th century. Stalin had said the previous year that they had to make a hundred years' progress in ten or the capitalist world would destroy them in a second attempt to abolish the first experiment in living without private business, unemployment, ethnic oppression and sexually unequal laws. He was right on the nose. Hitler attacked in 1941.

The Russians didn't need propagandists to tell them that Stalin was right in this. When he made that speech in 1931 it was only eleven years since they had emerged victorious but utterly ruined and hungry from three years of anti-Communist armed intervention on their soil by four-teen countries, including regiments of the U.S. Regular Army in east-ernmost Siberia and the European sub-Arctic. At one point the Soviet government's hold had been reduced to only one-ninth of the territory of the Russian Empire. To my fellow students at Moscow University, who were older than I, that intervention was a living memory. While they had been too young to fight, they remembered well the devastation, starvation, and disease the intervention had brought.

Moscow still harbored the last remnants of the packs of homeless children who had learned to survive on their own or die. My father's pocket was picked by them as we waited to march in the 1932 May Day parade. They were the subject of the best film released while I was there, the very first Soviet sound film. It is not known today in the West because it was not about the revolution or fighting oppression before it. That, this country can abide. But a film showing the Soviet government having done something good?—not likely.

The film was called "The Road to Life." It was a fictionalization of something everyone knew to be true. In the early 1920s the Communists had developed a program to round up these kids, de-louse, bathe, feed, and clothe them if possible, induce them to learn a trade and go to work. The film starred a marvelous untrained young actor, Tatar by national-ity, with Asian features, who played a character named Mustafa. Some scenes are as vivid in my mind today as when I saw it nearly three-quarters of a century ago. The film played a significant role in shaping my values. Mustafa, with one eye out for the cops, deftly razors a foot-square piece of sable fur from the seat of the coat of a businessman's wife as she wears it. Mustafa and his gang of teenage and pre-teen kids huddled against each other for warmth in their only clothing in the unheated basement of an abandoned building, singing the most heart-breaking and saddest of Russian folk songs, "I Will Die and No One Will Know Where I Am Buried." A sudden raid by police directed by female social workers rounds them up, and they are taken to a former church to be housed. The kids find a way to make white mule, get drunk, and wreck the tools and machinery of their workshop. A masterful dressing-down follows, with no punishment or incarceration, given them by the youthful head of this institution. There is a moment of unbearable suspense as he puts a wad of rubles into Mustafa's hand and sends him to a store for purchases. Will he take the money and run?

The boys had been exploited by an adult fence. He, deprived of his source of stolen goods, returns and sets up a saloon and whorehouse near the church to entice them back to their former life. Mustafa and the older boys come there, pretending to play along, and then trash the joint. The fence takes revenge. Mustafa, stripped to the waist and pumping his railroad hand-car along the spur line the kids have built, sings a merry Tatar tune, hits the gap where a rail has been pried loose, and is thrown to his death. The photography, the acting, and above all the meaning of that film stayed with every Soviet person of that generation who I asked about it on visits to Russia even sixty years after it premiered.

The spirit of the country in the early '30s was so upbeat that I was heartbroken to leave. But I brought with me to America a new interest. My courses at Moscow University had included one on algae taught by a distinguished prerevolutionary professor, one on calculus taught by a spirited woman of about thirty-five, and Political Economy, with Marx' *Capital* as the textbook, taught by an unpleasant character with an unclean rag always pinned around his neck as though for some primitive treatment of a sore throat. He could have been cast as a Hollywood movie version of a Communist intellectual.

Capital totally fascinated me. Our class was broken down into what were called "brigades" of six or seven each for purposes of study by discussion. Every member of a brigade was given the same grade, as a stimulus for the more able to assist the stragglers. I remember that Armenian foundry-worker who headed the Young Communist League sitting at discussions with his forehead knotted and lips pursed, trying valiantly to understand Marx' abstractions. But I just ate it up. In the first place, *Capital* dealt with the realities of *my* country's economic system— capitalism—and *not* that in which my fellow-students had already lived most of their lives. Secondly, I discovered that I was entranced by logic. Applied logic. I was bitterly disappointed when, because of the brigade system, I got my lowest mark, just passing, in Political Economy—although I didn't mind the fact that the same system got me the equivalent of an "A" in calculus, at which I was terrible.

So I entered New York's City College primed for action. They gave me credit for two of my Moscow University courses: physics (although I don't remember that course or its teacher at all) and calculus. Actually, I had a proper freshman's attitude. I was aware—perhaps too aware— of my physical limitations as the youngest entering student. The hazing by sophomores was mild, but you were certainly put and kept in your place. But the articulateness and capacity to think on my feet that are probably my only true gifts, and the sense of moral indignation that overwhelms my fears—both physical and of more authoritative and, in those years, of far older people—soon took pride of place.

CHAPTER 4

Education Terminated,
Life Begins

Fall 1932. Lecture hall of banked rows, City College, New York. The several hundred seats are all occupied. Others students squeeze in on the sides and back to support their leaders' speeches in protest of the firing of an English instructor, Oakley Johnson, because he is a Communist. Johnson had supported the students in their successful opposition to the introduction of tuition fees at the very bottom of the Great Depression. City police pour into the hall and clear it, clubs poking.

A week later, a meeting is in progress in the Great Hall of City College, its thousands of seats all filled. Dr. Frederick Robinson, the president of the college, has agreed to address the communist-influenced student Liberal Club, on the topic "Liberalism and the College." He will answer questions but student speeches are not permitted. I, a freshman, fifteen, come early enough to seat myself in the tenth row center. I catch the eye of the chair in order to ask the president a question that I had written out. It is in fact a speech about a minute and a half in length, but framed in correct grammatical form as a single sentence. As I wait, my knees actually shake and my hands tremble. I am called upon and read. I am not interrupted. In view of the consequences, I can only explain that by assuming that my voice already had the cadence and carried the conviction that enabled me to project a similar challenge nearly thirty years later when called before the House Un-American Activities Committee. My question, kept by my father for a lifetime, is:

"When Dr. Linehan, who termed himself during the recent Fees Fight the student spokesman to the administration and the administration spokesman to the student body, called in the city police and ordered them to break up a peaceful and orderly meeting of students in a room not being needed for any other purpose at the time; when the police used bodily force and the ends of their clubs to eject these students from this room; when, later, two police detectives who had come here at the call of the administration climbed into their car and provocatively drove it on the college sidewalk of St. Nicholas Terrace thru strolling groups of the students who had been attending the meeting; when one of those students could not get out of the way quickly enough, and one of the detectives got out of the car and punched him in the jaw; when these gentlemen, with whose character and tactics I cannot doubt that the administration—responsible for their being there—was acquainted; when these gentlemen commit such outrages, I begin to doubt, and I ask you, Dr. Robinson, whether such actions on the part of the administration are compatible with the theory of liberalism?"

The students responded with tremendous applause. When it died down, President Robinson answered in a single sentence: "I cannot imagine how any young man brought up in a decent home could have the insolence to expect an answer to so impudent a question."

As I think back, I have only one memory of my classes, probably because CCNY did not then offer a botany major. City College was designed to give poor kids training for professions in which a bachelor's degree was adequate. I took required courses in the direction of engineering, my father's profession. There were no electives for freshmen.

The memory I retain is of an incident in my English class. The instructor was a youthful Southerner with full lips and a superb liquid manner of speech. We were assigned to choose something to read aloud. I chose pages from Marx' and Engels' *The Communist Manifesto*—not exactly the done thing those days. It was simply unknown to most of American academe, unlike Europe. The instructor, Laidlaw by name, listened courteously, and properly confined his comments to manner of delivery and enunciation. Five years later he joined the Abraham Lincoln Brigade of Americans who went to Spain to help its new republic try to stop fascism. His body lies forever in Spanish soil.

Seven months after I hurled that brief challenge at Dr. Robinson, I learned directly from the dean of students that my question had ended my hopes for a college education. The administration simply waited for a seemingly legitimate occasion on which to act. They found it on Charter Day, the anniversary of the founding of the college. That day always brought a big celebration in the stadium. On May 29, 1933, President Robinson invited as guest of honor the general in command of the New York U.S. Army Corps Area. This was a deliberate slap at the students because of the campaign we had conducted all that academic year against the presence of the Reserve Officers Training Corps on campus.

Those students who held communist convictions were very edgy because Hitler had come to power in Germany just four months earlier. We were quick to regard the sweeping measures and what we thought was the social demagogy of the American president who had just taken office, Franklin D. Roosevelt, as fascistic.

Among other things, FDR had asked for an increase in military spending. We had been subjected, all our young lives, to newspaper, movie newsreel, and school assurance that if a second world war ever came— God Forbid— it would be against Godless Russia. We did not dream that he was arming America against Hitler's rearmament and also against Japan.

So we organized a counter-demonstration on Charter Day. Perhaps four hundred students participated. It was just a street corner meeting preceded and followed by marches with placards and streamers. As someone was orating, President Robinson arrived in his car with his guest, the general. The president was so outraged at this insult to his dignity and his guest that he had the chauffeured car stopped, got out, and physically waded into us, swinging left and right with his umbrella. We simply took the umbrella away from him.

Shortly afterward, I took the 9th Avenue train, and headed downtown to the headquarters of the National Student League. My trip ended little more than an hour after the actual umbrella incident, which had been covered by the press. The *New York American* was already being hawked with the screaming banner headline: "Guttersnipes! Says College Prexy." Within a day we had buttons made reading: "I Am A Guttersnipe." This event resulted in a student strike.

In response, a faculty investigating committee was established and a real star-chamber proceeding was conducted: just the professors and the hapless student, one at a time. My uncle, Simon Schachter, was a lawyer who later founded the New York chapter of the National Lawyer's Guild. He won the right to attend as a witness at my final hearing, on condition that he utter no word. I was surprised at the strange venue for the hearing, but at first thought nothing of it. It was held in a room under the flying buttresses of the Great Hall, twice as high as its small length and width. On the vertical wall behind the professors a sheet of canvas was hanging, extending its entire height.

The committee members asked me where I had been at the time of the demonstration. My response was that I had been in the yard of a public school playing handball, which would have been true just about any other day of the week at that hour. One of the professors walked to the canvas, which I now realized had been rigged as a drape. He pulled the cord. Behind it was an enormous blow-up of the bunch of us carrying our picket signs between two of the buildings as we had walked to the stadium. There I was, looking right at me, wearing the same sweater. A number of us were suspended, including me. I was forbidden to take final exams. Two more hearings were held, the last one a week after my 16th birthday. On my lawyer uncle's instructions, I made a handwritten memo of the proceedings immediately after we got home. Dad kept it.

"Prof. Mead asked why I 'had concocted the first story'," about playing handball. "I said that my business in the college is to receive an education, and thought I might succeed in staying in the college to continue receiving that education were that story believed. Dr. Gottschall [the dean] asked why I participated in such activities, since I was in college to receive an education. I replied that I considered such activity to be part of my education. Dr. Mead asked whether I had participated in the booing and shouting of slogans derogatory to the ROTC and calculated to disrupt a stated function of the college (meaning Jingo Day [our term for Charter Day]) as the parade moved down 138th St., adjacent to Lewisohn Stadium where these exercises were being held.

"I said that the shouting had been merely a vociferous statement of opinion on our part, and that I did not believe that those exercises should be a stated function of the college. Prof. Babor asked whether I would interfere with the running of the swimming pool if I thought that the swimming requirement were in some way unfair. I replied that the swimming pool was not a branch of the War Department, implying that it was not something foreign to the college.

"Dr. Gottschall said that the administration's viewpoint on the whole problem was that it was impossible for the administration to run a college under the existing conditions, where students interfere with stated college functions and defy college regulations with impunity. He then asked me to comment on this stand. My comment was that the administration might bother to find out the students' opinions on such matters—institutions in the college which they (the students) believe harmful to themselves. [Prof. Mead asked] what right I had to interfere with the taking of an elective course by students in the college. I answered that I thought that when such an elective might have results harmful to me, I thought myself bound to protest against it."

At this point, the dean asked whether I had participated in the earlier protest, and asked whether I had posed a question to President Robinson. This told me that they had been awaiting an opportunity during that whole period to ask me this question. The memo closes:

"Prof. Mead attempted to make clear to me, earlier in the questioning, that the committee was not in the least interested in my opinion on the ROTC (this in spite of the very pointed questioning and explanation on the subject), in fact, that I might have any opinions on that or any other subject, that I wished. I rejoined: 'Yes, but [I must take] no action.' Prof. Mead then said that no action which might be 'detrimental to the best interests of the college' should be taken by a student.

"The end of the hearing was as follows: Gottschall: 'Then you have no regrets for your action on the afternoon of May 29th?' I: 'No.' Dr. Gottschall: 'And you will not concede that your action on that afternoon was ungentlemanly?' I: 'Not at all.' Dr. Gottschall: 'Have you any further statement to make?' I: 'None.' And that was that." End of memo of 1933.

Twenty-one of us were expelled that spring of 1933. Some others who had been suspended, apologized (for their totally legitimate activity), and were let back in. Several who had been juniors or seniors made *pro forma* apologies a year or two later in order to get their degrees. I saw nothing wrong with that. At that time I had no desire to go back to school, because I believed, quite correctly, that there was nothing I could learn in the social sciences as then taught in college that I couldn't learn better by myself. Half a year later, under family pressure, I applied for reinstatement. The administration wanted an admission of wrongdoing, and I refused. Seven years later, when I was simply a kid workingman who had never even been mentioned in a newspaper, I phoned Dean Gottschall to ask about reinstatement. He had one question: "Are you still a communist?," he asked. I hung up the phone.

The next time I walked into a higher educational institution to take up a formal relationship was fourteen years after my expulsion from CCNY. The Hoover Institution at Stanford University had invited me to become a research fellow at post-doctoral level, with stipend equivalent to associate-professor salary, on the basis of the two books I had written by then.

At 16, I felt free, for the first time in my life, of the need to sit in classrooms taking courses that did not interest me from people who certainly were incapable of teaching me what I wanted to know: why 40 percent of my country's work force was unemployed and why people out of work through no fault of their own were being evicted; why lynchings not only continued but had doubled since the start of the Great Depression; why the U.S. Marines were in Haiti; why the Philippines were still held as a colony. Above all, I wanted to know what to do about this, and how.

The Communist Party maintained a political evening school in its headquarters on East 13th St., called the Workers' School. It had an enrollment as large as City College at that time: three thousand. Though it could offer no credits, of course, and didn't pretend to have that as its purpose. It did charge a small fee for each course to meet expenses. When the twenty-one of us were expelled from college, the Workers' School offered us free scholarships. I plunged into that, and in the academic year 1933-34 took everything they offered in Marxist economics, the history of the labor movement, dialectical materialist philosophy, and political science as Communists understood it.

I had seen the Party's work first hand. In 1933, the National Student League, of which I was a member, would ease its budget by renting its headquarters to other organizations for meetings. I was on caretaker duty one day when the hall had been rented by Big Six, the printers' union of New York's leading newspapers. These were chiefly men well on in years. I remember seeing many bald heads from my balcony vantage point. Members were chiefly German and Irish workers, highly skilled, who had earned very good pay until the depression hit. The union had hired this large hall to discuss the bill presented in Congress to institute a system of unemployment insurance in this country. There were invited speakers, pro and con. In favor was Louis Weinstock, a house-painter and head of the American Federation of Labor Rank-and-File Committee for Unemployment Insurance. Weinstock was a Communist. He had a very heavy Hungarian Jewish accent. Anti-Semitism was quite strong among the older German and Irish skilled workers of New York. His opponent was a silver-tongued Irish orator representing the official American Federation of Labor bureaucracy. Today this is hard to believe, but the A.F. of L. was officially opposed to unemployment insurance. Its well-paid leaders trumpeted, "American workers will never accept the dole."

But those printers had to eat. They had families to support and rent to pay. They set aside their anti-Semitism and voted to endorse the bill. Weinstock and his committee repeated this all across the United States, until finally a majority of the A.F. of L. membership was on record as in favor of unemployment insurance, and the leaders had to change their position.

My parents were having a very rough time then. Dad, unemployed for a full year since our return from Moscow, had gotten a job on a government make-work program at $18 per week, on which four people had to be fed and housed, and medical bills paid as they came up. I omit "clothed," because nothing was purchased until it had deteriorated beyond repair. The situation was remarkably like that which I found in post-Communist Russia in 1998. Dad would darn socks, because mother's vision could not be corrected sufficiently for her to do close work, but she could read, and would read aloud to him as he sewed. We had no radio.

My wife remembers me then—we met at seventeen, in 1934—as dressed in rags. I don't think it was quite that bad. She had a different perspective, being the daughter of a dentist. Though her family was not wealthy, had no car and lived in a walk-up flat, they did own a little summer cottage an hour from New York. Her father had lost his savings in the stock market crash, but people had to have their teeth fixed or pulled when they got too painful, so his practice kept going.

No longer a student, I had to find a job. Yet I was determined to devote all my time to the things I believed in. I resolved the conflict by selling radical reading matter in subway cars and after street corner speeches I made, and at picnics of leftist organizations. Rev. Harry F. Ward, professor of Christian Ethics at Union Theological Seminary in Manhattan, who had educated two generations of socially-conscious clergy, edited a very good-looking, large-format magazine called *Fight Against War and Fascism*. It sold for a nickel. I would think up a catchy why-you-musn't-miss-what's-in-this-issue slogan, short enough to be shouted from the middle of a New York subway car during its very brief station stops. Then, as it began to rumble noisily through the tunnel, I'd place a copy on the lap of every seated passenger. I'd circulate again and pick up the nickels from those who wanted to buy it, and the magazines from those who didn't. I had it timed to cover one car between station stops. This couldn't be done during rush hour, of course, when people were packed in like sardines.

For the street corner meetings I developed a partnership with a friend, "Chup" Dagen, a Jew from St. Louis who was married and had a baby, so he must have been about twenty to my seventeen. I generally associated with people older than myself. At eighteen, I looked twenty-five, and changed very little in facial appearance till I was forty.

I don't remember whether the first street corner meeting at which I spoke was in connection with this radical-reading-matter-selling enterprise, or whether it was an assignment by the Young Communist League, which I joined after being kicked out of college. But I remember the circumstances precisely, because I was scared to death. At the corner of 4th Avenue and East 12th Street in Manhattan, there stands what was then a nearly new clothing factory building. The meeting at which I spoke must have been a Young Communist League undertaking, because we would try to influence the largest units of employed workingpeople we could find. My fears were a combination of stage fright, fear of assault by the cops, and anxiety about coming face to face with the workingclass we placed our hopes in, without any idea of what to expect.

In fact, there were no problems. By this time the police were no longer routinely trying to disperse such meetings. There were too many of them, and people were too angry. The workers were neither pro- nor anti-Communist, but knew that the state of the nation was very bad, their own jobs were totally insecure, their union leadership was more conservative than the times called for, and that Communists had done good things in gaining what we now call welfare, as well as workfare jobs, none of which existed before the depression.

Chup and I had good times together. The Dagens' flat was in a tenement on 13th St., between Second and Third avenues. We'd walk down to the pushcart markets under the First Avenue Elevated train and buy the makings for a feast. I remember six pounds of sweet potatoes for a dime. That one item was all we could afford, plus butter to go with it. But we were young and had great appetites, and I felt full and happy afterward. When Tanya, my future wife, and I began to keep company, the Dagens would go out and let us use their apartment. I would read aloud Erskine Caldwell's short story, "Crown Fire," and it really turned us on.

Chup and I would travel, by subway and streetcar, to the public parks or private picnic grounds in the far reaches of the Bronx where the Communist Party, the *Daily Worker* , the Unemployed Councils, the International Workers' Order (Communist-led fraternal society with health-maintenance organization features), or one of the radical ethnic organizations (Jewish, Greek, German, Finnish, Lithuanian) held fund-raising picnics. He and I would sell our rich selection of radically-oriented creative literature, propaganda books, magazines, newspapers and pamphlets. We'd put them on boards over saw-horses, provided by the picnic sponsors, spin a large roulette wheel, and hand out books as prizes. The louder we shouted, the more people heard us over the din of food vendors, crying babies, yelling kids, shouting fans at the ball games going on, and friends hailing each other.

There were no public-address systems. Megaphones would be used at large rallies, but they reached too narrow a segment of the crowd for our purposes. I discovered that after a couple of hours of this shouting in the broiling New York summer sun, a glass of beer was a marvelous thirst-quencher. Prohibition was repealed that first year Roosevelt was in office. My mother had warned me off sugar-laced soft drinks from childhood, and Tanya, as a dentist's daughter, was even more adamant. My parents never touched alcohol, and it was many, many years later before I ever let myself get drunk. But that foaming cold beer!

The pamphlet-peddling finally did get me arrested, for the violation of a city ordinance against selling without a license, although the reason was political harassment in the purest sense. At the end of the twentieth century, which had seen three Catholic priests in the Sandinista government of Nicaragua, some bishops in the U.S. calling upon nuclear-weapons-workers to quit their jobs during the Cold War, and other bishops urging their flocks to go to the Soviet Union in Gorbachev's day and see what it was like for themselves, it is hard to imagine the rock-ribbed conservatism of the Catholic Church in the 1930s. Its position then can be fairly compared to that of the Christian Right, in this case Protestant, that arose half a century later and strongly influenced the Republican Party. Radio clergy were a dime a dozen in the 1990s. But one of the very first was Rev. Charles Coughlin, a Catholic priest broadcasting from his Shrine of the Little Flower in Michigan. He was a fascist demagogue in the true Hitler mold, railing against international money-lenders and strike-breakers on the one hand, but spouting anti-Semitism and outright totalitarianism on the other. Until Joe McCarthy a generation later, he was the most dangerous proto-fascist this country has produced.

A splendid popular pamphlet exposing him was written by the then-Communist journalist A.B. Magil. There were some real heroes who tried to sell that pamphlet in the Wall Street area. The combination of police zealousness in protection of the citadel of Big Business, and the Storm-Trooper attitude of kids from lace-curtain Irish as well as workingclass families who had the lowest-paying jobs down there made, it a highly dangerous place to be critical of Father Coughlin.

I chose Times Square, which was safer, relatively, to sell my pamphlets. In a voice always blessed by clear enunciation and good cadence, I would call out, "read the TRUTH about Father Coughlin." People on their lunch hours would hurry by, pay me their dime—I think that's what it cost—and hurry on. A plainsclothes detective or two, strolling by, even said, "That's a foin wurk yur doin', me boyo." But after a day or two—I must have been selling 50 to 100 per day, and clearing a full dollar or two for myself—either one of them actually read it, or someone else did and complained. More likely, word came down from headquarters, because arrests took place all over town.

I was taken in for peddling without a license, and the detectives on each side in the back of the car threatened to commit homosexual acts upon me. I was horrified.

The magistrate sentenced me to one day in jail—there was no jury trial or even the pretense of being entitled to one—and I got out that afternoon because of some burocratic rule about the day ending at the close of normal working hours. The next day I resumed selling, but was quickly re-arrested, given the same sentence, and I think I was in jail till late at night, but not overnight.

There was no point in continuomg. I was very conscious that I was trying to do what I had seen that hunchbacked Communist news-vendor doing in Hamburg within sight of Storm Trooper headquarters the summer before Hitler came to power. But, in Germany, the authorities recognized that selling printed matter was an exercise of freedom of the press, until the Nazis took office. In New York, and pretty widely across the U.S., the cops did not permit such civil liberties.

Americans were very conscious of Germany in 1933.Not only was Hitler disbanding all labor unions, outlawing the Communist Party that had just gotten six million votes in a country with one-quarter the population of ours, as well as the Social-Democratic Party, which had done even better at the polls, but he was also putting all activists into concentration camps. (His indiscriminate physical attacks against Jews, and even simply against their places of business, began five years later. Mass extermination was even farther down the road.) But the attention of the entire world was focused upon Germany by one of the most spectacular political trials ever held anywhere. This was before Stalin's show trials.

"Spectacular" is the precise word for it. The Nazis had burned down the Reichstag building—the equivalent of the Capitol in Washington—and blamed the Communists. Hitler's followers, and a large part of the world public, were too politically unsophisticated to realize that such an act made no sense from a Communist point of view. Hitler, to demonstrate an international Communist conspiracy—no, he didn't borrow that phrase from our Un-American Activities Committee; they borrowed it from him—put on trial three Bulgarian Communists who were then in Germany, plus a German Communist who headed the very large body of Communist members of parliament.

The American Civil Liberties Union and similar organizations worldwide demanded the right to send observers to the trial. Since Hitler had no military strength yet, and wanted to gain the time to create it, he agreed. The case was tried by Germany's Supreme Court.

The German defendant denied guilt but showed no initiative. One of the Bulgarians, George Dimitrov simply won the admiration of the entire world, with the exception of the ultra-Right. He proudly and brilliantly upheld his beliefs and cross-examined Hitler's flamboyant right-hand man, Hermann Goering, to the point at which the latter, leaving the courtroom, turned around and shouted from the doorway, "Wait till I get you outside!" That finished it. The court, all holdovers from the pre-Hitler period, found the defendants not guilty. Joseph Stalin, in a brilliant political stroke, conferred Soviet citizenship on the three Bulgarians, and demanded that Hitler turn them over to the USSR. In his politically and militarily weak situation, the Nazi Fuehrer complied.

Dimitrov became a hero to the whole world. In 1934, when socially-conscious theater suddenly sprang into being in the U.S., a great American actor, J. Edward Bromberg, later a victim of McCarthyism, declaimed Dimitrov's lines to the cheers of thousands in a one-act reconstruction of the trial. I was there. It was part of a double-bill with the pioneering labor-strike play, Clifford Odets' "Waiting for Lefty." And I resolved that if I ever found myself in a situation similar to Dimitrov's—after all, the Sacco-and-Vanzetti and Tom Mooney and Angelo Herndon cases were already part of my life experience—I would try to live up to his standard.

That new theater movement was one of the joys of life in New York in 1934 and 1935. The way in which I got to see plays requires a digression. At the end of the year during which I took a full load of courses at the Workers' School, its director invited me in and asked if I'd like to teach there. I certainly did. He asked my age and I said nineteen, which would have made me the youngest teacher by far. Actually I was seventeen.

I wanted desperately to be a good teacher, and judging by student attendance records, I was the second best among dozens. There were no required educational techniques. I employed what I later learned to be the Socratic method. I didn't know of its existence.

I wanted people to think for themselves and I was quite sure of my convictions. I believed that if I developed a sequence of discussion questions, then the students' daily lives plus our reading materials and simple deduction would produce what I regarded as the right answer, from which I would then proceed to my next prepared question.

The students were all older than I, some old enough to be my parents, except for one who was only six weeks my senior. I know her age because I'm married to her.

I am grateful that I have never been an academic snob in any context. I was the only teacher in that Workers' School who did not regard it as beneath my dignity to go downstairs to the *Daily Worker* pressroom after my evening's teaching was over, pick up the biggest armload I could tote, about fifty, of the next morning's paper, and go out to Union Square to hawk it. Strangely, the best location was in front of the one expensive restaurant off the square, an old German place everyone mispronounced so it sounded Chinese: Luchow's. Once in a while a patron would buy a paper from me, but most often it was the passing East Side working people who bought them. Evening-session students at Washington Irving High School, up the block on Irving Place, would come by for a paper. As in my subway days, I learned to develop the most saleable shouting headline from whatever was on the front page. Sixty years later, when I found homeless people in Berkeley unsuccessful in hawking their monthly paper at movie theaters, I reached back into memory to teach them how to find catchy headline slogans to shout.

While I sold my papers, the show began at Eva LeGallienne's Civic Repertory Theater, also on 14th Street, west at about 6th Avenue, just up from Greenwich Village. The last paper sold, I would dash the half-mile across town and generally managed to get into the threater free, because the third act was on. Sometimes I sold out early and saw the second as well. I recall "Black Pit" by Albert Maltz, who went on to become the second or third-ranking scriptwriter in Hollywood—so good that when he was blacklisted and moved to Mexico, he made a satisfactory living out of working for the American screen under assumed names. "Black Pit" was about a hungry coal-miner who betrays his fellow-unionists. Another who became a recognized playwright of the day was John Wexley, whose work for this theater was "They Shall Not Die," about the Scottsboro Case. One of the best shows was "Stevedore," about longshoremen of course, by Peters and Sklar.

Communists of those years were anything in the world but hairshirt hermits. We enjoyed life and all the arts. We contributed more than our share, as will emerge in chapters that follow. Most important, we upheld the specific outlook that art must serve the people. In the temper of the times, every creative artist in the country felt it necessary to take a stand on that issue. Most agreed with us.

Our main concern, however, was organizing the workingclass. As a member of the Young Communist League, I was given specific assignments. One was to help a strike of laundry workers who, then as today, consisted primarily of Black women. They worked under sweatshop conditions. The shop I went to picket very early each morning was in a semibasement in the Bronx, with small windows that barely poked above street level. We would be given the addresses of strikers or workers who were crossing the picket line, and would go to their homes to give moral support or persuade them to refrain from working, as the case might be. Our support was often much more than moral. We would collect money or canned food and distribute it to see them through the strike.

One of the picketers who showed up with great regularity was a very thin, leggy young woman with an absolutely round face, straight hair with a widow's peak and somewhat Asian brown eyes, straightforward and warm. She looked so young that the cop on duty would say, "Go to school, little girl." Although already seventeen, she would be getting into movies for kids' prices for years to come.

We must have belonged to the same Young Communist League club, because we saw a lot of each other for many months thereafter when we didn't yet particularly care for each other. Maybe we didn't belong to the same club, but I saw her because I had been going steady with one of her two best friends. Eventually we felt differently.

After we began dating, Tanya and I would sometimes go to a film to be together. But movies weren't much good. You couldn't get in for a nickel, which was about what I could spare, and the limit to what you could get away with in a movie were very much narrower than today.

We solved the problem in a very New York way. The cars on the old elevated trains had control cabins at each end, with a simple turning latch. Only one per train was in use at any given time, at its front. You could ride the subway and its El branches forever for a nickel, going way out to Coney Island even, and back. So we did our heavy necking in the control cabins of the El. Sixty-three years, three children, grandchildren, and a greatgranddaughter later, we're still together. That's true of a very high percentage of those we knew in the Young Communist League, who were all atheists. I'm a little tired of the nonsense that one has to be religious to have "family values." Likewise, the press accused the

Communists of practicing "free love." Reality was a close as possible to the opposite, given that these were healthy, normal young people.

The YCL was organized on a neighborhood basis for those not employed in some prevalent occupation or going to school. We had separate clubs for each industry to help deal with labor issues. Because New York City was a series of ethnic enclaves, our personal friends were all Jewish inasmuch as we belonged to the neighborhood branches. But our commitment was to internationalism, and we practiced what we preached. A nineteen-year-old African-American, Angelo Herndon, was arrested in Atlanta for leading an interracial demonstration for the institution of welfare. Conditions in the American South at that time were akin to those of apartheid in South Africa before Nelson Mandela. Herndon was indicted under Georgia's insurrection statute. Initially aimed at slave uprisings, this statute carried the death penalty. Because the white South believed its own stereotypes about Black people's fears, he was put in a cell with a man who had died. He kept his cool.

Arrested in the summer of 1932, Herndon was convicted and sentenced to eighteen-to-twenty years. Bail for release on appeal was set at $18,000, which might as well have been half a million, as far his supporters were concerned. Who could raise such money at the bottom of the depression? Yet it was collected, in pennies, nickels, dimes, quarters, at little house parties, raffles, street-corner meetings, and by collection can. It was 1935 before he was out on bail. When the money was brought down and accepted, there was a celebratory explosion of feeling that no superbowl game could possibly match.

We knew Herndon was to arrive in New York City by rail at Penn Station. In those years New York was one of the most severe places in the country as far as unauthorized parades were concerned. In my quarter-century of activism in New York, I can remember only two demonstrations without permits the police let proceed. The number of us who came to Penn Station that night was not massive by the standards of that city in the '30s, perhaps five or ten thousand, but our mood was such that the police commanders decided not to interfere. We were not looking for trouble. We had no weapons, no rocks, not even picket signs. But, man, we had *won*! We hoisted Herndon on our shoulders there on West 34th Street, and headed for our own turf, Union Square, a mile south and half a mile east. The cops stayed out of sight and, as was always the case in my personal experience when they did, there was no trouble. We had our parade, our triumphant rally, and went home.

As I recall all this, I ask myself: when did I sleep? Yet not only did I always get a long night's sleep—my way of making good what has normally been a very intensive day—but I also found time for a very unique activity in the America of that day. I skied. There was no such thing here in those days as separate cross-country and downhill skis. Perhaps there were jumping skis, but they were for the rich. There were no steel edges, no bindings of any kind. The ski was made of hickory, with a slot through which a short leather belt was passed, into which you would shove your toe. If you could afford it, you bought a kind of mocassin with turned-up toe that would stop you from sliding back out of that strap.

Still living with, and off, my parents, I had the deepest crisis of conscience when I took $10 that I had earned selling the *Daily Worker* and bought myself a pair of skis. I would wrestle those seven-foot monsters onto the subway, ride up to Van Cortlandt Park, and trudge up and slide down, trudge up and slide down. For my friend Chup, I nailed a strip of corrugated rubber onto each ski a couple of feet behind the toe belt, and we'd ride down tandem like two on a motorcycle and, of course, fall.

In the autumn of 1935, the Communist Party asked me to move to Cleveland, and a new life began.

My father believed all his life that when I left home at seventeen, I told him: "Dad, I've got to do this, because so long as I stay here I'm putty in your hands." Age sharpened his memory for things of the distant past, so I assume I did say that. If so, I must have been trying to find a phrase that would ease his hurt feelings. He certainly exercised an enormous influence on me, but he never ordered me to do anything. Rather, he transmitted his ideals to me. And he was unquestionably able to answer most of my questions about anything and everything; he researched the things he didn't have immediate answers to. Yet my decision to defy the authorities when I was expelled from college was entirely my own. My guess is that deciding to find an apartment when still in New York had more to do with the fact that I had a steady girlfriend, subsequently my wife, and that since I was out to make revolution, I really should not be dependent upon mama and poppa.

My income literally consisted of the pennies and nickels of margin on reading matter I sold in subways and at street corner meetings and picnics. The housing I could afford was rock bottom. And I couldn't even afford that, alone, so I had to find someone to share with. A college professor-to-be—as neither of us imagined at the time—and brother of immunologist Leon Wofsy, one of the more radical future professors at U.C. Berkeley in the '60s, became my roommate. Their father was the head of the Communist Party in Connecticut, and lived on the miserly salary that organization could afford, provided he could raise the money each month.

The kind of apartment we rented is well-described in a compelling book about the immigrant Jews of New York's Lower East Side, Mike Gold's *Jews Without Money*. It is vastly closer to the truth than Isaac

Bashevis Singer's mystical quasi-religious, semi-Zionist dream time, and infinitely more alive than Irving Howe's *World of our Fathers*. We moved onto the very block   Gold—I knew him decades later—names in his book, Cannon Street.

Cannon Street runs under the perpetually noisy approach to the Manhattan Bridge, which crosses the East River to Brooklyn. The street was lined by typical old-law tenements, so called because they were allowed to continue to exist after the city was compelled to adopt legislation forbidding further construction of buildings in which some rooms were ventilated only by air-shafts, with no windows to the street or the back yard. In our apartment the bathtub was in the kitchen and doubled as washtub for clothing. It had a fitted board cover so it could be used daytime for storage, ironing, rolling dough, whatever. The toilet was public—one per floor. Tanya and I have contrasting memories about the apartment in one respect. I think of the building as being too poor for cockroaches. She says that's my romanticizing imagination, and it was crawling with them. As she did the housecleaning—that's how our generation was raised, and no one I knew questioned it or even thought about it—I suppose her recollection is right. But mine is more fun.

There wasn't too much her parents could do about her coming down there, although we didn't live together. In the first place, she's at least as stubborn as I am. Second, her own parents, people as decent and proper as can be imagined, had never bothered getting legally married. They defied bourgeois convention not as Bohemians but as opponents of the notion that morality could be determined by whether or not one signed a piece of paper or swore in front of a civil servant or member of the clergy. Given this family history, it is no surprise that when I was sent to Ohio by the Communist Party, Tanya quit college shortly thereafter and joined me in Cleveland once and for all.

Tanya's folks and mine differed in one important respect that still reflects itself in a diverging outlook, and disagreements between us, on what our generation called the "Jewish question." My parents were secular and assimilationist. They never hid the fact that we were Jews, and one of Dad's three daily papers was in Yiddish. But they did not require my brother and me to learn Yiddish, never mind Hebrew, which was exclusively the language of religion prior to the founding of Israel. We spoke English at home and viewed ourselves as Americans of one particular ethnic origin.

Though coming from the same social stratum, Tanya's parents were what Jews call "Yiddishists." This meant they were determined to preserve the cultural values of their heritage and instill it into their children. They studied English diligently and knew it very well, but spoke with accents because they had come to this country after early childhood. Knowing that their children would learn English as a matter of course in school and with their friends, they deliberately and invariably spoke Yiddish at home. In consequence, Tanya spoke Yiddish before English. Likewise, she and her brothers were sent to what was then a very widespread institution in New York, Los Angeles, Chicago, and other major centers of Jewish immigration—an after-school system of secular education in Yiddish that continued through the high school level. Tanya is a graduate of one such *Mittlshul*—middle school.

After our daughter was born, Tanya's parents began to conduct a secular Seder, the Jewish Passover ceremony, since they valued its preservation of a part of the actual history of the people. The fact that the ceremony includes certain religious symbolism—such as leaving an empty chair at table for a supernatural visitation—didn't bother them. They regarded it as a natural reflection of the state of human thought at the time that ceremony originated. Tanya and I have never conducted a Seder, but she preserves another tradition, similar in nature. On another Jewish holiday, Hannukah, one candle of a nine-branched candelabrum is lit the first night, two the second night, and so forth. This, too, reflects an event in the history of the Jews, the victory of Judas Macccabeus over the king of Syria in 165 B.C. Although clothed in religious ritual, Tanya's celebration is based on happy childhood memories associated with that holiday, during which children receive gifts and play joyous games. The practical consequence of all this is that she is much more sensitive to and concerned with the preservation of Jewish culture, anywhere in the world, than I. Yet I believe that both attitudes are equally legitimate. One has a right to be assimilationist or preservationist, whether in secular or religious form. That applies to each of the hundreds of ethnic groups that have merged to form the American nation. I object, however, to those who force their attitude upon me, while I grant without argument their right to their point of view.

I wasn't sent to Cleveland to make the Revolution. The Party was entirely too realistic to believe that was about to happen. Nor would it send someone with absolutely no experience in working for an employer to organize the working class. I wasn't even sent to teach in Cleveland's small version of the Workers' School. Things were much simpler and more practical. I had a deep belief in the effectiveness and usefulness of the printed word, and had made myself an excellent salesman of reading matter that promoted our views. The Young Communist League maintained the post of Education Director at each level of its organization. I had held that post, unpaid, in what was essentially an assembly-district area in Manhattan, which included the tough gashouse district in the East 20s from Lexington Avenue to the East River. Such an area, which we termed a "section," would include several bottom-level organizations, called clubs. My section achieved the highest sales of printed matter in Manhattan, and perhaps the city. Given the wage levels and poverty of that period, it was remarkable that we would sell over $1,000 worth per month at a time when a hardcover book sold for a maximum of two dollars, and pamphlets and monthly magazines went for a nickel or dime.

My assignment to the smokestack industrial mid-West was considered a great honor in our circles, because that's where the proletariat, the heavy-industry workers whom Marxists regard as the key to moving toward socialism, lived. We expected the forces of law and order to be more repressive there. I had seen them at work in New York, and the thought that things might be worse out West frightened me. A particular event had etched their power sharply in my memory.

In an attempt to gain publicity here, Italy's fascist dictator, Mussolini, had sent over a large delegation of students. Yankee Stadium was booked for a welcoming rally by Italian-Americans, among whom he had mass support. Much smaller numbers actively opposed him. We Communists correctly perceived his militaristic rhetoric as threatening a second world war. A few months after the event I am describing, he invaded Ethiopia, and a year later sent a full division of troops to Spain to help Franco overthrow its republic and establish fascism there as well. Hitler had come to power only two years earlier in Germany, and fascism had been established in Austria under an independent dictator the previous year. The best-selling novelist, Sinclair Lewis, had just published *It Can't Happen Here,* projecting a fascist takeover of America and warning against complacency about what had happened in Europe and was occurring in Japan. A movie was made of the book the next year. We sought to help overcome complacency by blocking that rally in Yankee Stadium.

Thousands of us assembled a block or two east of the stadium. We were in a typical New York City block with tall apartment houses forming solid walls on both sides. The cops, mounted and pedestrian, in a show of massive force, bottled us up from both ends of the block and moved in systematically, bashing everyone their clubs could reach. I had come with Tanya and her two girlfriends. When the attack occurred, I took them by the arm, like a chivalrous young gentleman, and walked down the block at a normal pace, while everyone else was running and screaming. The cops must have thought we lived there, and left us alone. The same tactic of dignified behavior, and above all not showing fear, saved me in situations in later years. On the other hand, I have seen ordinary bystanders, in their dress and manner clearly not demonstrators, clubbed and arrested. That was particularly true in the 1960s.

I got to Cleveland by hitch-hiking. I had no money for any other means of travel. Freeways or even four-lane roads did not exist. Two-lane U.S. 6 was simply stunning as it wound through the lush fields of the Pennsylvania Dutch, with the striking sunburst designs painted on their great red barns to ward off the hex. Somewhere in that area a pudgy man in a suit gave me a lift, and we began a peculiar conversation. He asked if I had a big thumb. I looked at my thumb, and said, "I suppose it's standard size so far as I know." Suddenly it dawned on me that my thumb wasn't at all the organ he was interested in. I felt very uncomfortable, pulled down the front of my snap-brim fedora, squared the shoulders of my padded overcoat, and stared straight ahead in silence. No word was said for an hour or more as we traveled through the forests along the glorious Juniata River. Finally he said, "You needn't be angry with me." And with that, I made it safely to Cleveland.

CHAPTER 5

A Professional Revolutionary

Cleveland was something new. It has a lovely frontage on Lake Erie which, in those years, was rich in fish, although the swirl of floating used condoms near sewer outlets were a portent of the ecological near-death that lake suffered decades later—not from condoms but from industrial waste.

The East side included two Jewish neighborhoods, the colleges, Symphony Hall, a theater company that still exists, and an ultra-wealthy incorporated enclave called Bratenahl. Also on the East side was the Black ghetto, poor as everywhere, but different from New York's in that people lived in wooden three-story apartment buildings. The working class, largely Czech, Slovak, and Polish, as well as many skilled German-Americans, lived in small, often self-built houses chiefly on the West side. The dividing line was the Cuyahoga River. Great Lakes ore-carriers hundreds of feet long were maneuvered with remarkable skill up this narrow stream. Huge steel mills bordered the river for miles and cast marvelous tongues of flame upon the sky when the blast furnaces, coke ovens, or open hearths were being tapped. In later decades it was so polluted that it once caught fire.

On the east side of the river, at the point where it enters the lake, stood the main square, with its fine buildings, then quite new, probably erected just before the start of the Great Depression six years earlier. The main avenues ran east from the square. In the mid-'30s Cleveland had the look of a dying city. Stately mansions lined the avenues, few still in use as family homes. Most had been reduced to rabbit-warren boarding houses. Between them were auto sales lots, one after another, and the major movie house, complete with vaudeville act. A young Red Skelton would send us rolling in the aisles with his pantomime of a fat lady struggling into her corset. Male chauvinist? Of course. Funny? Uproariously.

I would be bawled out by my straight-laced older Party comrades not for enjoying Skelton but for arranging my time so I could take three hours off each Friday afternoon to catch that week's new flick at matinee bargain prices. Eleanor Powell in the "Broadway Melody" of each succeeding year was always something to look forward to. Her dancing, her teeth—I really mean that—and, of course, her legs. I didn't yet know that I had the makings of an exceptionally good dancer, particularly to jazz, swing, and big band music. In later years, I occasionally went out dancing by myself because Tanya insisted that she was hopelessly clumsy and wouldn't dance with anyone but me. And if a Black man asked her to dance and she refused, that could create an impression of racism reflecting on our organization, which it fought in its every manifestation.

The bookstore I ran also served as headquarters for my statewide sales efforts and was located below a much larger floor containing the Communist Party's city and state offices. A couple of rooms as well as the meeting hall and offices served, when not otherwise used, as classrooms for the local equivalent of the New York Workers' School.

That rather pleasant, but in no way entrancing, city was the backdrop for getting to know an entirely new kind of people. I was fascinated by their appearance and style. New York City in the poorest of times is nevertheless the center of the garment industry. People are clothes conscious. Cleveland's population, on the other hand, consisted of one-time European peasants and their children. The prevailing colors of men's clothing were, dark brown, black, maybe navy blue. Women's clothing wasn't much livelier. The entire attitude toward garments was utilitarian. One bought clothing as sturdy and cheap as possible, and in colors that required the most infrequent visits to a dry cleaner. There was no sense that shoes ought to be shined or pants pressed, which New Yorkers did in the worst of times. Footwear everywhere in the country was of leather. This was long before the '60s, when Americans learned to brag about their affluence by dressing as sloppily as possible, and blue jeans became the national uniform. Slacks on women were just not the thing, although you might see them in movies.

The faces of Cleveland were also different. New Yorkers in those years were Jewish, Italian, Irish, Black, and WASP. Not many Puerto Ricans had immigrated as yet, and there were few Asians. One was accustomed to the ethnic face of one's own neighborhood. New York was one of the two or at most three places in the country where the myth about the Communist movement being predominantly Jewish was locally true.

Cleveland was totally different. The faces were East European—solid. Huge hands, deep chests. These workers earned money in steel mills, or at Fisher Body and White Truck for the auto industry, or at Warner & Swazey and other plants making the machines that make machines, which Cleveland was rightly famous for. Automation was far in the future. What Cleveland, like all our industrial heartland, had was mechanization: machines to do much—not all—of the lifting and pushing and carrying that had earlier been done by human beings.

When steel came white-hot and flexible as string out of the bar mill, a man would grasp it with heavy tongs and swing it to where it was needed, hoping that the man at the adjacent mill wouldn't make a wrong move and snake his around him. At the truck and auto body plants, the heaviest parts were manhandled by brute strength onto the moving assembly line. Power tools did not yet exist. You drilled, hammered and sawed by hand.

The Communist Party leadership in Cleveland was a marvelous bunch who I realize now were very young, just past thirty at most—although, to me at eighteen, they were ancients. The head of the state organization was Johnny Williamson, blonde, blue eyed, balding early. He was the only Scotsman I've ever met who spoke with both a burr, the nearly Scandinavian pronunciation of "u", and a Jewish singsong, though he was not Jewish. He had been brought to this country at age ten—which gave the government the excuse to deport him during the McCarthy era. He became a radical just after World War I, and had a great deal of association with Jews, including his wife.

There were two women in the small top leadership. One was Maude White, a well-educated Black, originally a New Yorker, I think. I remember how shocked I was when I walked into a New Year's Eve party and saw Maude sitting in Johnny's lap. My shock had nothing to do with race. Rather, I had this wierd notion that our leaders were somehow above the mundane, like interest in the opposite sex. It was okay for me, because I was young and suffering—I thought—from a weakness of the flesh. But for old people over thirty?

On the other hand, I was always a bit stunned at the radiant beauty of the other woman leader, Helen Allison, married to an engineer my father knew from New York, Carl Winter. Helen was voluptuous without being heavy, and was tall and graceful. When Allison was a defendant in one of the Smith Act trials of the Communist leadership nearly twenty years later, and had to be pushed into the courtroom in a wheelchair, I was doubly sad, both because she was ill and suffering a most painful condition, and because I could not accept the notion that such beauty could wither.

Allison must also have been a feminist within our context. Although her father, Alfred Wagenknecht, was a famous old German-American socialist turned communist, she used the name of her mother, who had also been a socialist and, I believe, a feminist, of distinction. Later, between the Cleveland years and those of McCarthyism, she rolled up truly impressive votes running on the Communist Party ticket in another major midwestern city.

The Party's Education Director and my direct boss, Avrum Landy by name, was Jewish, and exquisitely handsome. In some ways he was a personification of the Jewish tradition of intellectualism combined with the vigor and purposefulness of the man of action. None of these people, with the possible exception of Landy, were local. They had been assigned to Cleveland as had I. Though I admired these leaders, it was the Midwesterners and also those active in my organization, the Young Communist League, who interested me most. Two became nationally known in later years. One was Gus Hall, who still heads the perhaps thousand people who call themselves the Communist Party. The other, Henry Winston, Black, became the organization's national chair. He was blind for the last thirty years of his life due to neglect, by federal prison officials, of a brain tumor he suffered while serving a long term of imprisonment for the crime of being a Communist.

It is not idealization of any of these people—I parted company with them politically forty years ago—that causes me to remember them as singularly attractive. Gus Hall, although not of a towering height, gave the impression of an Aryan giant out of Jack London's stories. His splendid posture was the resulting of having been a weightlifter and gymnast in a Communist sports organization in the iron-mining country of his native Minnesota. He had to wear short sleeves because his biceps were so big, or at least I thought that was the reason. His family name was Hallberg, of the Swedish Finns, and he was a real Scandinavian blonde with a mouthful of perfect white teeth and a huge and healthy laugh. In the years after I left the party he became a dictatorial martinet, a development apparently inevitable when one enjoys absolute power in any structure.

Winston was one of the sweetest individuals I have ever known. He came from Mississippi, which in those years is like saying he was from South Africa before Mandela. For a poor Black from that state—and there were none but *poor* African-Americans in Mississippi then—to have overcome the hatred and mistrust of all whites that those conditions bred in all Blacks, and to be able psychologically to work as an equal with whites in the first third of the 20th century in an organization of self-educated people of the working class, is an enormous achievement. It is also a compliment to the party's unending efforts to combat racism in its own ranks.

And then there was Andy Onda, that rough diamond of a Slovak workingman, square in body and face, with whom I had no choice but to get drunk when we were out campaigning for his election to the city council. Our knock at each door brought an invitation to come in, sit down, and have a glass of wine. That was an invitation no candidate could refuse. Nor did Andy want to.

Onda came within a hairsbreadth of victory under the system of district elections. The winner got 6,833 votes to his 6,452, a margin that was no accident. Unemployment among Cleveland's one million during the Great Depression had reached a quarter of a million: one-half of the city's labor force. Onda had led the Unemployed Councils, initiated by the Communist Party, to win "home relief" (read: welfare), and also to prevent evictions for non-payment of rent. The bailiffs would put the furniture out on the streets and the Unemployed Councils put it back. Pitched battles resulted. Five local Communists, including a young Black woman, were killed by police. The cops knew whom they were aiming at.

I should make clear that in the thirty years I was affiliated with the Communist movement I never saw a fire-arm in the hands of a Communist, except for one close friend, George David, who was briefly a New York City policeman. He was under Police Department orders, because it was wartime, to have his pistol with him even when off duty. Exactly once, I carried a piece of pipe for self-protection. I didn't have to use it. In my long personal experience, violence invariably came from the other side: the cops, the National Guard, employers' hired strike-breaking goons, or, on one occasion, actual fascists.

Onda's efforts won a far higher welfare food budget for the Cleveland unemployed than for those of any other town in Ohio. You couldn't exactly afford caviar—that budget was 22 1/2 cents per day—but you could survive. When Tanya and I were briefly on welfare at just about the time of Andy's campaign for local office, we existed largely on the free food-surplus prunes and terribly over-salted canned beef we were issued. I was once late to a meeting of the state officers of the Young Communist League because I had to walk several miles downtown for want of the nickel streetcar fare, and remember how embarrassed I was when our state leader gave me five cents out of his munificent $12-a-week salary so I could ride home.

Another Cleveland Communist, tall and dour E. C. Greenfield, organized a Small Home and Landowners Federation that attained a membership of twenty thousand in that one city. These solid citizens would build barricades at both ends of a block when the cops and sheriff's deputies came to evict someone who couldn't meet his mortgage payment. When the new Roosevelt Administration passed its Home Owners Loan Act, thirteen thousand of the thirty-three thousand loans granted in Cleveland to help people save their homes went to members of Greenfield's Federation.

The United Auto Workers, today one of the country's largest unions, was founded in Cleveland at this time by a worker in late middle age, Wyndham Mortimer, a Communist employed at the White Motors truck plant. At the founding national convention, he accepted the post of vice-president to avoid the divisive Red-baiting that would have resulted had he become president.

Although I had been brought in to Cleveland from New York because of my record in organizing sales of Communist-published or endorsed reading matter, my only connection with the activities just described was to go to the Communist Party clubs of the unemployed, the home-owners, and the industrial workers to promote this literature. The one exception, other than participating in that election campaign, was during the most critical and spectacular strike of that time. The steel industry had been regarded as immune to unionism since the breaking of a national strike in 1919 led by William Z. Foster, then an A.F. of L. organizer and subsequently head of the national Communist Party. In the '30s, Ohio had one-third of the country's steel-workers, and that industry employed 30 percent of all the state's workers in manufacturing industries.

A Steel Workers' Organizing Committee was set up by John L. Lewis, the beetle-browed president of the United Mine Workers, famous in all strata of society as a self-taught orator of the Winston Churchill school, and a Republican. But he knew where to find devoted and skilled organizers. Keeping the top posts for old-line unionists like himself, chiefly miners, Lewis went directly to the Communist Party to fill the organizing committee's two hundred paid posts, which his own union funded. The entire Communist Party and Young Communist League paid staffs in Ohio's one-industry steel towns were put on the payroll. Gus Hall headed the organizing drive in the most important, Youngstown, with tremendous success. Nationally (which meant essentially Illinois, Indiana, Ohio, and Pennsylvania) the union grew from eight thousand to half a million members in two years. "Big Steel", the United States Steel Corporation, caved in without a strike. But "Little Steel", three companies employing a total of sixty-five thousand, almost all in Ohio, would not consider a union. A strike was called. One day two hundred women participated in the picketing in Youngstown, and the police fired tear gas into their ranks. A six-hour pitched battle resulted, in which two strikers were shot dead.

I remember Youngstown at that time as virtually a movie set for industrial America. In Cleveland, a large city, you could remain unaware of the steel mills most of the time because they were crowded into the narrow flats along the Cuyahoga River. In Youngstown, however, the mills overshadowed the town the way the giant oil refinery I can see from my window in the Berkeley hills dominates Richmond, California. On one street homes and stores were crowded wall-to-wall —the Ohio River coal valleys left little room for building—and on the very next towered the immense blast furnaces, coke ovens, and open hearths. The nights glowed with light, roared with the hiss of gas, rumbled and clanked from the unending stream of trains bringing in raw materials and hauling out the finished products. Whistles shrieked. Hell has to be quieter.

Tanya and I and the other members of the Young Communist League did our picketing at the stupendous plant of Republic Steel in Cleveland. Killings occurred there as well. Fortunately, nothing happened when we were present, but that did not ease the fear of what had and might. We must have picketed during the graveyard shift, because although the strike took place during the summer, I remember pitch darkness because the plant was shut down. The giant windowless mill extended until it merged with the night. Only the oil-can fires maintained by the union pickets cast flickering shadows on walls, streets, and people.

At eighteen, I had become old enough to belong to the Communist Party, and joined, in Cleveland, while continuing membership in the YCL. I filled out my application under the eye of my boss, Landy. When I got to the line for "occupation," I looked up at him in puzzlement. He said, "You're a professional revolutionary, aren't you?" That was a term borrowed from prerevolutionary Russia. So that's what's on my application.

Being a professional revolutionary meant not only willingness to accept being sent wherever the Party felt you could best serve its needs, but also living a very hand-to-mouth existence on what it could afford to pay, whenever money was there. My salary as Literature Director for the state was $10 per week. That was the salary of every unmarried full-timer, as we were called, regardless of rank. When Tanya came out from New York shortly afterward—I remember her getting off the Greyhound bus in a green corduroy two-piece suit and large beret, very pretty—I was raised to the married person's $12 rate, and she was appointed my half-time assistant at the single rate, or five dollars. So we had $17 a week between us, about $385 today.

Being poor was taken for granted in the life to which we had committed. However, two years later the Party no longer wanted us in its employ, partly for reasons that will emerge, although we remained members in good standing. It eventually wangled jobs for me in Roosevelt's work program for the unemployed, first in Cleveland, then Akron, enabling me to devote most of my time to its activities.

In the interim we had to eat. The situation was quite serious. We had absolutely no money for rent. At one point a couple of kindly comrades let us use their attic room, and embarrassed the hell out of us ex-middle-class New Yorkers by calling our attention to the chamber pot stashed beneath the bed. There was no such thing as a two-bath home for working-class families in that day, and these were all two-story houses, with the bathroom on the ground floor. Earlier, when we had not yet sold for junk a wondrous jaloppy I had bought to do a traveling tour of duty around the state, and had nowhere else to sleep, we drove it out at night to the shore of Lake Erie. We discovered in the morning that we had driven to within a few feet of the edge of the bluff.

During this period of our rock-bottom poverty the Furriers' Union called a strike, and we were asked to picket for it, for pay. This was one of the most militant unions in the country, led by avowed Communists. Its workers certainly included the largest percentage of Communist Party members and supporters in any union. The labor force was almost entirely Jewish. So were the employers. The notion that they had any common interest because they were Jews was laughable, on both sides. This union was responsible for the fact that, years later, Tom Dewey of New York was the Republican candidate for president against Harry Truman. During Dewey's term as district attorney of New York, a mob of Jewish gangsters, led by a couple of hoods named Lepke and Gurrah (immortalized in a film by an Italian director that won the Cannes Prize in 1984) had been terrorizing the garment industry in New York with the cooperation of unscrupulous employers. They had taken over locals of other unions by strong-arm tactics.

One day they tried a similar assault on the headquarters of the Furriers in New York. Furriers were generally small, scrawny ghetto people. Their tuberculosis rate had been high before their union won decent pay and better working conditions. But these furriers possessed boundless courage. The next morning's New York papers carried photos of a score of the hoods sprawled against the front of that union headquarters, their legs stretched out in front of them, generally supporting themselves with one arm, their heads hanging to one side or the other, and their faces a mess. No one had been killed on either side, but the Lepke-Gurrah mob had been busted, by Communists, whereupon the cops booked the gangsters. Dewey then prosecuted them in a public atmosphere in which he couldn't lose, won a national reputation as a gangbuster, and rode this to the presidential nomination.

So there was this strike in Cleveland by a union we thought the world of, Tanya and I were broke, and we were offered jobs picketing. We had, in fact, met each other on a laundry union picket line in New York. We had picketed for the Ohio steel workers in a dangerous situation and would be on other picket lines thereafter. But to take money for picketing? It was axiomatic that picketing is the first duty of a worker on strike, for it gives him a feeling of participation. Moreover, from our standpoint, it would hopefully make him class-conscious. For outsiders to picket in support was an elementary principle of class solidarity. But to hire outsiders to picket? Had this not been a union in whose leadership we had absolute confidence, we would unquestionably have tightened our belts a notch. (That's an interesting male-chauvinist term, because women don't necessarily have belts with which to counter-irritate hungry stomachs.)

We took the job along with Irwin Laibman, a fellow Young Communist Leaguer with a great sense of humor. Bored to death, we would sing silly songs. I remember one from him: "I wish I was a fish, I wish I was a fish, I'd swim and swim in the deep blue sea, I wish I was a fish." Not exactly one of your stirring labor anthems. While this strike dragged on, Tanya found a job a block away painting live baby turtles.

Somehow I associate seeing my first DC-3, which happened in Cleveland, with the start of the Italian invasion of Ethiopia in 1935. Perhaps it was the same day. Imagine an all-metal monopolane, streamlined, with retractable landing gear, the engines actually built into the wings, capable of lifting twenty-one passengers into the air and carrying them from the East Coast to the Midwest without refueling! I've always been fascinated by technology, and in the McCarthy years made my living translating it for a decade after being driven out of my own field. But in 1935, when military planes were very rarely seen over our cities, that passenger plane put me in mind of bombers.

The fascist dictator Mussolini bombed Ethiopian villages from the air at a time when world morality had not yet degenerated to taking war against civilians as a matter of course, and the U.S. Marines were not yet doing practice landings in our own centers of urban poverty. A great debate raged in the serious American press, in liberal magazines, and even among Communists, about the attitude to be taken toward that war in Africa. Italy very openly used the standard imperialist argument that had always worked in white Europe and America until then, namely, that it was bringing civilization to the savages. Whites in general held the grossest racist beliefs and so accepted that logic. The American Black community rallied to Ethiopia's aid as far as it was able. Some African-Americans who fought in the Abraham Lincoln Brigade in Spain two years later did so to get back at Mussolini, just as the Jews in that force, comprising an extremely high proportion of its ranks, were particularly out to stop Hitler.

For us on the Left, things were complicated. Ethiopia was not only an absolute monarchy but also quite openly practiced slavery. How could liberals, radicals, much less Communists, support a slave state? It took very considerable discussion before we all accepted the notion that the overriding consideration was national independence: the right of Ethiopia or any other country to determine its own destiny. Certainly fascist Italy could not show Ethiopia the way to a better life.

But there was another, more ominous factor. During my year in the U.S.S.R., in 1931-2, the Soviet press repeatedly stated that if Japan were not forced to abandon the conquest of China then begun, it would lead to a second world war. When I returned to the U.S., that idea was simply ridiculed. By 1935 the situation was different. Hitler was in power in Germany, and talking more and more openly of a need for a world crusade against communism. President Roosevelt, regarding that as a pretext for a program of Nazi world domination, had finally established diplomatic relations with the Soviet government, which our government had withheld for sixteen years after the Communist revolution.

Hitler and Mussolini were establishing their Rome-Berlin Axis, and the later addition of Japan was already being discussed. To me, this was excruciatingly personal. I was just on the verge of military age, and knew perfectly well that a draft would be imposed in time of war. I was willing to take risks for ideals I believed worthy, but saw no reason for my life to be ended, ruined, or disrupted in a war that could have been forestalled by preventing Hitler from re-arming Germany and not shipping Japan the scrap iron that came back to us as bombs. Germany's occupation at the end of the war was achieved at the cost of millions of lives. This could have been accomplished before the war without bloodshed by making Hitler shut down military production, because when he came to power Germany hadn't the means to resist: it had been essentially disarmed when it lost the previous war.

I discussed the danger of war with Andy Onda, the man I later campaigned for. He demonstrated with impeccable logic—things did turn out exactly as he predicted—that if Italy were not stopped in Ethiopia, this appeasement of the fascists, after Japan's unpunished actions in China and the beginnings of Hitler's rollback of the conditions imposed upon Germany after World War I, could only encourage them to further undertakings. The rest of the world would find this intolerable, and world war would result.

My blood ran cold. I have never lacked imagination, which makes it a good deal harder to be brave. But meanwhile there was the work to be done for which I had been brought to Ohio. And here I had come up against a problem of conscience involving money. The Party had just taken a bold and risky step. In addition to the small-size *Daily Worker*, it now launched a Sunday edition, complete with color rotogravure section, a magazine section, and expanded sports coverage. While some sympathetic small businessmen would place ads which paid off handsomely, and a few Communist-influenced fraternal societies, ethnic organizations, and labor unions occasionally did likewise, corporate advertisers would not touch the *Worker*, not that it sought such money. The papers lived off subscriptions, newsstand sales, and endless fund drives, as public television and radio do to some degree these days. It was also clear to us that the very same people who would devote endless hours and effort to peddling our publications and collecting money would work just a little bit harder if there were some tangible reward as well.

At that time there was just one workers' state in the world, just one country without unemployment, the Soviet Union. There was no Red China or Cuba or Vietnam or North Korea to choose among as model, as happened with the young radicals of the 1960s. To see the Soviet Union was the dream of every Communist. So a trip to the Soviet Union was offered as grand prize to the person in Ohio who sold the largest number of subscriptions to the new *Sunday Worker.*

The subscription money passed through my hands. It was almost all in cash. Very few workingpeople had checking accounts in those days. Most of the money went on to New York. The prize was an Ohio project to be funded out of what we retained. The money to pay Tanya's and my combined $17 per week also was in my hands. It came from the profits on our regular literature sales. At the time in question, it just wasn't coming in. As a matter of fact, that's what I had been brought to Ohio to correct: their sales of reading matter had been very poor. I felt that I was entitled to eat, and I had to pay rent, so I went on paying Tanya's and my salaries, no more and no less. But when it came time to send the winner to the Soviet Union, the prize money wasn't there. I was hauled before the top state leadership of the Party, told that I had destroyed people's confidence in its word, and that if I weren't just a kid, I would have been expelled from its ranks. That gorgeous Helen Allison was probably the roughest on me. I was fired from my job.

The Ohio Party still had its obligation to the national office to achieve a stated level of subscriptions to the new Sunday paper. Everyone knew that I was good at selling printed matter in which I believed. I had done then unheard-of things like stapling the cover cartoons of our superb cultural magazine, *New Masses,* to telephone poles at eye level facing the street along the commute avenues to downtown. As people idled at red lights, they would take in William Gropper's savage and colorful renderings of the U.S. Senate stalling New Deal legislation, or of the emperor of Japan, which I remember particularly because Gropper couldn't help giving every face some slight tinge of his own Jewish origins. I had enjoyed this chance to be outdoors. And if the weather were hot, the buddy who helped me would go halves on a quart of ice cream of which we made our lunch.

So I was offered the job of traveling salesman for the paper. I took a stated commission for myself, essentially like a news vendor. This could not support both Tanya and me, and she had no alternative but to go back to her parents in New York. There just weren't any jobs, not even painting turtles. My job required a car. Dad couldn't help me with that out of his earnings on a government make-work program. Moreover,

Tanya, back in the city where we had long-established contacts, was the person who had to find the money. She couldn't ask my folks, who were still refusing to take our relationship seriously, although she had written them an extraordinarily mature and very beautiful letter describing her emotions and my very different ones quite accurately, which we recovered from Dad when he was already a centenarian. [After her father died in 1955, mine became a substitute in the deepest way.]

Tanya's parents, who were wonderful to us four years later, when our daughter Phyllis was born and they realized we were together to stay, did not yet regard me as family. She turned for help to our seventeen-year-old closest friends, Trudy and George David, who subsequently married and maintained their relationship until death did them part. Trudy, with talent as a painter, was very attractive. George was a heroically handsome blond in face and body, chiseled features rounded just enough to reveal his gentleness, dimpled chin, laughing blue eyes, the only Jew I then knew who had the kind of muscle that comes from being raised on a farm. I quite seriously recommended to him that he try out for the movies at a time when we Reds thought that was time-wasting trivia. He didn't. They provided me with their entire savings, $45, about $1,125 in today's value. [Their committed friendship continued in later life, when they helped me press a record of the tape of my hearing before McCarthy. George became a successful businessman before he was thirty. He provided jobs to several returned veterans of the Abraham Lincoln Brigade in the Spanish Civil War, including their commander, Milt Wolff, befriended by Hemingway and author of an autobiographical novel of that war, *Another Hill*. Milt, who presently lives near us in the East Bay, is a figure important to a very broad range of people of my generation.]

The kind of car that $1,125-equivalent would buy in 1935 was a 1927 Star-Durant, four cylinders, stick shift of course. My car had two very special peculiarities. Essentially it had no brakes, so I learned to stop it by carefully judging the distance to the car in front of me, on red lights. Then I would take my foot off the accelerator at a point that enabled me to hit him ever so gently. That brought me to a full stop. Cars were then built like tanks, and bumpers were not yet manufactured to encourage you to buy a new car if you hit something at over five miles an hour. However, the windshield was designed to open horizontally and admit air by use of a folding elbow hinge. Unfortunately the hinge pin was missing. When I stopped, tapping the guy in front —few women drove— my windshield would fly up and come down with a terrible clatter. The driver would dash out to see the damage, and go off more or less placated when none was to be found. Cincinnati had very steep streets, even a funicular. I'm afraid I chugged off after denting more than one fender there. To wait and pay was out of the question. What could I pay with?

Cincinnati was a very different place than Cleveland. It deserved the name, Queen City of the West, which Horace Greeley had given it a century earlier. Even though it sided with the North in the Civil War, some of the culture and elegance the slave-owners could afford rubbed off on it . People were clothes conscious, like New Yorkers, but just as broke as Clevelanders.

In Hamilton, a railway junction town west of Cincinnati, one of the names on my list of prospects was that of a tall, gaunt, unemployed railway worker whose only clothing were his work overalls and a clean pair of Sunday overalls. When I asked him to take out a subscription, which was two dollars for a year, he said, "Waal, I just been cut off relief, and I don't know when I'll see any cash again, so I guess I'd better take out that subscription now." Man does not live by bread alone.

CHAPTER 6

Being Red in Ohio

Sheets of driving rain. Lightning. Thunder. We take a tiny road, starting after dark for security, winding uphill from what passed for a highway in Ohio in 1936. Our goal an isolated shack next to the tipple of a shut down coal mine. In the big cities, Cleveland, Cincinnati, even Youngstown, Communists could function legally in the mid-'30s. In the coal country due west of Pittsburgh, being a Communist meant, at the very least, being thrown off welfare and simply starving. That's a much more effective form of terror than clubs, bullets, even jail. In jail they fed you, although your family on the outside might starve.

Nationally unemployment was dropping from the 40 percent peak of 1932, but in coal country it still crippled a good one-third of the labor force. The handful of local Communists and their supporters had gathered to hear my pitch for subscriptions to our new *Sunday Worker* in this poorest of homes. It consisted of two rooms. The bed was in one, with the couple's small children, about as many as could fit onto it. The hosts were Appalachian, though they called themselves "snakes," as they came from West Virginia, which sticks a narrow splinter of land between Pennsylvania and Ohio a couple of miles from this mine.

The meeting did not consist of more than ten people, including the local $10-a-week Party official who guided me there, and myself. The group was ethnically mixed, immigrants and native mountaineers. I don't remember Blacks on this occasion, but they were represented in the Party in full proportion to their numbers in the country's population. Ours was the only organization in the United States of which that was true. The Party insisted that the unions it helped organize—old ones like the miners', new ones like the auto and steelworkers'—abandon all discrimination against African-Americans, whether in barring them from membership or confining them to Jim Crow locals. Our reasoning was simple and effective: only the bosses benefit when workers are divided.

People at meetings like this one in coal country did come through with their $2.00 subscriptions, because I was able to put gas, at a dime a gallon, into my car from my commission. I'm not sure how much food I put into my mouth that way, because people like me would be passed from home to home, put up overnight and fed. I remember virtually nothing about the people who gave me food and shelter, though I do remember the meetings, however small, and individual responses to my efforts. I really had internalized the idea that my material welfare didn't matter, but only people's responses to what my organization had to offer. I must have eaten mountaineer food, Polish and Czech cooking, too, but remember none of it.

Only from Cincinnati do I recall some people individually. This is because the leads I was given for that city roused my curiosity when I met them, as they were a breed totally different from the workingclass of which I was a part in every way but heritage. They were academics. Because the Party concentrated its efforts in centers of basic industry, its contacts in other places were happenstance. My only previous contact with academics was in their professional capacities as professors in front of a classroom or, across a table, the faculty committee that expelled me.

But these Cincinnati college teachers were on the same side as I was. Perhaps since the few of them were isolated from like-thinking people elsewhere and also possibly because I had spent a year in the Soviet Union, of which they thought so highly then, they found me interesting. I suppose that's flattering, considering my age at the time.

They took me to meet either a professor or, I think for some reason, the president of Hebrew Union College in Cincinnati, the oldest rabbinical school in the United States. I had lived in the Soviet Union, and he was concerned about the status of Judaism there. To me the fact that pogroms were now unheard of and Jews were actually favored, to make up for previous discrimination, in gaining the education and entering professions from which tsarism had barred them, was what counted. In my eyes, his objections were academic nit-picking. Granted that my atheism was an obstacle to appreciating his point of view. I concluded, even from the academic contacts who shared my Marxism, that professors don't know much about the real world.

These Ohio academics also provided me with my once-in-a-lifetime ride on a genuine working Ohio River sternwheeler, which on weekends took people out to picnic at Coney Island, an up-river park. Incidentally, one Communist Party member in Cleveland was a retired Mississippi and Ohio steamboat captain of the generation that followed Mark Twain's. I. O. Ford by name, he repeatedly ran for office on the Communist ticket. He illustrates the fact, obvious to us who were in it, that the Party had its roots in every current of American life.

I visited Cincinnati repeatedly. Once I hitch-hiked to New York from there and back again. I got a lift from Cincinnati's outskirts to

Pittsburgh on a long automobile-transporting truck-and-trailer. The driver was constantly almost veering off the road, which twists along the Ohio River. It was not that he hadn't mastered the rig, but that this was his third Cincinnati-Pittsburgh round-trip without sleep. In those years, if there was work to be had, you did it on the boss' terms. Between those terms and the dictatorial, goon-squad type of union leadership like Jimmy Hoffa's gangster-connected management of the Teamsters' Union, you gladly chose the latter, because that union negotiated for you the chance to live a somewhat human existence. Think of the Russians' acceptance of Stalin for thirty years.

I was relieved when that rig had a flat on the bridge over which we rolled into Pittsburgh. The ride had become just a bit too hairy. Out of the Pittsburgh smog my next rides took me along that ever-beautiful Juniata River, this time in the immediate wake of the second most devastating flood in its history. The first, before my time, had produced the notorious Johnstown Flood, with much loss of life. This time, Johnstown, where a tributary enters the river and mountains rise sheer on all sides, had been flooded again, but with few, if any, deaths. Yet I saw mattresses in the tree-tops, and the river was still more like the Tuolomne flowing out of Yosemite than the bucolic stream I remembered.

The trip back from New York was in one sense a repeat of my first New York-to-Ohio hitch-hike two years earlier. Somewhere in the middle of Pennsylvania a guy gave me a lift, immediately took his right hand off the wheel, and began to feel for my genitals. I hollered, in an effectively angry voice, "Let me the hell out of here." It was getting dark, and I was lucky to have a truckdriver pick me up. I told him what had happened, and he roared with laughter. I interrupted the trip for a day in Cleveland, and spent it reading Sholokhov's splendid, honest novel of collectivization in the Soviet Union, *Seeds of Tomorrow.* Headed south the next day.

That night was one of the most miserable I have ever experienced. I was dropped off before dark, but hours went by without a ride. It fell dark, and a cold driving rain began. I got thoroughly chilled and was dog-tired by the time another truckdriver gave me a lift. I climbed into the cab and soon dozed off. A jab in the ribs woke me, and I heard a voice:

"What in the hell do you think I picked you up for?"

"I dunno," I said.

"To keep me awake, that's what." I stayed awake.

When that *Sunday Worker* founding circulation drive was over—in which Ohio did exceedingly well, thanks in some measure to my efforts—the Party used its connections to find me a job with the Works Progress Administration (WPA), the Roosevelt-era make-work program.

For some reason I was hired at the top pay that structure offered: $23 per week. Finally decent money! A skilled worker in private employ wouldn't get more than $40. So Tanya was able to come out again from New York. She became the local paid staff of the Friends of the Soviet Union. That country had not yet completed the Second Five-Year Plan to pull itself out from underdevelopment, yet Hitler was making public speeches saying that if Germany had the Ukraine and the Ural Mountains, it would be swimming in milk, pork, and honey. The Russians were in trouble.

The Friends of the Soviet Union did not raise money for the USSR. Its purpose was to bring knowledge of the only country in the world functioning without capitalism. Its membership was large, and its magazine, *Soviet Russia Today,* had a national circulation nearing a hundred thousand. Its editor, Jessica Smith, for whom I was to work a few years later, had been an active suffragist until American women got the vote, had lived in the USSR with her farm-expert husband, and had written the very first book on Soviet women in 1928.

My job on WPA (the Works Progress Administration) was in the printshop and bindery of the Cleveland Public Library. It involved the first heavy physical work I ever did, and also the danger of serious injury. I was taught to operate what the printing trades call a guillotine cutter. This is a heavy power-operated horizontal knife—about five feet long in the case of the machine I operated—used in the paper industry to slice hundreds of huge sheets at a time into pages. One's fingers get awfully close to the descending blade. At Cleveland's main library it was used for delicate trimming, one at a time, of bound well-worn books, from which I first removed the binding, so the pages would be fresh and square when new binding was applied. Using that monster on single books was like using an axe to trim one's finger nails.

The worst of it was changing the blade when it got dull. One would unbolt it from the traveling power bar above, raise the bar, screw a couple of large bolts in as grasping holds, and then lift it out to deposit in a box to go to the grinder's. At that point the fifty-pound blade was facing straight down over one's thigh, because one had to bend back to balance the weight. The floor had to be kept painstakingly clean of grease and oil, because a fall at that moment could result in grave injury at least. I never knew that to happen, although when I worked in commercial paper shops later in New York, every experienced worker had part or all of one or more fingers missing.

The changing of the blades aside, the job had its fun aspects. I was a very good checker player, and the boss, an Irishman in his 40s, loved the game. We'd play every day at lunchtime, and I would make sure to win two of the first three games. He'd then want to go to best out of five, and

I was more than happy to go along. The longer the lunch hour the better.

The work itself was interesting and involved skill. No two books were exactly the same size or thickness, and certain types of paper crumbled easily, so one had to know how to prevent that. Naturally, I enjoyed looking at books that were new to me. Angelo Herndon, the nineteen-year-old Atlanta Black we had carried on our shoulders from Penn Station in New York when we finally got him out on bail, had written a book. It came through for re-binding, and I had a chance to read it. (Half a century later I saw a copy again at the home of an acquaintance who was letting me go through her books to find source material for this one.)

I also took the risk of performing what I regarded as my revolutionary duty on what were, to me, dangerous books. No, I was not a civil libertarian then. This was the period of Stalin's purge trials, when Trotskyists were being accused of serving as spies for Hitler, and were executed. The establishment press assured us that these were frame-ups, but it was twenty years before Stalin's successor, Khrushchev, told us that indeed they actually had been. Meanwhile, even the U.S. ambassador to Moscow, a corporation lawyer, watching the trials from a courtroom seat, was sending coded cables to the secretary of state and the president assuring them that the Trotskyists had been fairly found guilty by the weight of the evidence. (You can find this in Ambassador Joseph Davies' book, *Mission to Moscow.*) So when an occasional Trotskyist book came by, my knife would slip.

I had my skis in Cleveland, and convinced Tanya to try them once. She was an absolutely fearless distance swimmer and canoer on rough water, but skiing intimidated her. She fell once, with no damage, but that was it. So skiing and softball were about the only things I did without her.

I continued my childhood habit of very long walks to absorb what a city had to offer. I would walk across town from Cleveland's Kinsman Avenue area, where we lived, to the 105th St. neighborhood near the lake, past the very attractive University Circle, with its Museum of Art, Symphony Hall, and gently rolling wooded parklands.

Our Young Communist League club would hike in the charming small gorge of the Cuyahoga River, and would canoe along the old canal and in Akron's Summit Lake. Once Tanya and I made love in the bottom of a canoe in a summer rainstorm.

The neighborhood club to which I belonged had its own headquarters, but we also made use of the Jewish community center a couple of blocks away. There we organized a production of Gilbert and Sullivan's *Trial By Jury.* It was a lot of fun, and excellent political satire. I would drop in on the rehearsals, and probably can recall the complete lyrics to this day, given a little help. The music is relaxing, and the words wield a real political stiletto. Unfortunately, Gilbert used more stanzas to make a point than permit illustration here. I think I knew the satirical arias in all their works. I also read poetry aloud at our meetings, particularly Langston Hughes, the verse of a poor-white Southerner, Don West, and Alfred Hayes' "To Otto Bauer," which, as literature, is the best piece of political poetry I have ever seen. All appeared in an extraordinary book, *Proletarian Literature in the United States*, 1935.

We also had picnics, and I remember Tanya becoming quite jealous of a vivacious young woman whom I flirted with. By remarkable coincidence, in view of my later career in Soviet affairs, this girl, Gail Davidow, subsequently lived in Moscow for many years as wife of the correspondent of the American Communist daily. She and her husband, Mike, had good personal reason to be excessively staunch supporters of the Soviet Union. They had an epileptic son who survived into adult life. As poor people in New York in the '40s and '50s, they endlessly battled unresponsive bureaucracies for proper care and education for their boy. But in Moscow they encountered marvelous, understanding, tender care. When they later lived in San Francisco I invited her to speak at a short course I gave at Antioch West, and I recall the respect with which the no-nonsense health professionals who were my students, including one recent immigrant from a Baltic Soviet republic, listened to her experiences.

The war in Spain began in 1936. The Party recruited people to go. I was not asked, possibly because I was younger than anyone who did go, at least from Cleveland. In any case, I was helpless without glasses. Unbreakable lenses had not yet been developed, and there were no opticians to serve the army of the Spanish Republic. But the bottom line is that I didn't want to die. Sometime during that period, I promised myself that if this country ever faced anything similar, I would not yield. And to the limited degree that the McCarthy period, the Peekskill assault on a Paul Robeson concert, the bayonets close to my chest during Ronald Reagan's martial law in Berkeley in the 60s, and incidents here and in the South have tested that resolve, I have kept my promise.

Since I will be tormented as long as I live by the fact that I was not in Spain, I must pay their due to those who were. One hundred and fifty Americans from Ohio joined the Lincoln Brigade. Half of them, including the son of the previous governor, were members of the Communist Party. And half of all those who went now lie buried in Spanish soil. One was Frank Rogers, head of our Young Communist League. He is seen in "The Good Fight," a superb documentary on the Abraham Lincoln Brigade made nearly half a century later. Joe Dallet, a Jew from New York, who had headed the CP in Youngstown, was also among those killed. Fifteen hundred people, Black and white, attended a memorial for him in that steel town. Speakers from the NAACP, the A.F. of L. Central Labor Council, and the Party honored him. The city's daily newspaper, the Youngstown *Vindicator*, which had denounced him in life, editorialized as follows:

"Those who have to do with public affairs frequently have found themselves disagreeing sharply with the causes which Joe Dallet championed, but all of them came to respect the rugged honesty of his character and some of them, at least, came to regard with real affection the earnest personality which looked so straightforwardly out of his brown eyes.

"Whatever may be said of Joe's ideology as a Communist worker, certainly he had a steadfast devotion to an idea, which he pursued without regard to the consequences for himself. That he should fall in battle for the cause he cherished, at the head of a charge which he felt was in behalf of liberty and justice to man, is thoroughly typical of his character."

It is difficult for me to imagine a Republican newspaper today (or any major Democratic one, for that matter) carrying such an editorial. It helps one to understand the atmosphere in the city to which I was sent next, Akron, then tire capital of the world, about forty miles south of Cleveland, where I was to head its hundred-member YCL. There, too, the status of the CP was widely acknowledged. When a writer who belonged to the Party wrote a book about that city at the time, it was featured in the main display window of the leading department store. The book was *Industrial Valley,* by Ruth McKenney, who later wrote the hit Broadway musical, "The Boys From Brazil." In its description of the kind of people who joined the Party, why they did so, how they conducted their activities, and their place in events, *Industrial Valley* is the best book ever about the Communist Party in the '30s.

Akron's daily, the *Beacon-Journal*, was nationally respected, and still is. Hardly a day passed between 1936 and 1939 without its political columnist, whatever the issue, speculating: "What does Jim Keller think about this?" The Party had sent Keller to head its organization in Akron after his release from jail in California. He was one of several imprisoned in the effort to organize farm workers, immortalized in Steinbeck's *Grapes of Wrath.* Jim was a Russian Jew with a heavy accent, but perfect English grammar.

Akron was a city primarily of former West Virginia mountaineers, poor whites from Alabama, and many African-Americans. When we were assigned down there I said to Tanya, "Your name is too Russian for that place. You really ought to find another." So she practiced answering to Toby. However, we discovered when we got there that Akron was one of the few cities in the country where the 15 percent of the working class that had been born abroad was largely ethnically Russian. There were lots of Vladimirs, Andreis, Sergeis, and Borises. So Tanya was okay.

That was 1938. In 1935 the Akron CP had only fifteen members, almost all Southerners, and chiefly white. By 1937, after an extraordinary strike was won that established the Rubber Workers' Union, five hundred to seven hundred fifty people attended Party meetings. Two thousand union members came to hear about the loyalists seeking to maintain the Spanish Republic. The president of the union, not remotely a Communist, was the main speaker at a "Save China: Boycott Japan" meeting prior to World War II. I was reminded of the conscious solidarity with underdogs worldwide that developed across Russia after the revolution. People there talked about and really believed the traveling electric sign above a very busy Moscow square near our home: "We'll tear the Scottsboro Negroes out of the hands of the executioner." In Russian, of course.

Tire manufacturers —Goodyear, Goodrich, Firestone, General Tire, Sieberling—were all in Akron or neighboring Barberton. Making tires was exceedingly heavy work, and required strong, young men. The employers themselves had instituted a six-hour day, because that was as long as a man could lift and throw tires, or pull back against the board with which he maneuvered each added ply of rubber against the spin of a core on which the tire was hand-built, layer by layer.

Three-quarters of the population was under forty, and the birthrate was very high. Tanya and I became friends with one couple, the Maxwells. She was a direct descendant of Virginia Dare, the first white child born in North America, in 1587, and that was her maiden name. Virginia was twenty-two, had five children when we knew her, and was girlishly beautiful. I asked her husband, also a Southern white, who was an active union member and a Communist, why they had a new baby every year. He said, "I work with rubber all day long. I sure as hell don't want to see it at night."

He might avoid seeing it, but neither he nor anyone else in Akron could avoid smelling it, except perhaps the wealthy on West Hill, which was up-wind from the factories. For the rest of us, the choice was only whether you lived near a plant working with virgin rubber, which didn't smell all that awful, or with reclaim, from which the stench of the chemicals used to reprocess it was beyond belief.

While their men made tires, women made condoms, which were the subject of endless jokes and practical tricks played upon each other with them. In those scarce times, they were also used around the house. They'd stretch amazingly, and you could carry or store a lot of liquid in one.

The CP had gotten a foothold in this All-American town in much the same way as everywhere else. It had led the unemployed, in the first years of the Great Depression, to demand government assistance. Unemployment insurance did not then exist. If a man was out of work for any length of time, the family literally starved. There was no second income to fall back on, as women did not work once they had children. The Communists had also led the national Bonus March to Washington, to demand that a promised cash payment to veterans of World War I, by now in their 30s, was disbursed. Finally, they had organized small home-owners to defend themselves, politically and physically, against foreclosure evictions.

Among African-Americans, the CP had won adherents by the same activities and, further, by the national campaign to save the Scottsboro Boys. By 1935 the depression had eased a little. Many of the Akron unemployed were back in the tire factories, among them the fifteen Party members. Workers were now in desperation over the endless speed-up of production. Weight output per man had risen nearly seven times in seventeen years. Over ten years, with an enormous increase in output, the number of workers had been "downsized" by over seven thousand. Kidney and back trouble was more prevalent than in any other industry, because of the particular physical stresses in tire-building.

When Firestone cut base pay 11 percent, the workers would no longer stand it. They sent a committee to listen to a story some had heard from a union printer who had immigrated from Sarajevo. He told them that in the old country, "we had an inside strike. We just sat around by our machines and, by God, nobody could come in and take our jobs and they couldn't arrest us either. We were on the job."

The committee asked: "Didn't the boss try to throw you out?"

The printer replied: "He couldn't. He was afraid of hurting his expensive machinery if there was any fighting inside." That night the first sit-down strike in American history occurred, in the Firestone Plant. The men won, and the union grew like wildfire.

There was a very special flavor to strike activities in Akron. Four thousand men would jam the biggest hall in town for a union meeting, with a thousand more outside. And while they waited for a proposed settlement to be thrashed out, they'd sing hymns as well as patriotic and popular songs. Ultimately seventy thousand workers in and around Akron joined the rubber union. The prestige of the CP was so high that meetings of strike picket captains would invite the county leader of the Party to address them and offer his opinion on union contract matters. His wage was supposed to be $15 per week, about half of what a rubber worker got, but the money often was not there to give.

Although union meetings uniformly opened with prayers and were interspersed with hymns, the Rev. Gerald L.K. Smith, a proto-fascist, openly anti-Semitic rabble-rouser from Louisiana, was a total flop in calling upon the workers to abandon the union. During the biggest meeting in the city's history, forty thousand workers decided to reject a later take-away proposal by Goodrich Tire. When Firestone was on strike, a parade rallied fifty thousand. A labor slate swept the Democratic Party, winning ten of eleven city council nominations. One woman elected on that ticket, a Southern white, was just short of Communist in her politics and world horizons. In 1938 several hundred people regularly attended meetings of the Democratic Club in her ward.

I was now twenty-one. On a personal level, I spent much time with two African-American brothers named Jones, sons of a rubber worker. We discussed politics and the Marxist-Leninist theories to which we adhered. Of course, we talked baseball, too, but I had to be careful not to one-up anyone with the fact that I had actually seen the Babe Ruth Yankee team a decade earlier. I'd love to know what happened to these Joneses. I recall them chiefly for a combination of fine character, dignity, and quick and deep intelligence. Today it is possible they might have acquired a higher education and become people of distinction, but for Black youths of that time and place, I doubt that their lives consisted of much more than working for a living, when there was work to be had.

Tanya and I lived from my earnings as a teacher on W.P.A. I taught classes in current events. Students, chiefly adults, attended my classes free of charge and were not limited by prerequisites. As I have found throughout my life, teaching people with experience out in the world is vastly more difficult and more rewarding than teaching university students who have known nothing but school.

I was not preaching to the converted. For all the upsurge of unionism and radicalism, Akron had elected a liberal Republican as mayor. He had managed to win on a platform including Red-baiting, because he had a clean labor record. And, despite the myths about the New Deal, there was little more than tolerance for communism or Communists. The difference between this and the later McCarthy period was that, in the 30s, people knew what Communists had done for the unemployed and the unions, as well as to combat racial discrimination. Communists were not automatically barred from teaching, and there was no up-front inquisition into a teacher's beliefs, at this time.

At one point a state-wide gathering of all WPA teachers was convened in Akron. "The Star Spangled Banner" was sung to open it, and everyone rose. Then an African-American teacher began to sing "Lift Every Voice and Sing," the Negro national anthem. All the Blacks rose, and so did I. I knew the words—all Communists learned it in the struggles against racism—and sang along. Whites were a large majority of those present. Some, perhaps most, had never heard the song before. Most were amazed that people, Black or white, would rise for it. A few sensitive white teachers straggled to their feet. The rest remained seated, with no sound or visible sign of disapproval. The following day, in the teachers' room of my own school, a Southern white teacher I had thought of until then as a pretty decent guy, referred to this and said, "Hell, where I come from we used to just roll them over and shove it in." It is a sad commentary on the state of race relations today that when, in the 90s, a Black schoolteacher living in the same Berkeley retirement home as my father sang that song, accompanying herself on the piano, and I joined in, she asked: "Where did *you* learn it?" She was clearly surprised that a white man knew it.

While I did my teaching, educating, and organizing, Tanya's next assignment from the Young Communist League was associated with an organization, the American Youth Congress, that brought Communists more directly into contact with the New Deal leadership than any other. At a time when experienced people were out of work, obviously there were no jobs for the young. Unemployment among white youth then was about what it is for Black youth today. Young people were deeply dissatisfied with their idleness. It was not boredom but outrage at not having enough to eat or a change of outer clothing.

Thanks to the activity of the YCL, it was impossible to refuse its national head, Gil Green, a seat on the national board of the American Youth Congress, an immense umbrella organization under Eleanor Roosevelt's direct sponsorship. The first lady was not just a letterhead name, but an active and direct participant. She used her prestige and the concessions she could gain in social legislation to prevent the Communists from becoming the acknowledged leaders of America's youth. The YCL sought to win support by demonstrating that it would work harder and better for the interests of youth and the American Youth Congress than anyone else. Tanya was assigned to visit organizations of young people, which were largely religiously affiliated, and urge them to send delegates to the Congress, which was to be held in Cleveland.

On the face of it, that may sound easy. A national convention of young people, just forty miles away, with the endorsement of Mrs. Roosevelt. However, America was a very provincial country then. Tanya's accent is unmistakeably that of a New Yorker. Many people of our political background found it very difficult to bridge the gap between our rather snobbish confidence that what this country needed was a socialist revolution, and the infinitely simpler and more practical outlook of most people, young and old, who focused on their immediate needs. Moreover, the entire Communist movement was just learning to adapt itself to the necessary change from the pre-Hitler perspective of revolution to one of unity against the danger of fascism and war. Finally, for principled atheists of Jewish origin, Christian churches were forbidding places. It was psychologically difficult even to enter them, let alone work in them. Anyhow, Tanya recruited about ninety delegates. Knowing her extraordinary personal shyness as a young woman, that was stupendous.

After some time with the American Youth Congress, Tanya led the successful effort to obtain a federal housing project for Akron. In those days, public housing was not looked upon as welfare slums, but as a necessary and desirable social advance. It provided working people, white and Black, with better housing, and at lower rent, than they could otherwise afford. Strangely, in view of Akron's exceptional social progressivism in all other respects, it was the last industrial city in Ohio to get such a project. This possibly had to do with the tradition of private homes, however small, among its recently rural population. Almost everyone outside the small center-city slum area had vegetable gardens. That must have helped them stay alive during the worst of the depression, as in Russia at this writing.

In any event, Tanya organized the coalition, meetings, petitions, delegations and hearings that won that housing development. I've always felt that it should bear her name. Consider that she was all of twenty-one.

For us, housing at that stage in life was always an adventure. In Cleveland we had rented rooms at two different times, spent that night in our jaloppy when we were homeless, and lived in three different attic apartments. The first was immense, so cold that one room had to be closed off, and gloomy with overstuffed furniture. The second was utterly charming. We called it the doll's house, because there was barely clearance for my head, and we enjoyed a separate staircase entrance overlooking a delightful garden. The last was a full five rooms on top of a brick home, which we furnished. In the midst of our relative poverty, we actually had a map room. In consequence of some replacement of school equipment, a friend gave us a huge set of large standing maps. The wooden stands themselves must have cost taxpayers a pretty penny. I had always been fascinated by geography, partly since I had voyaged to the USSR and back. But my interest was probably deeper than that, since, at ten, I had followed the progress of the Chinese allied nationalist and Communist armies north on my own war map.

In Akron, my $23 a week—equal to 20 times that today—enabled us to rent a decent three-room apartment in a small apartment house. It had a hideaway bed. We brought our furnishings from Cleveland in a friend's ten-year-old quarter-ton Ford truck, the first pick-up model ever made. With the load, it couldn't make the low hills between the two cities. The three of us had to push it over summits.

My father sent from New York an office-size second-hand Underwood typewriter— manual of course. There were none other. He packed it so meticulously that it took hours to pry apart the brackets and supports he had built into the crate to make sure it suffered no damage in shipment.

Tanya and I didn't drink then, although I wouldn't turn down a glass of wine or a beer at a friend's, but we used to joke about getting drunk just by looking at the wallpaper in our kitchen. It had a straight diagonal emphasis that made us feel we should list thirty degrees to port to be perpendicular to the floor.

Across the street was an Italian restaurant. For the first time in our lives we felt rich enough to eat out once a week. For us, an Italian feast was a heaping dish of spaghetti and meat sauce. A few blocks away there was a wonderful hamburger place, where a dime bought a third of a pound of excellent meat, topped with tomatoes and lettuce and all the rest. But it was in the shadow of the silos of the Quaker Oats plant. That grain cast a rich, heady aroma for blocks. While we were in Akron, Tanya became pregnant with our first child, Phyllis, and we had to stay as far away as possible from that Quaker Oats mill and, regrettably, the fine hamburger joint. She was able to abide the smell of the rubber factories during her pregnancy, but a whiff of the stored oats was catastrophic.

In Akron I had my first encounter with genuine American square dancing. There was a party at the home of one of the local Communists, Amos Murphy, originally from a Pennsylvania farm I think. Of course I thought of him and his wife as quite old. They may have been forty. So I was amazed, when the do-si-do got going, that Mrs. Murphy, who was neither tall nor large, swept me off my feet in the most literal meaning of the term. I was gangly in my early 20s, but not under a hundred sixty pounds. I've always enjoyed folk dancing, but not participating. It always seemed too rigid. I like to improvise as the music, the mood, and the body language of my partner suggests.

My big cultural memory of the year in Akron was seeing the first cowboy movie I regarded as art: John Wayne in "Stagecoach." "The Thin Man" also appeared that year. I had no idea that its writer, Dashiell Hammett, was a fellow-Communist. The one film with a liberal New Dealish line, "Mr. Deeds Goes to Washington," with Jimmy Stewart and Jean Arthur, didn't impress me much. I knew from experience that changing our society for the better required much more than honesty and naive good will. They certainly help, though.

We made excellent friends in Akron. The person I replaced as head of the Young Communist League was a local girl, Daisy Lolich. She and I became fast friends. She may have been no more than sixteen but, being Yugoslav, was big-busted, with a tiny waist, like a Mestrovic sculpture. She sparkled, loved to dance, and did not resent my being sent to take her place. Truly a good comrade, Daisy helped me learn the local situation and meet the people. Nor did she turn on me in any personal way, when I was dumped from leadership by a decision that came from Cleveland and New York, in my first-ever conflict with the Communist Party on a matter of principle.

At this time I was a member of the state committee of the Party at a time when that organization carried real weight. It had four thousand members in Ohio. I was also a member of the state "bureau" of the Young Communist League, whose operating leadership numbered a dozen or so. That organization held a national convention in New York in mid-1939, and I headed the small delegation from Akron. The organization was determined to become more than a junior Communist Party, by permitting other organizations affiliation to us if they wished. One proposal for our new constitution was that even an athletic team could affiliate, whereupon its members would acquire individual membership. Another article read that no member should have any contact, even personal, with Trotskyists.

I had no disagreement with the party's evaluation of Trotskyism. I faithfully believed in the truth of Stalin's trials of Trotsky's closest associates, who the dictator framed as Nazi spies and executed. Logic is to me an axiom of behavior, and I found those two proposed articles for our constitution conflicted with each other. So, while I thought Trotskyists were monstrous betrayers of the working class, I got up at that convention and said, "Look, we've agreed to admit athletic teams to our organization and give their members regular membership. Now, these people wouldn't know a Trotskyite from a hole in the ground. Therefore to require a ball team to have no contact with them, even personal, just doesn't make any sense." I voted against that article, which passed anyhow.

The roof fell in. A meeting of all Communist Party members in that Ohio delegation to the Young Communist League convention was called. The head of the state YCL, Bob Thompson, a Lincolnesque one-time lumberjack from the state of Washington and son of an old Socialist, denounced me with contempt. He said I was a half-baked intellectual, and so forth. Most important, as a member of a disciplined organization, the Party, I was bound to vote for its policy no matter what I personally thought. And it wanted that clause in that constitution.

When we got back to Ohio, I faced more of the same, but worse. I have a vague recollection that the whole ordeal was repeated before the full state committee of the Party. The psychological impact upon me was profound. I was a Marxist-Leninist who believed that the only solution to this country's problems was a revolution by the workingclass to introduce socialism, and that the Communist Party was the only entity that could bring this about. I had committed my life to that cause, for which I had abandoned formal education and consistent employment. The people who had passed this sentence upon me—removal from all posts of leadership—were flesh of the flesh and bone of the bone of the workingclass. They had given competent direction and appropriate form to many of the remarkable events that had occurred in this country during the preceding decade. Most of them had gone to prison or suffered beatings in the course of their struggle on behalf of the unemployed, the unorganized, the evicted, the African-Americans. Some were heroes in the strictest definition.

Thompson, head of the statewide YCL, had just come back from the Civil War in Spain, where he had been severely wounded and, after recovery, had gone back into battle. During World War II, he won this country's second highest military honor, the Distinguished Service Cross, for leading his men across a river in New Guinea in the face of withering machine-gun fire. It was public knowledge that he would have been awarded the Congressional Medal of Honor were he not an open Communist. During the McCarthy years, the Party instructed him to go underground. He hid out at Twain Harte in the Sierra Nevada, was captured, and served long years both under the Smith Act and for jumping bail to go underground. While in prison, some Yugoslav fascist smashed his skull with a pipe and he lived the rest of his life with a plate in his head, suffering excruciating headaches.

Thompson had a mind like a razor. Modest, he did not wear the ribbons of his decorations as was the general custom, at least on special occasions, in the early postwar years. He did not even wear a pin veterans called the "ruptured duck", identifying one as a veteran, which was universally worn. But because he did not understand that very few Communist Party members were capable of being as single-mindedly devoted as himself, he was hated in the New York State organization he later headed at a time when it had twenty thousand members.

Tanya hated Thompson for what he had done to me psychologically and because she regarded him as a cold and unfeeling person. I did not hate him. I've always been able to see people whole, at least as far as I am capable of understanding them. I did not love Thompson. But I revered his heroism and understood his value, then and later. He was one of three people I've known toward whom I had the conscious attitude that I would give my own life, if necessary to preserve their's. The other two were Paul Robeson and William L. Patterson, the Black Communist ex-lawyer who was Mr. Civil Rights in this country before

Martin Luther King came along.

Thompson was among the heroes of the workingclass who denounced me in 1939. And who was I? Just a half-baked intellectual. This incident completely destroyed my sense of self-worth for thirteen years thereafter, until I appeared before the U.S. Senate Internal Security (McCarran) Subcommittee in 1952. There, I defended my principles and my work of the intervening years, although a number of the people I had been taught to admire had caved in, crawled, or literally sold out and become stool pigeons during the period history knows as McCarthyism.

People who read or heard me, never mind any who knew me in those years, 1939-1952, would probably find the foregoing quite astonishing, because I did not behave either like a punch-drunk loser or an automaton. Not being permitted to function as a Communist other than in rank-and-file capacities was no dishonor in my eyes, and I did that loyally until expelled from the Party in the winter of 1952-3 on another issue of principle. Yet the events in Ohio devastated me at the time.

In 1940 I became a specialist in Soviet affairs.

CHAPTER 7

Eve of World War II

After I was removed from my leadership posts in the Communist Party and Young Communist League, I was instructed to persuade the YCL in Akron, nearly a hundred chiefly Black youth, that I was truly a bad man because of my refusal to accept the party's line at that convention, and didn't deserve to be their leader. To convince people to cry "mea culpa" and believe it themselves is a very old and harmful human tradition—a guilt complex I most strictly associate with religion. I realize today that communism was essentially a religion. It claimed to be founded on logic, but like all religions, it actually rested on articles of faith: that the workingclass would want to lead society and would act accordingly; that it would show greater solidarity with workers abroad than with employers at home; that if a party claiming to represent it came to power in some country, its leaders would not be motivated by the hunger for power and other personal interests that motivate other political leaders. As with all religions, faith produced both good and evil.

The members were bewildered by my self-denunciation, but I was persuasive, and they went along. The very same nice Daisy Lolich who I had replaced a year earlier resumed her old post. When Congress cut the annual appropriation for the Roosevelt make-work program to keep the number of unemployed high enough to hold wages down, I was laid off. Tanya was very pregnant with Phyllis. Both these things, plus the flap in the YCL, caused us to return to our native New York. We had no choice, economically.

That was in the late summer of 1939, and we were both twenty-two. With no money, we moved in with Tanya's parents in the Bronx. There was no extra bedroom, so we slept behind the dining-room table on a divan that opened into a bed for two. I was still determined to be a member of the workingclass, which I saw as this country's savior. A college buddy of Dad's was a union organizer and found me a job at my trade as paper-cutter. This place made writing pads, and my job was to lift enormous sheets, measuring three feet by four, five hundred at a time, into the machine, and slice it into the required pad size. Preventing that mass of uncut paper from flopping over and spilling all over the place instead of sliding onto the cutting table beneath my power guillotine took both skill and strength. Whatever muscle I have was probably developed on that job. My appetite was simply stupendous. I'd be hungry until Tanya upped the number of sandwiches she made me to six per night.

This night-shift job taught me how productive workers can be when there is an incentive to do so. It was not money. My pay was $14 per week, way down from my $23 on WPA in both Cleveland and Akron. The incentive was sleep. During the day a foreman was present, so workers moved at a pace that required exactly the eight-hour working day to cut the required eight lifts of paper. Each lift carried a five foot high pile of those 3'x4' sheets. At night there was no foreman. The work quota itself determined our output. None of us wanted to sacrifice the daylight hours to getting a good night's sleep. To give ourselves as much free time during the day as possible, we managed to get the eight lifts done in six hours, and would curl up in a storage area for the remaining two hours, usually halfway through the night. Neither the noise, the hard stack of paper we lay down on, nor the lights from the machine area stopped any of us from sleeping.

At one point a jurisdictional fight erupted between unions over that factory. Another union set up a picket line. To me a picket line was— and is—sacred, unless I have specific knowledge that it is phony. I didn't know the details of the disagreement, and therefore I didn't cross it. Not only did that put me out of a job, but it also made it impossible for me to go back to Dad's union-leader classmate for help in finding another, since his union wanted work at that factory to continue.

I found another job involving both paper-cutting and a task that brought me a back injury. This factory made party goods. Its products were cut and shaped from laminated sheets: shiny gold or silver, purple or pink, star-studded hats, bands, and ornaments sealed to stiff cardboard backing. Each of the components came in huge, heavy rolls that were glued together in a machine. When one roll, weighing at least a hundred pounds, was empty, we had to place another on the steel roller that held it. One day, while replacing a roll, I felt something give in my back. The injury was not bad enough to cause me to quit the job, but it was ten or fifteen years before the discomfort and minor disability it caused disappeared entirely. Workers with relatively light injuries, like myself, could not even think of looking into our rights under whatever workmen's compensation or temporary disability laws existed. They did not provide enough to live on. I think I was up to $21 per week on this job—$315 by today's standards.

During this factory job I spent my spare time trying to organize my fellow-workers into a union. The guy who gave me most help was a young Italian named Coppola. He lived with his parents and invited me once or twice for dinner in East Harlem. While Cleveland, and particularly Akron, were places where workers of different ethnic backgrounds mixed freely, that was not the case in New York. It was nice to be out of a Jewish milieu once in a while.

Our unionizing efforts did not succeed by the time the rush season of stocking up for the holidays was over. Layoffs followed and I was again out of a job. In my early life, to this point and beyond, parents and relatives were constantly upbraiding me for an inability to stick to anything seriously for a long time. In retrospect, I'm not sure they were right. In any case, that criticism could not be applied to the job-hunting effort I now undertook. Although unemployment had been reduced by a third since 1933, there were still about 10 million jobless in the country out of a total labor force much smaller than today's. Only World War II, which ruined the rest of the world, finally rescued the United States from the Great Depression.

The sensible thing was to look again for a job as power-machine paper-cutter at which I was skilled. So I went through the Yellow Pages of all five boroughs of New York City, and compiled a list of four hundred printers and paper houses that might employ me. To cover them by phone was financially out of the question. At a nickel a call, that would have come to a full week's wages. There was nowhere we could borrow that kind of money and have any hope of repaying it. Besides, employers didn't expect semi-skilled workers to job-hunt by phone. They wanted to look at you, judge your muscle and see whether you seemed at home in the surroundings of the work you claimed to be capable of doing.

So I filled a pocket-size loose-leaf notebook with the four hundred firm names and addresses. I arranged them in geographic sequence and began visiting them on foot. I covered all the industrial areas of Manhattan, block by block, plus those in the Bronx, Brooklyn, and Queens, in an effort to find a place that would hire me. It was fruitless, but I got to know one of the world's most fascinating cities even better than I had as a young boy.

I still have that loose-leaf notebook with the list of potential places of employment. Aside from nostalgia value, it had two very useful purposes. One had to do with my career as a lecturer. When the Cold War began upon the end of World War II in 1945, I pasted over those firm names the most pertinent paragraphs from stories in the *New York Times* and other unchallengeable sources to read aloud in substantiation of my views. They dealt with the reasons for using the atom bomb on Japan, or the building of U.S. bomber bases in Italy for use against what was then considered our brave and loyal Soviet ally, and so forth. Such revealing items would be carried by our "free" press exactly once, and would then be totally outweighed in readers' minds by a mass of material that, day after day, alleged the very opposite without proof. The other use to which I put that notebook was in raising our kids. When they were still at home and showed signs of insufficient resolve in one or another respect, I would take advantage of a parent's natural prestige, show them the list of firm names still discernable past the edges of the news clips, and say, "If your Daddy could do this, you can too."

I recall lecturing to a senior class in international relations at the beginning of 1948 at what was then the College—now the University— of the Pacific. I used those clippings to demonstrate that what they believed to be true about the origins of the Cold War was totally at odds with the facts. Years later, Professor Marshall Windmiller, who came to head the International Relations Deartment at San Francisco State University and earlier was an extremely popular commentator on KPFA radio, told me that he was one of the students in that classroom in 1948. He was enormously impressed by this portable source-book of mine and decided to make use of that technique in his own work.

But, eight years before that lecture, I was an unemployed working-man with a brand-new baby, living in his in-laws' living room. Our daughter, Phyllis, was born the day the USSR invaded Finland in November 1939. She looked precisely like her mother, in miniature.

In recognition of the invasion, I wanted to name our daughter Toivo, for a legendary Finnish Communist. Toivo Antikainen was a man who had conducted hundred-mile raids on skis a generation earlier during the Finnish Civil War, following the Russian Revolution. Tanya, fortunately, had more common sense than to burden the child with such a name. We agreed on one that began with the same sound as that of Tanya's birth mother. Phyllis is also the female version of the name of Tanya's baby brother, of whom she was particularly fond.

The war with Finland complicated the situation for Communists created by the Soviet Non-Aggression Pact with Germany a year earlier. In the mid-30s, Hitler had succeeded in convincing the leaders of Western Europe that he was the man to destroy the Soviet Union and the threat that its example might bring the end of capitalism worldwide. British Prime Minister Chamberlain sold out Czechoslovakia at Munich in 1938, specifically to turn Hitler's ambitions eastward. The Czechoslovak government refused a flat Soviet offer to come to its aid alone if need be. France, allied with Czechoslovakia, would not back resistance by her against Germany. This nullified a military alliance France had signed with the Soviet Union that had caused Communists worldwide much soul-searching: how could the USSR ally itself with a capitalist country?

Next, England and France shamelessly stalled negotiations for a joint alliance with the USSR to stop Hitler. Rather, these two governments pretended to engage in the alliance discussions because their people demanded it. Whereupon the USSR signed a non-aggression pact with Nazi Germany to keep the Soviet Union out of the coming war, if possible, or at least allow itself time to re-arm. The same West that had refused to ally itself with Moscow against Hitler—which military events compelled it to do two years later—now denounced Stalin.

Stalin invaded Finland in November 1939 to push the Finnish border beyond artillery range of Leningrad. France had built Finland's extraordinarily strong line of border fortifications, complete with battleship-size artillery capable of shelling the Soviet Union's second city and largest center of heavy industry. Stalin's five-month war with Finland had exactly the same impact on world opinion as Moscow's invasion of Afghanistan forty years later. When Hitler invaded the Soviet Union fifteen months after the Soviet-Finnish War ended, Finland joined him as an ally. Together, they besieged Leningrad, and nine hundred thousand people died of starvation and disease in that city in the nearly three years it was surrounded.

The Soviet invasion of Finland, on top of the Non-Aggression Pact with Germany, had catastrophic domestic effects for us American Communists. Many intellectuals who had either joined the Communist Party or contributed writings and art to its publications or money to its coffers abandoned it, often with fiery public denunciations. The press had waited for years to destroy the prestige Communists had gained for originating the drive for unemployment insurance that Roosevelt later co-opted and enacted as law. The media had a field day, inventing or popularizing words like "Communazi." These events revealed the fragility of the tolerance that had developed for Communists, and even the shallowness of the Party's support among the workingclass for which it had fought so hard.

World War II began, with England and France opposing Germany—whose rearmament they had facilitated through appeasement. Yet little fighting actually occurred for twenty-two months after Hitler started the conflict by invading Poland. In June 1940 he had also invaded France, which collapsed as fast as Poland, fundamentally because the French establishment preferred Hitler to the Communist-Socialist People's Front that was the alternative.

American Communist policy during those nearly two years of what was widely known as the "phony war" aimed to end to the conflict by joint U.S.-Soviet diplomatic action, backed up by the threat of force. Considering that that alliance, when it came, is what won World War II, it is probable that the threat would have worked, because Hitler had not yet had the time to organize the resources of conquered Europe into the war production and slave-labor machine that sustained his armies for four years. Tens of millions of civilians and soldiers would not have died. The Jewish people and Gypsies of Europe would not have been nearly exterminated. But the American mass media damned the Soviet Union for seeking to save itself, rendering a solution by joint diplomatic action impossible.

A witch-hunt began. The head of the Communist Party, Earl Browder, a native-born American, was sentenced to four years on a thirteen-year-old technical passport violation. The Party's treasurer got two years on a similar charge. The Communist candidate for governor of West Virginia was sentenced to fifteen years in 1940. Ten years were for allegedly failing to state what party he was collecting ballot petition signatures for, and five were added because he had been a pacifist conscientious objector in World War I. Eighteen Communists were arrested in Oklahoma and two were sentenced to ten years each. All this happened under the Roosevelt administration.

I was lucky to be living in the Bronx. The South Bronx was Irish, and anti-British sentiment was very strong for the same reason as when I write this nearly sixty years later. I remember participating in street corner meetings with a large, somber man named Tim Murphy, about forty-five and a veteran of the Easter Rebellion of 1916 in Ireland. He was a longshoreman, permanently disabled by an injury on the job. It is not generally realized that James Connolly, leader of that rebellion so honored in Irish history, was a Marxist, so Murphy's choice to have become a Communist was not at all strange. In that neighborhood, neither the people nor the police, overwhelmingly Irish, attacked us. Our slogan during that period was, "The Yanks Are Not Coming," and we had a rousing song that began with those lines.

This time was filled with contradictions. On November 5, 1939, after the Soviet-German Non-Aggression Pact was signed, but a few weeks before the Soviet-Finnish War began, a cultural event occurred that represented the absolute high point of Communist-furthered activities in the arts, and of the populism—in the very best sense of that word—of the New Deal. We heard on the radio at home the premiere performance of "Ballad for Americans," with Paul Robeson singing the solo. The composer of that cantata was Earl Robinson, then and for many years thereafter a Communist Party member. *Time* magazine reported that:

"In the studio, an audience of 600 stomped, shouted, bravoed for two minutes while the show was still on the air, for 15 minutes later. In the next half hour, 150 telephone calls managed to get through CBS' jammed Manhattan switchboard. The Hollywood switchboard was jammed for two hours. In the next few days bales of letters demanded words, music, recordings, another time at bat for 'Ballad for Americans'."

It was repeated on the air. Victor Records pressed it, with the original

People's Chorus, a Communist-organized group, singing behind Robeson as it did on the air. And in 1940 Robeson sang it at the *Republican* Presidential Nominating Convention. The nominee against Roosevelt, Wendell Willkie, a corporation lawyer, had defended the head of the California Communist Party before the U.S. Supreme Court without fee. He won on the very important grounds that the court recognized that the Communist Party had no intention of overthrowing the U.S. government by force and violence, but envisaged the use of such methods only in defense of a pro-socialist government elected by the people in case reactionaries sought to block the people's will by force.

I remember other voices from that distant time. One night in 1940 Tanya and I heard an extraordinary concert by three unknowns in a little upstairs space in mid-town Manhattan. One was Leadbelly—Huddie Ledbetter—one Josh White, also Black, and the third a white cowboy, Tony Kraber. Leadbelly's twelve-string guitar was then another entirely new experience, and it drove as hard as the engine in his "Rock Island Line." That evening I knew nothing yet of his life, or that he was just out of a penitentiary in Louisiana, but that peculiar nasal tenor needed no interpretation: "Out of our way, man—we're comin' down the line."

Josh White is a reminder that not everyone can take it when the chips are down. A fine blues guitarist capable of extracting a marvelous singing tone from long notes, with a silky voice that could acquire just the right roughness when the lyrics called for it, he was among those who caved in during the McCarthy years. During World War II there was an ongoing debate in this country over whether we really should be fighting on the same side as the Soviet Union, and particularly about whether to land in France to take pressure off the Red Army. Josh had this great song about "a little man sittin' on a fence, a-thinkin' and a-thinkin' about the national defense, while the Soviet Union goes rolling along."

The third man at that evening in 1940, Tony Kraber, did songs much needed in the days when the cowboy came to be equated with John Wayne, a particularly reactionary movie star. When Jesse Jackson said he'd rather have Roosevelt in a wheel chair than Reagan on a horse, I thought to myself how wonderful it would be if somebody would mount that would-be cowboy on Kraber's famous "Old Paint, the Horse with the Union Label," The boss tries to ride that horse, but

> "Paint, he just snickered
> 'Cause he knew the boss was a company spy,
> Which is why he landed in a tree nearby,
> And ran home cryin' for mama."

But the cowboy showed him his union card, and

> "Paint, he said:
> 'Climb right on, pardner
> I got plenty of room for a union brother'."

The tens of thousands of us who heard Tony over the years didn't need to read anybody's Ph.D. thesis to know that cowboys, too, participated in the class struggle. Those words are not used with quotes around them, or the slightest tinge of sarcasm. They are not quaint, or the least bit archaic. If they were understood today, as they were understood in the 1930s and 40s, workers would not be accepting declines in fringe benefits and real wages, take-backs, and mass firings prettified by the term "downsizing" in an era of the highest profits in history. The very notion of an employer proposing to pay newly-hired workers less for the very same work done by others longer on the job, the so-called two-tier system, was simply unthinkable in the years when millions of those who worked for wages believed that everyone else who worked for wages was his brother or sister, and that the owners who made money from those who work for wages were the enemy. A superb public relations job subsequently convinced labor that a certain level of wages had made it part of the middle class, and it lost the consciousness essential to upholding its own interests.

The songs of my youth taught much more complex lessons. Time after time, at Madison Square Garden, I would participate with 20,000 others in singing lines from Lincoln's First Inaugural Address, splendidly set to music by Earl Robinson:

> "This country, with its institutions, belongs to the people who inhabit it.
> This country, with its Constitution, belongs to those who live in it.
> Whenever they shall grow weary of the existing government,
> They can exercise their constitutional right of amending it
> Or their revolutionary right to dismember or overthrow it."

That's Lincoln, a decade before Lenin was born.

As I could find no job to keep me in the working class, I finally took one raising money for *New Masses*, the truly superb Communist cultural magazine. Its contributors included poet Muriel Rukeyser and Richard Wright, the first African-American to have written a best-selling novel, as well as James Agee, Federico Garcia Lorca of Spain, Langston Hughes, William Saroyan, Thomas Wolfe, Meridel LeSueur, Erskine Caldwell, John Dos Passos, Josephine Herbst, Dorothy Parker,

Ernest Hemingway, William Carlos Williams, Romain Rolland and Henri Barbusse of France, Theodore Dreiser, S. J. Perelman, and Ruth McKenney. Artists included John Groth, Reginald March, Gardner Rea, William Gropper, Ad Reinhardt, Adolph Dehn, Art Young, Hugo Gellert, Robert Minor, Fred Ellis, Jacob Burck, and Anton Refregier. Can even the *New Yorker* boast of such a list?

I was simply given a list of names of people who had made fairly substantial contributions and told to go speak to them and get more. The *New Masses* could not solicit big commercial ads. Big money knew which side it was on, and *New Masses* was not for sale.

I particularly remember two contacts . One was Rex Stout, creator of fictional detective Nero Wolfe. Stout was a pompous man with a big gray beard in a time when beards were rare. He lived in a typical Connecticut writer's cottage converted from a barn, actually not far from my in-laws' summer home. When I visited him, he denounced the Soviet-German Pact, the Soviet invasion of Finland, and sounded, in essence, like the academic neo-conservatives of the 1980s and 90s.

The other memorable visit was to a 6th-floor loft on West 45th St., between 5th and 6th avenues, where I was to find a Harriet Moore. The floor was occupied by an organization I had never heard of, the American Russian Institute. As I got into the elevator to go upstairs, Paul Robeson stepped out—the first time I ever saw him up close. He was in his prime, in his mid-40s, tall enough to have to bend his head to get out of the doors, broad enough to make one wonder if the elevator could hold two.

I got my contribution from Miss Moore, a skinny, large-nosed, vibrant Yankee, who, as I learned later, was then only twenty-eight. I asked if I could look around the place. It was a library of books about the Soviet Union in English and Russian, and of current Soviet newspapers and magazines. It published a scholarly journal called the *American Quarterly on the Soviet Union* as well as a monthly news bulletin, conducted cultural exhibitions and meetings, and maintained a card file of indexed news items in the Soviet press. The staff consisted of Harriet's friend Rose Rubin, who had her own business publishing the sheet music of Russian composers, and Rose Somerville, who subsequently became a professor at San Diego State. I told Harriet I knew Russian, had lived in the USSR for a year, and said, "I ought to work here." She tested me with a take-home translation of a long article on Marxism and physics, and hired me half-time in consequence. That, in mid-1940, was the start of my lifelong career as a specialist in Soviet affairs. I was twenty-three.

CHAPTER 8

The War at Home

Harriet Moore had graduated from Bryn Mawr a few years earlier with the highest academic average in the history of that elite college. I did not learn that from her. She was modest to the core. Her scholastic record appears in the autobiography of her friend and colleague, Frederick Vanderbilt Field, appropriately titled *From Right to Left.* He, a scion of America's top-ranking socialite family, became a Communist and served time in jail with Dashiell Hammett when they refused to give the government the names of those who contributed to the bail fund for Communist leaders on trial during Truman's presidency.

Aside from being a published scholar in her own right, and the only real academic mentor I ever had, Harriet was an organizer and manager of formidable talent. That emerged most fully after Hitler attacked the Soviet Union, when she founded, recruited impeccably respectable sponsors for, and ran Russian War Relief, which became the biggest charitable organization this country had ever known, bigger in that period than the Red Cross. In 1997, when Duke Ellington's long work, "Black, Brown, and Beige," was given its second performance ever, the press reported that the first had been under the auspices of Russian War Relief, in 1943. That was a reflection of Harriet's convictions on matters of race.

Half a century before a woman was named Secretary of State, I thought the country would be better off with Harriet in that post. The notion that a female could not do a job that hitherto had been held only by males was never part of my mentality. The reason I thought of her in terms of Secretary of State and not President was purely pragmatic. We had the President the times called for in Franklin Delano Roosevelt.

One of the marks of a great executive is the ability to judge people and use them to the fullest. When Harriet hired me onto the staff of the American Russian Institute I had no research experience and no training for the job. She assigned me to scan the half-dozen general and economic Soviet newspapers that came into our library, decide which articles and items in them deserved being indexed for reference purposes, and write ultra-brief abstracts on 3"x5" cards. I also scanned a dozen

Soviet magazines and scholarly journals for the same purpose. That work of over half a century ago now resides in the Bobst Library of New York University.

I took to this work like a duck to water. Each day I would expound to Harriet and my two other fellow staff-members my understanding of what various readings revealed about Soviet developments. This was a period of very fast-breaking and, in some ways, totally new develoments on the world scene, and they needed a lot of thinking through. For example, the Red Army entered the Baltic states — Latvia, Estonia, Lithuania — exactly when I was hired, one year before Hitler invaded the USSR. Those countries very quickly became Soviet, via mass movements witnessed on the spot by another female idol of mine, Anna Louise Strong. They were described in her book, *The New Lithuania,* and in another by a Latvian Social-Democrat, Gregory Meiksins, *The Baltic Riddle)* The fact that Lithuania, a Catholic country, elected indigenous Communists to head its government after becoming independent in the 1990s when Yeltsin destroyed the Soviet Union has its roots in this earlier period.

I tried to place those events of 1940 in the context of the theories of Marxism-Leninism in which I believed. With respect to the Baltic situation, Lenin's book *The State and Revolution,* was the pertinent text. I concluded, from the course of events in the Baltic, that the presence of the Red Army served to handcuff the repressive police and military forces of suppression at the disposal of these pre-Communist governments. This enabled grassroots democracy to bring about a social revolution by the workingclass and poorer peasants. I did not know that the Soviet secret police deported to Siberia almost the entire capitalist class and employing strata of the peasantry, virtually all pre-existing police, much of the professional officer corps of the army, and numerous intellectuals and small business people who opposed socialism.

Had I known that, it would not have changed my mind about the positive nature of this shift of power. Wealthy classes holding state power have been at least as brutal to the poor, everywhere in the world, to maintain their dominance. I believed it to be both inevitable and just that the poor would behave similarly to gain and control government. Besides, such a radical shift, including reversal of the role of oppressor, had occurred in every revolution that really changed anything: in 17th-century England, 18th-century France, and the American Revolution in which the Tories found it the better part of wisdom to flee to Canada. I did not know that the USSR had become a personal dictatorship, which had not been the case when I lived there in 1931-32. When I did learn that, in the mid-'50s, there began the very long process of revision of my thinking that ultimately caused a fundamental change in my views.

The American Russian Institute took no stand whatever on the developments in the Baltic or any other aspect of Soviet domestic or foreign policy. But I imagine that our discussions convinced Harriet that I had a head on my shoulders, and she very quickly moved me into research on specific projects. The first such assignment was to find and tabulate the statistics of Soviet foreign trade in the Far East, which she published as an appendix to her own Princeton University Press book, *Soviet Far Eastern Policy 1931-1945.* Next she sent me to the New York Main Public Library three blocks away to dig up Karl Marx' articles on the mid-19th century Taiping Rebellion in China. So I learned something about library research. Then she took the very bold step of asking me to write, for her bi-monthly journal, *The American Review on the Soviet Union,* the first study of the Soviet transport system ever undertaken in the United States. A professor emeritus at an Eastern institution of higher learning, Holland Hunter, spent his entire career studying that subject. His mother told me, when I first lived in Berkeley in 1947, that he got his start by studying my 1941 article. The statistical tables I developed for it were printed again in an excellent British *Geography of the USSR*, by Gregory and Shave. Not bad for a kid who had had only a year and a half of higher education in Moscow and New York.

Writing that article was a college education in itself. Harriet and I fought like hell. At that point, as a Communist Party member, I believed that when the Soviet Union set forth economic goals of any kind, they were unquestionably based on a sound understanding of the problem, of the human and material resources available, and on accurate and adequate statistics. I had grown up at a time when the Soviet effort to institute economic planning was ridiculed daily in our most serious newspapers. In a world accustomed to supply-and-demand, boom-and-bust economics, the notion that an economy could be planned was regarded as funny, never mind Utopian. Yet the Soviets had pulled themselves up by their bootstraps into the 20th century. They had won vast numbers of supporters worldwide simply by abolishing unemployment at the very time the entire capitalist world experienced the most catastrophic unemployment in its history. It would be half a century before the absence of the economic democracy of the market caused Soviet socialism to choke in its own bureaucracy.

Harriet had different ideas about proper research and writing. She told me, "You don't write a research article by saying that the Central Committee of the Communist Party of the Soviet Union and the State Planning Commission have decreed certain targets, and then by finding facts to support the advance conclusion that that will most certainly be accomplished. First you find the data, *all* the data you can possibly find in every available source. Then you put them under a microscope for reliability and accuracy. You examine the past record of accomplishment or failure. You look at the plans for the future. If new rates of development or different emphases are projected, you evolve an informed judgment as to the realism of such intents. And only then do you draw your conclusions."

When the smoke cleared, there was that article with my name on it, good enough to be accepted as the international reference source on the subject. This was no abstract academic exercise. The Western press was arguing that the Soviet transport system, then primarily railroads, was the Achilles' heel of the economy, and would be unable to stand up in time of war. My article appeared in February 1941, only four months before Hitler attacked the USSR. Very important decisions were then being reached in Washington based in part on estimates of how the Soviet Union would fare in the event of Nazi invasion. Virtually everybody— except Joseph Stalin, but that's another story —thought this was bound to occur.

The atmosphere in the United States during the four years of our wartime comradeship with the Soviet Union, 1941-1945, is something impossible to imagine for the subsequent generations of Americans who were raised to view the USSR as enemy. It does no credit to the majority of people of my generation that they permitted themselves to forget this atmosphere of comraderie—pun intended. If Soviet Communists are our allies against the worst monster human history has known, and if one can talk to the Russians and work with them, and make commitments for coordinated military actions they can be expected to keep, can't one deal in the same way with American Communists?

Being a Communist never really became legal, psychologically or otherwise, in this free country. But necessity took over. When the USSR was attacked, Roosevelt agreed to send Lend-Lease aid. He dispatched his right-hand man Harry Hopkins, Averell Harriman, and others to find out just what was needed—how much, where, and when—to supply the Soviet Union. This meant that our government acquired a sudden need for all kinds of factual data neither it nor the academic world had made any effort to accumulate.

There were three groups the government could turn to for information in that era before the CIA or think-tanks. One consisted of emigres from the Soviet Union who were supporters either of the overthrown tsar or of the overthrown capitalist-democratic Provisional Government of 1917. These people were absolutely certain that Communists couldn't do anything right, and that the USSR couldn't hold out. They didn't want it to, for how would they ever get back into power if it did? They knew Russian. They knew the country's geography and much else. But they were useless in understanding the Soviet Union. Then there were the American Communists as such, and organizations influenced by them, frankly favorable to the Soviet Union. One of these was the magazine, *Soviet Russia Today*, for which I worked half-time as research librarian before Harriet Moore found the money to employ me full time. However, the assumption was that those organizations couldn't be trusted for the facts because they had a stake in making communism look good.

Thanks to Harriet's insistence that we, the American Russian Institute, take no stand on any matter of opinion, but rather provide the facts and only the facts, we became everybody's accepted source of Soviet-related information. *Time, Life,* the United Press, and other significant entities paid us retainers as their information source. I still have a file of letters from government officials involved with USSR relations thanking me for digging up information essential to their work.

By 1943 Americans realized that our institutions of higher education must begin to inform themselves and their students about the Soviet Union. It had been totally ignored in curricula during its quarter-century of existence, but for about a dozen professors who had chosen on their own initiative to study Russian literature or history, philosophy or law. The Rockefeller Foundation provided money for the first intensive course on the subject, taught at Cornell in the summer of 1943. I have a telegram from the vice-president of that institution, de Kiewiet, later its president, in which he asked to interview me to teach a later wartime course for the U.S. Army on the subject of the USSR. When he discovered that I was very young and had no degree, despite my impressive list of publications, he was taken aback. By that date I had written fifteen articles on economic geography, ethnic matters, transportation, labor, and youth for our semi-monthly*Bulletin on the Soviet Union*

I had also written a long article, Soviet Central Asia," for a prestigious scholarly journal, *Pacific Affairs,* and another long study, "The Soviet Far East," in our own *American Review on the Soviet Union.* He knew that my first book, *The Soviet Far East and Central Asia,* was about to be published, and that it had been written, not on my own initiative, but at the request of the Rockefeller Foundation-funded Institute of Pacific Relations. In the academic world, acknowledgments, citations and quotations of one's work in books by others are important evidence of status and recognition of competence. The first of these had already appeared. At present writing, I know of over eighty. I did not get the appointment at Cornell, but held an identical one briefly at Syracuse University.

My lack of a degree meant that I faced academic snobbery for the nearly sixty years of my activity as a scholar of Soviet and post-Soviet affairs, which continues today. Consequently, expressions of confidence

in my knowledge by those in the best position to judge were very meaningful to me. Just before the war, a young Russian teacher, Masha, had
married, in the Urals steel town of Magnitogorsk, an American, John
Scott. *Behind the Urals*, John's eyewitness account of the building of that
steel mill, one of the key undertakings of the early five-year plans, in
which he took part as a rank-and-file workingman, is regarded as a classic by all Sovietologists, and was republished half a century after its first
appearance. He became a top editor of *Time* magazine, and presumably
used that as a cover for CIA work, because when I was desperately
unemployed in the 1950s, he suggested that I apply to them for a job.
His father, the great and staunch old radical, Scott Nearing, who
appeared in Warren Beatty's feature film, "Reds", when he was ninety-
nine, was heartbroken over the turn John had taken, and once said to
me wistfully, "I wish you were my son." John had been his only child.
He had dropped the surname of Nearing to become John Scott.

Although John was expelled from the Soviet Union days before
Hitler's attack for a dispatch reporting that it would come—Stalin
regarded that story as provocative of Hitler—Masha's behavior certainly did not indicate that John was yet an undercover agent, if she ever
knew. She was totally loyal to her native land and regarded that expulsion as just one of those things over-zealous flunkies could do. She
enrolled at New York University to obtain an American degree. Once,
one of her professors marked her wrong for certain answers she gave
with respect to the collective-farm system. She did a lot of her reading at
the American Russian Institute, and we knew each other well, so she
asked me whether she had been right. I said, "Masha, you come from a
collective farm. Why on earth do you ask me?" She replied, "Because
you understand our country so well." Masha's own opinions are the
basis of a book by Nobel-Prize winner Pearl Buck, *Talk About Russia
With Masha Scott.*

Right after the Battle of Stalingrad, something occurred that not only
enabled me to reach half of the newspaper-reading American public
daily from then until the end of the war, but also sheds a very sad light
on the manipulation of what is called news in this country. The United
Press (later UPI) phoned the Institute one day and asked us to spot a
couple of places on the map that had been named in that evening's
Soviet war communique as having been re-taken by the advancing Red
Army. I found them, moved the pins on my own war map as I had as a
child over fifteen years earlier during the Chinese civil war, and phoned
back. I asked, "Did the Russians really say they took..." whatever those
place-names were? UP confirmed that they had. I said, "In that case,
they'll retake the Dnieper Dam in a day or two."

The Dnieper Dam was as well-known to the world then as, say, the

Kennedy Space Center is today. That was the age of construction, and a hydroelectric dam was the biggest thing one could construct. Built between 1927 and 1932, the Dnieper Dam was the symbol of the First Five-Year Plan. Could those dumb muzhiks build such a behemoth? They did, and in record time. Moreover, the best U.S. dam-builder, Col. Hugh Cooper, had been hired as chief consulting engineer, and had come home with high praise for the workers' enthusiasm and their eagerness to learn.When the Nazis had taken that dam two years earlier, Hitler played the symbolism for all it was worth. And the Soviet destruction of its control gates and turbines before they retreated had been received by the world as a symbol that he would never gain anything from his conquest.

The day after I offered that prediction, the *New York Times* front-paged a story UP had written around it. That afternoon they called again, but this time the voice at the other end identified himself as Peg Vaughn, Night Manager. On a wire service that's the top operating executive, because it is the night operation that feeds the morning newspapers. He asked, "Mr. Mandel, how would you like to come to work for the United Press as our Russian Expert?"

I answered, "That sounds interesting."

"Be here tomorrow at 5 p.m," he responded.

I hung up the phone and called everyone I knew with the question, "How the hell much should I charge UP to be their Russian Expert?"

My hourly rate—I worked two hours a night, five nights a week—was higher than that of Walter Cronkite, who was risking his life for UP, flying with the American bombers over Europe, and higher than that of its Foreign Editor, Harrison Salisbury, who was with UP before he moved to the *New York Times* where he remained until retirement. It was taken as a matter of course that the Russian-front story was the most important during all four years of the war. Every once in a while there would be a battle in the West: El Alamein or Anzio or D-Day in Europe, or the Battle of the Bulge. For a week, maybe even as much as a month, that would get the primary attention, because our forces or the British were involved. Likewise, if a naval battle occurred in the Pacific, or if there were island actions—Guadalcanal, New Guinea, Okinawa—that would be news for a week or two. But on the Soviet fronts the most stupendous war in human history proceeded month after month. Individual battles involved numbers of tanks, artillery, and fighter planes several times larger than Eisenhower ever commanded in western and southern Europe combined. The Germans lost more men in a single sub-battle of the Battle of the Kursk Bulge than in the full year of fighting in France and Germany after the Normandy landing.

During the war no one doubted the overriding importance of that story. The key to the life-and-death struggle waged every day between the Associated Press and the United Press was whose story about the Russian front the *New York Times* would front-page the next morning. AP was Hertz, No. 1, and UP was Avis, No. 2, trying to replace it. Each day, UP would create elaborate reproductions of the *New York Times* front page, circling in red each item carrying the UP dateline for their salesmen to show newspapers across the country.

A month before I had been called in, a particular day's communique mentioned certain places as having been taken by the Soviets. Just as the United States has towns or counties named for Washington or Jefferson in many states, the Russians have multiple Petrovkas and Ivanovkas and Alexandrovkas. The UP's poor map-reader spotted the wrong ones that evening, and gave the Red Army a hundred-mile advance overnight. UP dishonestly put a London dateline on that geographic discovery by its New York office, and the next day's *New York Times* front-paged the story, with a big headline and map. That night's Soviet communique made clear that the story had been false, because the place-names in it were many miles to the East. The *Times* told UP that it would not run any Russian-front story of their's on page one for a month, no matter what. When I, ignorant of all this background, gave them that Dnieper Dam insight which was too important for that paper to pass by, it made the front page. That one bit probably meant more money to UP than everything they paid me in the two-and-a-half years I worked for them till the end of the war.

I would sit at the shoulder of the cable editor, and explain the significance of the bare-bones story our man in Moscow, Henry Shapiro, sent based on the miserly Soviet war communique. The Soviets felt the best way to prevent German intelligence from gleaning from the communiques anything it didn't already know was to make them as skimpy as possible. I used my then unmatched knowledge of the Soviet transport network and geography to interpret what they were up to and what was likely to happen. Inasmuch as the anti-Soviet commentators, columnists, and well-financed don't-trust-the-Russians organizations were constantly trying to drive a wedge between us and the Soviet Union, I used my position to respond. When they said we should send no more Lend-Lease aid because the Soviets would win anyhow, I emphasized the terrible losses of the Red Army, the destruction of industries and farmlands, the sufferings of the people. It happened that the Germans were able to mount a counter-offensive once that advanced briefly at Kharkov, second city of the Ukraine. Future cold-warriors argued that the Russians were going to lose, and our Lend-Lease would simply fall into Hitler's hands. I answered by pointing out that the Soviets had suffered far greater setbacks during the first five months of the war after

Hitler attacked them in 1941, and again in 1942 when the Nazis had reached Stalingrad and Grozny, capital of Chechnya, a thousand miles inside the country, but that at these critical points the Nazis had been stopped and turned back by the Red Army.

This stubborn, blind anti-Sovietism had created the situation which UP now called upon me to rescue it from. When the war began, the media quite naturally turned to our War Department—the merged Defense Department did not yet exist—for briefings. So long as the Germans advanced against the Red Army, things were going as our military anticipated, although it was taking surprisingly longer than the six weeks Hitler had proclaimed would suffice. When the Soviets turned the tide for good at Stalingrad, the officers in our War Department were at a loss. Everyone knew that Russians can't beat Germans and Communists can't do anything right. But it was happening. When, after Stalingrad, the Red Army ignored all the textbooks and sent its tank armies huge distances through and behind the retreating Germans, our briefers were simply flabbergasted.

My position with United Press included occasional signed articles picked up by papers in various cities, in addition to the unsigned daily war-front story. That brought me a lecture contract with the same agency that managed the biggest international names, later including Mrs. Roosevelt. This was important not only because of the large university and public platform audiences to whom I would speak, but because major newspapers —*Atlanta Constitution, Birmingham Age-Herald* — would interview me when I came to town to speak. Tens or hundreds of thousands would see my arguments favoring continued good relations with the USSR after the war. Each time I visited Canada for a lecture, CBC would run a long, prime-time coast-to-coast network interview.

My first two books got long and positive reviews in the *New York Times* Sunday Book Review and that of the then second-ranking paper in the country, the *New York Herald-Tribune*. This was despite the fact that the second of those books was published many months after the war's end, and Washington was already waging the Cold War. The reviewers were people of prominence, such as Foster R. Dulles of Ohio State, and Richard Lauterbach, a journalist of the highest distinction. Lauterbach wrote me personally, expressing the hope that my *Guide to the Soviet Union* (which was not a guidebook but an overall description of the country, its history, its system and its foreign policy) would be reprinted in paperback and find a mass audience. No such paperback appeared. The atmosphere was deliberately changed for the worse.

During the war, however, Raymond Leslie Buell, a top editor for the *Time-Life-Fortune* group, asked me to write a briefing paper on Soviet government for Wendell Willkie. It was presumed that he would again be the Republican candidate for president in 1944. Buell was a member of Willkie's brain trust. *National Geographic* asked me for an article, paid for it the equivalent of several thousand dollars in today's currency, but didn't print it. The *New Republic* solicited and published my views on Soviet policy in the Far East, and committed itself in writing to publish articles from a freelance journalistic trip to the Soviet Union that unfortunately did not come off. All this when I was 27-29.

It is interesting that the McCarthy-era witch-hunt committees a decade later, fed by the FBI names of people and activities to attack, did not go after me on the basis of my articles in popular periodicals and papers. What interested the committees were the writings that gave me standing in the academic world, which the general media regard as their source of authoritative information. In 1944 the *American Sociological Review*, for the first time in its history, published an issue entirely devoted to one country. It was called "Recent Social Trends in the Soviet Union." The editor solicited my help in deciding on the contents and credited me for that in print. Further, he published in that issue my article for the Willkie brain-truster. Eight years later, the McCarran Committee, and a year after that the McCarthy Committee, hauled me before them for that article, for my first book, and for a reprint of writing of mine in a collection by a Columbia University scholar.

The Communist Party made no attempt to influence or even familiarize itself with what I was doing. Contrary to myth, it vastly underestimated the importance of the Soviet issue in determining the future of the American labor movement where its greatest interest lay. The shoe was on the other foot. It was I who, regarding myself as a loyal Communist, tried to get my old leaders from Ohio, Johnny Williamson and Bob Thompson, at this time part of the national leadership in New York, to read my writings before publication. They never did. They took it for granted that a good Communist would propagandize for Soviet socialism. The notion of *thinking* about the Soviet Union never entered their heads. It most certainly entered mine. The Soviet paeans of praise to Stalin as an individual turned my stomach, as did the little-remembered fact that he ultimately acquired the title, Generalissimo. My article in the *American Sociological Review* took note of the postponement of regularly-scheduled elections, and of "repressive and...extra-Constitutional measures." I wrote that the change in the status of the church hierarchy had been made "partly in response to foreign sentiment." However, it would be nine more years before heresies such as these would bring my expulsion from the American Communist Party.

Intellectuals and professionals generally belonged to occupation-based party clubs or broader groups into which their work would fit. I, on the other hand, deliberately refrained from transferring out of my neighborhood club. I wanted to remain in touch with plain folk. At a Communist Party rally in New York's Madison Square Garden in the winter of 1944-1945, I spotted my comrade Johnny Vinnaccia from a decade earlier when I had been Education Director of the Young Communist League in the poor neighborhood that included the gashouse district along the East River. He was haggard, worn, sick-looking and literally old, although only just past thirty. We put him up for the night and talked for hours.

I asked him, "You fought in Spain. I worship the ground you guys walk on. But every time we've run into each other, there's been something extremely respectful in your attitude toward me. What's that all about?"

"What do you know about me?" he asked.

"You joined our club for unemployed youth and were a reliable, steady type."

"Then you nominated me to go to a political training school," Johnny interrupted. "You fought for that nomination. I was a three-time loser and New York had that four-strikes law. One more and I'd have gone to the big house for life. But you got me sent to that school, and it put me on a whole different track."

It was clear that he had to tell his story to someone he trusted, and that perhaps he was aware that he wouldn't have much longer to do so. He coughed constantly, bringing up phlegm into a big handkerchief. Johnny was of average height or less, thin to the point of being skinny. His face, with a huge nose, would have been hawk-like if not that it was broad across his highly-placed cheekbones. What lay behind it was not plain in the least. He began to tell his story.

"I was born in Sicily, 1912. I grew up around 14th St. and First Avenue." The Italian Lower East Side, Godfather country. "There was one way for an immigrant kid to get nice clothing, money in my pocket, standing with the girls. Cosa Nostra gave me little jobs to do. The first time I was caught, I stood up in court and told the judge I never had a chance in life, and wasn't to blame."

Johnny was still in his early teens and the judge gave him a suspended sentence.

"Ya ever read *Les Miserables?* That Javert. My probation officer was the same. I'd get a job, he'd tell the boss my background, I'd be fired. But as I was walking along the waterfront one day then, some guy yelled, 'Ya wanna ship out?'

"This was just before the Depression, and ships were looking for men. I jumped aboard. That freighter once put into Leningrad. There were damn few beggars, nobody I could spot for a whore, and absolutely no limousines. Guys who'd been there before told me about the

International Seamen's Club. I dropped in. Movies, lectures, non-alcoholic drinks and very nice girls. You been to Leningrad?" I nodded.

"There's an old palace a block long. Kids and teenagers like me were going in and out. I followed them. In one room boys, and even girls, were making model airplanes. There was an instructor and models of famous planes all around. In other rooms they were doing science experiments. There were game rooms, gyms, a movie running, a live kid show going on. When I left I thought that if I had had things like that to do as a kid I would never have gotten into trouble. When I got back to the States, the Depression had hit. I went back with the boys, got caught, and got sent to Welfare Island. You know about Welfare Island?"

"Some. But I never been there."

"Capitalism is corrupt, but Welfare Island beats all. A couple of big-time gangsters were in, but they had rooms in the prison hospital, liquor and food food from the outside. They'd take their keepers to night spots in Manhattan and pay the bills.

"The island was racist like everyplace else. Negroes were housed in the worst cells, with the worst crowding, and got the dirtiest jobs. Most white prisoners wouldn't mix with them. I did. People are people.

"The food got worse and worse. One day I began banging my bowl on the table and hollering that I wouldn't eat that slop. Everyone else joined in. The food got a little better.

"When I got out, there were still no jobs, and I didn't want to go back to getting money in the old way, so I hopped a freight west, dropped off in Cleveland, but hardly got out of the yards before a city detective stopped me. 'Whatcha doin'?' he asked. 'I'm a farm laborer, lookin' for work,' I told him. 'Lemme see your hands.' They were white and soft. Any calluses were long gone. So he put me on the next freight headed back to New York. Cleveland had enough jobless of its own.

"Back in New York, I found a place to flop at the fink house, our name for the Seamen's Church Institute. There was lots of us there, and we talked day and night. They treated us awful. Compulsory prayers and that shit. So one day there was a fistfight with the men who ran it. I started it. Some intellectual-looking guy had been hanging around the hall, and looked on at the fight. Couple days later he came over and said he was a divinity student. His professor suggested he learn about working people by assisting at the Institute. The guy said he told his professor about the fight and what it was about. The professor told him to ask if my buddies and me would come up and live at the seminary. The idea was that the students would get to know the kind of people for whom he wanted them to be ministers.

"I talked to the guys. I said, 'Let's go up there and give it a try.'

"We went. Every couple of days some representative of a movement that said it was out to help the people was invited to speak to us. The Socialist Party leader, Norman Thomas, came. He was a high and mighty preacher. The Communist Party sent Mother Bloor, Ella Reeve Bloor. She even knew Walt Whitman when she was a kid. She was married to a plain farmer. She talked our language. Jobs, now. Relief, now. We liked it.

"The college term ended, and with it our free meals and dorm. No jobs, no ships, that probation officer on my tail. I went back to the old life. It got me a conviction. Somebody in the same pen got the *Daily Worker*, and would leave it in the library. I read it. The guys called me the Red, but they knew I was one of them. Word got to some big-time mobster, whom they all regarded as their leader. He arranged to talk with me. Afterward he said: 'Kid, if I'd a known what you know when I was your age, I wouldn't be in here now.'

"I got out in 1935. No work. I went up to the Home Relief office on East 34th St. and waited in line for hours. People passed out from hunger. Guy looked at my application, 'No dependents? Sorry. There's no provision for relief to single men.'

"I jumped up on a table, pulled my prison papers out of my pocket, waved them around and hollered, 'I'm a three-timer. You want me to go rob somebody and go to jail for life so I can eat?'

"The supervisor put me on relief. Decent guy. Where there's a will, there's a way. When I left the office, there you were giving out leaflets for people to join the Unemployed Council. I did. So you got me sent to that leadership training school up at Camp Nitgedaiget. First Jewish word I ever learned: 'Forget Your Worries.' People treated me like a human being. Next year the war in Spain began. I hated what Mussolini had done to the country I was born in. I was ashamed that he was an Italian, too. Nobody had to tell me what fascism was. Bucko mates aboard ship, prison guards and keepers, the mentality of the gangsters I'd worked for. So I signed up with the Garibaldini, Italian anti-fascist exiles who came from France and everywhere else, and guys with the guts to find their way out of Italy just to get to a place where they could fight fascism openly. We beat Mussolini's tankmen at Guadalajara. I also met the men who went on to lead the partisans in Italy.

"When I got back from Spain, the National Maritime Union had won recognition. Shipping was picking up. I had steady work. When the war began, there was no problem. Capitalism works great in the killing-people business. Some of the runs were just this side of suicide. Like Lend-Lease to the Soviet Union at Murmansk. Higher losses among merchant seamen than among our soldiers in battle, in proportion to numbers. In Murmansk I found anti-Soviet Poles forging provocative issues of the *Moscow News*. I made my way to Moscow and tried to enlist in the Red Army. They turned me down. No foreigners. Stalin feared spies. On the way home, in Glasgow, I was beaten up by anti-Soviet goons."

I interrupted, "Strange place for that to happen. The Member of Parliament from Glasgow is a Communist, William Gallagher."

"I know. But he didn't get a hundred percent of the votes. Back in New York, I went up to the NMU [National Maritime Union] hiring hall to ship out, and the p.a. system announced that I'm to go to Blackie Meyers' office. Sitting in there are two characters who look like detectives, but better-dressed, smoother, better education written all over them. One says, 'Would you like to go to Italy?' You know, you never knew where you were shipping to, for security. I looked at Blackie, and he nodded to go along with them. Next question, 'You are a member of the Communist Party, right?' What the hell is this? I look at Blackie, a Party member like me. He nods okay. 'We're from the Office of Strategic Services.'" [In 1947 it became the CIA.]

"'You go down to Baltimore. Find the ship with Captain so-and-so. Tell him I sent you. You'll be in the crew of a ship to Italy. When you get there, contact the Communist Party. When you come back, tell us what you learned. You can also tell the U.S. Communist Party.' Blackie again signalled okay."

I had a very strange feeling, "Johnny, did you meet Dr. Eugenio Reale, the head of the Communist Party in Naples?"

"Sure."

"Late in 1943, the *Worker* carried an interview with him— the first description of the CP there in wartime and its plans after liberation. It was signed by a name I didn't recognize, but I somehow thought you wrote it, although if you ever wrote anything before I never saw it. I didn't know where in the world you were, although I knew you were shipping out. Did you write that article?"

"Yes."

"I suppose there was something of your personality and manner in it."

We paused. He had another coffee, coughed some more, and continued.

"I was smuggled across the front and wandered Italy behind the German lines, making contact with the partisans, carrying messages and so forth. This made me overstay my leave and I missed my ship. The O.S.S. straightened things out and put me on the next one back. This happened two or three times. But by then Italy was totally liberated, and they didn't need me any more. The next time I missed my ship, they had me arrested as a deserter and sent to a concentration camp. I was staked out in the sun. I got TB."

The next morning, Johnny went to see the woman he had married before his last voyage. We never saw him again. He died of tuberculosis within months after telling us his story.

All rise.

CHAPTER 9

William Faulkner Couldn't Get In

The national lecture circuit was fun. It yielded a handsome income as well as some truly exciting travel adventures, and was broadening in very real ways. I toured the entire country: The Deep South — Mississippi, Alabama, Georgia, Virginia; Texas, which is a world all its own; the entire West Coast plus British Columbia. In earlier years I had spoken in eastern Canada during the war, where I had been given equal billing with people like Norbert Wiener, founder of cybernetics; the famous China correspondent Edgar Snow, and others. I had addressed a conference of the Brookings Institution in Washington, with a U.S. Supreme Court justice and the vice-president in the front rows of the audience. I had been a guest on prime-time network radio in this country before television existed.

These experiences gave me contact with a level of society totally new to me. I was twenty-eight, and had been quite poor until just four or five years earlier. Sitting at home writing my first two books, or in the New York office of the United Press doing daily news analysis, or at the American Russian Institute providing background on the USSR to government agencies and major magazines were desk jobs that hadn't given me much of a picture of how the other half lived. As traveling lecturer I was dinner guest of the wealthiest local families. For them, ironically, it was I who added a touch of glamor. I remember the home of the Pisitz family in Atlanta, owners of its biggest department store. Meat was rationed during the war, and lamb chops like my mother used to buy were something I didn't see often. But the Pisitzes served lamb chops, thick and juicy. Actually, it wasn't the Pisitzes who served them, but their silent Black servants. I was not comfortable.

Although my announced subjects were on Soviet postwar foreign policy, I used my place on the platform to carry forward the battle against racism. For example, the *Birmingham Age-Herald* headlined a story about a lecture of mine in its December 17, 1945 issue: "Victories of Russians Attributed to Perfect Unity Among Peoples." The fact that this unity dissolved half a century later when Soviet citizens turned away from socialism had very little to do with the reality during World War II.

I had given the Birmingham talk eight days before Christmas, the first Christmas after the end of the war. The new president, Truman, was doing his damndest, through Russia-baiting, to keep our draftee armies in Italy, the Philippines, and other liberated countries. (There was no opposition to keeping them in Germany and Japan, which no one trusted.) A great outcry, including massive demonstrations by our soldiers overseas, demanded that they be brought home by Christmas. Truman yielded. That external circumstance, along with the vagaries of December weather, and the fact that my lecture management would provide both rail and air tickets for the same trip, just in case, led to a particularly delightful trip home.

A tremendous snowfall had buried Washington, and all flights terminating in that city were cancelled. There was no non-stop flight from Birmingham to New York, so I boarded an overnight Pullman. A landslide blocked the tracks at Winston-Salem, North Carolina, and the stationmaster said we'd be stuck for hours. Standing near me when we got the news were several veterans in a rush to get home. One, a Navy flight lieutenant returning from the South Pacific to his home in Boston, said, "Why don't we hire a taxi?"

Credit cards did not yet exist, and a cabbie was not about to accept a check on a New York bank from a stranger. I convinced the railroad ticket agent to give me cash for the next segment of my ticket. The four of us—the flier, an army officer, a sergeant from the Bronx, and I—hired the one cab available at that very late hour. It stood outside the station bar and the driver had been drinking. It was as disreputable-looking as any vehicle I had ever been in. One window was broken. We huddled for warmth. He took us 150 miles via snowy up-country roads. Tires, too, were rationed during the war, and when one of his baldies blew out in Danville, Virginia, he refused to go on. He needed the one spare to be sure to get home. But the trip had been gorgeous: full moon over freshly snow-laden pines in the Piedmont, utter silence. The blowout occurred near the tiny Danville airport, and the fly-boy said, "Why don't we hire a plane?" There was really no choice, if a plane were available. None of us wanted to spend the night there. A light was burning in the one small hangar, and we walked to it. There was the owner and pilot of the single plane in sight, a Waco biplane. The pilot was wearing fringed buckskins. A century late for Daniel Boone and twenty years early for the hippies. Yeah, he'd take us.

Except for the lieutenant when first trained to fly, and I for a single flying lesson I had once won, none of us had ever been on a plane so small. I'm not sure that the army men had ever been in an aircraft at all.

This little one went putt-putt-putt, not a reassuring vroom-vroom. The twenty-one-passenger transports to which I was accustomed had truck-sized balloon tires. This one had tiny doughnuts. We looked at each other. I don't know how the others felt, but my notion in those years was that if Uncle Sam licensed somebody and something to fly, I'd climb aboard.

The plane was a four seater, and there were four of us plus the pilot. He put the bulky sergeant up front with himself for balance, and me in the middle between the two others in back. They had safety belts. I had my arms around the shoulders of each of them as we took off. I was accustomed to planes that made a gradual ascent and then a gentle bank as they turned onto course. This one went, it seemed to me, straight up, and next I found myself looking down at the state of Virginia as the pilot stood it on its wing to head it in the proper direction. His radio was on, and soon we heard that the Washington airport had only one clear runway, with four-foot banks of snow on either side and a high cross-wind. The pilot said his lower wing offered no clearance and he wouldn't risk it. He put us down in Lynchburg.

Here, we found a pilot with a high-wing Stinson, but he would not take four passengers in a three-passenger plane. Whereupon the army lieutenant, just like in the movies, pulled out a billfold full of photos of attractive young women, showed us one who lived in Lynchburg where he had been stationed when in training, phoned her up, and was told: "Sure, come right on over."

The remaining three of us boarded the Stinson, which made the trip to Washington beautifully and uneventfully. I felt very V.I.P. as we heard the control tower put an airliner on hold to let us come in. I took a cab to Union Station, which was mobbed with returning soldiers, and I turned in the unused remainder of my railroad ticket for cash. The harried agent shoved both the original ticket, a ticket to New York and the cash back to me, and I dashed for the train, which was about to leave. In New York I cashed the ticket in again. I felt guilty for a long time over the possibility that the Washington agent might have had to pay for his mistake out of his own pocket. A fundamentalist would say god punished me right away. Dead tired, I had given myself the luxury of a parlor-car seat in which to sleep the rest of the way. It was daytime. No Pullmans. But the heater next to my seat had lost its mind. It stayed at well over ninety degrees. There was no empty seat to change to, and I squirmed and sweated all the way home.

Returning home from lectures was a lesson in the difference between life in New York, or any major city, then and today. Although I could afford cabs, I knew that the life I was living kept me separated from plain people, and I consciously sought not to lose the common touch. I would take the Seventh Avenue subway line to 145th Street, and walk uphhill with my suitcase to where we lived on 141st, between Broadway and Riverside Drive. Sometimes I'd be wearing a tuxedo, which was then still required by some lecture platforms. A white man in a tux, with a bag, walking through Harlem late at night No one ever touched me.

Another thing I did, to maintain contact with folks who did ordinary jobs, was just plain fun. The union to which I belonged in the 1940s, Local, now District, 65, had built a nightclub into the gloomy brick cube of its headquarters catty-corner to Cooper Union, my father's alma mater, in lower Manhattan. Then the union was of office workers, but today it is the powerful and influential organization of New York's hospital employees primarily. Leadbelly would sing in our union club, where on other evenings I would dance my ass off. I got more than my dues worth.

The lecturing itself began to require courage. My subject was relations with the Soviet Union. On March 6, 1946, four years before Joe McCarthy in the Senate decided he could further his career by witch-hunting, the House of Representatives' Committee on Un-American Activities, HUAC as people called it, cited Presbyterian Rev. Richard Morford for contempt of Congress. His crime was refusing to turn over the list of members of the National Council of American-Soviet Friendship. This was a totally legal organization employing the rights of free speech, free press, and freedom of assembly to head off World War III, which was already being propagandized for. He served three months in jail.

My management, in addition to sending me out on solo talks, set up a debate on Soviet foreign policy in which I toured with an opponent. Hallett Abend was a man whose articles I had read as a child and teenager when he was Far Eastern Bureau Chief of the *New York Times.* The agency wanted to title the debate, "Is Russia a Threat to Peace?", the same notion hammered at the American people for the next forty-five years. The title was simply an echo of Truman, the mainstream press, the body politic, and radio. I was outraged.

The Soviets had lost tens of millions of soldiers and civilians. We had lost four hundred thousand soldiers, one for every fifty deaths in the USSR. They had lost housing for 25 million in the cities and villages occupied by the Nazis—places that were deliberatedly destroyed by the retreating Wehrmacht when it had time. They had never had any paved roads other than city streets, and their railroads had been ripped up by the retreating Germans using special monstrous plows extended behind the last car of the last train, or cam devices that took a bite out of each rail. Their biggest power dam had been blown up. Their coal mines were flooded, blast furnaces and steel mills destroyed. People died from starvation there as late as 1947.

Fifteen years after the war ended, I committed an unforgiveable mistake in playing to Russian and Ukrainian Soviet graduate exchange students at Berkeley the most powerful song to come out of the USSR in that conflict: "May noble wrath crest like an ocean wave. We fight a people's war, a sacred war." Hearing it again turned them to stone. Fathers and brothers dead, homes burned, mothers and sisters starved, fields destroyed, cattle slaughtered, spent cartridges for toys, surviving pages from army manuals used for primers in school. That had been their childhood. I have heard its music used in films made after the collapse of the Soviet Union.

Let cynics who think World War II was morally no different than its predecessor listen to that "Sacred War," to the Jewish guerrilla song from Eastern Europe, "Never say that you have reached the very end," and to the song of the anti-Nazi Germans in Spain's International Brigade, with its unconquerable and incomparable upbeat, "Frei-heit!", leaving simply no room for doubt that "Free-dom!" would win.

It had won, but Truman radioed orders to ships on the high seas with Lend-Lease aid for Russia to turn around on the very day the war ended. Others prevailed upon him to cancel that, and he did. Both moves were vintage Truman.

The Soviets had never had much of a navy, and after the war it was virtually gone. They had no bomber force. The U.S. had the atom bomb and Moscow did not. Washington went on manufacturing it, despite queries even from Republican newspapers as to motive. Stalin also asked that question, and warned that the Soviets would have to make one too. Washington laughed. Those dumb muzhiks making an atom bomb!

I told my management that I would not debate under the title, "Is Russia a Threat to Peace?" because the publicity for these debates via newspapers, radio, direct mail and posters reached a constituency far beyond those who would actually attend. Debating such a topic would suggest to the public, less than a year after we had fought as allies, that Russia was a threat to peace.

Consequently we debated under an inverted title: "Is Russia a Force for Peace?" Interest was enormous. Our appearance in Wilmington, Delaware, was typical. One thousand people packed the theater. I still have the sixty questions they asked us. Some of them were hammered into people's heads by the mass media for decades thereafter. I quote the written questions sent up on that occasion: "To what extent is internal strife in so-called capitalistic countries Moscow-inspired or at least encouraged?" "Do you think that the Russian government with its goal of a world Communist state can have peaceful relations with the U.S. and other democracies?" "Is war with Russia inevitable?" Forty years later, Americans had not yet asked themselves whether those two generations of peace and absence of any attempt at Marxist revolution in western Europe, Japan, and the U.S. had not long since provided the answers to those questions. Apparently you can not only fool some of the people all of the time, and all of the people some of the time, but most of the people most of the time. There is more danger from the fact that the unstable Russia that succeeded the Soviet Union has ICBMs and stored plutonium for a hundred thousand warheads—more threat to peace, in my opinion, than there ever was from the USSR.

Perhaps my most interesting audience was in Oxford, Mississippi, home to William Faulkner, who was very much alive at the time, and also to the University of Mississippi. I was scheduled for a solo lecture. The railroad south from Memphis didn't pass through Oxford, and I had to take a bus from the nearest station. There were two lines to get aboard, one for whites and one for "colored" people. Among the African-Americans was a soldier just back from the war, with a chestful of ribbons. He looked at me with utter hatred, perhaps because I was the best-dressed white in a line of poor Southerners. An elderly Black woman was also in the line. I hung back, to make sure she'd have a place to sit. She hung back. It was not yet time for Rosa Parks, not by a decade and certainly not in Mississippi. I had no choice but to get on. I felt like two cents. There was a seat for her, in back of course, but that wasn't the point.

That incident is related to what happened at the university when I gave my lecture. I went to the office of the professor whose signature was on the contract. He wasn't there, but I saw a copy of a labor union publication, the *CIO News*, on his desk. In Mississippi? His name was Silver, and he became nationally known nearly two decades later in the Freedom summers of 1963 and 1964. Professor Silver was the lone Mississippi intellectual who took a public stand in favor of the movement to enable African-Americans to vote.

In the evening, as he and I stood outside the auditorium door while the audience filed in, I turned to him and said, "This room won't be big enough." He replied, "It's never been filled for a lecture." I rejoined, "They don't know me from a hole in the wall. But they want to know whether they're going to have to fight Russia."

The place was packed. The Fire Department closed the doors. William Faulkner showed up and couldn't get in. I remained in Oxford the next couple of days because I had no date till Monday in Dallas, and the faculty spent the weekend arguing in their homes over whether they were sorry their only nationally and internationally known citizen had been barred, or were glad because the s.o.b. had never tried to attend anything at the university before. The audience was painfully young. In Mississippi, whites didn't wait to be drafted, and many of the student veterans had obviously been below legal age when they signed up.

In Silver's class the next day, I told the story of the Black woman, the bitter soldier, and the bus. A large young man in back, who had plantation-owner's son written all over him, said, "She was a nigger, wasn't she?" But other young men in the class, and during informal talks later, put the notion in my head that their generation, or some of them, would be different. Consequently when Jimmy Carter, of that generation, became president thirty years later, I wasn't as surprised as most of my circle that he had a half-civilized attitude toward African-Americans, and that they found him acceptable. (I say half-civilized, because of his statement that housing should naturally be segregated, and the fact that his own church in Plains, Georgia, where he continued to teach Sunday school, remained lily-white.)

Until a date in the hard-coal town of Hazleton, Pennsylvania, at the turn of 1946-47, I was listened to with anything from normal courtesy to overwhelming enthusiasm. True, in San Bernardino, California, someone got up and asked me if I were a Communist. The chairwoman responded in a manner totally typical of that time, "Sir, Mr. Mandel is our *guest!*"

After my appearance in San Francisco, which I first saw as lecturer for the Town Hall of the West held in the huge Curran Theater—a very major platform in those pre-television years, where prime ministers, ex-presidents and world celebrities were the regular fare—its director wrote my management afterward: "Every American should hear Mr. Mandel's lecture, so that the fog of doubt concerning Russia founded in misinformation may be dispelled. The State Department would do well in appointing Mr. Mandel ambassador to the Soviet Union." I was twenty-nine. During the question period, I was handed a note on behalf of the Hoover Institution at Stanford stating that if I wanted a research fellowship there, it was mine for the asking.

I addressed a packed convention of the Bay Area Teachers' Association. There, I delivered a slashing attack on the American imperialism expressed in the clear intent to maintain troops indefinitely in and to dominate the Pacific and Western Europe, which had never previously been the case, in addition to maintaining U.S. power over Washington's satellite states in Latin America. That speech won the lengthiest applause I recall receiving anywhere. But the West Coast, particularly from San Francisco north to Seattle, was already alone in retaining a civilized attitude toward the world.

Hazleton, Pennsylvania, cooked my goose. There, I had been booked into the Presbyterian Church and the Kiwanis Club, with radio broadcast. The response was splendid, and the superintendent of schools asked me to speak to the junior and senior classes of the high school. A few days later the *Hazleton Sunday Times* carried a very lengthy letter by a Naval SeaBee. He wrote of my "active participation and campaign last November for the only Communist now seated in the U.S. Congress, Vito Marcantonio." Marcantonio, who I later knew personally, was never a Communist. He was the only member of Congress to vote against U.S. entry into the Korean War.

The Hazleton newspaper ran an editorial, which said, "A front page story in today's *Times* tells how one William Mandel...after delivering TWO addresses in Hazleton,...was permitted to lecture to the students at Hazleton High School, without even the pretense of proper rebuttal made available....[typeface as in the original] WE call on the Hazleton city school board...to investigate the conditions which permit an ostensibly tainted propagandist to be foisted on the faculty and student body of our school system, and to inform the public why the incident was at all possible and what will be done to preclude any recurrence."

The news story was a classic example of the technique we wrongly called McCarthyite— wrongly because it antedated his use of it by several years. I quote: "It has been learned through the offices of *Plain Talk*, a magazine for the purpose of disseminating information on Totalitarianism, that Mr. William Mandel, from 1945 to 1946 was an instructor at the Jefferson School of Social Sciences...New York City. This institution is definitely known as a Communist School and is under the auspices of, and controlled by, the Communist Party." That statement was true. The paper continued: "The Catalogue of the School indicates that in 1945 Mr. Mandel lectured on the 'Soviet Union Today' and in 1946, 'Soviet Union in Films.'" It went on to describe me as a member of the Research Staff of the American Russian Institute, New York, which it labeled "a semi-official Soviet organization for the purpose of providing propaganda for the Communist Party." That was a lie. The article then specified that my two books were used in classes of the Jefferson School and were sold currently in Communist book stores. That was quite true. They were also sold in every serious bookstore in the country. The later one was in use as a text at Yale, Stanford, and elsewhere. The earlier one had actually found its way into use at a university in South Africa.

The list of my sins continued. I was a member of the International Workers Order. True. That fraternal society offered health maintenance and death benefits, and was under Communist leadership. I had been a member of its Speakers Bureau. True, just as Hazleton had obtained my services through the country's most respectable lecture management. I had been mentioned twice in the past five months in the *Daily Worker.* Once was for a local speech I had given at a Communist-sponsored summer camp, the other for a statement I made on a national radio broadcast. In the latter case, I quote the *Hazleton Times*, I "very vehemently and emphatically demanded that United States troops be recalled from China and other outposts of the world. Everyone immediately recognized this kind of chatter as regular Communist Party talk." But it was also the view of the then Secretary of Commerce, Henry Wallace, who had been vice-president under Roosevelt and, earlier, his Secretary of Agriculture, and whose thirteen years in the U.S. cabinet amounted to more time spent there than any other non-president in American history before or since.

This extraordinarily editorial front-page news story concluded: "All indications are that he is a Communist." True, of course. Yet at that time I was engaged in conversations with a totally loyal Soviet person who was also a Black native-born U.S. citizen, conversations that led me to decide there were Soviet practices I could not accept. It was this that eventually led to my expulsion from the party, and my subsequent realization that it was not something I wanted to belong to.

Neal Burroughs had been born in the U.S. in 1922. His mother, Willianna, a Communist, had been fired from her teaching job in New York City for trying to organize a union. One was successfully established later. She went to Moscow with two of her sons, Neal, five, and Charles, eight. In the pre-war years, Mrs. Burroughs was the English voice of Radio Moscow. They had returned to the United States at the end of World War II, when she learned she was dying of cancer. Neal, like Dr. DuBois and Paul Robeson, had experienced no racism in the USSR. He was shocked and embittered that the only work he could find in his native land, despite his several years at Moscow University, was as an assembler of radios. Subsequently he got a job with the one book store selling Soviet printed matter in Russian. But they put him in the basement to fill orders, sort, and catalogue. A Black dealing directly with white customers was out of the question. Despit this racism, he did ultimately publish an essay on Turgenev in a Pocket Book of that author's work.

Neal and I became best friends. He was about twenty-five when we met. Neal was "Soviet man" to me, and he found me to be the American he thought understood the Soviet Union best, and therefore, understood him best. But we found there were things on which we disagreed, essentially because I was an American and he, psychologically, a Russian, despite being Black and U.S.-born. He spoke with a heavy Russian accent and lectured in my Jefferson School class as had his Russian professors at Moscow University, stalking back and forth with his hands folded behind his back.

With my egalitarian notions, I asked him why the Soviet Union had re-instituted epaulets for officers. He said, "We think they deserve it."

That way of looking at it had never occurred to me, and I accepted it. I asked him why Stalin had been given the title, "Generalissimo." His answer was the same. I was not satisfied, and asked, "How about the papers referring to him every single day, and on every single page, as father, teacher, Leader with a capital L? Everything good, or supposedly good, in the USSR is preceded by the adjective, 'Stalinist.' It's just like in the days of Russia's absolute monarchy."

He thought for a while, and replied, "Bill, sometimes a people needs a monarchy." The answer was frank, honest, totally rooted in the Russian mind set and historical experience. It was totally unacceptable to me and, I was sure, to the American people.

By that date there had been no convention of the Soviet Communist Party, or of the labor unions, for seven years, and none would be held for another six. That did not accord with my view of Marxism as a democratic philosophy based on faith in the people. I said so to Communist friends, which ultimately got me kicked out of the party. Meanwhile, the attack from the opposite end of the political spectrum in the *Hazleton Times* cost me my lecture management, and there were other evidences of sharply changing times.

There is a photo of me playing with my children in New York's Van Cortlandt Park. It shows a handsome young man with his arms folded rather oddly across his stomach, each hand gripping the elbow of the other. That was my way of suppressing the intense physical pain of what was then diagnosed as a stomach ulcer, although x-rays in later years showed no scar tissue. That pain was the price I paid for suppressing my passionate convictions in order to present my views in a manner that appealed to reason. I particularly remember the excruciating agony of an evening when I sat on an extraordinary panel brought together to debate the world scene for the annual meeting of the financial supporters of the New School for Social Research in January 1946.

The Cold War had not yet been officially embraced by President Truman, so interference for it was being run, very hard and very roughly, by liberals and one-time radicals. On that panel I found myself outnumbered five to one. Prof. Ernest Simmons of Columbia, an expert on Russian literature who was a member of the American Russian Institute board, was the seventh panel member. His bland neutrality that evening foreshadowed his subsequent retreat from active efforts to further good relations with the Soviet Union. One of the other panelists was Max Eastman, described accurately in the latest *Encyclopaedia Britannica* as a "leading radical who later became a militant conservative." He was a major character in Warren Beatty's feature film, "Reds." The others on the panel were James Carey, president of the huge International Electrical Workers' Union; David Dallin, a particularly embittered anti-

Soviet emigre scholar; Eugene Lyons, who had gotten the first interview with Stalin after the latter's rise to power and who, my father tells me, once dangled me on his knee; and a Czech diplomat I knew personally who was rapidly positioning himself to win the hospitality of the U.S. government.

What happened was best described in a letter to me from the president of the New School, Bryn Hovde. He wrote me on January 28, 1946, "I too was very much distressed at the useless and childish name-calling as it seemed to me mainly to one side of the argument....You spoke under about as difficult circumstances as I have ever observed and did it in a rational and decent way. My compliments to you!"

In private life at this time, I was a rank-and-file activist Communist. Tanya and I and another Communist couple in the building organized a rent strike among the sixty tenants in our lower-middle-class apartment house when the landlord raised the rent but would not replace the refrigerators. The rent control law permitted increases only if the quality of the housing and appliances were upgraded in some way that required added investment. In that effort we worked most closely with two of our best friends, a couple living in the same building, Communist Party members. But we fought bitterly with them over sending our children to the neighborhood school, which was overwhelmingly Black. The other couple felt the quality of their children's education came first. They felt that since a majority of the kids in the school were from families of low education, their children's schooling would be held back. Ironically, the wife was actually a teacher in that very school, an excellent one in the parents' opinions, and later a very hard-working activist in New York's wonderful Teachers' Union. As a teacher, her concern for Black children was splendid, but she found a way to send her sons to another public school.

Tanya and I were outraged. We were against segregation—no matter the excuse. Furthermore, the Communist Party undertook to serve as a model in race relations, and was quite specific that this applied to its individual members. Moreover, in a racist country we felt obliged to raise our children to get along with people of all races. Like all parents, we failed in some things—I took my frustrations of the period out on them—but not in this capacity.

In light of later events, it is fascinating that the right of this couple to remain members of the Communist Party was never questioned. We told our local Party club of this incident, but nothing happened. The teacher-mother-friend would not speak to us for a year. Then, somehow, we made up. Yet in 1985 this couple broke relations with us after forty-five years when I made a speech in New York critical of the USSR for its policies toward Jewish culture and history. The Soviet Union was not to be criticized under any circumstances. They belonged to the Party until its leader called Cleveland cops to bar dissenters from its national convention in 1990. But I was expelled early in the '50s because I developed areas of disagreement on an untouchable subject— whether everything done by the Soviet Communist Party was as it should have been. Fortunately, the invitation from the Hoover Institution, previously mentioned, provided me another year of broad acceptability before the McCarthyite long night closed in years before I was called before the witch-hunting committees themselves.

I arrived at Stanford in February, 1947, to begin the Hoover Institution research fellowship. The art gallery was then in the building adjacent to the Hoover Tower, which has always been called Hoover's last erection. Doubtless unfair. The president of the United States in 1928-32 wasn't all that old when it was built. He lived on campus.

A faculty art show was on and I wandered in. But for one painting, it was typical of academic work at that time: a competent, bland collection of decorative still-lifes, landscapes, portraits, strictly realist, and leaning heavily to watercolors and pastels. Not a thought in a carload—except for that one painting. Its strong but totally naturalist oils blazed across the room.

The painting depicted four Black men, working men in their go-to-church-on-Sunday suits, carrying a coffin in the middle of Market Street, San Francisco's main thoroughfare. A bulky policeman, standing with legs spread wide, each hand grasping an end of his club, stood behind them, watching. Over his shoulder shone the traffic light, blazing red. The title was "Anti-Lynching Demonstration." The artist's name was printed in clear block letters at the bottom: Victor Arnautoff.

At this time, the towns along El Camino Real, U.S. 101 bordering Stanford, had a policy that no African-American should be within their borders after the sun went down. A Black faculty member was simply beyond imagination. I remember no African-students, and find it hard to conceive that there might have been one, even aside from the financial barrier. Where would one live? In a fraternity or sorority? Incredible. In a dorm? But then whites would have to tolerate a Black sleeping in the same room. Out of the question.

We lived in liberal Berkeley, forty-five miles away, when I was at Stanford, because of the postwar housing crunch for families with small children. We had three. Berkeley had hired its first Black schoolteacher only four years earlier. She has written, "They made me teach kindergarten because it was the only grade parents did not *have* to send their children to. They told the other teachers that if they wanted to transfer, they would be allowed to. The principal actually took them up on it." The first year, none of the white teachers would speak to her. One teacher who wanted to befriend her said she could see her on the weekends, but could not talk to her at school.

I had accepted the offer of that Hoover Institution fellowship as both an honor and a responsibility, virtually a duty, but Stanford was not the kind of place where someone of my origins could instantly feel comfortable. The appointment was an honor on several grounds. Nineteen forty-seven was to be the first year of the first program in American academic history to study the Soviet Union, other than two wartime summer sessions at Cornell, and I was one of the first two people appointed to launch it. (A similar program was initiated at Columbia. Both were Rockefeller-Foundation-funded.) Second, I had no degree. Stanford, having taken the initiative in inviting me, accepted the two books I had published in lieu of M.A. and Ph.D., respectively, and granted me a stipend at post-doctoral level. The Ph.D. degree was not common then. Professors often went through their entire careers with no more than an M.A. In consequence, my remuneration was at the associate professor level. As grants were then tax-exempt, my take-home income touched the full-professor range. Finally, the Cold War had been launched, *an impossibility so long as Roosevelt was in the White House.* But Roosevelt had died.

How can I transmit the impact of his death to readers two generations removed from it? I remember on that day, April 12, 1945, walking past New York's Main Library at 5th Avenue and 42nd Street. I don't recall whether I first heard the news from someone in front of the library, or whether I saw a crowd suddenly gathering and falling still in front of a radio store across the street, where a loudspeaker was blaring. The President was dead, the only president in my time for whom I capitalize the "P."

But we had a party scheduled for the next day. And our friends would come, because it would be Tanya's birthday, her 28th. And besides, no one wanted to be alone under those circumstances. Except for the handful of modern Copperheads—a word originally used to define the northerners who favored the slave South in the Civil War—the entire country felt bereaved. This was the man who had led the country out of the Great Depression and to victory against Hitler, at this point clearly only weeks away. He had so won the loyalty of Blacks by his moves against poverty that they, having voted Republican from Lincoln's day on, had turned Democrats from his second election, in 1936, and remain so over sixty years later.

I went to a record store and bought a set of a cantata just out, "The Lonesome Train," by Earl Robinson, composer of "Ballad for Americans." His new work told the story of the train that carried Abraham Lincoln's body from Washington, via Baltimore, Philadelphia,

New York, Cleveland, and Chicago, for burial at Springfield, Illinois:

> A lonesome train, on a lonesome track;
> Seven coaches painted black;
> A slow train,
> A funeral train,
> Carrying Lincoln home again.

And the people, white and Black, came out and stood by the tracks in their hundreds of thousands all along the route to pay their respects to Franklin Delano Roosevelt just as they had for Lincoln. Burl Ives sang the lead. Robinson, who had belonged to the same Young Communist League club as I when I was a skinny kid and we looked like brothers, narrated the spoken passages himself. And so we marked Tanya's birthday by playing "The Lonesome Train." And then our guests went home.

World War II ended in May 1945 in Europe and in August in Japan. Yet on September 1, James Reston, Washington correspondent of the *New York Times,* wrote that several "tentative conclusions" had gained "general acceptance" in Washington. One was that the new Department of Defense, about to be established, "must be geared legally, mentally and militarily to strike the first blow without violating the Constitution, if that could be done, or by changing the Constitution if that is necessary."

Even though I was a product of Depression-era New York apartment-house upbringing and Stanford was a country-club campus par excellence, I felt it my duty to be where the prestige of the institution and of my own status there could add to my effectiveness in opposing the first-strike policy Truman had adopted. It was supremely arrogant and, as Reston had said, anti-constitutional. But I was sure lonely. I had no car and the commute from Berkeley to Stanford via four forms of public transportation took over two hours. My wife and children lived in Berkeley because people of our views had found housing for us there before our arrival.

Yet Stanford had a professor who dared to do that "Anti-Lynching" painting. Moreover, this was a professor with a Russian name. I sought him out. I would have done so in any case because of the painting but I was also desperately looking for a kindred soul on campus.

Arnautoff's office was in the far corner of the old quad. My knock brought a heavily Russian-accented "come in," and I found myself in the presence of a singularly attractive personality. He was a little past fifty, exactly the age of my mother at the time, and exceptionally handsome in the most conventional way: tall, slender, lean-jawed, straight-nosed, with a charming smile and laugh-crinkles in the corners of his eyes. He stooped slightly when seated, which created an impression of modesty.

I don't remember the conversation exactly. He must have known of my existence, because I learned that he was a member of the Russian-American Society, immigrants usually of anti-Communist background who had come to support the Soviets during World War II as defenders of the homeland. He also belonged to the American-Russian Institute of San Francisco, the pro-Soviet body through whose head the director of the Hoover Institution had forwarded the invitation to me. That single fact illuminates the stupendous difference between political alignments in academe at the end of World War II and when the Cold War shortly took over in every respect.

I told Arnautoff that I had been deeply affected by the painting, its craftsmanship, execution, and subject-matter. I gave him a copy of my recently-published book, as a token of respect, and inscribed it accordingly. He said that if I liked his work so much—there were a few other things in the office—Tanya and I should come to his studio in the legendary Montgomery Block in San Francisco (replaced by the Trans-America pyramid in our time) and see his entire opus.

Some weekends later, we managed to leave our children with someone, took the Key Train—long gone—over the Bay Bridge to San Francisco, and went to look at his work. It floored us. We had been raised on New York's Metropolitan Museum of Art, and that city's other great collections, and our standards were high, if conventional. This man was good. He was not only good, but his work also covered a wide range of human experience. His use of color was northern-California vivid and absolutely true, the draftsmanship superb. He loved color for its own sake, but believed in depictive realism. He put his passion for color into the red of the stoplight in the anti-lynching painting, the balloon tugging at its string in the hand of an unemployed seller who was the subject of another, the pastel of an arguing housewife's workaday shirt, the gold of the dry grass in a pasture, the California sky.

We oohed and aahed our enthusiasm. As we expressed our thanks yet again and started out the door, he said, "If you like them so much, why don't you take one?" I was utterly embarrassed, and made clear that was a degree of generosity I would not accept. He said, "But you gave me a copy of your book!" I replied: "The book costs $5 and your paintings are marked $100 and $150." He countered, "But it took you much longer to write the book than it took me to do any of the paintings!" And then knocked us over completely by saying, "You don't seem to know which you like best. Take one for a while, and if it isn't what you want to live with, bring it back and try another instead." We agreed.

My study in the Hoover Tower was spacious and had a superb view of the Coast Range with the fog eternally lapping over but never making it down to spoil Stanford's subtropical climate. In those years it was believed that a telephone would spoil a scholar's meditations, so I wasn't provided with one. One day a secretary brought me a telegram. It was from Tanya in Berkeley, and read: "Going nuts from loneliness. Must move near Stanford. Come home." I caught the next Southern Pacific commute train up to the old San Francisco passenger terminus at 3rd at Townsend, took some city transportation over to what is now the Bay Bridge bus terminal and then served the Key trains, crossed to Berkeley, and caught the street car that then climbed up the hill on Euclid Avenue, ending just a short block from our house on Cragmont.

I had been coming home on weekends and living during the week in the Palo Alto home of Professor Holland Roberts, a national authority on reading who later quit Stanford to head the California Labor School. What had made weekdays unbearable for Tanya was that it was June, school vacation time, and the neighbors had all moved to the Russian River for the summer. We couldn't for the life of us understand why anyone would ever want a vacation from the Berkeley hills. We thought they were paradise then, and we think so today, half a century later, after traveling over nearly all of Europe and the 15 republics of what was the Soviet Union.

Our first entry into Berkeley is, to us, still something out of a fairy tale. New Yorkers born and bred, with four years in the mid-West and, for me, one in Moscow, we were accustomed to winters being cold, messy, and, in New York, wet and nasty. Flowers bloomed for a short time in spring and summer, and there would be a few weeks of lovely leaves in the fall. That was all. We had moved from New York to Berkeley at the end of January. With three kids, one just a few months old, we flew in a DC-4 that had one engine die over the Appalachians and limped on to Cheyenne, Wyoming, where we had to change planes in bitter cold and with a long delay. Tanya got air-sick in those years, as did at least one of the kids. The coast-to-coast trip took twenty-four hours. It was miserable.

But at the San Francisco airport we were met by a nice lady from the American Russian Institute, who told us they had rented a house for us in Berkeley. There were no freeways then, and U.S. 101 crawled through the streets of South San Francisco and the industrial bayside cityscape. Our two-year-old, Bobby, looked at all the factories and docks, and said, "I don't like it. No trees here." Tanya and I realized that his New York and ours were quite different. We had grown up in the heart of the Bronx, and I had lived on the lower East Side of Manhattan. Neither were rich in trees. But to Bobby, New York was our apartment one door off Riverside Drive in Washington Heights, marking our ascent to relative material comfort.

The car then crossed the Bay Bridge, a wonder even to us who had lived walking distance from the George Washington Bridge across the Hudson. It then snaked through the Berkeley flats to Marin Circle, stood on its rear axle, or so it seemed to us, and climbed Marin Avenue, the steepest street we had ever seen. At Cragmont it turned right.

Heaven. Flowering plum trees planted by the city were in full bloom that February first. Grass was lush, gardens rich with flowers. The wonder of San Francisco Bay, the three bridges, the city, and Mt. Tamalpais spread out beneath and before us. The car came to a stop at what looked like a cozy, one-story tile-roofed pink cottage, with its own perfect redwood tree and a bank of immense cala lilies in front of a bay-windowed dining nook. I entered the front door, and it was no longer heaven, but something a full order higher: Hollywood, in Technicolor. The living room was thirty feet long, and the windows at the west end gave an unobstructed eighty-mile view from far above San Rafael in the north to a point not too far from San Jose in the south.

I don't know much Yiddish, but a phrase leapt into my mind: "vee kimmt es mir?" —how did this ever happen to me? The house was not one story, but three. The street level was the top floor, something you can't understand unless you know Berkeley and a few other perpendicular cities on the West Coast. Although our landlord lived on the floor below, we had the run of the garden at the bottom, with a flower-and-bird pool, and a tangle of a low earth-clutching tree with branches like the coils of a dragon.

The neighbors were as lovely as the neighborhood. We didn't know a soul, so were astonished when the phone rang at breakfast-time the first morning. It was the woman next door, saying, "I understand you have a school-age daughter. I'll be happy to watch the little ones while you take her to school."

So Tanya was able to make it alone, bearably, until the neighbors suddenly vanished in June. I came home, and next day we went back down to house-hunt around Stanford. We found a place in Menlo Park, walking distance from the campus. It was a well-proportioned large cottage with two bearing walnut trees out front, a plum tree against the kitchen door, and, in back, a couple dozen splendid rose bushes and a stand of blood-red cannas that towered well over six feet high. Inside, an immense living room with huge fireplace and an identical dining room with a door to the kitchen spread out before us. At New Year's we had a buffet dinner for fifty—all the grad students for whom I acted as teaching assistant, and the local Lefts I had met. They fit into one room, leaving the other clear for dancing. The vestibule was so large that a baby grand piano stood comfortably in it. The kitchen had a giant old half-wood, half-coal-burning stove. But the bedrooms were so tiny they barely held a bed and a dresser. There wasn't a painting or even a print in the place, nor a single bookcase or bookshelf, and there were things like a flat wooden three-or-four-foot high Black jockey holding an ash tray.

I phoned Arnautoff, described the interior horror to him, and made what I thought a very bold request. Instead of lending us one painting, would he lend us three or four to light up those awful walls? From them we would ultimately select the one he had offered us as gift. He agreed. In the course of visits to his studio, and hours I spent in his study on campus, I learned his life story.

Victor had been born into the lower ranks of the Russian hereditary nobility. His native city was Mariupol on the Sea of Azov, a very large bay of the Black Sea. Totally Russian in language and character, he thought he was of Greek descent. There has always been a Greek minority on Russia's southern coast.

When World War I broke out in 1914, Victor was a student at the Academy of Arts. He immediately galloped off to fight for tsar, god, and country as a cavalry officer. He must have made an extraordinarily dashing one in the stunning uniforms then worn. He fought gallantly through the war. When the revolution occurred, he naturally fought with the monarchists against the Communists, retreating all the five thousand miles across Siberia as "White" forces were gradually driven eastward. He was wounded eight times in the two wars. When the monarchists were smashed and forced out of the country, he found himself caring for the horses of Chinese Marshal Chang Tso-lin in Manchuria. In 1925, when the Chinese Revolution began, he made his way to San Francisco to study at the California School of Fine Arts. In 1929, his student visa expired, and he moved to Mexico, where he worked with and learned mural painting from Diego Rivera. In 1931, he and family— Russian wife, three sons—were admitted to the U.S. Rivera was a communist of the Trotskyist variety.

Arnautoff had stewed for years over the great puzzle of his side's defeat in the Russian Civil War. They had the trained officers. Artillery, machine-guns, rifles, munitions, even some tanks and planes, were all provided by the United States. The Communists had nothing. The West maintained a total blockade of Soviet Russia, permitting not even medicines and food to get through, the model for U.S. policy toward Cuba for nearly forty years to this day. Fourteen foreign countries, including the U.S., placed troops on Russian soil in the effort to overthrow Lenin. Yet the Communists had won. After years of agonizing—quite literally, for it resulted in an ulcer that ultimately cost him half his stomach— Arnautoff concluded that the people had been on the side of the Communists. And for the rest of his fairly long life they stayed there.

So this aristocrat and long-time monarchist officer decided that communism must be good for the people, and became one. He was a remarkable combination of Russian patriot and Communist internationalist. He learned the revolutionary traditions of the American people. This was evident in his murals in San Francisco's George Washington High School. He immersed himself in the history of African-Americans. On our living room wall is his splendid print portraying Harriet Tubman, the Black "general" of the Underground Railway. He contributed to the illustrated calendar put out by the Communist-led Graphic Arts Workshop, initially part of the California Labor School. Arnautoff is most easily seen in San Francisco's Coit Tower murals, where he painted an entire wall of city streets and people in the 1930s.

In the 1960s a car ran up on a sidewalk where the Arnautoffs were strolling, killed his wife, and drove off. Victor suspected that it was a political murder. When his wife was killed, Victor had had it with America. He returned to his native land. There he turned to a new form: huge tile murals. They were used in the Soviet Union to relieve the monotony of sheer concrete walls of apartment houses. He found a new and very pleasant wife, and had a good life until he died in his 80s well before the USSR collapsed.

CHAPTER 10

Fire-fog

My first impression of Stanford University in 1947 was of a procession of open touring cars leaving the campus on a balmy day in February, via the mile-long palm-bordered drive from the Quad to El Camino Real. They were filled with lightly-tanned, gorgeous, leggy girls. I'm sure there were boys, too, but why would I remember them? The cars all had skis sticking up from the seats, out the windows or were tied on, wherever. Ski racks didn't exist then.

I was long since a skier from my single year in Moscow in my teens, but couldn't understand for the life of me where they were going. I knew the geography of California. The nearest snow was 150 miles away as the crow flies, very much more by the roads of that time. Four-laners did not exist beyond the closest suburbs of big cities. On two-lane roads, with the endless curves in the Sierra Nevada and slow-downs because of logging trucks or snow, I figured it had to be five hours to ski country. It was. I simply did not have the Westerner's sense of space and time. Back East, no one drove more than two hours to ski, three at most, when there was only a weekend to spare. In New York and New England, 150 miles was virtually a trip to another country, psychologically.

My first look at Yosemite had a similar impact on me. Some graduate student had a pre-war car with a rumble seat. He packed it with food and sleeping bags, and we set off. First, we crawled across the old low-level, two-lane San Mateo Bridge. Then we zig-zagged slowly up the twisting predecessor of Highway 50 to the top of Altamont Pass. To me, the very notion of green hills in February was a wonder, fruit trees in blossom even more so. Neither Tanya and I nor either set of parents had cars in New York, so the natural bloom we knew had consisted of the early golden forsythias along Riverside Drive, the marvel of wistaria arbors in Central Park in late spring, magnolias in neighborhood parks in the Bronx, and wildflowers in Van Cortlandt Park. People who lived in the rare private homes not built right up to the sidewalks often had tulips. A few had roses. If one took the elevated subway lines to Brooklyn, where handkerchief-sized front gardens were common, one could see azaleas next to stoops. And of course there was the Bronx

Botanical Garden. But that was nothing like California.

The day we drove to Yosemite was clear, and at the top of the pass I was stunned by the snowy crests of the Sierra a hundred miles east across the valley. Down we drove to cross it, stopping for every red light. There were many, and no bypasses. The junction with Highway 99 was marked by the delicate pinkish white of a stupendous almond orchard. Having lived in Ohio, I understood farm fields of forty acres. But to see one a square mile in size, 640 acres, overwhelmed me.

Cars of the 1940s did not have the horsepower of today's, never mind the monsters of the 1960s. We puffed painfully up the fifteen-hundred-ft. rise to Big Oak Flat via the hairpin curves that are one of the few reminders of what mountain driving was like in those years. Car after car was steaming at the roadside with its hood up. Then came an hour or so of roller-coaster driving through arrow-straight Ponderosa pines taller than anything I had ever seen. Finally, at a very slow curve, a house-wide wall of red that went up, up and up. *Sequoia gigantea.* I giggled in disbelief. Its lowest branches were higher off the ground than the crowns of what I had thought of as giant oaks back East. A bit farther on, I took a curious and apprehensive gla nce at the turn-off to old Tioga Pass Road. It had so formidable a reputation that I still regret never having taken more than a mile or two of it before it was rebuilt into the very civilized drive it is today.

Next came Inspiration Point and the first view of Yosemite Valley. Why is it that I can remember the thrill of that first giant redwood, but not the emotional impact of that perfect Shangri-La panorama? Half Dome rising four thousand feet sheer from the valley, with Bridal Veil Falls in ideal photographic composition in the foreground? Yet after an absence of any time from home, my first glance at San Francisco Bay from the crest of the East Bay hills is as thrilling as Caruso singing "Pagliacci." Perhaps it's just that it is home.

That first trip to Yosemite must have been in summertime, because we slept on the ground up at Glacier Point. I opened my eyes at dawn to see the sun's rays precisely split by Half Dome. The first bears I'd ever encountered outside a zoo were rummaging through nearby garbage cans. They were healthy, large, beautiful, and frightening.

If visitors today can no longer try Old Tioga Road, neither can they see the firefall, that hokey but stunning immense pile of flaming embers built by the park rangers at sunset and pushed over the edge of Glacier Point to the valley floor well over half a mile below. And what was the background music they used to accompany that with: "Land of the Sky-Blue Waters?"

After Tanya and the children moved down from Berkeley to join me in Menlo Park, we would take very long Sunday drives in a pre-war

Chevy sedan loaned us by an elderly gentleman. Until very recently, driving, as far and fast as possible, on the hairiest roads I could find, was my chief way of relieving the mental tension that my work and public activities, and the controversial nature of my views, has brought me. To make it up Redwood Highway as far as Standish State Park above the junction of highways 1 and 101 on the Eel River, spend a couple of hours frolicking, and drive back the same day, was my personal insane way of staying sane. My strongest memory is of the logging trucks, each loaded with a single ten-foot-diameter segment of a redwood trunk. Others carried the higher, narrower portions and millable branches of those same trees. There was no need to bother with "small" stuff then.

On another occasion, the family and I made our first-ever trip to the top of Mt. Tamalpais, which dominates San Francisco Bay from the north. It offers a view more spectacularly varied than anything my extensive travels have ever offered. The Pacific is nearly three thousand feet seemingly straight down to the west. What appears from the peak to be unbroken forested wilderness extends endlessly northward. The bay and the East Bay cities are seen to the east. On a clear day, it seems as though one can touch them. In late afternoon, the sun behind one sets thousands of windows aflame. At night their lights glimmer like a horizontal Christmas tree. San Francisco, fifteen miles south, rises white or sunset-colored out of the water as did the mythical city of Kitezh in Russian folklore.

Getting up the mountain was simply delightful curvy driving, except where a wash-out had narrowed the road to one lane and a full-size tour bus came down at me after I entered that section. On the trip down I discovered that the borrowed Chevy would not stay in second gear. High gear was impossible: I was afraid of burning out the brakes. Low gear would have lined up a hundred honking Sunday drivers behind me. So I negotiated the curves with my left hand, my right firmly on the shift stick to hold the car in second. Because my attention was so tightly focused on each curve before me, I wrongly turned right toward Stinson Beach on the Pacific. A pea-soup fog rolled in. It was my first encounter with California fog, much denser than one encounters on the East Coast. I had to inch back to San Francisco at night on Highway 1, a stretch that twists, rises and falls more sharply than even the road from Sorrento to Amalfi. Safely back in town, we splurged—by our standards—in a Chinatown restaurant.

The Bay Area's fog can also be, quite literally, its crowning glory. On Skyline Drive between Palo Alto and San Francisco, there is a point where a valley falls from the very roadside to the Pacific. We got to that spot one evening when a sea of fog drifted around our car. The sun burnished it to gold and copper. Red wisps streamed within our reach. We stopped to drink it in, and the children tried to catch it. One of them cried, "fire-fog," and that's what it has been to us ever since.

On one trip with the children, without Tanya, having crossed Skyline, we started down to the ocean. Suddenly it was foggy and clammy. There was a very sharp left turn. I braked to slow down. The left front brake grabbed. The car veered into the left hand lane, and I hit an oncoming passenger car head on. Seat belts had not yet been invented. I was momentarily knocked out. As I came to, seven-year-old Phyllis was screaming, "Daddy, don't die! Who'll take me home?"

Driving was not the only pleasure the Peninsula offered. Menlo Park had once been orchards, and every fruit I knew of other than those of the full tropics could be seen in people's yards or fell from trees along the streets. Walking was a delight. A stream meanders to mark the boundary between the Stanford campus and Menlo Park.

Palo Alto had a surprising history of friendly interest in the Soviet Union, so that a movie house on El Camino played Russian films quite often. One Palo Altan, Ruth Kennell, had worked in Siberia in the 1920s with my father in the same "American Industrial Colony." Later Ruth served as tour guide around the USSR for author Theodore Dreiser, and wrote a book on Dreiser in Russia. The heroine of one of his short novels, *Ernita*, was modeled on her—the first literary treatment of a female American Communist. Ruth was a listener to my KPFA radio broadcasts from the time they began in 1958 until her death. She, Dad and I, in my capacity as Soviet expert, all appear in a documentary made by Siberians in 1996 about that would-be Utopia of seventy years earlier.

Anna Louise Strong, the great American journalist, who I knew from Moscow in 1931-2, maintained a home in Palo Alto. After an evening at our home in Menlo Park, she took her leave, went out to her car, returned in a couple of minutes, threw herself on a couch, and quite literally kicked her legs in the air and went into a tantrum like a baby. This was a person in her late 50s. I didn't know whether she was suffering a seizure of some kind or perhaps something monstrous had happened to her in our yard. I soothed her, she calmed down, and I asked what the trouble was. She had left her car lights on all evening, the battery had run down, and it wouldn't start. We took care of that minor problem, and she went on her way.

Anna Louise deserves her burial place in Tienanmen Square. When she died in the 1970s, I interrupted my regular broadcasting to do a special on her. But that incident in my home provided a confirmation of another story of her extraordinarily self-centered personal behavior told me, also in Palo Alto in 1947, by Albert Rhys Williams, a man of very generous spirit.

Anna Louise who, like Rhys, was the child of a minister, had first come to Soviet Russia with a Quaker relief mission in 1921. She worked in the midst of famine and risked contracting typhus. She lived then and later under conditions of unbelievable discomfort. Yet, said Rhys, she would not share with the fellow-members of her mission the chocolate bars she had brought with her from the West. We are complex, we humans.

Like Strong's, Williams' was a name tremendously honored for half a century in the USSR, yet simply unknown to Americans today. Warren Beatty's film "Reds" reminded us of the existence of John Reed, although his classic eyewitness account of the Russian Revolution, *Ten Days That Shook the World*, was known to students who took courses on that country. That book, simply a work of genius, written by the greatest American reporter of his day, overshadowed Williams' own superb eyewitness book, *Through the Russian Revolution*. Williams, a Unitarian minister like his father, actually organized an international brigade of foreigners in Russia to defend the revolution by force of arms. He was an extraordinary speaker, and his lectures on the revolution in 1918, in a day when radio broadcasting to the public did not yet exist, made him a national figure. On February 17, 1919, even before his book appeared, the *New York Times* ran an editorial about him that was a remarkable if unintended compliment: "We still think that the greatest creation of Bolshevism is not Trotsky's army, but Albert Rhys Williams, and the singular audiences that applaud him." His impact as a speaker, though not his style, was similar to that of Martin Luther King.

The Soviet Union remained grateful. There was a nationwide celebration of his 75th birthday in 1959. In 1983, on the 100th anniversary of his birth, the entire Soviet press ran tributes to him. In the 1930s he wrote a very successful factual book, *The Soviets,* and tried to repeat that during World War II with one called *The Russians*. Like most fine eyewitness reporters (Reed was an exception), Williams was not much of a researcher, so he came to me for factual data for that book. That Williams, with his ten years' experience in Soviet Russia, much of it among the peasantry, would trust my knowledge, was, like the earlier remark by Masha Scott, one of the things that sustained me through the very ugly early Cold War years.

Rhys—as everyone called Williams—came to Stanford's Hoover Institution on a short-term grant in 1947, when I too was there. He was supposed to be using its remarkable archives of the revolution for work on an autobiography. We would take long walks around the campus, chiefly talking about the problems, faults, and shortcomings of the Soviet Union, in a manner neither of us would share with those we thought would use that information as ammunition in the Cold War.

What we held private were our interpretations, not the unpleasant facts themselves. The very month of my arrival at Stanford, a review by Rhys of my just-published *A Guide to the Soviet Union* had appeared. In it he wrote: "Unfortunately, as Stalin once told a group of writers, 'the truth cannot be all sweet like candy or polished and shiny like a Tula samovar.' Alongside the glowing facts, Mandel realistically sets down many cold and dismal ones."

That year at Stanford was by no means an idyll of strolling conversations, trips to the Sierra, the Eel River, or over to the coast. Nineteen forty-seven was the bitterest year of the struggle to determine whether President Roosevelt's plan to cooperate with Russia and the Western allies in building a peaceful world would win out. Unfortunately, when Roosevelt died and Truman came to power, he, with the help of Winston Churchill, put us on the nuclear-bomb-building track that brought us to a minute before midnight in the Cuba Missile Crisis fifteen years later.

Roosevelt's longest-term cabinet member and strongest supporter of his plan for continued collaboration with the USSR was Henry Wallace. He was dropped for renomination to the vice-presidency because of the pressure of party conservatives, pre-civil-rights southerners primarily. But FDR made him Secretary of Commerce in his fourth term, and Truman had to keep him on at first to maintain the illusion of continuing Roosevelt's policies. Wallace felt there was no longer a place for him under Truman's get-tough-with-Russia policies, and resigned in 1946 to be free to fight them.

There is a myth that opposition to the Cold War was centered on those who shared— to any degree—the ideology of the Soviet Union. But it was Wallace, not an ideologue of any kind, who was the focus of that opposition. That was why the initiation of the Cold War had to be accompanied by a witch-hunt that pictured its opponents as outright traitors and silenced them. Nothing illustrated this more clearly than when Wallace came to speak at the University of California at Berkeley in 1947. I drove up from Stanford with a carload of graduate students who I sometimes instructed since I occasionally substituted for the head of the Hoover Institution, Prof. Harold H. Fisher, when he was away.

The University of California *simply denied* the immediate *past vice-president* of the United States the right to speak on campus! The university did not accuse Wallace of being a Communist or a traitor. He was simply too controversial because he opposed Truman's policy. The then mayor of Berkeley, a Reverend Cross, pastor of the Northbrae Community Church in its staid Thousand Oaks neighborhood, invited the former vice-president, secretary of agriculture, and secretary of commerce to speak from little more than a soap-box on the Oxford Street sidewalk that marked the edge of campus, at the head of University Avenue.

I walked around the entire campus to see what kind of crowd Wallace's presence would draw. Every student, his wife and baby (there were not many female students, and these were the returned veterans of World War II under the G.I. Bill of Rights), and, as far as I could tell, every office worker and professor was down there listening to Wallace, to the number of twenty thousand. Among them were Berkeleyans who remained active in peace movements till the end of the Cold War.

I used my status as Hoover Institution Fellow, author of then highly-regarded books, and former United Press Expert on Russia, to oppose Truman's policy. During my first month at Stanford, *Life* magazine, which shared with the *Saturday Evening Post* the status of America's weekly Bible in those pre-television years, carried a huge spread lauding the Greek Communists. They had waged such successful guerrilla operations against the Nazis that only four British Tommies were killed when Churchill's forces landed to take over from the Germans at the close of the war. The following week the president proclaimed the Truman Doctrine, which said its purpose was to protect Greece and Turkey from communism. *Life* did a flip-flop within a week to follow the lead of the president. For how many decades did we read of the "controlled Soviet press?" It is a sad commentary on the willingness of the American people to believe hogwash that cost us 300 *trillion* dollars in unnecessary expenditures in the forty following years before the Soviet Union collapsed.

I wrote a letter to the *Stanford Daily* denouncing Truman's policy. It was not the practice in those days for people with faculty status to deign to write in student papers. Here are its highlights:

"The reasons offered for the Truman Doctrine are three: Soviet expansion; the threat of Communism; the defense of democracy. The extension of Soviet frontiers ended 20 months ago, on V-J Day. Nowhere in the world are Russian forces beyond the lines they held then. Everywhere along their perimeter they have been withdrawn, although no power on earth could have forced them to do so against their will, short of full-fledged war by the U.S.

"Here is the record: complete withdrawal from Norway, Danish Bornholm Island, Czechoslovakia [to which they returned decades later, under totally different circumstances], Yugoslavia and Iran. Withdrawal from Finland and Manchuria except for one naval base city in each case—the only bases Russia holds beyond her frontiers in the entire world....The overall picture is that the USSR, second strongest power in the world, has less territory than decrepit Tsarist Russia on the eve of World War I. Its most distant military outposts are far closer to home than our own.

"What of the threat of Communism? Turkey is one of the very few countries in the world that have no Communist party, legal or ille-gal....Where, then, is the Communism which Mr. Truman allegedly fears?"

The letter was published April 9, 1947. There was no overall change in the Soviet military position from then until Gorbachev permitted the tearing down of the Berlin Wall in 1989. On the one hand, Soviet troops re-entered Czechoslovakia in 1968 and invaded Afghanistan a dozen years later. On the other hand, they withdrew totally from Korea and Austria, completed withdrawal from Bulgaria and Rumania, and gave up the naval bases in Finland and China. All this occurred under Stalin and his immediate successor, Khrushchev.

The mass media generally reported those Soviet withdrawals only on the day they occurred, usually as a small item on an inside page, and would then blandly go on writing about Soviet expansion, often in the very same day's paper. Consequently, the information in my letter was regarded as sufficiently sensational that the *Stanford Daily* republished it the next day as a news report of a talk I had given the previous evening to the local chapter of the American Veterans Committee. So did the *Palo Alto Times*. Not surprisingly there was a letter in the *Daily* attacking me. At a faculty reception where I was not present, someone asked the Hoover Institution director, Prof. H. H. Fisher, "What is Mandel doing here?" William Steele, who later became a professor at San Jose State, told me the next morning that Prof. Fisher snapped back: "He knows more about the Soviet Union than anyone in the United States." Academic study of the USSR then hardly existed outside this country, so he was saying I was one of the leading world authorities. In the subsequent half century, several thousand Ph.D.s were trained in this field to meet the needs of the Cold War. Each of them knew the minuscule sub-set of data on which they had done their theses better than I did. But it was not until the mid-60s that I gave up trying to know everything and focused my attention primarily on issues pertaining to women and ethnic groups. By then I had turned my attention primarily to using radio to further world peace and the domestic social agenda advanced by the youth and minorities rebellions of the 1960s.

Coming events cast their shadow before. When I had given a lecture three weeks earlier in the Palo Alto Children's Theater, people told me that the local police were quite openly taking down the license numbers of the cars parked outside. My subject was: "What is the Union of Soviet Socialist Republics?" Subversive, I suppose.

I recall lunching in the faculty dining room one day. A young profes-sor, his wife and child were eating at the adjacent table. The child was apparently not observing proper etiquette, for the professor suddenly hissed, "Eat properly! Do you want people to think you are a Russian?"

When I was the sole speaker at an event—as before the military medical personnel at Letterman Army Hospital in San Francisco's Presidio ("all duty officers, including nurses, *will* attend this meeting...By order of Col. Winn"), or the International Relations Section of the Commonwealth Club— the atmosphere was no different than in the glory days of the alliance with the Soviet Union. But when I attended academic conferences or spoke at events where I was not alone on the platform, I became aware of a sharp change in outlook on the part of others.

This occurred first at the annual meeting of the Western Historical Association. During World War II we had been told that U.S. war aims in the Pacific were purely defensive: to throw Japan back from conquered territories and prevent it from ever repeating that aggression. We would retain Hawaii—not then a state—and previous bases on islands in the western Pacific and the Philippines, simply as military outposts. Now suddenly academic papers argued for permanent U.S. presence in Japan and Korea and on mainland China, then controlled by nationalist Chiang Kai-shek, in the spirit of the imperialist Manifest Destiny argument propounded after the Spanish-American War. Half a century later we are still in Japan and Korea. When Mao Tse-tung threw Chiang out of China, the U.S. had no choice but to leave as well. There was no public support for a war against China.

Even more amazing was the tone of a round-table conference on the Middle East at San Francisco State, at which I was one of the four presenters.The speaker given pride of place in the *San Francisco Chronicle* report was an officer of the Arabian-American Oil Company, Aramco. Essentially he said that part of the world, too, should be our oyster. The *Chronicle* was so carried away by its desire to justify this idea that if flatly miquoted me:

"William Mandel, author of *A Guide to the Soviet Union* and a fellow of Slavic studies at Stanford University, said Russia eyes Middle Eastern oil because of her inability to produce enough domestic oil for her Five-Year Plan."

But I had read from a typescript, which reads:

"The competent officers of the Iranian government did initial an oil concession agreement with the USSR which covers an area so closely paralleling the Soviet frontier as to make one feel that Moscow's interest was more in keeping others' investments from its borders than in seeking oil." The Soviet Union did not drill for oil. "Yet, although the Iranian Mejlis has not yet ratified that agreement, Soviet troops have been entirely withdrawn." My speech continued, "Alone among the Big Four [U.S., U.S.S.R., Britain, France], the U.S.S.R. *lives* in the Middle East....It is the only one with home territory...in the Near East, and also the only one with neither army nor navy beyond its frontiers in that area."

A lecture management firm toured me around the state. I learned things about California, good and bad, that were not available in books, perhaps to this day. In Salinas, where I was sponsored by the American Association of University Women, the local high school principal drove me about to see the sights. He talked, and it emerged that the lettuce country had a distinct hierarchy of nationalities: whites on top, of course, then Blacks, followed by Filipinos, Chinese, and Mexicans last. Blacks were the top of the bottom clearly because they were not a serious factor in farm labor and not foreigners.

In another respect that same school principal represented something very positive in the West. He told me about Lake Tahoe, which I had not yet seen, and said matter-of-factly that he was able to spend the summers there because he worked as caretaker of the vacation estate of a wealthy grower. In the East, no man in his position would dream of taking such a job. If he did so to meet some catastrophic family need for additional money, he would never admit it. In the West, work with one's hands was still respected. On Fisherman's Wharf in San Francisco, I would see longshoremen in their distinctive white caps eating in the same places as tourists. Waitresses treated them with equal respect and a great deal more affection. Never in New York. The memory of the San Francisco General Strike just thirteen years earlier was very much alive. Labor had dignity.

Tanya and I fell madly in love with San Francisco. My first visit there, for that lecture the previous year, had almost been my last. I would spend a couple of hours exploring on foot any city I came to lecture in. I have always timed things very closely. Sometimes that, plus the walking habit, led to close shaves in my schedule. I remember walking in Boston from Roxbury to catch a plane to a very major date in Montreal. I arrived when the propellers on the DC-3 were already turning—they didn't warm up then for as long as larger later engines required—and the old-fashioned, manually-hauled passenger staircase had been wheeled away. They brought it back for me. Simply being an airline passenger made you a V.I.P. in 1944.

On that first brief stay in San Francisco I was house guest in the home of a wealthy orthodontist out in Sea Cliff, just inland from the Legion of Honor Museum at Land's End. The luxury of that neighborhood was like nothing I had ever seen except for the string of mansions that stood along lower Riverside Drive and on Fifth Avenue below the Metropolitan Museum of Art when I was a child. Luxury never impressed me, but beauty has and does. The white mini-palaces of Sea Cliff face the mile-wide waters of the Golden Gate far below, with the hills of Marin County rising to Mt. Tamalpais on the far side, the incomparable bridge framing Angel Island and the Berkeley hills as one looks inland across the sweeping bay.

No view anywhere in the world has ever thrilled me so, before or since. Sea Cliff can also be fog-soaked like nowhere else in my experience. The morning of my lecture I woke to find my pajamas sticking to my body, the sheets clammy, the tile walls of the bathroom dripping with condensation. It was mid-morning by the time I could decently halt a post-breakfast conversation with my hosts. The sun broke through the fog just as they had said it would. I dressed for my afternoon lecture— suit, tie, shined shoes—and got instructions for walking downtown. However, I began by heading in the opposite direction, to a path they had told me about, clinging to the cliffs near the golf course in Lincoln Park.

It had simply been described to me as a path in a park. In my Easterner's innocence, that meant something at least a couple of feet wide and probably asphalted. That it might be unsafe never entered my head. It proved to be of loose sand, narrow and narrowing, with sudden drops and climbs that required clambering. Here and there it actually passed through tunnels in which one had to hunch and stoop. I learned later that they had been dug to connect the coast-defense artillery batteries of World War II. Breakers pounded the shore far below. When I could actually see the end of the path turning safely back to the golf course, it grew so narrow that I had to lean inward and hang onto the sandy slope above me with my fingers. It looked deadly, and I learned later that it was. People slip from it to their deaths every year, although it is officially closed. My stomach still tightens as I think back and write these words. That one was close. But my hosts, fine and gentle people, were Westerners, and simply took it for granted that one was on one's own anywhere in nature.

My wife first saw the view of the Gate and the bridge the following year when I stayed home with the littlest ones and she took seven-year-old Phyllis across the Bay Bridge, and then by street car to the ocean. Tanya is one of the most psychologically stable people I know. Certainly then, as a young mother not quite thirty, nothing suggesting that she ever thought of her own death ever came from her lips. But as she stood at the base of the statue of El Cid outside the Legion of Honor Museum and gazed at the voluptuous green hills of Marin that day in early spring, the Pacific whipped in the wind, and the Golden Gate Bridge flaming red in the sunlight, she later told me she thought: "Here's where I'd like to be buried." The early Chinese in San Francisco in the previous century had had that same idea, collectively. Some of their gravestones may still be seen between the Monterey cypresses they must have planted around them on the golf course 100 yards away.

We would walk the city whenever we could find a baby sitter. To wander Nob Hill and Russian Hill before there was any tall structure in San Francisco other than the Russ Building on Montgomery Street offered a variety of views no kaleidoscope could match. Steps next to small townhouses or even low apartment buildings lead to back gardens. Walking just a few feet in along them, one found a young redwood, a palm, or both, as well as glorious roses and bougainvillea. The view of the bay was never quite the same from one such cul-de-sac to the next a block beyond. The gray-blue of the fog-tinted sky and redwood house sidings, painted white, chiseled by the rays of the sun, fixed themselves in memory.

San Francisco had more than physical beauty. It allowed me to live simultaneously in two worlds: academia, with its polite discussions and invitations to participate in symposia thanks to my Hoover Institution status; and the world of workingclass radicalism in which I had grown up and never had any desire to leave. At the California Labor School's dances I encountered for the first time a Mexican dance style in which one rocks way over on the outside of one's feet. The Labor School had a theater group from which Actor's Workshop, granddaddy of ACT, its most prestigious repertory company, evolved . We saw there the finest *King Lear* I have ever witnessed. The tragic old king was played by a young man—to do that successfully is a miracle all its own—who subsequently disappeared into the obscurity of high-school drama teaching. The school had a superb chorus. I still have one of its records: songs of the Spanish Civil War and of the Black movement long before Martin Luther King. There were art workshops and a writers' workshop, which at one point published a magazine contributed to by Alvah Bessie and others. Its visiting lecturers included Dr. W.E.B. DuBois, Paul Robeson, screenwriter John Howard Lawson, and African-American actress Beulah Richardson, before she won recognition outside the Left. I was invited to speak at a cultural conference it organized, where I was surprised to find myself listed as "historian." I dealt with the relationship of the writer of non-fiction to culture and its problems.

The California Labor School had been recognized by the federal government as one that returning veterans could attend and receive educational benefits under the GI Bill. In 1945 it had received a commendation from the U.S. Secretary of State for its help with the founding of the United Nations in San Francisco because it hosted the many delegates with labor backgrounds, people the State Department didn't know how to talk to. A couple of years later the Attorney-General proclaimed it subversive, though it had made no change in its politics. But the U.S. government had changed its.

This persecution, plus the sudden reversal of policy toward the Soviet

Union by the new president, supported by sensational stories in the media and the shifts in academe, caused bewilderment and a sense of insecurity on the Left. This expressed itself in a surprising incident. Late in May 1947, the American Russian Institute of San Francisco organized a folk dance festival. Unlike the organization of the same name in New York, for which I had worked, this was not a research institution but primarily a friendship society. Those who attended its events were largely workingpeople with Leftist convictions, including many longshoremen. The city was then primarily a port and manufacturing center, not the financial and tourist hub it later became.

Several hundred people were present at this event, most of whom were in their 30s. Whoever was calling the dances noticed that I was present, announced me, and I was given an ovation. These people regarded my book of the previous year, *A Guide to the Soviet Union,* to be a sheet-anchor of factual and moral support for what they believed to be true.

After the folk festival incident, I wrote my parents:

"Not only was this thing heartwarming...but it had a specific meaning to me. I often wonder if my work, taking me around the country and giving me little chance to sink roots, has any lasting effect. I am neither a [Henry] Wallace, symbol of a movement, nor a [Paul] Robeson, symbol of a people, possessed of great artistic talent and an awe-inspring physique, nor a [Leftist New York Congressmember] Marcantonio, with a hard-won record of delivering the goods to my constituents. I am merely an intellectual, undoubtedly well-informed in my field, and capable of presenting data with clear logic...and a certain emotional impact that stems from profound conviction. Therefore, to find that I command a certain personal following and loyalty is not only encouraging to me, but is proof that people appreciate an appeal to their intelligence, as well as to their emotions and material needs....My only other such experience was a class literally bursting into tears...after I had had them for a whole week."

That reference was to an event near Toronto in 1943, during the war. The Workers' Education Association Labor College, not a Communist institution and officially sponsored by organized labor, had decided to build its annual summer camp session that year around the theme of education about the Soviet Union. There was still a lot of British formality in Canada's culture then, and for the young worker-students to find their professor to be someone who was not only in their own age range, but who knew every labor and pop song, was a tireless and improvising social dancer, and played a fair game of softball, apparently had had an emotional impact. So, doubtless, was the fact that I placed no limit of time or place upon answering their questions. My then very recent experiences as a workingman and participant in labor struggles must have given my talks a relevance to them that might not have come from someone with an academic approach.

I was not to enjoy the West Coast long. Perhaps I should do without birthdays. Immediately before my 16th I was thrown out of college. On June 2, 1947, two days before my 30th, I was attacked by *Newsweek*, paving the way for my being blacklisted from the careers I had built in journalism, authorship, lecturing, and academe.

That *Newsweek* piece was a seven-page spread titled, "What Communists Are Up To." The people smeared included Charlie Chaplin, Orson Welles, the president's son Elliott Roosevelt, Senator Claude Pepper of Florida, and philanthropist civil libertarian Corliss Lamont, whose father had headed the banking house of J.P. Morgan & Co. None of them had ever been Communists. There were indeterminate leftists like Dorothy Parker, people of permanent Communist sympathies such as Paul Robeson, and others who were strong sympathizers at that time, like Langston Hughes. And there were those who were members for shorter or longer periods, including best-selling novelist Howard Fast, mystery writer Dashiell Hammett, playwright Lillian Hellman, and myself. In all, the article listed eighty women and men comprising a hall of fame of talent, decency, humanism, and courage. I have never been paid a higher honor than my inclusion in that group. And I was the youngest on the list.

The purpose of this mass fingering of people hated by J. Edgar Hoover, Director of the Federal Bureau of Investigation, was to remove from contact with the American people figures enjoying public standing who opposed the Cold War just inaugurated by President Truman, with the assistance of Winston Churchill. The witch-hunt worked. Chaplin retreated to exile in Switzerland. Senator Pepper was defeated for re-election, only to return as a member of the House of Representatives— years later, re-elected as long as he lived, and revered for his defense of the Social Security system. Hammett and Fast served prison terms for refusing to be informers. Robeson, as popular as Pavarotti forty years later, had his passport withdrawn by State Department fiat, thus preventing him from making a living abroad, and lost his concert and recording contracts at home.

The objection to me was very simple. I was "author of the pro-Soviet *Guide to the Soviet Union.*" Among dozens of books by the score of writers named, mine was one of only three listed by title. A second was by the son of the president just two years dead, describing his father's view of the world. It was condemned thus by *Newsweek*: "Elliott Roosevelt's *As He Saw It*, which is the way the Communists happen to see it now." I have never seen a clearer admission that those attacked by Truman and, later, McCarthy, stood for the policies of the only president the American people elected four times to that office.

The novelists and actors in its list were important to the witch-hunters for the prestige they brought to their causes. My importance was that I dealt with the very ideas they were trying to suppress: that the Soviet Union was a country it was possible and desirable to live with.

The Hoover Institution did not renew my fellowship. The official grounds were that its funds for the coming year were already committed. In fact, I had not been treated as someone who was expected to be gone when the academic year was up, and it actually became a practice at the Hoover to renew fellowships until they became, in effect, lifetime appointments. Moreover, although I no longer had any official status, I was told that I could retain my spacious private office-with-view in the Hoover Tower and go on using the research facilities! I did so for several months and left only because we couldn't live on air. Did Dr. Fisher privately hope that I could find some way to survive while he would be free of the criticism that would arise from keeping me officially employed? Or was this an exquisitely delicate charade to yield to the political winds while retaining the appearance of academic independence? Both? I did have the satisfaction of knowing that the person appointed to fill my slot was the very distinguished Edward Hallett Carr, who had joined the British Foreign Office the year before I was born, and who had just resigned from six years as assistant editor of the *Times* of London. He had written a marvelous small book with a huge title, *The Soviet Impact on the Western World*, which corresponded very closely to my own point of view. At this point in time, people with Carr's credentials were still unassailable in academe. His subsequent eight-volume *History of Soviet Russia* was chiefly ignored by official Sovietology because he regarded the revolution as quite within the natural order of things.

And so, without reappointment, we packed up the family and returned to New York for the next ten years.

CHAPTER 11

Cold War:
Which Side Are You On?

I wrote my parents to thank them for a gift on my 30th birthday, in June 1947: "At the present moment there is no news as to how I will make a living after October 31st, and in this case no news is bad news," I wrote them. "My lecture management finds local booking agents unwilling even to have the subject of Russia discussed from their platforms, so we are trying a new title: 'Wallace vs. Truman—What Are the Facts?' The Hoover Library says its fellowship money is all committed for next year. Maybe."

At that time, Harold Berman was at the beginning of a career that made him, as a lifetime Harvard professor, one of the country's two top experts on Soviet law. He was briefly also a Hoover fellow and came to me for some background information on the USSR. I provided it and then asked, "Why did you come to me?"

"Because you are the master in this field," he replied.

However, the chances of my being forced out of it were only too good. I wrote everyone I knew regarding appointment possibilities. One such was Prof. Frederick L. Schuman of Williams College. He was among the handful of top political scientists in the country. Schuman was one of the few academics of that day who enjoyed the same level of name recognition among the general public as, say, John Kenneth Galbraith in the 1980s. Schuman wrote me: "I have admired your work from afar for a long time....Investigate the present situation at the University of Chicago. To the best of my knowledge the late Sam Harper's chair has never been filled, although I believe it was once offered to John Hazard. It ought to be filled and I can think of no one better qualified to fill it than yourself."

Harper had founded Russia studies in the United States, in 1902, long before the Revolution, and led the field till his death in 1942. Hazard, at Columbia until his death in the mid-1990s, was its counterpart in the field of Soviet law to Berman at Harvard. So I could hardly have been ranked more highly.

A lot of good it did me. Everything depended on where one stood on the Cold War, and the last two jobs I was subsequently allowed to hold in my field, until twenty years later, came from top people who shared my general view of the Soviet Union. Neither was a Marxist, as I learned first hand when working with them. One was Vilhjalmur Stefansson, a world-famous Arctic explorer. He visited Stanford during my appointment there, and offered me a job writing on the Soviet North for his *Encyclopedia Arctica*, a project funded by the U.S. Office of Naval Research. I didn't take him up on it for over a year, for a reason best stated in a letter I wrote in December 1947, to Albert Rhys Williams:

"After seven years in this field, during which I have earned a fair professional-level livelihood in full accord with my political conscience, I now find a blank wall before me. There are no lectures in the East—they won't touch the subject. There are no jobs in the academic field— they won't touch *me*. There are no jobs with forward-looking organizations— they're broke. The only good thing that has come out of the extensive correspondence I have engaged in is the realization of exactly how high a standing I have attained in the field, and therefore how essential it is that I remain in it."

I felt it a duty to American political liberty—a foreshadowing of my testimony to witch-hunt committees in the '50s ande '60s—to continue functioning as myself, not as anonymous collaborator or writer simply for a reference work that would be consulted by only a few hundred specialists on the Arctic. I desperately sought to keep my head above water, and feed Tanya and the kids, by lectures. It is a measure of how completely Americans were kept in the grip of a fixed psychotic idea for nearly forty-five years that the following words in my set speech were regarded as worthy of direct quotation in the press in 1947: "I can say we will not have war with Russia this month, this year, or five years from now."

That was in Salinas, but once I got south of the Tehachapis the atmosphere changed. The House Un-American Activities Committee began its witch-hunt of Hollywood personalities that September. That month I gave a lecture in Los Angeles' First Congregational Church whose pastor, a Rev. Fifield, was of the same type as the Christian Right of the 1990s. He had apparently thought that my Hoover Institution affiliation defined my views. The reception I faced is best indicated by a letter to my management from someone who attended and wanted a copy of my talk: "It takes a great deal of courage and moral integrity to give the sort of speech which Mr. Mandel did....Tell Mr. Mandel for me that the world needs a few more clear-thinking straight-shooters like himself to save it from possible disaster."

In Eureka up north and San Diego on the Mexican border I received the same kind of documented Red-baiting that finished me as a lecturer in the East a year earlier. The San Diego case is the more interesting because it came from members of a sponsoring group one would have thought would be above that: the local American Association of University Women (AAUW). Admiral William Standley, who, after retirement, had been a Roosevelt-appointed ambassador to the USSR, came to hear me and took part in the discussion . He agreed with me that there had been enormous economic and social advances in the Soviet Union but differed on civil liberties, about which he was right. I had not been there since before Stalin's purges. Because our media lied to denigrate all progress in the USSR, I believed it was lying about repression. It was not.

The AAUW corresponding secretary wrote my management, citing six instances in 1946 and 1947 in which I had been referred to in the Communist *People's World*: two announcements of talks by me at the California Labor School, one at the Russian-American Society, etc. They also quoted just about the only two unfavorable sentences in the reviews of my second book in the *New York Times* and the *Herald-Tribune* Sunday book sections. But the two elderly gentlewomen in Piedmont who managed me wrote back acerbically:

"After re-reading the statements you copied [! - W.M.], we are inclined to believe they were taken from the Tenney Report [the California legislature's Un-American Activities Committee]. The Tenney Report is much on the order of the good (?) old *Red Network*, published several years ago by Elizabeth Dilling. Like the Tenney report it, figuratively speaking, listed as subversive almost everyone whose name even contained the letter 'R'."

The customer was not always right!

The Eureka situation is best described by excerpts from a letter of mine to the Humboldt *Times*:

"My lecture agency has been kind enough to send on to me a copy of the material appearing in your newspaper relative to my talk before the Travel Club....It is as perfect an example as one can hope to find of the freedom of the American press. My speech was reported in three inches of space under a one-column headline, but a hostile answer...got a full column on each of two successive days, under a heavy-type two-column head. What this amounts to, since the vast majority of your readers were not at my lecture, which you know perfectly well, is that my appearance served you as a pretext for some home-grown mud-slinging against Russia, in addition to that which the syndicated *calumnists*...provide every day."

At Stanford my public standing was unassailable so long as I remained there. In February 1948, Stanford's Institute of International

Relations held a three-day conference titled, "The UN and You." The speakers, other than myself, included U.S. Senator-to-be Alan Cranston, then a junior faculty member; a student named Eugene Burdick, later to be a UC Berkeley professor and co-author of *The Ugly American,* a worldwide best-seller, who was to be my opponent in a memorable debate in Berkeley a decade later; Eugene Staley, subsequently infamous for his development of the "strategic villages" concentration camps for the rural population of Vietnam; a future president of Mills College; and a future judge in Berkeley. England may have its old-school-tie network, but our elite universities are not much different as breeding grounds for the rulers, the officials, and the opinion-and-policy-makers of the nation.

A couple of sentences from my prepared remarks make clear that the world marked time for the four decades thereafter during which preparation for another world war outweighed all other considerations. "At the organizational session of the [UN] Assembly in London, January, 1946, Soviet Belorussia advocated UN action to secure the apprehension of Nazi war criminals who had found asylum in various parts of the world." The United States finally expelled a few of those people thirty-eight years later. It had refused to do so as long as they might be of use in a presumed American occupation government of conquered Communist countries after World War III. Now they were too old.

About the most recent General Assembly meeting, I said,

"Disarmament, advanced by [Soviet Foreign Minister] Molotov, was accepted as the chief issue of the day. While the final resolution lacked the teeth the Russians had proposed, it stated the most important principle they had advanced: that prohibition and elimination from national armaments of atomic and other weapons of mass destruction was an 'urgent objective'; that the Security Council consider a convention to outlaw these weapons (a favorite Soviet project); recommended the immediate withdrawal of armed forces stationed in member nations without their consent; and recommended a general reduction of all armed forces. The Russians agreed to UN inspection of the execution of such measures, free of the veto. The N.Y. *Herald-Tribune* , generally regarded as our leading Republican newspaper, in a joint summary of the session by the 12 members of its foreign staff, called this the 'greatest concession' made by any state, adding 'American and British concessions were minor compared to this one'....Also at this session, the USSR vigorously opposed the Union of South Africa's request for incorporation of the mandated area of South West Africa [Namibia], attacking racial discrimination....It was generally granted that the Soviet stand was decisive in the Assembly's action in condemning South African behavior toward Indians and refusing its mandate request."

The young war veterans who made up much of Stanford's student body wanted to think well of their recent ally, and I was well received. As is normally the case with in-house academic events, the presenters at that conference were not paid. Within that same month, I had one—final — professional lecture booked, at the University of Montana, in Missoula. All efforts to find another between there and Stanford were fruitless. Since the fee was $150—over $1,500 in today's money—and I badly needed every penny I could take home, I traveled by Greyhound bus.

It must have taken a day-and-a-half, perhaps two, each way. I had been to the Northwest only once before, somewhat less than two years earlier. But then I had been on the celebrity circuit and traveled by plane. I had spoken at a Sacramento forum series and was bound for Portland. It was a typical California winter day with the Central Valley buried in fog. The DC-3 flew low above it, the Coast Range peeking above it on the left and the Sierra Nevada higher on the right. As we approached the Siskiyous, the plane gained altitude, rising to perhaps seven thousand feet. But suddenly the fog-bank to the left rose at a forty-five degree angle, or so it seemed. Soon I realized that it was not fog, but snow, the sides of a mountain of immense mass, going up and up. It was Shasta, only a mile or two away, and rising in the brilliant sunlight another seven thousand feet above me. I have seen it many times since, but never again from the air beneath its peak, rising without warning from the fog. Today's planes fly far above it.

To avoid low clearance over the Cascades, the air route to Portland those days stayed east of the mountains, reaching the Columbia River at The Dalles. There, the plane dropped to a couple of thousand feet above the river and turned west. Mt. Hood towered to the left, Mt. Adams to the right. Clouds floated high above and sharp edged shafts of sunlight descended through light mist casting spotlights upon the river.

The bus trip two years later was equally memorable. I felt comfortable because it put me back among plain people. The bus-stop eateries were like the places I had known in Cleveland and Akron or, for that matter, New York when I didn't eat at home. At longer stops I would take brisk walks both to stretch my legs and to sightsee. Greyhound stops were never in rich parts of town, although they might be in business districts. These breaks gave me a chance to look at people, not just the houses and cars that are all one normally sees in residential areas in the West.

But I remember that bus trip chiefly for nature. I must have boarded late in the day, for I recall nothing specific until approaching Shasta. The night was spent rising to and circling around Shasta. There was no Interstate 5 then, but innumerable switchbacks. In those years, Weed was still a town out of a movie Western. No neon, but saloons, lumber-jacks, and cowboys who didn't have to try to look like what they simply were. Past Weed, I fell asleep again, and woke to see the mountain, white in February, rising 10,000 feet above the plateau to its north. I could not take my eyes from it until it was totally out of sight. Hours, perhaps.

As the two-lane roads snaked between walls of Douglas fir, I found a seat close behind the driver and mentally handled the bus. In another life I would have liked to have been an over-the-road bus driver. During the economically tough years that followed, I regretted that I could not apply for such a job, because people who wore glasses to drive were not accepted.

The audience was enormous in Missoula—attendance was possibly compulsory—and consisted chiefly of returned veterans of World War II. They wanted no more war, and I let 'er rip. Homesteading was still taking place in that part of the country. Populism was strong. A senator from neighborhing Idaho, Glen Taylor, became vice-presidential candidate on Henry Wallace's peaceful-coexistence ticket the next year. My attack on Wall Street imperialism as the real source of the tensions with the USSR suited these students fine, and I got a terrific reception. I have no memory of the people I met, but remember seeing Alpine glow for the first time in my life as the sun set and, in the morning, rose over the mountains, turning the snow red and pink.

The trip back was bad, with ice, a blow-out, long delays. My reception at the Hoover Institution was not good. Within a couple of days director Fisher sent someone up to my office with the message that he wished to see me. I went down. Fisher wore a waxed moustache and had experience in the world of diplomacy. It was impossible to read his face. He said, "The junior senator from Montana phoned President Hoover [one never said "former"], who phoned Secretary Wilbur [a Hoover cabinet member who was a member of the board of the Institute of Pacific Relations, which had asked me to write my first book], who phoned me about your having identified yourself as a Hoover Institution Fellow in connection with your lecture there."

The junior senator was an ignorant rancher who had just been appointed to fill a vacancy. The whole thing would have been a line out of a comedy if it weren't so damned serious. I excused myself, went to my office, brought back my correspondence with the University of Montana, and demonstrated that I had been very careful to specify that I was a "former" Fellow, and that I was not responsible for Missoula publicity and news people having omitted that. Regardless, it got me in trouble.

I had given my last talks in San Francisco a couple of weeks earlier.

They contain a paragraph or two that have meaning for arguments that still rage. One read:

"On February 2, 1946, the Associated Press carried a dispatch from Germany saying: 'Two of Germany's leading scientists said today that Germany knew the secret of harnessing atomic energy in 1941 but was industrially and financially powerless to apply the discovery in producing bombs...'We were told to continue our research...But Germany by then (the end of 1941, after the Battle of Moscow) had lost vast amounts of equipment in Russia which had to be replaced immediately. Money and factory facilities could not be given for research and production when they were needed to replace tanks, airplanes and guns.' In plain English, Russia saved us from German atom bombs, and gave us the time to develop our own, which we are now stockpiling against Russia!"

The Nobel Peace Prize winner of 1996, physicist Joseph Rotblat, said that he had quit the atom bomb project in 1944 when told that its purpose was to develop a weapon not against the countries we were then fighting but against our ally, the Soviet Union. Seventy scientists on the project petitioned Truman not to use the bomb because if the U.S. did so it would fail its "solemn responsibility" to avert the postwar spread of nuclear weapons. He used it.

Another speech of mine set forth my underlying view of the Cold War which motivated most of what I did for the forty years that it continued. "Moscow does not trust the sincerity of statesmen who say they fear Russian strength," I said. "This is because she is certain that they know facts which the common man does not, for instance, that Russia can produce, this year [1948], only about 17 million tons of steel, while America has a capacity of 85 million [five times as much]. Since we are the stronger power industrially, have the atom bomb, have a navy and an air force stronger than the rest of the world combined, have taken bases around the globe, and maintain troops abroad in non-enemy countries, she feels that it is up to us to demonstrate our peaceful intentions, and not the other way round."

But I spent vastly more time trying to find a way to make a living than in delivering lectures or even completing the one-man *Encyclopedia of the USSR* that was the official reason the Hoover Institution granted me a research fellowship. Unofficially, their invitation to me had not been conditioned upon any specific project. I applied for a Guggenheim grant and to another fund, without success. All such efforts got me was ego-support—which is damned important when trying to stand against the tide—in the form of remarkable letters of recommendation.

My hopes of hanging on as a Soviet authority on my own were finally dashed when my publisher, the John Day Company (later Stein & Day), wrote me in the frankest political terms that my encyclopedia, now complete, which I had started on an advance they paid me two years earlier, was unpublishable because of the change in atmosphere. Those who think there is a free press in this country will find the following excerpt from their letter of interest:

"I imagine that you realized when you sent the manuscript of your encyclopedia that it was coming at the worst possible time. The only worse time could be in the midst of actual war—and I still don't think there will be war." That last clause gives a notion of the delirium in the country at the time. The letter continues:

"Now we have come to a time when it is going to be impossible to sell enough copies of such a book to avoid serious loss for us or to reflect credit on you as the author. One would think that when a nation is worked up to hysteria about another nation, its public would want to read and learn all it can about the possible 'enemy.' But not so Americans. A year ago they were listening to lectures and buying books about Russia. Now they turn a deaf ear and a blind eye. I see no solution except to wait for saner days."

Over forty-five years later, that letter was part of the documentation which won me a Hammett-Hellman award from Human Rights Watch as an author who had suffered political persecution. The reason I had to wait so long is evidenced in a virtual duplicate of that letter I received thirty years later. Ramparts Press had granted me an advance to write a book on the non-Russian peoples of the USSR in 1977, when President Carter had not yet undone the Nixon detente. Two years later, when the book was ready, Ramparts told me that it could not proceed with publication for exactly the same reason that John Day could not in 1948. The head of Ramparts, the late Lawrence Moore, had become—and remained—a personal friend. But he simply could not afford to lose the money. Fortunately I had built a base of support in my radio audience, and the book was published on the basis of prepaid subscription.

The letter from the John Day Company was dated March 29, 1948. We moved back to New York on April Fool's Day, very appropriate given my situation. Despite the discouraging times, an unexpected and charming interlude soon gave me a couple of months of interesting work and the chance to get to know a fascinating personality, then world-famous.

One day the phone rang and a voice with a British university accent said, "This is Walter Duranty. Are you busy the next month or so?" I answered no. "I'm writing a book about Stalin and the men around him—his possible successors [Stalin would be 70 the next year], and I wonder if you'd collaborate with me."

Here was a man who had won the O. Henry Prize for best short story of the year and had won the Pulitzer Prize for journalism more than fifteen years earlier for his coverage of the Soviet Union for the *New York*

Times from 1920 on. He was the author of a published novel, of a best-seller on his years in Moscow, *I Write As I Please,* which went through more than a dozen printings, and of three other books on the USSR. I had read his dispatches from Moscow since I was ten, perhaps earlier. And this man needed a collaborator? And he was asking me? I responded, "Why me?"

He said, "I've read your books. You've come to the same conclusions from your scholarship that I have from my on-the-spot observations. In today's atmosphere I have to be dead certain that I am absolutely accurate on matters of fact. And I need documentary support."

This was a truly great reporter—he was as well-known in those pre-television years as the most famous major network anchor today, because Russia's attempt to build a non-capitalist society was *the* story of the years subsequent to World War I—but understood that he was not a scholar. (Albert Rhys Williams was also like that. Very few reporters understand that about themselves.)

So we worked together. It was delightful. Duranty had a suite in a hotel just off Park Avenue. I would sit at the typewriter and he would dictate, stomping around the room. Duranty was of middle height, quite bald, with a mouthful of false teeth, and an impish smile. One of his legs was shorter than the other because he had lost a foot jumping on a railroad train in France and wore an artificial replacement. He would order marvelous sandwiches for us from room service, and, true to journalistic stereotype, always had a drink in hand. I don't think I permitted myself alcohol when working, although I was not a teetotaler.

Every once in a while Duranty would ask for back-up information on something, and I would provide it, either from memory or from my *A Guide to the Soviet Union,* which had brought him to me. Despite the library of books written on the USSR by then, he directly quoted only two, mine and one by Prof. Schuman, mentioned previously, another member of our very small mutual admiration society.

I would interrupt his dictation with a suggestion or an objection, the latter usually on grounds of political interpretation. If he were sober, he'd say, "Bill, I'm no hero," meaning that he agreed, but the Cold War hysteria made it too dangerous to say what I wanted. If he were drunk, he would accept my point, and retain it when he re-read it sober.

My name did not appear in this book, *Stalin & Co.,* except as quoted source. I had a good feeling of getting even when *Newsweek,* which had listed me in its assault on Communists and fellow-travelers, gave Duranty's book a favorable review, nearly a full page, in 1949. Duranty, incidentally, was neither a Communist nor a Marxist, but, as an English citizen, was not even a Laborite. He always voted the Liberal Party ticket.

But he never got another book contract, and lost his contract on the lecture circuit, where he had been an absolute lion, and a lady-killer. It was simply that he truly loved the female sex, and women reciprocated. His experience proved the people at John Day right. Non-hostile books on the USSR were simply not saleable to the book-buying public.

CHAPTER 12

America Goes Nuts

The year, 1948, when we moved back to New York after my year at Stanford, was simply crazy. Imagine sending to jail a surgeon who had the courage to give up his practice and go to Spain to head the medical services of the American volunteers defending the Spanish Republic against Franco. That insurgent general was supported on the ground and in the air by Hitler's Condor Legion with the most modern arms and a division sent by the originator of fascism, Mussolini. What was this Dr. Barsky's crime? After the republic was defeated, he headed an organization which sent money to refugees of the Spanish Civil War, who were scattered all over the world. The House Un-American Activities Committee dared ask him and his board for the names of its contributors and of the Spanish Republicans in exile whom it helped. Dr. Barsky and his organization refused, asserting that this was none of the committee's business. They were also concerned that the names of the beneficiaries would unquestionably get back to Franco in light of HUAC's known sympathies, and their relatives in Spain would suffer. Franco had publicly promised to slaughter a million supporters of the republic after he won. He managed to find and kill about half that number, in a country with a population smaller than the state of California today. Genocide or no? The United States recognized his government in 1953. Cold War *über alles*.

The U.S. Supreme Court upheld this Alice-in-Hitlerland conviction. Dr. Barsky served a jail sentence, as did novelist Howard Fast and nine other members of the board. The first person actually to go to jail in this Truman-era witch-hunt, years before Joe McCarthy jumped on the bandwagon in 1950 and took its reins, was a lawyer, Leon Josephson. He had the heroism to enter Nazi Germany before the war to make contact with the underground. After the U.S. fought a war to defeat Hitler—a war in which several hundred thousand Americans died— Josephson, instead of being given the Congressional Medal of Honor, served a year in jail for refusing to testify on his pre-war action to the House Un-American Activities Committee. The Supreme Court refused to review the conviction. The convictions of Josephson, Barsky, and others were under federal law, and prosecuted by Harry Truman's attorney-general. Josephson went to prison in March 1948. Little wonder that no one dared to engage me as a lecturer any longer.

In my own field of activity, Rev. Richard Morford, a Presbyterian minister heading the National Council of American-Soviet Friendship, a man I knew well, was sentenced in April for refusing to give its files and the list of its contributors to HUAC. That was, in a way, my welcome back to New York. The Hollywood Ten were sentenced in May. At the end of the month, the American Russian Institute was put on the attorney-general's list of subversive organizations. I was the fund-raising speaker at its annual dinner six days later. I opened as follows:

"It has been my honor and privilege—may I repeat for the benefit of the attorney-general—honor and privilege, to be intimately acquainted with the work of the American Russian Institute for the past eight years, as a member of its research staff from 1941 to 1944 and as a grateful user of its remarkable facilities since then."

The physical and political scene that evening was simply bizarre. The dinner was in the most prestigious venue of the day, the grand ballroom of the Waldorf-Astoria Hotel, with seventeen hundred people present. General Walter Bedell Smith, U.S. Ambassador to Moscow, was also on the dais. He was soon to become Director of the Central Intelligence Agency! Others facing the audience included Andrei Gromyko, Soviet representative to the U.N. Security Council, who was later Soviet president and played a major role in bringing Gorbachev to power in 1985. Seated next to me was another Soviet ambassador, Jacob Malik, representative to the UN General Assembly.

The dinner was chaired by the president of Smith College. The Institute's Board of Directors was headed by Ernest Ropes, whom President Herbert Hoover had named, years earlier, to head the Russian Unit of the Department of Commerce. At that time the U.S. did not officially recognize the existence of the Soviet government but was quite willing to make money by trading with it. In 1945 Mr. Ropes had nominated me to the Colonial Trust Company to direct its efforts to build trade. Nothing came of that because I told the bank that the war-ruined Soviet Union couldn't buy anything from us unless Washington extended it a reconstruction loan, as it had to the other allies. It didn't.

Two weeks after that dinner at the Waldorf, the Internal Revenue Service withdrew the tax-exempt status the Institute had enjoyed for eleven years. When I was called before the McCarthy Committee five years later, unctuous Senator Dirksen, for whom the U.S. Senate office building is regrettably named, went on at great length about the fact that I had worked for this "subversive" organization. That no such blacklist had been issued when I worked at the Institute didn't bother him.

The essence of the foregoing is that the massive organizational structure erected among citizens at all levels of society in support of the U.S.-Soviet alliance of World War II still existed in 1948. Government was in the process of chopping it down by any and all means, from imprisonment to financial throttling to intimidation. Supporters of the New Deal and the notion of continuing U.S.-Soviet cooperation fought back. The issue was resolved in the 1948 presidential elections, in which that point of view was represented by the candidacy of Henry Wallace. In New York he got half a million votes. In California, then with little more than half the population of New York, he won two hundred thousand. In the rest of the country he was wiped out.

During the campaign I gave informational and fund-raising speeches and traveled on one occasion with Paul Robeson to a stadium rally in New Jersey where he was to sing. I was struck by the fact that Robeson, a master of standard English and serious student of twenty other languages, spoke Black English to the four husky, grim-looking African-Americans who were the other occupants of the large sedan. I learned later that they were gangsters who had offered him protection whenever needed, no questions asked and with no reimbursement. Although it would be another year before a mob attempt to stop a Robeson concert, that was already in the air. It is now forty years since he left the concert stage, but I hear him still in my mind singing songs of the Spanish Civil War, of the Chinese Revolution, of Welsh miners, Jewish laments and resistance songs, the spirituals of his own people, and above all "That old man river, he just keep rollin' ah-oo-uh-long."

I wrote much of the foreign policy section of the book-length campaign handbook used by Wallace activists nation-wide. A month before the election, I sent his headquarters an analysis of the world scene that is still relevant. This paper flatly disagreed with the position of the Communist Party, of which I was very much a member. That organization swallowed the government propaganda that World War III was just around the corner, despite the fact that Joseph Stalin himself publicly expressed the opposite view. More important, the belief in the imminence of war prevailed among the non-Communist majority of Wallace activists and continued to be the stimulus for the behavior of peace movements for the next 40 years. I concluded my detailed survey thus:

"All this leads to the conclusion that the Cold War is much more a struggle for position for a conflict still very much [far] in the future, as well as an ideal means of gaining public acceptance for Wall Street control of all the world outside the 'iron curtain,' and for reactionary economic and political measures at home, as well as vastly profitable arms contracts. Whatever the outcome of our elections, there is no reasonable indication of a change in this picture in the foreseeable future."

I wish I could forecast the course of events today with the certainty and accuracy of that prediction. The turmoil in the world since the collapse of the Soviet Union, the possession of nuclear weapons by more countries all the time, and the unwillingness of many small peoples to be intimidated, makes that impossible.

Other than via the Wallace campaign itself, there was virtually no way to reach the American people with arguments against U.S. foreign policy. On the strength of my previous contract with the country's number one lecture management, I was able to get another, with an impressive roster of speakers, to book speaking engagements for me. It found me only two during the entire year, and those were debates: no one dared have me speak without the opposite opinion being presented at the same time. But I had some unremunerated speaking dates that brought pleasant indications that I had not spent my previous years in vain, and that even echoed into the future. One was at Columbia University, in a lecture hall jammed with perhaps two hundred people. Among the graduate students who approached me afterward was one who identified himself as Lynn Turgeon. Lynn became a professor of economics, and the only one of radical—never communist—convictions to have believed, correctly, in 1980, that Reaganomics could be applied for several years without bringing the country to immediate economic collapse. Thirty years after that lecture at Columbia he presented me to speak at his own university, opening with the words: "I'd like to present a man who changed my life." I looked at him in astonishment. He explained that until that 1948 lecture he, a recent Navy veteran raised in California farm country, had firmly believed the cold war line about the Soviet Union, but the documentation I had presented from authoritative and unchallengeably respectable American sources had reversed his attitudes. Lynn died in 1999.

Another man came up after the Columbia lecture and said, in an impeccable Oxford accent, "I don't imagine you can guess what country I'm from." Odd gambit, I thought, but I couldn't guess, since it was a way of saying that it was not England. He was from South Africa, and told me that for the preceding four years he had been using my book, *The Soviet Far East and Central Asia,* in the courses he taught at the University of Natal at Durban. This was before apartheid, although Blacks and "Coloreds" were as totally excluded from power then as they were until Mandela became president nearly half a century later. They could still attend university, however. He had non-white students in his classes. Since I had used that book to document my belief, then and today, that the Soviet Union provided a model for the advancement of formerly colonial peoples, I was happy to learn that my fairly obscure research was reaching students in that country which, of all on earth, needed its lessons most.

Nonetheless, my recent experiences could hardly have left me with illusions about the academic world in general or, for that matter, that of journalism or lecturing, the other professions I had practiced. In November 1948 I wrote an article on the 31st anniversary of the Bolshevik Revolution for the magazine, *Soviet Russia Today,* in which I summed up my view of Establishment opinion-makers and youth-molders in language that unfortunately remains valid: "They talk of freedom, the pen prostitutes, the academic acrobats who document with equal facility the need for alliance with the Soviet Union in 1945 and war upon it in 1948."

I was most pleased when the nationally-respected pastor of the First Unitarian Church of Los Angeles, Stephen Fritchman, wrote to congratulate me on that article and order hundreds of copies to distribute to his activist congregation.

None of this moral support solved the problem of making a living for my family. Our children then ranged between two and nine years of age. So I took up explorer Stefansson's offer to work for him as researcher and writer for his *Encyclopedia Arctica.* He had come to know of me through Ruth Gruber, a regular user of the American Russian Institute library when I worked there during the war.

Ruth was the author of a book called, *I Went to the Soviet Arctic.* When President Roosevelt opened Alaska's Matanuska Valley to settlers, Ruth had been hired to supervise that project specifically because of what she had seen in the Soviet Arctic. During the war, when I gave a talk at the Brookings Institution, I looked her up in Washington, and she took me to a party totally outside my experience. The guests could have been the cast of a Hollywood spy movie, including the standard stunning blonde in a slinky black dress who could really shake it. They were exactly what they looked like: personnel of G-2, Army Intelligence. One man wore a magnificently cut silk uniform with the patch of the General Staff on his chest. I was told that he was the son-in-law of J. P. Morgan, the dominant figure on Wall Street. That officer looked at me more and more cross-eyed as his alcohol intake increased. Ultimately he and I found ourselves alone in the kitchen. He yelled: "I know you! You're FBI, and you're going to report that we got drunk!" He lunged for me. I dashed into the living room, grabbed Ruth, and split.

There could hardly have been a lovelier place to work than Stefansson's. His two old private houses—one of which served as his research library—were in the heart of Greenwich Village, looking out on a handkerchief-sized patch of trees and grass called St. Luke's Place. Shockingly to me, he was married to a woman barely older than myself. Evelyn was of Hungarian Jewish immigrant parentage, tall, slender, a classical beauty who had been a professional folk-singer, was a superb ballroom dancer, and was utterly devoted to her husband.

Stefansson had been one of my childhood heroes, exactly as astronauts were to the generation who were children when the Soviets put the first man in space in 1961. Stef—everyone called him that—had walked north of Canada onto the ice of the Arctic, alone, at the very beginning of the century, when it was assumed that white men would die there, as they generally did. He didn't, simply because he was not a racist. He assumed that Inuit were fully human beings and believed that if he ate what they did, he would not suffer the scurvy that had wiped out one party of explorers after another. (Vitamins had not yet been discovered; scurvy was simply a vitamin deficiency.) He was right.

My job with Stefansson provides a concrete example of how even research scholarship in obscure fields suffered under conditions of Cold War suppression in our society as in totalitarian countries. Nothing like his ten-volume *Encyclopedia Arctica* had ever been written. I contributed, in the form of articles, the equivalent of one thick volume—a good two hundred thousand words. Among other things, I wrote about agriculture in the Soviet Far North, government departments, scientific institutions, schools. I also contributed a dozen long articles on the geographic administrative districts of the Soviet Arctic including what interested me most: those organized along ethnic lines for the indigenous Paleo-Asiatic peoples and Mongolian Sakha (whom the Russians called Yakuts). I also wrote on esoteric topics such as the "biographies" of Russian ships famous in Arctic exploration and the histories of drifts. From early in this century, cases had occurred in which ships, icebound in the high Arctic, had thus drifted for a year or even two. Crews and explorers survived in some cases, and made vast numbers of scientific observations.

My imagination refused to be confined within the limits of assembling and organizing factual data. At the Stefansson Library I grappled with a major controversy I discovered to exist among Arctic scholars, which directly bore on my writing. It was up to me to decide, subject to Stef's approval, just how far south the Soviet North went. I discovered that specialists couldn't even agree on what the Arctic is. Everything north of the Arctic Circle? Huge areas south of it are just as cold. Murmansk, to the north, is a large city with normal urban life, thanks to the warm Gulf Stream that keeps its port open to shipping year round. The tree line? But immense territories anyone would regard as Arctic are heavily forested, while there are areas in both Canada and the USSR where treeless tundra stretches far south of the Arctic Circle. A temperature line? But a very different boundary emerges if you trace the mean annual temperature than if you draw the line wherever July temperatures do not exceed fifty degrees Fahrenheit. The permafrost line, where underground ice never thaws? But that dips far south into Mongolia, which certainly isn't Arctic.

So I applied the philosophy I adhere to, dialectical materialism, and decided to define the Arctic in terms of change in material circumstances, meaning the level of human interaction with nature. Edmonton, for example, Canada's northernmost great city, with 850,000 people, had been a tiny outpost till little over a century ago. Until the railroad reached it in 1891, it was regarded as Arctic. I came up with this definition: the Arctic is everything north of the continuous railroad network and year-round water communication. The Associated Press came to our office one day to do a feature story on us. They wound up with one about my theory, published nationwide under such headlines as: "Scholar Offers Idea of Shrinking Polar Circle," with four maps they had drawn to illustrate my reasoning. I never submitted my notion to any learned journal.

In those years before coffee machines became a workplace standard, we would have virtually ceremonial coffee breaks. The bookkeeper would make it in a distinctive New England style: pouring the coffee into a saucepan of boiling water, letting the grounds settle, and carefully decanting the brew. Two full-time staff writers worked for *Encyclopedia Arctica* other than myself, both immigrant women in their 50s, one German and the other Russian, neither of whom were Jewish. The German was reserved and coy, as proper upper-middle class, well-educated ladies of her generation were supposed to be.

The Russian's name was Yevgeniya Olkhina, but she had been born Volkonskaya. That is, she was of the princely family thinly disguised in Tolstoy's *War and Peace* as the Bolkonskys who gave the book one of its two major male characters, Andrei. The real-life Volkonskys (Volkonskaya is the female form of the name) were a most extraordinary family. One had been a general in the war against Napoleon. Another, also a general, was a member of the earliest revolutionary conspiracy aimed at overthrowing the Russian monarchy, for which he served thirty years at hard labor in Siberia. His wife had the courage and devotion to follow him into Siberian exile. They all bore the rank prince or princess, at the very top of the aristocracy. Another Princess Volkonskaya was one of Russia's first women writers, and the subject of poems and stories by Pushkin and others.

My colleague was probably also a princess, but nothing could have interested her less. Her family had naturally migrated to the West after the Revolution, but she, like my San Francisco artist friend Arnautoff, also an emigre of the nobility, had become a Communist. For a person of her background that ideological move took not only open-mindedness but extraordinary strength of character. She had been in her early 20s at the time of the Revolution. The high nobility all went to France, where they established a tightly self-contained community with rigorous adherence to rank and station, even though some made their livings as taxi drivers or doormen. To dissent meant ostracism or worse. Russians of any political persuasion living abroad are extraordinarily nationalistic. They simply do not want to blend into the general population. So our Volkonskaya learned to keep silent and, when she spoke, to express her dissidence from accepted views among the emigres by acid, sarcastic remarks that pricked the bubbles of their beliefs.

The most vivid memory I have of the stories she would tell me from across our facing desks in that serene, high-ceilinged 19th-century house in Greenwich Village was of fleeing from the Nazi Army as it swept across France early in World War II. I had read of planes strafing civilian refugee columns, but to hear it from someone who had been in the fleeing mass was another matter. She had spent days standing in a cold, barely-moving freight car packed to crushing in November 1942 when the Germans extended their military occupation to the part of France they had previously been content to treat as a satellite.

Her experience as a dissident aristocrat and an anti-Nazi in occupied France caused her to confine frank expression of opinion to only a very few people in the America of 1948 and 1949, which was then deporting non-citizens suspected of sympathies to communism or the Soviet Union. Yevgeniya spoke with pride of only one thing in her family's immediate background. There is a five-story bookstore in Leningrad— as very many there still call it, although it is officially St. Petersburg once again—called the World of Books. Her parents established and owned it until its nationalization after the revolution. To Russian intellectuals, books are the highest of human achievements.

I lost track of her after I left Stefansson's employ. I learned later that she returned to the Soviet Union some time in the 1950s. There, she wrote a small booklet in tribute to him, detailing how his—our— *Encyclopedia Arctica* had been blocked from publication because of Stefansson's opinion of the USSR. In those times he could hardly have survived the evidence of his own printed words unless he chose to renounce them. He was not that type of man. In his Introduction to Ruth Gruber's *I Went to the Soviet Arctic*, he had written:

"When war came there was in the vast country such a union of sympathy and purpose as the world had never before seen in an empire of comparable size and population. And this was a unity...of all the peoples that compose the Soviet Union—from the Karelians in the north to the Georgians in the south, from the White Russians in the west to the Chuckchis and Eskimos in the farthest east....If finding the one hundred and fifty or so other nationalities, of whatever race, standing in war shoulder-to-shoulder with the Russians was to the Western democracies not the greatest revelation, then it was probably to find that the women of the Soviet Union took so large a share in the war....More than three out of every four students in the medical colleges are women;...how that can be, and how it can strengthen a nation...you will understand when you read in this book the story of Igarka, a city of the Arctic whose 'mayor' was a woman."

Stef was no male chauvinist.

In desperation he finally arranged for his immense and unparalleled library of the Far North, including the encyclopedia manuscript, to become part of the Dartmouth College library, with his wife as curator and himself as consultant. Thirty-five years later, a friend gave me a book by a Canadian scholar, *Discovery in Russian and Siberian Waters.* I scoured it in vain for any reference to the immense work, including my own, done for Stefansson's unpublished encyclopedia. Today, of course, even unpublished work is listed in computerized information banks and such an unclassified government-funded effort would be on the Internet. But at that time there was no such thing, not even duplication by microfilm or micro-fiche. So our work is lost, even though the type-script exists in the archives of the Arctic Institute in Calgary, Alberta.

In 1992 I saw a portrait of Stef in the Montreal Museum, where he was described as a "Canadian explorer." Actually, he was from North Dakota, of Icelandic immigrant parentage, and the Canadian government ceased funding his expeditions after World War I, when Canadians acquired national pride. He saw no conflict between his own ethnic pride and his obvious internationalism. Baptized William Stevenson, he found himself the butt of chauvinist remarks by the overwhelmingly Anglo-Saxon student body of Yale when he entered it. In response he officially changed his name to what it would have been in Icelandic.

While I worked for Stef the Soviets tested an atom bomb for the first time, on September 23, 1949. The phone began to ring at the Stefansson Library from people who wanted to know where to retreat from the bomb, and assumed the North would be safe. Others came in person with the same request. I was assigned to handle them. As an opponent of nuclear weapons who wanted to see people spend their time trying to do away with them rather than saving their individual skins, I got grim pleasure out of pointing out that the only place north of the U.S. to which one could flee on the assumption of escaping the bomb would be north of Canada's populated areas, because it was an American ally and would also be attacked. The one way to travel north of Canada's rail was along the Alcan Highway, which remains the only overland connection between Alaska and the lower forty-eight states. I called their attention to the fact that that road would naturally be a prime Soviet target for bombing, conventional or nuclear. There was no hiding place. There still isn't.

Stef was eventually forced to fire me. Dr. Herbert Aptheker, the Communist historian, whom I had never previously met, invited me to lunch one day and asked me to write an article on the Soviet Arctic for the cultural magazine, *Masses and Mainstream,* of which he was an associate editor. I did so. One day two crew-cut types passed in front of our library window. I recognized the magazine in the hand of the one nearer me. They went into Stef's basement office, which opened onto a garden in back. After an hour or so, he rang and asked me to come down. He was alone. He asked: "Did you have an article in this Communist magazine?"

I said I had. He responded: "I've just had a visit from Naval Intelligence. They said: 'Your work is funded by the U.S. Office of Naval Research. Do you want the Navy investigated by the House Un-American Activities Committee?'"

I was dumbfounded—not by the fact that the witch-hunt had reached me, but by their words. This was little more than four years after the end of World War II. The armed forces enjoyed tremendous prestige among the American people in consequence of the successful war against Hitler and Japanese imperialism. The political conservatism of the military was legendary. The notion that the Un-American Activities Committee would even dream of going after them was beyond my comprehension. But Naval Intelligence knew the atmosphere in Washington better than I did. While HUAC never did make that move, Joe McCarthy did, in his investigation of the army five years later.

Stef said he could no longer retain me in the Navy-funded job, but switched me to another project of his, translating permafrost materials for the Army on a freelance basis. That is how I entered the profession at which I earned my living continuously until I retired thirty-two years later. In other words, my career as professional writer, researcher, journalist, and lecturer was terminated forever by mere fear.

In a book written decades ago I find, next to a mention of General George Marshall, my handwritten note: "to whom Stefansson talked about whether he should fire me." Marshall was then Secretary of State.

Leaving the Stefansson Library in Greenwich Village to do my translations in the isolation of our apartment in Washington Heights was unpleasant not only because of the switch from creative to technical work, although the next year brought the highest earnings of my lifetime. Nineteen forty-nine was also not a year to escape world politics.In March a large group of this country's most eminent intellectuals had convened an American Cultural and Scientific Conference for World

Peace. They invited towering figures from every country. One was the Soviet composer Shostakovich. He was denied an entrance visa. This led to a tremendous outcry in protest, and the visa was finally granted. Whereupon the *New York Times* did the most despicable thing I can recall in the twenty years I had read it up to then. It knew that most of those attending such an event would be *Times* readers. It devoted a story starting on page one and covering *most* of page two to the preparations to cart away those who would supposedly be injured in consequence of pickets blocking the entrances to the conference. Fifty ambulances would be present, it said. It scared me sufficiently that I stayed away from the opening event.

But the effort at intimidation of large numbers failed. The meetings were full—at Carnegie Hall, the Waldorf-Astoria Hotel, and a major rally at Madison Square Garden. Most important, the few hundred pickets, vastly outnumbered by those attending, were, by appearance and accent as they shouted slogans, overwhelmingly recently-imported Europeans. They included pro-Hitler trash and collaborators from Eastern Europe and the western USSR when it was Nazi-occupied in World War II. It was officially admitted many years later that they were deliberately brought here to create potential governments-in-exile and support forces for re-infiltration.

To counter the impact of the conference, the CIA founded, as revealed in 1966, the Congress for Cultural Freedom, headed by composer Nikolai Nabokov. It sponsored art shows in many countries, particularly promoting abstract expressionism as a counter to the pointedly anti-war and socially-conscious realism that had been strong in the '30s and '40s.

Just before the year began, on Christmas Eve 1948, I attended a party at the home of a next-door neighbor. There was a paperback book in an unusual kind of binding, not used in this country, on the arm of an overstuffed chair. I picked it up. It was *Africa - Britain's Third Empire*, by George Padmore, published in London. Padmore was a Liberian and the co-founder of Pan-Africanism thirty years earlier with Dr.W.E.B.DuBois. This was Padmore's eighth book. He had at one time been a Communist, and resided for several years in the USSR. Communist parties denounced him, as they did all who parted company with them if they sought to advocate and/or organize on some different political basis. But a passage I found as I leafed through the book indicated that he refused to reply in kind. He continued to express his admiration for positive things he had seen in the Soviet Union, although he found it necessary to cite authority in his support.

"While it is considered not only improper," he wrote, "but positively indecent, in official Colonial circles and certain Labour [Party] quarters to refer to Russia's achievements in Central Asia, I am prepared to run the risk of incurring the displeasure of these hidebound Soviet haters (and perhaps even be denounced as a 'Moscow agent') by quoting the testimony of an unimpeachable American authority.

"In his most authoritative report, *The Soviet Far East and Central Asia,* Dr. William Mandel, an outstanding authority on Asian affairs, compares education in Uzbekistan and Sweden. Nothing illustrates more strikingly the phenomenal cultural change which has taken place in Uzbekistan, a territory formerly as backward as any African colony." Padmore had lived in Uzbekistan. He then quoted a long paragraph from my book.

I was blue, on that Christmas eve, because two other books of mine, both written on publisher's advances, could not be published in the rising Cold War atmosphere—and in fact never were. I had entered a thirteen-year period in which no publisher would accept any proposal bearing my name. Padmore's book gave me the satisfaction of knowing that my first published book was still at work, far beyond the bounds of this country.

Jawaharlal Nehru had been released from prison in 1945 by the British rulers of India. Independence was clearly imminent—it came in 1947—and his becoming prime minister was a certainty. A fellow-Indian friend of his living in New York came to me for a copy of that same book to bring to Nehru in the hope that it might help in the framing of India's ethnic policy. Nehru, like Nelson Mandela, was an admirer of the Soviet Union, and educated his daughter, Indira Gandhi, who succeeded him as prime minister, in that spirit in a series of letters he wrote her from prison, later published as a book.

Nearly a quarter century after my book's publication, it was quoted repeatedly in an academic work by a professor in India who spent nearly four years in the Soviet Union studying Central Asia. And in England in 1951 a couple who had written eleven previous books on the Soviet Union quoted me repeatedly and at very great length in their book on Central Asia. This was at a time when the generation of American Sovietologists trained in the Cold War spirit had chosen to forget that work of mine. They were helped, of course, by Joe McCarthy, who targetted that particular book as the reason for subpoenaing me.

The continued use of my work was very important in giving me a new sense of self-worth, and of maintaining my morale, in years when nobody was listening here at home . To be more exact, those who controlled access to the public eye and ear isolated me as effectively, if not as completely, as if I had been in prison—in some respects even more so. There have been cases in this country when books written in prison have been published and reached substantial, even immense audiences.

But in the Cold War and McCarthy years, one could be free and even earn a satisfactory living one way or another, but no publisher dared touch one's work if it dissented from what became the American religion, anti-Sovietism. In my case that applied on both sides of the political fence. Although it was never my first choice, I had submitted projects and manuscripts to the Communist house, International Publishers, when publication by one with broader access became impossible. Yet after the 1920s, International would never publish anything that differed in any way from official Soviet policy and interpretation.

I was personal witness to the shaping of public opinion at the time. When still salaried by Stefansson, I spent my three-week vacation in 1949 filling in for others taking their's from the United Nations at Lake Success, Long Island. I was assigned to the Economic and Social Council, chaired by Eleanor Roosevelt, the president's widow. She sat facing me, perhaps ten feet away, as did the other delegates, in a circle around us. I took long-hand notes of everything said in Russian and French, and then typed them up as an English synopsis.

The delegates to the council represented the United States, the Soviet Union, Britain, France, Australia, and a couple of Latin American countries. They were drafting the Covenant of Human Rights. The 1955 *Encyclopaedia Britannica* describes exactly what I observed: "Some members insisted on the inclusion of economic and social rights, while others insisted that only political and civil rights should be protected." Specifically, the U.S.S.R. wanted inclusion of the right to a job, a legally limited working day, and paid vacations; the right to maintenance in old age, sickness and disability; the right to education; equal rights for women; and equality for all races and nationalities. The U.S. opposed including these, and sought to avoid discussing them separately by insisting that none of them had any place in the document. Mrs. Roosevelt, although privately an advocate of all these things, was a loyal representative of the Truman administration, and upheld its policy of excluding them. She used, as I was able to observe, every parliamentary trick and steamroller tactic in the book.

The behavior of the other nations was an education to watch. Britain had a Labour Party government, but it was dead broke in consequence of the war and totally dependent upon official U.S. charity in the form of Washington's Marshall Plan. Its representative did whatever Mrs. Roosevelt wanted. Australia was the ultra-Left opposition. Whatever the Soviet Union proposed, Australia would offer a more radical formulation. Was that a deliberate effort to show that Moscow did not deserve to be regarded as the leader of social progressivism? The final wording was always somewhat to the right of the Soviet proposal. The Latin Americans would vote one way one day, somebody would reach them overnight, and they would reverse their statements and/or votes to accord next day with the U.S. position.

If, in early 1949, the threat of violence at the Cultural and Scientific Conference for World Peace proved empty, by Labor Day we faced the real thing.

CHAPTER 13

They Shall Not Pass

Tanya's parents had built a small and simple summer cottage in the 1920s at a place called Golden's Bridge, about forty-five miles north of New York City. It was part of a genuine cooperative erected on a one-time farm by professionals and skilled workingclass people from New York, primarily Jewish and largely radicals of one sort or another. Several such co-ops existed within a belt extending some twenty miles westward to the Hudson River at Peekskill. A week before Labor Day 1949, the Millsteins—Tanya's parents—agreed to mind our three children for a weekend to give us our first vacation without them in the five years since our second had been born. We were thirty-two.

Lacking a car, we hitch-hiked 150 miles north to Lake George, where we rented a charming motel cottage and hiked to the fire lookout atop the nearest peak. The next day we rented a canoe. Out in the middle of the lake a gale sprang up, and we paddled like crazy for shelter. Altogether a wonderful weekend. We caught a Greyhound bus the last stretch of the way home. As we got off, we saw the *New York Daily News* on a stand, an extra edition. The entire front page was a blow-up of Paul Robeson's face, distorted and ugly with anger, under a headline "Red Riots At Peekskill."

By 1949, Robeson, who was long since a Broadway and international star and followed Isadora Duncan in establishing the tradition of liberal and then left activism among top-rank American entertainers, had vast political experience all over the world. He sang to the Abraham Lincoln Brigade in the Spanish Civil War, when the shooting literally stopped because, as the International Brigades had hoped, both sides wanted to hear the voice coming over the loudspeakers. Yet even he, according to his granddaugher's lovely pictorial biography, had no notion of the violence that would erupt when he was scheduled to give his fourth annual open-air concert near Peekskill for the benefit of refugees from that war that fascism had won.

The newspaper picture we saw caught his outrage as he described the assault waged by a violent mob of three hundred against forty men and boys who came early to serve as ushers. Among those forty, who gave a good account of themselves in a really bloody fight with fence-posts and rocks, was Tanya's younger brother, Fishie, not long back from wartime service in the U.S. Navy in the south Pacific. Fishie is the affectionate diminutive of Fishl, his name in Yiddish. He had gone to the concert-grounds in an open truckload of children, women, and a few men from Golden's Bridge. During the battle, the truck was used as a defensive bulwark, with the women and children behind it, and the men, including novelist Howard Fast (who had grown up an orphaned New York street kid) slugging it out in front.

My reaction to seeing the photo and hearing Fishie's account was, I later learned, identical to that of thousands of others: the concert must be re-scheduled and held, or intimidation by physical violence against citizens—in other words, fascism—would blanket the country. That remains my judgment nearly half a century later, despite the academic whose Ph.D. thesis on the two weekends of the Peekskill riots concluded that they were of no lasting historic significance. After all, fascism did not triumph, he reasoned. The fact that by stopping fascism physically, and shaming the country to its senses, we nipped it in the bud, was beyond his comprehension.

The day after the initial riot, sixteen hundred people gathered—with four hours notice—on someone's large lawn near Peekskill, and decided to invite Robeson back. The new date was the Sunday of Labor Day weekend, one week after the first attempt. That Saturday I had an afternoon open-air lecture date scheduled at Camp Unity, a culturally marvelous Communist-run summer camp less than an hour's drive from Peekskill. My lecture was to echo years later. One of the particularly notorious professional stool-pigeons of the McCarthy period, Harvey Matusow, was in the audience, and used that occasion to identify me at one of the witch-hunt hearings. Matusow was extraordinary in that, after ruining dozens of lives by his informing, he had the courage to decide that behavior was wrong, and admitted publicly to having lied on the government's behalf. Whereupon the FBI thanked him for his services by having him tried on that perjury charge. He served several years.

It is a measure of the racism that pervades this country that I had to summon up all my courage to say to that friendliest of audiences that I would like to live to see the day when a Paul Robeson could be elected president of the United States. The Communist Party had, for the past five elections, named an African-American as its vice-presidential candidate, which no other party would do. Many of the people listening to me had put their bodies on the line, more than once, for racial equality, and would do so again the very next day at Peekskill. But to fly in the face of prejudice to the degree of challenging the American people to put a Black in the country's most important office was something no party could yet conceive of doing. The ultra-liberal Progressive Party, in its anti-Cold-War election campaign the previous year, had followed the standard rule of naming white Anglo-Saxon Protestants, male of course, to both top posts. I had no reason to fear even criticism, much less physical reprisal, for my advocacy of Robeson. But it took all my will to make myself utter words that were, to my knowledge, unprecedented.

That evening the camp offered its usual stage show and dance. The drummer in the big swing band, Elayne Jones, then a very young woman, later became the first African-American female tympanist in any American professional symphony orchestra, San Francisco's, and a close acquaintance. The show offered that evening was "Finian's Rainbow." It was very well done, with an exceptional performance by a light-skinned Black man barely past twenty. I think encouragement is helpful. It certainly is to me. So I asked the young man's name, and went backstage, stuck out my hand, and said, "You're really good, Mr. Belafonte. You ought to stay in this business."

That day volunteers were sought to build a defence force for the new Robeson concert to be held on the grounds of an abandoned country club, some twenty-five miles west of Camp Unity. The recruiting was officially done through several labor unions and the defense was announced to be headed by an officer of the Furriers' Union, Leon Strauss, himself a war veteran. Actually, the organizing was by the Communist Party under the head of its New York State organization, Bob Thompson, former commander of the Lincoln Battalion ["brigade" is a misnomer: the Lincolns were part of a larger brigade] in Spain and winner of the Distinguished Service Cross for heroism as a U.S. infantry sergeant in the South Pacific in the war against fascism. The reason for the deception was that Thompson was currently on trial, with the rest of the state leadership, for the crime of being a Communist, for which he was later convicted and served eight years. He was out on bail, and his presence at Peekskill might be regarded as violating bail terms.

I did not join the early-morning group. This was not the only time in my life when, facing physical danger, I hung back at the outset but later did what had to be done. I went in mid-morning, in someone's car. Tanya had remained in Golden's Bridge with the children that morning, but also went to the concert later by car. The children were not brought along but could not help but hear the next day, and for many days thereafter, of what had become a terrifying event.

Arriving at the long, narrow, two-lane road leading from the public highway into the improvised concert grounds, we found ourselves hemmed in by 950 uniformed men, as the press later specified. Most looked like Keystone cops, but the situation was not funny. They were the constables of every summer-resort and commuter town in

Westchester County and the police from larger places like Peekskill itself, which had a population of fifteen thousand. Two hundred were New York State troopers. Traffic guides, our people, showed us where to park. Huge chartered buses from New York City arrived in a steady stream, and my impression of their parking arrangement was that someone with a knowledge of military defense must have set it up. We got out and converged with the crowd—the minimum estimate later was fifteen thousand—moving toward the meadow where the concert was to be held. This was a Sunday crowd, chiefly young couples. African-Americans were present somewhat in proportion to their numbers in the population: about ten percent.

A man I had not seen for several years—it turned out that he was one of those the Communist Party had sent underground in its belief that fascism was around the corner, a belief I did not share—approached and asked me: "You see anybody around who is totally dependable for a security job?" My mood had changed. The massive police presence, plus the fact that the fascist riff-raff—officially the war veterans organizations of Peekskill—had called for fifteen thousand to turn out against the concert, made it clear that this was a put-up-or-shut-up situation. So I responded: "How about me?"

It turned out that a small group of bodyguards for Robeson and Thompson was being organized. I was assigned to Thompson. Part of our job was to make sure that no one got close enough to his small hilltop command post to see him, and of course to keep our mouths shut subsequently. The prosecution at his trial never learned he had been there.

That assignment caused me much less tension and danger than a great number of others. On our side, twenty-five hundred men, virtually all war veterans, formed a nearly shoulder-to-shoulder defense ring a long stone's throw, in the most literal sense of that word, within the boundary of the rented venue. Outside the ring, the mob of fifteen hundred fascists—all they could assemble—paraded wildly back and forth on the road, screaming racist filth and shagging stones. Each man on our side had a baseball bat behind him in the grass, but they were never used. Years of discipline in the armed forces stood our guard force in good stead.

At one point the police demanded that our defenders draw back to what would have been the edge of the crowd of concertgoers. That would have destroyed their lines of sight and would have left no room for retreat in case we were attacked and had to regroup. The defense command refused, and the police retaliated by withdrawing from the grounds. Good riddance. They had not protected the forty defenders the previous week, and we had no reason to believe they would be any better this time.

Thompson's command post was, in one respect, poorly chosen. We could see everything except the entrance to the concert grounds. Latecomers, particularly Blacks, were beaten all day long. There are photos of the first African-American aviator in World War I, Eugene Bullard, being clubbed to the ground by uniformed state troopers and police. Bystanders subsequently testified that a fascist had spat in his face and he had spat back. (He had flown for France. The U.S. would not dream of allowing a Black to fly in World War I.) Later in the day, two African-American Marines in dress uniform had the guts to escort their mother onto the grounds.

The civilian fascists were working themselves into a frenzy, particularly as the forces of law and order would take no action against them. They repeatedly attacked our men at the entrance. On the newsreels the next day I saw a rabbi who was a friend of ours standing guard at the gate like Samson. He was a physical giant who, while helping us to move on one occasion, had carried a steamer-trunk by a handle in one hand. Another time, while picnicking with the family, he wielded a bat for the first time in his life, and slugged a softball farther over my head than I have ever seen one hit before or since.

Robeson and Pete Seeger sang, although the police helicopter hanging over their heads made it less than a triumph musically. However, our purpose was accomplished. The concert took place. Buses loaded up and left. Cars followed. Thompson said that was it, and so we walked down the hill. A car came along with Yank Levy, the Camp Unity sports director who was, I believe, a veteran of Spain. I got in the back seat between Yank and another man.

Although there was a crossroads at the exit, and one should have been able to drive left, straight ahead, or right, the cops would only let us go right. The fascists had heaped up, in plain view of the police and at intervals of a few yards, piles of stones so large that their intent could only have been to commit murder. Actually their size saved anyone from losing his life. Cars in the early postwar years had small windows, rather high up, and the rocks steadily hurled at us were so heavy that few could be heaved high enough to hit side windows. Shatterproof glass did not yet exist. Many, many windshields were splintered, but in most cases that slowed or stopped the rocks themselves. Tanya, sitting in the back seat of another car, got home covered with blood from a person in the front seat who had been badly cut by shattered glass. Hospitals admitted 161 persons, nearly all on our side. Many times that number took their cuts and bruises home or to private physicians. One young man, whom I got to know, lost an eye to what a wartime reconstructive surgery physician said was the most devastating non-fatal wound he had ever seen. The young man was Jewish, but he told me that the doctor who watched over him day and night when he was in critical condition was a German Nazi, a recent immigrant, who placed his Hippocratic oath above his anti-Semitism.

During the running of the gauntlet, which for some continued intermittently for fifteen miles, as the fascists had stationed themselves on overpasses and at traffic lights all the way to Tarrytown, our side showed extraordinary, spontaneous discipline. Novelist Howard Fast, in his *Peekskill, USA,* wrote that he responded to the rock-throwing by driving onto the shoulder of the road and scattering the attackers. I did not see a single driver do that, even though I saw hundreds of cars. Any of us could have done it, but that would have risked killing or seriously injuring one of our opponents. At one point, when we were stopped, Yank and the man at the other door wanted to leap out and fight back. I grabbed them both and said, "Our job was to hold that concert, not to give the authorities any excuse to blame this on us." They subsided.

Twenty-three years later, radio station WBAI in New York did a documentary on the Peekskill events. The producer went up there to talk to locals. He asked the sports editor of the local paper, who had been present: "What do you think of the rock-throwing?"

"What rock-throwing?" the editor responded.

"Here, look at this photograph. Isn't that man heaving back to throw a rock?"

"Could be an ice-cream cone, for all I know."

"How about the cars you see here smashed and turned over?" asked the producer.

"Heck, there were no more than 25 or 30 turned over."

The WBAI producer spoke to the chief of police, who had then been a sergeant. He said of us: "It was staged to provoke a riot. They wanted an incident in this area." He did not deny the rock-throwing but said: "I don't think I would espouse this kind of action, but in this particular instance it was very effective."

Night had fallen when we got back to Camp Unity. We sat in the huge social hall and waited for the cars to come in. As the hours wore on, the radio reported admissions to every hospital for miles around, and spouses, relatives, friends were still missing. Hysteria began. One of the most affected was a prominent union official, the wife of the man who had recruited me as a bodyguard. She had good reason. This weekend was the first time she had been with her husband since the Communist Party had sent him underground in anticipation of fascism.

People made crazy and conflicting proposals. I took charge, and demanded that we wait until things became clearer. I do remember learning from a phone call that six hundred of the defense force —about one-quarter—had been trapped on the grounds by the 950 armed police and were being beaten. I know from my brother Gene, who returned to Peekskill that night from New York City, that the Communist Party quickly reoriented itself and organized their rescue. But I cannot remember whether what I did next was on my own initiative or in response to that phone call.

I asked for volunteers with cars to go back to the concert grounds to get our men out. Those who responded were not only physically courageous but also took a financial risk. These were young people who now owned their first cars. New York City working folk didn't grow up with automobiles. After the war these people, chiefly veterans, bought cars so they could take rides in the country or go to summer cottages. And not one car had gotten back from Peekskill without badly dented wheels, fenders, and side panels, never mind broken windows.

I recruited sixteen drivers plus one additional man to ride along in each car, for protection. The remaining seats were for those we were to bring home. I put myself in the lead car, because is was night and I knew those small back roads very well, having hitch-hiked and ridden them for the fifteen years since I first visited the Millsteins' place. The car, a small Austin, belonged to Bob DeCormier, Belafonte's music arranger.

As we started out the camp entry, the management thoughtfully left a barrel of plumbing handy. We each took one piece of lead pipe and stashed it under the seat. But when the leader of the hired dance band, an African-American who had not gone to Peekskill for the day, opened the door of his fine Packard to get a piece of pipe, someone spotted a rifle under his seat. I had DeCormier stop our car, went over and said: "No guns." I don't remember his words, but essentially they were that he wasn't goin' into no trap where a bunch of honky cops were armed to the teeth and he had no firearm. I must have argued with him a good five minutes, and finally said that if he wouldn't leave the gun, we wouldn't move the caravan and nobody would be able to go. He gave the gun to someone to hold for him, and came along without it.

The drive back was as scary as anything in my experience. From the radio we knew that we could be ambushed anywhere, as had happened to many others. Occasionally we'd pass a house. One after another carried the banner that had been posted all over the county against us: "Wake Up, America! Peekskill did!" "Wake up, America" was a direct translation from Hitler's slogan: "Deutschland, Erwache!" All day long we had heard yells: "Jew-kikes," "nigger-lovers," "niggers," "Go back to Russia!".

By the time we got to the concert site the cops had let the remainder of our guard force go. Most had been picked up by cars from New York. Some had been spending the weekend at one of the three Left summer camps in Dutchess and Westchester counties or at the summer home "colonies," as they were called. We picked up one guard, Louis Weinstock, a Communist house-painter and elected leader of his union. He is the man to whom Americans owe the existence of unemployment insurance more than to any other individual, save his associate Herbert Benjamin, leader of the Unemployed Councils during the Great Depression. I described Weinstock's activity in an earlier chapter.

I had never spoken to Weinstock before. The tension was over, and we chatted about family. Soon we began to talk about how people of our beliefs should deal with the situation our children faced in school, where passing exams meant writing that communism was slavery, the Soviet Union wants war, and so forth. My daughter, soon to be ten, had already come up against such propaganda, and it was to take a much more severe form for her in the next couple of years. Weinstock was a member of the National Committee of the Communist Party and, like Thompson, a Smith Act defendant. He later served time under that law for the "crime" of teaching a course on unionism at the Comunist-led Jefferson School in New York. Responding to me, he said that he told his son attending CCNY to give whatever answers they wanted, get his degree, and get out. As I had been expelled from that very institution on political grounds, and had never gotten a degree because I refused to apologize or abandon principle, I was thoroughly shocked. I know nothing of Weinstock's son's subsequent politics, but I do know that many Left parents, including courageous ones, suffered very sharp, heart-rending breaks with their children because of seeking to protect them from the very things the parents themselves had fought so staunchly against. In some cases the cause was the opposite: children, particularly teenagers, resented facing isolation and hostility from their peers because of parental involvement in things "unpatriotic." In those cases, such as ours, where parents succeeded in transmitting their values and beliefs in substantial measure to their children, this did not save them from deep and lasting psychological scars. It did keep us close and mutually supportive for a lifetime.

Because—and only because—we had held the line at Peekskill, the Establishment attacked those who had rioted against us. The *Christian Science Monitor* editorialized: "This is the Fascist pattern of violent suppression. The Ku Klux Klan pattern of lynch law..." The American Civil Liberties Union, which had expelled its one Communist national board member, Elizabeth Gurley Flynn, in 1940, and whose co-national counsel, Morris L. Ernst, had been cooperating with the FBI since 1942, felt compelled to conclude, in its investigation of the Peekskill events, the following:

"There is no evidence whatever of Communist provocation....While the demonstrations [against the concerts] were organized to protest against and express hatred of Communism, the unprovoked rioting which resulted was fostered largely by anti-Semitism, growing out of local resentment against the increasing influx of Jewish summer residents from New York....The local press bears the main responsibility for inflaming ...Peekskill residents to a mood of violence....Terrorism was general against all who advocated freedom of speech, freedom of assembly and preservation of constitutional rights....There is strong indication that the initial violence was planned and was carried out according to plan. Terrorism spread over the whole area and included threats against private individuals, against their safety, lives, property and business....The Westchester County police permitted the assault upon the Robeson supporters....Transcripts made by radio reporters at the second riot record a new and fearsome epithet, 'White niggers,' shouted at Jews seen associating with colored people."

Veterans of fascist violence in Europe drew direct parallels, like this testimony from Tim Murphy of the Bronx: "I was born and raised in Ireland. I saw the Black and Tans at their worst. Last Sunday I saw the same thing happen in Peekskill, only more vicious." A refugee from Nazi Germany testified: "I saw in Peekskill a repetition of the day in November of 1939 when I was finally driven from my home in the Rhineland town of Andernach....The howling mobs came in the evening with great piles of stones which they threw into our homes....There was the same rock-throwing with intent to kill at Peekskill as there was at Andernach. But even more striking for me was the psychopathic hatred, the hysteria of the hoodlum mob. Both acted and looked exactly the same. There was, too, the same obvious organization from bigshot officials using the backward, ignorant, bigoted sections of the population to do their dirty work....In both cases, too, the official instruments of 'law and order' stood by approvingly while the mob did its murderous work."

That is why I have used the word "fascist" to describe Peekskill. And it is why, when we defeated them—and no similar large-scale attempt was made during the four worst years of governmental McCarthyism that followed—I concluded that there would be no fascism in this country during that period of history. That conviction largely explains the tone of dominance in my testimonies before the McCarran, McCarthy, and House Un-American Activities committees. Those who thought we were doomed, including people with records of battlefield and civilian courage, were defensive.

Though I escaped without a scratch, the stress must have affected my resistance to disease. I came down with viral pneumonia the next week. It resulted in my only hospitalization in half a century. During that hospitalization in 1949, my Communist Party club sent me, as a get-well gift, A. L. Morton's *A People's History of England.* That was the first human gesture of which I had been a recipient in all the twenty-two years of my activity in the Communist movement. The person who initiated the gift, I learned, was Dr. Morris U. Schappes, formerly an English professor at CCNY. He had served a year in jail because he refused to reveal the names of the other Communists on faculty there during the flare-up of anti-Soviet hysteria in 1939, after the USSR signed a non-aggression pact with Germany. He and I were, on his initiative, the only white members of the Association for the Study of Negro Life and History in New York City at that time. Later, we were bitter political enemies because of his Jewish nationalist attitude toward the status in the Soviet Union of the people from which we both spring.

No sooner had I recovered than I found myself in the middle of a literally explosive controversy having to do with that country. The USSR tested its first nuclear bomb at the end of 1949. This shook the U.S. out of a complacent and arrogant mood of superiority that had existed for the four years since it had made the only use ever of that mass-murder weapon, in the attacks on Hiroshima and Nagasaki. Washington believed it could dictate to the world because of its A-bomb monopoly. Suddenly that monopoly was gone. The Soviet vice-minister of Foreign Affairs sought to channel the world discussion in a constructive direction by a speech to the United Nations in which he said, with respect to peaceful use of nuclear explosives: "We are razing mountains; we are irrigating deserts; we are cutting through the jungle and the tundra."

Hyperbole, obviously. But the world wanted to know whether this was so. And it was important not only in terms of whether nuclear energy truly could be used for non-military purposes, but also in terms of what became a forty-year debate over whether one side could gain nuclear arms superiority. I had discovered an article by a Soviet military engineer describing the use of directed blasts of extraordinary power unknown in Western engineering practice. He described the moving of a mountain in this way. I wrote an article on this, associating it with the statement before the UN about nuclear explosives. The *Daily Compass*, a New Deal-ish newspaper then existing in New York City, devoted its entire front page to a headline for my story: "What Russia is doing with the atom—and where" with the sub-head "SOMETHING TO MAKE OLD ATLAS GREEN WITH ENVY: *See William Mandel, p. 3.*"

The next day the Paris correspondent of the *New York Herald Tribune* reported that a single atom bomb, as then known, would raise a million cubic yards of earth, a figure beyond imagining in Western engineering. Whereupon the *Compass* gave me the front page a day later for an article in response to this assertion in which I pointed out that, nearly three years earlier, the Russians actually had moved that much earth with a single blast at a dam-construction project in Azerbaijan. In 1976, more than a quarter-century after this controversy, Mark Gayn, a nationally prominent Soviet-affairs journalist, reported the digging of a lake in Soviet Central Asia by an atomic blast in an article in the *San Francisco Chronicle*. The event occurred eleven years earlier but was only then revealed.

The day after my first article ran, the editor of the *Compass* devoted his full-column editorial to an open letter to the head of the Atomic Energy Commission, in which he enclosed a copy of my piece and asked for a public report on U.S. intentions, if any, in peaceful applications of nuclear energy. Finally, the *Compass* carried a third article by me, in which I reviewed a book, *Atomic Energy and Security*, by James Allen. The burden of my article is contained in its title, "The People Could Use the Atom." By strange coincidence, three years later, Mr. Allen and I, who had never had any personal contact, were both called before Joe McCarthy on the first day of his book-burning hearing. These articles got me a contract with the *Compass* for a series of articles on the Soviet economy, which they paid for handsomely but did not use.

When Stefansson yielded to Naval Intelligence pressure and switched me, at the end of 1949, from research and writing to technical translation, I sought some way to continue in Soviet-affairs scholarship and participate in the permanent debate over our relationship with the USSR. In 1948 I had approached the Rockefeller Foundation-funded Institute of Pacific Relations, which had commissioned me to write my first book four years earlier, suggesting that I now do a book on Soviet foreign policy in the Far East. They agreed to a much more modest undertaking: that I would compile Soviet documents and journalism in that sphere.

I finished that project at the end of 1949 and approached them again with the idea of a book. Not only did they reject that, but they published my collection in a most peculiarly shame-faced fashion, reflecting the fact that the institute was now under attack by the Far Right. They got an anti-Soviet scholar in England named Max Beloff to write an introduction, and published it. The cover and title page both read as follows: "*Soviet Source Materials on USSR Relations with East Asia, 1945-1950*, with an Introductory Survey of Soviet Far Eastern Policy Since Yalta, by Max Beloff." My name did not appear at all, not even on the table of contents, which indicated a "Compiler's Preface," with no indication of who the compiler was. That preface itself was signed not with my name, but only my initials! My name did appear in a foreword written by the Secretary-General of this institute, William L. Holland, who had engaged me to do the job.

I went down to his office, essentially banged my first on the table, and told him what I thought of the cowardice this revealed. He solved the problem with diplomatic finesse. The cover of this nearly three-hundred-page volume was of a paper that would take a rubber stamp. He had one made, reading, "Selected and compiled by William Mandel," in a typeface indistinguishable from the printed original. It was painstakingly applied, though to this day I do not know whether only the copies sent to me were so stamped!

I still had hopes that the West Coast would be more liberal. After all, I had had academic standing and a public reputation in the Bay Area just two years earlier. So I wrote the leading Sovietologist—that word didn't actually exist yet—at U.C. Berkeley, a Prof. Kerner, expressing interest in a position. He too had a diplomatic response: what they had open were research assistantships at $1,200 a year, about ten times that in today's dollars. He knew very well that with a wife and three young children, I could not accept such an offer.

But 1949 did close with an event that gave me a great deal of satisfaction. In addition to African George Padmore's quotation from my first book as authoritative support in one of his, in September I had been among those who made possible the successful Robeson concert. Now, in December 1949, I found myself fellow-panelist with the third of those three greatest Black world personalities of the day, Dr. W.E.B. DuBois, at a Congress on American-Soviet Relations. I began by turning to him and expressing the honor I felt for this chance to be in his company. He was fifty years older than I.

Subsequently our paths crossed in a variety of ways. The next year we ran for public office on the same ticket, headed by him. The year after that I had to try making a living as an interior decorator. He and author Shirley Graham had just been married, and they bought a fine old town house in Brooklyn Heights. I sold them some furnishings. While I was there installing, they asked if I would place an oil portrait of him over the mantlepiece. I did so, and he noticed that it was slightly off center, which I hadn't. Little wonder that he was functional until his death at ninety-five.

Functionality covers a multitude of activities, one of which is sex. When he married Shirley, whom I knew longer, people could not help thinking: what can a man of eighty-three do for a woman forty years younger? I wonder if their season's greeting card that year, of which I was a recipient, may have been a subtle answer to that question. It was a color photo of him on their recent visit to the West Indies. He was simply in bathing trunks, standing ankle deep in water. His arms were spread wide in an unaffected gesture of friendship. But that pose pulls up one's pectorals, of course. He had surprisingly muscular arms and legs, probably from the wood-chopping that went with being a country schoolteacher in his youth and the walking that a low income in those times required. Despite the moustache, goatee, bald head, and scholar's stoop, the photo gave the impression of a man far younger than his calendar years. Tongues stopped wagging.

In 1952 he was kind enough to mention in his book, *In Battle for Peace,* my defense of him when he was under federal indictment for heading the circulation of a peace petition . Finally, in 1962, when I, no longer a Communist, took the affirmative in a debate before an overflow audience at U.C. Berkeley against the then leader of the Christian Right over whether Communists should teach there, I used DuBois' awesome academic career as my strongest practical example. He had joined the Communist Party. By this time, we had differed very sharply in print over what I regarded as Joseph Stalin's very repressive role in his later years.

Nineteen forty-nine had been quite a year, and when it ended I badly needed a break. I went skiing for a week at Whiteface Mountain overlooking Lake Placid in the Adirondacks. Lacking a car, I went up by Greyhound bus, which did not go to Whiteface. During the long wait for the local bus, I learned of something new in American culture. The bus station had several bookracks of paperbacks, a relatively new phenomenon of the post-World War II years. I browsed through them and found a remarkable number of literary classics, good current literature, and worthwhile nonfiction. This was one of a number of things from which I learned that America's development in the 1950s was not all materialistic and not all downhill.

The 14 million Americans who had been abroad in the military during World War II had been tremendously broadened by that experience. Under the GI Bill of Rights, some millions had gone to college who would never have been able to do so before. Previously higher education had essentially been confined to the elite, plus strivers from among the poor and those ethnic groups, at that time primarily Jews, in whose culture education was one of the highest values. The veterans' travels and their postwar education had given them a taste for reading. In very many cases it was not for trash. The firm that was published my next book many years later when the blacklist withered away, established itself in the market by betting, in the postwar years, that people would want to read literary classics in the public domain, on which no royalties had to be paid. It won that bet and paperbacks took off.

Ski resorts circa 1950 bore little resemblance to those of today. True, the runs at Whiteface had been laid out by Hannes Schneider, a great Austrian name in the sport. They strongly resembled those of the present day at June Mountain, part of the Mammoth resort in the Sierra Nevada. There were no chair lifts, however. You slid uphill seated on half of what was essentially a pick-axe, while holding onto its cable support. Safety bindings didn't exist, but things had improved over when I learned to ski in Moscow in 1931. Now, instead of galoshes, you wore ankle-height ski-boots redesigned from hiking boots to have an inflexible sole. There were bindings instead of a mere toestrap. The bindings were not called bear-traps for nothing. There was no release, so a bad fall meant injury. I had only one in over 60 years of skiing, probably because all of us early-day skiers learned to fall relaxed. We certainly fell often enough.

In those days I would ski until I was utterly exhausted, six or more hours per day. I liked to show off, and would aim at a tree, skidding away in the final inches. Either I had quick reactions or I was just lucky. I quit only when a late-afternoon fall would result in a severe abdominal fatigue cramp. We slept in unisex dormitory barracks at the top of the mountain, heated by a huge pot-bellied stove. I was scared to death of fire, but nothing happened.

It exhausts me just to look at the list of things I did in 1950. I've never lacked energy, but that year was almost beyond belief. Making a good living at home from the steady stream of translations for Stefansson was easy. We were able to put money away for the first time in our lives. I made a little money through low-fee lectures for liberal and Left forums and organizations, as well as from selling my 1946 book, and also sold a few articles to obscure papers and magazines. I was fast enough, at that wordage-rate translating, to be able to schedule just about anything else I wanted to do.

Determined to go on expanding knowledge of the Soviet Union, I organized a six-week cross-country tour for myself through contacts I had from pre-cold war years. Instead of hotel housing, I was put up by like-minded people, which is nicer anyhow. In San Francisco I was still respectable enough to be invited to address the Commonwealth Club's International Relations Section, as I had two years earlier. I stayed at the home of a lawyer living on Washington Street just uphill from Powell. His apartment had a balcony. After putting my bags in the closet, I walked down to Market Street, bought myself a fresh whole cracked crab, with it a loaf of French bread and a bottle of Dos Equis, and then went back to the balcony and enjoyed, with the cable cars clanging beneath me and an unobstructed view across the bay—no Trans-America pyramid, no Embarcadero Center, no Holiday Inn, which have since destroyed that panorama.

Across the bay something brand new had emerged: the first radio station financed by its listeners, KPFA. It was in its first year of operation and invited me for an interview. My Communist friends said not to participate because there were—they claimed—Trotskyists associated with the station. I asked them what kind of idiots they were. The entire thrust of the past four years had been to isolate people of our views from the public. In the '40s I had guested on major network radio in this country and in Canada. Since my forced return to New York, I had been on the air only four times in two years, one appearance being on that brand-new medium, television. All were local shows.

It happens that that first appearance on KPFA—eight years were to pass before I appeared on it again to start my show that lasted half a life-time—was the day after the Soviet Union and China signed a twenty-year treaty of alliance. An amusing description of that interview appears in Matthew Lasar's *Pacifica Radio: The Rise of an Alternative Network*. A quarter century later I thought I'd give KPFA listeners a chance to laugh at my naivete by playing that broadcast in connection with a fund-raising marathon. I hadn't listened to it in the interval. It stood up amazingly well as serious listening. I had not foreseen the subsequent split between Mao and Stalin, but my forecast of what the impact of that alliance would mean to the world as long as it lasted—and it lasted ten years—was remarkably accurate.

On that exhausting tour in 1950, I would lecture for an hour on some theme, answer questions for an hour, and take an hour's break before the next one. During the break I refused to speak to anyone, but would go for a brisk walk. That was fine in San Francisco and Los Angeles, but this was mid-winter. The walks in Salt Lake City, Denver, St. Louis, Minneapolis, Chicago, Ann Arbor, and at the University of Iowa were kind of nippy. People smoked a lot in those years —I never have—and the fresh air was essential.

I remember one such seminar at a house on the beach in Ventura, California. That night we went to a bar with a dance floor, and I learned of another way in which high culture was reaching the people. One of the records in the juke box was the saber dance from the Soviet Armenian composer Khachaturian's ballet, "Gayane." Frothy though it may be, it was light-years ahead of what juke boxes had provided in earlier times. My own culture was broadened that night in a different way. I learned for the first time what a margarita is. I had a sweet tooth. The fact that this was supposed to be a woman's drink never bothered me. Sometimes one's convictions—in this case, simply that women are people too—can make life more pleasant. And I danced my butt off. It was a marvelous way to unwind after eight hours of lecturing and answering questions.

Eighty people attended my seminar in Los Angeles, one of them a retired general, Holdridge by name. The Journalism Department at the University of Utah invited me to address its students. At the University of Colorado the head of the Philosophy Department, after hearing me at a public meeting, asked me to address a score of faculty members and

advanced students, of diverse political views, about intellectual controversy in the Soviet Union. The oldest African-American paper on the
West Coast was the *California Eagle*, published in Los Angeles. After
hearing me speak, its editor, Mrs. Charlotta Bass, who was to be the
Progressive Party's vice-presidential candidate two years later on a ticket headed by Vincent Hallinan, requested permission to serialize my
book, *A Guide to the Soviet Union.* Mrs. Bass was particularly interested
in urban problems, and also ran articles of mine on Soviet cities. On
June 1, 1950, she wrote an editorial on the closing of a public library in
the Los Angeles ghetto and the likelihood that the 28th St. YMCA would
have to be closed. On which she commented:

"This in America where billions are being spent on WAR, in keeping
alive a cold war that long ago would have frozen to death had it not had
a constant stream of dollars...pumped into its veins! One cannot help
but contrast this tragic condition in Los Angeles with the accounts of
what is happening in the cities of the Soviet Union, as described by
William Mandel and which are being published each week in the
California Eagle....Just this week in the story of the Uzbek Socialist
Republic...with a population of a trifle more than 6,000,000, we have:
'There are 1,596 public libraries'....In Los Angeles County, with a population of about 4,250,000, there are less than 100.

"Whose fault is it if we make these comparisons? How are we going
to prevent those terrible Communistic thoughts from creeping into our
minds, when we have the figures right before us?"

A pleasant surprise awaited me on my return to New York. I had met
Prof. George Renner, head of the Geography Department at Teachers'
College, Columbia University, when he was at Stanford for a period during my year at the Hoover Institution. He had arranged for me to be
inducted into the national professional geographical fraternity, Gamma
Theta Upsilon, on the basis of my work on the Soviet Arctic. Although
acceptance was certain beforehand, each candidate was required to
undergo a friendly oral quiz. I flunked mine, because I was asked to
identify the place with a name descriptive of my politics, but could not
think of any. The desired answer was the city of Liberal, Kansas. I have
no apology to make. "Liberal" was not my definition of where I stood.

There was a tragic aftermath to my acquaintance with Renner. He
was Geography Editor for Thomas Y. Crowell, a major textbook publisher. Late in 1955 he arranged for me to write a geography of the
Soviet Union. Renner said that it would have to carry his name as co-
author because mine carried no weight among geographers although he
knew that I was the person to write that book. I agreed without hesitation. That would have broken what was by then a ten-year blacklisting
of any possible volume carrying my name. However, I wanted to make

sure that nothing in that book would violate my beliefs, since he had editorial powers, and I wrote him to that effect. In response he poured out his soul to me in a letter in which he said that his mildly liberal front was a fraud necessitated by the academic climate of the day, and that his views of the Soviet Union did not differ from mine. He mailed the letter, had a heart attack, his first, and died. Thus he joined movie star John Garfield, stage actor J. Edward Bromberg, journalist George Marion—a personal friend—and others who died immediately or shortly after they had torn from themselves confessions of faith in this time of great stress, or had their careers destroyed by the witch hunt. There were also several suicides.

CHAPTER 14

The Pits

In February 1950 Senator Joe McCarthy, Republican of Wisconsin, burst onto the national scene with a speech claiming that he literally held in his hand a list of 205 Communists employed by the State Department. Eventually it proved to be totally phony. That made no difference at the time, because it brought the witch-hunt launched by the Democratic Truman administration to white heat. In that year's midterm election, conducted amidst the panicky hysteria over the Korean War, which had just begun, I ran as a peace candidate for Congress. This was at the request of a well-established third party in New York with significant backing by organized labor. Each major party tried to outdo the other in Russia-baiting and, as a corollary, domestic Red-baiting. That resulted in a rash of loyalty oath requirements passed by state legislatures and local governments. At the Berkeley campus of the University of California, for example, a majority of the faculty took such oaths as an insult. Most of them ultimately gave way, and twenty-six of the refuseniks were ordered dismissed while thirty-seven resigned. Forty-seven professors from other universities protested by rejecting invitations to teach at Berkeley. Forty courses had to be dropped. Not one faculty member in a total of four thousand was found to be a Communist.

My own career at the time offered almost a mathematical measure of the change in atmosphere. Having signed four contracts to write books, all with cash advances, in four years during and right after World War II, no publisher would touch me for the fifteen years starting in 1946. After my stint by invitation at Stanford's Hoover Institution, twenty-two years were to elapse before another university would give me paid employment. Having entered journalism at the top, with national distribution of my articles, I was out of salaried journalism forever. Likewise with salaried research, at which I had ten years experience and a formidable reputation.

This was totally a consequence of the national atmosphere and my opinions. I have never been called before a grand jury or a court as a witness, never indicted for a crime. Even the witch-hunt committees had not yet gotten around to me. Yet my professionally-managed lecture appearances dropped from forty-two in 1946, enough to provide a living even were this my only source of income, to three in 1950.

People like me were to be un-personed. I had no intention of yielding and organized the lecture tour previously described. It provided no net income, but I sold five hundred copies of my most recent book, although it cost five dollars, equivalent to at least $40 today. What I had to say was reported in the the newspapers of Chicago, Minneapolis, Salt Lake City, San Francisco. The commercial electronic media would no longer interview me.

At Roosevelt College in Chicago a member of the Board of Trustees financed my appearance, and made sure that two deans and many faculty attended. One professor, who had had me address his students, subsequently wrote me a courteous letter saying that he was "personally convinced that the Stalinist regime will result in the total destruction of Russia." Forty years later, with Stalin long gone, it pretty nearly did, but in his lifetime it flourished. History is not simple. Another, Abba Lerner, who had some national prominence, forgot his academic cool in a letter to the student newspaper in which he described my talk as "a disgraceful piece of Soviet propaganda." He continued in language that demonstrated very neatly the kind of objectivity he brought to his listening:

"Soon after I got into the room I saw the director of the Council of American Soviet Friendship. I began to suspect some communist propaganda....The suspicion was deepened when I saw a pile of *Soviet Russia Today* on sale."

Back home in April, the mail brought a copy of the last article of mine any learned journal would print for the next fifteen years. Appearing in *Arctic*, it was titled: "Some Notes on the Soviet Arctic During the Past Decade." The North American Newspaper Alliance service had someone rewrite it as a feature story, published as nearly a full column in the *New York Times*. My name was unmentionable.

I had never harbored illusions that academe or the Establishment press would uphold academic freedom or civil liberties or a rational foreign policy if that were against the desires of those who paid their salaries or bought their advertising space. My hopes continued to rest upon bringing what I regarded as truth to working people, for as a Marxist I regarded them as the engines of social change. So I went back to Chicago in May for a month of speaking to people in organized labor. Local people organized this of course. It had a very practical significance. The official leaders of the American labor movement at this time took the position that expression of the belief that we could have peace, friendship and understanding with the Soviet Union identified one as a traitor to the United States. This was the position of President Truman.

Those leaders were in the process of expelling from their ranks a dozen national unions with a combined membership of a million, whose officers and whose convention resolutions on foreign policy regarded peaceful coexistence as desirable and possible. Under all the verbiage, the leaders of the American Federation of Labor and of the Congress of Industrial Organizations, then separate organizations, were saying to working people: "If you believe us, that we have to get ready to fight and defeat Russia and support candidates for public office who take that position, there will be large military appropriations and you will have jobs. If you disagree with us, and vote the other way, the military budget will decline, and you'll be back where you were ten years ago in the Great Depression." My side argued that there were plenty of things the country needed built and produced at home, and that government appropriations for those purposes would create jobs just as well, if not better.

Where the situation in a given union did not permit a full speech by me followed by a question period, I went along with whatever could be managed: fifteen or twenty minutes at a regular meeting of a local, its executive board, or of the shop stewards. I appeared as invited guest at unions including the Packinghouse Workers, the Great Lakes division of the International Longshoremen's and Warehousemen's Union, the United Electrical Workers, and the Mine, Mill and Smelter Workers. The very leftist Furriers' Union was afraid to touch the issue, because it was facing difficulties due to the Supreme Court's rulings with respect to the Taft-Hartley Law, which forbade certification of a union as representative of workers in a place of employment unless every officer of the union files an affidavit that he or she is not a Communist. Political freedom, anyone?

The meeting that left me with the most pleasant memory was one of thirty-five shop stewards of the Mine, Mill and Smelter Workers. After working in hot die-casting shops all day, they travelled from all over Chicago—a sprawling city—listened to a forty-minute presentation on a subject other than what unionists call pork chops (although I certainly made every effort to demonstrate the connection), and then asked every conceivable question for another hour and twenty minutes. I had quoted from my book. Two workers came up afterward and asked where they could buy it. I called out that it was available for sale, and five people bought it, although one could go to half a dozen movies for the price in that day. That, and the fact that not one of these exhausted blue-collar people dozed off in the course of the evening, left a very warm feeling.

Some people at these meetings represented the average level of consciousness of that day. At a regular local meeting of the Packinghouse Workers, I was asked whether women were nationalized (public property) in the Soviet Union. I also addressed workers in unions under hard-line anti-Soviet leadership, where access to any official gathering was denied. Despite this, I spoke to steel workers in Gary and South Chicago, auto workers in South Bend and Chicago, and machinists and office workers in Chicago. These meetings were in private homes, taverns, or the halls of ethnic fraternal societies.

That letter by Prof. Abba Lerner after my February visit resulted in a formal debate between us at Roosevelt College in May. The dean of students presided, and the attendance was the largest at any voluntary gathering that semester. The applause at this essentially African-Americn, inner-city campus favored me by a wide margin. A Black student set up a meeting in his home to discuss the ethnic situation in the Soviet Union. I shared the platform with Moscow-raised Charles Burroughs, brother of my close friend in New York, Neal. Charles' wife, Dr. Margaret Burroughs, founder of Chicago's DuSable Museum of Afro-American History, read poetry at a meeting where I spoke on Soviet culture. Artists and dancers were among the hundred people attending. Then there was a talk on Soviet medicine before a dozen people in that field, one on law to a score of attorneys including a state legislator, and another on women before a dozen Black and Jewish middle-class and workingclass women in Gary.

At this time a new, very real source of hysteria came into being. McCarthy's rantings and the government's loyalty oaths, jailings of reluctant witnesses before the House Un-American Activities Committee for contempt of Congress, and the on-going trials of Communist Party leaders had already begun. The Alger Hiss case for perjury in connection with alleged espionage and direct spying-for-the-Soviets cases also colored the national political consciousness. Mr. Hiss, who had been a top-level State Department official, was still trying to clear his name when he died in 1996. The people had been convinced that Moscow could never have developed the atom bomb unless somebody gave or sold them some secret. Space stations, anyone?

At this time Tanya and I and the children had just moved to a new apartment for the first time in seven years, a big one with six rooms, meaning that I had a real study of my own. It cost $72 a month, less than ten percent of the very good money I was earning at free-lance translation. A three-block walk west brought one to a magnificent overlook above the mile-wide Hudson River with the sheer Palisades on the New Jersey side and the George Washingon Bridge another twenty-minute walk upstream. A stroll the same distance east led to a similar overlook above Harlem and the Harlem River a mile away. Those three blocks of brownstone houses and apartment buildings constituted what African-Americans called Sugar Hill, where Blacks who had good steady jobs and the few who had made money lived. We were on the Mason-Dixon Line.

Everything west was white; and everything east was Black. Just two blocks north of us was Audubon Ballroom, where Malcolm X was to be assassinated many years later.

The Korean War jolted us out of the relaxing bustle of settling in to a new apartment and helping our children, then ten, six and four, adjust to a new neighborhood. Truman clearly implied that this military conflict was the Russian aggression he had been arming against. In fact, Moscow had withdrawn its troops from North Korea two years earlier, never to return. Some Soviet fliers did secretly participate in the war, entirely in defensive operations over North Korean territory, so their presence could not be detected if they were downed. I myself learned of this only thirty years later, when I saw in a Moscow home a photograph of a family member lost in that war. Our forces had not—and have never—left South Korea.

To make the atmosphere worse, North Korea almost won the war in the first six weeks, destroying the South Korean Army and driving the Americans into a small corner around Pusan. President Truman's Secretary of the Navy, Mathews by name, actually called for war on the USSR and found a public-relations phrase to describe that: "We would become the first aggressors for peace." It got the front page of the *New York Times*, of course.

Gen. MacArthur then counter-attacked with fresh U.S. troops from Japan, with great success. So the panic of an unprecedented near-defeat was followed by the hysteria of what looked like quick success. Nearly thirty-five thousand Americans were dead before the fighting ended in a stalemate three years later.

On July 20th, four weeks after hostilities began, the American Labor Party called a street-corner meeting about the war at a very popular corner for such things, 181st at Broadway, and invited me to speak. That party had been founded fourteen years earlier by the city's major trade unions to provide a line on which workers could vote for Franklin Roosevelt without casting a ballot for either of the bosses' parties, as Republicans and Democrats were both widely designated in labor circles in the depression years. The neighborhood where the meeting was held was a focus of old-line Irish Catholicism, including the kind of overt anti-Semitism expressed in a then very recent incident in which the beard of an old-country Jew trapped in the subway station at that corner was plucked out.

Our meeting was severely heckled, reaching the very edge of violence. As I stood on the ladder-like speakers' stand, a middle-aged Irishwoman, very poor in appearance, grasped my trouser cuff and tried to pull me down. Did she have a son in the army whom she thought I was stabbing in the back? I knew that police are accustomed to taking orders. I put on a voice of command, ordered them to protect a meeting being held with a proper permit and, in the same voice, instructed one of my supporters to go to the nearby precinct station and get the commander. The ploy worked. They restored order. I even saw one cop slap his club on the back pocket of a disorderly drunk, breaking the bottle within.

However, Police Inspector McVeigh, in charge of the area, used this incident as excuse for an edict during the election campaign that the Korean War was not a permissible subject for discussion, and that if street speakers talked about it, the meetings would be dispersed. That kind of arbitrary violation of the First Amendment was characteristic of the times. Trying to fight it in the courts of that day would have been preposterous. All the defense attorneys in the trial of national Communist Party leaders were ordered to jail by the judge for contempt of court because they insisted on their clients' legal rights. One of those lawyers, African-American George Crockett, later served as a judge in Detroit and many years as member of Congress from Michigan until voluntary retirement.

Shortly afterward I spoke at another street meeting, in the Bronx. Italian youths threw a barrage of tomatoes and rotten fruit at us, to the point at which we decided we'd better pack up our stand and retreat to our headquarters, a couple of blocks away and fortunately up a steep and narrow flight of stairs. The hostile crowd outside worked itself into a frenzy. Things might have gotten worse if not for the fact that two courageous men could defend those stairs. They were only wide enough for two attackers to climb at a time. It took six police squad cars to get past the mob and rescue us.

I had not been a community activist, but the American Labor Party asked me to be its candidate for Congress against liberal Republican Jacob Javits, subsequently long-term U.S. Senator. I probably was chosen to run because foreign affairs was regarded as the day's chief issue, I was a good speaker, and it was known that I kept my cool in tight situations. My reason for accepting the nomination was essentially identical to that given by Dr. W.E.B. DuBois, in his book, *In Battle for Peace,* for agreeing to head the ticket as candidate for U. S. Senator:

"...this campaign would afford a chance for me to speak for peace which could be voiced in no other way....Because of my support of the Progressive Party in 1948, my acceptance of an honorary and unpaid office with Paul Robeson in the Council on African Affairs, and my activity in Peace Congresses in New York, Paris and Moscow, I found myself increasingly proscribed in pulpit, school and platform. My opportunity to write for publication was becoming narrower and narrower, even in the Negro press. I wondered if a series of plain talks in a political campaign would not be my last and only chance to tell the truth as I saw it."

He was eighty-two. Another line of DuBois' is also pertinent to me: "I went into the campaign for Senator knowing well from the first that I did not have the ghost of a chance for election, and that my efforts would bring me ridicule at best and jail at worst."

Perhaps it is worth recalling that his stature had been such that he had been a special U.S. Minister Plenipotentiary to Liberia in 1923, when according diplomatic status to any other African-American was inconceivable.

He described the situation in which we were running in a pithy sentence of his set speech: "The most sinister evil of this day," he said, " is the widespread conviction that war is inevitable and that there is no time left for discussion." He was referring to war with the Soviet Union. There was one final respect in which his description of his campaign corresponded exactly to mine. DuBois wrote: "[Presidential candidate] Dewey could afford to spend $35,000 for one day on radio; when friends of mine the nation over sent $600 to further my campaign, it represented more honesty and guts than all the millions spent on Lehman and Hanley," his major party opponents.

Before the campaign was over Dr. DuBois was indicted by the federal government for failure to register as a foreign agent because he headed the campaign in the United States for signatures to the Stockholm Pledge. It read: "We consider that the first government henceforth to use the atomic weapon against any country whatsoever will be committing a crime against humanity and should be treated as a war criminal."

Washington's opposition to that petition was the frankest possible admission that its strategy was first strike. In that fear-filled year of 1950, the Stockholm Pledge nonetheless gained 2.5 million signatures. World-wide it obtained half a billion signatures, as well as x-marks and thumbprints of the illiterate to whom it was read, on all five continents. Nothing in world history, before or since, has won the individual support of that many human beings. Thirty years later its principles were adopted by overwhelming vote of the UN General Assembly. Yet Dr. DuBois was tried in federal court for advocating this.

My campaign was even more poverty-stricken than his. We had some mimeographed leaflets and a number of street meetings, at which I beat Inspector McVeigh's edict by reading aloud the *New York Times'* reports of isolationist Republican Senator Taft's speeches on the Korean War in that body. I also sought to help constituents with their problems, such as writing the appropriate authorities on behalf of a nurse who had practiced for over twenty years, but who was denied re-registration under a new law requiring an exam in general school knowledge. I asked how many physicians twenty years out of college would be able to pass exams in high-school algebra, history or geography.

The courageous sound man who set up the amplifiers for my street meetings was Saul Sherman, member of a poverty-stricken Jewish immigrant family. He lived with his mother and two siblings in a one-bedroom apartment. Saul later became an electrical engineer and moved to Berkeley. I had the unhappy honor of speaking at his very well-attended memorial service when he was killed in an industrial accident in the 1970s.

The absence of money for my campaign was due not only to fear but also because whatever money was available to people of our views was going into the bottomless pit of court costs and publicity in the endless political cases the government was then prosecuting. I had only one piece of printed literature. It was in the form of an open letter by a then popular writer, Earl Conrad. It said of me:

"Mr. Mandel fights for his neighbors. He led a successful rent strike in his apartment house. Mr. Mandel stands with the most oppressed. He helped maintain a day nursery in public school so that Negro mothers can earn a livelihood for their families. Mr. Mandel fights for civil liberties. He has filed suit in Federal Court for an injunction against the McCarran Act. Mr. Mandel is incorruptible. In the past 17 years, sticking to his principles cost him his college education (1933), his top-flight newspaper job as United Press Expert on Russia (1945), his contract with the country's leading lecture agency (1947), and his position with a famous university (1948). No one can buy off such a man."

The best campaign leaflet drafted was never issued. I came home from a hard day's campaigning one evening to find the following clearly-lettered and only slightly-misspelled sheet written by my eleven-year-old daughter, apparently helped by my six-year-old older son, for it read:

"The American Labor party is sponsering someone for Congress. this person is Mr. William Mandel. He will try to make the U.S. better than it is. He has written two books. He will try to bring peace to the U.S. He will try to make it so that when your *children* grow up they will not have to go to fight at war.

If You Want

a

good person for congres

Vote for

William Mandel

Made by

Phyllis and Robert

MANDEL"

I keep a xerox of that permanently on my study wall. The original is put away where the light cannot fade it.

Phyllis took her principles to school. She suffered for them very severely as a thirteen-year-old because she refused to write accepted answers proving the Soviet Union an the evil empire. Instead, she cited the opportunities it gave women and minorities and the absence of unemployment. On another occasion she refused to hide under a desk in a drill for supposed protection against atom bombs. The principal came into class to dress this child down before all her peers. Tanya went to school and gave the principal a dose of his own medicine. I would have loved to have been there.

I challenged Javits to debate me on streetcorners. As a smart politician, he declined. Why build up an opponent lacking the means to reach the entire electorate on his own? The previous year he and I had debated each other, once on radio and once on TV. When I came home from one of the debates, Tanya said, "Bill, you lost that one." I had been a gentleman and scholar while the politician-lawyer Javits had hogged the mike. That experience taught me not to be polite in that regard.

We did have indoor debates during the election campaign, one sponsored by the Jewish War Veterans and another by the League of Women Voters. After the election there were those who said: "Javits won the election but Mandel won the debates."

The one thing this campaign did accomplish was to uphold civil liberties. The local American Legion and Veterans of Foreign Wars informed the police officer in charge of issuing permits for street meetings that they objected to any that might be held by the American Labor Party. This cop told my campaign manager that if these people arrived— and he was sure they would—and if they yelled at all, our meeting would be stopped and no further permits would be granted! I wrote a letter to *The Daily Compass*, which gave it a fine two-column head: "Candidate for Congress May Face Speech Ban!" In it I asked readers to write the police precinct captain.

We were able to hold the meeting—a test case of this issue. I proposed to our congressional district committee that we climax our campaign not with a rally but a Paul Robeson concert: "a Robeson concert...under present conditions...represents our reply to the attempt to gag the magnificent voice of one of the world's greatest vocal artists due to his political beliefs (cancellation of commercial concerts and refusal of passport), barring him from earning a livelihood abroad," I wrote our committee. "With serious Negro artists finding it so difficult to obtain bookings in any case, defense of the right of the greatest of them to pursue his art, by presenting him with a concert platform, is an act of struggle for Negro rights, and will be received as such. In that connection, I propose that we do not ask

Mr. Robeson to sing gratis, as at a political rally, but request him to set a fee commensurate with the size of the hall [1,500 capacity], the prices we believe we can charge, and our desire to make some money for the A.L.P. out of the affair."

The manager of Audubon Ballroom, the hall we rented, was so worried about what might happen to his property in light of the incidents at Peekskill the previous year that he called the downtown headquarters of the hostile veterans' organizations. They claimed they would not interfere but said they could not be responsible for the actions of individuals. The manager of the ballroom increased our rent for the evening by $200 (over $1,500 in today's money) and paid it as graft to the mayor for police protection. He provided 150 cops, plainclothed and uniformed. A dozen mounted police were kept out of sight behind the building to break up any possible mobs . In view of police behavior both at Peekskill and earlier in my campaign, I didn't trust them at all, and used labor connections to obtain my own defense force of dozens of union seamen and furriers.

It would take a Charlie Chaplin to do justice to that concert, because it was a combination of high comedy and pathos. I dashed from one side of the hall to the other, telling my workingmen protectors that the burly men in business suits were not attackers but city detectives, and then going to the latter to tell them that the grim men in dungarees were my boys.

My father insisted many years later that when I introduced Robeson I broke down and cried. I don't remember that but have no reason to doubt it. My emotions lie close to the surface, although I am capable of controlling and channeling them completely when necessary. I would most certainly not cry when up against the witch-hunt committees. After the concert—the hall was packed to capacity—Paul (everyone called him by his first name) stuck our his hand, smiled that overwhelming smile, and said: "Thanks, Bill." That was one of the high points of my life. One of the pictures on my study wall is a photograph of him we sold as a souvenir of that concert. The situation in the country was such that he had only two other performances that entire year, one in the church of which his brother was pastor, the other in that extraordinary little city in California, Berkeley, which lived by principles of civil liberties long before the 60s.

On election night I committed a faux pas. I had, for the first time, received an invitation from the Soviet Embassy in Washington to attend a reception on the anniversary of the Revolution, which had taken place on November 7, 1917. In 1950 that coincided with our election day. Having, in traditional American style, campaigned to exhaustion—I would come home, lie down on the floor in the first room inside our door, and fall asleep—I wanted to unwind. I also felt it was important to attend that Embassy event because it was being boycotted by all high administration officials as part of the Cold War. So I went down. The next day my most loyal campaign worker, a printing trades unionist, phoned in a fury. How could I dare abandon my headquarters during election returns? I replied that I was certain I would lose, so what was the point? He replied: "You never know!" I was amazed. This was a very sober, mature individual. Hope springs eternal.

I ran against Javits again two years later, on the issue of ending the war in Korea, and just as predictably lost again. Our names appeared together only once in subsequent years. In 1967 my publisher sent me a copy of a bonehead English text for college freshmen, titled *Improving College Reading,* brought out by another publishing house. It consisted of some forty excerpts of writings on everything under the sun, with vocabulary and texts. One was several pages from the chapter on Soviet women in my book, *Russia Re-examined.* Another was from a book by Javits. Other selections were from J. Edgar Hoover, writing on Joseph Stalin, and from people who could no longer protect themselves against bad company, like Mark Twain. American eclecticism in the guise of liberal education.

A World Peace Congress was held in Warsaw in November 1950. I was told that I would be included in a tour of the Soviet Union would follow. I had not been there for nearly twenty years, and the USSR had not yet re-opened its doors, subsequent to World War II, to foreign travelers. Yet I decided not to take advantage of this opportunity. I knew by now that no one there would talk freely with a foreigner about developments that disturbed me, which I had listed to Neal Burroughs five years earlier. I had not yet realized that Soviet citizens did not dare any longer to discuss them freely with each other. I did not want to face being lied to. At that point I still saw such lies as aberrations, not as necessities to maintain the Communist monopoly.

My chief concern at the close of 1950 was much more mundane. The funding for the translation project had run out, and I had to find a way to make a living. It was not until Sputnik six years later that the country was jolted into recognition of need for knowledge of everything and anything happening in the Soviet Union, creating an insatiable market for translations.

I sought employment in a fury of correspondence. I wrote detailed, thoroughly-thought-out projects for a broad spectrum of books. To Angus Cameron, the famous editor at Little, Brown & Co. who had supported the Wallace campaign, I proposed one titled *What Russia Wants in Asia*, to rest upon my collection of documentary material for the Institute of Pacific Relations. To the Conservation Foundation I suggested a study of conservation efforts in the Soviet Union. I had previously provided its head, Fairfield Osborn, the information for a chapter on the environmental situation in the USSR for his book of 1948, *Our Plundered Planet*. My later writings on that subject in the 1970s had deeper roots than some might have guessed. I wrote the head of the Hoover Institution in the desperate hope that, despite the rise of McCarthyism, something might again be available there. I also wrote Holland Roberts of the leftist American Russian Institute in San Francisco, re-opening a previous invitation from them to become its executive director, but they could not guarantee my salary any more than before.

We did have some money in the bank. So when, at the end of January 1951, the Communist Party asked me to join a mass pilgrimage to Richmond, Virginia, to try to stop the executions of seven Blacks for an alleged gang rape of a white woman, I agreed. This was known as the Martinsville Case. As in previous situations in which probable physical danger was evident, I went because I could not find an excuse for not doing so to myself or those who approached me. Absolute apartheid, Jim Crow as it was called, still existed in the American South, and we would have to violate it simply to conduct our protest.

Open, frank Jim Crow was not confined to the South, where it was law. People from Chicago, Detroit, Boston, and New York came in chartered buses, and by sheer numbers were able to command human treatment until reaching Washington, D.C. But a carload of five from Denver had an experience more typical of a racially mixed group in those years. They had driven three days and nights over frozen roads in a convertible with a torn top, and had lived on candy bars because none would eat where any were barred. One of them, a white woman of seventy-three, had fallen and broken her hip as she stalked in rage from a restaurant in Kansas City that had refused service to the group. She insisted that the others leave her in a hospital and go on. An African-American clergyman in that group, Rev. McNeil by name, had done most of the driving and his right foot had been frozen so badly by the air coming up around the pedal that for a while he feared gangrene.

The Greyhound bus station in the nation's capital was totally segregated. We did not try to integrate it because our purpose was to get to Richmond and not be diverted by possible arrests en route. When we left Washington for Richmond, I realized that I, at thirty-three, was older than all but a handful on that bus. I knew that I was cool in crises and so, remembering the stoning of buses and police behavior at Peekskill, I very reluctantly hauled myself out of my seat and up alongside the driver to deal with whatever came. When I sighted Richmond police squad cars coming toward us on the outskirts of that city, I thought: "Here goes!" But nothing happened. When we disembarked at the bus station and there was no mob awaiting us, I flashed back on the young white war veteran students I had addressed at the University of Mississippi four years earlier and my conclusion that some of them wanted a new South.

Our headquarters in Richmond was to be the Negro YMCA, which violated Jim Crow by the mere fact of accepting us. None of the well-established Black churches in this, the former capital of the Confederacy, would have anything to do with us at the outset, though the [Black] National Baptist Convention of twenty-three thousand churches and 4 million members opposed the death sentences in this case of alleged rape. They were NAACP legalists, and the NAACP at that time had not come around to understanding the need for mass action to pressure the courts. When the civil rights movement of the '60s arose a decade later, this caused young people to reject the term "Negro" as a self-designation, because they associated it with those who could not abandon the caution learned from decades of lynchings.

Our delegation had been organized by the Civil Rights Congress (CRC), which believed in mass action, as did the movement led by Martin Luther King later in the decade. Opposition to the death sentences was also voiced by six national labor unions, plus numerous huge locals of the auto and steel unions. Half of the 517 members of the delegation were from unions, and 35 were official representatives of churches and ministers' associations of good-sized cities. There were 23 from Virginia and 40 from North Carolina.

William L. Patterson, a Communist and head of the CRC, directed the Richmond action from New York. This Black man's deputy in charge was Aubrey Grossman of San Francisco, a lawyer and one-time UCLA football star, Jewish.

The defendants had granted the NAACP the power to conduct their legal defense. It refused to touch the issue of guilt and therefore whether the case was intimidation of African-Americans as a whole. It confined itself to the issue of equal justice: that Blacks should not die for a crime no white had ever suffered death for. The pilgrimage's intent was simply to have a mass of people fill the seats in federal court when it heard this issue. Since it was a federal court, Jim Crow did not apply. Our mass walk to and from the court was phenomenal because many of us, particularly women, were arm in arm, Black and white.

The authorities filled every second seat with newly-sworn deputies. This actually made our presence seem larger, because the majority of us could not get seats, and so we spilled out into the halls and the streets, maintaining perfect decorum. There was no chanting, no picket signs. The court turned the defense argument down, and the men were headed for death.

The YMCA had no auditorium big enough to hold the people who had converged from all over the country, but a minister newly arrived in Richmond from the deep South had a church large enough to accomodate us. He allowed us to meet there. Our integrated crowd was sensational in itself, and the Black press carried pictures of the meeting nationwide. We discussed what to do. Most of us had to return home immediately to hold our jobs, but we agreed that those who didn't have to should remain and fight the case down to the wire, while those going home would organize a barrage of telegrams and phone calls, and try to break into their local press and radio. Despite not having been in bed for days, they stopped in Washington on the way back and picketed the White House, demanding that the seven men not be killed.

On that day, January 31, 1951, the United States government granted clemency to twenty-one Nazi war criminals who had been sentenced to death. They included six former SS men convicted of shooting 142 unarmed American prisoners of war at Malmedy, Belgium, during the Battle of the Bulge. One of those whose life was spared had been the commander of that SS unit. The U.S. needed Germany as an ally in the envisaged war with the Soviet Union. The American most active in the successful demand for clemency was Senator Joe McCarthy. I spent that day commuting between the front of the White House in Washington and the State House in Richmond, participating in picket lines and a prayer vigil in a driving sleet storm and twenty-degree weather.

Three dozen people remained in Richmond for the week, including me. Another dozen were willing to, but there was no money to feed them, never mind pay their fares back home other than as passengers on the chartered buses that had brought most of them. We could only afford to rent three rooms with three beds each in the Black hotel and the YMCA, enough to accomodate one fourth of those who stayed, so we slept in hot-bed shifts. In fact we were so busy that the beds were not always occupied.The days that followed were among the most thrilling of my life for the confirmation they provided of my conviction that the most downtrodden have nobility and courage when given a sense of support, and that there was more decency than racism in the plain white people of the South when compelled to confront their consciences.

The local defense committee was headed by a youthful African-American half-crippled by arthritis, James Smith, whose livelihood depended upon his job as a delivery "boy" for a pharmacy, white of course. Another member was a stupendous Black woman—in spirit, energy, smarts—Mrs. Senora Lawson, the middle-aged wife of a railway worker. Most symbolically, she had been born literally in the swamps when, in 1898, the Ku Klux Klan wiped out the elected populist inter-racial government of Wilmington, North Carolina. She knew that story by heart from family tradition and later related it to me in full detail. With that background, cooperation with like-minded whites was entirely conceivable. She had actually gotten a very substantial vote in a run for the state legislature the previous year. Had she won, she would have been the first African-American in state government in the modern South.

Non-Blacks on the local committee included a stunning redhead. This twenty-six-year-old mother of three was an Appalachian white and the wife of a carpenter. There was also a couple who looked like swarthy whites but were Lumbee Indians, a physically assimilated but ethnically self-aware group. They had a tiny farm, owned a small truck, and did odd jobs. There was also a Jewish couple, Communists. Two white medical students, brothers, with an aristocratic name, were most active.

We decided to continue the prayer vigil round-the-clock on the lawn of the State House. A more symbolic action could hardly be imagined, for the building had been designed by Thomas Jefferson, and the lawn was studded with statues of generals who had fought for the maintenance of slavery, in the Civil War, and lost. The police limited us to four people at a time. That worried us greatly, because half a dozen Klansmen could have hurt us badly. We didn't know whether to be glad or sad that no police were assigned to the vigil.

We conducted this, too, in accordance with principle. The four always consisted of a Black woman, a white woman, a Black man and a white man. That got us sustained and nasty heckling, but no violence. We huddled around an oil-can fire beneath what we later christened the Martinsville Tree, for the town where the alleged crime was supposed to have occurred and which gave the case its name. The temperature dropped to seven degrees one night. I learned more of the contents of the Bible on my shifts in the days that followed than in all my previous life. We had a large lettered sign: "Join Us In Prayer for the Martinsville Seven."

The convicted men were scheduled to be executed in two groups after the weekend. On my proposal, we decided to call everyone in the phone book, which meant chiefly whites, both because the city was mainly white and because few African-Americans could yet afford phones. We asked if they thought Blacks should die for a crime no white had ever been executed for. If they thought not, we asked them to phone the governor for clemency.

Someone walked into the lobby of Slaughter's, the Black hotel where our women were housed (no white hotel would rent to a mixed group) and asked people to phone. One man ran out and got five dollars worth of nickels—a call cost five cents—and a second read off the numbers to be called. A third of the people in the crowded lobby lined up to make the calls. The hotel keeper brought out a free lunch for the man who started it all.

A couple of others in our group went to the Black movie house and asked the manager to stop the show and tell the audience to send wires and phone calls. He did so. When these things were reported to a midnight meeting of our committee, I realized that something new was happening. With eight hours to go before the first execution, I proposed that we call a mass death watch in front of the state house at 6 a.m., despite the police limitation to four people. Some white delegates felt we would get no response, rousing folk in the middle of the night. I proposed that the committee guide itself by the opinions of the Richmond Blacks present. "Sure, the people will come out," they said.

At 2 a.m., we started making lists of names to call. We out-of-towners could call only those people we had gotten to know. I phoned the one African-American owner of a taxi company, and asked him to radio his cabs and spread the word that we were violating the police limit to four at the vigil, and would they spread the word. He did.

Then I tested a wild experience. A white mountaineer who made his living as a pool shark had approached us one midnight at the vigil, said he thought the Martinsville Seven were guilty but should not die because no white man had ever gone to the chair for rape in Virginia. He told me that he had been foreman on a jury in a like case a few years earlier, except that it had involved seven white men. None had gotten more than four years. One had been acquitted as having been too drunk to have gone through with the act. That man was now an announcer on a major Richmond radio station. If I wanted any cooperation from the radio announcer, I should give the name of the one-time jury foreman. I phoned the station, knowing that announcer was on duty at this early morning hour, mentioned the foreman's name, and asked him to air a straightforward announcement of the mass vigil with the earliest news. He did so.

In the wee hours of Friday morning—the court hearing had been on Monday—a dozen of us were in one of the rooms the "Y" had made available to us as headquarters. Those who had just come off the prayer vigil were huddled around the gas heater. Others, for whom there was no bed space in our rented rooms, were lying on chairs with coats thrown over them in place of blankets. Light shone in from the other office. We heard the clicking as James Smith dialed yet another number. He had worked at his job all day Thursday and would again on Friday. He had been phoning for hours. Elder Warner, unpaid preacher of a storefront church who had been an industrial worker in the North, was using the phone downstairs. Mrs. Lawson was calling from her home. So was Mrs. Vaughan, who ran the Black driving school in town, and her son, owner of a repair garage that had customers of both races. Mrs. Lawson's niece and another young woman were phoning from Slaughter's and a hotel around the corner.

The white Richmond people had long since finished calling the few friends who would come to the square. One couple had gone home to tend their babies and catch a couple of hours sleep. The Lumbee man was hauling us to and from the vigil in his truck. Others, too tired to go home, or too far from home to get there and back by six, had stayed at the "Y." It was a moment of pause, and for perspective. We New Yorkers were lucky. We had slept Sunday night before starting for Richmond. The Detroit and Chicago people had left home a day earlier. The carload from Denver had started three days before that, driving day and night.

Someone said that this was the story-telling hour. I said that I wanted to know what had caused each of us to come to Richmond, and why those who had stayed beyond the court hearing did so. A voice said: "I'll tell you," and I took out my notebook. Tape recorders were not yet for sale. A xerox of those notes is in my papers at the State Historical Society of Wisconsin. I have retained the original.

The voice, mild, Southern, and with a touch of a lisp, was that of James Goodman. An African-American of about thirty, tall, well-built but not noticeably powerful in appearance, he had been one of the quietest participants all week. Earlier in the evening, however, he and a young Jewish boy from New York had gotten the white male manager and the white female band leader at the huge city-owned dance hall, where it was "Negro night," to stop the music every half hour and ask the crowd to phone the governor to stop the executions. Other than that, we had known him only as a delegate from Brooklyn who had appointed himself guardian of the oil-can fire that kept us from freezing as we sat with our Bible outside the State House. By appearance and speech, he was a workingman.

"I was born in Panama. My parents moved to Nashville, Tennessee, when I was a boy. But I was old enough to remember Panama. My father was one of the three Negro locomotive engineers in Tennessee. He also had a farm.

"When I was fifteen or sixteen I worked in a grocery. One time I made a mistake in an order. The boss said: "'Nigger, don't you know what to do?'

"I said: 'Don't call me nigger, you know my name.'

"He come back: 'We kick dumb niggers around here,' and he kicked me.

"I hit him with a coke bottle. He called the cops, and they came to take me to jail. One cop said: 'Who did you hit with a bottle?'

"'Robert E. Miller.'

"'Look, nigger, when you talk to white people you gotta say, Sir. When I get you to the station house, I'll teach you how to talk to white men.'

"At the police station, one of them kicked me in the pants, and the other hit me in the jaw. Then they tossed me in a cell, and said: 'This is for niggers and dogs.'

"I would have got two to five years in reform school, but my father paid $500 graft and got me out.

"I kept on asking him to go North or to Panama. But we couldn't leave, on account of his railroad job. I was unhappy about the schools. The whites had brick schools and recreation grounds. The Negroes had frame schools, and they were cold. There were two coal heaters in each room, and we sat around them, instead of keeping class the right way. There was no recreation at all.

"Then the cops were very nasty, too. They would stop any Negro walking through the white section and question him. If they didn't like what he said, he'd get a beating and six months on the rock pile.

"One time I was working as house boy for a white family. I was about seventeen but big for my age. The man's daughter, she was nineteen, she liked me. She told her father: 'When I get to be twenty-one, I'm gonna marry Jimmy.' He went to my father and made me quit that job.

"My mother took me to Chicago. The living conditions, schools and recreation were better than in Nashville. I wanted to stay, but my mother took me home to Tennessee.

"At eighteen I packed my case and went on my own. During the war I was in the Navy. After basic training, I was at Yorktown Navy Mine Depot, not very far from here. I was base electrician. Once there was a wrong circuit in the recreation hall. Civilian white workers were called in, and they couldn't fix it. My C.O. told them he had a man who could fix anything that could be fixed, and he sent me over. One of the whites said:

"'Where did a nigger learn that type of work?'

"I said: 'Don't call me no nigger.'

"We had a scrap, and I got thirty days in the brig on bread and water."

I interrupted to say that it must have made him pretty weak.

"No," he continued. "I didn't stay there long enough. The brig was a hut with a cyclone fence around it. I pried it apart with my hands until I could get my feet in. Then I worked it open.

"I drew a suspended sentence for breaking out of the brig, and the C.O. told me to build a new one that prisoners couldn't get out of so easy. He gave me a detail of 12 men, and I built it of steel and concrete.

"Then I went on liberty. The bus to Richmond was crowded. There were two seats up front. Another boy and I sat down. The driver refused to move the bus until we got out of the white section. We wouldn't get up. There was a riot, so he started the bus. The fight in the bus kept on all the way from Yorktown to Williamsburg. There I was picked up and brought into camp. They held me for mutiny. I asked for a general court-martial. I beat the case.

"I told them the bus driver had no right to give me orders, so how could that be mutiny? They had to agree, and they freed me.

"Then we were shipped to New Guinea, and from there to the Philippines. A couple of our officers were Southerners. One was from Mississippi. One day I was on guard duty. Afterward, I started to cut across the white camp over to the Negro camp. The Mississippi officer stopped me. He said: 'Niggers got no right to go through the white camp.'

"We had an argument, and it became a fight. I was arrested. The C.O. told me I had no right to argue with an officer or with any white personnel. I was put in the brig again, and then sent to the psychiatrist. He said I had battle fatigue."

I interrupted to say he hadn't told us about any battles.

"I'd been at Iwo Jima with the 20th Amphibians. I operated an LPC boat, carrying twenty men to land. I was hit by shrapnel. I've got a plate in my head. They put me in the crazy stockade. I was there for ten days. Then outside camp and back to the States. That was in 1945. They sent me to St. Alban's for treatment for battle fatigue."

I said they didn't know what kind of battle he was fatigued of.

"They sure didn't. I got a medical discharge in 1946....[Then] "I settled in New York. I worked at Bethlehem Steel and Todd Shipyard as an electrician, and studied electrical engineering at night under the G.I. Bill. Sometimes I did longshoremen's work. So I joined the Longshore Club." He didn't say "of the Communist Party," but that was the only organization on the New York waterfront with that name.

"I picketed Ryan's office when they tried to squeeze Negroes off the waterfront." Ryan headed the International Longshoremen's Association. "I picketed Bethlehem in the 1948 strike. Then I worked in the Henry Wallace campaign, and in the Ada Jackson and Hattie Brisbane campaigns," African-American women running for office on the same American Labor Party ticket I had run on.

He stopped, and after a brief silence Fern Owens spoke up. A white woman undoubtedly in her late thirties, for she had come to Richmond straight from her daughter's wedding, she looked a good deal younger. She had a strong nose and a set to her mouth that was the only indication of the person within. Her English was clear and clipped.

"My maiden name was Pierce, and the president of that name, a slave-owners' stooge, was an ancestor of mine. But some of my ancestors were Utopian socialists, in Owens's colonies, and I heard something about that in childhood from a brother, the only radical in the family.

"My father was a sharecropper outside Oklahoma City. I walked to school in town through the Negro community. The lies about Negroes being shiftless didn't impress me, for I saw their homes through the eyes of a cropper, and not of a white of higher class.

"There would be fights. The white boys would stone the Negro girls. That rubbed me the wrong way. One day the white school was surrounded by Negro boys in retaliation. The principal told us to stay in our seats. After a while he and the principal of the Negro school got together, and the Negro boys were called off. But this incident built up my respect for them.

"When I was in sixth grade, a girl in my class had an affair with a boy. They were intimate. Her parents found out, and she was terrified. To get out of it, she said she had been raped by a Negro. A lynch atmosphere developed. Only the fact that the truth was well-known in school prevented some innocent Negro from losing his life. I could never forget this, and this is one reason I'm trying to save the lives of these Negroes framed on a rape charge.

"Later, the Negro neighborhood spread until it completely surrounded the school I had been going to. The white parents didn't want their children to go through a Negro section, and so the school was closed. It was not made into a Negro school, because it was considered too good for them, and the authorities felt that if they had one such school, they would want more. I was terribly shocked when I heard that, because I had had my schooling in snatches when my father didn't need my help, and I appreciated schooling greatly.

"I heard of the Scottsboro Case when it began in 1931. I was still in Oklahoma City, and I went to open air meetings in a park where they talked about it. I believed what they said because of my own experiences in school.

"The Depression got very bad about then. There was much actual starvation. People were evicted and set up a 'Hooverville' under a bridge, Negro and white intermixed. There was an almost spontaneous organization of the unemployed, with both races together. The Unemployed Councils played a role.

"There was no city relief [welfare], and one day there was a march on City Hall to demand that something be done. En route we passed a very well-stocked food store. People left the line of march and raided it. The police came with clubs and tear gas.

"A Negro woman near me had taken a ham. A cop came up and said: 'Put that down.' She set the ham down carefully at her feet, then seized a can from the counter at which she was standing and bashed the cop over the head. He dropped in his tracks. She calmly picked up the ham and walked home.

"Afterward, the cops set out a dragnet for my brother, thinking him the ringleader, although he was not. He had to hide, and it was a Negro family that offered to take him in, difficult as it would have been for them to explain the presence in the house of a white man.

"In later years I married a Negro. I don't want my husband or my son to face what these men are facing. I think I can understand how Mrs. Grayson feels." Mrs. Grayson was the wife of the only married man of those awaiting death. They had five young children.

(Fern Owens divorced, and married another African-American, Henry Winston, who became National Chairman of the Communist Party.)

Jeri Wynne was the next to speak. She was a nineteen-year-old very light-skinned Black woman who had been on her own for two years. "I was born in Cleveland. My father was one of the few men to study electronic engineering before the war. When Western Electric had an opening in this field, there were only three applicants, and he was the only one who qualified. He didn't get the job, being a Negro. This embittered him terribly, and he withdrew into himself.

"My mother's story is similar. Although a graduate of the Cleveland School of Art, she managed only now and then to get some commercial work.

"From the time I was four until I was eleven I lived with my grandfather in Mobile, Alabama. He was of a Cuban Creole family, and enormously rich. He owned much of the city. His money came originally from cigars, but he owned entire streets of real estate, and a whole island.

"He had a twenty-room house, and there were lots of kids around. He knew how to handle kids. He was the stingiest man I have ever seen, but on Saturdays when he lined the kids up to give them a nickel to go to the movies, he had a way of making each of us feel wonderful.

"He bought a new black Packard every year, and the family was outraged when, after his death, his daughter bought a Studebaker intead. The five Creole families of Mobile and New Orleans were as aristocratic and snobbish as the Cabots and the Lodges.

"I didn't know that I was a Negro. In color, the family ran from blue-eyed blondes to my color." In a white family, Jeri would be taken as white, and in a Black as Black. "I found out later that my family had been outraged when my mother married a dark Negro. But meanwhile I didn't know, for we children went to a Catholic school for Creoles, where the French patois was spoken. And I hated niggars —we pronounced it to rhyme with cigar. My parents were separated, and I hadn't seen my father since I was four.

"When I was nine, the whole family, with all the children, made a pilgrimage to Macon, Georgia, to visit my greatgrandfather Faustina, who had a thirty-room house out of town, with Negro servants. One day, shortly after we arrived, we children were playing near the railroad track that ran past one end of the place. We heard a lot of noise, and a group of men came along, dragging a Negro. They took some spare ties, stood one in the ground, tied him to it, drenched him with kerosene, and burned him alive.

"For some reason, I just stood there. Greatgrandfather had been watching from the window, for when it was over and we went home, he gathered the whole gang of us in the drawing-room. In the presence of our elders, who were outraged at his destruction of what they had worked a generation to build, he said: 'We are all Negroes here. It could have happened to any one of us,' and he told us the family background.

"I turned and fled to my room, and stayed there for two weeks. When I came out, I was a Negro, and no longer a Catholic, for no God of Mercy would let things like that happen in the world."

It was now a quarter to six, and time to go to the square for the mass vigil.

A hundred African-Americans showed up on that short notice. A Black restaurant owner gave up his early breakfast business, closed up shop, posted on his front door the handbill our people were distributing, made huge jugs of coffee and trucked them down for free distribution to the people standing outdoors with the temperature at fifteen degrees. The first four men were executed that Friday morning, and the other three were scheduled for Monday. After the first executions, a Black taxi driver drove a young Black Detroit steelworker and myself at night the 225 miles to Martinsville to offer our condolences and help to the families. It was hairy. Scheduled buses had been cancelled because of icy roads. When we became hungry, the driver parked the cab away from the lights of a roadside eatery so no one could see that there was a white among Blacks in the car. He went in, bought sandwiches, and brought them out. African-Americans could not sit down to eat. I felt ashamed, miserable, and demeaned, as I had when required to board that bus in Mississippi in 1946 ahead of an older Black woman.

Death by violence at the hands of government and police was not new, and the parents of the executed men were calm, at least by the time we arrived. Mrs. Hairston asked if there was any hope for the three remaining boys. One home was no more than a room, a bed with a patchwork quilt, a kerosene lamp, and newspaper pasted to the wall to prevent the wind from howling through between the boards.

Back in Richmond on Saturday night the story-telling resumed. Charles Childs, sandy-haired with pale blue eyes, was twenty. His mother had been a textile worker in Tennessee. A strike occurred. She refused to scab, and moved to North Carolina with her five children. There was no husband. Charles remembered how happy he was the day his mother got a job in High Point. She thought she had a good boss, because he let her work overtime.

The children would pick up coal along the railroad tracks. The locomotive firemen would deliberately push some over the edge of the tender for them, and did not discriminate between African-American and white children. His mother had died just ten months earlier. The family now consisted of five. He lived with his two sisters, one deeply religious, the other anti-union.

Four years earlier, when he was sixteen, he got a leaflet urging workers to attend a meeting planned by the United Furniture Workers to organize for a five-cent-an-hour raise. Charles made notes about the contents, and showed it to people. He went to the meeting and listened to Mike Ross, a legendary figure in Southern union organizing. He remembered Ross talking about "surplus profit."

In 1948, less than three years earlier, Charles was active in Henry Wallace's campaign for the presidency. He had been drawn in because he was opposed to Universal Military Training, the draft. Meanwhile Charles had managed to get into college. His English thesis was on an "ideal society." He had drafted a Utopia. Charles was sharp.

After the executions of the Martinsville Seven, one of the Black spiritual advisors to the condemned men said to his fellows: "I sure hope the families can get the bodies for a decent burial. There's a rule here that 'rapists' bodies are given to the university medical school."

Another clergyman asked: "That white man they also electrocuted this morning really committed rape, didn't he?".

"Yes, but no white man has ever been executed for that. He died for murder."

"And murderers' families get their bodies?"

"Yes."

When one of those clergymen repeated that story to us a couple of hours later, Charles drew the obvious conclusion: "First they reserve the death penalty for rape for Negroes. Then they reserve for Negroes only, therefore, the privilege of being dissected by medical students."

One day Charles and a young woman had been assigned to distribute a leaflet on downtown Broad Street. She said that a degenerate-looking drunk began to berate him. Most people took the leaflets, saying nothing or "thank you," and putting them in their pockets after reading a line or two. The drunk hollered: "nigger-lover!" Charles ignored him, and kept on handing out the leaflets with Southern politeness: "Here you are, ma'am...one for you, sir." The drunk kept it up: "Damyankee! Ought to fry right next to them niggers."

"I was born and raised in the South," Charles said, for the benefit of the passers-by. "Never been away in my life." A Black soldier came along, took a leaflet, walked along slowly reading it, turned around, came back to Charles, and said: "Mighty fine thing you-all are doing."

"I appreciate that, mister," Charles responded.

The drunk exploded: "*Mister!*" he screamed.

Four years later, when North Carolina Communist leader Junius Scales, a white man, was tried and convicted simply for membership—the only person to serve a sentence on that basis—he was fingered in court by Charles Childs. On cross-examination it turned out that Childs had been an FBI informant for years, paid in the form of a college education. He had told me that government should pay for higher education. In his case it did.

On Sunday morning we decided to organize, that very afternoon, a mass memorial march from the church services to Thomas Jefferson's austere and beautiful State Capitol building. The police were neither asked nor notified. All nine hundred mourners who had filled the church marched, including forty whites. Half a dozen of them were local: working people and aristocrats, none from the middle strata. The parade was headed by two local women, one Black, one white, carrying a wreath. Six clergy followed, of whom one was a white Episcopalian from Chicago. As the parade crossed Broad Street, Richmond's main thoroughfare, the traffic—white Richmond out for a Sunday drive—stopped to let us pass.

The next morning there was another prayer vigil till the last three men's deaths were reported. This time the crowd seemed on the verge of hysteria. So, for the first time in my life I raised a prayer. It was for interracial unity and couched in religious terms: we are all the children of one father. To that I added: "I want to offer a prayer for the day when all men will truly be brothers, and the color of a man's skin will mean nothing. My prayer is for the day when there are no masters or slaves. Abraham Lincoln said: 'If the Lord wanted some men to be slaves, and others to be masters, he would have made some men all hands and no mouths'."

But that night, back in the "Y," although we had planned a mass memorial service, it was clear that it was all over. Someone tuned the radio dial away from the customary search for news and found good dance music. A couple began to dance. All did, interracially of course. Most were in their twenties, often early twenties. The tension had broken.

Two days later there was a final interfaith funeral service in a ghetto church. Two thousand people jammed the church and the streets. A local white workingman known to all for his efforts mounted a soap-box. Police arrived. The crowd would not budge. The police left. Inside, the presiding clergyman paid tribute to the national delegation and asked if any of us wished to say anything.

I felt we should explain our motivations to the people who would come to the service and typed a statement in the expectation that there would be an opportunity to present it. The pastor paid tribute to us from the pulpit, and asked if any of us wished to say anything. I rose in the balcony and read my statement: "I am moved to offer a word of explanation in answer to a question many have asked: 'Who are these people? Why did they come here?'

"As for the Negroes in the delegation, their very presence speaks for itself. For myself, I came because there can be no true freedom for the mass of the white people in this country when the Negro people are downtrodden. When you cannot vote...men are elected to the Senate and Congress who do not represent the common people of your state. Therefore, when I want government aid for education for my children, the votes of these men from the southern states deny that money. So I suffer, and all my people, whether they know it or not, because your people are held down....

"So, we did not come down here to be patronizing or nice to somebody else. We came here because we know that our own freedom, our own lives, our own livelihood, depends upon you having freedom and equality.

"That is why I am grateful to you for being here today. You are standing up not only for your people, but for mine, when you assert that you must have an equal right to life and liberty.

"I admire your courage. You have to stay here and face the music. We can go home, away from Virginia justice.

"I want to say one more word. I am not of your faith. I am a Jew. My grandmother can recite from memory over fifty members of my family who were done to death in Hitler's gas chambers less than ten years ago. My people suffered Martinsville a million times over, for 6 million of my faith were exterminated. I know that so long as the idea of racial inequality exists, I face the same fate as the men of Martinsville, for the Jews of Germany were of the same white race as Hitler.

"That is why, for my own sake, I do what I can in a case like this—for my children, and for my country, of which I am bitterly ashamed when something of this kind happens. When we go North and West and South again, we will not forget this. You have taken us into your hearts and homes. I welcome you, for all of us here, to be our guests and friends when you come to our parts of the country."

A couple of days after returning to New York, I was riding home in a subway train. Two Black sleeping-car porters were talking to each other.

One had just arrived on a run from Richmond, and he was telling the story of what I had experienced the previous week.

Three years later came the Montgomery bus boycott that propelled Martin Luther King to fame. One of the top leaders was a sleeping-car porter, local rank-and-file organizer for the union.

CHAPTER 15

That Desert Year

I have never kept a diary, but once in a while have written down all the events of a day either when it was particularly satisfying or, on the contrary, when I wondered where it had gone. A notebook entry dated November 8, 1950, falls into the latter category. I was unemployed, and Tanya was supporting us by bookkeeping at a neighborhood hardware story in Washington Heights. Phyllis was eleven and Bobby six, so I presume they took care of themselves physically, because the entry reads as follows:

"Finished breakfast, dressing Davey [then four years old], fixed bed leg by 10:30 a.m. (took 1 hr. 10 minutes). Buy milk, butter. Find out from Tanya what to buy. What to wash: What goes to laundry. What to make for supper, and how." One could base an entire essay on how that journal entry reveals the continuing responsibility of a woman for a home even when the man is househusband, as I was then. The note went on to deal with job-hunting: "Mimeo translation record; send to all agencies. Phone McGraw-Hill re translation."

I had just completed my run for Congress, focused against the Korean War. I obtained only six thousand votes to the winner's hundred thousand, and so the note continues: "File election expenses. Get election materials." I was working on an idea for a book on foreign policy, and the note ended: "For book, use Progressive Party Handbook, back file of *National Guardian,* back file of *In Fact,* back file of *Daily Worker.*"

A month later a source appeared that would have been vastly more persuasive than some of those I listed. It is a remarkable indication of how the most impeccable conservative credentials cannot win more than a passing news report when the current Establishment, including government, mass media, and the educational system, is determined to push through an official line. Former president Herbert Hoover had just returned from a tour of Europe. He gave a speech on national network radio, which was carried by the *New York Times:*:

"Even were Western Europe armed far beyond any contemplated program, we could never reach Moscow. The Germans failed with a magnificent army of 250 combat divisions and with powerful air and tank forces, as contrasted with the 60 divisions now being talked about [for the United States]. Equally, we Americans alone with sea and air power can so control the Atlantic and Pacific oceans that there can be no possible invasion of the Western Hemisphere by Communist armies. They can no more reach Washington in force than we can reach Moscow. In this military connection we must realize the fact that the atomic bomb is a far less dominant weapon than it was once thought to be...

"We have little need for large armies unless we are going to Europe or China. We could, after initial outlays for more air and navy equipment, greatly reduce our expenditures. The prime obligation of defense of Western Continental Europe rests upon the nations of Europe...We cannot buy them with money. Our policy in this quarter of the world should be confined to a period of watchful waiting without ground military action....Otherwise we shall be inviting another Korea. That would be a calamity to Europe as well as to us. Honest difference of views and honest debate are not disuniting. No promise should be made...to land any more American land forces in Europe until the American people and the Congress have had an opportunity to explore the whole question."

The Republican ex-president was paid no more attention than the liberal Democratic former vice-president Henry Wallace, who had been driven out of public life for expressing virtually identical sentiments. Nor was any serious consideration given to the views of former Ambassador Joseph Kennedy, father of the president-to-be of a decade later: "Half of this world will never submit to dictation by the other half. The two can only agree to live next to each other because for one to absorb the other becomes too costly. What business is it of ours to support French colonial policy in Indo-China or to achieve Mr. Synghman Rhee's concepts of democracy in Korea?"

Rhee was already notorious for his dictatorial conduct. He had been flown in by Gen. Douglas MacArthur, commander in the war. In Korea, MacArthur ignored President Truman's policy and drove north to the Chinese border, although China warned that it would not tolerate an approach closer than twenty-five miles. China invaded massively and inflicted a resounding defeat on the U.S. forces on November 5th, 1950. In response, MacArthur wanted to escalate further, for which the only available means was another American use of the atom bomb. Yet China and the USSR were bound to each other's defense. World war would have been the outcome. This resulted in the first of several occasions in life in which I rose to the level of statesmanship. By this I mean understanding the real state of international or internal affairs earlier than others, and proposing the necessary solution. When, on March 24, 1951, MacArthur went over Truman's head to the American public via a letter to a congressman, a Communist-baiting columnist in the mass-circulation *New York World-Telegram and Sun* wrote: "William Mandel...a few months ago demanded Gen. MacArthur's summary retirement."

He doubtless believed that this would help destroy criticism of MacArthur, who had almost god-like status with the American public as commander of U.S. ground forces in the Pacific in World War II, reinforced by his remarkable flair for publicity. Truman fired MacArthur in a matter of weeks, obviously not because I recommended it, although the possibility exists that someone who had his ear saw that story and thought it the proper course to take. To me, what is important is that I understood the need for an action that was seemingly unthinkable when I proposed it, given MacArthur's towering prestige. I rank that foresight with my published conclusion early in 1953 that Joe McCarthy could be defeated, when that ran counter to the view held in all parts of the political spectrum, and with my wires to Khrushchev and Kennedy proposing precisely the solution to the Cuba Missile Crisis of 1962 that they adopted, although in that case as well I do not know whether my messages played any role.

There was no significant support for the views of former President Hoover or Ambassador Kennedy within either major party. Organizations holding similar views were being systematically suppressed and disbanded. Some were declared subversive by the House Un-American Activities Committee. The tax-exempt status of others was cancelled by the Internal Revenue Service. When this failed to destroy them, their leaders were indicted, jailed, or, when foreign-born, deported. Under these circumstances, the Cold War and McCarthyism rolled on in seemingly invincible fashion.

Since there was no way I could reach the public with a direct attack on these policies, I pursued my ideals in other ways. Participation in the struggle for the Martinsville Seven was one. But as a scholar, I felt as I feel in writing this autobiography, that helping others understand what had gone before would assist them in finding ways to deal with issues of the time. So I approached the great Congressman Vito Marcantonio, who had had the courage to cast the single vote against the Korean War, with the idea of writing his biography. Although regularly in the national news, he was also beyond the pale of the publishing world in the atmosphere of the time. I proposed to finance publication with advance subscriptions solicited in the clubs of New York's American Labor Party, which he headed and on whose ticket I had run. He approved, and I sat unobtrusively in his office as he received constituents.

The congressman was an impeccably honest man, but his style was that of the padrone, even though he lacked the physical equipment. He was slender and of medium height. Yet in his gray-black striped business suit, with his thumbs often hooked into the arm-holes of his vest, he exuded an air of total confidence. With his set jaw and rapid-fire disposition of any issue, he was dominant and impressive. He knew local housing, rent, welfare, and health regulations as well as tax matters and the ways of Congress, and was often able to be of help to constituents despite lack of a patronage machine.

That biography project resulted in my writing a money-soliciting letter to a big farmer in Colorado that records pretty well my notion of who I was and sought to be. The previous summer I had spoken in Denver in the kind of hall that had probably seen IWW and Western Federation of Miners meetings in previous decades. There I made the acquaintance of H.B. Sprague, a lean, leathery, somewhat wizened man, born about 1870, who had homesteaded in easternmost Colorado at the turn of the century. An intense, remarkable correspondence resulted. A letter from him of less than two thousand words was rare. Most of the time they were on the blank backs of radical, atheist, or single-taxer literature. He would discourse shrewdly on local and world affairs, tell me about the weather and the crops, and detail his business affairs with such precision that those letters could unquestionably have served the IRS as evidence of tax evasion if it had been that agency reading my mail instead of the FBI.

His life story emerged from a few sentences: "I used to walk and guide the plow behind a yoke of cattle in Nebraska and plow an acre and a half [per day]. Last summer I drove one of the big rigs and did a much better job, and plowed 75 acres in five hours...We have just weaned 460 calves....Raise and fatten 500 hogs. A good normal crop of grain is 100,000 bushels. A nice well-bred string of saddle horses. And Shetland ponies....We have paid over $140,000 in taxes during the past 12 months."

Yet this same man would read and circulate among his neighbors the Information Bulletin published by the Soviet Embassy in Washington. He was not a communist but a single-taxer, believing that land was the sole source of value, and conceived of himself as a socialist. Knowing that Tanya and I were having a very rough time, economically, he wrote me the following in March of 1951:

"I am going to surprise you by asking you to bring your family and join us here on the farm. At least we do not have to go hungry. You would have to work for $90 a month and the wife for that figure and 'found.'" So he valued a woman's work equally with a man's. "We all share in the farm produce, such as three to five kinds of meat, milk, butter, eggs, fruit and vegetables....We have the usual communist features of Post Office, Rural [mail] Delivery daily, children hauled to and from school, and good community roads.

"If you were to come, your first job would be to cook for your family and from two to three men....In harvest time we have 20 to 25....We would want the children to learn to cook and serve and pay them something as we are now doing with the kids that are here. Mostly, take care of the chickens and cows, and I give two of the grandchildren here a dollar a case to help with the eggs.

"If men like you could be paid for what you can do and know, and not as now only the ones who can lie about Russia and Communism get five-figure incomes, I would believe your place should be in writing and speaking and teaching. As of now, you're lucky to be out of a concentration camp or in prison." Consider the atmosphere that had to exist in the country for a highly successful self-made farmer and rancher in the classical American tradition to have written that last sentence.

He concluded by saying that he wanted me to help him change minds in his farm community. I replied, March 21, 1951:

"I am not going to run away either from the possibility of hardship or of jail. Each of us has the business to contribute to progress in the best way he can. I am best at writing, research and speaking. Cooking on a ranch is perfectly honorable work, and your objective of having me influence the few hundred people of Amherst and vicinity is quite admirable. But for a person like myself, who has been able to influence thousands by his books, tens of thousands by lectures, hundreds of thousands by radio talks and, for a brief period, millions through the newspapers, it would be moral and physical cowardice for me not to go on trying to do what I have been doing.

"Vito Marcantonio has authorized me to write his biography. The idea was mine, and I want to do it for several reasons. One is that I want to see him back in Congress next year. Barring a greater change, let the people have at least one voice crying out the truth from that rostrum, one fighter who will stand up against the gang. Another reason is that no one has yet written a people's history of the New Deal. The discouragement, apathy, cowardice and cynicism so widespread today must be dispelled. It can be, if the people are reminded about the way they themselves fought farm foreclosures, fought for the soldiers' bonus, fought for unemployment relief and insurance, fought for the Scottsboro boys, fought for peace, only ten to 15 short years ago. They can do it again. I have seen examples, myself, most recently in Richmond, Virginia. Marcantonio has been involved in all these things, as the people's watchdog and spokesman in Washington. I want to use him as a peg on which to hang this story of the people's fight. *The National Guardian* (75,000 circulation) and the N.Y. American Labor Party (150 established clubs and 200,000 votes) will sell the book when written, but they can't feed me while I write it. Will you invest $3,000 in this? What good is your money otherwise? Who remembers a rich man?"

I received no response for quite a while. Finally he wrote: "I believe you can do a hundred times more good writing and influencing prominent people in the right way than you can writing biographies, no matter who the individual may be. Just my idea. Not dictating to you. If I get a holt of some money I will give you some without any strings on it, I think you would be well paid if you come out and see this wheat country at its best."

That summer he did send us the fare, and Tanya and I spent a week or two on his stupendous working farm and ranch. I learned more about American agriculture sitting on a huge Caterpillar as it disked an unbelievable acreage in a single day, and riding ninety miles to their foothill ranch in a semi to round up cattle for market than a decade in a library would have taught me.

Meanwhile the Marcantonio project had fallen through, for political reasons. For all my admiration for him, I would not yield my right to disagree in my capacity as the leader of his party in my state assembly district. When he sought a change in party organization that would give him absolute control, I was among those who opposed it. So he cancelled the book project. It would be thirty years, and him long dead, before someone else's biography of him was published. He deserved it, and there is much that politicians and organizations for the people can learn from it.

I did one piece of writing that desert year that had an effect on the few hundred people it reached in mimeographed form from me or via further duplication by the recipients. It was a lengthy, raging poem about Martinsville and its outcome, "New Trial in Richmond." A minor poet, Hugh Hardyman, wrote: "I was surprised and pleased to see that someone besides myself remembers and likes Whittier these days....I gave your piece a hard try-out, reading it aloud to a group at dinner last night—my family are highly critical of verse, having been largely prejudiced against it at schools where the teachers did not know what poetry was—and to my surprise they all liked it, without exception....The opening four stanzas are so much better than most all the verse I see today...."

There was also a very generous but less specific postcard from Langston Hughes: "...stirring poem....I hope you're doing more poems as effective for recitation and reading."

I did several, all within those few years when America scraped bottom. One was "To My Children, for Dr. DuBois," which I wrote when the government indicted him. It brought an interesting letter of criticism from a very fine recognized poet, Tom McGrath, who lived into the 1990s: "Don't think it is as good as 'Trial'....I don't doubt that the poem has moved people, but isn't it likely that they responded to the *idea* (the abstraction) more than to the *poem*? I suppose the job of the poet is to rescue life from all the death cliches—including saving the great things in which we believe from the good and valiant people who have been taught (by false education, newspapers, etc.) to let even their best beliefs become infected by the death that transforms them into the cliche and the stock response."

This is why I don't quote any of my verse here, although I think that in "Trial" people responded to the rhythm, which pulsed, a kind of Whittier rap.

A resolution to end the war in Korea was introduced into the U.S. Senate on June 25, 1951, the first anniversary of that conflict. As co-chair of the congressional-district organization of the American Labor Party, I wrote every leader in the community urging them to communicate with President Truman to make a truce. Within one month thereafter, thanks to such messages from all over the country, he instructed the generals to begin truce talks, but it took two more years and a new president, Eisenhower, to bring the war to an end.

A letter on another subject was fruitless. When the U.S. Supreme Court upheld the jail sentences of eleven Communist leaders, I wrote about a hundred community leaders asking them to protest. My key sentence read: "When the Communists are outlawed, if a man wants free speech, an end to discrimination, lower prices, a different foreign policy, higher wages, shorter hours, he is called a 'concealed Communist,' he is clapped into jail and his organizations are disbanded." That was a reasonably accurate description of the atmosphere that those prison sentences actually did produce during the two years that followed, in which McCarthyism reached its height.

As a result of Tanya's activity in the Parent-Teacher Association, I was aware of the inadequacies of our country's education system. I have a note of mine from 1951 which reads: "Conditions at P.S. 169 needing attention: totally inadequate lunchroom facilities with at least 85% of the children eating lunch in school. No auditorium. More than 30 children to a class. Inadequate teaching staff for the kindergarten resulting in only a fraction of the children eligible for kindergarten being accepted. The playschool and afterschool center does not meet the need of working mothers. It has a tremendous waiting list. It is the only center in the entire Washington Heights community."

While Tanya was the schools activist in the family, as is usually the case, I remember thinking and saying to her: "All this is well and good, but you and I believe that there can be no real solution to all these problems until we have socialism. What is being done to present *that* idea?"

Yet under the atmosphere of the day it was not possible for her to do

anything on that score. Any such public advocacy would bring accusations of communism from opponents of whatever reform one proposed,
however unrelated to fundamental social change. People shied away, if
only because of fear of McCarthy and the FBI. In that sense I was fortunate. As a Soviet affairs scholar, I was able to discuss events in a country I regarded as socialist even if I had to tack it on to an activity having
some base in the public, as happened next .

During World War II each new work by the Soviet composer
Shostakovich was copied, as soon as the ink was dry, to be rushed to the
U.S. by American diplomatic courier for performance by our greatest
orchestras so as to build warmth toward Our Great Russian Ally. But
when the Cold War began, Shostakovich became an unperson. In 1949
he wrote a very melodic cantata, "Song of the Forest," on an environmentalist theme: Stalin had decreed the planting of shelter belts in the
windswept steppes of the Ukraine and south Russia.

A record of the cantata was pressed in France. No American company would import it. The industry was following the lead of the government, which had denied him a visa. The American people were to forget
that anything positive could ever be created under the Communists. The
excellent music critic of the Communist *Daily Worker,* Sidney
Finkelstein (whose book on jazz is still worth reading) obtained a copy
of the record. I heard it in his home. Meanwhile, the chorus of the
California Labor School in San Francisco was preparing the premiere
live performance of that cantata in the U.S., and invited me out to introduce it with a talk. Although no speakers' bureau would book me any
longer, I used my personal contacts from earlier professional lecturing
years to organize a small tour. I would simply get up on the stage with a
phonograph, at the Chicago Art Institute, for example, or the University
of Wisconsin, or wherever, play the record, and entertain questions on
the musical scene in the USSR. College newspapers would still provide
press coverage; the metropolitan dailies would not. Questions asked me
were quite heavy. Stalin was then stifling anything that could not be
grasped by popular taste—in music anything beyond the Romantics—at
the same time as the U.S. was barring Shostakovich on straight political
grounds.

The musical lecture and associated courtesies took three, perhaps
four of my waking hours. I spent the rest of the day on the activity that
made the tour possible. It was promotion of *We Charge Genocide*, a book-
length petition to the United Nations edited by William L. Patterson,
San Francisco-born son of a slave who occupies the chronological space
between W.E.B. DuBois and Martin Luther King as leader of the struggle for civil rights. Patterson is forgotten because he was a Communist
to the end of his days. He was impressed by the way I conducted myself

in the South during the Martinsville Case, and asked me to promote the book to Black leadership, where his name was then an open sesame, and to such whites as could be reached, primarily people in those Left-led labor unions that had not yet been smashed.

Americans had been brainwashed into believing that genocide means only mass murder. In fact, the UN Genocide Convention reads: "In the present Convention, genocide means <u>any</u> of the following acts committed with intent to destroy, in whole *or in part*, a national, ethnical, racial or religious group, as such: (a) killing *members* of the group; (b) causing serious bodily or *mental* harm to *members* of the group; (c) deliberately inflicting on the group conditions or life calculated to bring about its physical destruction in whole *or in part*; (d) imposing measures intended to prevent *births* within the group; (e) forcibly transferring children of the group to another group" [emphasis added].

Every time a cop kills a Black when he would not kill a white, that is genocide: killing *members* of a group. For that reason, the U.S. Senate, led by Southern die-hards, refused to ratify the Genocide Convention for nearly forty years. The American Bar Association was a major ally, saying frankly that indictments could be brought within the United States if it were ratified. Now ratified, it is part of the law of this country. My promotion of *We Charge Genocide* represented what I could do to combat discriminatory violence and to break down the walls of the ghetto that, to this day, cause life expectancy among African-Americans to be substantially lower than among whites.

Two films shown that year in neighborhood theaters presented issues of conscience. One was "The Desert Fox," glorifying the Nazi General Rommel. The other was "Oliver Twist," with Dickens' evil Jew, Fagin. I participated in picketing them, to protect the minds of a new generation of youth who already then, only six years after World War II, did not remember Hitler or know the damage done by anti-Semitism. We kept those pictures out of a number of theaters in the neighborhood. In Germany, abstract adherence to civil liberties had helped bring to power a regime that instituted death camps. Consequently, after Hitler was defeated, that country and many others in Europe outlawed, for example, publication of assertions that the Holocaust had not occurred. Those prohibitions are still in effect.

Despite the fact that I was househusband while Tanya brought home a weekly pay check in this McCarthyist year, the difference between her civic activities and mine reflected the standard division of gender roles. I was unusual only in not regarding that as foreordained, in thinking and ultimately writing about it as it pertained to my field of interest.

A quarter century later, in 1977, I attended the founding convention of the Women's Studies Association, held in San Francisco. After I had said something from the platform (Doubleday-Anchor had recently published my book, *Soviet Women*), someone who looked as though she were approaching forty came up and asked: "Are you the man who wrote *Man Bites Dog*?" I said I was. She went on: "I was brought up on it. My parents had it in the house."

I tried to appear calm. We had a little chat, and went our separate ways. In fact I was thrilled. *Man Bites Dog* is a small pamphlet of only twenty-four pages, which consists of my testimony before the U.S. Senate Internal Security ("McCarran") Subcommittee in 1952, the year before McCarthy called me. And here was someone of my own children's generation, who could only have been entering her teens at the time, remembering it twenty-five years afterward. And now she was of an age to tell her own children about it.

In that first confrontation with McCarthyism I was an amateur. I was naive enough—a mistake I did not repeat when subpoenaed by the other witch-hunting committees in 1953 and 1960 —to think that if I conducted myself as a scholar, which I am, and a gentleman, which I hope I am, and concisely presented documented fact and offered a challenging evaluation of the committee's methods and purposes, then I could reach the American people via the press. After all, the hearing room was jammed with reporters. Every major newspaper was there, every wire service, every national magazine. They crowded up afterward, asked questions, and scribbled diligently.

Not one word appeared in any publication outside the Left, and very little surfaced there. I had forgotten that it is not what you have to say that counts, but how important you are perceived as being. And I was not a celebrity. True, I had had two books published, and it was specifically for the crime of writing one of them, *The Soviet Far East and Central Asia,* that the committee had subpoenaed me.

I worked hard in preparation for the McCarran hearing, and was entirely successful in manipulating my interrogators. With my background as journalist, it was clear from the behavior of the reporters present that they thought they had found a real story. Their editors unanimously engaged in self-censorship by killing it, in response to the five years of intimidation launched by Truman.

The hearing itself was a psychological wrestling match. Unlike the McCarthy and the Un-American Activities committees' hearings, which were held in courtroom fashion, all parties in McCarran Committee hearings sat around a huge rectangular table. Only one senator was present that day, Homer Ferguson, a Republican from Michigan, who had been a judge and would later be ambassador to Mexico. I was lucky that McCarran himself was not in attendance. McCarran's behavior was known to be downright erratic. McCarthy, playing for public support, tried to appear judicial, which I took advantage of. McCarran, from gambling and legal-whorehouse Nevada, didn't give a damn, and would throw uncooperative witnesses out of the hearing room.

Senator Ferguson sat at the head of the table. I was placed around its corner to his left. Facing me across the table were his inquisitors, the subcommittee staff, who had prepared the case against me and were to do the questioning. One of them was also surnamed Mandel, but totally unrelated to me. (Mandel is in fact an abbreviation. My grandfather had been Mandelman, and the innumerable Mandels one encounters today had, a generation or two earlier, been Mandelbaums, Mandelbergs, Mandelowitzes, Mandelstams, and so forth.)

David Caute, in his definitive work, *The Great Fear,* writes of this man with whom I shared my name: "The Senate Internal Security Subcommittee also succeeded in luring from [the] House Committee on UnAmerican Activities its celebrated director of research, Benjamin Mandel." Sitting next to him and doing most of the questioning was the committee's counsel, Robert Morris. He had been a New York municipal court judge and in later years became president of the University of Dallas.

The power of these men was such that the Secretary-General of the United Nations, Trygvie Lie, heading a supposedly independent international body, actually consulted with Morris and with McCarthy's counsel, Roy Cohn, after Congress threatened to slash the U.S. appropriation providing 40 percent of the UN budget. Lie then fired forty-five American staffers the witch-hunters had declared subversive. The moral stresses were such that the general legal counsel of the UN, an American and close friend of the Norwegian Secretary-General, took his own life by jumping out of a window. He had been brought to despair by being forced to dismiss employees who had merely invoked a constitutional right in refusing to testify.

I decided that the way to get Senator Ferguson to let me say what I wanted on record was by creating an atmosphere in which he and I were equals—two gentlemen in a club— and by treating the others as flunkies. When replying to questions from Morris and Benjamin Mandel I deliberately ignored them, but faced and looked to my right, across the table-corner, at Ferguson. He went along with my tactic, engaging me, and disregarding the others. There was not the slightest sympathy between us, but he clearly felt that he was in a verbal duel and had to win. I couldn't have asked for more.

Before we got into this, I started on a prepared note of belligerency. I'd be damned if I'd let that committee present itself to the public as an objective body seeking data on the basis of which to draft legislation— the stated reason for the establishment of committees of Congress. I wanted the public to know it was simply a punitive body. When Counsel Morris opened with the routine question as to what my occupation was, I responded: "Due to the blacklist resulting from the activities of this committee and others, I am not able to pursue my occupation as a writer and researcher and translator, so I am trying to make a living as a furniture merchant."

They were stung, and Ferguson gave me exactly the opening I hoped for. "Will you make a further explanation as to what you mean by being blacklisted?" he asked, defensively. "Certainly this committee has issued no blacklist?"

I came back: "The climate of opinion that has arisen in connection with persons who, as I do, deem it possible to live in the same world with the Soviet Union, at peace; that climate of opinion, to which I believe the conduct of this subcommittee and others has contributed, has made it impossible for persons such as myself to earn a livelihood in our accepted professions."

Ferguson: "Do you claim that you have been harmed by virtue of the fact that you have advocated the proposition that America and Russia should be able to live in one world?"

I: "Precisely, sir."

He continued on the same theme. "Let me say, as far as I know, nothing has ever been said in this committee in derogation of that right."

I plunged ahead: "To the degree that I am informed of the testimony thus far, and I have read a good deal of it quite carefully, the line of questioning pursued has been such, particularly in the light of the overall events of the past year [the Korean War and China's participation on North Korea's side], as to indicate that anybody who does not believe we ought to go to war with China is a communist. That is my interpretation of the testimony and the questions with regard, for example, to gentlemen like Mr. Lattimore."

Owen Lattimore *was* a celebrity, the country's most famous expert on the Far East and head of the school of diplomacy at Johns Hopkins University. He was also associated with that Institute of Pacific Relations the committee was out to destroy. Lattimore was ultimately able to continue his career only by moving to England and taking an appointment at a secondary university, Leeds.

Committee Counsel Morris decided it was time to rescue the senator, and asked a question that played on the public mood. During the Korean War then in progress, China had surrounded six entire U.S. divisions—90,000 men—and came within a hairsbreadth of destroying them totally. There was no more flag-waving a question than the one he now posed: "Would you shoulder arms against Red China?"

"*If* Red China attacked us, which is an *utter* impossibility, I certainly would," I replied. "The very question indicates to me what I said earlier about the purpose of some of the persons doing the questioning before this committee in seeking to create an atmosphere in which anybody who opposes war with China is shut up. *Obviously* China cannot attack."

In response to another provocative question regarding Korea, I was finally able to say the following, which I hoped would reach the American people: "The important thing today is *to end the thing before it gets us ALL into it,* rather than to argue out questions to which, at best, I can offer an opinion only, and anyone else can also offer an opinion."

Here, Senator Ferguson displayed real interest, because a presidential campaign was about to start which his Republican Party would win when its candidate, Gen. Eisenhower, promised to end the war. "How would you *settle* that?" Ferguson asked.

I: "Stop the fighting where we are and settle all other questions afterward."

He: "And move out?"

I persisted: "Stop the fighting where we are, and then let our side and their side argue the thing out. Let the negotiators get stomach ulcers, [just] so [long as] we don't kill any more men." I am happy that that is precisely how the Korean War ended a year later.

Ferguson then asked an utterly unconstitutional question of political opinion, though in an area I was more than delighted to address. He asked: "Do you believe that the Smith Law, under which the 11 Communists were indicted and tried, is a good law?"

"My answer is that it is not, sir....It goes counter to the letter and the spirit of the Constitution and, what is more important than that, I think it is very bad for this country to have any legislation that tends to restrict people's expressions of opinion in any way."

He asked whether I thought those tried under the Smith Act had gotten a fair trial. No, I said, I did not, because the juries were weighted "disproportionately against working people, Negroes, and other minorities. Since these men put themselves forward as defending the rights of working people, Negroes, and other minorities, it is obvious that they might have expected, or might have had some reason to expect a different kind of verdict if such people had been on this jury."

Next they tried to bring the aura of espionage into the hearing by asking if I had contributed to the defense of Alger Hiss. I said that I had not, but deliberately volunteered that I had indeed contributed to the defense of Dr. W.E.B. DuBois, the Black intellectual then in his eighties who had been indicted specifically for circulating a petititon affirming that the next country to use an atom bomb would by that deed brand itself a war criminal.

Toward the end of the hearing, it became clear that what the committee held against me above all was a stinging letter of mine published in the *New York Times.* Morris asked: "You wrote a letter to the *New York Times* that appeared on the editorial page on Oct. 29, 1951?"

"I did, sir."

"Did you write that at the request of anybody?"

"*No, sir.*" He had one paragraph read into the record:

"If the Institute of Pacific Relations is guilty of something or other because it sponsored or published my work, then so are all the others listed above, which makes everybody out of step but McCarran and McCarthy. If the dicta of that group are permitted to stand, and if the Federal and State governments are not influenced to drop the prosecutions of Dr. W.E.B. DuBois and [M.I.T. math] Prof. Dirk Struik, the principle of guilt by association will be used to hound and whip into line all who...ever permitted free discussion and scholarship in the field of foreign policy or anything else."

Ferguson: "Is that a fair statement of what you said?"

"That is *exactly* what I said."

I regret that the Committee did not enter into the record the closing paragraph of the letter, which reads:

"The greatest sufferers will be not the scholars and molders of opinion, who are, after all, few in number, but the mass of the people whose lives, living standard and liberties are at stake where foreign policy— peace or war—are concerned. It is to the people at large that I look for defense of our liberties and whom I urge to realize that the liberty of scholars to write and speak freely is literally a matter of life and death to every American."

Incidentally, the *New York Times* had phoned and asked me to delete my defense of DuBois and Struik, because in the public mind they were Communists. I refused to do so. It ran my lengthy letter anyhow, because it wanted occasion to editorialize against the McCarran Committee, and I had provided the paper a hook on which to hang that opinion. But to let its readers know word one about my own subsequent testimony before the committee was not news fit to print.

As with the subsequent McCarthy and HUAC testimonies, this hearing garnered approval from across the social spectrum. Gen. Philip Faymonville, who had been military attache at the U.S. Embassy in Moscow in the 1930s and on-the-scene administrator of our Lend-Lease there during World War II, wrote me from his home in San Francisco: "I hope the plain unmistakeable expression of your views gave the committee some of the postgraduate instruction they seem to need so badly."

A retired judge in San Clemente wrote: "I wish to congratulate you on your courage and clarity in dealing with the committee. This should lend much support in 'times that try men's souls'."

But the letters that meant most to me at the time, and helped to build

my confidence—a very important consideration in that depressing period—were from those who had themselves been called before the witch-
hunters. Prof. Ralph Gundlach of the University of Washington, a member of its Psychology Department since 1927, was called before that
state's Un-American Activities Committee in 1948, and fired without
severance pay the next year. After his twenty-year academic career he
was forced to retrain for four years and became a psychologist in private
practice. He was very successful, and acquired a Park Avenue address in
New York City. He wrote me: "Mrs. James, who with her husband,
Burton, was also convicted of contempt of the State of Washington's
Canwell Committee, is now living with us. And she was quick to say
that what a different outcome there would have been in our cases if we
had had your example before us at that time." Dr. Gundlach had also
served a prison sentence for contempt for refusing to answer unconstitutional questions.

Yet such trials, and more serious ones involving longer potential sen-
tences, were still in progress. I was particularly moved by a letter from
Honolulu, in which a Japanese-American, Mrs. Aiko Reinecke, a dis-
missed school-teacher, wrote: "As a wife of one of the seven Hawaii
Smith Act victims, I wish to distribute your excellent pamphlet [*Man
Bites Dog*] among my friends. Please rush this order. The Hawaii Smith
Act Trial is set for Sept. 29, 1952."

A quarter-century of hardship followed for Mrs. Reinecke. She was
finally legally vindicated, recovering not only her accumulated pay and
pension rights—she was now too old to teach—but also substantial
damages. A mutual friend told me in the 1980s that Mrs. Reinecke was
blithely giving this money away to the downtrodden and oppressed and
to movements working on their behalf.

All this signified the entry of an entirely new element into my life.
Hitherto I had been, and had been regarded by others, as a scholar, a
communicator, and a rank-and-file activist. The mail quoted above
could, however, have produced a grossly inflated ego. Fortunately, as a
student of history, I have always had the keenest appreciation of how
small an individual's part is, unless he is the leader of a movement capable of transforming humanity's destiny, the deviser of a new way of
looking at nature or at society, or an artist whose work transcends all
time and place. I knew that I neither was nor had the potential to be any
of these. But I also believe that each of us is responsible for helping make
the world, or at least one's own country, a place where one need not die
in war or from its consequences of disease, hunger, and cold; where one
can develop one's abilities unhindered by birth into poverty or disad-
vantaged by one's race, ethnicity, gender, or sexual orientation; and
where one can select a partner in life across any of those lines without

negative consequences.

I had to evaluate that fan mail of 1952 for what it meant in terms of my new-found social and political influence and what components of society I had acquired meaning for. I needed to take stock of the standards I now felt responsibility for living up to, because I would hurt that which I believed in if I disappointed those who now saw me as a model. Yet I was fully aware that I was known to only a small fraction of the American people and, under the circumstances of the day, had very little expectation of becoming known to many more. But the people who were consciously resisting McCarthyism and the drive to war were the salt of the earth. The country's history and, because America was so powerful, the world's, depended in good measure upon how skilfully and determinedly that fraction of the population spoke out.

It is amazing how many individuals who were really important at that time vanished without trace from public life. Those who turned coward, or who gave up the fight because of discouragement, cynicism, or contempt for the people, are a different matter. Of course, human abilities vary. People can be held responsible only for not using to capacity their individual gifts. The chief problem with those I am thinking of has been an inability to see and adapt to new developments, such as the shift from labor to youth as the engine of social change that occurred in the 1960s. I take particular pride in a picture in a 1984 issue of LIFE magazine in which I appear as one of a group brought together to illustrate an article on the Free Speech Movement at the University of California twenty years earlier. My pride lies in the fact that I understood that shift very early on, was able to bridge the gap between the movements of the 1930s and the 1960s, and find language and forms in which to transmit some of the experience of the former to the latter.

My life at the beginning of the '50s did not consist solely of fighting McCarthyism, the Korean War, and the various forms of oppression of African-Americans. Tanya and I have always been avid theater-goers. We had become friends with two playwrights and directors, Barney Rubin and Herb Tank, who founded a theater called New Playwrights.Their first production was Rubin's "Candy Story," about life in and around a Jewish momma-and-poppa candy store in a New York neighborhood. As Communists, opposed to racism, they had no hesitation in casting the superb Black actress, Alice Childress, as the Jewish mother. That simply was not done in those days. Yet theater is based on suspension of disbelief, isn't it? And Childress had the capacity to convince you she was the character being portrayed.

Rubin did another play involving a court-martial. He wanted me to play a Marine colonel on that court. However, at the time and for decades thereafter I failed to understand that performing artists could influence people to a degree very few dealers in fact and logic could ever hope to. So I declined that offer. Actually, New Playwrights offered the most concrete proof of how success as a performer can put one in a position to be influential in public affairs. I have a hard-bound volume of its most successful play, "Longitude 49," by Herb Tank, in which the end-paper photos show Sidney Poitier in his first professional role, long before going into the movies. His later star status made him a significant voice on behalf of the causes that concerned him.

During that period when there was no public outlet for what I knew and could do best— writing, lecturing, broadcasting on the Soviet Union— I did what I could to help other cultural workers. Tank's wife was a fine photographer and a great dance partner. It was she who took the photo of a woodcarving of a clothes-presser I described earlier. The carving was the work of Zuni Maud, elderly member of a family that ran a Leftish summer resort in the Catskills. He had done a splendid fresco over the entire ceiling of the dining hall, in a style similar to Chagall's. I hope it has survived. As Zuni rode New York's subways, he always carried a block of wood no more than six inches high, a knife, and a bag for the shavings. Nearly every piece he did was on the labor trades of immigrant Jews: carpenters, tailors, house-painters, printers. Though small, these wood sculptures were truly monuments. I borrowed half-a-dozen and tried to sell them for him, but the only purchaser I found was the clothes presser in the tailor shop on the ground floor of our apartment house.

I wondered how culture could be used to spread anti-McCarthyist, anti-war, pro-labor, anti-discrimination ideas. Toward this end I researched union and progressive publications to find out what cultural activities were currently being conducted or sponsored by labor organizations. My findings were astounding: art shows and forums, musical pageants on labor history, serious theater, reviews and circulation of creative literature, night clubs featuring truly folk songs. But this could not endure when the sponsoring organizations themselves were forced out of existence. McCarthyism, by destroying the dozen national labor unions under Communist leadership and driving people of broad perspective out of the others, decimated more than political and organizational opposition.

By June, I had been nominated to run against Congressman Javits again, and also did some speaking upstate on behalf of my party. In Syracuse the city's newspaper reported my talk:

"The Progressive Party [the national party to which we were affiliated] will select its own presidential candidate this year because major party candidates believe that the war in Korea must continue....Mandel named two major differences of opinion on policy which makes it impossible for Progressives to endorse either Democratic or GOP candidates.

"He called the Korean conflict an 'endless, grinding slaughter' and said the Progressives stand for a quick peace settlement, with negotiations afterward....He pointed out that 90 percent of the national budget is for war expenditures—for the current conflict or preceding wars [to pay off their debts with compounded interest].

"Taking issue with Gen. Eisenhower's statements, Mandel said the general's ideas on tax reduction could not be enforced and still carry out his program for government operation....Mandel called attention to President Truman's recent action in approving one *million* dollars for domestic flood relief and in the same week setting aside one *billion* [a thousand times as much] for an H-bomb plant.

"Mandel observed that wars do not necessarily bring prosperity on the home front. He cited the 'textile depression' apparent in several cities today, and said that today's war production involves small quantities of expensive items manufactured in many new plants."

Shortly afterward, the Progressive Party named its candidate for the presidency. Somewhat earlier, its national committee had met in New York City. I was not a member, but as a party candidate was welcome to attend and speak. The atmosphere of gloom was virtually tangible. The people we hoped might run either didn't want to go down in embarrassing defeat, or left the impression that they would do no more than go through the motions. However, a nattily-dressed lawyer from the West Coast spoke with hope and ebullience.

In those days minor parties would no more consider a Westerner for the No. 1 slot than would the two major parties. Too few votes out there. The shift of population to the Sun Belt had not yet occurred. Having lived in California for a year during my Hoover Institution fellowship, I had a sense of its vigor that most of the others present did not. I got up, pointed to this San Francisco lawyer, said that he had the spirit to keep us afloat and should be our candidate. That's how Vincent Hallinan got to be nominated for president. He was no ordinary attorney. Having been the top criminal defense lawyer of the San Francisco region a decade earlier, he was now under sentence of contempt for the vigor of his defense of longshore union leader Harry Bridges. At the national convention itself, Hallinan was nominated in absentia, for he was serving his sentence in a federal prison. His wife, brilliant and beautiful Vivian, a workingclass woman who had made them wealthy by shrewd real estate dealings, carried the campaign for him, and spoke at my closing congressional election rally. The candidate for vice-president was an African-American woman, Charlotta Bass, editor of a paper in Los Angeles which had earlier serialized chapters from one of my books.

August 1952 found me back in Richmond, Virginia, as the invited house-guest of another Black woman, Mrs. Senora Lawson, whose extraordinary life story I thumbnailed briefly earlier. The purpose of the visit was to gather material for what I hoped would be a book on that struggle. When it became clear that there was no chance whatever for publication of a non-fiction work of that nature in the atmosphere of the day, I wrote it as a biographical novel with her as the central figure, but never completed it.

Upon arriving in Richmond I found that, instead of doing a leisurely series of interviews, I was plunged into exactly the same kind of case we had fought eighteen months earlier. The story is told in a leaflet I wrote, mimeographed in unadorned typescript as follows:

An Appeal to White Virginians
Let there be no more 'Martinsville' cases
HALT THE EXECUTION OF ALBERT JACKSON

"22-year-old Albert Jackson, Jr., Negro, is scheduled to die on August 25th, a week from Monday, for alleged rape of a white woman. However, the white policeman who made the arrest testified in court that the woman said: 'Where's my five dollars?' Clearly, where money was involved, what happened was not rape....

"THERE HAS BEEN NO EXECUTION FOR RAPE SINCE THE MARTINSVILLE CASE, a period of 18 months. We are convinced that that was a result of the protest made at that time....A standard of justice for Negroes taken from the time of slavery endangers justice for whites. Some day we will realize that the poverty and backwardness of the white South, which we all regret, results from suppression of the Negro.

"LET YOUR VOICE BE HEARD! This Monday at 3 p.m., Governor Battle will hold a hearing for commutation of sentence in this case. Sign your name to this leaflet and mail it to the governor TODAY so he gets it Monday. Ask your pastor to pray for justice in this case on Sunday, and inform the governor of his opinion. Let him send a telegram or phone the governor. Do so yourself. Attend the commutation hearing Monday at 3 p.m., to express your interest. That is your right. SAVE THE HONOR OF VIRGINIA.

What happened subsequently is described in an article I must have written about five days later. It reads:

"The skies fell on Richmond yesterday. Governor John Battle...yielded on six hours notice to an unceremonious demand by a Negro drug store clerk that Battle receive a citizens' delegation seeking commutation of the death penalty....This had never happened in Virginia before. Bear in mind that this was a delegation of local people, chiefly Negroes, unsupported as yet by the spotlight of national or world opinion....

"I have seen a police cruiser on a Sunday morning break up a group of Negro men passing the time of day on the corner. I have heard a bus driver, in his idea of a joke, tell a Negro that it cost 25 cents extra to get on at a certain corner, and the man deemed it the better part of valor to pay and go on to the back of the bus. The same driver earnestly urged a young Negro boy to go to church. Turning to me, he said: 'It's good for them.'

"It is against this background that you have to understand the whirlwind protest campaign that compelled Gov. Battle's action....Richmond today is not the place that it was before the electrifying 24-hour-a-day midwinter Death Watch on the [state] Capitol lawn in the Martinsville Case, and the unprecedented, unauthorized memorial parade which capped that struggle 18 months ago.

"Last Thursday evening, James Smith, arthritic young drugstore clerk, reconvened the Martinsville Committee. That very night, leaflets were handed out at a Negro dance in the city auditorium. The distributors needed no exhortation. One of them is brother-in-law to a man arrested for 'rape' just last week on a fantastic charge levelled by a white neighbor jealous of the Negro family's property. A 14-year-old girl distributor answered a question from me: 'Why am I giving out these papers? I think, suppose Jackson was my brother?'

"On Friday, the Richmond dailies refused to carry the Committee's press release. The people got the news anyhow. Negro newsboys had tucked a leaflet into every paper they sold. The Committee was penniless, and managed to scrape together only $28 for leaflets, postage, stationery and everything else. But no leaflet was wasted, and one did the work of ten.

"A candy store keeper posted one on his counter, and I saw customer after customer read it and go out to pass the word. A laundry owner stapled one to every package for delivery. A clergyman brought 500 to a state-wide Sunday School convention of the A.M.E. Church, and other ministers present pledged to spread the word from the pulpit, and to wire protests from their congregations. Boy Scouts and deacons passed them out at services this Sunday.

"Meanwhile, a white house painter and a laborer distributed

'An Appeal to White Virginians' in the heart of the shopping district. Within an hour, the committee had phone calls like this one from an utter stranger. He told the housewife who answered the phone: 'I am a white man. My name is J.J. Hughes, and I operate the frame shop on North Second Street. I am completely opposed to that man being executed, and I will do everything in my power to help.'....

"On Saturday evening, steps were taken to organize the delegation. Mrs. Senora B. Lawson, who has come closer to election to the State Legislature than any Negro since Reconstruction, volunteered to lead it. And on Sunday morning James Smith posted his letter to the Governor. It did not plead for the courtesy of an interview. It said: 'This is to inform you' that a committee would call. It condemned the sentence as 'lynch justice' designed to terrorize the Negro people. And the last sentence read: 'We will not be terrorized.'

"A Negro journalist and radio announcer looked at that letter, shook his head, and said: 'I know John Battle. He'll go through the roof when he sees that letter.' James Smith did not agree. And Governor Battle, with the specter of the Martinsville demonstrations before him, saw the delegation—25 people, in addition to the three lawyers he had expected to receive as supplicants. He listened carefully."

Albert Jackson was not executed. I was an intimate participant in planning and carrying out every one of the measures described above. I take particular pride in having drafted the letter that James Smith felt he could and should mail. That is to say, I was able to grasp the mood and enjoy the confidence of the most militant Black leadership.

When I returned to New York I found myself in an Alice-in-Wonderland situation. On the one hand, leaders of the Communist Party were studying my testimony before the McCarran Committee as a model of how to uphold one's political beliefs and principles before the courts. One such leader was Jack Hall, head of the Longshoremen's and Warehousemen's Union in Hawaii, who had managed to bring eight thousand pineapple plantation hands and twenty thousand sugar workers out of conditions resembling colonial peonage into a life of decent pay, a health plan, and vacations. At the same time, the New York Communist Party put me on trial, secretly, for having a mind of my own. I had told close friends in the Party that things were happening, and not happening, in the Soviet Union that were totally contrary to what we believed in. One such friend, a classical true believer, reported my "heresies" to Party officials.

I don't know what would have happened in normal times, but the atmosphere of McCarthyism created fear in the land that readers today cannot imagine. A worker had been thrown out of a factory window by his fellow-workers for collecting signatures for that DuBois anti-nuclear petition. Nearly a hundred national and state leaders of the Communist Party had been sentenced to prison terms, were in jail under extraordinarily high bail or were only free after months of effort to raise such bail. Two hundred and seventy-five foreign-born persons, many of them brought here as infants or young children, had been arrested for deportation for belonging to the Communist Party or other organizations designated subversive. Persons who had been driven out of their professions or fired from their jobs, among whom I was one, numbered in the thousands.

"In the District of Columbia a man was refused a license to sell secondhand furniture because he had invoked the Fifth Amendment about Communism. In Indiana professional wrestlers were obliged to take a loyalty oath," wrote David Caute in his classical book on McCarthyism, *The Great Fear.* In Utica, New York, a woman was granted an annulment of her marriage solely on the ground that her husband was a Communist, and the official referee who issued that decision then boasted to the press that it had never before been done .

Under these circumstances, the principal Communist Party leader, William Z. Foster, drew the conclusion that fascism was imminent. Under those conditions the Communist Party would have to go deep underground. Therefore it had to rid itself of all who might be untrustworthy, i.e., anyone who showed any doubt about its beliefs or what amounted to articles of faith. One such article was that anything the Soviet Union did, internal or external, had to be right. Another was a Communist version of guilt by association: no Communist was permitted to have even social contact with any follower of Leon Trotsky—the issue on which my dissent in 1938 had brought permanent removal from leadership. Contact with Zionists was almost as bad.

Naturally, there was no legal compulsion upon me to appear at that Communist Party trial in which I was the defendant. Nor was there intimidation. Simply, as a loyal member of an organization in which internal discipline was a principle of organization, it was taken for granted that I would show up. I did. The only thing I can say in favor of that trial is that it was presided over by a Black woman. Another member of that court was Dr. Doxey Wilkerson, one of the very few Black academics of that day, who later left the party himself. There was no other majority-white organization in the United States at that time in which it was conceivable that Blacks would sit in judgment upon a white.

In some respects, the trial was funny. The McCarran Committee had wished to demonstrate my association with Communists. The

Communist Party sought to demonstrate my association with my mother-in-law. Tanya's mother had been a clothing worker in her youth and was now the very earthy wife of a dentist. She was not deep, politically, but proudly regarded herself as a socialist. Her vague mix of notions unquestionably included some nuances of Zionism and Trotskyism. Exasperated at some of the questions about her, I snapped: "I'll trust Sabina Millstein over some leaders of the Communist Party." That proved only too true. Some of its officers at state levels crumpled or sold out, becoming FBI informers and government witnesses. The overwhelming majority did not. But my in-laws stood by us through the McCarthy years, both when we needed financial support—they were not wealthy—and when I was the focus of publicized hounding by the witch-hunters.

One question posed to me simply took my breath away: "Who *told* you to become an expert on the Soviet Union?" I was dumbfounded and made no answer. They simply could not grasp acting on one's own initiative.

The party had taken itself so deep underground that it never told me the decision in that trial. Yet for the next four years I tried to pay my dues and attend meetings, but no one would accept the money and no one would tell me where the meetings would occur. I quit the Party permanently in 1957, prompted by events that had not yet occurred in 1952.

It wasn't only adults who were whipsawed by high politics in those years. On November 8, 1952, the New York *Teacher News*, publication of the Teachers' Union, carried the following letter from me:

"One more for your file of anecdotes on suppression of free thought among school children. You may recall Corliss Lamont's story at your annual TU conference recently about a 12-year-old who was reprimanded for quoting [former President] Herbert Hoover (in reinforcing her argument against civil defense). That was my daughter. Since then, she had the experience of being asked, as an examination question, to show why the Soviet Union was undemocratic. She replied that it *was* democratic because of absence of discrimination on the basis of nationality, opportunity for women to enter any field, and equality of opportunity regardless of parents' wealth or lack of it. She was marked wrong. Since she wants to enter a special high school, her marks are very important. Thus, a child has to choose between fulfilling her ambition—following the bent and inclination on which her heart is set and at which she works hard—and stating her true beliefs on a very fundamental issue of our times.

"Thus, we train liars—or break kids' hearts."

Under the pressure of the times, I contributed to her difficulties. When I was already elderly, son Bob reminded me—or rather told me, because it was completely absent from memory —of an event a little later in that period which contributed to his and Phyllis' need for therapy decades later. The IRS had shut down the Communist paper, the *Daily Worker,* on tax evasion charges. These charges were preposterous, because the paper was always money-losing and survived only by appeals to its loyal supporters. Party members would donate a week's wages. On this occasion, the paper called for a special effort at street sale as an act of resistance, to demonstrate that it would not quit.

Phyllis and her boyfriend, Keith, whom she later married, went out to sell it and came home rather late at night. I remember most clearly that, ever since they had begun to keep company, I was fearful—Bob as a child under ten could not know this—that she might become pregnant at a time when abortions were totally illegal and the cost would have devastated us, while if a child were born the financial burden would have been still worse and her life would have been totally sidetracked. Bob tells me that when she came home that night I banged her head against the floor. He says that the general mood at home in those years was that of a day when one never knew when clouds would suddenly block out the sun. His parents were constantly fighting, and he particularly feared my capacity to verbalize contempt.

I do not believe my failure to remember the incident was denial. Just weeks before Bob told me that story, Tanya reminded me that I had gone out of my way on behalf of a family member in a purely personal matter involving some legal risk. I had not only forgotten this incident, as with the other one, bit I also could not recall that later event even after she related it to me. The fact is that, until the collapse of the Soviet Union and, with it, my faith in Marxist socialism, family was always secondary in my consciousness. Trying to change the world came first.

My children are unstinting in their praise for what they call my mellowing in the past decade. Bob even calls me "sweet" and "laid back." To me it is much simpler and, in a way, sad. There is no longer a Utopian ideal I believe in. My time must no longer be devoted to bringing it to reality. For example, my father, in his last years, increasingly needed my help. There was no reason to think that such a diversion of my energy would in any way postpone the millenium. Likewise with Tanya. Today I am a very attentive and caring husband. I am sure I would have been regardless of politics, as the demands of her declining health necessitated. But I would have been conflicted, if a specific revolution were still to be made.

CHAPTER 16

One on One with Joe McCarthy

In 1953 the countryside seen from a train window between Washington and New York was still chiefly pastoral. But in March the bare branches of the trees, the dark brown of the fields, the black of the asphalt roads, and the cold gray of the sky, deepened by early nightfall, corresponded to the mood of the nation: gloomy and fearful.

I felt the same way. I should have been elated. I had gone to Washington in response to a subpoena from Sen. Joe McCarthy and had been determined to do as much as any single person could to destroy him. Now, convinced that I had damaged the senator severely, I was scared. I was sure he knew that he had lost, and badly. This was borne out by a personal attack on me in his newspaper column five weeks later, after dozens of other witnesses had been called, many of them national figures, as I was not.

I had had no doubt before being called, and even less after confronting him personally on consecutive days, that his was truly a fascist mentality. And fascists use physical violence to dispose of their opponents. He was immensely powerful, having brought the State Department to its knees and having already attacked the former head of this country's armed forces, Gen. Marshall. Prime Minister Clement Attlee of England said to Parliament that year that he sometimes wondered whether it was Gen. Eisenhower or Joe McCarthy who was really president of the United States.

Back in New York that evening, I learned that the most sensational parts of my attack on him had been carried on national TV news, in addition to the complete live coverage during the day. Later, NBC pre-empted its very popular national radio show, "Music at Midnight," to rebroadcast the extremely defensive brief testimony given that day by the former head of the Communist Party, Earl Browder, as well as forty-five minutes of my own. My friend George David, who possessed a wire recorder—ordinary citizens didn't yet have tape recorders—made a splendid copy of it. The next day, my testimony was front-page news in the *New York Times*, which wrote: "Mr. McCarthy became the principal target of bitter comment, angry charges and personal attack that at one time prompted him to call a Capitol policeman to stand ready to eject Mr. Mandel. Mr. McCarthy reddened at times."

The crudely anti-Semitic handling of the witness preceding me by another member of the committee had put me in a mood of towering rage. Further, I was disgusted that a fellow Jew, the unspeakable Roy Cohn, was willing to serve as prosecutor for McCarthy, who had sought to protect Nazi S.S. murderers of American prisoners of war against punishment. The *Times* continued: "Later Mr. McCarthy paid tribute to Jews and contended that the witness [myself], while apparently trying to speak for them, did not. 'Every race has its renegades,' Mr. McCarthy said. 'It certainly does,' snapped the witness, glaring at Mr. Cohn [the Committee's counsel]....Senator...Dirksen...attempted to smooth the ruffled feelings and bring the inquiry back to base [asking]: 'If you were a member of this subcommittee, assigned to find out why libraries designed to combat communism contained books by Communists preaching their philosophies in countries where we have problems, would you feel that our work now was an improper exploration?'

"'If I were a member of the subcommittee,' Mr. Mandel responded, 'I would first try to find out how Senator McCarthy was able to save 175,000 bucks while making a salary of $15,000 a year'."

That line tickled writers' fancy across the political spectrum. *The Nation* editorialized: "Telecasts of recent inquisitions have brought a new understanding of the ugly menace of McCarthyism to thousands who were formerly indifferent or uninformed. A large audience heard one witness demand that the Senate find out how McCarthy 'was able to bank 175,000 bucks while making a salary of $15,000 a year'."

In its own distorted way, even the coverage in *Time* magazine told me I had accomplished what I had set out to do, and further circulated my arguments. It wrote: 'The week's most agitated performance came from a blazing-eyed New York advertising copywriter" and then quoted the exchange about Jewish renegades and my accusation: "This is a bookburning. You lack only the tinder to set fire to the books as Hitler did 20 years ago." It is a mark of the times that *Time* chose to identify me not as a scholar subpoenaed because of his books, but by the work to which I had to turn for a livelihood after I was blacklisted.

The Hearst press put in bold-face my words: "You, Senator McCarthy, murdered [Major] Raymond Kaplan by driving him to the point where he jumped under a truck."

UPI, for which I had been Russian Expert during World War II, reported, "Mandel was the most outspoken of the three" witnesses that day. This story reached subscribing newspapers all over the world, and included coverage of the bookburning, the murder, and the Jewish-issue exchanges.

I read these articles with a sense of satisfaction, of course, but also with a feeling of contempt for the press. A year earlier, when subpoenaed by the Senate's McCarran Committee for the crime of writing my first book, *The Soviet Far East and Central Asia*, not a single word of my testimony had been reported, because I had used moderate language to express views the press was not interested in circulating. But because, learning from that experience, I had now chosen to hang it by its own petard, sensationalism, my words were news.

The only section of the press that attacked me was that of the country's official Jewish leadership. *The Reconstructionist*, magazine of the American Jewish Committee, not only carried an article on the subject but circulated it as a separate reprint. The *Jewish Day* , a Yiddish-language daily published in New York, was also critical of me. The underlying issue is best explained in the book, *Naming Names*, by Victor Navasky, publisher of *The Nation*. He wrote:

"It was the heritage and the style of the Jewish establishment to work with the internal-security establishment...When McCarthy's hearings about the Voice of America and the USIA program were telecast on March 25, 1953, featuring a hostile witness named William Mandel, the response of the A[merican] J[ewish] C[ommittee] was not to attack the investigation as misplaced, not to question what valid purpose was served....Rather the AJC's reflex was to ask whether something couldn't be done to prevent giving witnesses such as Mandel, whom they regarded as an embarrassment to the Jewish community, a forum. Mandel, pointed out the [American Jewish Committee] staffer Morton Clurman in an internal memo, was 'an extremely unpleasant, evasive, unctuous character who reinforces every stereotype of the Communist Jewish intellectual'."

The AJC's attitude was identical to that of the Jewish establishment in Germany a quarter century earlier. They believed that keeping silent would protect them against Hitler. Others reacted differently to my attack on McCarthy and Cohn. A few weeks later when I spoke to a Bronx neighborhood group—strangers to me—in the very modest apartment of a clothing worker, a toil-worn immigrant woman said to me: "Du bist der bester Yid in die gantse Velt" - you are the best Jew in the whole world.

I went into work the day after the hearing, and my employer at a Madison Avenue medical advertising agency told me to stay home for a few weeks, and that my salary would continue. I dropped into a bar to watch the noon news before getting on the subway, and there I was on the tube yet again, slamming into the committee. When I got home, a telegram had arrived from a fellow-employee with whom I had never had any association except at work. It read: "Dear Bill The following is my telephone number Plaza 35198. The following is my address 153 East 51st. If I can be of any service to you please call. Anna M. Santoro."

At home, my phone rang. It was a friend since our teens, an engineer at a huge military aircraft plant on Long Island. He told me that workers had been talking in the cafeteria: "Did you hear that Commie give it to Joe McCarthy last night?" Their evaluation of my politics was unimportant. What counted was that they had learned it was possible to beat McCarthy. I began receiving letters from total strangers who had gotten my address from media reports as well as from acquaintances.

William A. Reuben, a thrice-wounded infantry lieutenant in World War II, had had the courage to write, in the left-New-Dealish *National Guardian,* the first articles to challenge the assumption of the guilt of Ethel and Julius Rosenberg when even the Communists wouldn't touch that case because they feared the nuclear espionage charge rubbing off on them. He wrote me:

"Bravo! Bravo! Bravo! When even the *Times'* and [New York *Herald-Trib's*] accounts make you seem like a hero, you can be sure that you really *were* good. Reading their accounts of your appearance before the Committee was, even for such a jaded 'subversive' as me, wonderfully inspiring; and in doing so, I was awfully proud that I know you and am a part of the same movement. Congratulations. You've certainly established a new high for progressives who might be called, to emulate, and have given encouragement and confidence to *millions* of *others.*"

There was also antagonistic mail dated that very first day after the hearing. One, signed by a woman with a Ukrainian name in Chicago, was sent to me care of the McCarthy Committee, which dutifully forwarded it. It contained a very interesting sentence: "You can see there is a temptation to get violent with your type of people." But she was puzzled. "What makes you tick? You fascinate me!" It was not a stupid letter, and had some very pertinent things to say about lack of civil liberties in the Soviet Union. But most of the letters were concerned with our own country's situation. One said specifically: "You deserve the warm thanks of all Americans who treasure their civil liberties."

The compliments were certainly nice to read, but what interested me most was the effect of my testimony in a very discouraged time, particularly out in places where there was not much chance of contact with like-minded people. A man in Richmond, Indiana, wrote: "We listened, late in the evening, to an hour or so of testimony. And your courage and manhood made us so happy that we actually jumped up and down in our chairs." He added that he hoped I wouldn't lose my job, and wanted to write my employer, but couldn't get the address as it went by on the air. I needed support, because my employment status was not yet settled, and sent him the address. He did write that letter, and sent me a copy. In a large, bold, sweeping, almost 19th-century hand, he made a particularly fine statement about the nature of the fight against McCarthyism. He wrote that I had defended my: "basic American privilege of writing books and putting into them what he feels is the objective truth, as he sees it. To me, this attitude (freedom to think and speak), plus the bravery and courage to defend it, constitutes the true American way of life... that the authors of our Constitution and Bill of Rights envisioned....The true democratic situation should be such that all Americans, regardless of their financial or social position, should feel... completely free, to speak their honest thoughts on all subjects....It was in this spirit that Jefferson and his co-founders of our nation created the political democracy which unfortunately is under such fearful and terrible attack today."

The man also hoped that my "way of making a living would not suffer." A lot of good it did me. At this time I was writing prescription drug ads for publication in the *Journal of the American Medical Association* and survey articles on treatment outcomes for a proprietary magazine sent directly to physicians.When McCarthy had insisted that I identify my employer on the air as the condition for letting me express my opinion of his committee, I did so, and then added:

"It was known to the members of the committee who were present yesterday [at the executive session], and everyone here now knows this, that my present employment has nothing whatever to do with the purposes of this committee. I asked the committee yesterday, in the spirit of fairness, *which I doubted it had,* not to place my job in jeopardy, for that reason. One of the committee members...then indicated that I should be willing to pay the price for the activities in which I engaged. That was an admission by the committee that it has arrogated itself the right to exact punishment, although it is not a court of law and thus deprives one of due process of law."

The manner in which my boss reacted was fairly typical of the period. My employer, L. W. Frohlich, canvassed all his clients—Parke-Davis, then the major drug manufacturer, Parkside Laboratories, Heublein, which was non-medical—and asked whether I should be fired. None supported doing that, but neither did they urge my retention. They wanted no problems with McCarthy. Who knows what he might investigate next? After my month's paid leave, I was fired and paid *another* month's salary as severance pay, although I had been there only a year. Conscience money.

I now proceeded to give what further lectures I could get in my own field. No management dared to represent me any longer. But the fan mail inspired the idea of circulating my testimony in the form of a phonograph record. The first version was 78 rpm, and therefore had to be very abbreviated. Fortunately, the country's very first tape editor,

Tony Schwartz, had emerged. He transferred my friend's wire recording to tape, and then physically suspended tape strips just like film editors did in cutting rooms, before taping them together. Tony was also Pete Seeger's editor for record production, and that was where I met Pete for the first time. He had already been blacklisted without having yet been called before any of the witch-hunters.

The 78 rpm recording went well, and the response revealed that many more people already had machines that could play 33 rpm LPs than I thought, so I put out a forty-five minute record—essentially the entire hearing. Since my live copy was from that NBC replay, I didn't possess the end, which contained some of the sharpest exchanges, particularly when I accused McCarthy's counsel, Roy Cohn, of being a renegade to his Jewish heritage, discussed how to end the war in Korea, attacked the Smith Act under which Communists were being jailed, challenged McCarthy on the unexplainable size of his bank account, and said that the committee was out to pressure librarians to take books off the shelves. And the AJC researcher quoted by Navasky had called me "evasive"! That still rankles. To make this portion of the record, I found a professional actor to volunteer his services in reading the McCarthy, Dirksen, and Cohn passages from the official transcript, while I re-enacted my own testimony.

That was my one experience as a theatrical director. I learned from it something that did not at all surprise me—that I am not an actor. It is one thing for me to ad lib both statements and responses, and to do so with a keen sense of how to reach my audience and how to force a benchful of opponents to play my game. But to *act* — to psyche myself into re-reading my very own words with the electricity and nuances of the live original—was something I didn't quite achieve.

Yet, in 1953, that LP of my McCarthy testimony served a useful purpose. A stranger who had seen it on TV once told me me that he thought it would prove the turning point against McCarthyism. I choose to think of it as more meaningful than radio icon Ed Murrow's highly-publicized broadcast against the senator, or attorney Welch' marvelous turn of phrase the following year when McCarthy was investigating the U.S. Army: "At long last, sir, have you no shame?" Neither Murrow nor Welch came to grips with the basic issue: that this junior senator from Wisconsin had attained enormous power to terrorize—a Columbia professor and a journalist I knew both died of heart attacks immediately upon forcing themselves into expressions of opposition—by carrying the Establishment's own anti-communism tactics to their logical extreme. I faced him down on exactly that issue.

Some of the mail in response to my phonograph record was very humbling, because my life was physically comfortable, for all its tension and uncertainty. I'd get letters like this one from Detroit:

"I am a member of Local 600, a worker at the Ford Rouge plant and a former editor of *Ford Facts* (65,000-circulation weekly paper of the local union)...We are going thru a terrible ordeal, Bro. Mandel, and your example is a model for all true Americans to emulate - and a source of encouragement to all of us who may have to follow in your footsteps. I am concerned about how you and your family are getting along as a result of your recent experience....Please take care of yourself. Our country needs people of your mold. Best wishes to you and your wife and children."

That kind of man I had to know. So I wrote him. He replied as follows:

"How did I know you had children? A man *without children of his own* could not have fought like you did. As I listened to you over TV that night, I said to myself, 'here's a man who is not only defending his ideology and personal integrity as a man—he's defending his own flesh and blood.' By remarkable coincidence, I too, have three children, Lila, 15, Nancy, 10, and Jackie, 7. Having children seems to give us a bigger stake in this struggle; we're fighting for something tangible, our very children's future no less. That is not to say that a man or woman without children cannot make a good anti-fascist. But I am saying that people like us fight with more feeling, greater depth and personal meaning...and better understanding....Unlike Gracchus I think they can be beaten now, not in some remote faraway future. But I definitely do not believe they can be beaten by staying on the defensive. We have to go on the offensive, Mandel style."

The writer of that letter, Leo Orsage, had been one of the founders of the union at Ford. That meant he was willing not only to stand up to beatings by company thugs, but also had the strength to attend meetings and distribute leaflets before and after a working day in which Ford sought to extract every last bit of energy. He had been fired, and it was three and a half years before he got his job back by order of the National Labor Relations Board. He sent me a printed leaflet from his campaign for election to the local's bargaining committee. It carried his picture: a worn face, sunken eyes, but openness, kindness, generosity writ large.

Two national labor unions, the United Electrical Workers and the Furriers, bought my record for use at their meetings. So did the Longshoremen in Hawaii and even the A.F. of L. Trades & Labor Council of Yellowstone County, Montana. The *National Guardian* published the text as a pamphlet, *Mandel vs. McCarthy*.

Despite the immediate pressures of the day, a number of letters revealed a sense of history. Another letter from Detroit, accompanying an order for the record, referred back to the actual hearing, which the writer had watched. "I very quickly had the sense of listening in to something that had the authentic historical ring to it. I felt that I had accidentally tuned in one of the decisive statements of our times."

A young woman in New York whom I had met at a summer camp wrote: "I will give this record to play to my children some day, as a sign of these trying times, and the courage of these times. I have no doubt that this record will one day become a collector's item." More important to me is that, forty-three years later, the night before I wrote these words, a young listener to my radio program phoned in to say that he had taped a broadcast of the record a couple of months earlier and had made copies and distributed them to friends. I would like to think that an acquaintance of one of my brothers-in-law was right when, after my 1953 McCarthy hearing, he wrote me, "There will most assuredly be a time...when the records will be opened again and the Cohns and McCarthys as well as those who grovelled before them will be revealed before the eyes of an awakened and irate populace. At that time I'm sure that your actions will be remembered and revered by the people—which is the highest reward for men of principle."

In light of the award of an Oscar for lifetime achievement in 1999 to movie director Elia Kazan, who had named names and destroyed the careers of fellow film people during the witch-hunt years, I wonder when that time will come.

My main satisfaction lies in what I know I did for people in what Lillian Hellman dubbed "the scoundrel time." From Shreveport, Louisiana, a Jack Hooper wrote me. "Any time that I become depressed, due to the operations of the Nazi-Fascist McCarthy Committee, I play your record and I truly get a 'lift'." I heard a former YWCA secretary in China, Maude Russell, say of her own speaking tour across the U.S. at the time: "I would also play Bill Mandel's record, and you should have seen people's backs straighten up."

While it was good to feel I was keeping people's spirits up, it was important to me—very conscious that I was an intellectual—that I had gotten through to people who lived by their hands, and to Blacks. Orsage in the Detroit Ford union local was proof of the former. As to the latter, I received a painfully-scrawled letter from the chairman of the Fair Employment Practices Committee of Missouri, in St. Louis. If the writer's handwriting was uncertain, his ideas were not. He wrote: "I need the record for all my Christmas meetings at my headquarters....We say put McCarthy out in '54. Elect the Progressive Party...The truth should be told about the Rosenbergs."

Cohn had asked me about that last, in the most classic of all illustrations of McCarthy's true purpose. The senator was not at all interested in whether the State Department had exercised bad judgment in acquiring a few copies of my work on Soviet Asia for its Overseas Libraries, but in squashing dissent. I suppose I could have responded by asking what relevance the Rosenbergs had to the stated purpose of an investigation into book purchases by McCarthy's Subcommittee on Government Operations—which is all that the senator officially controlled. I had never been a government employee. But that would have been perceived by the nation glued to its television screens as dodging and weaving—defensive. I was very deliberately out to instill a consciousness that McCarthy and Cohn could be brought down. So the exchange went as follows:

Cohn: "Has the *National Guardian* been conducting quite a vigorous campaign in defense of the convicted atom spies?"

Mandel: "Who are you referring to?"

Cohn: "Julius and Ethel Rosenberg."

Mandel: "I wanted to make that clear. The convicted *what* ?"

Cohn: "Atom spies."

Mandel: "*Do you know your law,* Mr. Cohn?"

Cohn: "Well, I prosecuted the case. I think so."

Mandel: "What were those people convicted of?"

Cohn: "They were convicted of conspiracy."

Mandel: "*Exactly,* and conspiracy is not espionage."

Cohn: "Do you think the Rosenbergs were guilty?"

Mandel: "Unlike a great many people who are taking an active part in that campaign [to release them, which he had asked about], and who have read the transcript of the trial from beginning to end, and who have drawn the conclusion that they are not guilty, I, as a scholar, will not offer an opinion, because I have not read the transcript from beginning to end. However, I do think that the offering of a death sentence in peace time is unjustified."

In the course of further questioning pursued by the committee, I added: "It is rather typical of the situation existing in this country that the first two people ever to get the death sentence in peace time for this crime happened to be Jewish."

Incidentally, over forty years later, my view of the case remains the same. The Russians had naturally used espionage to speed their development of a nuclear bomb. A German scientist, Klaus Fuchs, freely admitted when arrested that he had transmitted information on American bomb work to them, and proudly proclaimed his belief that his deed had furthered the prevention of World War III by helping break the U.S. monopoly of the bomb. He was tried in England and served a long term, but he did not name the Rosenbergs. A post-Soviet book published in Russia has been cited in the West as doing so. But the author, an anti-Communist military historian named Volkogonov, denied this. In very recent years, an American Bar Association moot court retried the case on the basis of the evidence presented in the original trial, and the jury of law professors found the Rosenbergs not guilty. Few people are aware that the U.S. Supreme Court never reviewed the evidence in the case, but only whether procedure was correct. Later revelations of prosecutor Cohn's illegal consultation with Judge Kaufman during the Rosenberg Trial, and his behavior in other cases, make it clear that no one he ever prosecuted, guilty or not, ever received a fair trial.

On a personal level, my McCarthy hearing brought satisfactions not reflected in fan mail. Those who heard the proceedings or read the news stories had no way of knowing what had gone on in my heart and mind in preparing for it. When I was handed the subpoena by a process server who rang my doorbell at about noon on a Saturday, I was packing an overnite bag in preparation for a lecture that evening at a synagogue in New Haven, Connecticut. I had been invited to speak by the rabbi who married Arthur Miller and Marilyn Monroe. The subpoena demanded that I appear on Monday at 2 p.m. How was I to find a lawyer in Washington from New York City on a Saturday afternoon? Fortunately, my lawyer uncle, Simon Schachter, knew the home number of a good attorney in Washington, Joe Forer. I reached him, and that was taken care of.

I weighed alternatives: should I go to New Haven to carry out my speaking engagement? Logic indicated I should cancel the date to give myself maximum time to think through how to handle McCarthy and to assemble necessary documentation. But there was a higher logic. The purpose of such subpoenas was to silence the people to whom they were served. To fail to meet my lecture date would be, in that regard, a victory for McCarthy. I went to New Haven, spoke, came home, and spent Sunday making notes. Having already been called before the other Senate witch-hunting committee the previous year, I had carefully followed the changing Supreme Court findings on what one could and could not legally say. Yet I wanted to smash the wall of media silence that had followed my previous hearing. With a wife and three young children, six, eight, and thirteen, I wanted to avoid a contempt citation and jail sentence. Every additional person who went to jail added to the atmosphere of fear of McCarthy himself and McCarthyist practices. So did everyone who stayed out of jail by caving in. I wanted to destroy McCarthy and yet avoid imprisonment. I felt the people hated him, and that someone who spat in his eye, figuratively speaking, and got away with it, could turn the situation around. That's what I set out to do.

The hearing was to be televised. I knew from his previous investigations that McCarthy did not permit logical discussion, so I would have to jab, cover up, and hit him with a hard right when opportunity offered. Naturally, this would not look like a prize-fight. I was perfectly aware, and from his behavior so was he, that this was theater. My job was to be the dignified scholar, which I was, and prosecutor when I got a chance. The senator knew that people were very dubious about his methods, and wanted to look and sound judicial. That meant that, by proper demeanor and deftness I could force him to let me say what I desired to, as he would look the villain if he silenced me.

All this was ahead of me, but very clearly in mind, as I sat in my lawyer's office. While we were there, former New York Congressman Marcantonio walked in. He asked, "What are you doing here, Bill?" I replied, "Old Joe has subpoenaed me." Marc flashed back:"Why don't you ask him when he's going to get that Christine Jorgensen operation?"

In today's atmosphere of struggle for gay rights, that sounds awful. Jorgensen was the first American to undergo a sex change operation. There were rumors that McCarthy was homosexual. I don't believe he was. But in the America of that day, to pose that question would have done me more harm than it would have done McCarthy. Homosexuality was simply not something "decent" people discussed. Anything like the public airing of the intimacies between President Clinton and Monica Lewinsky was absolutely inconceivable. But I understood that Marcantonio's snap remark represented the instinctive reaction of a brilliant politician that something truly sensational had to be said. So I decided to accuse McCarthy of murder.

A military communications engineer, Major Raymond Kaplan, had thrown himself under a truck after being browbeaten by McCarthy because a Voice of America short-wave transmitter proved unable to reach the USSR. Siting an antenna properly in the United States for that purpose was then at the very cutting edge of technological possibility. A very poignant letter to his wife and son had been found on Kaplan's body, and the *New York Times* had published it. I decided to use it to back up my charge.

I feared that my lawyer's office might be bugged, because Forer had represented many "unfriendly witnesses," as we were called. Therefore, I wrote out my questions in clear longhand and handed them to him instead of stating them out loud. I asked whether I could query McCarthy about the relative size of his savings and salary. My list of possible challenges to him continued: Why did you defend Nazis who murdered U.S. prisoners of war? Why do you want war with China?

I set out for my lawyer what I thought I could legally do: "Judging by the Los Angeles un-American [Committee] hearings, the foregoing does not constitute contempt, provided that one answers their questions, within the limitations of law. Nor is it contempt to say: 'I have nothing but contempt for this Committee.'" Another of my queries was: "Several years ago, a San Francisco witness waited until he had been dismissed from the chair, and *then* shot his accusations at the Committee, as a private individual in the hearing room. Might I do that BEFORE I am sworn in, to catch them off balance & throw it my way? I would prefer it to be part of the sworn record, however."

Forer confirmed my belief that all these tactics were permissible, even during the hearing and on the record, if I could find occasion to say them. Contempt of Congress consisted solely of refusal to answer questions posed by the committee, unless I protected myself by recourse to the Fifth Amendment. Also, I could not refuse to answer a question if it flowed logically from my own answer to a previous question. This would be a chess game. I had to avoid checkmate—put in a position where I would have to name other individuals or go to jail for refusing to do so.

From the vantage point of today's legal situation, the committee's very subpoena to me was a violation of freedom of the press, but U.S. Supreme Court rulings at that time on appeals by previous witnesses had been such that I could not refuse to honor it. Specifically, I was called as one of the witnesses on the first day of an investigation into how books by "bad" people like me and Dr. W.E.B. DuBois, who was subpoenaed to appear on the same day, found their way into U.S. Embassy Information Office libraries overseas. The others subpoenaed that day were the current and previous heads of the Communist Party, Browder and Foster, and the head of the Party's publishing house. It was obvious that McCarthy was out to discredit the movement against first use of the nuclear bomb by attacking its leader, Dr. DuBois, and the notion that the USSR could be lived with, in my person. DuBois' attorney, former Congressman Vito Marcantonio, called Roy Cohn beforehand and asked: "Do you really want the whole Negro population down on the neck of the committee?" DuBois' subpoena was withdrawn.

The committee knew that the books in question had been ordered by the State Department from our publishers. I had no notion that my books were in those libraries until Cohn announced it in the hearing. But that didn't concern McCarthy. He was out to smear the State Department for even daring to maintain diplomatic relations with the USSR, by showing that its libraries contained books by radicals. Frankly, this didn't concern me either. I was out to cut his balls off.

Chiefly, that was for what he had done to my country and was threatening to do to the world. It was also for what he and his support team had done to me and my family. Today it is documented fact, thanks to the Freedom of Information Act, that the FBI, supposedly part of the distinct executive branch of government, was constantly feeding McCarthy material. Despite this symbiotic relationship, I did not know whether he had strong-arm men of his own. Fortunately, it turned out that he did not, and that he hoped to run the country by causing existing governmental mechanisms to do his will, not by establishing storm troops a la Hitler.

To the general public, the FBI and its boss, J. Edgar Hoover, were national heroes. To me, it was fundamentally a political police. The Bureau's persecutions had put people devoted to the public welfare in jail or forced them underground. My barely teenage daughter and her boyfriend of the same age had their own personal FBI tail—presumably on the assumption that they might lead them to the boy's father, whom the Communist Party had sent underground when it was made illegal by the McCarran and Smith acts and trials of its national and state leaders. This terror had serious effects upon Phyllis and Keith, her husband-to-be, all their lives. It caused thousands of people to lose their livelihoods in consequence of FBI visits to their employers, although, with very few exceptions, the people thus hounded had jobs in fields unrelated to national security. The FBI was anti-labor, anti-Black, anti-Semitic, and obviously anti-Soviet. It was anti-gay despite, or perhaps because Hoover was homosexual, which became public knowledge in the 1990s.

Prior to my McCarthy hearing, a telephone caller identified himself as an FBI agent and asked me to come down to see them. I said no, thanks. That was apparently not a common response, because he retorted, surprised and arrogant: "But we want to see you!" Bureau agents were all required to be graduate lawyers and knew perfectly well that a citizen was under no obligation to speak with them. I found myself choking with anger and spit out my reply: "But *I* don't want to talk to *you*," and slammed down the phone. It was only then that I realized how totally outraged I had been by the FBI's behavior over the past several years. They made further attempts to see me, at home. The fright it caused in our children was expressed in irrational fears for years to come, requiring a period of hospitalization for one of them. Finally, the FBI said to Tanya: "Tell your husband that if he doesn't cooperate with us he'll be a defendant in a major case." This was when the Rosenbergs were in the death house.

I was an ideal candidate for a frame-up. I was a specialist on the Soviet Union, had lived there, and had associated with Soviet people, although incomparably less then than in subsequent decades. The last time I had spoken to a Soviet person was over four years earlier, and that was to their United Nations ambassador when we were both speakers at a banquet. Nothing could have been more public. The fact that no Soviet person had ever identified himself to me as being involved in intelligence gathering meant nothing. Perjured identifications were rife in those days. Both of the witnesses who identified me as a Communist Party member were proved to be perjurers in other cases. One, Harvey

Matusow, served a long term for that. The other, Louis Budenz, was actually the named cause of the U.S. Supreme Court throwing out an important conviction because the defense had so thoroughly exposed him as a tainted witness.

That was the kind of cooperation the FBI wanted of me. Since they wouldn't get it, I had to think of how to protect myself against the dangers of refusing. So as soon as Tanya told me of that visit, I called up everyone I knew and informed them about it. If I were arrested and held incommunicado, they would know what had happened to me. And if the threat proved empty, then peoples' fears would be reduced: they would know that an empty threat had been made. The threat did prove empty. The Bureau made one more attempt to talk to me at my front doorstep. They never tried to do so again until fifteen years later, when one of my sons applied for conscientious objector status during the Vietnam War, and it was the FBI's job to determine whether his request was justified. (He was a pacifist affiliated with a Quaker youth organization—but he wasn't granted that status.)

Put simply, when Senator McCarthy subpoenaed me, I was a very angry man.

The hearing on Monday afternoon proved to be an executive session, at which the committee tried to size me up and hopefully recruit me as a stool-pigeon. I, on the other hand, hoped to persuade them that it would be in their interest not to call me in open session. I assumed that they were familiar with my previous year's testimony before the McCarran Committee. I thought that if they were, they might not regard it as wise to give me access to a microphone and cameras. If they so decided, it would save my livelihood. I told them that if they insisted upon my appearing in public session, I would do my best to expose them. That stung McCarthy. He brought my threat up the next day at the public hearing.

After the executive session, I made the acquaintance of another witness, James Allen, author of pioneering books on African-American history. He was white. We tried to relax by going to see "Oklahoma," then on the stage in Washington. I don't know whether it worked for him, but it didn't for me. I got very little sleep that night. In the morning I dashed over to the Library of Congress and copied the highlights of Major Kaplan's letter from the *Times*. Aside from being heart-rending, it was significant in that it gave one a flavor of the period. He wrote his wife and child that he was committing suicide for their sake, since "if I don't, I am afraid you too through absolutely no fault of your own will be continuously hounded for the rest of your lives."

It was that mood of utter long-term pessimism, widespread throughout the country, which made it necessary for some witness to conduct himself in a manner that would say to the people: "the king is naked."

I set myself a complex series of objectives. Sheer defiance to break the pall of fear was only one—even that would not work if I were merely obstreperous. I would have to conduct myself so as to win the sympathy of as large a spectrum of the population as possible. I knew that the live audience would number in the millions, and that if I did my job well, I would also make the news shows. I had no intention of leaving the impression that McCarthy was the only anti-Semite in government. Contrary to the subsequent attack on me by the American Jewish Committee and the *Jewish Day* on the grounds that I had "dragged in" the issue of anti-Semitism, the need to deal with it had emerged from the day's proceedings before I was called to the stand. James Allen immediately preceded me as witness. That, at least, was the name under which he lived and wrote his books, and it was the name under which the questioning began. Midway through the public hearing, Senator Mundt, knowing the answer he would get, because it was already in the record of the executive session, asked him to state his real name. The reply was: "Sol Auerbach." The entire audience gasped. The meaning of that gasp was unmistakeable to any Jew: "That dirty kike, hiding behind an Anglo-Saxon name!"

I was standing in the back of the packed hearing room waiting to be called. I grew livid, but understood that I now had the chance to rally the country's Jewish community behind me. So when Roy Cohn, the committee counsel, opened with the routine question as to my full name, I shot back: "My name is William Marx Mandel, and to save you the trouble of bringing out any possible pseudonym, as you did in the matter of Mr. Auerbach, I would like to make clear that I *am* a Jew."

Cohn, totally flustered, had no meaningful rejoinder: "That you are what?"

"That I *am* a Jew."

Cohn: "So am I, and I don't see that that is an issue here."

I replied: "A Jew who works for McCarthy is thought of very ill by most of the Jewish people in this country."

McCarthy was finally reduced to saying, "If you put on a campaign against the committee, you will not put on the campaign within the committee room."

I responded: "Poor Senator McCarthy. You can dish it out, but you can't take it. O.K."

CHAPTER 17

We Bury The Rosenbergs

In some respects, I take greater satisfaction in a lecture I delivered in May 1953 than in my behavior before the witch-hunters. Thinking is harder than articulating defiance. The manner of my defiance was a consequence of a distinct personal view of the times, best set forth in that lecture before a Leftist fraternal organization in New York. The text survives because my uncle Si Schachter was editor of its printed newsletter, in which he published the transcript of my talk. Although historians have had forty-five years in which to analyze the downfall of McCarthy, I believe my evaluation eighteen months before the U.S. Senate worked up enough guts to condemn him still stands:

"The American people have demonstrated in absolutely unmistakeable terms that they are not willing to act as fascists against anybody here at home. Peekskill was a fiasco for the fascists, and no attempt has been made to repeat it. Mass lynchings rarely occur in the South [any longer] and have had to be replaced by 'legal' executions, police killings, and private murders....

"Fascism cannot be brought about by legislation. Many feared this when the McCarran Act was passed in 1950...But by 1953, when the McCarran Board handed down its very specific list of organizations to register on pain of tremendous fines and long years in jail, there was no similar fear reaction at all....

"Today, after seven years of [the] Taft-Hartley [Law], there are 17,000,000 union members—the largest number in history....In 1929 there were only three million...Today the Negro people have reached a state of organization and political consciousness sufficient even to have elected, recently, a few city officials in the South."

There was great confusion over where the new administration stood relative to McCarthyism. Eisenhower, just a few months in office, was the first Republican president in twenty years. "The Administration group is deeply aware of the moral authority it enjoys," I wrote, "so long as the American people believes it has a free choice at the polls and that government reflects that choice at least to some degree. It is quite willing to use the Smith Act, the McCarran Act, the McCarran-Walter Act, the Taft-Hartley Law, spy trials and Congressional witch-hunts to suppress...militant organizations, but recognizes the importance of maintaining the appearance of legal forms as long as possible." While Hitler had come to power by winning a plurality in an election, his Storm Troopers had used forced to reduce opposition votes, and he was quite open about his intention to exercise totalitarian power.

My view of the world scene at this juncture was not the then common one of gloom and nuclear doom: "Why has Churchill so sharply changed his attitude, so that he who initiated the Cold War with his Fulton, Missouri, speech of 1946, now demands a conference with the Soviet Union for the settlement of world problems?....Now that the McCarthyites bent on the final folly of extending the [Korean] war to China through blockade demand that London surrender one of its few remaining sources of income abroad [carrying freight to and from China], Churchill has decided that it is time to break free before it is too late. In so doing, he bids for the creation of a new grouping, involving all of western Europe and Japan—all the countries which find that...American restrictions deprive them of trade with the...people living between Berlin and Shanghai."

That grouping ultimately came about with the establishment of the European Union and the introduction of its euro currency in 1999. Only foreign policy specialists remember today that up to the time of my lecture the U.S. had simply forbidden Europe and Japan from trading with the Soviet Union and Red China, on pain of losing the Marshall Plan aid that raised them out of the ruins of war. Now the countries it had assisted were somewhat revived and wanted to pursue their own interests.

If I did not share the general pessimism, I was by no means a pollyanna, thinking that things would take care of themselves. "The urgency of the moment is to stop McCarthy before the power of government is effectively in his hands," my talk continued. "He has no intention of waiting for an election to become president. He is trying to exercise full power now. He tried to break relations with the Soviet Union by blocking the naming of any ambassador to that country. He attempts to blockade China through blackmail of Greek shipowners and the threat to sink British ships. Yet the president yields. Clearly, only the people—you— can stop McCarthy. He *can* be stopped, but he can be stopped only if all Americans, setting aside political prejudices and disagreements, unite to do that job."

For the most part, other witnesses who refused to become informers were governed by the psychology that they were on a sinking ship, but that they would not abandon or sell their principles as the price of rescue. My view was that the ship could be saved. When, in 1996, I rebroadcast my testimony before McCarthy over a station with a generally youthful audience, listeners phoned to ask how I was able to speak out in that manner at a time when people were committing suicide in the belief that he was here to stay. The answer lies in the view I held of the country's situation at the time I was subpoenaed.

But the issue that dominated public discourse the month after my lecture was painfully concrete: whether or not Ethel and Julius Rosenberg should be executed. In March I had made my position on that clear in my exchange with Roy Cohn at the McCarthy hearing. On May 25th the U.S. Supreme Court rejected a motion for a new trial. Execution was set for June 19th. The Committee to Save the Rosenbergs called for a death watch on New York's 17th St. off Union Square. Thousands gathered, including many for whom participation in a demonstration was a very rare occurrence, including my mother. We stood in a family group: my parents, my brother and his wife, Tanya and our daughter Phyllis. I described what happened next, and a little of the immediately preceding events, in an article written in white heat the next night, after the funeral.

In writing an autobiography one learns much about oneself. As I read the written record of 1953, I see three very different sides of my character. That lecture in May surveying the domestic and world situations was the calm work of a scholar. Then, there is the sharp debater and improvisational actor of the hearing in Washington. But the article on the Rosenberg execution is pure soul. Were I to try to write about that event today, I doubt that I would be able to recreate my emotional state. Nor are my opinions precisely the same. But that article does present the feel of the times even though my passion led to hyperbole. It also describes a moment in history otherwise lost.

New York, Sunday night, June 21.

This is the story of the people's anger.

I love my city. I love the people it produces—the Rosenbergs who are dead, and the ten thousand living Rosenbergs who this past week demonstrated the futility of trying to gag a nation with an electric chair.

The New York of the past ten days is again the militant, passionate, fearless, surging people's city of the Thirties—only more determined, vastly better organized, unbelievably disciplined.

Before I go on, let no one say—what about the other seven million? Ten thousand people don't behave as these did the past ten days unless they feel the support of vastly greater numbers. I could offer a hundred incidents —let me cite but one.

On that fearsome Friday afteroon, <u>after</u> the six black-robed prostitutes and the general in the White House had turned thumbs down, three young girls—one of them my daughter [aged 13]—stationed themselves at a subway exit. This was no ordinary subway exit, but one which older and "wiser" heads would avoid, because it might be expected to produce as hostile a crowd as could be found in New York. It is used almost exclusively by middle-class suburbanite commuters dashing out of their offices in our crowded city for the buses to take them to the cool lawns of New Jersey.

The girls distributed the leaflet with Prof. Urey's telegram to Eisenhower, and cried out: "Wire the President to phone Urey for the facts." [Physicist Urey was a key figure in the development of the atom bomb.] In two hours time twenty-seven commuters stopped in their headlong rush, signed the wire, and gave the girls 75 cents each [equal to $6 in 1999] to send them.

This was the kind of support on which the people acted. And what were the results?

The world knows how, last Sunday, seven or eight thousand New Yorkers (and thousands from other places) made their way 250 miles to Washington. Some stood in the crowded trains all the way—both ways. Hundreds drove....Several people called me Saturday, asking if I knew of a lift to Washington. I could not help them. Yet I saw every one of them on the picket line in Washington next day. Somehow they got there. Did I say picket line? That was a wall, a sea, an avalanche. But no army was ever better disciplined.

From Monday on, the city [Washington] was swamped with leaflets and petition gatherers. Thursday was the Day of the Mothers. Do you know what it means to take kindergarten-age children for a 500-mile train ride, leaving downtown New York at 9 p.m. and returning at 5 the next morning? [Actually the morning after the next.] When [Chief Justice] Vinson the Bourbon called his murder caucus after [Justice] Douglas' brave act, a train had to go to Washington. This was midweek, and husbands were working. So the mothers went and took their children with them. For they had hearts for another mother and her two children. Hearts—and anger.

Oh, there was anger. On May Day New York was forbidden its parade, but seven weeks later there was a parade—the first unauthorized parade in nineteen years which the police failed to disperse.

Let me tell you about that parade. Shortly after 8 o'clock Friday the Rosenberg Committee announced from the sound truck that Ethel and Julius were in the execution chamber. [Next we heard that they were dead.] A wave of agony found voice in the people, and the police, thinking that terror had won the day, cut off the power line to the sound truck.

Slowly, at the pace of deepest sorrow, ten thousand people moved west out of 17th Street. As we reached the corner, someone called out: "Let's march down Fifth Avenue." [That was me.] We moved around that corner like the tide. A voice rose: "Long live the Rosenbergs!" [That was Tanya,] and in a moment the whole canyon shook with a people's coronation: "Long live the Rosenbergs!"

At 14th Street we swung East, and at the South end of Union Square a Negro friend said to me: "Let's head for the East Side. Pass the word back." My daughter raised a placard: "We are innocent" high over her head, and took a place at the head of the line that none sought to make her relinquish. It was proper that the clear wrath of a child should speak the people's soul. It was proper that a Negro, whose heart bore the sorrow and the lessons of a thousand black Rosenbergs, should have started that parade. It was proper that a mother of three should cry out over and over again, in a voice that permitted no answer: "We shall avenge them!" [That was Tanya. again] It was proper that a ski-trooper hero against Mussolini and Hitler, and a clear-voiced man of middle age, both with personal memories of the days of the Storm Troops, should also have been in the front rank.

At first the police were dumbfounded. They had killed us at Sing Sing minutes ago, and we were surging past them as though they didn't exist. Then a mounted patrol formed behind the first hundreds of us, but the people simply stood their ground in a tremendous disciplined dignity which said: "This is our city. These are our streets. They are our dead. WE are the city. You just don't count."

Those behind just overflowed down 13th and 15th streets. Soon the line of horse was meaningless, and took itself away.

A squad car began to move parallel to the head of the line. There was no further effort to stop us. One of the police called out to me: "Where are you going?" I replied in scorn: "We're going for a walk."

That was some walk. We had listened and we had worked. Now we would cry the truth in our hearts: "The Rosenbergs were innocent. Their memories shall not die!" Over and over again, in a roll of thunder up and down the line: "The Rosenbergs were innocent. Their memories shall not die."

Between 7th and 8th streets, along Second Avenue, where the scum which served Hitler in Eastern Europe now clusters, swinging windows of second-story "social" clubs pushed open, and astonished fascists, who have terrorized this neighborhood for months, saw the corpses of Auschwitz and Dachau rise before their eyes, take on flesh and march toward a time of reckoning.

The Rosenbergs were Jews. The Rosenbergs were killed as Jews—rushed to death in a horrid witches' Sabbath before sundown brought the Sabbath of the Jews. And that parade on this bitter Sabbath night was chiefly of Jews, who were giving their warning: Never again do we wait for them to build their gas chambers. We shall not wait for others in our country graciously to grant us the right to live. Fighting for ourselves, we fight for all America. None can part us from America, and none can part America from us. [In the margin I made a note to myself: "On this I take my stand."]

That was Friday night—five thousand, ten thousand—who knows? But I know that the police who tried to bar our way on 14th Street stopped traffic to let us pass, on Houston and at Delancey. I know that when we finally deigned to let them know that we were going to Straus Square, they rushed to route traffic away from the Square so we could have it for ourselves. And I know that for two hours, over a distance of three or four miles, we marched where <u>we</u> chose, and shouted what <u>we</u> chose, and infused strength into ourselves and the troubled people of the East Side who had smelled the acrid smoke of the crematoria when the switch was thrown at Sing Sing.

But there were those for whom the pall did not lift: my daughter's friends, young girls in the spring of life, for whom death is unbelievable, and the premeditated murder of a couple in love [as the Rosenbergs' death house letters made clear], a mother and her husband, is the unforgiveable sin. One lovely child pulled away in the subway station, tears in her eyes fixed as for eternity, and said: "I wish I were dead." And, looking for an answer which could not satisfy: "Why did they have to kill them?" And another, who had worked as only youth can work, sat as though stunned, expressionless and empty-eyed as 16 has no right to be. For this, oh rulers in Washington, we shall never forgive you.

On Saturday I looked impatiently through all the papers for a report of our parade. Most papers said <u>nothing.</u> One or two said we had been stopped by the mounted police on 14th Street. Yet press photographers had been with us all the way.

The picture was clear. They wished to bury the Rosenberg <u>Case</u> with the Rosenbergs. But saints are remembered forever. [They were treated as saints in a 1992 national TV docudrama, "Roy Cohn."]

Sunday, the day of the funeral, the fires of hell seared the streets of New York. Heat-tortured people, forgetting modesty, had slept nude with windows wide open and shades up. [Only the rich had air conditioning in 1953.] Few rested through the night, many not at all. But by nine in the morning, through the furnaces of the subways, on foot over baking sidewalks, and by car and bus under the raging sun, people came to file past the bier. Here were another ten thousand, by manner and appearance mainly working people of Brooklyn, where the funeral was held. At 1:30 the doors were closed, and for the next two hours the people paid homage, while the services were held and the blessed Manny Bloch stripped naked the harpy that is American jutice. [Bloch, not the best of lawyers, was *the only one in America with the courage to take the Rosenberg Case. Literally everyone with a reputation had been asked.*]

As the hearse started for the cemetery, here again the people flowed around and over police barriers to possess themselves of their streets. Then, from every alley for blocks around, cars formed a line behind the cortege to the cemetery thirty-two miles away. The highway police estimated 7,000 automobiles in the line, a fabulous figure. If this was exagerrated, and included many simply out for a Sunday drive, the police have only themselves to blame, as I can testify. For as we came to a point three miles from the cemetery, a police car blocked the road and we were waved off in the wrong direction. Soon it became clear that we had been misdirected—the authorities wished no great demonstration of strength at the cemetery. Again angered, we turned back to the barred turn-off, waving the rest of the cortege to join us.

America's mechanized way of life can be the people's weapon. These hundreds of cars in the hands of week-end drivers made a simultaneous U-turn on that highway that would have shamed many an army for precision. Reaching the turn-off, we stopped and asked the patrolman to permit us to proceed. When he refused, we blocked the highway four lanes wide and dozens of cars deep, in yet another remarkable demonstration of spontaneous organization, determination and discipline. It was explained to strangers caught in the jam that we simply wished to pay our respects to people we believed unjustly executed and desired to cause no inconvenience, and that the highway police had it in their power to open the jam by letting us proceed.

It was this, causing a tremendous back-up of traffic, which may have caused them to think that 7,000 cars sought admission to the cemetery. With the arrival of additional police, the blockade was forced upon, but the police had to inform us of a route to the rear entrance of the cemetery. This was barred by a gatekeeper, but the cars pushed open the gates and we gained entrance, too late for the services, but in time to demonstrate our presence and file slowly around the fresh mound heaped with flowers.

Back in New York, I bought the morning papers, and read them with a feeling of grim satisfaction. "Ike Called Murderer at Rosenbergs' Funeral Rites," screamed a three-column head in the *Daily News*. The Republican *Herald-Tribune* reluctantly restored the case to its front page. "10,350 at Service. Rosenbergs Eulogized as Martyrs at Funeral."

At one point someone had said to me: "Let's keep it quiet, or the cops will break it up." Somebody else said: "No slogans. This is a procession of mourning." I answered: "Mourning, hell. That's what *they* want.

What *we* want is to fight back. Come on, everybody: 'The *Rosen*bergs were *in*nocent. Their memories will *never die.*'

So long as Ethel and Julius Rosenberg were alive, the third convicted defendant, Morton Sobell, was essentially forgotten, because he had not gotten the death penalty. Therefore, a couple of days after the executions, I wrote an ad, "Free Morton Sobell!", and got the same discount store that had run previous unsigned political ads of mine to to buy space for its appearance in the *National Guardian* as what the trade calls institutional advertising. It reads:

Ethel and Julius Rosenberg are dead.
But Morton Sobell, convicted in the same trial whose evidence the Supreme Court admits it has never read—Morton Sobell is alive, condemned to jail for 30 years, a life sentence.
Alive? He is on Alcatraz, that fogged-in rock in San Francisco Bay, a Devil's Island so bad that the Director of the Federal Bureau of Prisons urges that it be closed down.
But he keeps Morton Sobell there.
Why? For exactly the same reason they kept a telephone line open to the execution chamber in Sing Sing until the deed was done: they hoped that the Rosenbergs would "cooperate."
Today those whom Manny Bloch called the 'animals' in Washington know that there is only one thing that will lay the ghosts of the Rosenbergs - a 'confession' from Morton Sobell....
Decent America—and two weeks ago in Washington and New York we thrilled to learn how much there is of decent America—<u>must free Sobell!</u>...
To free Morton Sobell means to expose the frame-up and vindicate the names of the Rosenbergs as Sacco and Vanzetti were vindicated. <u>It means to compel the Supreme Court to read the record of the Rosenberg-Sobell Trial.</u>
For his sake and for ours, let us not wait 23 years as Tom Mooney had to wait."

Mooney was a San Francisco union organizer framed in 1916, and freed in 1939 by a governor who had made his freedom a campaign pledge. Mooney was to American labor what Nelson Mandela was to Africa half a century later, and also got worldwide support.

I was active for a period in the campaign proposed by my ad, and got to know Sobell's wife, Helen, and his mother. Both women were simply indefatigable.

Morton Sobell served 18 1/2 years, most of it on Alcatraz, although he was a first offender. He always maintained his innocence. I met him for the first time in 1993, a quarter-century after his release, and marveled at how so mild and unassuming a man could have lived through those monstrous years with no obvious psychological effects.

After I was fired by that medical advertising firm because of having been subpoenaed by McCarthy, I found another where the readers were much less demanding than the physicians who read my articles written for that earlier employer. On the new job, I was essentially selling aureomycin to cows, vaccines and such to hogs and chickens. I never could get myself to put in a full day writing such great literature as "Safeguard pigs! Tell your farmer friends to <u>Vaccinate with ROVAC!</u>" for publication in the *Agricultural Leaders' Digest.*

Fortunately I had a private office, and the advertising agency had a splendid collection of serious farm journals and U.S. Department of Agriculture annuals and other publications. The Soviet leader, Khrushchev, who had just succeeded Stalin, revealed that Soviet livestock head had fallen in Stalin's last year and that peasants were uprooting fruit trees to get out from under unrealistic taxation. He later embarked on a policy of opening the dry plains of southern Siberia and northern Kazakhstan to grain growing. I decided that I had to find out why Soviet agriculture was not doing its job. So I used the agency's library, closed the door of my office, with an ear for the bosses' footsteps, and gave myself an education in modern farming. I could fool them only so long. I got fired.

With three young children and a wife whose one out-of-the-home skill was bookkeeping at the small retail level and who was already being plagued by chronic illness, I had to take whatever I could get. I found free-lance work translating technical German and French into English. There were also the labels of German wines, worded to mislead the customer as to the actual quality of what he was buying. Since my knowledge of these languages was limited to what I had gotten in a fine New York public high school and one year in college, my piece-work earnings initially worked out to about a non-union dishwasher's hourly pay. Later, I subcontracted work from Russian from Navy and Air Force contractors. For nearly a decade I had to swallow the bitter pill of doing work whose ultimate consumers were those whom I regarded as the most dangerous elements in the country—once McCarthy had been defeated. Fortunately, the fact that I did not seek and obviously could not obtain security clearance meant that everything I translated consisted of material the Soviet Union published in unclassified technical sources anyone anywhere was free to read.

I was constantly writing letters to research organizations in the hope of getting a job that would make use of my formidable experience. But anyone who had been before McCarthy had no chance with a main-line research organization. I tried the few unions and labor-oriented publications that shared my point of view, but they were being pressed to the wall by the same sort of attacks I suffered from. It was hard enough to pay their existing staff, much less hire anyone new. In an effort to get back into the medical-writing field, I wrote the heads of the firms that had been the clients of the agency where I worked at the time of the McCarthy hearing, stating in these letters:

"No government agency has found any reason to proceed against ANY of the author-witnesses called in connection with the Overseas Libraries 'book-burning' a year ago. No witness, 'friendly' or 'unfriendly,' mentioned my name before the committee in ANY connection whatever, before or after my appearance. No charge of <u>any</u> kind was made against me by the Committee."

I was trying to get them to understand that the hearings sought only to terrorize by quarantining from employment and, particularly, from their special fields, those who were called before the TV cameras. I am sure they did understand it, because none had replied to my employer's request to them for advice as to whether to fire me. But they feared guilt by association.

I thought up all kinds of ideas for books about the USSR: conservation, sports, trade, Far Eastern policy, worked these projects out in detail, and submitted them to publishers large and small. This was how I had gotten three of my four book contracts before McCarthyism. No publisher I approached would now touch me with a ten-foot pole.

So I translated, and thought up a new idea for reaching people. Since the LP record of my hearing before McCarthy had been successful, I sent out a mailing proposing to do a monthly half-hour commentary on a record, which could be listened to at home gatherings in this time when people feared to meet in public places and hall-owners refused to rent to groups they did not know to be innocuous or conservative. There was no such thing as a Left or non-Red-baiting liberal funding foundation at that time. I sent out a fund-raising letter to get money with which to advertise.

I asked for advance subscriptions for three months, and got enough to get started. The number was in fact preposterously small, but the places they came from made the effort worthwhile: Decaturville, Tennessee; Squire, Missouri; Yellow Creek, Pocanville, and Saskatoon, Saskatchewan, in Canada; Buffalo, Oklahoma; Holtville, California; Puerto de Tierra, Puerto Rico. There were individuals whose orders I regarded as an honor, such as that from Scott Nearing. Thirty years later, and approaching his hundredth birthday, Nearing was the articulate leather-faced "witness" in Warren Beatty's "Reds."

Comments came in with the orders. From New Mexico: "Thanks for the opportunity to listen to a liberal—truthful, honest, non-bickering, non-mud-slinging against our neighbors"; from New York: "with cataracts in both eyes, listening will supplant reading. For me this is a life-saver." Lens replacement was unknown as yet.

Listener mail gave me a clear notion of what the country was thinking. On the one hand there was still fear: "We regret to inform you that we wish to have our name removed from your mailing list. Wishing you well—and success in your endeavor." That was on personal stationery, and from a very upscale New York suburb. From Los Angeles, a man running a private rental film library wrote: "People seem so panicky that they will not give much attention to speeches or music....We will show the film 'Peace Will Win' and others..., but people are actually afraid to be seen in a group looking at them....I fear things will go like they did in Germany. People do NOT protest. They simply crawl under the bed and those who speak out like Mr. Mandel do not get the backing they should get." A personal friend who was a German Jewish refugee reported the same fears but would not quit: "I have found...your records to be most effective on people who will not come to meetings, but who will listen to them in their homes."

I was most encouraged by the painfully-written letters from those to whom fear was irrelevant, and who doggedly spread the word. From Fond du Lac, Wisconsin, in McCarthy's home state, came this one, full of misspellings, wrong capitalizations, and grammatical errors. So what.

"My machine is a 45-78 but I have a friend that has a 33 rpm. We played them on his. He and his company that was there thought they were fine. Last night we took them to my son's. My friend brought his portable machine to play them on. We plan on taking them to North Fonddulac to a frined out there, also to a friend of mine that is an officer of the Fur and Leather Workers' Union....

"America is too great a country to be destroyed by McCarthyism, Lincoln said that Freedom takes eternal vigilance."

Lecture audiences were what was left of the Left: branches of the International Workers' Order fraternal society, remaining clubs of the American Labor Party, Compass clubs originally founded to support the short-lived New Dealish newspaper of that name. But the atmosphere of the times outweighed everything else, and the record venture died.

I didn't have to cast about for something new to focus on. It came to me, and absorbed my attention and my passions for the next three years, with echoes for the next forty. Nineteen fifty-four marked the 15th year since I had become a professional student of Soviet affairs, and while it was now five years since I had been able to make a living at that profession, my interest had in no way decreased. There was both the fundamental need to remain at peace with the USSR, and my hope that in some way it would serve as a socio-political model for a better world.

After Stalin's death in 1953, things began to be published in Moscow that lent support to the doubts that had led to my expulsion from the Communist Party just months earlier. Because what is called de-Stalinization is usually dated to the famous "secret speech" made by his successor, Khrushchev, three years later, it is not realized that the Soviet people were gradually being prepared for that for at least two years before it occurred, even though the speech was not published in the USSR until the late 1980s. In the mid-1950s that led, for all who hoped that the USSR pointed the way to a better life, to excruciating soul-searching and profound psychological turmoil as well as to the break-up of friendships, marriages, families, actual deaths.

That should not be cause for surprise. All human beings everywhere know that we survive very far from Utopia. A minority cynically accept that and seek only personal gratification, at whatever cost to others. I don't envy such people, because they essentially strip themselves of what makes us human—morality, a conscious quality possessed by no other species. Human beings find it necessary to find a rationalization in morality for even the worst things they do, at least do collectively. Churches, for example, have usually—though not always— blessed the armies of their particular countries. How God can possibly be on both sides of a slaughter is beyond my comprehension.

But religious people really have it easy. They can claim their morality to have been established by a source that is not human, and they can therefore cling to beliefs on faith alone, with no need for proof.

Marxists chose a much tougher row to hoe, in the belief that human beings are totally responsible for their own behavior, and that all ideas, including religions, are no more than that— ideas. But being only human, Marxists shared with all others the desire for a model to emulate. The religious have Jesus, or Buddha, or the less tangible Allah or, in the case of the Jews, the Book. But for a great many that becomes tangibilized in a geographic locale where ideals seem to have been realized. Several countries have played that role in recent history, France for one, whose slogan, "Liberty, Equality, Fraternity," inspired millions worldwide for more than a century from 1789 on. The phrase, "human rights," is simply the currently popular translation of the French phrase that used to be rendered as "the Rights of Man."

The United States was, and to many still is, another such country as model. But as the injustices inherent in the economic system prevailing in France and the United States and the rest of the capitalist world became clear, and a government was established in Russia committed to abolishing them, numbers of people everywhere, vast in some countries, came to regard it as the wave of the future. Large movements, Nazism the most obvious example, were founded to uproot that belief by force, first at home and then by war against the USSR. McCarthyism was a much milder American version of the same thing. The fact that the capitalist world did succeed in climbing out of the Great Depression, largely thanks to the market created by the great destruction accompanying the slaughter of World War II, and subsequently learned to moderate its economic cycles, was a factor reducing the attractiveness of the Soviet Union in the developed world. The inability of the USSR to attain a living standard equal to that of the advanced countries played a very major role in its demise. So did the fact that severe restrictions upon freedom, even when not bloody, proved to be required to run a non-market system. These last were the principal factors in causing its peoples ultimately to abandon Marxist socialism.

But for those who, until the collapse of the Soviet Union, saw its problems as rooted only in its heritage of backwardness, its sufferings in two world wars, and the forced diversion of its resources by a cold war in which the West was at fault, it remained a model. The very author of the American policy of containment, U.S. diplomat and historian George Kennan, publicly regretted in 1996 that his notion of *political* restraint upon the spread of communist rule, which he felt had been achieved with the rescue of Europe by the Marshall Plan in 1947, had been replaced in Washington by a policy of *military* confrontation.

Not content with the fact that Soviet economic and social achievements were without precedent or parallel, some in the absolute sense, others in terms of the rapidity of Soviet progress, Communist parties nearly everywhere saw it as an ideal of government as well. No one who was truly an adherent of the Marxist concept of dialectics, that the only thing permanent in the world is change, could regard the Soviet Union as perfect. I for one had written of specific shortcomings in government even at the height of American euphoria over Our Great Russian Ally during World War II and much later had expressed the doubts that resulted in my exclusion from the Communist Party. But I still did not regard these phenomena, individually unacceptable, as having fundamentally damaged that form of government as a model, so long as it seemed to release the energies of the people more effectively than any other. That, to me, was the ultimate test of democracy.

But in August 1954, that is, about a year and a half after Stalin's death, the house organ of the Soviet Communist Party, *Party Life,* with national circulation, published an article that revealed a situation opposite to democracy, one that throttled popular expression. My life for the next forty years in the highly-charged sphere of interpretation of Soviet developments was constantly affected by the degree to which the situation the article described had and had not been corrected, or could be, under Marxist socialism. The article stated:

"Propagation of worship of an individual [usually mistranslated as "the cult of personality"] has adversely affected the training of personnel, has led in a number of cases to depriving the local organizations [of the Soviet Communist Party] of responsibility, and has doomed the large, skilled staffs of republic, province and district administrative agencies to passivity and inertia.

"Under these circumstances officials have appeared in various Party, Soviet and economic agencies who have bureaucratic mentalities and who have made it a habit to follow the 'letter of the law' and who do not move a step without instructions from above. The outlook of these chairwarmers is aptly expressed in the familiar lines: 'Why look further? / Sit and wait / for instructions: / We never have to think / if the leaders think'."

Russian poetry has lines for all situations! The article continued:

"When Party democracy and the principles of collective leadership are violated, incorrect relations between Communists inevitably arise—they begin to regard each other as higher and lower-ranking personnel rather than as equal members in a militant union of ideologically united Communists. This creates soil favorable to the growth of such repulsive remnants of capitalism as toadying, obsequiousness and careerism."

Unfortunately, other Communists who read the article preferred not to confront the fundamental issues it raised. This preference for accepted faith over fact and logic resulted in political and psychological turmoil for Communist parties and their members that governed much of what I did during the next three years. My immediate reaction was that not only did this specifically bear out the criticisms I had offered and for which I had been ostracized but that it depicted a much more serious situation than I had imagined. Most important, it demanded that those of us who believed in Marxist socialism as the solution to America's problems take this fully into account, both in our vision of a better future and in explaining our position to the American people.

Fortunately, at about this time I had been engaged by the fine humanist philosopher and civil libertarian, Corliss Lamont, to research the Soviet scene for a revised edition of his book, *Soviet Civilization*. I had done a similar job for the original edition a couple of years earlier. If I could not get books out over my own signature at this time, here was an opportunity to contribute to one by a man I totally respected. He was, in fact, the only person whose understanding of the essence of the USSR I regarded as superior to my own, even though he was not a Soviet-affairs specialist and I was.

Corliss, who lived into the 1990s, came from the very topmost stratum of inherited American wealth. His father had succeeded J. P. Morgan as head of the bankers' bank. Corliss never ran away from his wealth, but neither did he flaunt it. He was one of the few very rich Americans—Frederick Vanderbilt Field was another—who had the humanism to understand the built-in injustice of the system that produced the money to which he fell heir. He was an advocate of a democratic socialism most of his life and was also the very sensible kind of person who does not expect perfection anywhere and knows that the practical consequences of social theories differ from what is envisaged on paper. Therefore, Lamont supported the Soviet Union for its social achievements, yet consistently criticized its very restrictive political system and restraints upon civil liberties. But his attitude was not holier-than-thou. He observed in a book: "Here we are well over 200 years after our birth as an independent nation and we still have to fight tooth and nail, day in and day out, for the preservation of our democratic liberties as expressed in the United States Constitution and Bill of Rights."

The up-to-the-minute knowledge I accumulated in reading the current Soviet press for the Lamont project found an unanticipated outlet. In 1954 the head of the Canadian Communist Party, Tim Buck, a man whose record of fighting for welfare and work projects for that country's unemployed in the 1930s deserves admiration, returned from a visit to the Soviet Union and published nonsense to the effect that the USSR would have as many cars as we the day after tomorrow. He claimed that it was already giving its people more education than we, and that they had greater access to culture. Buck's report impelled me to rewrite my findings for Lamont as an article, "Common Sense on the Soviet Union," which was published in 1955 by *Monthly Review*, a socialist magazine of international reputation that is still in existence. I had first offered it to the Communist Party's magazine, *Political Affairs,* which turned it down. I was torn between my voluntary adherence to Party discipline—in that paranoid time no one would inform me that it had stricken my name from its rolls—and my certainty that the Communist Party had destroyed its credibility by adhering to a Utopian view of the Soviet Union that everyone else in the West knew was false.

My faith in Lamont's integrity and good sense caused me to submit the piece to *Monthly Review* despite the fact that the Communist Party hated that magazine as it did all who advocated socialism but did not adhere to its particular brand. Far from wanting to expose the Party, my hope was that members reading my article would press it to emancipate itself from the blindness I criticized. That piece proved to be extremely important to my reputation on the Left for independence as well as for understanding the Soviet Union, for it anticipated by a year, in print, much of what Khrushchev had to say in his bombshell de-Stalinization speech. People remembered that I had taken that position earlier. But the Canadian Communist Party was so infuriated by my lèse majesté that it implied strongly that I was a CIA man. Letters poured in to *Monthly Review* not only from the U.S., but from Scotland and Communist-governed Czechoslovakia, the latter written by an American woman who, with her husband, had found it a refuge, and staunchly defended her dream of the USSR. The magazine devoted a section of a subsequent issue to publishing them and a rejoinder from me.

As any religious person who has abandoned the faith in which he was raised knows, the emotional stress of my apostasy was enormous. We needed a getaway trip. I had burned out the 1951 Kaiser by not satisfying its enormous thirst for oil. I replaced it with a 1953 model of the same car. At three years old, it's the newest car we've ever owned. The difference in price between a new car and one three or four years old has repeatedly paid for trips overseas.

We headed down the spine of the Appalachians. In those lonely days for Lefties, particularly in the South, I figured there would be people willing to talk to kindred souls they'd never met. I wrote people who had purchased the record of my McCarthy hearing by mail. One reply, from a Bill McGirt in Winston-Salem, North Carolina, provides a sense of the time, place, and feelings:

"I hope you will plan to eat with me....There isn't a bath here in the house (sink and commode), but there is a double bed. If you are pushed on finances (as what progressive isn't these days??!!), you can stay here, too...The work you have done puts you high on my list of people to be admired without serious danger, as I see it, of any downgrading!....I'm eager to see you and only wish more Northern people would visit South so they could actually <u>see</u> the good and the bad. This will be a great place to live some day. And it will take a lot of history-making."

I have no recollection of the trip till we got to Harper's Ferry. John Brown is one of my heroes, and to walk where he had was deeply moving. Its location at the confluence of the Shenandoah and Potomac fits the dramatic events that occurred there, and the preservation of its appearance as of a century earlier heightens the impact. As we proceeded up the river, we sang "Shenandoah" of course. It goes totally with the countryside. There is a grist mill that, even forty years ago, was already no more than a working museum. Yet farms were generally small and poor and lived up to one's image of Appalachia. At one point we picked up a young Black man, and had him with us for several hours. My attempts to draw him out on the situation of African-Americans, by reference to the Martinsville Case and other things I'd been involved in, were in vain. Whites were not to be trusted, Northern accent or no.

We had a destination, a "cove" in local usage— meaning a narrow valley where a mountain stream takes its origins. This was up high just east of Erwin, Tennessee. A one-time professor at Duke University, Ernest Seeman, lived there with his wife, in two houses they had built with their own hands. As writers, they found that living separately prevented distraction. The Seemans had purchased the pamphlet of my McCarran Committee hearing, and responded like McGirt to my request for an invitation. To reach them I had to drive, for the first time in my life, over a bridge consisting of two ordinary planks, separated by empty space precisely the standard width of a passenger-car axle.

Professor Seeman had made the mistake of being critical of the tobacco industry in his published research. That was not exactly the way to make a career at an institution bearing the name of, and funded by, the clan that had made more money out of cigarettes than any other. So he had been fired. That was the end of his academic vita. As they slowly built additional houses in their cove on the banks of Tumblin' Creek, they rented them out as vacation spots to people from lowland areas of the South. He had completed a novel based on the Duke family, *American Gold.* More than twenty years elapsed before it was published, to high critical praise.

For me 1955 to 1957 was one furious, unending political debate involving every personal friend, every adult family member, and my children insofar as they suffered from my internal turmoil, as well as an endless stream of things over my signature in Left magazines and newspapers. The debate was not over what most would recognize as an American problem, although I saw it and see it today as precisely that. It was over what one was to think of the Soviet Union in the light of the revelations about the Stalin period. Only Americans committed to socialism could be so concerned with what was happening in a foreign country that called itself socialist.

How concerned they could be is best told in the tragedy of a seemingly hard-boiled newsman and next-door neighbor in New York, George Marion. In 1955 George, an excellent professional journalist, was still a member of the Communist Party, as was I. But I had been following the Soviet press subsequent to Stalin's death two years earlier. While the 1956 revelations of monstrous injustice and mass murders had not yet been made, all the other distortions resulting from one-man rule and its imitation at lower levels had been published. George Marion and I had argued day after day, week after week, month after month. Finally, one day, he sat down to write an introduction for an edition of a book of his to be published in Communist-ruled Czechoslovakia. He was engaged, of necessity, in self-publishing, and had just returned from a lecturing-and-selling tour of the mountain states and far west. On this tour he had been subjected to vigilante victimization at house meetings, even though the Army-McCarthy hearings that finished the senator were already a year in the past. Yet the fact was that he had been able to publish his book, dissenting against our society, and sell it. Therefore he forced out of himself and onto the typewriter page the assertion that there was more civil liberty in the capitalist United States than in the socialist world, and fell off his chair, dead. He was just past fifty. His paralyzed wife, Betty, crawled to my door and banged on it. I dashed in, found him beyond saving, that preface in the typewriter, and his Communist Party membership card in his pocket. Perhaps he had been looking at it. The preface was never published in Czechoslovakia, of course.

Establishment opinion-makers in as well as out of government welcomed the Soviet revelations and gave them inordinate publicity and interpretation in academe and the media as a means of arguing the invalidity of the social system with which we had been competing for the previous forty years and would for thirty more until it finally collapsed.

One mainstream paper in the country would carry my opinions at this time, the *Gazette and Daily,* of York, Pennsylvania. On October 30, 1956, a period of turmoil in Eastern Europe, I wrote in that paper:

"Will the Soviet peoples watch the Poles and Hungarians gain a free press, academic freedom for students, and outspoken parliaments, without trying to do the same for themselves?....The Polish and Hungarian Communists have shown that they don't want to be ruled by holdovers from the Stalin era. Do the Russians?....Is it logical to suppose that the Russians want a rubber-stamp parliament (the Supreme Soviet) any more than the Poles or Hungarians? Do they wish to be kept in the dark about events, so they are caught completely unawares by the Polish and Hungarian development?"

I thought the answer to these questions was "no" and I therefore expanded on this in an article in *The American Socialist* which I titled "Trouble Ahead in Russia?" The correct answer was "not yet," for over 30 more years. Several months earlier I had shown what time has revealed to be a better understanding of reality. That was before the Polish and Hungarian pots boiled over, and I had not yet been put in a state of euphoria by the hope that democracy would be added to socialism. In a letter to the editor of the *Daily Worker,* published June 14, 1956, I had written:

"It is apparently still not recognized [by the U.S. Communist Party] that the problems of the Soviet Communist Party and of American friends of socialism are not the same, even as far as information on the Soviet Union is concerned....On Stalin's death, the Central Committee [in Moscow] had to warn publicly against 'panic and disarray', so completely had Stalin's leadership and everything Soviet been identified as one, to the Soviet people. Had anyone then said what Khrushchev says now, the internal repercussions would have been a great deal worse than 'panic and disarray'; the new leaders would have been seen as traitors to the accomplishments under The Great Stalin. The job has had to be gradual, with Khrushchev's speech going by word of mouth to the Party, until word comes back that the people are ready to take the full shock. The *Daily Worker* must learn that the demands of American political life often require opinions on Soviet matters before the time is ripe for public statements in the USSR."

The *Daily Worker* never learned that lesson. But in the eighteen months of 1956 and 1957 that the *Worker* did permit untrammeled discussion, I was able to get into print things in which I take much satisfaction. I often used pseudonyms so the opposition could not contend that I was getting too much space. During that period, it was the freest paper in the United States. The rest of the press kept the American people well-informed on the negative aspects of Soviet life, but not on the positive. The *Worker* printed both. On April 29, 1956, it ran a long article of mine saying, for the first time in any Communist publication in the entire world, that: "Stalinism—one-man rule in a socialist country—was bad in every field of life: labor policy, the farmer-labor alliance that is the bedrock of the Soviet government, policy toward minorities, science, culture. It must be bad, because it violates the dignity of man, holds back his powers of creation, and contradicts the very nature of socialism."

I was able to get the article published because it opened by setting forth the positive consequences of Soviet history during Stalin's thirty years in power.

I ultimately concluded that democracy was understood in Europe only as far east as Napoleon had been able to carry the ideas of the French Revolution nearly a century and a half earlier. He had been defeated in Russia, and his body of law, the Code Napoleon, had never been established there. Russians take enormous pride in having hurled him back. I think that was a tragedy for Russia but not Russia alone. For decades, that country was referred to as "the gendarme of Europe," an appelation it fully deserved.

Defeating Hitler was progressive. Defeating Napoleon was reactionary, as proved by the fact that triumphant tsarism was able very easily to crush a rebellion of officers in 1825 who wanted to bring to Russia the advances of the French Revolution they had witnessed when serving in the occupation force in Paris. And to lump the victories over Hitler and Napoleon together under the heading of patriotism, as Russians do, is nationalism. I concluded that Stalin's form of dictatorship was a Russian phenomenon. I described it as "Stalin's Russian monarchist autocracy" at a lecture in the summer of 1956. Three years later, when

I visited the Soviet Union for the first time in twenty-seven years, and people would use the stock phrase, "worship of an individual" to describe it, I would contradict that and call it, in Russian, "an old-fashioned Russian autocracy." No one there ever challenged the accuracy of that statement, although support for Soviet socialism was still overwhelming. But it was not until 1991 that I realized that Stalin's dictatorship was just the Russian answer to the problem posed by Marxist socialism. Abolishing the market, it requires an economy run by command. This in turn demands dictatorial government, which is why Castro, Mao and the rest were Stalinist in forms reflecting the histories of government in their countries.

That summer of 1955 Phyllis was sixteen and found a job as junior counselor at a camp outside Montreal. Tanya and I wanted to see her and needed a break from the furor. So we drove up along the Hudson, Lake George, the Adirondacks, to Montreal, down the St. Lawrence to Quebec, and back via the coast of Maine. In the decade since World War II, Canada had suddenly discovered itself as a nation vis-a-vis the United States, now that it was fully free of British rule. Phyllis and the one or two others from our country were made to feel this very sharply by the Canadian teenagers, so on July 4th they deliberately dressed up in red, white, and blue. It was an interesting lesson in nationalism, occurring at a Leftist camp where the parents were professedly internationalists.

We were able to have a vacation without the younger children because of the existence of a Communist-influenced children's camp, Kinderland, where we placed ours for three summers. It still exists, although I have no idea what politics, if any, prevail. The friendships and loyalties it produced were such that people who are now grandparents have reunions to this day in remembrance of those wonderful summers.

Tanya and I are not the kind of married people who don't talk to each other. However, we are capable of keeping silent in each other's presence. And both of us love the experiences of travel: new sights, walking, swimming, boating, the pleasant distraction of choosing a meal or a motel, although sometimes the latter can be irritating. That trip to eastern Canada and New England was a real vacation from the uproar in the international Left and even in the family caused by my article in *Monthly Review*. Both Tanya and my father had been reduced to blank despair by my original draft. They didn't want to believe what I said. They argued, probably rightly, that it could only destroy all contacts with other Communists and pro-Communists. This was a year before Khrushchev's speech confirmed my conclusions.

Tanya entered the hospital for an operation, as planned, immediately after that trip. It was the week before that lecture in which I defined Stalin as a traditional Russian autocrat. It was probably in response to a query from me as to what she thought I should say that she wrote the following notes on the back of the bill for surgery:

"1) Anyone believing in socialism must, of necessity, start with the thesis that socialism exists in [the] Soviet Union and is being built in China, etc.

"2) Must have a real knowledge of the socialist sector [of the world], including positive and negative (cite how this has actually been available to us all along, in detail).

"3) Must not base methods and ideas in our own country on those in [the] socialist sector [of the world] but use only such methods and experiences which actually do apply.

"4) Must be free to criticize faults in socialist sector from the viewpoint of socialism and humanism (such as: Jewish question, lack of correct trial procedures, etc.)."

In November, she wrote a letter to the *Daily Worker* which evokes the flavor of the times: "Friday night I attended a city-wide New York section leadership meeting called to discuss the Hungarian events." Soviet military intervention was crushing, in bloody fighting with thousands dead, a government of reform Communists. "A majority of the speakers and the audience opposed the position of the *Daily Worker* and the resolution of the National Board on the Hungarian crisis." They had criticized the USSR.

"Several people spoke scornfully of 'emotionalism' and demanded we support proletarian interntionalism by supporting the Soviet Union's action in Hungary.

"I answer - yes, I am emotional: I'm emotional on behalf of the workingclass of Hungary, and of the Hungarian people. I am a Communist, but first of all I am a human being. The supporters of the Soviet action say it had no choice but to bring in troops to save 'socialism.'

"What kind of 'socialism' did they have in Hungary, that after twelve years the workingclass of Hungary, the youth of Hungary (raised under 'socialism') felt it had to take up arms against the government, and is still fighting and striking after two weeks of bloodshed, hunger, and all kinds of promises and threats?

"I have been a member of the Communist Party for 19 years and a member of the Y[oung] C[ommunist] L[eague] for five years before that. When the 'Stalin revelations' broke last Spring, many members felt this would be the end of the C[ommunist] P[arty]. I felt there was still hope, that if we really analyzed and corrected all our mistakes we could still become the party to lead the American people to socialism.

"But now I do not want to belong to an organization whose members feel socialism should be imposed on the end of bayonets. That is not the socialism I worked for and dreamed of.

"I do not feel the speakers or audience at the meeting reflected the majority of the Party. I urge all our members to speak out and write to the *Daily Worker* in support of its stand."

The italicized paragraphs of Tanya's letter were quoted thirty-two years later by Maurice Isserman, a man we did not know, in his *If I Had a Hammer*.

The world reacted to the Soviet intervention in Hungary in 1956 as it did to that in Afghanistan in the 1980s. The *Worker* had taken a position in opposition to the use of Soviet troops. The United Nations voted to condemn Moscow's action. But in 1956 the major non-Communist Asian countries abstained: India, Indonesia, Burma (Myanmar), Ceylon. They had all been colonies less than a decade earlier. I felt that that abstention said something important about the situation in the world. England, France, and Israel had invaded Egypt in an attempt to seize the Suez Canal at the very time the Soviets invaded Hungary. In an article for the *York Gazette and Daily* I wrote:

"The Anglo-French and Israeli actions in Egypt give part of the answer [to the question of why the Asian countries abstained from criticizing the Soviet action]. None of the newly-independent states has lost, for a minute, its fear that the old empires would try to turn back the clock....But shouldn't Russia be feared, particularly after the suppression in Hungary?....There is not one Russian unit outside her frontiers in all of Asia....The Russians have been building steel mills for Asia, buying rice and cotton surpluses, and sending technical help....We send track stars to impress the Indians. The Russians didn't believe it beneath their dignity to send the two most important men in their country, Khrushchev and Bulganin.

"We laughed at the funny fat Russians in Indian costume clumsily imitating Indian gestures of courtesy. The Indians felt they were being treated as equals, and turned out in demonstrations bigger than [Mahatma] Gandhi, [Premier] Nehru, or their own independence day had ever been given....From Asia, Hungary is a pimple on the far side of Russia....And if [Moscow] wants to keep her troops flung out in that direction [westward] when the European powers have again shown their perfidy, Asia can only gain if Russia thus compels them to keep forces on guard in Europe. So goes the reasoning."

The fear that the West might try to turn back the clock was manifested again forty-three years later when China, India, and Indonesia supported post-Communist Russia's opposition to the U.S.-led NATO bombing of Serbia in 1999.

Agonizing over events in the Soviet Union and its intervention in Hungary had not prevented me from seeing that that was not all that was happening in the world. There were very emotional, personal components to this time. I had earned my very first money by writing articles for the *Moscow News* when I was living there at fourteen. That paper was edited by Anna Louise Strong. After World War II, Stalin had thrown her out of the USSR as a spy. It was now clear that she had been falsely attacked, and I wrote a letter to the *Worker:*

"She was accused of betraying the very meaning of her life—by those who had themselves betrayed theirs, and feared her probing for the truth. No iota of proof was offered, but people believed. I include myself. But has there been an apology to Anna Louise?....Personal apologies are needed as a matter...of common decency..."

At that very moment Strong was writing a book whitewashing Stalin, *The Stalin Era,* because she felt he had been right, on the grand scale, despite her personal humiliation. The Communist cultural magazine, *Mainstream,* asked me to review it. I wrote: "a reviewer is compelled to treat her book in terms of whether it advances or retards the cause of socialism in this country." I concluded that it did the latter.

Mainstream was co-publisher of the book along with Anna Louise herself, and it called me in. The head of its publishing division was present, and said: "How can we publish your review? We can't afford to lose our investment." I replied that I hadn't undertaken to do a puff job. I didn't add that, after thirty years in the Communist movement from childhood on, I was utterly shocked at the kind of ethics his words reflected. The magazine editor asked what I proposed they do. I said I was sure they could find someone who would support the book as sincerely as I opposed it. They found Dr. DuBois. So the front cover read:

"THE STALIN ERA" — Two Views
W.E.B. DuBois
William Mandel

The exhausting, years-long struggle over the implications of the revelations about Stalin to the future of socialism in America came to a climax and, thank goodness, an end, at the Communist Party's national convention in February 1957. One day in the spring of the previous year, shortly after Khrushchev's speech, I opened the door to the ring of a stranger who was almost the stereotype of a New York City detective in body build and facial appearance. Even his name was Irish, McCloskey. He succeeded in convincing me, however, that he was the new "section organizer" of the Communist Party for my area—the lowest grouping of clubs, often covering a State Assembly district. He came to inform me that my ouster of three years earlier had been cancelled, and to invite me to re-join.

I was extremely hesitant because I thought the party was hopelessly in the hands of Stalinists or those who would not make the clean break without which I believed it had no future. He himself, a high-iron construction worker, not a detective, shared my views and pleaded that my previous year's article in *Monthly Review*, along with my behavior before the McCarran and McCarthy committees, had given me a prestige that might help. After discussions with Tanya and friends I agreed to give it a go, but for not longer than until the convention scheduled for 1957. If we didn't win then I was sure the party would be a corpse, and I wanted no part of it.

So in 1956 and 1957 I had fought, with the considerable energy, the knowledge and eloquence I possessed, to turn the U.S. Communist Party toward a socialism compatible with this country's contribution to civil liberties and governmental democracy, although my personal experience of blacklisting and persecution the previous decade would have made a cynical attitude understandable at least. The very first statement proposing such a turn published in any Party-controlled publication was a "communication" of mine in *Masses & Mainstream*. It got attention in the country's leading Republican paper, the *New York Herald Tribune*.

I was a delegate to that 1957 convention. A veteran of the Lincoln Brigade, Al Lannon, said aloud as I passed: "Something stinks around here." But I was accompanied to and from the mike by a self-appointed bodyguard of Buffalo steelworkers, organized by McCloskey. Despite the seething emotions, no violence erupted at any point in the convention. Between sessions, Lorraine Hansberry and her husband, both of whom belonged to the Communist Party in our neighborhood and held views similar to mine, joined me in bemoaning the way things were going.

My speech was an unequivocal farewell. The officialdom got even with a nasty piece of business. While most other speakers who had to make a living outside the Party in private employ were identified in the published convention *Proceedings* as "a delegate" or by initials, I was one of several identified by name. That would have given the government legal grounds for jailing me for contempt had it subpoenaed me in any proceeding and asked me to identify others present at the Convention, which I would not do. Never mind the problem of livelihood: outright blacklists of all sorts were very much in use at the time.

When the *Proceedings* were published as a book, the *New York Times* gave it a column, including "William Mandel of New York was quoted as...predicting that 'after the constitution of the full national committee [those who opposed far-reaching change] will be in full command.' Two years later, Prof. David Shannon, in his book, *The Decline of American Communism*, wrote that I had "made a prediction at the convention that turned out to be remarkably accurate. While the convention chairman was declaring him out of order and trying unsuccessfully to get him to sit down, William Mandel...told the delegates that....The fully independent element will be the distinct minority in the full National Committee."

That was the end of my affiliation with the Communist Party—a personal as well as political matter. It became impossible to maintain friendships with those who had been on the opposite side of the fence. The organization fell apart for all practical purposes, showing no significant revival until the trial of Angela Davis for murder a good fifteen years later, after which it entered its final decline.

I felt trapped in New York. As my free-lance translating work was done by mail in any case, we could live where we chose, and chose Berkeley. A decade later Berkeley became the center of the 1960s universe, but this was only 1957. There was an element of the political in our choice, although the city's natural beauty was a very major consideration. The spirit of freedom in Berkeley was unique, as we knew from our period of residence there ten years earlier. It had had a Socialist mayor early in the century, and he had left as legacy a police force that, although entirely white, was described by Black friends then as not practicing discrimination. Regrettably, that later changed.

Immediately to the south is Oakland, with streets common to both. Oakland had a general strike in 1946. San Francisco workers had waged one a dozen years before that. A respect for labor—even the individual workingman or woman, not simply the unions—permeated society locally in those years before the student rebellion and the Black Panthers. Men in work-clothes and without ties could eat in the kind of places that would never admit them in New York.

But first the Mandels and their chattels had to get to Berkeley. And that was a trip.

CHAPTER 18

Berkeley Was Not the Bronx

Tanya's father, Moisei, died in 1955. He was a neighborhood dentist with wonderful laugh-crinkles around his eyes and a short moustache which bothered her when she kissed him.

Her mother, Sabina—stepmother, actually, because Tanya's mother died giving birth to her—ran the family. Moisei didn't mind, because she respected his space—his office was for years a room in their Bronx apartment—his time, and his work. Tanya's maternal grandmother and her two sisters were still very much alive. Bubbi (Grandmother) Lisenco had been a revolutionary in her youth in the Ukraine, with views that combined socialism and Zionism. By the time I knew her, she was staunchly pro-Communist, and so she remained. Her husband had died of cancer at quite an early age, and she supported herself by operating boarding houses consisting of one, or sometimes two, multi-bedroom apartments. She kept herself very well-informed, was an interesting conversationalist, and the soul of kindness.

My father-in-law's savings went to his widow, naturally. It was only at her death five years later that the property, including a small country cottage, was divided between Tanya and her two brothers. But because she was the offspring of a first marriage, he had bought a tiny insurance policy with some fraternal organization with Tanya as beneficiary. This came to just enough to buy a four-year-old Kaiser. Thirty-five years later son Dave bought me a tin-plated showroom sign for that model, with the slogan "the world's first 'safety first' car." Maybe it was. In any case it was our first automobile since our return from Ohio nearly twenty years before.

I love constant changes in scenery, and as always relaxed by navigating twisting roads. We explored the Catskills, Connecticut, New Jersey. There were no freeways or thruways, all roads were two lane, and most were just paved wagon trails. So I got plenty of relaxation. The mainland side of Long Island in wild rhododendron time was a favorite.

The sense of isolation that led to our decision to depart via Kaiser to Berkeley in 1957 was not solely a consequence of my leaving the Communist Party and being blacklisted by the Right. There was also the problem that the same Left which preached contempt for the Establishment in fact regarded acceptance by the academic world as proof of competence.

Our cross-country odyssey was a gas and an ordeal. We left in a wonderful mood. Brecht's "Three-Penny Opera" had just been put on in New York for the first time in many years, with the star of the original in Germany twenty years earlier, Lotte Lenya. I remember thinking that she must be a very old lady: twenty years! We saw it a couple of nights before departure. A single gesture from that performance has stayed with me forever: one of the plug-ugly gangsters crooking his little finger in imitation of the manner of the rich he both despised and envied. The music, then new to me, fixed itself in memory, and, whistled or hummed, kept me going on that endless drive across two-lane America as I poured sweat in July.

Our trip Kaiser had a roof carrier on top, Tanya and the two boys inside. Phyllis, our eldest, then seventeen, chose to remain in New York, where she had a boyfriend she soon married and a grandmother to rely on.

In Iowa the temperature hit 104 degrees, and humid. We had no air-conditioning. I drove in shorts and Tanya was constantly sponging me off with a wet towel kept soaking in a playpail. She doesn't drive. The engine heated up so it wouldn't start after a stop unless given a long time to cool off. After this happened a few times we grew impatient . At a gas station, some bright character said he'd give us a push. I didn't know any better—it's amazing how much I don't know about cars even now, after sixty-five years of driving—and I agreed. As the car started, I heard something give. Later I learned that the piston rings had expanded with the heat and stuck in the cylinders. When the push compelled the engine to turn over, one ring broke.

We had friends in Laramie, Wyoming, the sculptor Robert Russin and his family. He had grown tired of teaching in a Manhattan high school where the woman heading the art department thought fashion design was a useful thing for the kids to learn but was contemptuous of "impractical" sculpture. Offered the job at the University of Wyoming, Bob leapt at the chance to move west.

So we pushed on the six or seven hundred miles to Laramie. In Nebraska the corn really was as high as an elephant's eye. A ferocious but refreshing thunderstorm relieved the monotony. The car ran right along, except for a little knock until it warmed up in the morning or after long rests. The Kaiser made it up the continental divide at nine thousand feet, and then to Laramie. There Russin had his mechanic look at it. The verdict was that the engine would fall apart any minute, and we must not go on.

Continued on page 337

Max Mandel (father) at thirty-two in Kuzbass, Siberia, 1926.

Dora Mandel, mother, shortly before her death, 1960.

Tanya as a child with her parents, Moisei and Sabina Millstein, New York, 1920-21.

William Mandel, rear, nearly seven, with brother Eugene, and friend. 1924.

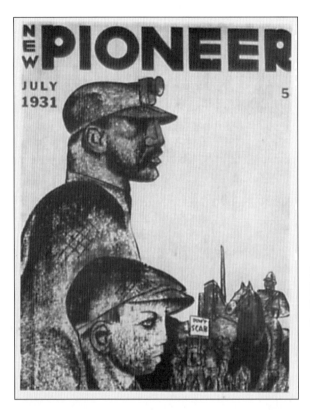

Magazine of Young
Pioneers of America,
Communist children's
organization.

William Mandel, far right, in Moscow with performing group of
Leningrad-resident U.S. and Canadian children of foreigners who came
to help "build socialism." Moscow, 1932.

Tanya and William Mandel at eighteen, starting out together.
Cleveland, OH, 1935.

Tanya at twenty, 1937.

"Dangerous Subversives": Young Communists, in Greenwich Village,
NY, 1939. William Mandel is front row far left; Tanya Mandel is rear
row fourth from left.

Grandmother Schachter left, with Grandparents Mandel, New York, 1942.

William Mandel, Golden's
Bridge, NY 1943

With American Russian Institute friends in Greenwich Village, NY 1943

In Palo Alto, CA, during Hoover Institution Fellowship at Stanford. 1947.

Tanya with daughter Phyllis, Camp Unity, NY, 1949-50

Leaving Paul Robeson concert at Peekskill, New York, August 26, 1949 (Courtesy of UPI.)

Speaking against the Korean War during his run for Congress with Dr. W.E.B DuBois, New York, 1950.

Mandel in front right. Paul Robeson right rear at Soviet Embassy celebration of anniversary of revolution, Nov. 7, 1950, Washington, D.C.

They Pleaded for Martinsville 7

"Some of the nearly 500 delegates of both races in the 'Crusade to Richmond' sponsored by the Committee to Save the Martinsville Seven on the eve of the electrocution of the seven men in the Virginia capital. Nearly every State in the union is represented. Photo was made at meeting in Leigh St. Methodist Church after Federal District Judge Sterling Hutcheson had denied petition for writ of habeas corpus for each of the me. Note that colored and white are sitting side by side and not in segregated sections as they did at the recent Marian Anderson concert at the Mosque Theatre."

The Richmond Afro-American, Feb. 10, 1951

Saying no to power. Subpoened by Senator McCarthy, Mandel declares "This is a book-burning! You lack only the tinder to set fire to the books as Hitler did 20 years ago, and I am going to get this across to the American People!" 1953

Death watch for Ethel and Julius Rosenberg, June 19, 1953. When executions were announced, Mandel led these thousands in parade without a permit for miles through lower Manhattan. African-American with glasses, lower left, is William L. Patterson (see photo, p. 326). To his right with glasses is Earl Robinson, composer of "Ballad For Americans."

"THE VOICE OF 500"

New Trial In Richmond*

BY WILLIAM MANDEL

"The South alone," my host had said
"remembers its dishonorable dead."
His arm swept round the ordered Square
to mock the statues frozen there
of generals whose armies bled
that white might eat the black man's bread.

But never had these marbles seen
assembled on this quiet green,
the slaves' descendants, in a mass,
with their brothers of the working class,
demanding that the murders cease,
that Negroes live their lives in peace.

Despite police and jails and chair
the people had foregathered there
to warn that patience tugged its chain
that this Seven must not die again
nor six, nor four, nor two, nor one,
that Justice must, in truth, be done,

That Court will come, one day, to sit
beneath this Tree, a monument fit
with green and growth and shade and life
to honor Grayson and his wife,
the Hairstons, Milner, Taylor, Hampton,
who went with dignity and pride
seeing the People at their side.

And I shall sit on that Court some day
not with bowed and bended head to pray
as we did through many a winter night
beneath that Tree, in a losing fight,
but, lessons learned and battle done,
Our Court shall call them one by one,
Governor, President, judges gray,
whose hands took seven lives away
to keep a people bound in fear,
to hold the line that awful year
when Negroes fought a kindred race*
and bound themselves to a lesser place.

---

*Introduction to an epic poem about the
Execution of the Martinsville Seven.—Editor.
*reference is to Korean War. (handwritten)

Langston Hughes wrote Mandel
complimenting him on this.

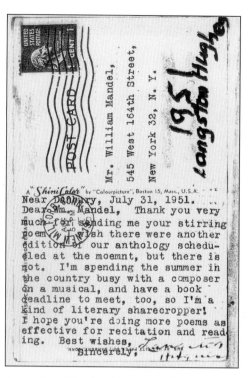

Langston Hughes's postcard.

Tanya and William Mandel, with sons Bob and Dave, singing at Vincent and Vivian Hallinan Estate, Marin County, CA.,1958.

Tajik students, their Russian friends, and William Mandel on a parapet facing Moscow University, 1959.

Mandel testifying before HUAC, 1960: "If you think I will cooperate in any way with this collection of Judases, of men who sit there in violation of the United States Constitution—if you think I will cooperate with you in any manner whatsoever—you are insane!"

William Mandel on KPFA during fundraising marathon, Berkeley, CA, 1960.

Advertisement for "Operation Abolition," Bakersfield Californian, September 1960.

Talking with KPFA supporters at gala event honoring the Pacifica Network, one month before the HUAC hearings began. 1960.

Cartoon in Chico State Wildcat, February 6, 1964.

At Republican National Convention in San Francisco, holding a sign that says, "Protect My Kids in Mississippi." Son Bob who was in Mississippi for the voter-registration drive, had disappeared the night three other students were murdered. Fortunately, he had only been arrested. San Francisco, CA, 1964. Photo credit: Lorin Gillette

Free Speech Movement, University of California, Berkeley, 1964-5. Police photograph carries names of identified leaders.

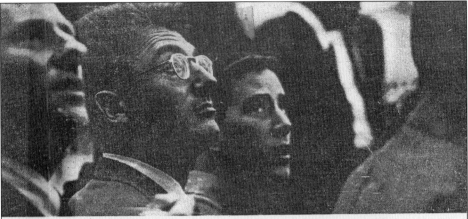

LIAM MANDEL, a member of the Communist Party, served as a middle aged mem-
of the Free Speech Movement Executive Committee, indicating that the FSM was far
an innocent student movement.

"William Mandel, a member of the Communist Party." A lie at the time.
Published in Berkeley right-wing paper during Reagan's campaign for governor, 1966.

With Tanya and Russian, Ukrainian, and Belarus Soviet exchange students.
1966.

At fifty-one, taking part in "liberation" of Telegraph Avenue, Berkeley, on Independence Day, July 4, 1968.

Daughter Phyllis leading International Women's Day celebration in Berkeley, CA, March 8, 1968.

In KPFA studios during fundraising marathon, Berkeley, CA, 1968.

The Creative Alternative From 1949 to 1979

Photo: Phiz Mozesson

On April 15, 1949, America's first and only listener-sponsored, non-commercial, and non-governmental radio network was born. It was called **Pacifica Radio.**

It all began with one station: **KPFA-FM** in Berkeley. And this year, as **KPFA** celebrates its 30th anniversary, we would like to tell you about these last 30 years of broadcasting with an exciting slide-tape presentation: **"Playing in the FM Band."**

In the **1950's,** McCarthy and his buddies created a climate of fear during the Cold War. **Pacifica** radio had the courage to speak out.

In the **1960's,** college campuses and the nation's ghetto's exploded in rage against a senseless war abroad and injustice at home. **Pacifica** gave them a voice.

And in the **1970's** the U.S. government did its best to cover-up during Watergate. Once again, **Pacifica** provided the news coverage people could trust.

Since 1949, **Pacifica** has also provided a voice for the arts. All forms of poetry, music and drama— whether traditional or *avant garde*—have appeared on free speech radio.

Through historical images and sounds, **"Playing in the FM Band"** brings back the 'fifties, 'sixties, and 'seventies as the show looks at some of the most important events in our recent history. In a way that only free speech **Pacifica** radio can tell it.

Photo: Jeffrey Calhro

After more than twenty years on KPFA, Mandel's popularity was still such that this picture of him, singing at an early fund-raising marathon, was chosen to celebrate the station's thirtieth anniversary.

The Oakland Seven in '67 (left to right): Steve Hamilton, Jerry Cannon, Reese Erlich, Bob Mandel, Mike Smith, Frank Bardacke, Jeff Segal (inset) was in prison for draft refusal at the time of the photo.

William Mandel in Moscow conducting interviews and research for his book, *Soviet Women*. 1973

Son Dave, Vietnam War draft resister in exile,
Canada, 1969.

Tanya Mandel, center, with major creative artists of Kyrgyzstan, including
actor in "Dersu Uzala," playwright, TV film-maker, assistant movie director.
1970s.

With Central Asian friends. She is a Ph.D., Ob-Gyn; he is an encyclopedia writer; daughter, standing, is a musician. Alma-Ata, Kazakhstan, USSR, 1979.

With John "Paka" Meachum, Soledad Prison, Soledad, CA 1980.

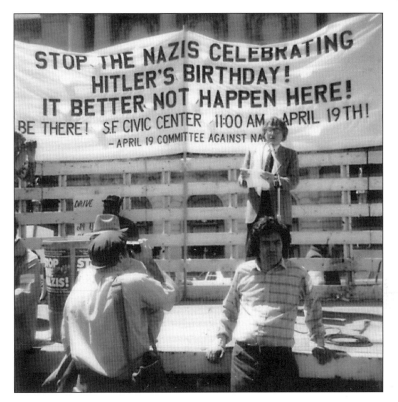

Speaking at San Francisco demonstration organized by son.
1981.

Back at Chico State, California,
1982.

Dancing at 20th anniversary of Free
Speech Movement, Berkeley, 1984.

At the grave of William L. Patterson, the son of a slave. He entrusted Mandel to travel the country promoting his book, *We Charge Genocide*, to Black leadership and such whites as could be reached in 1951, during the bottom of the McCarthy years. Chicago, 1985.

With Larry Pinkney, a Black Panther who served nine years in jail for a burglary frame up. Mandel visited him in jail, supported him on the air, and drove him home upon release from prison. St. Paul, MN, 1986.

At 70. KPFA gathering. Berkeley, CA, 1987 Photo credit: Susan Elizabeth

With wife and daughter of hydrology officer who stayed up all night to develop these pictures. Peace Walk, Novgorod, USSR, 1987.

With democracy proponents from Novgorod, USSR, 1987.

Selling his books at KPFA
fair. Berkeley, CA, 1988

Group of Soviet and American peace walkers singing "Star Spangled
Banner" as U.S. flag is raised in Ukraine, USSR, 1988. Mandel to right of
microphone.

Standing in front of a 1931 tractor, the first ever in this Ukrainian city, 1989.

William Mandel shaking hands with a veteran, thanking him for helping to save the world from fascism. Ukraine Peace Walk, 1989.

On the road during the Uzhgorod - Kyiv Walk, Ukraine 1989.

With Jewish ritual butcher in *shtetl* in West Ukraine near his maternal grandmother's birthplace. Taken during American - Soviet Peace Walk, 1989.

1990. Kyiv with hiking club of Youth Housing Complex. Original frescoes on Ukrainian themes. Actress Irina Horobets resting against table.

William Mandel talking with Angie Frabasilio at Young Pioneer camp near miners' health resort, Kazakhstan, 1990. Photo credit: Rhoda Evans

Answering questions about America posed by Youth Housing Project work-er-residents in the compound's ballet studio. Kyiv 1990.

Left to Right: Correspondent who since emigrated to Canada; Horobets' child, Mandel, Liubov Kovalevskaya, a poet and reporter who blew the whistle on Chernobyl in advance, and has since died of cancer; Irina Horobets, a movie star at 18 who became the culture director of the Youth Housing Project. Kyiv 1990.

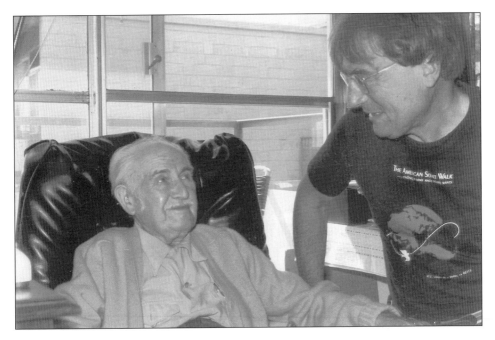

With Max in his 90s.

With another former peace walker at anti-Iraq War parade, San Francisco, 1991.

1958. Five generations of Mandels: Max, William, Tanya, Phyllis, great granddaughter Alana, grandson Dan, Dave's partner Traci Eckels, left to right in top row. Below: grandson Kevin, son Bob, his wife Cheryl, son Dave.

Max speaks at 100th birthday celebration, 1994.

Radio Legend Off the Air Waves

KPFA suspends host Bill Mandel

By Ryan Tate
Contributing Writer

[handwritten: 80 by count]

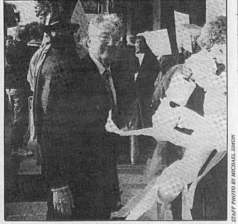

More than 50 loyal supporters of local talk-radio host Bill Mandel picketed and later entered the Berkeley offices of KPFA-FM on Wednesday, demanding that the political commentator who was suspended last month be allowed back on the air.

Shouting "Hey! Hey! K-P-F-A! Bring Mandel back on Monday!" the protesters, including station subscribers and long-time Mandel listeners, urged KPFA managers to reinstate the radio host after he was dismissed from the listener-sponsored station April 30.

"They should put him back on the air," said picketer Dolores Plum, who has been listening to Mandel for 30 years. "He is one of their living treasures."

According to protest organizers, during a KPFA advisory board meeting on Wednesday station managers said Mandel was on a five-week suspension and could reapply for his job early next month.

Station managers are on a two-day decision-making retreat and could not be reached for comment.

Mandel has worked for KPFA for more than 38 years and said that in the late 1960s he invented the current talk-radio format.

Topics on Mandel's show usually revolve around issues pertaining to the former Soviet Union. Mandel was called before Joseph McCarthy's House Committee on Un-American Activities in the 1950s.

His defiant response to the committee's questions regarding his political affiliations is featured in the opening to the film "Berkeley in the '60s," a documentary on the Free Speech Movement.

"If I've held an audience for 38 years, people must like me," Mandel said. "(KPFA) used an excuse to get me off the air."

Mandel, whose show originally aired every Monday afternoon, said he recently agreed to switch to Monday mornings in exchange for an additional afternoon show every other Sunday.

Then, last month, KPFA discontinued Mandel's morning show, citing tardiness and a lack of adequate preparation, among other factors, according to Mandel.

The commentator then used his Sunday afternoon show to blast station management for taking him off the air, claiming that he did not need to arrive as early or prepare as thoroughly as his producers wanted him to. Mandel also said on his show that station managers' true complaints were that he failed to stick to his primary topic, the former Soviet Union.

In accordance with KPFA policy, which prohibits the discussion of station business on the air, Mandel's Sunday show was discontinued, leaving him without a show or airtime.

Mandel said "the minimum" concession he would like from the station is a weekly half-hour show.

Bill Mandel and supporters protested at KPFA Wednesday.

William Mandel at protest organized by his supporters after he was taken off the air at KPFA. Berkeley, CA 1995.

Vital at 79.

William Mandel with Lester Radke and a Russian host in Siberia, 1998.

Mandel picketing in support of KPFA broadcaster, Robby Osman, dismissed for breaking the gag rule, June 1999.

We took it to two more mechanics, both of whom offered the same opinion. Finally, Bob said he had a student who tinkered with cars. This football player turned out to have a Cadillac, a big Chrysler and a Lincoln, each bought dirt-cheap and fixed in his own shop. His opinion was similar to mine: we could make it. But to make sure, he called in yet another expert tinkerer, who thought the same. The two of them decided to let the local night-shift radio announcer, also one of Bob's students and car fixer-upper, give his verdict. After all, the car was the most valuable piece of property we owned, and we hadn't the cash for other transportation. Credit cards were not yet part of life.

So that night we drove to the radio station in the high desert outside of town. The d.j. spun some wonderful old-time jazz and then started a music broadcast while we all went out to the car. He lifted the hood, started 'er up, listened, and the three experts went into consultation. I nodded wisely and Bob threatened to flunk any of them if they steered me wrong, while pinching their cheeks in affection (they weighed about two hundred pounds each and were married war veterans with families). Suddenly the recording going over the air (and piped outside the station by loudspeaker on the veranda) ended. The d.j. broke all records for the ten-yard sprint and fence vault to get to the mike in time for some more announcements.

When he came back he agreed with his friends and said that the car ought to take us to California if I didn't push her too hard over mountain passes. So we drove on. We did fine through Wyoming. The Snowy Range was still snowy in July. I badly needed a break, and climbed a thousand feet or so up the rubble of a mountain alongside the highway. Our box Brownie camera recorded the immensity and grandeur, and the happy faces of Bobby and Davey in brand-new cowboy hats. They hadn't been happy at all in the soaking heat of the Great Plains.

Utah brought a down-grade I thought would never end, and sawtooth snow-clad mountains outside Salt Lake City. I made a mental note to ski them some day. It was nearly twenty years later before I managed to. Then a hundred miles of glaring white salt flats, and on to Nevada: vast, dull brown, dull gray, dull green, legal slot machines and fine food.

The road that is now Interstate 80 was then U.S. 40, and the difference lay in more than the designation. West of Reno it hung between heaven and earth, and was being relocated and made a four-laner by incredibly brave and skilful construction workers. We had to crawl along at ten miles an hour behind some very frightened drivers as the twisting, cliff-hugging road rose from four to six thousand feet. That driving in low gear did the engine no good.

We cut off to see Lake Tahoe. In those years what is now the walking trail down to the water's edge in Emerald Bay was open as a one-way road, probably as steep as any in service. We could see boats down below making wakes around that perfectly centered islet, whose size and mini-mountain shape are precisely in harmony with the bay. We found out it was possible to rent a power skiff. There was a division of opinion over whether to drive down. I don't recall whether the condition of the car was an issue. Anyway, Tanya and Davey insisted on going down, and we did so. We took turns steering a boat and had a marvelous time.

Getting back up to the highway again required driving in low gear. Up top, I asked a California tourist which was the easier road west, U.S. 40 over Donner Summit or 50 past Echo Lake. He said 50, perhaps because of the construction on the other.

That last thousand-foot climb to the pass was the beginning of the end. The car was now knocking all the time, but lightly. As we started downhill, the California driver in a Ford truck ahead of us took curves at well over the marked limits. I tried to keep up for a while—I have a competitive streak—but then decided we might as well live a while longer.

Down at the foothill level it got hot, and in the Central Valley it was no better than New York or Iowa in midsummer. There were no cuts to level out the last hills, and each time the car had to take an upgrade it sounded as though we'd never make it to the top.

We didn't find a motel with room until eleven p.m. This was the height of tourist season. But what we found, on the strip just west of Sacramento, offered unimaginable luxury compared to everything we had encountered before: free room TV (black and white, of course, back then), free continental breakfast, a large swimming pool with diving board, and huge oleander bushes in bloom all round. Tanya was feeling very sick, but snapshots in the pool show her the picture of health. She always was a water baby.

The following morning we frolicked in the pool. I knew it would be unbearably hot and that the car was on its last legs, so I felt we ought to start in the best mood possible. The engine clanked like a knight in armor, but it was kind to us—until we passed right in front of the door of the Milk Farm, which still serves tourists. At that moment a connecting-rod went through the block, and that was the end.

There was a phone right outside. I called folksinger Malvina Reynolds (who wrote "Little Boxes") and her husband Bud in Berkeley. We knew them from a visit they'd made to our next-door neighbors in New York. When our car broke down, Bud had just been to Detroit to buy a new car cheap. He had been an auto worker there for many years. He was not willing to use the new car to tow us, because the law forbade a line more than eight feet long and if he had had to make a sudden stop, I would smash his rear end. He drove out to pick up Tanya and the boys, and I had to figure out what to do with the car.

As we waited for Bud, sipping malted milks, a truck driver hauling an enormous flatbed trailer stopped by. He sat at the next table, nibbling, and commented on the car in the pool of oil outside. I said it was ours. He offered to carry it on his trailer if we could get it up onto the bed. I assumed he wanted to make a few extra bucks, told him a $20 bill—$140 in present purchasing power—was all I had on me, and he was welcome to it. He said he had moved to California twenty years earlier during the Great Depression, and knew what making the change was like. He wouldn't take a dime. This was my first encounter with the truly neighborly spirit typical of California in that remote time.

We attached the car to the truck by a tow-line and set off to find a ramp to get it up onto the truck, which we eventually found.

The man was a driver for the state prison system, and half his flatbed was covered with semi-finished chairs from a workshop at some other pen to be finished at San Quentin. As we reached Richmond, he told me we could not make it to Berkeley in time for him to drive back for his delivery before nightfall, when it would be against the rules. So my first visit to a prison—I had twice been in New York City jails to serve one-day terms—was not through the visitor's entrance, the warden's office, or with a lawyer, but right into the big yard.

The guards passed us, probably assuming that the man in the horn-rimmed glasses was a supervisor. We were up in a high cab, and they couldn't see from below that I was wearing nothing but shorts. As we parked at the loading dock, I reached for the door-handle to get out and help the driver. He grabbed me and hissed, "Stay put. They'll rape you!" I was, as Muhammad Ali used to call himself, pretty, and didn't know whether the truck driver was serious or not.

So while the truck was unloaded I got a good look at the yard population. I was shocked. I knew that northern California was then over-whelmingly white. Yet half the prisoners were African-Americans, and many of the rest were Chicanos. One elderly white man, with the visor of his cap turned up, looked as though he had been sent by Central Casting to play the stereotypical old con. Unloaded, we headed out the gate. The trucker joined me in a great sigh of relief. It turned out that the gate guards were men he had never seen before.

Arrived in Berkeley, we headed for the Reynolds' back-yard mechanic. He offered to find and install an engine at a reasonable price. I invited the driver to bring his wife sometime and be our guests for dinner. He said "sure," but never did. In subsequent years I found equal friendliness when in trouble on the roads only from Latinos.

We spent a week or more, all four of us, in the front room of the Reynolds house on Parker Street. They found a place for us thanks to the bulletin board of the Consumers' Co-op on University Avenue. To us that was a marvel. Imagine a whole supermarket run on cooperative principles! Of course we knew that co-ops existed. I remembered the co-op cafeteria on Union Square in New York a quarter century earlier, where I first saw the twin pines symbol. But for a co-op market to be a significant part of the available food supply was a new experience. Its location in the heart of the Berkeley flatlands reflected the fact that it had been founded largely by Finnish workingpeople, the class I, as a Marxist, then hoped would lead this country to a society run in the interests of the common folk.

And to be able to find a place to live without paying off real estate types, through the friendly device of a free bulletin board! Our house was on 10th Street off Cedar. It belonged to a young Jewish longshoreman, Leo Kanowitz, and his peach-pretty southern WASP wife, Libby.

Raised in that nest of radicalism the Cooperative Apartments in the Bronx, Leo was then studying law at Boalt Hall, UC Berkeley. The couple was going somewhere for the summer. We became friends after their return, and remained so for many years. When Leo published his first book, *Women and the Law,* perhaps a decade later, I told him what I knew, which by then was considerable, about promoting and selling one's book. In 1969, when he was a professor at the University of New Mexico, he supported a Black teaching assistant fired by direct resolution of the State Legislature for distributing to the students in his English class poems by Lenore Kandel, one of which dealt explicity with oral sex. I gave what help and encouragement I could in circulating the book he wrote on that ordeal, *Poem Is a Four-Letter Word.*

In 1975, when my *Soviet Women* was published by Doubleday, I sought Leo's endorsement. His name carried weight among feminists because of his pioneering first book. I got a lawyer's tactful turndown. I guess a book having anything favorable to say about the USSR was not something he wished to be associated with, although we had no disagreements over its contents, which we discussed in depth.

I happen to be a very loyal friend, and expect equal loyalty from my friends, whether or not we see the world in the same way. And when I find that not to be the case, I don't see such people any more.

The house we rented from the Kanowitzes was part of a new way of life to us. Imagine, a whole house to ourselves. Moreover, it was built around a courtyard, so I could feel isolated from the world. I am very sociable in company, but also treasure being, and feeling, alone. I work alone, and value a sense of total privacy in my workplace. I spend a lot of time, even when seated at the typewriter or today the computer, in what used to be called reverie. But it was always all right for the kids to break into it. I remember once playing catch with Davey in the street. He threw wild and the ball went into a tree. I wrote my parents: "I reached into the leaves, thought I had caught it, put my right hand into the gloved left hand to throw the ball and glanced at it. Slight error. In my hand was a peach. That's California for you."

The house on 10th Street brought another sense of Berkeley that I liked very much: "As I had a catch with Bobby...I saw a white woman stop to have a few laughing words with the Negro man watering his lawn next door. The kids play together with utmost freedom, and many of the white kids have accents marking them as from the South or Southwest."

In my letter to my parents at the end of our month in the Kanowitz', I still hadn't gotten over that: "Moving 'up the hill'...will take us out of a neighborhood with the most remarkable race relations I've ever seen. It is perfectly normal here for the door to ring, and a Negro girl to ask, 'May I borrow Bobby's bat?' And an hour later it will ring again, and a white child will return it. Our neighbor on one side is a Negro, and when we chat, he automatically calls me 'Bill,' in the normal American fashion, and not 'Mr.' The neighborhood we are moving to is lily white." One reason for returning to Berkeley was that, when we had come to the Bay Area a decade earlier, knowing nothing whatever about where we wanted or could afford to live, acquaintances had rented for us a house in the Berkeley hills with an 80-mile view from north of San Rafael to south of Palo Alto.

In my letters to my daughter in New York I simply unwound. She has kept two from that time. The first went on for two single-spaced typed pages simply describing that trip across the country. The second, a week later, was one such page. Then I turned it over and scribbled: "This side of the page is blank because I have to return to earning some rent and pay-back-debts and postage and haircut and accordion-payments-for-a-boy-who-doesn't-want-lessons...money. Believe me, imagination time comes high..."

We found a house at $135 per month—well below the 25 percent of income that Americans then thought financially bearable to commit to housing. The house was at almost exactly the altitude of the top of the Empire State Building, with view to match, provided you spent your time in the bathroom!

Only a Berkeleyan could be less than satisfied with the view from the front. Facing San Francisco, it was interrupted by a stand of a dozen red-wood trees planted on the grounds of a sprawling pueblo-type home. What had probably been intended as the front entrance of our house, judging by the neo-Gothic Maybeck-type peaked entryway, faced a wonderful thicket of a twisting, ground-hugging tree. Beyond the thicket towered young redwoods rooted in the uphill neighbor's yard, maybe fifty feet above us vertically. When there was wind and fog, the waving branches at the tops of those redwoods were hypnotic.

The rent was low because the house was an impractical monstrosity within. One bedroom was 8x10, another 8x8, the third a normal size. The house dated from the time—probably the late 1920s—when northern Californians kidded themselves into believing they enjoyed San Diego temperatures. Only the dining room and master bedroom were heated. I worked in that glass-enclosed porch, the window casements decayed and leaking air, the unheated living room between me and any heat. On sunny days, I'd move myself and lightweight desk out onto the patio, strip to the waist, and pretend I was warm. Being young is nice.

Up the block on Poppy Lane stands Cragmont Rock, where students from the university still come to practice rappelling and other mountaineering techniques. Altogether, the surroundings were ideal for casting off the stresses of the bitter ideological struggle I had left behind in New York. Even forty years later, after all the urbanization that has occurred around San Francisco Bay, that magnificent body of water and the splendid belt of inter-county regional parks within a fifteen-minute drive from inner-city slums provide extraordinary opportunities for relaxation in nature. We'd drive in San Francisco to one of its separate hills: Potrero, Russian, Nob, Telegraph (there are fourteen in all), or to Sea Cliff where the Golden Gate meets the ocean. We'd park and walk for hours, rejoicing in the pocket gardens, the endless variety of architecture, and the wonderful light. Other day trips from home took us to Sutter Buttes, that archaic residue of a mountain range that once comprised islands in the inland sea that is now the Central Valley, or the Feather River Canyon. Less often we would drive down to Monterey and Carmel, where one could rent a room reasonably in a lovely gabled inn right on the waterfront. Or up to Dutch Flat in the Sierra Nevada where Alden Bryant—yes, named for his ancestor John Alden—let us stay in his minimally-furnished clapboard second home, virtually unchanged from when some gold-miner or pioneer farmer had put it up.

Sputnik rose into the sky only two months after we arrived in California. Like everyone else, we stood outside to watch the second man-made Soviet star cross the night sky a month later. Washington realized that Moscow's fanciful statement that it had an intercontinental ballistic missile to trump our long-range bombers was true. And I understood that the day had come when I could again make use of my professional knowledge of the Soviet Union. But how?

When we moved to Berkeley in the summer of 1957, a unique aura of freedom pervaded the San Francisco Bay area. Murals dating from the New Deal years had been covered or destroyed elsewhere in the country if they made pro-labor, never mind radical, statements. This was not only true for publicly-funded properties but even Diego Rivera's privately-commissioned work in Rockefeller Center, New York. Such things had not happened in San Francisco, despite campaigns to destroy the Coit Tower murals, including a huge panel by my Stanford friend Victor Arnautoff, and those in the Post Office Rincon Annex by an acquaintance, Anton Refregier. They were both Russians and Communists.

Berkeley boasted the country's, probably the world's, first listener-sponsored radio station, committed by its charter to free speech and world peace: KPFA. And comedian Mort Sahl was ripping Joe McCarthy in San Francisco's "hungry I" when no other night club in the country would dare to book such an entertainer. Moreover, the club hired a veteran of the Lincoln Brigade and Hollywood Ten screenwriter jailbird, Alvah Bessie, as in-house publicity man, doorman, and general factotum.

The Bay Area was the regional capital of what had been the country's last frontier of pioneering on the basis of individual free enterprise and the political system founded thereon. It was the only place in the United States where the New Deal coalition of labor and intellectuals had never been crushed. The key labor union in the area at the time was the Longshoremen's. It had never surrendered to or been smashed by Red-baiting. It enjoyed extraordinary prestige among all other unions as well as other segments of the population—a result of the successful San Francisco General Strike in 1934.

After our first months in Berkeley, we began to uncover its cultural riches. "There are several night clubs featuring *jazz and poetry*," I wrote my parents. "This is the only city in America where the reading of poetry aloud is accepted mass entertainment." An elfin bookdealer named Sol Mandelblatt, another veteran of the Lincoln Brigade, had set up his second-hand store in an abandoned cold-storage block just west of the University. On Saturday evenings he scheduled poetry readings and hootenanny guitar playing, and artists displayed their works on the soaring walls above his bookcases. I would take our boys to the guitar fests, and remember being struck by the extraordinary use of obscenities in the work of Ken Spiker, a poet who played and read in Berkeley for many years afterward. He anticipated Haight-Ashbury after the summer of love, although it was still nearly a decade in the future.

When living in Berkeley ten years earlier, I had been impressed by the free intermixture of cultures in recreational folk dance groups. In New York, Cleveland, Akron, cities in which we had lived, each nationality did its own dances in its own ethnic dress. But by the time European migrants reached the West Coast, the nationalist factor must have receded because I found people dancing the dances they liked, whatever their individual ethnic origins, in the costumes that appealed to them individually.

In addition to Malvina and Bud Reynolds, and to our longshoreman-landlord, we quickly became friends with Virginia and Clinton Jencks, stars in the underground film of the '50s, "Salt of the Earth," by black-listed Hollywood Ten director Herbert Biberman. Clint had been an organizer for the Mine, Mill & Smelter Workers, left-controlled heir to the famous Western Federation of Miners founded by the IWW's Big Bill Haywood in about 1900. When the witch-hunt convinced the top Mine-Mill leaders that it would be destroyed, they decided to dump "Red" ballast like Clint, a move they thought necessary to gain admittance into the larger and more powerful Steel Workers Union. Clint came to Berkeley shortly before we did. He had just won a landmark U.S. Supreme Court decision granting defendants access to FBI files. He had been falsely testified against by the same perjured witness, Harvey Matusow, who had named me in 1952.

Clint found a job as rigger, a heavy-machinery installation skill. I wrote my parents that Clint's "current employer came across his name and picture in one of the major magazines recently after the Supreme Court decision, and told him all this made no difference: he was a good workman." As that shop was organized into the Steel Workers, Clint had the grim satisfaction of finding himself a delegate to the national convention of that union, while his own, which had rid itself of him, was still on the outside looking in. Shortly afterward he learned that a Woodrow Wilson Fellowship in economics was available, and asked me what I thought of him applying for it. I knew he had graduated as an economics major some twenty years earlier, and pointed out that the field had undergone a fundamental revolution: he would have to master math of kinds utterly unknown to him, plus the then-new mystery of computer work. I have never met anyone of greater tenacity. He went on to a master's and a Ph.D., putting in unbelievable hours at odd jobs. He beat the Red-baiting that dogged him in the academic world by sheer charm and the kind of honesty that would melt stone. Then he went to England and crawled through its coal mines for his thesis on the Labor government's nationalization of that industry. Finally he became a professor of economics at San Diego State. Poetic justice: the Steel Workers Union made him official custodian of the papers of the Western Federation of Miners and its successor union, Mine-Mill, so he subsequently spent his research time on the very union that had forced him out.

When I visited Cuba just before the CIA-sponsored Bay of Pigs invasion in 1961, Clint gave me scripts of "Salt of the Earth" in Spanish. In Havana I met the leading Mexican actress, Rosaura Revueltas, who had played the female lead in "Salt." For this she was permanently blacklisted in Mexico by a government that automatically toadied to Washington. Red-baiting and blacklisting was the official policy of our government, and not merely of the point men comprising congressional investigating committees. The U.S. film projectionists' union cooperated with the government by refusing to let its members show "Salt." The decade-old film, which initially had virtually no distribution, only re-emerged in the latter half of the '60s when the new women's liberation movement discovered that its high point was Chicanas taking over the picket line when their husbands were barred from it by injunction. For several years "Salt" was *the* feminist film. They gave no thought to the fact that it had been written by men and directed by a man, and that its positive portrayal of women reflected those men's Marxist convictions.

With friends like the Jenckses we were not lonely in Berkeley. But a purely personal life was not fulfilling. As soon as school opened in the fall of 1957, I wrote a teacher of a Russian-language high-school class that had been written up in the *San Francisco Chronicle,* and offered to address his class on the theme of technical translation from Russian. When the first two sputniks went up, in October and November, I wrote the chancellor of U.C. Berkeley, Clark Kerr, proposing that it pioneer in teaching technical translation. He replied, saying he'd bring my suggestions to the attention of his academic advisory committee. That was the last I heard of it. In 1999, with the USSR long gone, American scientists were pleading for such courses in an Internet chat room on Russian affairs. The Soviet heritage of scientific achievement required that a significant number of Americans possess that Russian technical translation capability.

A measure both of the impact of the sputniks and of the unique political atmosphere in the Bay Area is provided by a symposium held in November, 1957, on the theme, "The Sputniks, Science, and Capitalism." It was arranged by the Berkeley Socialist Forum, and organized by a prominent local actor and poet, George Hitchcock, who had left the Communist Party shortly before. The symposium was remarkable for the fact that a major solid-state physicist and a rocket-propulsion expert, both U.C. professors, agreed to discuss the subject along with me. Nowhere else in the country would scientists speak under announced socialist auspices at that time. I said that the major significance of the launching of the space age was that, in some extremely remote future, humanity's descendants would be able to leave a dying earth for a more hospitable heavenly body. The only real obstacle to that would be destruction of human and probably most other forms of life on earth in a nuclear war. I anticipated Star Trek, without its intergalactic wars. Already today, space research is seeking water on planets in our own solar system with the notion of development of agriculture. Won't it be nice if, a zillion years from now, some being would discover this book on disk (paper doesn't last) and react: "This guy knew what was coming"?

I rejoiced: "Immortality for mankind; not for each human being, of course, but for the race or its successors. This is the meaning of the satellites. The whole world should be on holiday, celebrating—and thinking. But instead of immortality, those who shape our thoughts—or try to—would have us think of death. I have heard the president speak twice in the past week in answer to the people's clamor for enlightenment....And all I have heard is death: missiles of twenty-eight different varieties, bombers, nuclear 'deterrents'."

A friend suggested that I try to start a regular program on KPFA. I talked to its president and manager, Harold Winkler, a former U.C. Berkeley teacher of political science dismissed for refusal to sign the loyalty oath, who turned out to be a neighbor. I proposed a program on Soviet science, since I was doing science translation for a living and the country was in a tizzy over the "miracle" of sputnik: those dumb peasants beating us into space. For all my feeling that Berkeley had the freest atmosphere in the country, I apparently didn't appreciate the full depth of its commitment to freedom of thought, for I didn't dare suggest a series closer to the essence of Soviet society. But Winkler, never a Communist, countered by proposing that I do a weekly review of the Soviet press, since they then had similar programs on the British, Swedish, and other press. I was delighted, and I broadcast for 37 years.

When KPFA got a Peabody Award just months after my program began, mine was one of the series invariably cited in press stories about that honor. Because I have always preferred answering questions to lecturing, I proposed that phone-ins be part of the program. The notion that ordinary citizens might be heard on the air without pre-censorship was unheard-of at the time. But KPFA was strongly civil libertarian. So was I as a consequence of my mental evolution after the Stalin revelations.

Consequently, I'm the inventor of the "talk show." I checked this out long ago with people older than myself and with lifetimes in radio, and have established that, before my broadcast series, such a format was never previously used in this country. Listener participation had been limited merely to phoning in contributions.

Within months of starting the radio show, I approached KQED-TV, San Francisco's public channel, with the idea of doing the same thing on video. At the time, that station was a closer competitor of commercial TV, in the public mind, than in any other city in the country. In those years it originated more public-network broadcasting than any other. They approved of my idea. We called the show "What the Russians Are Told," and they too accepted the phone-in idea. I want to collect an Emmy for that someday.

I gave the program visual quality by having a Moscow newsstand prop, which I decorated with Soviet magazines having illustrated covers. I'd walk over to the rack, pick one out, riffle through to the article I planned to use, have the camera zoom in on pictures, and take it from there. Cultural exchange between our two countries had just begun, and people who had visited the USSR were rare. Our government gave preference on such trips to the bitterest Russia-haters. Professors going there had to be cleared by the CIA. I would invite them as guests on the show. But I also committed the sin of inviting Australian-born Harry Bridges, avowedly pro-Soviet head of the longshoremen's union, whom the government had sought to deport in trial after trial for sixteen years. KQED, pressured strongly by the Reaganites-to-be who had taken over Stanford's Hoover Institution, suspended my program over this and another invitation I had extended to Albert Kahn, biographer of cellist Pablo Casals and ballerina Ulanova. Before World War II Kahn had written the last of the American pro-Soviet runaway bestsellers, *The Great Conspiracy*. But when the next broadcast year began, I was back on KQED.

The television and radio shows, both unpaid, had to be done after my day of earning a living as technical translator. I did an enormous amount of reading in Soviet papers and periodicals for them, spending four evenings a week plus all day Sunday at the UC Berkeley library, plus all day Monday writing script. The next year, 1960, KQED paid for subscriptions, so I could do my reading at home. The list of Soviet publications I received, skimmed, and translated from for the broadcasts is exhausting. I subscribed to periodicals such as (titles translated into English): *Crocodile* (humor and satire), *Life of the Blind, Jolly Pictures* (for littlest children), *The Peasant Woman, The Recreation Center, Soviet Consumer Cooperatives, Soviet Literature, Social Welfare, Family and School, Rural Life,* and a daily newspaper *Izvestia*.

I would take Saturday off with the family and spend one evening with Tanya at a film, concert, or play. We took in a lot. In a letter to my parents at the end of 1958 I described our recreation. One weekend we went to a dance in San Francisco to benefit SANE, the Committee for a Sane Nuclear Policy. The Beat atmosphere was strong: "a girl of 20 was sentenced to jail the other day because she chose to walk down the street barefoot, and fought back against the cop." At the dance, the kids "wore things like green leotards with very short skirts over them, broad-brimmed flat sailor hats....Very interracial....Some weird Bohemians, including a man of about 70 who danced with the youngest girls he could find....That was Friday. Saturday went to Golden Hind's production of 'Marriage of Figaro,' to benefit Jewish Community Center....Very good costuming."

We went to Davey's school for a concert by the children, with an "orchestra so good you won't believe it." And we heard then-Soviet pianist Ashkenazy with the San Francisco Symphony on one of the few freebies my broadcasts got me. We heard Isaac Stern in the UC Men's Gym, "so you know why I think the American people are developing a taste for culture."

During our second year in California I began visiting prisoners. This continued, intermittently, for decades. In this case it was the nineteen-year-old son of blinded Lincoln Brigade veteran Bob Raven. I went down to see him at Soledad, south of Salinas, a three-hour drive each way, every three or four weeks.

Although I was already past forty, people usually thought I was twenty-five to twenty-seven. My youthful appearance was hereditary: both parents had it. In my case it probably was helped by daily swims in Berkeley's Lake Anza from May through October (I still do that) and by a week of skiing each year. I discovered Sierra skiing the winter of 1958-9. I'd ski a full six hours, then have legs enough to wash dishes as my share of the cooperative set-up at the University of California bunkhouse to which a friend had access, and then dance as many hours as there was music. Ah, youth!

In my head I knew perfectly well that ultra-violet rays are powerful and dangerous at eight or nine thousand feet. But one day the temperature was simply balmy. I stripped to the waist, and skied without a hat or goggles or sun-screen lotion. My face was simply peeling off as I drove back to Berkeley, and I also had an excruciating torso sunburn. I was afraid to face Tanya, from whom I would get a loving bawling out, so I dropped into the Pot Luck. It was the forerunner, by a full decade, of the Berkeley gourmet ghetto, and was run by a friend, Ed Brown, in partnership with pioneer American wine connoisseur and Lincoln Brigade veteran Hank Rubin. The Pot Luck was a marvelous place— genuine, original funk—in a huge converted boxy house. The California wine industry ought to erect a monument to Rubin. He was really the person who won the Berkeley intelligentsia, previously cocktail, hard liquor and beer drinkers like everyone else, to the notion that a meal without wine was naked. His cellar was superb.

Brown, who was such a Spanish Civil War buff that I took him also to be a veteran, thought I was somebody special because of my broadcasts, and would stand me to drinks. I preferred dark beers, of which they were early importers. The Pot Luck later moved to a spot not far from the East Bay hangout of the Beats, the Steppenwolf. It was run by Max Scherr, bearded (not common then), pot-bellied, near-sighted, much older than the people who frequented his bar and, if I recall correctly, a lawyer who'd gotten tired of that life. Max went on to deserved fame as founder of the first, best, and biggest of the "underground" papers of the '60s, the Berkeley *Barb*, which reached a hundred thousand circulation nationally.

For a period, anything I chose to write, or said in lectures, would be placed on the front page of the *Barb*. I'm particularly proud of an article titled, "The Whiteness of the University," in which I analyzed the racial composition of the faculty, which was literally 99.9 percent white. I pointed out, department by department, what the students would gain by the presence of professors who could contribute the standpoint of the African-American and other minority experience. I'm reasonably certain that no one of whatever race had treated that issue before, anywhere.

Nineteen fifty-nine brought a very interesting reminder of family heritage that I was surprised not to have known about. The only role I was aware that my mother's lawyer brother, Simon, through whom my parents had met, had played in my life was his presence as observer during my CCNY hearing that got me expelled me from college. Twenty years later he had found me the attorney who represented me during the McCarthy hearing. Simon had a fault deadly in our family: he was quiet. So while everyone else talked and sang he would simply sit there, and I learned nothing about him. Beyond that, in childhood and early youth I didn't care for lawyers. Either they dealt with criminals, who were bad, or with businesspeople, who were worse. It was not until the McCarthy period that I developed a real appreciation for the kind of lawyers who defend civil liberties, victims of discrimination, and opponents of wars.

But in 1959 Si turned sixty-five, the New York *Guild Lawyer* ran an issue on his retirement, and I learned some remarkable things. I knew that he had started life as a manual worker when he came to this country at fifteen. But I did not know that at nineteen he helped organize the Millinery & Hat & Caps Union, where he held the post of Secretary. He had entered medical school and simultaneously attended the Columbia School of Journalism, which evidently was possible then. He gave these up for a paid job leading five locals of the Furriers Union, from which he was forced out by reactionaries. While there he led a strike detailed in historian Philip Foner's *The Fur and Leather Workers' Union*. During the post-World War I Red Scare, when J. Edgar Hoover, then just appointed to head the FBI, led the so-called Palmer Raids that brought deportation to large numbers of militant immigrant workingpeople, Si was Secretary of the Workers' Defense Union. That required courage. Later he was again a labor official, managing the Suitcase and Bag Workers' Union. After working in trade newspapers, he became Night City Editor of the *New York Daily News,* an important job on a major paper.

Meanwhile he got his bachelors' and master's degrees in law, and became a clerk of court, preferring that to practicing law. When the Lawyer's Guild was organized in 1937, he became the founding editor of the *Guild Lawyer*, and he headed the Guild in New York for eight years.

Among the tributes to him from colleagues, I liked this one best: "A ded-
ication to a cause...can sometimes bring about an erosion of one's sense
of humor or cheerfulness. To such a blight, Si has been entirely
immune." I realized that I had never seen him gloomy, and remembered
a slow smile that he always saved for others' appreciative reaction to his
wry remarks. What struck me most was the unfairness of a child's judgments. True, my father stimulated my intellect and, in fact, Simon's.
But, on balance, Dad had only twice actually put his money where his
mouth was: when he went to the Soviet Union in 1925-6 and 1931-2 to
contribute to the building of socialist society. Uncle Si had been on the
battle line all his life.

In 1959 I was able to obtain a lecture management for the first time
in over a decade, and found myself getting V.I.P. treatment when I
passed through the San Francisco airport. There was then just one terminal building, and a surprising number of its personnel watched my
show. I remember taking a cab home from the airport once, and the driver turned out to be a fan who got me into a discussion about Tolstoy.
The cabbie was not Russian.

My TV audience must have been really large. When the phone-in
question period was instituted, the station did not yet have equipment
to take calls directly, so they'd be written down at the switchboard and
handed to me. On one occasion early in 1959, my thirty-minute show
prompted eighty-three calls. I still have that sheaf of questions. They
covered everything conceivable: archeology and genetics in the USSR,
education, juvenile delinquency, living standards, the Berlin crisis, airline pilots' pay, space travel, architecture, what I thought of American
press coverage of the USSR, ballet, personal freedom, religion, travel to
the Soviet Union, classical music, insurance, counter-intelligence.

The show resulted in long-lasting friendships with exceptional people, and won remarkably enthusiastic response from newspaper media
columnists until the anti-Sovieteers got to them. Guy Wright, later a
general columnist with the *Chronicle,* was then TV and radio editor of
an afternoon daily, the *San Francisco News.* He devoted a column to me:

"Successful statesmen must know more than the facts. They must
also know what their opponents believe the facts to be....That consideration alone should make it worth your while to watch KQED's new
series, 'What the Russians Are Told.'....Don't let that throw you. It's also
a darn fascinating show.

"Did you know Russians like science fiction? Did you suppose their
largest-selling magazine is some scurrilous propaganda sheet? Well, it
isn't. It's a Russian version of *The Woman's Home Companion*, with the
usual dress patterns, recipes and homemaking hints.

"You didn't know these things? Well, neither did I till I watched

William Mandel a week ago on the premiere of 'What the Russians Are Told.' I watched him again last night when he started to trace the way Russian newspapers have treated the Middle East crisis. Time ran out before he got very far, but if you think they've been splashing it all over page one, you're mistaken.

*"KQED allows the program only 15 minutes, which is entirely too short. It deserves 30....*KQED is fortunate to have Mandel for this series....He is that rarity among experts on Russian affairs, a dispassionate scholar who keeps his facts separate from his moral judgments." That one sentence of his in italics won me a thirty-minute spot.

A competing afternoon paper, the *Call-Bulletin,* said that I gave "an accurate picture of what the Russians are told through Soviet publications." The *Chronicle* published a separate news story on me and its media columnist for 30 years, Terrence O'Flaherty, plugged both my TV and radio shows repeatedly. Viewer and listener mail was overwhelmingly similar to the opinion of columnist Wright, particularly stressing what the audience regarded as my objectivity. There were a few exceptions. A letter to KQED from Sanatorium, California, high above the Napa Valley, read, "I doubt that the communists themselves could have engineered a more effective means of getting publicity for their stuff in this country." Coming subpoenas cast their shadows before.

Anti-Semitism must have a deep impact on me, because there was one real shocker that remained in memory before I started through my mail for this autobiography. The writer was a post-revolutionary emigre from Russia, who identified himself as having been editor of a pre-revolutionary paper in Irkutsk, Siberia. He wrote: "Your American-english is Delancy St. Yiddish-intelligentsia-english....You are an abominable egotist promoting yourself for a fast buck even if it means placating native and immigrant white guards." White Guards were the Russian contras. So the man had become pro-Soviet without losing his Russian anti-Semitism. It was not until I made my first post-war visit to the USSR in 1959 that I realized that combination existed there as well. But the man did have style. He ended: "One of these days you'll produce enuf [sic] of your poisonous saliva to drown yourself in it. With profound contempt," followed by signature in Russian.

Pleasant experiences resulting from the TV series far outweighed the nasty ones. The fact that the station asked the national Educational TV & Radio Center, forerunner of the Corporation for Public Broadcasting, to fund my going national, was one, even though the proposal was not accepted. The purely personal elements gave me the greatest satisfaction. One day the phone rang, and a very childish voice said, "My name is Liza Hirsch. I'm in 3rd grade in San Jose. My teacher said things about the Soviet Union in class that I don't think are true. I told her I know a man who does a TV show about that and asked her if you could speak to the class if you would come. She said yes. Will you come?"

Of course I came. I've always loved speaking to the youngest children, and am very proud that I can hold their interest. One of my most treasured memories is speaking about the Soviet Union during World War II to an auditorium full of allegedly retarded Puerto Rican children in Spanish Harlem. It quickly became obvious that they had been shunted off simply for being difficult or due to home conditions. Although their questions revealed tabloid information backgrounds, they were just as bright—or dumb—as those put to me by the highly-educated parishioners at Rev. John Haines Holmes' Community Church on Fifth Avenue. I held these children's attention for two class periods.

I had known Liza's mother, Ginny. She was a workingclass Muir from Altoona, Pennsylvania, greatgrandniece of John Muir, the black sheep of his clan who abandoned his family to become the poetic explorer of the Sierra Nevada. Ginny had been secretary for the American Slavic Congress in New York during World War II. I then assumed she was Slavic, because of her high cheekbones and heroic build. She later married a Jewish plumber, Fred Hirsch, who had been a schoolboy in Peekskill at the time of the assault on the Robeson concert, and had the guts to crawl through the surrounding fascist lines to carry messages.

Fred was a hero routinely, first driving truckloads of supplies to the Mississippi voter-registration drive in 1963. Subsequently he did the riskiest jobs in Caesar Chavez' farm-labor organizing campaign, bringing him both beatings and a near-fatal auto accident. He was beaten again in his own Plumbers' Union local when he spoke out against the Vietnam War. But in 1998 a new president of that local was among the hundreds at a sixty-fifth birthday surprise party for Fred, still active as ever, in the San Jose Labor Temple. The party was Fred's dream come true: labor united, from Dolores Huerta of the Farm Workers to representatives of the Teamsters, who had been battling Huerta's union for representation of cannery workers.

In the early '70s, when the CIA was something no one dared talk about, Fred had taken the dangerous step of writing a booklet, based on his own research, on that agency's use of the AFL-CIO top leadership to run unions in Latin America. This was before ex-agent Agee exposed *The Company*, as his book was titled. The CIA had not yet lost its virtue in the public eye. Later Fred founded NICH—Non-Intervention in Chile—and spent time in Mexico.

The Hirsch family was a center of Left activity in San Jose.

Liza, who was in the third-grade at age five, already deserves a biography. An unspoiled, truly modest genius, she was the most dependable 4 a.m. picketer for a solid year when her family moved to the Central

Valley to work with Chavez. Picket shift over, she'd go to school and get straight A's. When Chavez came up with his most brilliant stroke—the national grape boycott campaign—and assigned staff to various cities to run it, he said to Liza, "You take Chicago."

She said: "I'll have to ask my mother."

"How old are you?" Chavez asked.

"13." She looked like a mature young woman.

Liza speaks perfect Chicano Spanish. On one occasion, kids in her class in San Jose High began to stay away from school because a fine teacher was transferred out. Liza simply took the whole class down to a public meeting of the Board of Education, and these supposedly inarticulate kids spoke very intelligibly indeed. When her high school undertook an affirmative-hiring program for teachers, the astute principal thought he could co-opt Liza by having this schoolgirl draft the questionnaire candidates would have to answer: Black and Chicano history and a number of situational tripper-uppers. She gave me a copy. That questionnaire was used. The teachers were not told who wrote it. Of course she was valedictorian at graduation, and a family friend videorecorded it, more or less idly. When she was done, he realized he had something totally out of the ordinary, and sold it to the Huntley-Brinkley national TV prime-time news show, which used it.

Her speech had been an unpretentious and profound lecture to the older generation about the meaning of the youth rebellion of the '60s, then just over. It goes without saying that she got into the elite college of her choice, Reed, in Portland, with scholarships from a union and a bank. It was I who had suggested Reed: our Bob had gone there. Her fellow-students, spoiled upper-middle-class types heavy into drugs, bored and outraged her. She graduated ahead of schedule despite having to hold a job and being flown to Sacramento by Chavez every time he needed briefs prepared for legislative hearings. When the union held its founding convention, she coordinated the myriad organizational details, although she was still in her teens. She applied to law school, was worried stiff about getting in—her modesty is simply irrational—and found herself able to pick from the country's best. But Chavez convinced her that the union needed her more, so she took a longer time than normal to complete her education. At just past twenty, she was negotiating and signing contracts for the Farmworkers with growers who had never had to deal with a woman as equal, and had led and won its first strike in her area in southern California.

Liza's love for those who have not gotten a fair shake from life is evident on the personal level as well. For several years she lived with a man with a hereditary degenerative disease. Subsequently she married a leading New York political liberal with cystic fibrosis, who did not survive his fifties. That husband died. Liza was then the attorney for New York's Musicians' Union and its very major hospital workers' union, District 1199. Later she became the attorney for the unionized musicians of all the major orchestras in the country. Today she is married to a Chicano union officer whom she knew from her teens when he was a farmworker. She dropped her previous practice. She is still barely into her forties, and has taken time out to raise their new child.

My TV show also brought letters that gave me a sense of truly deep accomplishment. A woman wrote: "We rarely miss one of your programs. Actually I feel that I am beginning to have a picture in my mind of modern Russia from what you have presented and emphasized, as *War and Peace,* (after three readings) made old Russia live and breathe."

For all that, no program based on the current press could provide a systematic knowledge of the USSR. I had no illusion that mine could do so. As the academic world showed no signs of giving me a chance to do that, I conducted a course under the sponsorship of the Socialist Workers Party, which was willing to run it despite their awareness that I did not share their Trotskyist convictions. Attendance at that small class included people ranging from Bogdan Denitch, bitterly anti-Soviet and subsequently a professor in New York, to Carl Bloice, later editor of the Communist Party's *People's World* and already then a member of the Party. Mike Miller, head of the UC Berkeley student political party, SLATE, also attended. He was, and is, a middle-of-the-road citizens' action type reformer for "proximate goals," as he put it.

In 1959 I found myself in a new milieu. Quakers were very strong among KPFA staff and supporters. The American Friends Service Committee (AFSC), a Quaker organization, also had a high-school program. I was invited as resource person for a weekend at a camp in Marin County and then for a week at Lake Tahoe. A remarkable proportion of the musicians who created the San Francisco sound of the '60s came from among these kids. My younger boy, Dave, a good guitarist and better dancer than his father, grew up with the members of the first top bands. Joan Baez, then nineteen, and a major singer for decades thereafter, was one of the students at that summer camp.

The camp fostered an atmosphere of love entirely new to me. I wonder if it did not spread from the Quakers to the entire youth culture of the 1960s. At week's end, we all linked hands and sang "Cum By Yah." Everyone was asked to speak on what, if anything, the week had meant to himself or herself personally. I don't recall what I said, but I remember vividly the words of the late Bill Bailey, an Irish longshoreman and veteran of the Abraham Lincoln Brigade, whom I admired even before that for having torn down the swastika flag from the German ocean liner, Bremen, in New York harbor in 1935. It does credit to the

Quakers' breadth of vision that he, too, had been invited to the camp. Bill became widely known in the 1980s and early '90s for his humanism and morality, as he reminisced in the documentaries "The Good Fight" about the Spanish Civil War, "Seeing Red" about the Communist Party, and "The Men Who Sailed the Liberty Ships," of whom he was one, as well as a film on the San Francisco general strike of 1934. His autobiography, *The Kid From Hoboken*, should be better known.

In the late 1950s Bill, like myself, was for the first time in his adult life without a political home. Neither of us could live without being part of some activity aimed at a better life for humanity. So when it came his turn to speak, he said, "I'd a cum up here if I'd a hadda crawl on my hands and knees all da way from Frisco to Lake Tahoe." I felt the same way. In that politically dull time of the late '50s, the Quakers were one of the three things going in the United States—the others being Martin Luther King and KPFA.

In the non-religious sphere, the Quakers founded two organizations, AFSC and the Friends Committee on Legislation (FCL). The latter was headed in California by Trevor Thomas, a non-Quaker former gold miner and later liquor salesman who was eventually a manager of KPFA, subsequently a KQED news reporter, and finally a documentary film-maker. He died in 1999 and I stimulated commemoration of his life.

One of the biggest names in American writing in the late '50s was Eugene Burdick, co-author of *The Ugly American.* He had been a student at Stanford when I was a research fellow there and then became a professor of political science at U.C. Berkeley. Thomas, as FCL head, asked me to debate Burdick on U.S. foreign policy, by which I learned that I had achieved stature in the Bay Area. To comment on our presentations he invited a panel consisting of U.C. political science Prof. Paul Seabury, who later became chancellor of the Santa Cruz campus, and a young professor at San Francisco State, Marshall Windmiller. At the time of the debate, Marshall was a highly popular commentator on KPFA and a power in the thriving California Democratic Clubs network, a real grassroots organization.

I wrestled with myself over how candidly I could characterize U.S. policy toward Southeast Asia, Cuba, Europe, Japan, and the Near East. I decided I would risk employing a term that had been unusable for a decade upon pain of isolation from public discourse: "imperialist." The six hundred people packing the auditorium of International House at U.C. were comfortably middle-class, academic in part, and middle-aged. The '60s had not yet come. From the applause I was obviously the winner, but my use of the forbidden word, which was totally accurate, labeled me. Until then I had been a very respectable citizen of the Bay Area, invited to speak even at Republican clubs. The Democrats wouldn't have me: they were fearful of being thought soft on communism if they had a speaker who would not damn the Soviet Union. The essential prohibition of the use of the word "imperialist" to describe the United States remains in effect forty years later. In 1997 a minister in the Palestinian cabinet welcomed an American envoy's cancellation of a trip to Israel, saying, "You are imperialists, even now. All the world forgets this word, but I do not."

In the summer of 1959 I visited the USSR for the first time since boyhood. I paid my way by leading a tour for a respectable local travel agency. Nearly half the tour were KPFA listeners. But I almost didn't get to go. The State Department had denied me a passport for a decade, in implementation of a policy that had been defeated by a U.S. Supreme Court ruling only the previous year. The court found that the department could not establish political qualifications for issuance of a passport. Nonetheless it stalled endlessly over issuing me one. Finally I phoned longshore leader Harry Bridges. He got onto my member of Congress, Jeff Cohelan, an only-in-Berkeley combination of former Rhodes scholar and Teamsters' Union official. The passport came through at the last moment.

The tour group was fascinating: a contractor, about eighty, and his wife (he had erected the Kaiser hospitals, was related to Caterpillar Tractor money, etc.); a shrink and his wife from highly-prosperous Left family backgrounds, in their early thirties. The aged couple, utterly practical and probably Republicans, concluded from the trip that Russia was going to make it. They remembered America when it was no more materially advanced than the USSR, and saw no reason why the Soviets couldn't make equal progress. In their lifetime that expectation proved out. They could not have lived to see the collapse of the Soviet Union thirty years later.

The young Leftist couple was completely turned off by the USSR. They couldn't understand why Soviet kids were so well-behaved. The wife, determined to show her solidarity with the peasantry, walked barefoot into a childcare center in the major city of Kiev. Soviet parents were scandalized and demanded to know whether she would do that at home. I translated dutifully. Also on the tour was a Philadelphia travel agent who had guessed, correctly, from the announcement folder that she could learn something valuable about leading tours to Russia from me. She was quite obnoxious in contradicting my first-timer handling of tour problems.

The Russians were very new to the tour business then, and that didn't make things any easier. The Soviet guide who accompanied us started out by revering me as a hero when he found out about my experiences with McCarthyism. He wound up undercutting me because I relentlessly insisted that we get the first-class accomodations for which my group had paid. A very traditional Russian sloppiness pervaded the manner in which the Soviet tourism monopoly worked. In dealing with a ship's purser—part of the trip was a Black Sea cruise—I learned the Russian trick of hollering, stamping, and then when matters are settled, sticking out one's hand for a shake and calmly saying: "It's a deal."

In New York on the trip home I went to see my parents and my mother-in-law, who died unexpectedly only weeks later. Mothers-in-law are often not fond of each other. Our parents were no exceptions. I wanted my mother to know, once and for all, how I felt about Sabina, and wrote: "I became very fond of her over the years. Faults? I have a few too. I'm very glad I went up to see her at Golden's Bridge." Tanya flew east for the funeral and remained for a couple of weeks to be with her brothers and other close family. I stayed to care for the boys, and took them to Lake Tahoe for two days. In September that lake at six thousand feet is finally warm enough for swimming. David, then twelve, drew Emerald Bay. He had taken a summer art course at our insistence, and the results showed. But he developed another talent that surprised me greatly, and I wrote my mother about it: "Last week he baked a banana cream cake that would have done credit to a really good chef....Two days later...Davey baked lasagna as dinner for our guest (and us). She had a second helping. First rate. Mother, these are *not* mixes from a package. He shops and cooks from scratch. For our trip, he borrowed sleeping bags, air mattresses, a camp stove and gasoline from a neighbor, shopped for the food, etc. Out at the lake, he set up the stove & cooked, cleaned up, and next morning packed everything very carefully in the car....Can we eat in that mountain air!"

I needed those breaks. Freelance translating was not fun. Tanya wrote my parents in December about my feast-or-famine work situation. Currently I was rendering about thirty-five thousand words of Russian technology into English per week via tape recorder. A couple of months after the Tahoe weekend I was able to take four days off with the kids during their Thanksgiving break. We drove sixteen hundred miles. We went up the California and Oregon coasts, reaching Portland the second night, all on two-lane roads. Then we followed the Columbia River. We started at 6:30 each morning and I'd drive till two hours after dark. Tanya wrote: "The rest of us, of course, enjoyed the trip very much....Seeing what has happened to Oregon's coastal forests showed us the need for conservation. Mountain after mountain with not one tree left on it. Old whitened stumps looking exactly like gravestones, they are so many & so close together." After sixty miles on the Columbia we curved around Mt. Hood to head south. That required climbing to an altitude where there had been an overnight freeze. I hit a patch of totally clear ice, spun around completely, but stayed on the road. I stayed put for an hour or two until a maintenance truck spreading sand came by, and crawled along behind it. The mountain blocks moisture-laden clouds from the east, of which Tanya wrote: "The desert area is an Indian reservation and it is quite obvious that no one could possibly make a living off it." On the final day we saw Mt. Shasta, the beautiful and stupendous dam that made Lake Shasta, and the powerhouse with its overwhelming turbines.

Nineteen sixty was to be a very stormy year, but it started in the most mundane of ways. Tanya's mother had left us $5,000, which in that dream time was enough for a down-payment on a house in the Berkeley hills. We'd have bought the place we had been renting for the past 2 1/2 years on Poppy Lane, but no bank would lend on that property because of slide danger. One year during that decade a severe rainstorm did destroy several homes in the hills by mudslide. Since then engineers have made enormous progress in learning how to build under these conditions, and homes have stood stably for a quarter century on lots no one would have dared to use earlier.

While I pounded away at my translations for work and the broadcasts, Tanya went house-hunting. We agreed that we must have a view of the Bay, there had to be an essentially sound-insulated room in which I could work, and it would be best if the house were one-story to make it possible for my mother, with very high blood pressure, to visit, and naturally it had to meet the needs of our two growing boys.

One day Tanya came home and said she'd found a house I would like, although the room that could be used as a study had no view of San Francisco Bay. Architecturally the house is the most standard kind of one-story, three-bedroom, two-bath late 1940s redwood ranch-style home. The location, however, is spectacular. It stands on the crestline of the Berkeley hills. The front view is of the Golden Gate Bridge across the bay, with San Francisco on its left and the Marin County headlands rising to Mt. Tamalpais on the right. Because we stand right on the narrow ridge-top, there is nothing behind our rear patio but the valleys and hills of the seemingly endless East Bay Regional Parks.

From my study and the bedrooms the view eastward is uninterrupted. In high-fog season a solid wall of gray greets one in the morning. As the sun warms it, patches burn away, wisps drift high. One piece of the ridge behind us becomes visible, then another, then the mass drifts and visible curves change. There are two sunsets, one to the west over San Francisco Bay, the other its reflection on the hills to the east, a few hundred feet higher than we. In the dry season, when the grass turns brown, the reflection is virtually alpine-glow.

To the west, particularly in winter when sunrise is late, San Francisco rises from the water as mysteriously as a mountain island in the South Pacific, but with lines, lights and shadows. Sometimes the towers of the Golden Gate Bridge pierce upward through a solid mass of fog.

But the back view to the east is best at night. In a full moon, the true proportions of the hills are visible. They are gentle, and the absence of artificial light in the park make them infinitely soothing. No matter how tense a day has been, I need only step out onto that patio at night and I am a million miles from nowhere. There is no traffic at night on our dead-end street. Deer wander onto it from the park or even the reservoir lands beyond. Raccoons scurry across the street at night or stare boldly at us from our patio, their eyes shining bright as they converse in their language of clicks.

Thirty-one years later the mortgage was finally paid off, and the house actually is ours.

From February, 1960, when we moved in, I had three months enjoyment of this idyll. It was made additionally pleasurable when our daughter and her new husband moved out from New York. We would refresh our own first appreciation of the region by watching their reactions as we played tourist guide. But one day in early May, driving on Spruce Street just a few blocks from home, I was pulled over by Berkeley Police Chief Beale, who handed me a subpoena to appear before the House Committee on Un-American Activities in San Francisco's City Hall.

That closed chapters in my life, ending permanently my TV show and my budding renewed career as professional lecturer. But it opened a new one, projecting me into a role as a founding member of the youth movement of the '60s, although I was as old as its participants' parents. It gave me an association with that generation that continues in the 1990s, when some of the actuality film of my HUAC testimony was used in the Oscar-nominated "Berkeley in the '60s." When San Francisco's official autumn fair of 1985 was held, one of the '60s people phoned to tape me for the Antenna Theater, performing a piece on the city's history that would include my appearance in front of HUAC. In 1997, at the huge memorial to poet and fearless '60s activist Allen Ginsberg, I found the cameras of half a dozen people trained on me. Inasmuch as I was merely a member of the audience, as were the picture-takers, some of whom I knew, I could only understand that behavior as fallout from having lost an icon. They were desperate to latch on to someone still alive who symbolized that period to them.

A few weeks later, a stranger, selling his organic strawberries at Berkeley's farmers' market, recognized me and refused to take payment for his produce. Days thereafter, a prominent photographer asked me to write a couple of pages about HUAC for his anthology of photos of the '60s for which a Pulitzer-winning historian was writing the preface. For my 80th birthday, also in 1997, an artist who had been a young naval officer when I appeared before that congressional witch-hunt, and who insists that my words changed his life, went to considerable expense in converting the documentary footage of both the HUAC and earlier McCarthy testimony into a form that would make it usable should anyone wish to make a film about me.

CHAPTER 19

"Honorable Beaters of Children"

In May 1960 I was subpoenaed by yet another witch-hunt committee. This was no replay, although the House Un-American Activities Committee doubtless hoped it would be. In 1952 and 1953, each intended victim had prepared for the hearing alone. To meet beforehand with other subpoeaned witnesses would only make it easier for the committee to demand that one name names or go to jail. But by 1960, the public's attitude toward the Committee had changed, especially in Northern California.

This committee hearing was held in the ornate Supervisors' Chamber atop a sweeping marble staircase in San Francisco's magnificent city hall. Forty-six people had been subpoenaed. A meeting of the prospective witnesses was called, and twenty-two showed up. I do not know whether fear accounted for the absence of others. We agreed to issue a press release, which I wrote. The *San Francisco Examiner* carried a fair portion of it. This marked a change from the earlier period, when subpoenees could reach the public only by spectacular testimony or by becoming informers. My release provides a picture of who we were:

"Most of the individuals present found themselves utter strangers to each other. They discovered themselves to be a cross-section of the community—workingmen and professionals, rancher and housewife, salesman and student. Two groups predominated: teachers, of whom there were 11, all but one having been subpoenaed [also by HUAC] last year, plus one of the attorneys who had been active at that time, and manual workers active in their respective labor unions.

"Seeking to determine why they had been subpoenaed, they discovered that no officer or spokesman of the Communist Party had been called by the Committee, despite the announcement of its chief investigator, Mr. Wheeler, that the hearing had been called to expose the activities of that organization during the past several months.

"They did find, however, that a great many are currently active in picketing stores refusing service to Negroes in the South, and they noted that two of the three members of the Sub-Committee here are Southerners, including chairman Willis [of Louisiana], who delivered the [House] Judiciary Committee minority report against the Civil Rights Bill recently passed by Congress.

"Further, they found that the only civic activity engaged in by some of the persons subpoenaed consisted of urging abolition of the Un-American Committee, and concluded that those subpoenas were reprisals pure and simple. Lastly, in at least two cases, the Committee was continuing its policy of harassment of persons in journalism and related professions, which boomeranged when it went after *New York Times* staff members four years ago. The prospective witnesses expressed gratitude to the several Bay Area newspapers that are pursuing a policy of not publishing names of persons subpoenaed."

Personally, I faced the problem of paying a lawyer. Having just moved into the first and only home we've ever owned, we had naturally saddled ourselves with time payments for essential appliances and such, and had no savings. The lean years due to my earlier harassment by the McCarran and McCarthy committees were in the very recent past. I was told that I'd have to pay $200—well over $1,000 in today's money—for a lawyer. I wrote my old friend, millionaire philosopher Corliss Lamont of the Bill of Rights Fund, asking if they'd provide the money.

"There is no doubt in my mind," I wrote, "nor in that of persons with whom I have spoken at KPFA, that I have been called in order to embarrass that station in the FCC [Federal Communications Commission] hearings envisaged over whether to renew its license. The fact that I am the only KPFA person called relates, I believe, to the fact that the HUAC is notoriously opposed to any accomodation with the USSR, and that I most strongly favor such an accomodation....There is no reason to believe that KPFA will take me off the air as a result of the hearing. Unfortunately, my KQED TV program [also in its third year] is scheduled to end, at least for the time being, at the end of May, and supporters of the Committee (HUAC) will doubtless read a victory for it into this termination."

In fact, the program director of KQED, the man who had initially put me on that station's air, told me, "Bill, I am not a very courageous person." The program never was renewed, despite tremendous viewer demand for a solid year thereafter in letters of which friends at KQED kept me apprised. My testimony before the committee in connection with broadcasting reads:

"I refuse to testify on the grounds that as a radio and TV public affairs broadcaster, active in those capacities today, the subpoena issued to me interferes with the right of my stations to schedule informational programs on their merits and is thus a direct violation of the First Amendment guarantes of freedom of speech and of the people's right to hear."

In the activities against the committee before the hearing, I naturally did the things I know best. I drafted a leaflet:
"UN-AMERICAN COMMITTEE—WHO ARE YOU?

"Rep. Willis of Louisiana. You are Chairman of this Subcommittee. Who are you to investigate Un-American activities? You come from a district with 300,000 population, but only 8,000 people voted for Congress - and you got every single vote! Is your district in America, or in Nazi Germany? How many Negroes are allowed to vote in your district?

"Mr. Richard Ahrens, Chief Counsel of the Committee....You admitted you take $3,000 from Wycliffe Draper, who finances studies to prove that Negroes ought to be sent back to Africa! What do you know about Americanism?

"Rep. Francis Walter, Chairman of the full Committee: You are supposed to be engaged in upholding the laws. But last time your Committee came to California, you televised the hearings despite orders from House Speaker Sam Rayburn to stop the TV. The State of California told you it wasn't interested in your phony evidence, but you ignored it and sent it to the local district attorneys to pressure school boards to fire teachers."

My leaflet on the eve of the hearing reconstructs the atmosphere of the time: "You order process servers to give people subpoenas not in the privacy of their homes, but on their jobs and in their employers' offices, in the hope that they will be fired.

"WHO HAVE YOU SUBPOENAED?

"An old man of 70 who went broke raising chickens in Sonoma County and now works in a tailor shop. Is he a danger to America?

"A boy of 18 studying at the University of California to be a teacher....Is he un-American?

"A dozen school teachers who teach their children that the *whole* U.S. Constitution is good. *Including* the 14th and 15th amendments that grant Negroes the right to vote. *Including* the First Amendment that guarantees freedom of speech. *Including* the Fifth Amendment that protects you against being a witness against yourself and a stool-pigeon against others.

"GO HOME!

"say the Episcopal Diocese, 520 professors at the University of California, Stanford, San Francisco State and San Jose State..."

In Berkeley that bounced back hard. A news story in the Berkeley *Gazette* said: "Working before a highly-emotional, foot-stamping crowd of 1000, the Berkeley Board of Education today voted to retain on its teaching staff one of two teachers subpoenaed by the House Un-American Activities Committee....The hissing, booing, foot-stamping crowd literally shook the huge auditorium and on many occasions completely drowned out board-members armed with microphones.... A significant portion of the audience was composed of young adults, college students and a surprising number—perhaps 150—of children under 12."

None of this eliminated the problem of how I should conduct myself before the Committee this time. I had no desire to appear. My hearing was set for May 12th, on which I had a contract for a paid lecture before a club of prosperous women whose husbands were influential in San Jose. I wired the committee for a postponement to the following day, which it granted. May 13th proved to be tremendously exciting. Actually, it was historic, for it launched the mass movement of white students of the 1960s. Black students were already on the move, primarily by sitting at lunch counters in the South and demanding to be served on a par with whites. Support of these Blacks was one of several issues that had caused white students to begin to organize and protest even before the HUAC demonstration.

Immediately prior to the HUAC hearing, a freshman, Fred Moore, had gone on hunger strike against the Reserve Officer Training Program (ROTC) on campus, resulting in seven thousand signatures being collected at Berkeley and UCLA to abolish compulsory ROTC, the very issue that had resulted in my expulsion from college in New York.

HUAC made a fatal error in including an 18-year-old UC student, Doug Wachter, among the subpoenees. While the rest of us prospective witnesses were organizing our own meeting, the leader of the liberal Berkeley student political party SLATE and another student who had headed the Student Civil Liberties Union, called a meeting to organize a protest against the HUAC hearing. About fifty students showed up. They got two thousand signatures on a petition to cancel the hearings and abolish the Committee, and also organized a picket line outside the hearing and a mass rally in San Francisco.

While I was in the hearing room waiting to be called on the 13th, the police turned hoses on and viciously beat the mass of students. The next day, the *San Francisco Chronicle* immortalized the occasion by devoting its entire front page to nothing but a photograph of the City Hall rotunda with the students being washed down its staircase.

I had not yet been called to the stand half an hour before the usual end of the hearing day. I turned to my attorney and said, "My subpoena specifically says the 13th. If they don't call me today, do I have to show up tomorrow?" He said "no."

Tanya had told me as I left the house, "Let someone else do the hero bit this time." I agreed with her totally, although I still resent her phrasing. I hadn't set out to be a hero before the McCarran and McCarthy committees in 1952 and 1953, but felt that other witnesses had not taken full advantage of the opportunity. I was committed to communicating our opposition to McCarthyism to the public at large.

Within minutes of my lawyer's reply, my name was called and I took the stand. What happened then was best described in a letter I wrote the following day to James Aronson, editor of the *National Guardian*. His paper had published as pamphlets my testimonies in those other hearings seven and eight years earlier. I wrote:

"The police attack upon the persistent student demonstration almost swamped out reports of the truly remarkable conduct of the witnesses. I would say that after years of <u>witnesses</u> holding the fort, <u>popular</u> indignation has taken the offensive, and quite properly we who were called to the stand become <u>secondary</u> when matters reach this stage.

"Nevertheless, much of the testimony is worth reporting. My own, although drafted to be quiet and dignified, with an eye to my radio and TV work and preservation of my livelihood, took on the passion of indignation as news came to the hearing room of the events right outside....I made comments on the police and the Committee which had the result that, when I was asked to step to the mike at a Cal student emergency rally at 11 p.m. that night (attendance 800: *Chronicle* estimate), I was greeted by the only standing ovation it has ever been my privilege to receive.

"These supplementary remarks were as follows: 'Honorable beaters of children, sadists uniformed and in plain clothes, distinguished Dixiecrat wearing the clothing of a gentleman, eminent Republican who opposes accomodation with the one country with which we must live at peace in order for us all and our children to survive—my boy of 15 left this room a few minutes ago in sound health and not jailed solely because I asked him to be in here to learn something about the procedures of the United States government and one of its committees. Had he been outside, where the son of a friend of mine had his head split by these goons operating under your orders, my boy today might have paid the penalty of permanent injury or a police record for desiring to come in here and hear how this committee operates'."

Those were my words as taped. Because they were ad libbed, I didn't remember them precisely the next day. That bears on my next sentence to Aronson, which is very interesting psychologically: "The rest I don't remember, although the *Examiner* quotes me as saying in response to a further question: 'If you think I will cooperate in any way with this collection of Judases, of men who sit there in violation of the United States Constitution, if you think I will cooperate with you in any manner whatsoever, you are insane'."

So I didn't remember the single sentence that brought an interruption of the hearing by an ovation both within the hearing room and from the students listening outside the building via loudspeakers—a sentence that has been used in five documentary films, numerous TV specials, and a video over a span of 39 years! Three days later, when I came into KPFA to do my weekly broadcast, a volunteer there, student leader Mike Tigar, subsequently a very prominent law professor and criminal lawyer—he defended Nichols in the Oklahoma Federal Building bombing massacre—greeted me by swinging around in his chair and declaiming that passage to me. I would like a psychologist to explain to me why I didn't remember it the very next day.

Of course, I was enormously fatigued. After appearing at the student rally, which ended at midnight, I found at home our dear friends Virginia and Clinton Jencks. They had brought with them the distinguished British historian Eric Hobsbawm. They asked me to play for him the phonograph record of my 1953 hearing before Joe McCarthy. I did so, but uncontrollably stalked the full depth of the house, front to rear and back, over and over, for the forty-five minutes it ran. It would be another twenty years before the immense turmoil of that event and time would recede far enough into the background for me to remain calm when it is played.

My letter to Aronson continued: "My entire testimony, prepared and ad lib, constitutes part of an amazing KPFA tape, an hour long edited from fifteen hours of material, that in my opinion deserves a Peabody Award." It got it.

I added a one-sentence postscript: "We _have_ come out of the woods."

That was not only a cry of rejoicing. It was also a bitter comment on a seven-year-old battle with many components of the movement against McCarthy. In 1953 Aronson's paper carried an advertisement I had written and convinced a small businessman to place, entitled: "Time to Come Out of the Woods." My purpose was to turn around the mood of despair about McCarthyism. When that same man also bought space for it in the Communist _Daily Worker,_ that paper printed the ad because it desperately needed the money, but, for the only time in its history, the _Worker_ ran a disavowal along with it.

People still ask how I managed to go on the offensive before the various committees. I believe I had a deeper confidence in the American people's devotion to democracy in those years than did others. That confidence was based not on emotion but on analysis. In a word, our immigrant forebears had found greater liberty here than in whatever country they had come from, while World War II had taught my own generation to hate all dictatorships. Even Blacks, still under Jim Crow, felt that half freedom was better than no freedom at all.

My son Dave, reading this chapter in manuscript, offered another view of my conduct at the HUAC hearings. "You're a strange laddie: while this paragraph is accurate, it's an example of how you can be arrogant and appear egotistical on smaller matters but are often truly humble on the most important ones. You challenged and beat the committees on their turf by allowing outrage to overcome fear (and that is the essence of bravery) and by totally outsmarting those scum!"

A follow-up letter from me to Aronson a week later gives the flavor of the moment: "Times have changed," I wrote. "Of all the 46 subpoenaed, one salesman, one workingman, and half-a-dozen teachers have lost their jobs. The worker, despite being shop steward for four years, actually faces possible lifting of his union card by his very old-line outfit. Steps are now being taken to settle this quietly, so I provide no particulars. The salesman's friends down Santa Clara way have pledged $100 a week for a minimum of three months to keep him in groceries while he scouts around. The teachers have the resounding support of the Calif. Fed. of Teachers and even the Calif. Teachers Assn., so some or all of the jobs may be saved.

"One worker (warehouseman) returned to the job to find the whole large shop lined up in salute! Another, leader in the Teamsters' rank-and-file movement [against the gangster-linked and Red-baiting leadership], found the boys calling him 'Khrushchev' and was able to settle brewery beefs on his first day back on the job, with no questions asked. A woman draftsman was informed of a raise by a very major corporation (presumably decided before the hearing, but nevertheless—). An elderly woman assistant cook came back to a hug and a kiss from her immediate superior.

"The wife of a teacher received a call from a woman who said: 'Will my children be safe there with a man like your husband as teacher?' She replied: 'Are you a Communist?' Caller: 'What?' 'Are you a Communist?' 'Of course not!' 'Prove it.' 'Why—I can't prove it—but this is ridiculous!' 'Exactly!' The caller came over, spent hours with the teacher's wife, and phoned the next day to say that a friend of hers 'who has a big mouth' is going all over town telling everyone what fine people you and your husband are, and what a terrible thing the committee is. The teacher himself, *whose contract was terminated as of the end of this term*, said he had never had such attention and respect from his students."

The letters I received took my breath away. One read: "'Congratulations' is far too tame a word. I wonder what the Virginia Burgesses, the ring of 'if this be treason' still in their ears, said to Patrick Henry as they shook his hand." A Petaluma chicken farmer wrote: "As my wife said, 'I just heard the true America speak'."

Another: "I have discovered that patriotism can be a heady brew and twenty-four hours after listening to you....I still feel so elated that I may be slightly incoherent. For too many years now that word, mouthed by McCarthy and the current Un-Americans has become, for me, anathema."

My own experience was fantastic relative to the entire preceding decade. The Federation of American Scientists at UC Berkeley, of which Nobel physicist Owen Chamberlain was the guiding spirit, asked me to address their meeting the following week.

A professor in the natural sciences, living across the street, with whom I had had exactly one conversation as a neighbor, knocked at the door. He opened by saying he had watched my TV show the night before on a crisis that had just occurred in U.S.-Soviet relations, and said I "had handled it beautifully." Then: "On this other unfortunate matter last week, I must say that I am a conservative in many ways, but I abhor that committee." I replied that, no matter how strong my own feeling that I had done the right thing, I was very happy to know that I had support. He said that that was the thing he had come to say, and took his leave.

The TV columnist of the *Chronicle,* who had not mentioned my program for a year or more, gave it a big bold-face plug. At least a dozen kids in each of my sons' schools (junior high and high school respectively) offered congratulations to me through them. A Berkeley high school teacher replayed the KPFA tape of the hearing and police attack on the students in the faculty room at lunch time. A physician in State employ, having the same first and last name as myself, who was confined to quarters in the Army for a period after *my* McCarthy hearing in 1953 solely because of the name coincidence, had the courage to write his congressman on this hearing and to raise money for legal defense of arrested students. An important Democratic Party leader subpoenaed was given a 59-to-1 endorsement of his behavior by his organization.

Just as Senator McCarthy had gone after me personally in his newspaper column a month after that earlier hearing because he realized I had damaged him, so HUAC now felt that same sting. It was totally taken aback by the massive student outpouring. So it lashed out by making a movie of these events, including some of my words and the defiant behavior of Archie Brown, an avowed Communist, longshoreman, and veteran of the Lincoln Brigade. The film, *Operation Abolition,* was given enormous audiences—18 million total—by the cooperation of the largest corporations and the nation's police departments. It briefly made me a national figure among youth. My testimony often had an effect opposite from that intended by the film-makers. Thirty-five years later, an aging San Francisco street poet told me that he, a student in Minnesota, went with his buddy, named Zimmerman, to see the film. It turned them against the Establishment. His friend became known to the world as Bob Dylan.

All this was actually a lull before the storm that burst over the heads of students and myself with the first showing of *Operation Abolition.* HUAC had subpoenaed the TV footage, plus KPFA's audio footage of the hearing and demonstration. A mysterious Washington company produced the movie within two months of the events. HUAC filed it as a report to Congress, thus protecting it against libel suits. It needed that protection, because it was an outrageous piece of falsification by editing. Time sequences were reversed so as to suggest, for example, that Longshoremen's Union president Harry Bridges had incited the students to riot. In fact he was having lunch in a restaurant and didn't get to City Hall until the police riot was over. "Police riot" is a phrase the students invented to describe the events that occurred. The movie libeled individuals, including me, referring to me as a Communist. I had left the party three years earlier, before moving to California, a fact the FBI unquestionably knew. The courts had already found the designation "Communist" damaging in a libel suit by a TV personality. I had, under pain of perjury had I testified falsely, denied Communist membership at the HUAC hearing, although in very careful phrasing so it could not imply condemnation of anyone who *did* choose to be a member of that party.

The American Civil Liberties Union soon made a film titled *Operation Correction*, devoted solely to exposing the falsehoods in the Committee's movie and its editing. I was told that a midwestern liberal Catholic group—in those years "liberal" and "Catholic" were still a contradiction in terms in the minds of most people—made its own film supporting the students. Finally, an opponent of the committee, Hollywood producer Robert Cohen, made the best of the anti-HUAC films, despite its deadpan title: *House Committee on Un-American Activities*. It is still used in higher education.

I spent much of the next four years responding to the furor created by *Operation Abolition*, and participating in the counteroffensive the hearing and movie stimulated. The first two showings of *Operation Abolition* were on TV in Los Angeles, introduced by a former governor of California. Someone told me about it. I responded with a letter accusing the show and those associated with the film of defamation of character, slander, and libel. My letter was read on a subsequent broadcast in that TV show, with disparaging remarks about me. So I sent another letter. The host went after me again. A viewer taped it off the air, transcribed it, and sent it to me. It was clear that the Right had been stung. The host said, in the course of a long tirade: "William is the fellow that before this House Committee said that he was very proud when people walked up to him on the street and congratulated him as the man who killed Joe McCarthy....And he called the members of the Committee that were sitting in San Francisco Judases....It's high time that the Congress of the United States enacted legislation that would protect the committees from such abuse as was...directed toward it by William Mandel and Archie Brown of the Longshoremen's Union....By next year there will be some protection afforded the Committee so these men can be cited for contempt when they act in such a manner and dunked into the pokey for an extended period of time."

Five days later another letter from the same viewer made the matter seem serious: "You seem to have been selected out of many candidates to receive Tom's right-wing ire. Last night, Aug. 23, Tom commented on a photostatic copy of KPFK's *Folio* [KPFA's sister station in Los Angeles]....He read a series of the titles of your programs....It could possibly have serious repercussions....He has devoted viewers...and a letter campaign could develop against you....I don't really think I'm exaggerating the effect on his rabidly patriotic and conservative followers."

The writer was afraid KPFK would be successfully pressured to take me off the air. That did happen, the first of several times, later in the decade, but it was due to Zionist, Maoist, and Trotskyist objections, not those of the indigenous Far Right.

Operation Abolition had its first showing in our area at the end of September. The *Daily Californian,* newspaper of the UC Berkeley students, ran a statement by me: "The film is exciting, which makes it dangerous...with its present commentary. The danger...is its attempt to divide and weaken opposition to the committee by the use of a 'red herring'."

The showing had been on that same public TV station, KQED, that had just taken me off the air. It was presented on a regular weekly program conducted by Caspar Weinberger, later President Reagan's super-hawk Secretary of Defense. I wrote the station saying that I would sue KQED-TV for libel unless it ran my full testimony, which contradicts the film script. The results were triumphant and hilarious. My full testimony was available only in audio form. Weinberger sat at a desk and said that a couple of weeks ago he had shown a film containing a portion of the testimony of William Mandel, and that the audience would now hear Mr. Mandel's full testimony. And so for fifteen minutes the future most-powerful cabinet member sat stone-faced under a huge blow-up portrait of me the producer had provided, as I ripped into HUAC. I'd love to have a print of that broadcast.

The Los Angeles TV commentator's type of attack did have some dangerous consequences. A month later, an incendiary bomb was thrown against the building of the Citizens Committee to Preserve American Freedom, in Los Angeles. It was headed by Frank Wilkinson and was the adult organization seeking to abolish HUAC. A man of classically respectable upbringing and background who had been a public housing administrator, Wilkinson had been convicted of contempt of Congress and served a year in jail. First, however, he had a truly triumphal speaking tour at campuses across the country, including one at UC Berkeley with an audience of five thousand. A couple of months later, a lunatic walked into the office of English professor Tom Parkinson, as rational and decent a man as could be found on the Berkeley campus, blew the side of his face off with a gun, and killed a graduate student. When captured, he said that this was an anti-Communist act and he had hoped to start World War III. He was clearly insane, and was institutionalized. The fact that his mental illness took this violent political direction reflects the incandescence of the times.

Attacks, not lethal but politically more dangerous, came from presumably saner quarters. The *Saturday Evening Post,* the weekly middle-America trusted, with 6 1/2 million circulation, editorialized about student protests: "Those Mobs Are Part of the Kremlin's Plan," and said: "Directions for these disorders...were printed in *The Californian,* UC student newspaper, and circulated among the rioters." That was a lie, and the *Daily Californian* forced the printing of a retraction.

The letter from Los Angeles about that TV show was the first of a steady stream I received from all over the country for years to come about *Operation Abolition..* People would see me in the film, be outraged, decide I could help them in their efforts to fight the Committee and the local reactionaries who were promoting it, and wrote me either for suggestions or to come and speak. My home address was in the official proceedings of the hearing, which were widely circulated by both sides.

A nationwide mass movement now arose to abolish HUAC. The silent acceptance of McCarthyism during the preceding decade was a consequence of belief in the inevitability of war with the USSR. This belief demanded that all Americans close ranks. That the United States would beat the USSR even in a nuclear war was taken for granted. Then Sputnik went up in 1957. This proved the Soviet claim to have developed an intercontinental ballistic missile, because they clearly had rockets capable of boosting payloads beyond the pull of gravity. The small minority of citizens who had hitherto been vocal opponents of nuclear arms swelled into a mass movement embracing people from all strata of society. Americans now realized that this country too would be destroyed in such a conflict. In that sense, Sputnik, opening people's eyes on all these issues, contributed to the anti-HUAC movement.

The week after I appeared before HUAC I received a letter from an elderly chemistry professor at Chico State, Courtney Benedict. He informed me that he and his wife had been listening to me for the three years I had been on the air and that they had been on the picket line outside the San Francisco hearing. He had taped the KPFA broadcasts of the hearing. They were now being used in history and political science classes, adding, "Over 100 students so far have signed a petition to abolish the Committee." Particularly interesting was this sentence: "Actually we went to San Francisco to attend the Little Summit Conference *which had a news blackout* even tho it ended in 2,000 marching from Opera House to Union Square and 3,000 in Union Square to hear...[Nobel-winner] Linus Pauling."

There was a direct connection between the two events. Five months later, the U.S. Senate Internal Security Subcommittee investigated Californian Pauling's circulation of a petition to the United Nations calling for a cessation of nuclear bomb testing, a petition signed by more than eleven thousand scientists. A letter in the *New York Times* on behalf of forty-one members of the Rutgers University faculty, including *all* the law professors, read: "We oppose especially the attempt by the committee to force Dr. Pauling to disclose the names of other scientists who helped him circulate the petition. We urge the committee not to cite Dr. Pauling for contempt for any failure to make such disclosures." Berkeleyans, including our family, were a very large proportion of the first mass march on UC's Lawrence Radiation Laboratory in Livermore, where each new nuclear weapon was designed. Dr. Pauling addressed a packed meeting in the town's biggest hall.

Berkeley students could not abandon their opposition to HUAC even if they wanted to, which they didn't. Sixty-eight people, primarily students, had been arrested the day I appeared. One British graduate student, a veteran of the Royal Air Force, was harassed by the Immigration and Naturalization Service. Students now organized to oppose HUAC and to defend themselves legally. They were particularly outraged by the accusation that they, who had stood still in the face of fire hoses and gone limp when dragged down City Hall's staircase, had started a riot. A committee was established, which I attended. I proposed that it follow the example of those of us who had faced witch-hunters in earlier years by making an LP phonograph recording from the audio record of the event. That was done: it is called "Sounds of Protest."

The students' behavior was highly principled. When offered dismissal of the charges against them on condition they file no suits against the police, they agreed, provided the judge would also dismiss charges against non-student demonstrators. He did so. One student, Robert Meisenbach, was separately indicted and tried for starting the riot. He was acquitted when his attorney produced an enlargement of a photo in *Life* Magazine which showed this young man standing completely across the huge hall from where the hosing was in progress.

That summer of 1960, SLATE held a weekend conference in the redwoods at Mt. Madonna State Park, south of San Jose. One hundred and forty participated, from every major California campus and colleges all over the country. I attended, quite certain that this student activity marked a new wave of citizen participation in the country. I was amazed that not a single American faculty member at U.C. Berkeley chose to attend, although a number had actively supported the arrested students. One visiting Scandinavian professor, Christian Bay, did so. We hadn't previously met, but he had written me, with a copy to KPFA, because prominent sociologist Seymour Martin Lipset, who claimed to support the students and was a fellow-broadcaster on that station, had used his air time to imply that I was a Soviet spy. Lipset had said that I took the Fifth Amendment at an earlier hearing when asked about espionage and sabotage. He failed to mention that my use of the Fifth was before Joe McCarthy. That would immediately have put listeners on guard. Nor did Lipset tell his listeners that when McCarthy used my answer to imply that I was a spy or saboteur, I had immediately shot back, under oath: "No, sir!"

The Mt. Madonna Conference confirmed my hopes that a new student movement was really under way. When Students for Agricultural Labor, a Berkeley group devoted to arousing student support for the farm labor organizing drive, asked for volunteers to work in the fields as hands, several dozen did so, in the hundred-degrees-plus heat of the California summer sun. Some had never done any physical labor. I was astounded.

When the fall 1960 semester opened at UC Berkeley, the campus was humming. There were tables out representing BASCAHUAC, the Bay Area Student Committee to Abolish the House Un-American Activities Committee, which led a massive national campaign for the next four years. A lifelong bond formed among us. Other tables promoted Students for Agricultural Labor, the Young People's Socialist League, and the Young Republicans. Also active were the Fair Play for Cuba Committee, the Student Civil Liberties Union, NAACP, Students for Racial Equality, Young Democrats, and SLATE.

I have on several occasions recognized major shifts in the political atmosphere and significant new movements earlier than anyone else, as far as I can determine. In October, just weeks after U. C. Berkeley's fall semester began—the HUAC hearing had occurred immediately before the spring semester ended—I wrote to Bill Sennett, a veteran of the Abraham Lincoln Brigade, then living in North Hollywood. He had invited me to speak to his discussion group about the split between the USSR and China that had just occurred. My letter tried to convince him to change the subject of my talk. I wrote:

"There is one phenomenon in current American political life—and current American political <u>movement</u> —with which I am intimately associated and highly familiar, and which I believe is more important to your group than this Sino-Soviet business.

"I refer to the student movement, and in particular student opposition to the Un-American Committee. The seriousness with which this is taken by the opposition is indicated by the fact that 1000 (one thousand) prints of the movie *Operation Abolition* have been made. This is the film giving the Committee-FBI version of the San Francisco demonstration, and trying to discredit the student movement as Communist-led....

"It is important for your group to know that a new movement is under way that, I am absolutely convinced, will have a major impact on American life in the years just ahead. I was present at a week-end encampment of the new campus political parties this summer, which so impressed the head of the official National Student Association, who was present, that he endorsed its opposition to the J. Edgar Hoover report on the San Fran demonstrations, and also endorsed its call for national student commemorations of the anniversary of [the American nuclear bombing of] Hiroshima....This is not a movement led by any traditional Left party, although these students obviously have very advanced ideas in the major areas of social life. A very special characteristic is the fact that red-baiting has been absent and is rejected in advance as a matter of principle...."

A month later a pamphlet called *Campus Rebels* appeared, written by Al Richmond, editor of the Communist *People's World*. He had interviewed me and quoted me anonymously, thus:

"An older radical, who is acquainted with student leaders, said this movement might well spearhead a progressive democratic revival in American life, filling a vacuum that he believes has been created by the abdication of labor leadership and the ineffectiveness of existing radical groups."

My view was at odds with conventional wisdom, Left, liberal, and Right. The Left believed that any movement not led by the working class could not be of significance. Liberals quickly recognized that something was happening, but did not know what to make of it. As for conservatives, an article in the *Wall Street Journal* titled "Campus Radicals" was subtitled "Increasingly, They Are Right Wing, Drawn to Goldwater." Exactly the opposite was true in the '60s.

While I was busy with the HUAC aftermath, the earliest development of a potential socialist society on the American continent had occurred. My appearance before the Committee was five months after Fidel Castro had won in Cuba. Propaganda for invasion of that island was downright frantic. My intention to vote for John F. Kennedy (his opponent, after all, was Richard Nixon, who was the ex-HUAC member and co-author of the bill that became the McCarran Act) was cancelled by Kennedy's Cincinnati campaign speech promising to overthrow Castro. (However, I told my friends that he'd get my vote anyhow if I thought the Catholic issue would defeat him: I immediately regarded his election as a historical step forward for American democracy in that the Presidency was no longer reserved for Protestants alone. It was only in the late 1990s that I found that view expressed in historical writings.) Among radicals and students, who were rapidly freeing themselves from the attitudes of the 1950s, Cuba was a subject of intense curiosity and debate. An opportunity for me to go to Cuba was provided by the Fair Play for Cuba Committee. I went, over the 1960-61 Christmas holiday, in what turned out to be the last "legal" visit by Americans for a long time.

We rode a public bus the six hundred miles from Havana to Santiago de Cuba, and talked with every conceivable person en route. I didn't know Spanish, but that was no problem in the Cuba of that day. Among every half-dozen bus passengers someone had lived in Miami, worked on U.S. ships or in the offices of U.S. firms or at the Guantanamo Naval Base, or had served American tourists.

My notes from that trip would still make a colorful book of its own. I recall the female militia company that drilled itself into the best marching order in the parade before Castro on the anniversary of the revolution, countering pervasive male contempt for women soldiers. I see a young, deeply religious Methodist woman taking the bus to her assigned place as volunteer teacher in that year's literacy campaign. The female aristocrat, also on the way to teach country folk to read and write, who proudly described herself as "latifundista y tipografista"— landowner and printer. Her Spanish, and Castro's, I could understand thanks to my French. But the average Cuban's dropping of consonants made comprehension impossible to me.

The night of December 30th we reached Contramaestra, gateway to the Sierra Maestra, where Castro's guerrilla movement had begun. Thousands of peasants were gathered, rifles on their backs, for distribution of deeds granting them land. The speakers' platform was decked with all the flags of the Americas, including our own. Cuba's leading writers were among the speakers. One of them presented a check to the army on behalf of the country's writers in an amount sufficient to purchase a fighter plane. An idiot American, ultra-Leftist, pledged to the crowd, in utter hysterical sincerity, that the American working class would defend the Cuban Revolution, arms in hand. So I asked to speak, and said that as one whose weapons were the voice and the pen, I would fight for Cuba's independence by every means available to me. I kept that promise, although in that atmosphere of raging fever about "Communism 90 miles from home," it wasn't easy. Eventually two or three TV shows and at least half-a-dozen radio stations other than my own interviewed me, and I broke into some newspapers.

But first I had to get home. When we had left Miami, self-exiled anti-Castro Cubans, supporters of the butcher, Batista, whom Castro had overthrown, harassed us at the airport. Police stood by. Their leader was a blowsy woman with blue hair and blue eye shadow. Our return to Miami from Cuba was quite late at night. As we passed through Customs, the officer reached into my opened bag and removed the thick handful of Cuban newspapers and magazines I had deliberately put on top, in plain view. I said, "You can't take that." He waved me to a sequestered area. I went through the ceiling, emotionally. I don't believe that even my hearings before witch-hunt committees had offended my sense of dignity as a free American with the right to read, as much as that did. The people with whom I had spent two weeks in Cuba, many with long radical backgrounds but quite subdued by the McCarthy years, went through Customs like good children. Only one boy in his late teens said to me, "Mr. Mandel, is there anything I can do for you?" I said, "Yes, get me an ACLU lawyer. They've got to be listed in the phone book. Get him out of bed if necessary."

I was taken to a small room by plainclothesmen who had none of the appearance or manner of city detectives. They had an air of education and were neither beefy nor crude. I insisted I would not leave without my reading material from Cuba. A nasty Customs man tried to intimidate me within legal limits: examining my arms for needle tracks and so forth. Finally, before daylight, the chief of the operation, whatever agency he was with, was brought in from his home. I repeated that the importing of non-pornographic material was not illegal, nobody was going to tell me what I was going to read, I was not leaving until I had my papers and books, and that I had asked for the ACLU. I scrunched down on a window seat as though preparing for a long stay. They finally returned my printed matter and I left. When Kennedy's catastrophic Bay of Pigs invasion of Cuba came just a couple of weeks later, the reason for the extraordinary atmosphere of that airport became clear.

CHAPTER 20

Traveling Gadfly and Diplomat

In 1996 the San Francisco Film Festival offered the first public showing of a documentary on Dr. W.E.B. Du Bois. In the discussion afterward, the film-maker dealt with the problem of creating an interesting movie about an individual who was, above all else, an intellectual. I was present, and that struck a sympathetic chord. How am I to transmit to you, the reader, the excitement of being re-admitted to the ranks of published authors after fifteen years of being untouchable?

In 1961 I received a letter from Lawrence Hill, a long-time acquaintance who was now a partner in Hill & Wang, saying "it's about time" they had a book by me on their list. They asked that I do an overall book on the Soviet Union similar in scope to my big book of 1946, but in size and style suitable for high-school use.

I thought they were crazily optimistic about the chance of a non-cold-war approach gaining significant acceptance in American high schools and that they were probably affected by Camelot euphoria: Kennedy had just become president. The history of the manuscript bears me out. The book was written in a year, as contracted for. In the interim, the Cuba missile crisis had occurred, and public hostility to the USSR had again become extreme. The partners decided to seek an outside reader's opinion on the manuscript, and got Harrison Salisbury, as Hill told me years later, to read my book. Salisbury was a Pulitzer-Prize winning Moscow correspondent for the *New York Times,* who later attained major editorial responsibilities on that paper, and is best known for his book on the siege of Leningrad, *900 Days.* His comments on my manuscript were sent on to me, unsigned of course, and I was extremely puzzled. On the one hand, the reader obviously knew me personally: "Bill says this," "Bill says that." We had worked together at the United Press during World War II. On the other, he displayed a most peculiar combination of schoolboy ignorance about events in the USSR prior to World War II and obvious first-hand knowledge of certain details of later happenings that I did not possess.

Wang also could not accept things like that the USSR had essentially abolished prostitution. Yet this was true. (So much so that, immediately before the downfall of the Soviet regime, a retired female schoolteacher there with whom I was corresponding rejected as an insult to Russian womanhood my prediction that post-communist collapse of the living standard and of guaranteed employment would bring prostitution back.) I convinced him by finding words to that effect in the bestseller, *Inside Russia,* by pop-expert-on-everywhere John Gunther. It was humanly impossible for Gunther to have learned as much about that country in his visit to gather material as I had in my twenty years, by that date, of scholarship on the Soviet Union. I dealt with Salisbury's criticisms by accepting things on which his observations rang true and rejecting some that it was possible to disprove by reference to such acceptable sources as the *Encyclopaedia Britannica.* One such was his incredible denial that the tsar's defeat of the 1905 Revolution was followed by, as I put it, "extermination with ruthless cruelty of what remained of the revolutionary movement."

After the delays caused by all this, my *Russia Re-examined* was published in 1964, when our relations with Moscow reached their best level since Roosevelt's death. Although only elite high schools used the book, it was quite successful thanks to purchase by the general public and use in college courses including graduate-level work at one law school. The professor's reasoning in that case was quite simple: how could he teach his course in Soviet law to students who hadn't the vaguest notion of what the USSR was all about, never mind its government? There was a revised edition in England the next year, and a further revision in the U.S. in 1967.

I must have had an awful lot of energy. The publisher's advance was not large enough to support us. In addition to writing the book, I ran my unpaid radio program, and I had to continue translating full time, because the salaried job I found in 1962 depended upon my translating twenty-four academic journals per year. I also spoke widely in response to the "Operation Abolition" movie, mentioned earlier.

The film gave me the first chance to get a sense of America outside the San Francisco area since my last lecture tour a dozen years earlier. From the English Department of Ohio State University I received an invitation to speak at a showing of the film and comment on it. It was signed with a most marvelous name, Henry Orion St. Onge. From its style I pictured a white-haired Yankee who looked like Emerson. When I arrived I learned that the reason he had invited me was because of my use of the English language in my testimony. The tape was, in fact, used in numerous English, Speech, and Rhetoric classes across the country for years. St. Onge turned out to be a brand-new Ph.D. in his mid-30s, but I was right about where he came from: New England but of French-Canadian workingclass origins.

Opposition by the John Birch Society, the most influential nation-wide far-Right organization of that period, caused the university president to withdraw permission for my appearance. There was much faculty support for St. Onge. When the Birchers tried to put the governor of Ohio on the spot over this in a press conference, he responded in a way that hadn't been heard for 15 years. He said he thought the students were mature enough to make their own judgment on what the speaker would say.

As it turned out, I spoke in St. Onge's back yard, from his kitchen steps, to an audience in which plainclothes types equalled students in numbers. He had posted a sign above his steps: "The Thomas Tusser Society Presents William Mandel." Afterward I asked him who Thomas Tusser was. A 16th-century English pastoral poet. And what was the Thomas Tusser Society? Well, in the cafeteria one day he had rejoiced at discovering one other grad student in English who had heard the name, so their coffee klatches thereafter had been dubbed the T.T. Society. Since I had been denied any kind of official sponsorship by the university, and was, he said, "in the classical English tradition of verbal utterance" (I made a note of that!), I deserved to be presented by the T.T.S. And besides, finding out who T.T. was would give the Birchers and the FBI something to do. Subsequently he had someone who could do fine calligraphy make me a "certificate of honor" from the T.T.S.!

That evening, I had an indoor lecture at the Columbus Unitarian Church, so packed by students, eight hundred or so, that they were quite literally hanging into the windows. The ruckus over my appearance went on daily in the student newspaper for a month thereafter. The faculty senate was still dealing with its aftermath a year later. In retrospect, it occurs to me that the ongoing debate among Ohio State students can only be explained by the times. Educated youth felt it had to face its conscience and convictions. Up to then, anti-communism as presented by the House Un-American Activities Committee and the FBI had been the holy writ upon which their schooling in civics and government had stood. And now they were grappling with the possibility that the king was naked.

My Ohio State contretemps became an early part of the history of student activism in the '60s. It was described in an article in *Atlantic Monthly,* later in an Atlantic book, also in a paperback on the John Birch Society. St. Onge was fired from a teaching job at a Nebraska university for which he had received a contract just before the incident. The matter went to the American Association of University Professors, which published a long report in its journal three years after the event, censuring Nebraska's Wayne State and compelling it to reinstate the contract or reimburse him. Meanwhile, St. Onge, out of work, took his family to

New Zealand to be out of the way of the H-bomb war he and a very large percentage of Americans expected. I did not. His wife, a folk singer, wrote me from there that the Kiwis were as dull as the sheep that covered the hills. Not the New Zealanders I knew a generation later. The Ohio State incident was also treated in the 1970 book, Foster and Long's Protest! *Student Activism in America,* 1970. Fourteen years later, a woman living a block from us brought over a visiting high school teacher from Seattle who had attended Ohio State in 1961. Our neighbor had told him beforehand that I lived nearby and he had carried down photographs of me speaking from St. Onge's back porch, and said I had affected his life ever since. I said nothing new on that occasion, so this must have been the first time he encountered the ideas I was expressing, or at least in a fashion that got through to him.

St. Onge was not the only academic to lose his job for sponsoring me. Monterey Peninsula College (MPC) in California had had for years an evening public lecture series whose roster of speakers even put me in awe. My other speaking dates after the HUAC hearing, whether in California or the Midwest, were all about the witch-hunt, with the Birchers putting out a finely-printed four-page brochure on my background. It was distributed to all audiences when their efforts to bar me were unsuccessful. They picketed me with wonderful signs like "Brainwashing: By An Expert." Monterey Peninsula College, by contrast, invited me to deliver three lectures on my own subject, the Soviet Union, at fees higher than I'd seen in fifteen years.

No sooner had the contract been signed in the summer of 1961 for my lectures the following spring than the one local paper, the Monterey Peninsula *Herald,* began a virtually daily assault on Dean Leavitt of MPC, the school board (this was a junior college under school board administration), and me. It continued for months, with the school board meetings providing copy.

At year's end I was in New York at my dying mother's bedside. A stroke had felled her. Her hair was virtually free of grey at sixty-six and her flesh had the color and firmness of a young woman's. She heaved with silent sobs, tears flowing. In terror? In frustration at her inability to respond to me? The phone rang, and it was Dean Leavitt, terribly apologetic. He had phoned me in Berkeley, learned why I was in New York, and gotten the number. The pressures on him had become too strong. Would I consider surrendering half the lectures, and switching to a debate with me having one evening, an opponent the next, and the two of us face to face on the third? If so, he would leave it to me to suggest an opponent.

Just as I respected Hill & Wang for having broken the publishing blacklist against me, I respected Leavitt. A complete stranger (he told me he was a listener to my broadcasts), he had, by his invitation, said in effect that I belonged at the top as a lecturer in my field. I not only had no desire to squeeze him, but also felt that his proposal would still make it possible to strike a blow for free speech. As opponent, I proposed Stanford political scientist Prof. Robert Carver North.

North had won the Best-First-Novel-of-the-Year award in 1949 for his *Revolt in San Marcos*. It had been written in 1947 while he was a graduate student at Stanford and I was a fellow of the Hoover Institution. He and I had been close friends. North was a veteran of World War II in the Pacific, which he had gotten to participate in by artificially reducing his high blood pressure before taking the entrance physical. Although actually an Air Force officer, his job was to go in with the very first waves of infantry or Marines as islands were assaulted and to talk dive bombers down onto enemy bunkers. But as an officer and Air Force man he was resented by the very dogfaces whose exposed positions he shared.

North had given me the manuscript of his novel about the war to read: a marvelous action story, good pyschological portrayal, and very fine description of political attitudes. He described a fascist-minded American officer of a kind I had never seen in any novel about the U.S. armed forces, and a climax of extraordinary tension as the Japanese all but succeed in overrunning the divisional headquarters. Unfortunately, Norman Mailer's *The Naked and the Dead,* with identical setting, had been published (1948), and the trade didn't think there was a market for two novels on World War II! I thought North's book distinctly better.

His published novel was the first ever to deal with modern political realities in Latin America, including Communists and Trotskyists. In light of North's later political evolution to centrist Democratic views, there's a bit of wry in the fact that I, then bitterly anti-Trotskyist, told North as I read his first draft that he had pictured them as two-dimensional monsters, and that they had to be understood as human beings, particularly in a novel. North reached real heights in describing the local Indians. When asked how he was able to describe so convincingly a totally different culture, he told me that he knew Mohawks from upstate New York. He had worked with them as a high-iron bridgebuilder, if my memory serves me correctly. His wife of those years was Native American, but her father was a Yale graduate. So she was hardly typical. North also did a stunning job of describing the smells and sights of a Latin American marketplace from the eye-and-nose level of a small boy. When I asked how he managed that, he told me that his father was a lecturer who would go to Mexico to gather material and take him along. *Revolt* did not appear, however, until over a year after I moved back East subsequent to the Hoover Institution stint. North had not sent me the final revisions to read, which would have been normal if he had continued to regard me as mentor, as he had at Stanford. In published form, the book describes the Indian central figure, now a liberal politician, breaking with the Communists.

In the fifteen years during which we had grown apart, North had become an expert on China, producing dull academic works, and a loss to literature. He was a pioneer in content analysis, which is essentially a sophisticated computerized adaptation of what I had done with the Soviet press since 1940. When we returned to California in 1957, he visited our home once, but it was clear that we were not on the same wavelength. He had become a cold war liberal, and that made my nomination of him as my opponent in that three-evening debate entirely legitimate. The only thing wrong, which was beyond my control, was that he was a dull speaker and I the opposite whenever the situation was challenging. However, he had the public state of mind going for him, while I had to fight it.

The debate accomplished exactly what I had hoped. The audience lived up to my faith in American attitudes, as has every audience that has ever heard me out. After the months of drumfire in the paper, the Birchers distributed their brochure on me, which people took to their seats, read, and then set aside. The auditorium was packed for each of the three evenings. In the final face-to-face appearance, North was particularly impressive when he raised his voice just a bit, set his angular jaw, and closed: "Hang on to that democracy!"

That was perfect. To me, the debate was not over the merits of the two social systems, nor did I believe I was going to make a dent in our country's foreign policy. Rather, it was over whether the people of Monterey and, by extension, the country, had *the right to hear* a dissenting viewpoint—whether we would finally put an end to McCarthyism. But a price was paid. Dean Leavitt was forced to resign. He had become a controversial figure in a school system that had many interests to balance. I was not invited to speak in Monterey again for fourteen years.

Driving home from Monterey after one of that series with North, I picked up a couple of hitchhiking Cal students. We exchanged names, and when they heard mine they told me that they had written in my name for president in the 1960 presidential election in consequence of my conduct before HUAC. If that is no more than an indication of my standing among students during the first half of the '60s, a president-to-be actually did inject himself into the controversy roused by my appearance. The far-Rightists who had wanted me barred had consistently insisted that I be required to answer the questions on which I had taken the Fifth Amendment in the HUAC hearing. Shortly after my talks, Richard Nixon came to Monterey. At a press conference, a student asked him, "Do you feel that a college should be an open forum for ideas, having the right to choose speakers of any belief if they choose to?" He replied, "Speakers who...refuse to testify before congressional committees should not be hired by tax-supported institutions to express their views." But I took pleasure in the fact that that semester's professor-in-residence at Monterey Peninsula College was James Baldwin, and the next speaker in the series of which I had been a part was Eleanor Roosevelt. Good company.

Prior to my Monterey debate, I had one on the Berkeley campus during this period that was of public importance. In 1962 Stanford students asked me to debate on campus a Dr. Fred Schwarz, an Australian resident in the U.S. who was the founder and head of the Christian Anti-Communism Crusade. To me he was simply primitive, but it is a measure of how far and fast campuses moved later in the '60s that at the beginning of the decade he was able to fill the largest auditoriums and have organized support groups among students. It was they who had contacted me. The strategy was to ride my drawing power because of "Operation Abolition," and to mousetrap me with the proposed subject: "Resolved: That Communist Professors Should Be Fired," with me taking the negative. The subject posed no problem for me: in 1962, thanks to McCarthyism, there had long since been no Communist professors in the United States. It would not have been a problem, either, to show that fact was a consequence of the witch-hunts, and that Schwarz was setting up a straw man so as to further intimidate administrations and faculties.

It is a measure of the times that Stanford's administrators refused to permit me to appear on campus, even though I had been a post-doctoral fellow in its then best-known research institution. They had no objection to Schwarz, a physician who made no claim to academic qualifications. To me, no chance to lash out at would-be fascists was to be missed, particularly since Schwarz was getting maximum publicity and attracting very substantial audiences.

When Stanford barred me, I phoned the U.C. Berkeley student party, SLATE, and suggested they run the debate at Cal. I counted on the fact that, aside from the issues involved, the permanent Stanford-Cal rivalry would influence them: imagine putting on a big event that Stanford students couldn't! One day before the debate, SLATE called to say that Dean Towle (ex-head of the U.S. Marines' female entity) had decreed the debate could not take place under the announced title, because that alone would convince the public that the university did have Communist faculty. Instead, she insisted upon the opposite title: "Resolved: That Communist Professors Be Hired," with me taking the affirmative. That did present a problem. I was in favor of such hirings on grounds of civil liberties and to enable Americans to know at first hand the basic thinking of the competing social order from its advocates. But I was absolutely determined not to be isolated again from a generation that was beginning to think things through, by taking a stance too far out for acceptance. I remembered how my use of the term, "imperialism," to describe U.S. policy, had set me back in the aftermath of my debate with Eugene Burdick in 1959.

I spent a hard couple of hours mulling over Towle's edict and decided that students were indeed ready for the position I had been asked to uphold. I phoned to say I'd go ahead, and concluded that I had to do something very risky: speak from a prepared text. My radio experience reading my scriopts aloud, plus the fact that I respond well to existential situations, saved me from being dull.

Aside from the arguments capsuled above, it was clearly necessary to prove that there indeed were Communists who could meet any academic standards. I presented by name and credentials historian Herbert Aptheker and economist Hyman Lumer. Although my personal attitude toward them at that time for their opposition to Khrushchev's expose of Stalin, their support of Moscow's invasion of Hungary, and their unqualified defense of the Soviet Jewish situation, was one of contempt and hostility, they did help prove the larger point. I saved for my peroration a career which was the equal of any in American academic history, for this scholar's publications and their recognition, for his years on faculty, and for public service including a diplomatic appointment. I concluded that review: "You can read his books on this campus, but you are not allowed to hear him speak: Dr. W. E. Burghardt DuBois!" Members of the Communist Party, which he had joined not long before, were specifically barred as speakers, never mind as faculty. The tape records only scattered applause at this point from an audience that had repeatedly interrupted me with general applause and sympathetic laughter. It was clear that in 1962 most of a University of California audience of fourteen hundred, primarily students but including many faculty, had never heard the name of DuBois. I verified that later with those who came up to speak with me. I have never encountered a clearer indication of racism in education and the effects of the witch-hunt in purging textbooks.

When I concluded, the audience rose in a prolonged standing ovation, only the second in my then twenty years as a public speaker. Americans were a reserved people before the '60s. I have a news photo of that event in which student David Horowitz, then a radical but subsequently a leading ideologist of conservatism and supporter of Ronald Reagan, was applauding me like crazy. Schwarz ended his rebuttal period by turning toward me and saying into the mike: "If noise means anything, I have to admit you've won." Son Bob commented afterward: "shredded Schwarz."

My speech was printed in an influential publication, the *Liberal Democrat,* which then set the tone for the Council of Democratic Clubs, a state-wide organization that in those years drew thousands at its annual convention. It was reproduced in student newspapers from conservative Chico State in California to Oregon's Reed College. But the University of California, which had taped the debate, refused to release it for broadcast when KPFA requested it, or even for classroom use, until years later.

That was no accident. The years 1960-1965 marked an about-face in the willingness of Americans to defend civil liberties. Before the San Francisco HUAC hearing of 1960, the rules set by Truman's Loyalty Oath and McCarthy's witch-hunt governed. Neither media nor the educational system permitted dissenting voices in policy and politics to be heard. The tiny Pacifica group then of three radio stations—KPFA in Berkeley, WBAI in New York City, and KPFK in Los Angeles—was the only exception. It was my good fortune to possess the gift of logic and passion that, at the 1960 HUAC hearing, set fire to the tinder that had built up among students no longer satisfied with conformity. From then until the Free Speech Movement at the University of California began in the fall of 1964, I was in the forefront nationally in breaking the ban against hearing the other side. If I battled the far Right in the Berkeley debate with Schwarz in the spring of '62, I was fighting the world-wide official far Left in Moscow that summer. The Soviet Union hosted in the Kremlin a Peace Congress initiated by its wholly-loyal World Peace Council. I had been impressed by Soviet leader Nikita Khrushchev's peace moves subsequent to 1956 and, more important, so were the Quaker-led movements to which I was closest at the time. This 1962 Congress was the first such event under essentially Soviet sponsorship to offer advance guarantees that opinions other than echoes of Moscow's would be heard, and to seek actively to involve non-Communist peaceniks. The Committee for a Sane Nuclear Policy was present, as was British philosopher Bertrand Russell's Committee of 100, famous for its civil disobedience. Similar movements throughout western Europe were represented. Distinguished editors like that of *France-Observateur* were present.

Premier and Communist Party chief Khrushchev was the main speaker at the opening assembly of six thousand. He announced that the USSR was going to resume the testing of nuclear weapons, which it had earlier stopped unilaterally. The United States had followed suit, and a moratorium was in force. Panels followed. I attended one on bomb-testing, where I was astounded by the number of monks in saffron robes. Not Hare Krishnas, but the real Asian article. I said that Khrushchev's argument that the Soviet Union, being a socialist country, could not possibly start an aggressive war, would be utterly meaningless in the U.S. I also argued that his resumption of testing would destroy the American peace movement. I proved wrong on that latter point. I continued, correctly in this case, that the American people's response would simply be: "If the Russians resume, we have to also." At a meeting of the fifty or sixty participants from the U.S., most of them, Communists or Party sympathizers, would have gladly thrown me out. That was particularly true of the San Francisco area contingent, for they were responsible for the invitation to me. It is fascinating that the name of the late leader of that delegation, African-American Dr. Carlton B. Goodlett, is now borne by the street fronting City Hall, and therefore decorates all official stationery. He more than deserves the honor.

Next morning my phone rang, entirely too early. I had been partying. A voice in Scandinavian-accented English said a delegation was waiting on me, and might they come up? I asked for a minute to brush my teeth. When a handful of people filed in, it turned out that they had been authorized to represent the entire non-Communist contingent from western Europe, Canada, and the U.S. They had heard my remarks at the bomb-testing panel, and asked me to speak for them at the plenary session. Later I learned that there were two other reasons for their asking me. The first, a precondition for the second, is that a lifetime of indoctrination with fear of the KGB by our mass media had somewhat intimidated these very courageous people. I can understand that, because I was fearful each time I went to the USSR in the pre-Gorbachev years. Although I never engaged in any illegal activity, I operated on the principle that I'm a free man. When a cop at a bridge once confiscated Tanya's film because he thought the camera was pointed at a power plant, I insisted on being taken to police headquarters, where I bawled out the chief of police. I'd think twice about doing that at home. Who knows what they would think to slap me with, just for harassment? Our police regard themselves as sacrosanct unless one has connections.

The second reason I was asked to speak for the West had to do with the party the night before. An Englishman who had been a graduate student at Berkeley at the time of the HUAC hearing had asked me to read my opening statement on that occasion. I had brought it in case anyone accused me of being an American agent (later the Chinese actually did). He told the western delegations that if they wanted to have someone present a minority view who could handle a maximally hostile situation, I was their man.

It all ended in a fiasco. I took it for granted that the Soviets knew what was going on in our preparation. Therefore, when I wrote the brief speech I would give, I presented it to the press, including the *New York*

Times man, Ted Shabad, to whom I'd given some assistance when he was an undergraduate. One Soviet to whom I handed it was a then unknown young man, Vladimir Pozner, who became famous in the Gorbachev years for his frequent interviews from Moscow on American TV and his regular participation in the then top-ranked Donohue show. He is today a major national TV personality in post-Communist Russia.

I went to the great auditorium, submitted my name, and waited to be called to the platform. By mid-afternoon the need to urinate was too strong, and I stepped out to the john. Obviously I had been watched: my name was called as soon as I left the hall. Somebody on my side dashed down to get me. I zipped up, hurried back, and walked to the platform, where Rev. John Endicott of Canada was in the chair. The speaker at the moment was Carlo Levi, author of *Christ Stopped at Eboli*. Endicott said he was merely calling out names as the secretariat handed them to him. My turn was passed, but I could try to change the mind of the secretary. One look at him and I knew it was hopeless, although I tried. He was a Bulgarian with Stalin written all over his face. The two words were then regarded as interchangeable (although I met a Bulgarian scientist who, on a visit to Berkeley, said to me, "Stalin is the worst thing that ever happened to communism.")

The key passage in the prepared speech I was prevented from making was: "When Mr. Khrushchev...argues that it is the western tests that have outraged the conscience of the world, he does absolute damage to the peace movements of the West, where the people say: 'what kind of idiots does Khrushchev take us to be? Everyone knows that the Soviet Union broke the moratorium first, and that the United States followed. If he talks like this,' they reason, 'how can we believe him on anything?' The intricacies of Mr. Khrushchev's argument that the German crisis necessitated these tests are simply lost upon the people who still have to be won for mass action for peace."

The Congress had its memorable sidelights. Erich Fromm was one of the Americans present. He was then at the very height of his popularity, known to every student in the country. He wanted me to introduce him to Soviet delegates of prominence, intellectuals, and equals. I sought such people out. I translated. He had absolutely no interest in knowing what they thought about anything whatever, but spent his time lecturing them. Not on particular matters: just on general principle. Sometime thereafter I greatly shocked my radio audience by condensing for it a lecture some group had asked me to give on Fromm's *Marx's Concept of Man*— absolutely the worst book I have ever read on the subject, and that covers a lot of territory. Ignorant as hell, essentially he made the same mistake as the Communists did about major figures, but in reverse order. They refused to recognize that Marx, Engels, and Lenin evolved, and therefore

tied themselves into knots trying to make the early writings of those figures undifferentiable from their later ones. Fromm, on the other hand,
tried to reduce Marx to his philosophical manuscripts of 1844, when he
was obviously not yet a Marxist, and was only twenty-six.

Another sidelight. The Soviet delegation gave a private reception for
all the Americans. It was chaired by Khrushchev's son-in-law, Adjubei,
whom the leader had made editor-in-chief of the second most important
newspaper in the USSR, *Izvestia*. The Russians sang, as a group and
individually, very well. They have marvelous stage presence, and are
unselfconscious in such situations. I called for a song of the First Five-
Year-Plan period, 1928-32, of which Soviets active at the time were very
proud and had deeper feelings about than any other time, save World
War II. Adjubei struck up one from the Civil War period a decade earlier, and the older Russians tittered: he was too young to know the difference. They were pleased when the Americans' turn to entertain came,
and I did a song of the period I had called for. Fortunately, Russians
helped out.

That evening I was seated at the same table as a very attractive young
man with an open face and brows scarred by boxing. It was Yuri
Gagarin, the first human in space, who was killed when testing a new
plane a few years later.

A particularly heart-warming personal encounter, because of the
memories it revived, was part of the otherwise tense Congress. At the
opening session, I had walked up the center aisle of the auditorium on
the off chance that I'd see someone I knew. Seated there in an unmistakeably Soviet suit was a little man, gray, balding, but with square
shoulders and a distinctive impish smile. "Harry!" "Bill!" It was the
schoolmate of my childhood in the Bronx, Harry Eisman, organizer of
Young Pioneer activities at P.S. 61. Harry had been deported from the
United States while still a juvenile. The Soviet Union accepted him. So
when the Mandel family arrived in Moscow in 1931 we were looked up
by Harry, then seventeen, short as he would always be, but decked out
in a superb Red Army officer's uniform, with that unique pointed hat
Trotsky had designed and the handsome floor-length greatcoat of those
years, pinched in at the waist. He was the mascot of a regiment, and literally a household name to children of the Soviet Union through newspaper interviews and radio talks.

Harry became a Soviet citizen, and during World War II battled for
the right to fight in the Red Army. The fear that foreign Communists
might be intelligence agents under deep cover was extreme in those
years shortly after Stalin's Great Purge. He finally got his way, and spent
three years slogging through the mud, a Jewish Rumanian-American-
Russian putting his body where his mouth was. He was seriously

wounded, and like many other Soviet veterans, married the nurse who took him through his convalescence. His proudest day came at the end of the war when he was assigned to guard a bunch of Nazi supermen taken prisoner. His saddest was earlier in the war, when as a lieutenant—he had been promoted from the ranks—a Ukrainian girl introduced to him by one of his admiring soldiers in a village they had just liberated refused to believe he was Jewish. "Jews don't fight," she said.

When the war was over, and Anna Louise Strong came from the West in her effort to reach Communist China by rail, she did not realize that the free and easy times she had known in Stalin's earlier period, when a foreigner could go anywhere and talk to anybody, were gone. She phoned Harry and asked him to see her in her hotel room. He knew it wasn't wise, but he was a loyal friend. However, contact with someone Stalin dubbed a spy made him a possible subject for recruitment into espionage. In consequence Harry served five years of exile in Siberia.

In 1966, long after Stalin's death, Harry wrote his one book, reminiscences of that early Communist children's movement in the United States. The preface was written by the leading female Russian revolutionary still surviving, Yelena Stasova, then in her 90s, who had worked for years on behalf of political prisoners in the capitalist world.

When I returned home from the Peace Congress, the *San Francisco Chronicle* ran an interview with me about it. But an event occurred almost immediately that made everything else that rich year pale in significance. American nuclear missiles had been stationed in Turkey, right on the Soviet border, for years. Now, however, American spy planes discovered Soviet missiles in Cuba. President Kennedy announced a naval blockade against Soviet ships en route to that island, a flat violation of freedom of the seas, which is a long-standing, universal principle of international law. Its acceptance would mean Soviet surrender to domination of the world by the United States. Moscow could not accept that. The world was on the verge of nuclear destruction for the first and only time ever.

On the day the blockade was announced, I phoned KPFA manager Trevor Thomas and told him that on my broadcast that evening I would abandon my Soviet-press format and would attack the president for placing the existence of humanity at risk. Did Thomas want me to read the script to him? He said no. Considering the circumstances, and the government's known plan to incarcerate dissenters in long-maintained concentration camps if it came to war, Thomas' reply was the finest act of support for freedom of speech I have ever encountered.

The crisis began on Monday. Wednesday of that frightening week was our wedding anniversary, and we had tickets to Moscow's Bolshoi Ballet at the San Francisco Opera House. I cannot imagine a more surreal situation. I had wired Kennedy: "Tamper with Russian ships and you will have a war," hoping that the deliberate arrogance of the wording would cause someone to think the sender knew something, so it would be passed to a high level.

I had also wired Premier Khrushchev: "In the name of peace, could the Soviet government speak thus? The present acts of the U.S. government do not include invasion of Cuba. In view of the admission of intention to overthrow the Cuban government, this means Kennedy understands an invasion of Cuba would be disastrous for the United States. The Soviet government is satisfied that its arms to Cuba have already caused the U.S. to realize this. For world peace, the Soviet government therefore believes it possible to order the return of Soviet ships now bound for Cuba as a temporary measure to permit negotiations and UN action for withdrawal of the U.S. blockade. The USSR won't permit Cuba to go hungry or defenseless, and will resume shipments whenever urgently necessary."

All of San Francisco society was at the opera house. The performance was splendid, the ovation stupendous, and in the intermission people chattered as usual. What else was there to do? Their destiny was not in their hands. I am reminded of the ball of the dead in Bulgakov's *The Master and Margarita*.

I dropped everything for the week, even my inhibition from the depression years against lengthy long-distance phone calls. I did whatever I could think of to save the world. I use that phrase with no embarrassment or sense of cliché. It was not that I had illusions about my influence, but simply that I had to try. My older son, then at Reed College, was going out with the daughter of a top AFL-CIO official who was very close to Bobby Kennedy. I phoned that man, told him that the Russians could not tolerate any violation of international law on the high seas such as the boarding of one of their vessels, and urged that he transmit that immediately to the highest people he could reach. For once in my life I was glad that cold-war paranoia caused some people to think I was a Russian agent and therefore might be a back channel for diplomatic contact.

I phoned the same message to a retired Yale divinity professor who had been at the Moscow peace congress. There he told me that a former student of his, McGeorge Bundy, Kennedy's National Security Advisor, had asked him to report on the meeting. The professor asked me to brief him on my judgment of the conference. I had done so at length, in his Moscow hotel room. That's probably in Soviet intelligence files. I assume we were all bugged.

My younger son was going with a daughter of a former State Department official then living in Berkeley. This man, John Carter

Vincent, had been fired in consequence of the McCarthy witch-hunt because he believed that the Chinese Communists were going to remain in power. He had broken up an earlier relationship between my older son and his older daughter because we are Jewish and I a radical. I phoned him, said the matter at issue overrode anything of a personal nature, and said I assumed he still had personal entree to former associates in the department. I urged him to transmit the same message. Finally, Henry Shapiro, then still the UPI correspondent in Moscow as he had been during World War II when I put meat on the bones of his dispatches at the head office in New York, was in the Bay Area visiting his sister, a professor in the Soviet field. I phoned him with the same request.

To all, I said that the matter could be settled if we would leave Castro alone. I also said we should give up the U.S. naval base in Cuba, Guantanamo. Shapiro said that wasn't in the cards. When all the papers on that crisis are made public, I'd like to know if I had any input. President Kennedy, in his American University speech of June 1963, calling upon us to "re-examine our attitude toward the Soviet Union" (which I think got him killed), described damage to the Soviet Union in World War II by a comparison right out of my book of 1946: "a loss equivalent to the destruction of this country east of Chicago." One of Kennedy's university professors, Russ Nixon, shared my views and admired my book. But I have no idea how that comparison got into the speech.

The crisis lasted just under a week. On my broadcast the following Monday, I read my wires to the two leaders and commented: "I believe that telegram to Khrushchev is an exact description of the events that followed and of the situation as it now stands."

John Carter Vincent's attitude toward my teenage sons would have been normal or not too far out in other parts of the U.S.. In Berkeley it was an anachronism. At Berkeley High my older boy's other best friends had been the daughter of the head of the Communist Party in Northern California and the son of hydrogen-bomb hawk physicist Edward Teller. The parents knew who the visiting kids were in each case. None of them made any objection to the friendships. That would have been simply inconceivable anywhere else in the country at that time.

In public life, however, there were still those who were affected by the McCarthy-era extension of guilt-by-association to one's parentage. In September 1964 Bob was to be one of four veterans of the Mississippi voting-registration effort to address the Democratic State Committee of California in Sacramento in support of a resolution favoring the Freedom Democratic Party in Mississippi over the racist official party. A newsman asked him in unfriendly fashion whether he was the son of the Mandel of "Operation Abolition." The very sincere man in charge of lobbying for the resolution asked Bob to withdraw as a speaker. So did the legislative secretary of a state assemblymember who was really pushing hard for the resolution. Neither of them had anything against Bob or myself. They feared that Red-baiting might be used against the resolution. Bob spoke. When the resolution passed the next day, the full state committee of nine hundred politicians rose in a standing ovation for the kids.

CHAPTER 21

"Don't Trust Anyone Over 30."

Poets know that emotion can often explain things that logic makes turgid. Thirty years after the Free Speech Movement [FSM] at the University of California, of which I was a part, my daughter Phyllis wrote a reminiscence of that event after attending its anniversary commemoration. With her permission, I reproduce it, with her emphases:

And the rockets' red glare, the bombs bursting in air gave proof to the night that our flag was still there... and in a rage at our government's disgrace of our flag, (Viet Nam War period) people tore the flags down and burned them.

The FSM was a result of off-campus organizing and the desire of young people all over the country involved in civil rights and civil liberties, to organize. It wasn't Freedom of Speech for anything, it was Freedom of Speech for many things: for wanting to end hunger, poverty, lack of housing, lack of or poor education or educational opportunities, and later freedom of speech against the Viet Nam War. It was the RIGHT TO THINK FOR ONESELF AND TO ACT ACCORDINGLY!

I want to thank all the stars of the FSM, the spokespeople, and the unknowns who sat there that day while Jack Weinberg was in that [police] car [surrounded by students who wouldn't let it leave] and vindicated *my rage* at my McCarthy anti-red witch-hunt period education during which I was penalized for my outspokenness... The FSM tried to "Let America Be America Again"—a poem by Langston Hughes, African American poet, that my parents in their wisdom provided me outside of my public school education to read.

I grew up in NYC in the '50s. "What did you learn in school today, dear little child of mine?", a line from a Pete Seeger song: I learned that Negroes supposedly liked slavery, and that a black young boy whom I liked hung himself by his tie in the boys' bathroom, that a senator named McCarthy was good for our country because he was protecting us from "communists" and that my Dad of course was a bad guy, because he was one of the folks being witch hunted. I learned that it was OK to execute two Jews for "conspiracy to commit espionage" and that a 12 year old child (*me*) should "go back to Russia" (where I wasn't born) for standing up for them. I learned that Paul Robeson, one of America's greatest African Americans, shouldn't be allowed to sing because he was a "known communist," and I learned that it was OK for six kids to live in one room with rats and roaches. My public school was 85% Black, my junior high school was 80% Black, 15% Puerto Rican and 5% white.

Somehow after I graduated high school in the year 1957 (the year our government instituted the "under G-d" in our Pledge of Allegiance, a violation of our country's separation of church and state) I couldn't stomach school anymore, and there I found myself that November of 1964, sitting in Sproul Plaza [the beginning of FSM] with my five month old son in my arms, weeping in gratefulness that a lot of white middle class kids who got to go to the uptown schools and got their books at the beginning of their semester, while I got mine two months down the road, seemed to be pretty outraged at our most respected institutions making a farce of our constitution and beliefs in Freedom of Speech and Freedom to Assemble, and in fact, Freedom to Learn. I never was a good student after I graduated high school, I kept dropping out. My grades weren't good enough to get into the illustrious university and my anger at anything that was authority or that told me lies in my class was so strong that even when it wasn't there I thought it was...

THANKS AGAIN FSM'ers!!!

Yours for a better life for all!

1964 marked the beginning of the highest wave of student activism in thirty years. Tens of thousands of students had seen "Operation Abolition," in which my defiance of the House Un-American Activities Committee (HUAC) invariably brought applause. They essentially adopted me. Here was a rare bird: someone their parents' age who was not content to color within the lines. So the Berkeley chapter of CORE, the Congress of Racial Equality, requested that I write something for its magazine, *The Campus Core-Lator.* I was the only member of my generation asked to contribute to its pages. One of the principal figures in it was that young man, Jack Weinberg, that Phyllis wrote about. Decades later Jack told me that he had invented the slogan, "Don't trust anyone over 30"—which became one of the hallmarks of the '60s nationwide—specifically against me. He had nothing against me personally, but wanted to counter the allegation that they were being manipulated by older people, particularly of Communist persuasion.

The year started quietly enough. A young reporter from Cincinnati who had moved to Berkeley and was working on a book on HUAC came to our house to interview me about it. This was Jerry Rubin, whose later spectacular and courageous street-theater antics in the movement against the Vietnam War made him a household name nation-wide and is perpetuated in a 1999 feature film about his rival, Abbie Hoffman. In the latter half of the decade, when Jerry himself was subpoenaed by HUAC, he came to my home again to ask what I thought of his plan to show up there in American Revolutionary War uniform. I was of the opinion he should not, in the mistaken belief that such behavior was past its time. He did so anyhow. His device made it possible for him to get his views onto network TV and into all the papers.

A student organization at San Jose State University, TASC, asked me to teach a course on the Soviet Union in the fall of 1964. That represented something totally new: a conviction on the part of students that they should have a right to determine what courses should be given and who should give them. It was a harbinger of the general rebellion against the materialism and acceptance of things as they are which they regarded as typifying their parents' generation. A widely-ballyhooed ABC-TV miniseries on the '60s in 1999, which persists in videocassette form, was factually highly accurate but failed to deal at all with this rejection of existing curriculum, administrators' and professors' attitudes, and teaching methods. It therefore left viewers at a loss to understand what white students were so angry about before the Vietnam War, other than their support for Blacks in the South. As far as I have been able to determine, mine was the first student-sponsored course of the '60s anywhere in the country.

Among the four who invited me was Luis Valdez, who also became a national name, but more enduringly, with his Teatro Campesino and his films, of which "Zoot Suit" was the first. He was already theatrical enough, wearing a beret with a red star, smoking big cigars, and looking as though he had just flown in from Havana. Another of the organizers was Frank Cieciorka, an excellent artist whose muscular fist emblem became the symbol of all the movements of the '60s and must have been reproduced on pins and in print hundreds of thousands, probably millions of times. I have a signed copy of the original ink drawing, modestly titled "Hand," on the wall of my study.

Early 1964 also brought the first occasion since the Martinsville Case in Virginia a dozen years earlier when I was willing to engage in a voluntary action that might bring arrest. For me that was always a very serious, carefully weighed decision. In responding to witch-hunt subpoenas all that was voluntary was the decision to uphold one's dignity. CORE and others were conducting demonstrations to get African-Americans hired by the hotel industry in San Francisco, which had until then refused to employ any at all. Mass picketing of the Sheraton-Palace Hotel was followed by a sit-down in the lobby. I would have been willing to be arrested. However, Tanya had been badly injured in an auto accident, spent months in a wheel chair and then on crutches, and her leg gave out while we were still picketing. So we went home before the arrests. Among the arrested was Terrence Hallinan, who thirty-five years later was San Francisco's elected District Attorney. He had been in Cuba at the same time as I, and was the son of the man I had proposed for the presidency in the 1952 election.

The incident that launched the Free Speech Movement at Berkeley in the fall was simply whether students might set up card tables on their own campus to collect money for the Mississippi project (consisting of students, including son Bob, who went there to help Blacks gain the right to vote) or anything else that moved them as concerned citizens. The administration wouldn't let them. It is no accident that Mario Savio, who emerged as the movement's prime but not only leader, was a veteran of Mississippi. Such students could no longer be treated as children under the silly formula, *in loco parentis*, meaning that college administrators substituted for parents. Several of the voting activists had been killed down South. Furthermore, Savio was a very rare exception at that time: a student of workingclass parentage.

One evening in the fall of 1964 I was handed a leaflet on Telegraph Avenue, the students' main drag. It invited non-students to come to a meeting to organize in support of students. The conveners actually had ex-student youth in mind rather than older people, but had no objection when a very few individuals their parents' age showed up. On the strength of whatever it was I said, plus support articulated by younger people who referred back to my HUAC hearing as well as my KPFA broadcasts, then very widely listened to on campus, I was elected the body's alternate delegate to the Free Speech Movement Executive Committee. The reason was best described in a term paper on FSM sent me a dozen years later by a graduate student who planned to expand it into his thesis. The context made clear that he was not of radical background. About me he wrote: "His brilliant denunciation of the House Committee at the [1960] hearing led to Mandel's becoming something of a cult hero in the eyes of politically active students."

In FSM, while the students themselves learned the routines of organization amazingly fast, and devised non-elitist, participatory-democratic forms entirely new to me (and themselves), I was able to serve as the voice of experience. Very early in the movement, Art Goldberg, who became a voluntarily-poor people's-advocacy attorney in Los Angeles, almost tore the whole thing apart over whether he had the right to put the word "fuck" on an FSM placard. The Establishment used this to dub us the Filthy Speech Movement. I was able to stop the controversy at an Executive Committee meeting, much more on my prestige from HUAC than by whatever argument I used.

A major issue throughout FSM was that of essentially anarchic behavior by a small outraged group versus an effort to win the broadest possible student and outside community support plus that of as much faculty as could be gotten to take a stand. When the famous sit-in was being planned that resulted in the arrest of seven hundred—as far as I know the most massive arrest in U.S. history to that day other than in labor strikes and round-ups of African-Americans—I opposed it because I knew how much energy needed to raise funds for bail and lawyers would be diverted from the movement. People would be hurt (beating of white students had not taken place in thirty years). I argued repeatedly for a general student strike instead. In retrospect, it is clear that the entire student body would not have struck had it not become outraged by the arrests and beatings that took place at the sit-in. No one dreamed that, thirty-five years later, UC campus police would hold open the eyelids of students in another sit-in and inject Mace. The night of the FSM event I went home, only to be roused by a phone call from son Dave, who was a troubadour of the movement, one of several who wrote and recorded songs and jointly made a record sold to the entire student body.

I went down, and at perhaps two or three in the morning a very pregnant young woman was permitted by the police to leave Sproul Hall. She came to me and told me of the decision of the Steering Committee: "O.K., Mr. Mandel, you have your strike." The next morning the university was shut down tight. Faculty, which had hung back from supporting the students, drove out by the hundreds to Santa Rita county jail, 20 miles away, to bail out the students and bring them home.

Attitude toward faculty was something on which Savio and I had had sharp differences. He, a truly gentle, sweet, kind kid, had come to refer to faculty as "rabbits" for their timidity. One one occasion—I think it was on this issue—he snapped at me at a meeting: "That's stupid." Far from being insulted, I relished that moment because it meant I was being treated as an equal, a participant, not some queer old duck. These were youth in their late teens and early 20s, and I was a father and grandfather. But on another occasion, when Mario and I were on the same side, and my motion won, he beamed at me and announced: "The voice of reason triumphs again."

I think Mario's fineness of character was as responsible as anything else for the psychiatric problems that set in soon after FSM and affected him for a number of years. He was a hero and just didn't want to be. Adulation wasn't his thing. The strain on him was enormous. Here was an undergraduate negotiating one-on-one with Clark Kerr, the president of the university, and then having to justify his own decisions, which usually were excellent, before an executive committee of a hundred whose individualism and immaturity were second only to their idealism and guts. He married one of the young women on the committee. Before the women's liberation movement, which largely arose in resentment against the macho behavior of movement "heavies," Mario was cooking, minding the baby, shopping, and generally behaving like a civilized man. When he died at fifty-three in 1996, he was a white-haired professor at Sonoma State University, regarded as perhaps the best teacher on campus. His words and manner at the 30th anniversary of the FSM made me regret that he had not become a priest, for he would have made the kind of pope the world needs badly. His sensitivity to the possibility that any deed or gesture of his might hurt an individual or group was truly extraordinary. A letter from another FSM-er reminded me that I, an atheist, actually called him "an angel from heaven, and it's a blessing to know him."

Those qualities did not prevent him from articulating very principled and forthright positions. That anniversary event was followed shortly by the decision of the ultra-wealthy Rightists comprising the University of California Board of Regents to abolish affirmative-action programs. Mario quietly played a leading role in organizing faculty state-wide against that decision. That was his final public activity.

Lenin once made a speech assailing "Communist arrogance." Although my years in the Party ended four decades before Mario's death, his brother's remarks at the funeral made me realize that I suffered that fault. I unthinkingly assumed that only hereditary Communists like myself and my children were raised in the tradition, coming from my father, that working for the welfare of humanity, as we understood it, was a normal part of life. But Mario, it turned out, came from a similar family tradition. There was actually a St. Savio in his ancestry. Two of his aunts were nuns who devoted themselves to the poor. His mother, working in a five-and-dime store, found that an African-American woman was being paid less than she for the same job. Mrs. Savio told the owner that she would "stop the store" unless he corrected that injustice. He replied that he was doing what everyone else then did, and raised the woman's pay to equal level. Perhaps the most revealing story was that when Mario, as a boy, asked his father, a blue-collar punch-press operator, why he was sure he was right over some issue, his father replied, "I have a pure heart. It tells me what's right and what's wrong." Mario inherited that.

The other nicest person among the FSM leaders was Bettina Aptheker, 19 years old at the time, daughter of the prominent Communist historian Herbert Aptheker and herself then a Party member. She must have heard of my publicly-expressed distaste for her father because he had been unwilling to confront the realities of Soviet repression at home and particularly in the invasion of Hungary, about which he had written an entire book of apologia. His deserved prestige for his contributions to African-American history had been used to obstruct reforming the American Communist Party away from automatic endorsement of anything Soviet. Bettina's relationship with him was excellent. Nonetheless, she and I got along very well on the executive committee, because we both believed in a course of action that would involve the largest possible number of students rather than spectacular do-or-die behavior. We both felt that every effort should be made to win over the faculty. We saw the need, beyond FSM, to change the governance of the university, bringing students, faculty, non-whites and non-wealthy people onto the Board of Regents. After FSM she devoted a lot of energy to that last objective, publishing a book on it. Bettina certainly deserves much of the credit for the presence of representatives of those groups on the board. (Unfortunately, they remain a token minority, automatically outvoted by the money-bags.)

Bettina and I often supported each other's positions on the executive committee, although we never had private discussions. Aside from being modest, she also had the exceptional stability, for so young a person, not to permit criticisms by me in print to disturb our relationship. At one point, after FSM, when she was still a student and very big on campus, the *Daily Californian* published a letter of mine pointedly asking her about the Communist Party's failure to challenge the Soviet Union on certain aspects of its treatment of Jews. On purely psychological grounds, it speaks extremely well of a young person to react with complete objectivity to criticism by someone a great deal older and certainly much more prominent than she before FSM began.

Today Bettina is a professor at UC Santa Cruz, long out of the Communist Party, a feminist and out lesbian, with two children from an early marriage. On the very best of terms with her parents even when they were still in the Party, she delivered a speech of wonderful warmth in tribute to them, splendidly received at a huge rally at UC Berkeley in 1984 marking the 20th anniversary of FSM.

I failed to get that movement to understand the need to end institutionalized McCarthyism, expressed in the fact that people like me continued to be barred from teaching. The students were so committed to rebellion against academic authority in general that, while they could relate to me as a fellow FSM-er, they could not understand why anyone would want to be a professor. They were devoted to improved and "free" teaching. (Of course, a disproportionately large number of them later became professors, or are married to such.) But that they wanted to learn was excitingly obvious.

In the spring of 1965, immediately after the victory of FSM, the left-liberal campus political party, SLATE, organized a series of lectures for me. Originally it was to have been delivered in the quiet of a lecture hall, in the late afternoon. But when the late President Kennedy's brother-in-law, Sargent Shriver, spoke outdoors in Lower Sproul Plaza and a large crowd turned out, I felt that I could draw as well, and asked that my lecture be in the same spot. When I came for my first talk in this series on Soviet Social Thought, six hundred were waiting. I set forth my philosophical premise in the opening lines:

"One does not have social *thought* unless one has social *problems*," I began. "In a perfect society, man will not have to think about improving it. But perfect societies are impossible: man would have to stand still for a society wholly adequate to his being at any given time to be attainable. As long as man and his activities change, his societies will also have to."

One of the most satisfying things I wrote at the time was an article, "The Free University or Freeing the University," which I originally delivered as a kind of valedictory at the final FSM executive committee meeting. It was published in the university's *Daily Californian,* which, for the full decade of the '60s, provided space and prominence for my writings. In retrospect, that is the clearest evidence of my standing with the students. In 1966 a banner headline read: "Mandel Describes Russian Visit." In 1967 the paper gave a full page for five consecutive days to serializing an essay of mine, "Reflections on the Soviet System." I do not believe that any professor on the university's faculty, any student or outsider has ever been paid a similar honor. Likewise, the headline across the top of the seventh issue of the *Berkeley Barb,* voice of the movement, read: "Mandel Raps Anti-Soviet Vigil." In 1967 it front-paged my detailed department-by-department analysis, "U.C. Profs 99.9% White." In 1968 it ran a continuing debate between Yippie leader Stew Albert and myself, essentially over anarchism vs. Marxism. Stew was a prominent character in the feature film on Abbie Hoffman made thirty years later.

The FSM won the right to have courses taught for credit on campus by others than faculty members. In the Bay Area, that came first and most smoothly at San Francisco State. In 1966 I taught a course at its Experimental College. Either I or the professor required to sponsor it posed the question of the students getting credit. A couple of days later the phone rang, and the voice at the other end introduced himself as the head of the Sociology Department of S.F. State, Don Gibbons. "You don't know me, Mr. Mandel, but I know you. That will be a three-credit course." I taught it for three years, and Tanya commented wryly, "The kids get credit but you get no cash."

The *San Francisco Bay Guardian* is the longest-established independent weekly in that city. A man named Burton Wolfe was its crack muckraking reporter when I did that teaching at SF State. He was also freelancing for *Amerika Illustrated*, the U.S. government's slick-paper monthly published in Russian in the USSR in exchange for their circulation of *Soviet Life* here. He had the idea of including my class in an article for *Amerika*. Describing a course quite friendly to the USSR given freely in an American university would score very legitimate propaganda points with Soviet readers. But when the security idiots in Washington learned the name of the teacher, they cancelled the thing. I keep a 1967 letter from Wolfe on my study wall to look at when I'm down: "Many thanks for permitting me to attend your wonderful class. I believe it is the most important in the Experimental College, and I think it could become one of the most important at S.F. State if it were included in the regular curriculum. It is a pity that the classroom is not packed for your course."

There was lots of mail like that from students there and elsewhere. But this was from a mature man, a practicing Catholic, former editor-and-publisher of an independent magazine of his own, and, in that capacity, one of the more solid citizens to come to the defense of the student bystander tried (and acquitted) in the 1960 HUAC affair, and of those subpoenaed.

In 1968 some dozen professors in half-a-dozen departments at U.C. Berkeley authorized undergraduate and graduate credit for students taking a course I gave there. They included the chairman of the History Department, himself a specialist in Russian history. He wrote a letter describing me as an "established scholar" in the field, although carefully dissociating himself from my interpretation of events. He told his secretary, whom I knew, that he had been using my 1946 survey volume, *A Guide to the Soviet Union* , since he started teaching in 1949. Inasmuch as I did not think of myself as an historian, and each discipline guards its turf most grimly, I took satisfaction in the endorsement of my competence by academics across the board. I know of no other case in academe, here or abroad, of anyone being honored by acceptance as qualified in so wide a range of disciplines.

In 1969 I finally got a formal appointment in the Sociology Department at Berkeley. As one of the senior people in the field, I wanted full-professor salary, pro-rated of course, since I taught but one course and had none of the non-teaching duties others carried. When the appointment came, the remuneration was at associate-professor level. I couldn't be too angry, because my sponsors felt they had to compromise on salary in order to get the appointment through. Yet I'm still insulted when I think of it. Twenty-two years earlier, at Stanford, my fellowship had already been at associate-professor level in net value, because fellowships were then not taxable income. And in the interval I had published another book, which had wider use in higher education than the previous ones. With thirty-five thousand copies sold, it was a solid success by American publishing standards.

My course was Contemporary Soviet Social Thought, and the text was the just-published *Social Thought in the Soviet Union*, to which I was a contributor and unofficial co-editor. Hopefully, my course might cause a few young Americans to think about the USSR in terms other than the forty-year outcry about their imprisonment of a Swedish diplomat, Raoul Wallenberg, who our press finally admitted in 1996 had been an American spy reporting on Soviet troop movements, exactly as Moscow had claimed all along. But in 1997 it forgot that admission, just as at the start of the Cold War, Soviet troop withdrawals had been reported the day they occurred and then forgotten because they destroyed the excuse for U.S. continuation of nuclear-bomb production.

Although my teaching drew no criticism, I was not re-appointed at U.C. Berkeley. The reason goes back to 1966, when Ronald Reagan was elected governor. His campaign advisers told him, "attack Berkeley," and so I found pictures of myself on the front page of unofficial Reagan literature in company with student FSM figures. "Middle-aged juvenile delinquents on campus" was a campaign-speech phrase of his. Reagan's election gave him control of the Board of Regents by 1969 as the terms of earlier appointees ran out. He announced that the professors had better be good or they would get no raises. In consequence, the university let Angela Davis go at the southern end of the state, and me in Berkeley. My status offered no legal recourse. She had been on a tenure track. As Black, female, and a Communist Party member, Davis was the obvious person to command support in that era, which strongly favored affirmative action and civil liberties.

People have always regarded me as a much better-than-average teacher. Yet my courses, whether at the Free University organized by FSMers and drop-outs or later in more formal settings, showed only a little less drop-off in attendance than did those of others. I understood why, and it didn't bother me. I was teaching about the Soviet Union. It had ceased being an ideal for me a decade earlier, but I felt that the more we knew about it the better. The U.S. arms budget of $300 billion per year in peacetime was based on the belief that the Soviet Union presented a threat. But my students were idealists, and it was Utopia they were looking for. At least, those who were doing so dropped out of my classes when they realized that I didn't believe that the U.S. could resolve its problems by patterning itself after the Soviet Union. They turned to Utopias elsewhere.

A few became hippies in the deep sense and/or supporters of the far underground grouplets which turned to bombings. A very few became

Maoists or Trotskyists. But the Communist Party, which had had two members on campus in 1960, picked up fifty or sixty in the course of the decade. Doubtless there were always one or more FBI, CIA, military intelligence or local police informers. Very early in the decade I received a letter from a young man who had attended the course I had taught sponsored by the Trotskyist Socialist Workers' Party. He wrote that he had been an informant. He apologized, saying he was convinced that I was a thoroughly patriotic American although he disagreed with me fundamentally. The next day he was found in his car on Grizzly Peak Boulevard, dead. The engine was running, the windows closed, and he had run a hose from the exhaust into the body.

All my books have been required reading in major educational institutions across the country. I was acceptable as guest lecturer. I was permitted not only to deliver papers but to organize panels at academic conventions. I have been published by invitation in symposium volumes in political science, sociology, behavioral science, and English. Yet once the student pressure let up, no one let me teach a full-term course after 1969 but for a single semester in 1978 when I taught Soviet jurisprudence at Golden Gate University Law School in San Francisco.

After fifteen years when nothing bearing my name would be touched, my return to publication in academic journals in 1965 sheds interesting light on the reflection of the Cold War in scholarship. A high school history teacher who listened to my broadcasts, Gene Bergman, had sent me a booklet consisting of a translation into English of the article about the United States in a volume of the *Large Soviet Encyclopedia.* The booklet had an introduction by a then-famous liberal Democrat who had been his party's candidate for the presidency of the United States, Adlai Stevenson. It also contained extended comments on the Soviet article by prominent American historians, including the then president of the University of Wisconsin and a U.C. Berkeley winner of two Pulitzer prizes. Published by a major textbook house, it was supposed to indicate to U.S. high school students what Americans looked like in Soviet eyes.

The translation was illiterate linguistically, historically, and politically. The distinguished Americans made fools of themselves due to their lack of knowledge of Russian by criticizing what the Soviets did not say, but the translators did. I demonstrated this in broadcasts over KPFA. A U.C. Berkeley history professor, Reginald Zelnik, phoned me and said my commentaries should be published, suggesting *Slavic Review,* the interdisciplinary organ of the Soviet and East European Studies field. I asked whether he thought they'd print anything with my signature, and he said times had changed.

They did publish it. In the next issue of the journal, the editor referred back to my article, saying "there is much to learn from that piece" and commenting on how often the "translations we encounter" indicate "shakiness in the command of the language of origin." This, with reference to academic experts whose interpretations of Soviet statements influenced U.S. policy. The classical case is Soviet leader Khrushchev's supposed statement, "we will bury you," while the meaning of his Russian was actually "we'll be there at your burial" in the sense of "we'll outlive you." A simple statement of conviction, not a declaration of war. But since I had a great deal more to do with radio than with academe in subsequent years, my satisfaction lies in their recognition that the level of scholarship at which I conducted my broadcasts merited academic publication. That happened repeatedly over the next twenty-five years, including the incorporation of one radio script into a very widely used volume of readings for Western Civilization courses in 1991.

Nineteen sixty-five brought a request for an article that involved a little drama. Twenty years earlier my brother-in-law, just out of the army, had brought to the house a fellow World War II veteran, Samuel Hendel. Sam, recently discharged, was planning his career and sought my advice: how to become a Soviet-affairs specialist. He already had two bachelor's degrees, one in law and one in government, and wanted to continue in those disciplines. I told him to go for a doctorate under John Hazard at Columbia, who had been associated with the American Russian Institute when I worked there.

Hendel did so and became a professor at CUNY. In those very dark early '50s my daughter and his found themselves classmates in junior high and became friends. Yet her father never communicated with me in any way. Too risky. He went on to head Graduate Slavic Studies at CCNY and became chairman of the national academic freedom committee of the American Civil Liberties Union.

After twenty years of silence, I received a letter from him in 1965 stating that he and another professor were doing a book for Knopf on half a century of the Soviet regime. They had gotten a list of distinguished contributors. Would I write for them too? The proposal had a special twist. The articles on individual internal aspects of Soviet society were each to be written by a single authority. But those on foreign policy and on overall evaluation of the society were each to be done by two people, chosen for holding opposing views in these most controversial areas. I was asked to write on society as a whole, opposite Bertram D. Wolfe, who had published, in 1948, *Three Who Made a Revolution*, about Lenin, Stalin, and Trotsky. This was *the* cold war classic, reprinted endlessly. Few American college students who took a European history course or even a government course during the next forty years did not find that book on their reading lists.

Although Wolfe's path had crossed mine before his book appeared, we met in person for the first time at an academic conference at Stanford in 1969, and were introduced by a conservative mutual acquaintance. Wolfe, of my parents' generation, barged right in: "You know, I read for Dial Press the manuscript of your *Guide to the Soviet Union* in 1945." I did know. During World War II, Wolfe, who had previously been a Communist of high international rank, was convinced that the USSR would fall apart under Hitler's attack. For that reason, he had a hard time making a living during that period. The United States and the Soviet Union were allies, and our government didn't want defeatist views publicized. One of the things he did to earn a living was read manuscripts for publishers. He certainly had the qualifications to read mine. His interest in Russia dated from the year I was born, he had lived in Moscow for two years working for the Communist International, and he had met Stalin, Trotsky, and everybody else.

Wolfe continued: "I'm something of a literary lawyer. I showed them how they could get out of the contract and not print it." There was no humor in his voice. Chutzpah? Maybe he invented it. But he was aware that we were enemies over matters we both regarded as critical to the destinies of the world. My book was published despite him, and made my reputation.

So in 1945 I was at the top of the heap, as United Press Russian Expert, lecturer under contract to the country's top management, and author. He was at the bottom. Five years later the situation was more than reversed. With the Korean War, he became Director of the State Department's Ideological Advisory Staff, which he established and headed for four years—the very worst of the McCarthy period. I, of course, was called before the witch-hunters twice in those years and scrambled to live as furniture merchant, translator, and antibiotics copywriter. But when, in 1965, Hendel put the two of us on a par as contributors to that book, Wolfe, for all his standing, did not decline to accept me as opponent. He knew that, to the student generation then seething, he was simply someone whose book they had to read for class, while I, through HUAC and FSM, had caught the interest of many of the most capable of them. My article opposite his in the Hendel and Braham book was subsequently reprinted in a political science reader.

Wolfe died in 1977 when his bathrobe caught fire. When I heard this, I couldn't help thinking of the napalming of Korean civilians, which his propaganda excused.

In 1966 Tanya accompanied me to the USSR—her first visit. Much more a believer than I, she had been more deeply disillusioned by the revelations about the Stalin era. She developed a bitterness toward the American Communist Party that I did not share. I simply thought it was useless, but had no problem with cooperating with members when we were on a parallel course. As a practical matter, so did she, because some fellow-members of Women for Peace, with which she remains involved, were Communists. Because of the difference between her parents and mine over whether children should be taught Jewish culture, she was more deeply concerned with matters Jewish. As a woman, she was naturally a good deal more sceptical than I about Soviet claims to have solved aspects of the problems of gender inequality. But for both of us, fairness is very important.

When we got to the Soviet Union for a very extensive trip in its European republics, including nine days on a Volga steamer, she went to work on those two problems. (She can make herself understood quite well in Russian.) Wondering whether women really wanted to hold jobs—this was the year of the rebirth of feminism in the U.S. —she was impressed by the answer Soviet women repeatedly gave her: "how can you sit home and look at the four walls all day?" Nobody said: "We can't live on my husband's pay alone." (This attitude, documented in my book of 1975, *Soviet Women,* persists unchanged in post-Communist Russia, according to British scholars Sarah Ashwin and Elain Bowers, writing in *Post-Soviet Women,* a 1997 Cambridge University Press book edited by Mary Buckley.) Low as the Soviet level of living was by Western standards, it was vastly higher than before. And from Jews, she got the feeling that economic opportunity was more important than ethnic culture for many. A mahogany craftsman: "I've got six suits. How many does your husband have?" The young director of Kiev's major Park of Culture and Recreation: "As you can see, no one has stood in *my* way." The fact is that, at present writing, eight years after the collapse of Soviet society and thirty-five since the intensive Zionist campaign to get Jews to leave that country began [openly and directly financed by the U.S. Congress,] three hundred thousand still remain there.

On that 1966 visit I made actuality tapes of ad lib, person-in-the-street interviews, something that no one had done before. A nineteen-year-old fishing in the Moscow River and awaiting induction into the army was willing to fight us in Vietnam: "One must help the weak, right?" (The same attitude was expressed by men of that age thirty-three years later when the U.S. bombed Yugoslavia.) A female Azerbaijani woman vacationing in Moscow was so angry about Voice of America treatment of the USSR that she felt like ripping her radio from the wall. A youthful mother appealed to me, as a father, that our countries never fight.

The Vietnam War had now become a very real thing. Drop-outs undertook acts of very wild courage. One young woman sat on the tracks in lotus position waiting to be run over by a troop train passing through Berkeley, but was snatched away at the last second by a city detective.

I sought to work with the university faculty, and was pleased when a large turnout of professors—a couple of hundred—accepted my proposal to launch a nationwide petition for a million signatures requesting the end of bombing of Vietnam. At the other extreme, young people editing *The Movement,* the Bay Area monthly of the Student Nonviolent Coordinating Committee (SNCC), invited me to join its editorial board. Ours was the one area in the country where this movement of Black activists would still accept broad white participation. The editorial board was too white, however, although I was again very proud to be called upon by people my children's age. I sought to get them to understand that their objectives were reachable only if they got the support of labor, and urged them to get industrial jobs. Some did, and at least one became and remained a militant union officer. Another is a steel worker presently nearing retirement.

Nineteen sixty-seven saw war, again, between Israel, Egypt, and Syria. It resulted in Israel's greatest conquests and expansion. I have always favored Israel's existence, because of the failure of the Western powers to save Europe's Jews from holocaust when that was still possible. Jews had to have a place in which they could safeguard their own existence. I believe, however, that world peace depends upon barring any acquisition of land by force. Make an exception for one nation, and one cannot deny it to any. As most countries exist in whole or in part on lands taken from other peoples at some previous time, I apply the no-expansion rule as a practical matter to anything occurring after post-World-War II boundaries were established. Israel's attitude, however, can be capsuled by a paraphrase of the notorious Dred Scott Decision of the U.S. Supreme Court before our Civil War: "Arabs have no rights that Israel is bound to respect." When I spoke at a rally in UC's Sproul Plaza in 1996, protesting the Israeli shelling of Lebanese refugees in a UN camp, Prof. Laura Nader of the Anthropology Department informed me of a calculation by another UN entity that, from the time Israeli-Arab hostilities began in 1948, there were a thousand Arab dead for every Israeli killed, including military and civilians on both sides in both formal and guerrilla warfare.

It happens that the daughter of the Jenckses of "Salt of the Earth," described earlier, was scheduled to marry an Egyptian in Berkeley within days after the end of the brief war of 1967. We were invited. So were many Egyptian students. They knew me from university-related events, the Vietnam movement, and radio. They were utterly distraught by the loss of the Sinai, which is Egypt proper, and clustered round during the wedding: "Mr. Mandel, what should we do?" I replied: "Organize guerrilla warfare." Actually, it had already begun on a small scale, but the news had been successfully suppressed, and I was unaware of it. To me as a Jew, it is particularly outrageous and shameful that the people from which I spring, who had so suffered from disregard of its ethnic existence and even the right to individual physical survival, should have denied the rights of the Palestinians to a land of their own. I am proud that when the Berkeley student Arabs overcame their despair and also their sheer fear as foreigners, with revocable visas in a country officially on Israel's side, and organized a public protest shortly afterward for the first time, I was the one Jew they invited to speak.

In 1968 son Dave, twenty-two, was drafted. He was a total pacifist and had joined the anti-draft project of the American Friends Service Committee highschool organization years earlier, before he was old enough to be called and before U.S. ground forces were sent to Vietnam. When he was drafted, Dave and his girlfriend handcuffed themselves together and reported to the induction center. He said, "Where I go, she goes. She's my lady friend."

In the processing of his appeal for conscientious objector status, an FBI man came to the house. In the McCarthy years I had refused flatly to talk to the FBI. This time I felt I had no choice. Inasmuch as I always assumed they knew more about me than I can remember about myself (I found later that some of their information on me was wildly and amateurishly inaccurate), I explained Dave's position by contrasting it to my own. His request for CO status was denied.

In those years, when I said that I could understand his being drafted only as a reprisal against me for their inability either to jail or silence me in the preceding twenty years, I sometimes detected a lifting of eyebrows. Now that the vindictiveness of the FBI and, more important, the fact that it has always had a domestic and foreign policy of its own has been publicly documented, I no longer encounter that reaction. Dave thinks he was denied because he was not a member of any organized religion in which thou-shalt-not-kill is an absolute. That was the officially-stated reason. Yet the following year, when son Bob was one of the Oakland Seven tried for their demonstrations seeking to shut down the Oakland Induction Center of the U.S. Army, the prosecutor tried to convince the jury that Bob should be convicted because his father was such a bad man. That prosecutor is currently a federal judge in Oakland, with a lifetime appointment.

Dave was indicted for violating the draft, and went to Canada. When Dave had left home four years earlier to lead the complete hippie life, crashing in Berkeley basements and garages, we told him that we were perfectly willing to support him if he wished to go on with his studies at the university (he had dropped out as a freshman), or to hunt seriously for any kind of employment. If he wished to be a hippie we would respect his choice but he would have to support himself. Of course he would always be able to have dinner and/or spend a night at home.

He lived for a while in Toronto and worked as road man for small-time rock bands. His job was to make sure they got up on time, got stoned on time, got equipment set up on time, and got to gigs on time. Afterward he moved to Vancouver, which made it easy for us to visit him. Variously a singer-guitarist, competent maker of crafted leather goods, and hash-slinger, he also had a fine green thumb, and for several years was a union landscape gardener.

His first marriage was to an Anglo-Canadian. Their wedding in 1974 was out of Bertolt Brecht. At twenty-seven, he had been into the total hippie lifestyle for nine years. Now he had found the young woman with whom he foresaw spending his life, and she wanted the symbolism that went with it. She was a non-practising Baptist, and he an atheist Jew. They agreed on a Unitarian minister, whose thick glasses and full beard delighted Dave because they answered his image of a rabbi. The clergyman wore a stunning Arab burnoose given him by a couple he had previously married. The church was handsome, simple-modern, with impressive abstract decoration. Dave, a bit of a bantam rooster in appearance—short, cocky, touch of a swagger, slender then, erect—found himself a fine tuxedo jacket, had trousers made to go with it, and wore a ruffled shirt.

If the guests at that wedding and the characters in Brecht's "Threepenny Opera" were not quite interchangeable, they certainly would have understood each other. The best man was a boy on welfare who got up in the morning with a can of beer or a bottle in his hand and put one down alongside his bed when he went to sleep at night. In his 20s, his face and body showed no effects of alcohol as yet. There was an immense, hawk-nosed fisherman, Dave's other best friend. Lumberjacks, film-makers, people into music, craftsmen, gardeners, drug dealers were also present. One husky boy with four or five front teeth knocked out and, as I saw the next morning at Dave's, an ugly unhealed sore on his arm from a contaminated needle, had the filthiest mouth I have ever encountered. He was irrepressible, smiling and drunk at all times, with an endless repertoire of dirty and usually funny jokes—ethnic, scatological, whatever—but told entirely without malice. Most of this emerged at the dinner after the service, and particularly at Dave's the next day.

Everyone's eyes were on the visiting Mandels from the States. Dave adores his mother, liked to brag about his father, delighted in his tiny, peppy granddad, then in his 80th year. We had driven up, together with my father's companion of the time, a woman of seventy who had been a folk dance teacher. She still danced well enough for me, an utter snob when it comes to choosing dance partners, to enjoy dancing with her immensely. I was more than a dozen years her junior, and then still very trim, not looking much different than in 1972 when Dave saw me for the first time in a semi-mod, semi-hippie ensemble, and said, "Hey man! From the rear you look like a French-Canadian lumberjack of 30 in for a week-end on the town." I glowed of course. I was fifty-seven.

At the wedding we broke them up when the music began. My father wore the very proper suits you would expect of a retired engineer who was also the son of a tailor, but was utterly unpretentious. Knowing he can't dance, he moved around the dance floor arms akimbo in the manner and style of "Fiddler on the Roof." His companion wore a truly stunning thrift-shop gown and craft jewelry in excellent taste. My wife is simply everybody's mother. It's written all over her face, and when others are happy, she's happy. Virtually all of the crowd, Dave told us, came from broken homes. The notion of a family, all three generations of it, driving a thousand miles to the wedding of one of their own, and turning out to be regular people despite being intellectuals and Jews, put his friends in a mood of protective warmth toward us. It was lovely, also sad. I was reminded of the day at the induction center when Dave was drafted, and we were all there handing out a leaflet in his support. Some poor drafted kid on his way to the bus that would take him the first mile to Vietnam took a leaflet from my father, who had said, "I'm his grandfather." The draftee glanced at it and murmured, "I wish I had a family to back me up like that."

Nineteen sixty-nine was a flashback, a climax, and an end. One day an old friend from New York, when he was briefly a pitcher for the Dodgers—and also a law school graduate who never practiced—phoned up. Sam Nahem had for many years been a worker at the immense Standard Oil refinery downhill in Richmond five miles from us, and was one of the leaders of its union local. He is Syrian Jewish. He and another friend, Tony Russo, Italian, from the classical steel-industry mills in Pennsylvania and Ohio, were now working at the same plant, were getting ready for the first strike ever at Standard Oil. Sam said, "Bill, we want you down at the picket line at 5 a.m. tomorrow when we go out."

I had not worked in a factory for nearly thirty years, and was by now as typical an intellectual as one can find, but not in appearance. My clothing did not identify me as a desk person. Here were two workingmen, like myself past fifty, taking on one of the most powerful corporations in the world in what was essentially a company town. These men were totally aware of the tensions in strike situations, the need for instant decisions, the fact that most of the workers they were leading were young, entirely inexperienced with strikes, possibly hot-headed, and that the police would of course be on the company's side. Yet they felt that I was the kind of person who would be able to relate to workers, workers a generation younger than me, and that I could be counted on in such a situation. I was thrilled to tears.

I showed up, walked over to the picket-site in the pre-dawn darkness, and those thirty years rolled back as though they had never been. I was simply at home. I was aware of this, and amazed at my own reaction. It was like my experience on the picket line at Girdler Steel in Cleveland in 1936, when strikers were killed at other plants owned by that firm. The stupendous plant extending to infinity. A really big mill or refinery cannot be appreciated from a moving vehicle. You have to stand down there, feeling utterly dwarfed. An oil refinery, particularly, is surreal, because instead of buildings there are vast chemical retorts—towers, snaking pipes, tanks, wild patterns of dim lights—and endless empty roads.

Cops came and were nasty, but had no orders to be violent. Some young strikers hollered at them, and at least one talked about doing things that would have been provocative. I found myself totally calm, talking to them in language that did not mark me off as intellectual, cooling things, explaining what should be done and what not, and why. That was all there was to it. Nothing happened. Later during the strike Berkeley activists showed up on the picket line. Once Barbara Garson came, with her new infant strapped to her back. Barbara was then famous for her slashing satirical play on President Lyndon Johnson, "MacBird." I went over and told her she was crazy, and to get the baby out of there. A strike picket line in heavy industry can become a confrontation at any time. The company may desire a provocation to discredit the union, the cops may receive orders to break the picket line physically, anything. What was she going to prove with her baby there? A child of ten can learn something from such an experience, if that's what a parent wants. But an infant can only be injured. The strike was settled.

But 1969 in Berkeley was heavier than most strikes. One hundred and ten people were shot in one day by police and sheriff's deputies. Of the victims, one was killed outright, one blinded for life. This is recorded in the '60s-in-Berkeley mural at the Telegraph Avenue corner near where the murder occurred. Intelligently, the muralists, who rendered everything else of that decade in color, did the killing in black-and-white, exactly copying a published photograph, so they could not be accused of exaggeration.

The murder was committed during the one-sided "battle" of People's Park. A half-square-block had been cleared of homes that had been rental housing for students. Hippies, street people, and students had planted sod, trees, bushes, flowers, and vegetables, making a park by volunteer labor. By 1969 the University of California was despised as a symbol of the System. The university administration wanted to construct anything on this spot to drive the decade's rebels from their base near campus. When the university tried to rip up "People's Park," as its builders had dubbed it, the youth resisted bulldozers physically, but totally without weapons or even picket sticks: just by hands and bodies placed against them. The Alameda County sheriff's department and the Oakland police moved into Berkeley to aid local cops, and simply opened fire. The massacre—what else does one call gunfire striking that many people, including numerous individuals simply walking around the many square blocks south of campus?—had the effect one would expect: utter intimidation.

Late that night, our son Bob phoned on behalf of his group of radicals of assorted views. The assault had forced to set aside their differences. H said they had decided that the mood of intimidation had to be broken, and asked if Tanya and I would participate in an illegal demonstration midday the next day. It was illegal because Gov. Ronald Reagan had proclaimed a "state of emergency"—martial law—and the city was occupied for two weeks by the National Guard, armed to the teeth.

Tanya and I felt that civil liberties had to be restored, and that the only way to do it was to practice them. So we showed up the next day at the little open triangle where Shattuck Avenue divides, in the heart of Berkeley, one block from the university. I deliberately wore my utter-respectability uniform: a charcoal-gray suit which I'd bought for my medical advertising job seventeen years earlier, white shirt, somber tie. It was the same suit I'd worn the night the Rosenbergs were executed, when I led that illegal mourning parade through the Lower East Side of New York. I'd also worn it at all three of my witch-hunt hearings.

The Guard was ordered to disperse us. Tanya was a couple of blocks away, handing leaflets to Guardsmen and seeking to explain the issue to them. But where I stood, a platoon advanced on us with bayonetted rifles. From the grim and totally certain looks on their faces, it is quite clear the murder of students by the National Guard at Kent State, Ohio, and Jackson State, Mississipi, the following year would have happened in Berkeley if such had been their orders. Relatives and friends of mine have been wounded and killed in wars, sunk on ships, beaten to pulp by police, but for me it was one of the more dangerous moments of my life.

I was the only person of mature years in a crowd of youth. Some of the young women were quite literally offering flowers to the Guardsmen as gestures of peace. Nothing could have been more futile. I yelled to the crowd: "Don't turn your backs. Don't run. Face them. Back up slowly." The bayonets were no more than a couple of feet from our chests. But we did not break. After a while, I turned around and walked away at a normal pace. The Guard had done its job of dispersing an unauthorized gathering, but we had held our demonstration.

Once again, luck was on my side. Just a couple of blocks away, the Guard and deputies rounded up six hundred people, including a post-man on his route and Robert Scheer, later prominent *Los AngelesTimes* newsman and author. Both in Berkeley and later, when hauled out to Santa Rita, Alameda's grim county jail, formerly an Army camp, the arrested people were treated exactly like prisoners of war: spread-eagled on the ground in hot sun, without water, for hours. They were kicked if they moved. Bettina Aptheker, who I had worked with in the FSM, was raped. She speaks of that publicly in her classes.

The following day, the U.C. Berkeley professors decided to conduct a procession of silent mourning for James Rector, the man killed in the mass shooting. He, the blinded man, and my close acquaintance Tom Luddy, today an established movie producer and then manager of a the-ater, had been watching the events from its roof. The Alameda sheriff's deputies simply fired at them. No charges of any kind were leveled against Tom and the blind survivor. Nor were they taken into custoday. The university faculty planned to walk across campus, with students permitted to follow in their wake, and parade silently through city streets. No placards, no slogans, no shouting.

I was a faculty member in the Sociology Department that year. I wanted to go on teaching, both as a symbol of the smashing of the black-list, and also because I would be able to present, to whoever chose to reg-ister, a civilized view of the USSR. In the hope of staying out of trouble that would kill chances of re-appointment, I put myself at the very rear of the faculty contingent of several hundred. When the procession reached the edge of campus, it was blocked by the Armed Forces. There was a battalion of National Guardsmen with bayonetted rifles, armored weapons carriers, machine-guns on the roofs of buildings. The profes-sors up front found that sweet reason got nowhere, and the whole thing dissolved simply into a crowd of people. The students swallowed us up and silence was broken. Extremely hostile shouting and screaming began, led by people who would later become the violent Weathermen faction. They were former activists in a strike at New York's Columbia University who had gravitated to Berkeley— where the action was.

The professors had no experience with this kind of situation. They were useless to control what I sensed was potentially the worst situation yet of that crazy week. I hunted for recognized student leaders but couldn't find any.

The wild ones had climbed on top of a car in the large semi-circular driveway that is the campus entrance on Oxford Street, and were haranguing the crowd with inflammatory rhetoric. I indicated that I wished to speak, and did so. Under the circumstances a calm voice would simply have been ignored. It would not have been heard, either: we had no public address system. So I deliberately used a most unacademic tone of voice. Police tried to shove through the tightly-packed crowd several times to get at me. I responded by shouting that I was a Berkeley taxpayer, had not been arrested in thirty-five years, and then only for selling a pamphlet against a fascist radio priest, that if I were arrested I would sue the Berkeley authorities for a sum so large the taxpayers would drive them out of office because of the bill they would have to foot, and that I was the kind of witness a jury would believe. The police stopped short. I closed by calling for withdrawal of the "Alameda sheriff's murderers...identification and prosecution of the killer," and by saying: "It is obvious that *the* People's Park has got to be reopened as James Rector Park."

I thought I had succeeded in quieting the situation, but unfortunately the next speaker was the elected head of student government, who made the mistake of calling for the crowd to march in protest to the home of the chancellor, on campus. Whereupon we were tear-gassed, massively and continuously.

I walked out, headed for Sproul Plaza to leave campus at Telegraph Avenue, and found another crowd running pell-mell toward me, away from a very low-flying helicopter that was spewing tear-gas. (Again and again in 1969, the odor of tear-gas overwhelmed Berkeley's normal aroma of flowers and trees in bloom. Many children in their school classrooms in different parts of town were affected by it.) Either that or the following night, a mass meeting was called at Berkeley High School auditorium to decide on next steps. Again I felt that a voice of reason would not be heard unless it were couched in a theatrical framework. So I hung round my neck the framed 5"x7" drawing of the clenched-fist symbol by my former student at San Jose State, and went to the meeting.

A future underground Weatherman made the lunatic proposal that we march on the City Hall a block away. The place was surrounded by National Guardsmen with their ubiquitous bayonetted rifles. A march would have been suicide in the most literal sense. The mood of madness was enhanced when nationally-known activist Tom Hayden, at this writing a state senator of long seniority, came on stage with a rifle and hollered: "Power comes from the barrel of a gun!" A line straight out of Mao Tse-tung. When I got the floor, I said that we needed to appeal to the citizens of the state outside Berkeley, and could do so, because the students came from all over California and elsewhere in the nation and world.

The Berkeley High School authorities demanded we leave their building. The discussion continued at a hall in Oakland. That neighboring city was not under martial law. In Oakland, both my son Bob and I were among those who spoke. We took sharply differing positions. I called again for appealing to the people of the state, he for something more militant, but not of the Weatherman variety. I was under a severe handicap: the front rows were full of bandaged people who had been peppered with buckshot on the day of the mass shooting. They tried to hoot me down. I don't yield, but neither did I carry the day.

By this time the general public had recovered from its shock, undoubtedly helped by our various refusals to give into martial law. Some committee called for a protest parade in Berkeley on May 30, and it was the biggest by far in the city's history. The lowest attendance estimate was twenty-five thousand people. Sympathizers came from all over the Bay area. I walked along with my friends the Hirsches from San Jose. As we passed a knot of Berkeley cops, one of them said to the others: "There goes Mandel." But in my forty years in Berkeley, my only personal encounter with police power, other than traffic tickets, was when the chief stopped my car to hand me the HUAC subpoena in 1960.

That one semester when I was permitted to teach as a U.C. faculty member also witnessed a strike called by students of color in support of a teaching appointment for Eldridge Cleaver, author of *Soul on Ice,* and of demands that ethnic studies be established. I would not cross a picket line to teach, but neither did I wish to provide an excuse for not renewing my appointment. So I met my class off campus, in the YMCA. That accomplished nothing. I was not re-appointed. Perhaps that was contributed to by an action of my own, a risk I took consciously because I wanted the public to think about the matter at issue. I had agreed to be interviewed by a Sacramento TV station in connection with my appointment, which had also been reported in the *San Francisco Chronicle.* The academic world doesn't like its curriculum and appointment decisions to be placed in the context of the need for information for practical purposes, such as maintaining world peace.

1969 was one of several years in my life that it exhausts me just to think back on. I did my translating job, my unpaid weekly broadcasts, participated in the People's Park events, the Standard Oil strike, taught both at UC Berkeley and at San Jose State. There the official Associated Students funded me, at pro-rated full-professor salary for one course. I taught in the Philosophy Department, whose chairman announced that students would receive normal credit. The university president then announced that they would not, whereupon the chairman told friends he would resign from the university. I told him the place needed people like him, so he resolved the matter in his own conscience by taking a sabbatical in protest.

The one thing I didn't find time to do that year was to attend the eleven-week trial of my son Bob and the other Oakland Seven defendants who had organized the week-long roving demonstrations of some ten thousand people that sought to shut down the U.S. Army Induction Center. Those demonstrations were the climax of five years of protests against the Vietnam War, which, in our area, began with the mass attempt to stop troop trains. Our Bob had quit an accelerated-Ph.D.-track program in History that U.C. had put him on, to become a full-time anti-war activist. Both my father, then seventy-five, and my wife, took part in the demonstrations outside the induction center. I was out of town on a lecture tour organized through the contacts established by my public activism.

The defendants, their friends, associates, and families, including myself, were convinced that the Seven would be convicted. Only two people thought differently: defense attorney Charles Garry and my father. Garry, now deceased, was a marvel at the questioning of prospective jurors, which is always helped by advance scouting of the persons summoned to be on the panel from which the jury is selected. My father retained a faith in the fairness of Americans that I thought was misplaced given the evidence.

When the jury was selected, I thought the defendants were finished. There was a retired U.S. Marines colonel, who at one time had been second-in-command of the Corps. In his time the Marines were very sparing with the rank of general. The jury foreperson was a young man with top security clearance at Lawrence Livermore Laboratory, where nuclear bombs are designed and laboratory-tested. But Garry called a stunning array of character witnesses to present the defendants' motivations. Garry actually convinced that jury that assembling massive crowds to block access to the induction center was a legitimate exercise of freedom of speech under the First Amendment! Hatred for that war certainly ran deep.

Tanya attended every day, for the nearly three months of the trial. She phoned home one day to say that a verdict was expected. I dropped my translation and drove down. The scene when I entered the courtroom was conceivable only in the Berkeley area and only during the '60s. As the jury was out, court was not in session. Bob's then wife was playing with another defendant's young child on the judge's bench. Lawyer Garry, bald, in suit and tie, was standing on his head in a corner doing yoga. The defendants, with years of their lives in the balance, were outside, playing touch football, barefoot, in the park across from the courthouse.

When the jury announced "not guilty," and the judge declared court dismissed, I rose, unplanned, to thank them and the judge, saying that perhaps it would restore the defendants' faith in the workability of American justice. It did not: they all became radical opponents of capitalism. Downstairs we waited quite a while for the jurors to emerge to thank them personally. Meanwhile the defendants sent someone shopping. Judge Phillips, a small man, eventually came out of the elevator, carrying a huge jig-saw puzzle. He came up to me, a pleased smile on his face, and said, "Look what the kids gave me!" He had been very much against them in his early rulings, but Garry's brilliant line of defense, and the clergy and professors called as character witnesses changed his mind.

Nineteen sixty-nine was also the year when our daughter Phyllis, with feminist Laura X and some others I don't recall, had organized the first International Women's Day demonstration to be held in the United States since not long after her birth thirty years earlier. I take pride in having celebrated that day on my broadcasts each week of March 8th from the time I began my radio program, eight years before the new feminism appeared in 1966. Most certainly in the Bay Area, and among late 1960s feminists who spent time in this region, the knowledge that such a holiday exists came from me. Since the Cold War began, it had been known only to Marxist socialists.

The year was also specially meaningful to me because of a very particular acknowledgment line in someone else's book. That was a time when the new generation of Black militants was very stand-offish with respect to whites. I suppose I could have been satisfied with the positive quotation of my first book in 1948 by the Liberian and co-founder of African nationalism, George Padmore, and the positive reference to me by the other co-founder, Dr. W.E.B. Du Bois, in his book of 1952. But the 1969 generation was at the end of a decade in which Blacks had taken their destinies into their own hands, accepted white support, but rejected white opinion—much less analysis of African-American history. I was very surprised when a young scholar, Robert L. Allen, whom I knew only by name as a writer for the weekly *National Guardian,* phoned to ask if I would read the manuscript of his book, *Black Awakening in Capitalist America: An Analytic History*, which Doubleday published in 1969. Allen was, and is again at present writing, editor of *The Black Scholar* and author of additional books, well-received.

I went over his manuscript. When the book appeared, he wrote: "I am especially indebted to Bill Mandel, who evaluated and criticized the manuscript with professorial diligence, offering many valuable insights in the process." I would take great satisfaction from that alone. But inasmuch as the book sold fifty thousand copies, has been assigned in Black studies courses uninterruptedly, and was re-issued more than twenty years later, I feel that I have played some small role in informing the whole first generation of college-educated African Americans subsequent to the '60s. Of more than a score of books whose authors have credited me for manuscript criticism or other aid, none has been more generous. In 1997 Allen, by now a member of the board of the Bay Area Book Council, had me invited to chair the panel on books about the '60s and '70s at the San Francisco Book Festival, the region's major annual literary happening.

Nineteen sixty-nine closed with an event in which commitment to the advancement of Blacks required physical courage. Early in December, Chicago police conducted a pre-dawn raid, murdering Black Panther leader Fred Hampton in his bed. This was part of a nationwide pattern in which that organization's leadership was physically decimated. Later that month word came down that a similar raid would occur upon the founding Black Panther organization, that of Oakland, although its headquarters was actually a couple of blocks over the line in Berkeley. Whites were needed to stand guard around the building, in the hope that police would not shoot randomly into them. Tanya and I went down, and found about 50 other whites there. Most were 1960s youth, but there were others in their 50s, chiefly old-time radicals like ourselves. By the close of the '60s, would-be world-changers were divided into at least half-a-dozen warring sects: Maoist, Trotskyist of several varieties, pro-Soviet Communist. After the fashion of religious sectarians from time immemorial, they would not even speak to each other, and there had been a couple of violent incidents. In the aftermath of the People's Park military occupation and mass shooting, willingness to be at Panther headquarters that night was a litmus test of sincerity. I felt a surge of warmth to all present. They were the core who meant what they said.

CHAPTER 22

After the Storm

The 1970s began with old friends invited over for New Year's Day. Eric Fenster, of our children's generation, had first looked us up because we had been friends of his father, an auto-worker and Young Communist League activist with us in Cleveland in the mid-1930s. Eric graduated from UC Berkeley, and was a cancer researcher as graduate student at Stanford. His political genes eventually took over, and he later devoted his life to helping workers with full-time jobs to get higher education via TV courses and weekend colleges conducted by universities. This invention of his is now an established feature at many institutions.

Allan Isaksen, tall and rangy, who also joined us on New Year's, was a carpenter when we met him in 1947 in Berkeley during my tenure at Stanford. He shared our views and was attracted to me because, "imagine, this guy had actually lived in the Soviet Union." He had been a very good friend, and was a fellow-witness before the House Un-American Activities Committee in 1960. When he went back to college a decade later, he wrote a term paper on that event which is the best description anywhere of the political environment in which it occurred. Subsequently Allan became a successful builder, but still detested capitalism.

Glenna Bryant was also present. She, too, is someone we knew from that earlier stay in Berkeley. Glenna was born to be a linguist. She had learned more than a dozen languages, but grew up when women were taught to make a proper marriage and raise kids. That was particularly true of her upper-class American Jewish background, in which the rule was to assimilate and for gods sake not stand out in any ethnic way. She had lived by that, but during the early feminist revival got a divorce, became a teacher of Russian, found she had organizing abilities, and later enjoyed a career as college administrator.

Ethel and Stephen Dunn, too, shared our company that day. Both had cerebral palsy. Ethel is Jewish, Stephen New England Yankee. Ethel was one of the early M.A.-equivalent graduates of Columbia University's Russian Institute. Stephen's Ph.D. thesis was about the Jews of Italy, though he was not Jewish. In the humanities and literature, he was the most erudite individual I have ever met. She is practical, a demanding house-manager, a determined scholar. He was the classical academic, immensely thorough, cautious, gentlemanly, but utterly firm in upholding conclusions once arrived at, without ever being untactful. He was the more severely disabled. Both lived in wheelchairs, but enunciation required great effort for him, and his hands had limited function. The prejudice against "cripples" lost America a great professor in barring him from teaching.

Although I know of upwards of a hundred books by others in which I appear, the fact that Steve quoted me as authority on Marxism in his highly-specialized *Fall and Rise of the Asiatic Mode of Production* gives me special satisfaction because of his very high standards. Once, when I had assailed him for something in a letter, Steve wrote me that his feeling for me is as close to love as it can be toward any male.

Feminist Laura X rounded out our New Year's celebration. She should not write an autobiography, because she wanders even more than I do. But a book should most certainly be written about her, in addition to those in which she has already found mention. Laura comes from very wealthy WASP and German parentage. She decided in the '60s that Malcolm X was right in not using his slave name, and believed that women were fundamentally no less subject than slaves to their fathers and husbands. So she borrowed his X and helped found the field of women's history by collecting every possible news clipping, leaflet, and periodical of the feminism that revived in 1966. Untrained as a librarian, she filed them in accordance with her own weird and wonderful notions, i.e., "Women as Bitches." Astounded by what she discovered of the role of women in 19th-century Russian revolutionary organizations, she started SPAZM, the Sophia Perovskaya and Andrei Zhelyabov Memorial *Co-educational* (her emphasis) Society for People's Freedom through Women's Liberation. The seventeen people she invited as founding members included three Mandels—Tanya, Phyllis, and myself. One-quarter were males. That was early 1969.

This 1970 New Year's gathering became focused on discussion of an article in a socialist magazine, *Monthly Review,* which said women are a reserve labor force in *all* industrial societies. I held that was not true in the USSR, where their role, particularly in the professions, continued to rise after the shortage of men caused by World War II had ended. I am in total agreement with Laura's unwillingness to be satisfied with anything less than total equality for women, the remoteness of which is indicated by their virtual absence from the top positions in the Fortune 500 companies today—nearly 30 years after that New Year's Day. Nor has a woman yet been nominated for the presidency by either major party.

The argument became heated, and a grand time was had by all. Steve put in that if the choice were between ruling women and being ruled by them, he preferred the former, but he did not want that choice. I compared Laura's wing of feminism to the Black Muslims ("all whites are devils") by contrast to the then significant Black Panthers, who regarded white working people as potential allies. (In retrospect, it would be more fair to say that Laura believes that while in human society men have generally exploited and ruled women, there are exceptions.) This led to a discussion of just what kind of social entity African-Americans constitute. Steve saw them as did the pre-Communist American Socialist Party, which thought of Blacks *only* as poor members of the working class. It did not understand the issue of race.

The party ended, as all New Year's do. The next day I sent a proposal for a book on Soviet ecology to a publisher. It got nowhere, but the following year I had a roaring debate in print over the environmental situation in the USSR with a Harvard professor, Marshall Goldman. He had written a standard everything-over-there-is-bad book on that subject. The leading magazine in the field, Prof. Barry Commoner's *Environment,* asked me to review that book. I did, Goldman responded in the following issue, and we both had at it in yet a third. The essence of my argument was that it was just not possible for the environmental situation there to be as bad as here, for three reasons. First, the total output of industry was substantially lower than in the U.S. Second, the number of automotive vehicles was a tiny fraction of ours. Third, as the Soviet Union was nearly three times as large as our country, there were vastly larger volumes of air and water to absorb emissions. His response ignored those factors.

I differed with Commoner, too, because he placed equal value on ecological wisdom and economic and social justice. I wrote him: "Has a non-fertilizer ecology ever been famine-free? What is your explanation of the rapidly lengthening life-span of women during the very period that labor-saving materials and machinery (using energy, of course) have become available on a mass scale? It is under 'natural' technologies that women's lives are shorter than...or equal to men's... and men's are shorter than under modern technologies."

That week I also shipped off to the State Historical Society of Wisconsin the first copied batch of the William Mandel Papers. They had asked me for them the previous year for their Social Action Collection. I replied that I wasn't dead yet, so they provided a copier which Tanya spent many months feeding stuff into. At the end, she said, "You never stopped trying." I needed that. The Chief Archivist of that very highly respected repository, F. Gerald Ham, wrote me in 1974: "Several of my staff have commented about the richness of the research material you have sent....Hell, Bill, if Nixon could ripoff nearly $600 grand for his crap, think of what we might have gotten for the Mandel Papers."

I rejoiced in the regard shown by people whose side I had taken in difficult situations. Moslems in the United States have never had it easy. The American oil barons do not want Near Eastern countries to control their own petroleum. Sympathy for the Jews in Israel was a handy cover for this. Three years earlier, I had publicly opposed Israeli seizure of parts of Jordan, Syria, and Egypt in the face of manic behavior on the past of American Jews, who regarded me as a traitor to my origins. Thirty years would pass before Israelis admitted massacring hundreds of Arab civilian prisoners in that war. So I was very pleased when a Pakistani student requested that I moderate a forum on war crimes at U.C. Berkeley's International House.

My activities in the '60s—and the fact that that wide-open time made it possible for me to go far beyond the Soviet Union in answering questions on the air—led to invitations to participate in all sorts of things. I was asked to go to the Central Valley in support of Cesar Chavez' organizing of farm workers. I did go, but only to bring food and participate for a day in the pilgrimage.

I engaged in affirmative action for Blacks as opportunity offered. Melvin Whitfield had been high school leader of the Mississippi Freedom Democratic Party. That party was founded when the white leadership of the regular Democratic Party sought to bar African-Americans. Upon graduation, Whitfield came to the San Francisco area. He lived with friends, including us, and I was of some assistance in getting him into college. At that time there were no Blacks in the field of Sovietology. I encouraged him to take courses that would enable him to take over my radio broadcasts in the future. He preferred public health, a field with which he could be of help in Africa, and acquired a couple of M.A. degrees and a doctorate. When he left the Bay Area, African-American friends organized a farewell party, well attended, on the Peninsula. The tributes were very warm. Apparently he had been of much service to the local Black community. Twenty years later, we stayed with him and his wife during a week's vacation in Washington, D.C. It struck me that this was only the third Black home I had ever been housed in, in a lifetime. How utterly segregated American society still remains.

When Chicano self-awareness arose, I helped as I could. The first Chicano group ever to visit the USSR consulted me before departure. This was in 1971, after my brief stint on the Berkeley faculty. I was now conducting a less formal student-sponsored course, and members of that group spoke there on their observations after they returned from the Soviet Union. My standing with minority students was such that in

1969 Dr. Paul Wong of the university's Ethnic Studies Program invited me to fill the post of Visiting Scholar. Although the university had other plans, to me that expression of confidence in an old white male was a high honor.

Many scholars asked for my assistance until President Nixon's policy of detente was ended by his ouster via the Watergate scandal. A biochemistry professor wrote on the assumption that I knew about research in his field in the USSR. I did not, but was able to guide him to sources. Leo Kanowitz, then teaching at the Law School of the University of New Mexico, asked me to review the manuscript of his second book before publication. Howard Sherman, in the Economics Dept. at UC Riverside (I had played some role in nominating him for the job) did likewise, with respect to his *Radical Economics.* Noel Mottershead, Chair of Philosophy at Chico State in California's Central Valley, proposed it set up a pilot study program in the USSR with me heading it. It didn't eventuate.

I often made single appearances in courses taught by others. Bob Cirese had been a student of mine at Berkeley. One day he had me speak to his Labor Economics class at Golden Gate University, consisting overwhelmingly of workingclass people. The majority stayed an extra hour after class, several stayed yet a third hour. One said he would be two hours late for work. I came home and cried. I do love to teach.

A friend, Virginia Franklin, who won a variety of high school teaching honors and also taught in junior college, would invite me to speak to her classes year after year. Virginia was a big, hearty blonde, classical golden girl of the West, with a huge laugh and a tremendous zest for life. She told of nude swimming with her students in white-bread agricultural Northern California during the hippy '60s. African-American militants in Oakland during the Black Panther period paid her the enormous compliment of listing her as the only white teacher they wanted to continue at Merritt College. She required her students to read my books in her courses on government, to provide them with a notion of a system other than her own. She would send me their term papers. To one of her students at Merritt I wrote:

"No one before you has ever written 23 pages on that book [my *Russia Re-examined*]. I am now writing another book. You cannot imagine what an effort that involves. But the thought that, eight years after it is published, someone may be affected by it as strongly as you were...is, without any sentimentality or phoniness, the kind of thing that gives one the strength to go on."

Much later, Virginia's son, Warren, became a major figure in the special effects end of movie making. In 1970, when he was in his mid-20s, I wrote to back his acceptance as a member of an American youth delegation to travel in the USSR: "I believe it more important that Warren go than any other individual. American youth today are *not* responding on a mass scale to political militants of any persuasion whatever. Film is *the* medium that turns youth on. So when one has a young person who is already an established film-maker and who is even interested in going to the USSR, one should grab the chance to have him go." When Virginia died in 1992, Warren asked me to preside over the memorial, held at San Rafael High School. I was shocked and depressed that only one of the students to whom she had given so very much showed up.

Oakland Tech is a ghetto high school. After an appearance there, an African-American teacher wrote me: "You really were the highlight of the session for the students, and they relied more on your presentation for material for their work than on any other source. The final product of the group was a very amusing tape made by the students doing 'on-the-spot' interviews with Russians and Americans. It was not only entertaining but reflected a great deal of thought. It also showed that they learned very much from your talk."

I was always happiest teaching people who wanted to learn for its own sake, with no discipline enforced by the need to make grades, be marked present, or to justify parental support while studying. When Angela Davis was on trial for murder in 1971 for allegedly having provided weapons used in an attempted prison break, I conducted a class for the Bay Area United Committee to Free Angela Davis. The subject was "How to Read the Newspaper," and its purpose was to equip activists, mostly young and Black, to do their own research in the most easily available sources and use their findings in their activities. I wrote a leaflet to attract students, reading in part:

"Last week we started out rapping about: the Attica Prison Massacre and why the Establishment press would print the coroner's report that the hostages had been *shot* after they had printed the lie that the prisoners had cut the throats of the hostages. Does this mean that the Establishment press is fair and impartial? We ended up talking about: who owns the newspapers? Who advertises in them? Who goes to prison in the U.S. and why? And what is the capitalist interest in the working class?"

A year after my appearance in Cirese's class at Golden Gate University I received a letter from him: "As an elected faculty representative to the Selection Committee for the Dean of the [new] School of Public Affairs...I would like to invite you to submit your resume for consideration by the Committee." I did, only because he was a friend. I knew I wouldn't get the job.

At the end of January, 1970, Prof. Ralph Anspach of San Francisco State phoned to ask if I would teach the Soviet economy in its

Economics Dept. I said yes. Within a week of his first call, Anspach told me that, although all three interviewers had approved me, and the whole Economics Department had voted for me fifteen to three, someone turned to an "outside" person—the president?— who vetoed it. The faculty didn't want to fight, I was told frankly, because of exhaustion from its long strike the previous year. Anspach said, "Guess who will be teaching it? Howard Sherman," who was on sabbatical from his regular professorship. Howard had gotten his first knowledge of the Soviet Union from me when he was in college. I phoned him and said taking the job would be scabbing. He agreed not to take it.

Within two weeks of the San Francisco State fiasco a Prof. Braunstein at the California College of Arts and Crafts phoned. Like Anspach, he was a stranger to me. Did I want to head their Sociology Department then being established? I spoke to the dean of Humanities there and told her I was not interested in general sociology teaching. I suggested Ethel or Stephen Dunn or the African-American scholar Robert Allen. None of them got it.

Another African-American, Prof. Bill Brown, geographer then teaching at UC Santa Cruz, volunteered efforts to get me an appointment there to teach Soviet geography, a field which I was one of the first to publish. But this was a year after the offers described above, and academe was that much farther removed in time from the student pressures of the Vietnam era and the civil rights movement. He ran into a blank wall, as did Cirese at Golden Gate with his nomination of me for a deanship.

Quite naturally, the roughest treatment came from the discipline specifically created to wage the Cold War, Sovietology. The *New York Times* wrote, April 3, 1965: "The second advance" in academic study of the USSR, "was said to have been correlated with the deterioration of American-Soviet relations, the intensification of the cold war, and the Soviet technological achievements beginning with the sputnik." Many sovietologists directly served the CIA. That was publicly admitted when interest in that field began to decline and it began to plead for money, pointing to that service as one reason to meet its needs. In *Slavic Review*, journal of the discipline, Prof. John Kautsky wrote, in March 1967: "The government's need for information about Communist countries and the mobility of personnel in this field between government agencies and universities have bent some of the scholarly work in it in the direction of intelligence work."

The American Association for the Advancement of Slavic Studies was dominated by sovietologists. In 1972 I delivered a paper, "Urban Ethnic Minorities in the Soviet Union," at its convention in Dallas. The paper was the first ever to point out that Russians were the largest such minority in cities of non-Russian republics. This fact became quite a political issue in the '90s when the newly-independent republics began to force Russians out of all kinds of jobs. More copies of that paper were picked up by attendees than of any other. The general session was offered a resolution condemning the Soviet Union for its treatment of dissidents. I offered a friendly amendment, adding a paragraph, in exactly the same language, of criticism for American academe's treatment of dissenters like Angela Davis and myself.

The chairman, Prof. Holland Hunter, was courteous. It would have been difficult for him not to be. His mother had told me twenty-five years earlier that he had chosen the field of Soviet transport economics as his specialty after reading my very first published paper, "Soviet Transport Today and Tomorrow," which appeared in 1941. At least one distinguished figure at the convention, John Hazard of Columbia University, this country's first expert on Soviet law, had greeted me earlier with: "Bill, it's been forty years!" Actually, it had been nearly thirty since we'd seen each other, but certainly a long time. However, neither he nor any other academic present I had known said a word when the hall responded to my amendment with shouts of: "Shut up!" "Sit down!" These were the same people who had been outraged when concerned students found they had to express themselves vociferously in the '60s to get a hearing for the notion that they, too, were part of the university, not only the professors and administrations.

Nonetheless, my academic recognition did continue for another couple of years, until the intensifying of the Cold War that followed Nixon's ouster in 1974. After that juncture, association with someone of my views became entirely unsafe. That year I participated by invitation of Ohio State professor ZumBrunnen in a panel on Ecology in Banff. Also in 1974, Prof. George Breslauer, political scientist at UC Berkeley, who had audited my course when he arrived there in 1969, sent me an article of his for comment, as he had done on previous occasions. After I read it, we had an hour-long conversation by phone. He said, "I'm getting an entire education." I confess that I would write such things down immediately afterward because I had to be able to look at them to convince myself when things got bad that I really belonged in there against an army of opponents.

In that peak year of recognition, 1974, before the long night of my enforced silence in academe closed in, an article of mine on Soviet ecology brought requests for reprints from universities in Sweden, Mexico, Australia, Czechoslovakia, Israel, and a government department in India. No World-Wide Web yet existed to help scholars to discover such articles. In this country requests came in from university departments of geography, rural sociology, political science, psychiatry, and a jet propulsion lab. A single collection of essays, *Soviet Politics & Society in the 1970s*, carried seven citations of my article, "Soviet Women and Their Self-Image."

I took the initiative in advancing equality for women in the ways available. The simplest was by lecturing. The opening of one presentation at San Jose State University in late 1970 makes my position clear:

"Has any woman here ever been denied a job because of her sex? Changed her educational plans because she knew the field she wished to enter is closed to women? Anyone here have a pre-school child you would like to place in a nursery but can't? Have you previously postponed returning to school because of that? 3rd World people ditto all above? Has anyone here *never* paid for medical or dental care? Has anyone dropped out of school for want of money to live on?"

In 1969 I proposed, on the air, that KPFA carry feminist programming, which did not exist anywhere. The then manager's outraged reaction that I urged this in public was identical to that which finally got my program cancelled a quarter-century later. In both cases I followed this course of action because I had learned that it was the *only* way to move top management off the dime.

In 1970, I submitted a proposal for a panel on women in the Soviet Union at the next Far Western Slavic Conference, which I had been asked to organize. I invited a majority of female panelists. That was utterly unprecedented. Ethel Dunn was among them. I managed to get the male chair replaced by Prof. Olga Matich of the University of Southern California. From a letter to her: "As I wrote professors Dmytryshyn and Berton [both male], to have a panel on women in which both the organizer and the chairman are male is to reinforce the very situation that women today are protesting against. That applies to me as well. In letters to women here and in the USSR, requesting information for use in my paper, I stated: 'This paper should preferably be done by a woman....I'm doing it because it has to be done, and there is no woman in Soviet studies out here who wishes to undertake it." The paper I presented, "Soviet Women and Their Self-Image," was well enough received that I was allowed to go on for forty minutes, more than twice the time allotted. I later offered it for publication first to *Slavic Review* and then to the weekly *National Guardian.* Neither would publish it, quite typical in my experience: I was too Left for one and too Right for the other. Later it was published in the *American Behavioral Scientist* and a separate book reprint of that issue. One-third of all the instructors of women's courses nationwide in 1971 ordered copies of an offprint from me. An association of women in the field of Slavic Studies came into being some twenty years later. In 1971, the team of young female faculty preparing the first women's studies course at Stanford had invited me to meet with them beforehand to discuss it and then called upon me for a lecture.

The upsurge of the women's movement won the proclamation of 1975 as International Women's Year. I was the only male among eighteen invited panelists at the huge conference marking it, organized by the United Nations Association of San Francisco. The rebirth of feminism and, to a lesser degree, the rise of academic interest in it, made me feel it was time for me to write a book. In 1975, Doubleday published my *Soviet Women,* contracted for during the period of detente. Getting *Soviet Women* out wasn't easy. I wrote my Moscow friend in that field, Yuri Riurikov, about the editors assigned to it:

"In typically American fashion, she has no sense of history whatever, and no understanding of the point of view of workingclass women....Both editors are influenced, sincerely and stupidly, by the current American belief that China is the new Utopia. As you see, things do not go as fast in America as you might think."

Reviews in periodicals of the young and still radical women's movement were overwhelmingly favorable, but the review I treasure most was that by my boss of thirty-five years earlier, Jessica Smith, who had been a suffragist when I was born and had written the first book on Soviet women half a century before mine. She wrote: "One could not ask for greater sensitivity to women." And a lifetime of activist participation in the struggle for equality for African-Americans brought its reward in this regard. When Angela Davis wrote a fine review for *The Sun Reporter*, San Francisco's Black weekly, its publisher, Dr. Carlton Goodlett, an acquaintance of mine since the 1940s, suggested that I send a copy to the Executive Director of the National Negro Publishing Association. "You are to say that Dr. Goodlett has asked you to send the review and that he requests publication in all of the NNPA papers." All 140 Black papers across the country did carry the review.

I had many Soviet friends, including one woman, Raisa Tselikman, who was totally fearless in private conversation. But when entrusting her thoughts to the mail, which might be opened, she, in long, frequent, meaningful and beautifully-written letters, would offer ideas on the situation in her country only by commenting on my descriptions of what was happening here. Rarely, she would use Aesopian language, such as referring to her own surname as "unbecoming" in referring to the fact that it was unmistakeably Jewish. But she insisted on using it, not that of her husband, the fine sociologist of literature Vladimir Kantorovich. Only with respect to life in earlier Soviet times would she spell things out. She was an unreconstructed early 1930s feminist, totally contemptuous of young Soviet women of the '70s who wanted wedding gowns and rings, in which they were supported by officialdom.

Because of that, I took particular satisfaction in a letter from her after we had known each other for five years, both through two visits of mine to Moscow and regular correspondence:

"Since you are such a defender of women, I am proud of you, only you! I never congratulate anybody about anything, and have trained all my friends and acquaintances not to offer [meaningless] congratulations, but I congratulate you on the occasion of [International] Women's Day!!! Live for the joy of us all, write about us, hail the easing of our lives, fight for our rights: that is a worthy and good cause! Because we have so many enemies! Even my son said to me in a demonstrative fashion: 'the world is rolling down hill—the [British] Conservatives have chosen a woman as their leader' [Thatcher]. And that was so that I would hear that and know my place."

That son, who emigrated well before the Soviet system collapsed, and was a great admirer of the United States, reflected in that remark the psychology of the very leaders whose overall ideology he rejected. My position was precisely the opposite on both counts. As early as 1954, two years before Khrushchev's denunciation of Stalin compelled Communists everywhere to understand that the Soviet Union was less than perfect, I wrote in a book proposal to editor Angus Cameron of Little, Brown & Co.: "When there is as yet no single woman among the top leaders of the Soviet Union, [this] must be regarded as [a] reflection of the persistence of male supremacy, while the fundamental value of socialism in striking at the roots of sex inequality is illustrated by the mass attainment by women of posts and professional occupations still largely closed to them beyond the socialist world." That was a dozen years before the new feminism appeared in 1966.

Knowing that I had the approval of so staunch a feminist, and of *every* Soviet woman who has read my book, I did not hesitate to confront the lioness herself, Gloria Steinem. I had met her through Laura X. When *Soviet Women* appeared, I wrote Steinem: "Obviously, I'm waiting to see how *Ms.* will review it....In your first 31 numbers you carried exactly one article on women in Russia, and it dealt with the persecution of Jewish women...seeking to combat emigration restrictions....I personally am aware of four letters to the editor...one from me (the only male) saying that there is a great deal else that Soviet women are doing...that *Ms.* readers should also know about. None of the letters were published."

When no review appeared in the next three months, I wrote the magazine's book editor, with a copy to Steinem at her home address. *Ms.* had published a full-length review of a book critical of the status of women in Czechoslovakia, while the book editor had informed me that mine would get a "capsule" review. I wrote: "A paragraph to the Soviet Union and columns to Czechoslovakia? And Gloria assures me that 'there is no strong anti-Soviet feeling here' [at *Ms.*]. With your only article on the USSR thus far on the mistreatment of dissenters? How naive can one get?" I guess that worked. In any case, *Ms.* published a review long enough to catch a reader's eye, and considerably more favorable than unfavorable.

The worsening atmosphere in American-Soviet relations intimidated liberals as usual. I wrote Carey McWilliams, renowned editor of *The Nation*:: "The failure of *The Nation* to review my book (even negatively) simply reinforced my conviction that your attitude toward the USSR is identical with that I describe on the part of most of the Stanford conferees in my enclosed comments. But then I think, Carey McWilliams did once write *Factories in the Field*. So maybe one can get through to him."

He replied: "It is an odd experience to be charged with anti-Soviet attitudes in view of the long years in which *The Nation* has been charged with exactly the contrary stance." None so blind as those who will not see. It is a matter of record that in my fifty-nine years of publication in the broadest possible range of periodicals popular and scholarly, I have never appeared in *The Nation* except by the courtesy of the letters editor. Friends think of me as a knight *sans peur et sans reproche* against the far Right and the doctrinaire Left. In fact, liberals accepting the taboos of the very structure they inveigh against have been a significant obstacle over a lifetime, in publishing, politics, and academe.

Prof. Gail Lapidus, then at U.C. and subsequently at Stanford, utilized a totally unique set of Soviet research papers I had brought back from the Soviet Union and loaned to her when she wrote her book, *Women in Soviet Society*. She made no acknowledgment in her book, which followed the chapter organization of mine. Clearly, her book was written as an attack on mine, without specifying that. Her book, appearing in 1978, served the purposes of the Cold War, whatever her personal attitude toward that may have been, as mine served detente.

She wrote Professor Roberta Manning, teaching at an Eastern university, asking why the latter was using my book as required reading in her course instead of her's. Manning sent me a xerox of Lapidus' letter, but denied me permission to cite this in a letter for publication. I wanted to charge that it was a violation of ethics. She explained she might have to work with Lapidus in the future. Just a year earlier, Lapidus had asked me to review a paper of her's—not the first time— and we had had lunch to discuss it after I wrote her my comments. It was titled "Modernization Theory," and my letter to her, January 13, 1974, offers a concise summation of my disagreement with Establishment scholars:

"Soviet per capita industrial output is below ANY European country but Portugal, Albania, Bulgaria (I'm not sure about Spain without checking). If one disregards that continuing relative underdevelopment, it becomes impossible to understand the level of persistence of peasant attitudes in the self-image of each sex, and that opens the way to unhistorical put-downs of what has been accomplished there re women, and what as-yet-insufficient change in the material base has not created the foundation for."

In mid-1975 I had been a discussant at the conference at Stanford on "Women in Russia". Laura X subsequently told me that at a post-mortem meeting of the conference organizers, Prof. Martin Malia of UC Berkeley, a bitter cold warrior, said that I should have been barred. In fact, as one of the three founders of the sub-discipline, study of Soviet women, it was preposterous that I had not been invited as one of the seventeen presenters. Malia's expression from the standpoint of the dominant political trend of the day may explain why the discussion paper I had read was omitted from the book, edited by Lapidus and another scholar, of materials from that conference. But there were four citations of me in other contributions. Malia was a man I had invited onto my TV show fifteen years earlier in full knowledge that he was at the opposite political pole. Thanks to the emergence of the Internet, it was possible for me to take him on in 1999 by posting in a chat room of Russian-affairs specialists. He had appeared on the Op-Ed page of the *New York Times,* a publication that has been closed to me since it ran my letter against McCarthyism in 1951 and then discovered that I was a radical. Technology can be a force for democracy.

I had no illusions about why things like the Stanford incident happened. Four years earlier, I applied for a Phi Beta Kappa Bicentennial Fellowship. The theme set by that body was "Man Thinking in America." I proposed to study "Continuing Crippling Effects of Anti-Communism on Man Thinking in America." I stated my proposal thus:

"My thesis is that, in the past half-century, anti-communism has become almost irretrievably interwoven with American culture in the broad anthropological sense and with academic culture in particular, and that its effects continue to be devastating. With that as my working hypothesis, I will make an across-the-board examination of social thought, cultural expression, and the behavior of the intellectual community, to determine the degree and identify the evidence of anti-communism as the factor that has stultified our progress and crippled our sense of responsibility and morality as well. If I fail to prove it, I believe my career is a singular demonstration of the intellectual honesty required to admit that. In any case, others would no doubt be able to find the holes in my argument. If my hypothesis is correct, I will have made a contribution to the purpose for which these Fellowships are granted."

That I did not get the fellowship came as no surprise.

I did several lecture tours to publicize *Soviet Women.* In Kansas City an extremely intelligent female reporter interviewed me, and asked the most profound questions, even about whether I thought real women's liberation is possible under capitalism. She wrote the story absolutely straight. As a consequence, the roof fell in, not from her bosses but in letters from readers.

The lesson from my treatment by academe was clear. No one known beforehand to be an opponent of the Cold War and to strike at its foundation by demonstrating the falsity of the Evil Empire paradigm was to be allowed to teach, once the organized student demand for free access to information had died down.

While I fought with outrage the denigration of real social progress in the USSR, I was equally outspoken in assailing its shortcomings to audiences of its defenders. Perhaps more so, because I was then still of the belief that if it would only straighten up and fly right it could become a beacon for humankind. I would make such statements particularly in the presence of Soviets, with the hope that this message would be taken home. A delegation of perhaps twenty of them attended when I addressed the Los Angeles Association for Cultural Relations USA-USSR in 1971. I criticized the then head of the Soviet Union, Brezhnev, for "crude economic determinism," in still using steel production as measure of economic advancement in the age of plastics. This was before computers and entry into the information age became the proper criterion.

I was brutal in the realm of foreign policy: "The Soviet leadership obviously believed that its position would be stronger as a consequence of the invasion of Czechoslovakia. The notion that the hostility of 14 million people who previously were grateful to and respectful of Moscow is more significant than forced adherence to Moscow's version of socialism by the power of half a million troops is apparently beyond the understanding of today's Soviet leaders."

Neither was I kind to my own government: "Similarities in the behavior of the leaderships in Washington and Moscow extend into other areas as well. Both show a significant, and politically important, disregard for world public opinion. The attitude of the entire world toward the U.S. intervention in Vietnam, for years now, has been too well known to require discussion."

Few in the audience were pleased. Someone present informed me that the organizers railed at me in a post-mortem meeting. It was five years before that organization invited me again. When they did so, it was because even they could not fail to realize, from listening to my broadcasts carried in Los Angeles by KPFK, that my fundamental purpose was to combat the Cold War, and in the course of so doing to call attention to many things in the USSR I looked upon favorably.

A few months earlier I had a head-to-head clash with a man I regard as a tragic figure. Aaron Vergelis was a Soviet Jewish poet, veteran of World War II, and editor of the Yiddish-language cultural magazine, *Sovetish Haimland,* which he had politicked tirelessly to get permission to launch in Moscow. Even the editor of our State Department's *Problems of Communism*, himself a Jewish scholar, thought very highly of the literary qualities of Vergelis' magazine. But Vergelis functioned in an atmosphere of fear that Soviet people traveling abroad might by "turned" by the CIA, Zionists acting in Israel's interests, or whoever. On a visit here by a quasi-official delegation, including other literary people, he got up at a reception to read one of his poems. Claiming that he had forgotten to bring it in its original tongue, he read his translation of it into Russian. That was unquestionably so the KGB informers in the delegation would not think he might be offering unapproved thoughts.

By not reciting in Yiddish, he provided ammunition for the tireless anti-Soviet campaign in the American Jewish community. I was present and said wrathfully, first in Russian then English, that there was no such thing as a poet in Russia who did not know his own work by heart. Upon returning home, he attacked me in his magazine, ascribing words to me that I simply had not uttered, as everyone present knew. The attack was translated into most of the languages of the world when published in *Sputnik,* the Soviet equivalent of *Reader's Digest.* It was sent me by Nils Wessells, then a junior researcher at the conservative Foreign Policy Research Institute in Philadelphia. He wrote: "Anyone who has detractors in the Soviet press *and* at the Foreign Policy Research Institute must be doing something right."

That latter organization published a magazine, *Orbis.* Despite my knowledge of its bias, I submitted an article on foreign policy, which was rejected. I was getting tired of that sort of reception, so I wrote its editor: "If you read the chapters on foreign policy in my *A Guide to the Soviet Union,* Dial Press, 1946... you will find that it offers a rational explanation of what Moscow is doing today in world affairs, despite the fact that there is much on which I was either naive or just plain wrong. I challenge you to point to a volume of that date representing the views that came to govern American foreign policy which paints an at-all recognizable picture of reality today, a quarter century later."

KPFA remained the center of my activities. Its long-time program director, Elsa Knight Thompson, was fired in 1964, and a strike ensued. The basic issue was that which simmered for another thirty years, when first I and then dozens of other programmers were ousted. In the earlier struggle, it was claimed by the national board of Pacifica Foundation, which held the broadcasting license, that the station "needs professionalism." I presented a paper, "Headline Mentality, Utopianism, Ethnocentrism," to the first board meeting after the strike, pointing out that the board's own report said KPFA produced the best original programming of the then three stations in the chain. But I, too, was critical: "Its public-affairs broadcasting and news coverage show very strong signs of the headline mentality and ethnocentrism that are characteristic of this country, and the Utopianism that typifies those who would like a better world in a hurry."

One way of relaxing from all these stresses was by annual day drives to the almonds and to later-blooming cherries, redbud, poppies, apples. Tanya and I generally did not have the radio on. We would keep totally silent for an hour or more at a time and just look at the scenery. Then we'd stop for long strolls under the blooms, hug and kiss. The silence was not a planned therapy. We certainly knew each other well enough, and would speak only when something had to be said, or a thought arose. That's still true.

Tanya was the organizer of our cultural recreation. Fortunately, our tastes are quite similar. We both love opera, but have been able to afford it only since becoming old enough to qualify for senior rush prices. For years we would dash across the Bay Bridge for the one-hour free lunchtime Brown Bag Opera at which the finest young prospects could be heard. We had been raised on records of the very best voices, and in my case live performances of the Bolshoi heard regularly during my year in Moscow, 1931-2. Consequently, we had little patience with any organized company but the San Francisco Opera and Donald Pippin's Pocket Opera.

With the Music Department at the University of California in Berkeley, and the Conservatory in San Francisco plus the Music Department at San Francisco State University, there was never a lack of exciting instrumental music. Living only fifteen minutes' drive from UC Berkeley, there were years when we would attend the free noontime concerts at Hertz Hall quite regularly. Low-cost venues such as the Capp Street neighborhood music center in San Francisco's Mission District, the Old First Church, and free offerings at San Francisco State and the Conservatory made frequent concert-going possible.

Music, or at least music in modern societies, seems to be the only art delicately responsive to the sequence of generations, and even to decades and single years. The monotonous thump of rock and roll is primitive to our ears, as is its notion that the louder and shriller the better. But our children respond to it, as do virtually all of their generation.

Jazz is cross-generational. In the mid-'90s, a branch of the Oakland Public Library in one of that city's poorer neighborhoods became the official site of its African-American history museum. That branch library launched a cultural program that reminded me, although on a very much more modest scale, of the magnificent Houses of Culture that used to exist in every city of the Soviet Union. Today the library has, among many other things, free Sunday afternoon jazz jam sessions. We attend regularly. The participants range from early teens to late sixties, Black and white, female and male, straight and gay: the American mix at its very best.

Black friends have said to me, literally: "you got rhythm," when I sang their music. But the social meaning that characterized the songs of our generation is either gone or watered down or obscure in current songs. The exception is rap, but neither of us hears well enough any longer to make out the words.

As a should-have-been professional dancer, I have always seen all the dance I can. Tanya shares my fondness for this art. We are humanists with complete confidence in the capacity of any people whatever to develop its folk expressions to high art.We saw that phenomenon launched in dance by the Soviets' Moiseyev company, generously funded there specifically due to belief in that capacity. So we take great pleasure in seeing nationalities emerge on the dance scene. Most recently, in San Francisco, the Filipinos have done so.

Tanya is immoderately modest in everything, and in recent years insists that her memory is failing. Certainly not where theater is concerned. In our forty years in Berkeley, plays have been a bigger part of our cultural life than either music or dance, museum or gallery visits. It is only to theater that we buy full-season tickets. I enjoy the plays and acting immensely when they are good, but usually forget them immediately afterward. When they are poorly produced, or offensive to my taste, I am quite capable of getting up and walking out. It is very rare for Tanya not to stay to the end. Yet our final evaluations are generally, not always, quite similar. But she remembers plays, actors, productions. I do only rarely.

I was endowed with gifts in music and dance of which I made almost no use. The successful histrionics of my witch-hunt committee hearing testimonies suggest I might have done well in theater. By contrast, I have never had the slightest desire to paint or sculpt. Yet painting, drawing, and sculpture can move me more than any other cultural expression. We began visiting Europe west of the Soviet Union in 1974, and have been to Italy four times. On each occasion Florence and Rome were in the itinerary. Invariably I stood in front of Michelangelo's David and wept. His Moses in Rome is visible only by artificial light which is turned on by dropping a coin in a timer. I come with loaded pockets and remain there until I have spent them all. Ravenna is to me the extraordinary dark-blue star-studded mosaic vault of Galla Placidia's tiny 5th-century church. It also means standing in front of Dante's tomb and reading aloud his long passages carved in stone for the sheer pleasure of the sound. I understand little more than half his Italian.

My interest in art brought friendship with the oddest couple. Hela Norman grew up a member of the Hitlerjugend—Hitler Youth—as a matter of course, being a teenager in Nazi Germany. Irving Norman, her husband, was a Lithuanian-born Jewish-American and lifelong Communist. He had fought in the Abraham Lincoln Brigade in Spain. At the end of World War II she was eighteen, and emigrated to the U.S. shortly after. They met on a city bus in San Francisco. He was attracted to her, pursued her, married her. He was nearly twice her age.

Norman was a painter, and won his first recognition only in the early 1970s, late in his career. Hela was trained as a gardener in Germany. In California's Half Moon Bay she was so successful that her employers sent her with an entire four-engine cargo plane full of plants she had selected for the new palace of the Queen of Iran. Hela put in a remarkable garden around the house they had expanded from the isolated country shack which was all they could afford at marriage. She had an amazing ability to attract wild small birds, which would eat out of her hand.

I had met the Normans through Irving's interest in my broadcasts. He defended me against all attacks, bought my books, and contributed financially to KPFA. But we had sharp differences. We first visited their home in 1972, the year before he won that first recognition. I was appalled by his paintings, and said so. His composition, draftsmanship, use of color (although they too reflected pessimism) were superb. His style was unquestionably original. He called himself a social surrealist. His theme was always human beings, en masse. When it was a gathering of the rulers of the nation, his obvious hatred for them was understandable in light of his politics. But often it included, or even consisted of, numbers of common people. The blank, expressionless uniformity of their faces seemed to me utterly at odds with what I regarded as the humanism of Marxist socialism. I told him that. He was an admirer of Joseph Stalin to the end. Ironically, Stalin would at the very least have had him barred from the Artists' Union for his paintings, because they lacked all optimism. It is clear, in retrospect, that his work shared the dictator's view that people would have to be dragged kicking and screaming into the projected heaven on earth.

Before that first meeting, Norman apparently thought me a cold logician. The next day, he wrote me a letter: "Sorry to have disturbed you at some points. You are quite a combination, a man of science, and of deep—very deep—feelings. I consider it very beautiful." We remained friends. Since Irving's death, we drop in to see Hela every time we spend a day enjoying the redwoods and shore south of San Francisco. Her devotion to his memory and work is heroic. In 1996 she persuaded the de Young Museum in San Francisco to put on a major show of his work, with eighteen large paintings. There, I asked her how the creator of such angry art could have been so pleasant and stable an individual. She replied that he worked out his rage in his paintings. Reviews, lauding his painterly mastery, put his work down for its negative view of society. I wonder whether he won't gain popularity for that very fact.

Film is *the* art of the 20th century. My internationalist upbringing and convictions were a blessing in attracting me to European films as soon as they made an appearance here. Subsequent to World War II, I saw the films of India, Africa, Japan, and other lands as they mastered that art.

The producer Tom Luddy started as manager of a repertory house in Berkeley and went on to found the excellent Pacific Film Archive at the University of California, before making films on his own. We have known each other since the activism of the '60s. On a few occasions, I was asked to give introductory talks when new Soviet films were shown at the Archive. I was amazed that professors teaching about the USSR at the University almost never attended. I myself never failed to learn something from those films, whatever their quality as cinema. Through them I got to know some interesting Soviet figures. One was the legendary war documentarist Roman Karmen. His physical courage was limitless. He had covered every revolution and war from China's Long March to Chile's Allende and Castro's Cuba, and was the head of the Soviet teams filming the Russian front in World War II. He himself was up where the fighting was fiercest.

He told me a great story. During the Cuba Missile Crisis in the last week of October 1962, he was on his way to the Caspian Sea to work on a film on the offshore oil fields. The phone rang, and the voice at the other end was that of Anastas Mikoyan, the number two man in the Khrushchev administration. "What are you doing, Roman?" "I'm packing to go to the Caspian." "How would you like to come with me to Cuba?" "When?" "Tonight." "But I don't even have time to get my equipment." "It's already on the plane."

They flew to Cuba, where it was the job of Armenian Mikoyan, by far the smoothest member of the Politburo, to break to Castro the news of the withdrawal-of-missiles deal. Karmen filmed. Then they flew on to Washington, where Mikoyan was to dot the i's and cross the t's to render ironclad President Kennedy's promise that the U.S. would never try to repeat the CIA's Cuban-exile invasion at the Bay of Pigs and would soon withdraw nuclear missiles from Turkey.

Mikoyan was ushered into the Oval Office. After a while, someone came out and called for Karmen, who was in an ante-room full of the very top U.S. and world news and camera people. As he picked up his tripod and followed the official, the room exploded: "Who the fuck is this little shit who gets in there, and we can't?"

Real reality—not its reflection in film or whatever—requires that one understand one's place in it. I have often had to force myself morally. I don't like to be hurt physically, suffer the indignities that go with jailing, or put my life in danger. So when such risks existed, my convictions, what Europeans call civil courage, have carried me into and through them. It was only fairly late in life that that kind of response became automatic. There is a newspaper photo of a picket line at the Oakland Airport during a demonstration, organized by our son Bob, to demand that a CIA airline supporting contras in Central America be forced out of that city-owned airport. I was then about seventy. The picture shows motorcycle police hemming us in. I am closest to the cops. That was no accident, yet entirely spontaneous on my part. I was outraged by their arrogance in seeking to intimidate by using their vehicles to try to herd us. Yet before the demonstration I had thought very carefully, as always, about the possibilities of police violence and arrest.

For the twenty years of my salaried job, I would do the things that really interested me from morning to mid-afternoon, and the translations from 3:30 to 11 p.m., with a break for supper. The freshness necessary to keep that schedule was maintained by daily swims from mid-May to October in a lake five minutes drive from us, and twice-weekly climbs of the ridge behind our own the rest of the year, even more than by our cultural forays. I still do that, but don't climb as religiously.

Has anyone studied why it is that humanity is so widely agreed that one day in seven is needed for rest? I certainly need it. For each day off Tanya and I spent with the arts, probably two were given over to long drives. In earlier years I would head eastward to the high Sierra on fourteen-hour sunrise-to-late-night outings, most of which were consumed by driving. I had superb reflexes and was an outrageously fast driver. I once burned out an old six-cylinder station wagon by pushing it to ninety miles per hour on the way home from the Sierra, reaching a hundred on downgrades. With my eye on the mirror, I never got a ticket away from town. Tanya was invariably scared to death. I got no pleasure out of frightening her—or anyone else, ever—but fast driving and making it on difficult roads for many hours and fording risky streams was my way of accomplishing what others turned to drugs, alcohol, or cigarettes for. Tanya hated the virtually non-stop driving, and made me quit this practice sometime in the '70s.

The quiet loneliness of the coast north to Bodega Bay or even as far as Mendocino was also a great attraction. Southward, however, we would dash non-stop to Santa Cruz, if not to Monterey and Carmel. In recent years we rediscovered beauties closer to home. An east-west road joins coastal Highway 1 at Half Moon Bay. Immediately south of that town, blacktop Purissima Road runs inland toward the unattainable crest. It snakes up following arroyos and gullies, but finally gives up and hairpins back to the coast farther south. Precisely at that turn, giant coast redwoods, elsewhere far above the road, line it for a hundred yards. The road was built a century or more ago to log them, and a tiny parking lot occupies what must have been the loading area. It offers access to an easy trail ascending very gently a hidden canyon lined with 150-foot second-growth redwoods along a lovely stream. Until very recently, Tanya could still manage that, bad heart, accident-caused limp, tremor and all. We would walk a very slow mile and then turn back.

CHAPTER 23

Being Me

Until the USSR collapsed in 1991, the overriding consideration in my life after World War II was contributing my knowledge of that country to help prevent nuclear war between it and the United States. KPFA and two other of the stations then carrying me are controlled by Pacifica Foundation. In 1964, I asked its Board of Directors to name me Pacifica's correspondent in Moscow, unpaid of course. My employer, a New York firm, agreed to let me do my job of social science translation from Moscow as I had been doing it by mail from Berkeley. I was named correspondent in December 1965. But now the Soviets refused to accredit me, because that would unbalance the exact numerical equality of American reporters in the USSR and their's here. As part of the Cold War, the U.S. refused to accept any additional correspondents from Moscow, and the Soviet Union would not grant Washington the right to have more of them there than they could send here

I eventually lost patience and wrote the editor of the Soviet Embassy's English-language magazine: "I am sick and tired of a situation in which every goddamn cold-war professor is allowed by your government to stay in the USSR under the cultural exchange program; every filthy liar from our major media.... Lots of Communists who have no influence in the U.S. whatever...can make long visits; but a person like myself, who has influence with students, with the academic world, and a substantial radio audience and readership for my books, and who has fought the Cold War uncompromisingly from the beginning, is not accredited as a correspondent.

"I don't know what stupid bureaucrat is responsible for this, and I don't care. This is an angry letter, intentionally so. I know that you do not make the decisions in such matters. But I know very few Soviet people. You at least are in the newspaper field. You understand something about these things. You are also in the exchange journalism field. So I ask you to do whatever is necessary to get a decision on this matter—quickly."

I never was accredited by the Soviets as a correspondent, so I continued to make visits of no more than a month each. They were both helpful and misleading. Our trip in 1970 included a visit to Stalingrad, where the tide of World War II was turned. Aboard the same Volga cruise vessel was a German who had fought there, when it was destroyed as no city of modern construction has been since, anywhere. He said that he had thought it could not be rebuilt in fifty years, and here it was, bigger and better than before, in half that time. I had no way of knowing that the time of our visit was precisely when the inherently burocratic nature of the Marxist economy would make it begin to run out of steam.

That 1930s feminist, Raisa Tselikman, gave me insights into other aspects of Soviet life. She described how she spent her first half century in communal apartments in which one knew every detail of everyone else's life, and regarded that as quite normal. That was important to me, for it helped me understand that people then judged their condition by comparison to their own past, and not what they read about the outside world or the pre-revolutionary nobility. About our first encounter she wrote me: "I'm afraid that that was the first time I had seen a live American!!! And I was very pleased that you were utterly natural...and were dressed so unspectacularly that you immediately won my confidence. And besides, you praised the dinner very highly and declared that my apple cake was just like American apple pie!"

In another letter: "To read—in a foreign language—the thoughts of a person who lives so far away, in an entirely different society, but who has seen so much and given so much thought to so many things—this is the first time in my life this has happened to me, and is more interesting than a dozen books." Subsequently she not only read *Soviet Women,* but translated it orally, word for word, to her husband. A third letter retains its significance in terms of our understanding of what occurred in the Soviet era:

"Is Soviet Russian literature really so little known in the U.S.? For we love American and read it so much!....This year I've managed to read no less than 30 books in English....It is hurtful to think that Americans do not know our contemporary writers. There is no question but that a splendid literature has been written here these nearly 60 years. And it will be studied for a long time to come."

I wrote her in 1975 that a Soviet exchange professor was teaching their literature at San Francisco State University, and that only a single person had registered. "Do you know why?", I queried. "'Freedom,' American style! Our 'free' press and radio and television and damn-fool writers (I am thinking of a very prominent survivor of the Hemingway group I know personally) [Kay Boyle] have convinced the American people that there is only one significant writer in the Russian language today, and he lives in Switzerland." The reference was to Alexander

Solzhenitsyn, who had not yet moved to the United States. My omission of his name was a way of getting around Soviet lack of freedom: mail censorship. "And frankly," I continued, "I am suspicious about who that one student is. There is another, secondary reason, in my view [for the non-enrollment]. Only in the last few weeks have most Americans of student age become aware, because of articles in our press, of the fact that the FBI and CIA pry into the lives of ordinary citizens. Do you think the effect of such an 'expose' is greater freedom? For most people, it is greater fear! After all, a student wants to get a job upon graduation, right? And if his record shows that he took a course from a Red Russian Communist professor? Ai, ai, ai! Yet in your country, when our Prof. Bridgman recently taught at Moscow University, was there any lack of students wanting to hear him? Perhaps there is less fear in your country? Ah? [This] story is a measure of how effective my own life's work has been in changing American attitudes: zero."

In view of the value Russians place upon friendship, and of Raisa's very independent nature and uncompromising views, one letter left me walking on air: "We have many friends, but you have taken your place among them. Somehow, it is very good to feel that far, far away there is a good person who sometimes—more than that is not necessary—thinks of one, wishes one well, respects one and one's work."

Viktor Kantorovich, her husband, had yet another heart attack at the end of 1974. Raisa wrote us a most moving letter about him. I sent a wire in which I informed him that I was translating one of his essays for publication in the American quarterly, *Soviet Sociology*. She wrote in reply: "This gave him much satisfaction. After all, man is weak: one always wants to believe that one really is of use to someone."

That described my life exactly.

Her letter about his illness called forth a response. I addressed them both: "Raisa, when I read to my wife your words about your 'most worthy, very special, very thinking friend, the man I love,' she cried, as I had when I first read them myself. That is very, very beautiful. Vladimir, you are a very lucky man to have such a wife....I always like to write about 'serious' matters, but after all, what is really more serious than relationships among human beings?"

Upon recovery, Viktor wrote me: "You even said that literature still needs me. That is the kind of exaggeration only a friend can indulge in, but it is balsam for the soul."

Vladimir died in the late '70s. I stupidly broke relations with Raisa in the early '80s, because the gap between us in understanding each other's countries had become too wide. I was emotionally not capable of accepting the truth of her picture of what had happened to Soviet society, for it logically led to the conclusion that the system was corrupt beyond reformation, a reformation I devoutly desired.

The Kantoroviches introduced me to Yury Riurikov, his wife Rita, and their then very young child, Sveta, who also became close friends and tireless correspondents. Yury was the one Soviet writer on love, and made it possible for me, working on *Soviet Women,* to have the first-ever frank discussions with Russian women about sex since puritan folk attitudes were imposed upon the entire society in the 1930s. His best book, which exists only in Russian, is called *The Three Attractions.* He inscribed it to me, in his native tongue: "To Bill Mandel, American womanologist, from a Russian historian of amouristics and sexonautics. P.S. Better three-time-three attractions than three infections."

But the Riurikovs were very serious about helping me understand their country. For one thing, they fed me as they would feed themselves, not with the host-impoverishing luxury that is Russian tradition. He also had me meet people from whom I could learn things totally censored out of the Soviet press. His upstairs neighbor had one of those names suggesting "progress" that the early post-revolutionaries inflicted upon their helpless children: Radium Fish (!), son of the prominent Communist journalist Gennadi Fish. Radium hated the regime with a fervor I did not encounter elsewhere until people of his views began to set the country's intellectual tone during the Gorbachev period. He was an infantry veteran of the Far Northern European front in World War II, had been an Arctic seaman, and was a distinguished scholar of the Islamic peoples of the Soviet south. This was a man whose opinions deserved attention. He managed to get published, jointly with a Tajik scholar, a book on the history of the Soviet period in that remote country on the border of Afghanistan that enabled me to understand the bitter rebellion and civil war which occurred when the USSR broke up. That event in the 1990s finally forced me to accept that Soviet ethnic policy, designed to bring medieval peoples to a position of real equality with the more modern, had been forced down the throats of some of them against their desires.

On another occasion, when Riurikov invited me to dinner, a man who had been sent into Czechoslovakia with the Soviet invasion of 1968 as a propagandist was also present. He immediately realized that the Czechs didn't want the Russians there, and quit. Contrary to the Western propaganda image of instant and savage retribution for such behavior, he was simply brought back to the Central Committee of the Party in Moscow, severely lectured, and turned loose when he would not renounce his convictions.

Mail from KPFA listeners told me who was listening to the picture of the USSR my broadcasts presented. In 1970 I received a greeting card reading: "Happy New Year. Old Black Drifter." The sender had enclosed a clipping from the *Christian Science Monitor* he thought I'd find interesting. An African-American just starting in life wrote: "I am a 15-year-old high school student. I'm black and my parents are upper middle income educational administrators....I would sign this, but my parents are afraid of government reprisal. I have listened on Sunday mornings, while preparing for church, for two years over WBAI." That was long after the McCarthy era, and not sent from the deep South before Martin Luther King, but from New York City. And people wonder why I am contemptuous of those who think in absolutes about America as the land of "intellectual freedom" and the Soviet Union as representing the opposite. For that matter, when a friend died in 1998, his widow was instructed by a granddaughter not to have anything "political" said at his memorial because the young woman was afraid this might cost her her position in Los Angeles' educational system.

I made it a practice to digress from Soviet subject matter on my broadcasts when significant people I had known passed on. People asked for copies of the program I devoted to Paul Robeson when he died. Another such brought a letter from feminists: "We are grateful for your eulogy of Anna Louise Strong. I hope this morning's broadcast reached many of the younger generation who will have learned of a great American woman."

On the other hand, a Communist listener objected to my saying that the Soviet leadership had treated reformist Party chief Khrushchev as an unperson from his ouster to his death in 1971. She made some reference to the Soviet Constitution. I wrote her: "Bluntly, you're naive. The top leadership pays absolutely no attention to the Constitution, and I'm not talking only of what it says about freedom of assemblage, speech, and the press. Time after time, the Party changes laws as it wishes, and the Constitution is (or is not) amended after the fact."

Listeners began to give me presents. In 1971 a Fannie R. Williams in Los Angeles, KPFK listener, "old and disillusioned," wrote: "I am not affluent, but I'll give you my most prized possession." She was seventy-nine. She described it: "a Chinese bowl of the Kung Dynasty, about 962 A.D., bluish green with crackled veins." I wrote her: "I've put your bowl where I can look at it when I feel 'disillusioned'." Sometime later in the '70s my brother brought from New York a splendid artist's proof of a large lithograph. The artist, a member of my audience on WBAI, the Pacifica station there, sent the message that he wanted to express appreciation for the broadcasts in that way. His litho depicts a street in Palermo as he saw it when a soldier in World War II.

In the 1980s the wife of a maker of furniture that had been shown in museums phoned before Christmas to say: "Eben is making something for Bill." The Haskells and I knew each other only as listeners and broadcaster. We had visited them up in Grass Valley, once a gold-mining town, when I did an autographing session in its book store, which advertised in the KPFA program guide. I imagined perhaps a table-top reading stand, and was greatly flattered. Just before the holiday, a panel truck pulled into our driveway. Father, mother, and daughter staggered in under the weight of a loveseat of exotic South Pacific and California woods with fixed chamois and leather cushions, standing on a short, knuckle-like post supported by five slender rough-hewn branching legs of uneven size. Sounds awful, but looks magnificent because of its fine proportions and irregular but harmonious design. Its great weight is the consequence of being built around a wrought-iron skeleton totally hidden by the wood, enabling the seats cantilevered to either side of the post to be used without supports at the far end.

However, I value most a speaker the station itself gave me at the end of my third year on the air, 1960. It was part of the state-of-the-art equipment at the 1940 San Francisco World's Fair which the station had salvaged to start its operations a decade later. Twenty years old when the chief engineer built a sound box for it and hung it near my study ceiling, it still functions perfectly, well over half a century since manufacture. To me it is a reminder of a time, very long gone, when KPFA was a family, though not without its squabbles.

But no material gift meant more than some letters. A younger woman wrote from Los Angeles: "I am a working mother, with husband and 3 young, under 12 years, children. My radio listening is very rationed....I choose your program as very special and a must....I know nothing about politics but I love people....It is because I understand human conditions and want to learn about them that I listen so attentively to what you say on your programs."

Gifts went both ways. Hale Zukas is disabled by cerebral palsy to the point of having to communicate via a stylus strapped to his forehead with which he uses his computer. His voice is so distorted that only those in daily contact with him can understand him. Yet he graduated from U.C. Berkeley with a major in math and a minor in Russian, and has been organizationally effective on behalf of the disabled to the point of having been appointed to President Carter's national body on that problem. He listened to me all thirty-seven years I was on KPFA, since his teens. At one point his helper called to ask how to get a Russian-English technical dictionary. I bought it for him. He wrote me: "I appreciate—another much-abused cliche—the thought involved. Gifts such as this, made when an opportunity happens to arise, make much more sense and are more meaningful than those made as part of some ritual occasion."

In 1971, WBAI dropped me for the third time in four years. In 1967 its reason had been that, in that year's war with Arab states, which resulted in Israel's greatest expansion, I did not accept its position as automatically correct, as virtually all Jews did. So did most Americans, partly because of anti-Arab prejudice, and partly because of U.S. government policy in that area, based on controlling Middle Eastern oil supplies by using Israel as a lever. In the eyes of WBAI management, functioning in the city with the largest Jewish population in the world, my position naturally made me a Soviet spokesperson, since Moscow took the same stand. This presumed Soviet association made it unnecessary for the station to ask itself whether it was violating the principles of free speech to which it proclaimed adherence. The second time it had dropped me was when WBAI acquired a new Public Affairs director, the most politically naive in its history. Since my program most often consisted, openly and deliberately, of readings of my translations from Soviet publications, to this person I was automatically a propagandist. I responded: Does reading from official U.S. government statements, a normal aspect of the news broadcasts, make the station an agent of Washington?

On this third occasion, the station had gone ultra-New-Left in its outrage against the Vietnam War, and saw the USSR as selling out Vietnam and the R-r-revolution in general. So I wrote the program director, with copies to the station manager and the national office of Pacifica, informing them of fan mail from New York listeners in 1969: the editor of *Natural History* magazine had asked how to obtain the author's permission to publish an article by a Soviet geographer I had read on the air; the attorney for an environmental organization wanted to know how to sue the USSR for whale hunting; the editor of *Film Comment* wrote regarding a broadcast in which I mentioned a Soviet magazine interview of him; a Columbia University sociologist inquired about a broadcast I had done on differential social mobility for a paper being written by internationally-renowned scholars for UNESCO; a listener at Monmouth College, N.J., sent pages on the USSR from a 6th-grade textbook, asking my comments and that I provide a list of materials for a social studies unit on the Soviet Union.

This flow of information went both ways. A listener corrected an oversight in one of my broadcasts regarding the length of the workweek in the USSR. Another informed me of articles in Paris' leading daily, *Le Monde*, and in *France-Observateur*, contending that the average Soviet citizen was probably the world's most cultured. And there were the eternal questions: Is the USSR progressing to a true socialism?; Will it be a democracy by 1980?; and Are there slave labor camps in the USSR?

As on each previous occasion when I had been dropped from the station, listeners demanded my reinstatement. Many sent me copies of their letters. One schoolteacher wrote: "If our station means what it says about avoiding the broad-based middle to bring in *all* of the unheard voices, where else is there a William Mandel, bringing an immensely scholarly, first-hand, objective yet friendly view of contemporary Soviet life?" With the copy, he sent me a covering note: "If it was BAI's choice [no announcement had been made regarding my not being on the air—I just disappeared], I would not renew my eight-year-old subscription, for you represent that rare combination of vast first-hand knowledge and different viewpoint which the station *must treasure* to preserve its function. And I told them that in my letter."

WBAI put me back on the air for another three years. When it dropped me yet again in 1974, one of the letters it received contributed a new perspective: "Having just returned from a year's work and study in Hannover, Germany, has strengthened my appreciation of WBAI. Dropping William Mandel would be disastrous. There is nobody in America or Europe who reports in such depth and with the integrity that can only come of intelligent and dedicated research. And his contribution has not been small—the *extremes* of right and left political thinking that are otherwise foisted upon us leave no room for the hope of peace in a better world. Please keep Mandel on the air!"

Such things led to a totally new phenomenon: the publication of radio broadcasts of mine as articles in scholarly publications. I know of no previous case of that happening in the history of radio. In 1967 *California Social Science Review,* issued at Stanford, published my broadcasts analyzing the horribly biased textbook treatment of the USSR in high-school textbooks used in the state. In 1968, *Issues,* organ of the American Council for Judaism, published my broadcast, "Soviet Jewry Today." This continued into the '90s.

In 1975 I tried to convince Hill & Wang, the publishers of *Russia Reexamined,* my most successful book, that I should do another revised edition. Arthur Wang now protested that my attitude was uncritical. I compiled several pages listing quotes to the contrary from the earlier edition. Wang's change in attitude from the time of publication of the first and second editions was a reflection of the fact that the U.S. was now in the years when a sing-Johnny-one-note named Solzhenitsyn was trumpeted to the American people, and those of the entire NATO world, as at least the successor to Tolstoy and Dostoyevsky. The unending publicity given him by every U.S. government agency here and abroad, plus the mass media, led by the *New York Times* and the *New York Review of Books,* earned him $6 million in royalties. His was the official Western Truth about the USSR. This praise lasted until he was invited to address Congress (see what a cultured country we are? we invite a *writer* to speak to our law-makers!) and lectured them upon the fallacy of democracy and how it would be better if the Orthodox Church ruled. In the early post-Communist period, when anything approved by the U.S. was taken by the all-too-gullible Russians as the word of God, Solzhenitsyn's return to his native land was publicized there like the Second Coming. But he was off their front pages long before his intentionally slow journey by rail westward from Vladivostok reached Moscow. Not even Yeltsin wanted a theocracy, and the public heard nothing from the returning exile that addressed their bitter practical problems except that corruption and crime were bad.

Listener letters dealt with related concerns, but in concrete form. One wrote, in 1970: "I am trying to put together a research course in the study of art and art education and how they relate to political and social issues." I sent a thorough, lengthy response, including a bibliography, and recommended that he consult a scholar at New York University. I took the opportunity to deal with the decades-long debate over "socialist realism" versus abstract art.

"I don't think it is good for art or for anything else for the exhibition of non-representational art to be suppressed," I wrote. "I don't think any art is purely utilitarian. I think it is one of the things in human life that is a value in itself. Artists are not remembered for what *any* ruling class or party thought of them, but for whether they are good artists....I don't think Soviet artists are helping to bring about social change even *within* the objectives and program of the Communist Party. Look at contemporary Soviet posters. Truly incredibly dull. Then look at the wonderful things done in that regard in the early years of the revolution, until the Political Bureau set itself up as art critics....I am certainly not putting down what is done in the USSR to give the mass of the people a desire to look at art."

My listeners covered the spectrum of political views. A man with a German name wrote: "We simply believe that all evidence shows that the Russian people are a simple-minded and cowardly lot. The rest of the Soviet nationalities have been carrying the dead weight of the Russian garbage for 53 years. Many people are already convinced that stupidity is now genetically fixed in the Russians and Russian refusal to react to renewed [American] bombing and invasion of North Vietnam is making us feel that way too about their obvious cravenness." I disagreed. Moscow managed both to avoid world war and, by its economic and military aid, to save Vietnam from U.S. domination.

A listener to a Seattle station carrying me wrote it that he would subscribe if they took me off the air. The manager sent me a copy of his stinging response: "I gather that you listen to KRAB frequently. For this privilege you pay nothing and in fact sponge off the community whose financial support makes KRAB possible. We assume that the people who support us financially do so because they value freedom in broadcasting. They listen to the programs they like, not the ones they dislike. KRAB advocates free access to the media. If we did take programs off the air because certain listeners dislike them, we wouldn't have anything left to broadcast. Fortunately for KRAB, there are people in this community who recognize the value of freedom in broadcasting and are willing to support a station that practices it."

In addition to individuals who disagreed with me, the Establishment had not ceased trying to use my broadcasts as an excuse for silencing Pacifica. In April 1970, *Barron's Weekly* editorialized against renewal of our license: "Herman H. Kahn of New York expressed concern about a WBAI broadcast of a news report from Moscow consisting of verbatim quotations of *Pravda* and *Izvestia* concerning the assassination of Dr. King." Kahn was a grey eminence of the Cold War. But a white downtown church in Berkeley reprinted that broadcast of mine for its parishioners.

My past was always with me. Senator Javits of New York forwarded to the Federal Communications Commission a Jerseyan's complaint about WBAI, quoting *Barron's*: "During the 1963 [Senate Internal Security Subcommittee] hearings [on Pacifica radio], William Mandel was identified as a frequent writer for the Communist *Daily Worker*....[Untrue even when I was a Communist, and totally false since, which included all my years on KPFA. I had indeed written letters to the editor.]....At the time Pacifica emphasized that he was a regular broadcaster but not a commentator. Today, it lists him as a regular commentator and 'authority on the USSR'."

Few listeners were troubled. If there were such a thing as a "median" attitude in the mail, it came through best in the following letter: "Your basic humaness [sic] is almost palpable. I hope you are teaching young people. It would be very good in many ways."

Some compliments just made me feel good. I had spoken at a home as a premium to someone who had made a large donation in KPFA's fundraising efforts. A letter came: "In a personal vein, I must say you were so different than I had imagined listening to you on KPFA. I had visions of you as short, stocky, bald with a rounded nose—a Khrushchev-type figure. So when this young-looking athletic man walked in—surprise!" I had just turned fifty-four.

For all the positive words, there were listeners whose gut feel for what was happening in the USSR was better than mine. A Canadian-born New Yorker of my age wrote in 1970: "God damn—the Russian system is dull! It won't last, despite what you say. You think the Russians will suffer 'the clerks of the Kremlin' into 1974?" He wasn't off by too many years, as history is measured. "I've got ten bucks here says, by then, the intelligentsia will have kicked out the clods. Where are the Russians who look beyond Russia into the possibilities of man and beyond? Where are the real men among the livestock?"

But while I could not dream that the Soviet system would collapse, my belief in socialism did not blind me to facts. In 1971 a listener wondered why the guides in the museums of the Revolution in Moscow and Leningrad made no mention of either Trotsky or Stalin. I replied: "The *omission* of historical facts is very widely practiced in the Soviet Union, particularly with respect to political figures whose views those presently in power believe would mislead the people at large, were they permitted to know about them. This is true of Trotsky and Khrushchev, who are now entirely 'unpersons,'....*Distortion* of historical facts is also widely practiced....Of Communist leaders throughout the world, I know of only two who were essentially honest with the people: Lenin and Castro."

To another listener's question I responded: "What happens in Russia to pacifists?....Contrary to the Soviet Constitution, such a person cannot hire a hall, get on the air, hold a street corner meeting, or print a publication advocating pacifist ideas. Refusal to serve in the armed forces is punishable by imprisonment, which is in fact suffered by religious conscientious objectors....If by pacifism is meant a policy of peace, Soviet people will staunchly contend that this is what their government has always pursued, under Lenin, Stalin, Khrushchev, and today." Only the Afghan War in the 1980s affected my perception of Soviet foreign policy to any degree, and then not fundamentally.

The 14th International Congress of Historical Sciences took place in San Francisco in 1975. A small delegation of top Soviet scholars was there, headed by an ethnic Korean and including a Jew. Its women played a more active role in the presentations and discussion than women of any other delegation. I spoke and criticized the Soviets for unwillingness to re-examine the Communist canon on a matter of grave importance: the definition of fascism. The official position adhered to in the USSR was that formulated in 1935 by the Bulgarian Communist Georgii Dimitrov, then a hero to the whole world, despite his politics, for his behavior in court when tried under Hitler for allegedly burning the parliament building. I disagreed with his definition. Monopolies do not openly dictate in fascist countries, as his wording had it. Fascism is not openly terrorist to the mass of the people, but makes unprecedented use of social demagogy. I offered my own notion of its distinguishing characteristic: fascism requires that a politically decisive mass of citizens is willing to use force to deny democratic expression to fellow-citizens, and organizes storm troops to do this. I revived an old Russian term, "White terror," originating from the tsar's White Guard, to define the governments of Pinochet in Chile and the colonels then ruling Greece. I was wrong only in saying that "White terror can generally be predicted as having less stability and a shorter life than fascism." Pinochet, then in power only two years, lasted until he decided to permit elections.

The first discipline in which opponents of capitalism became strong enough to organize and form a recognized entity within the national body was economics. A Union of Radical Political Economists (URPE) had come into being, and was part of the American Economics Association. It, too, had a convention in San Francisco in 1975. URPE asked me to be a discussant in a panel on whether the Soviet Union had gone capitalist. That is ludicrous to think of today, after its collapse in 1991 and subsequent headlong rush toward capitalism, but rather a measure of the childish infatuation with Maoism that then prevailed among academic Marxists. My speech came down hard with the combination of documentation, Marxist theory, and the thunder and lightning that was my hallmark when I wanted to shake people loose from cherished superstitions. (I was yet to discover that I needed some of that for myself.) No one left the hall— 150 to 175 were present—until the hotel management came in and said they had to change the room configuration for its next use. I had requests for my prepared remarks, so I offered them for publication to the *Review of Radical Political Economics,* to which I wrote: "My point of view is one that radicals have not been permitted to hear. [URPE attendees] asked me whether it would be published, and I replied, wearily and accurately, that I had not intended to submit it anywhere, because it adheres to no one's line." The *Review,* both Maoist and scholastic, did not print it. A sympathetic listener wrote at this time: "It must be hard to keep reporting on the USSR in these times—but when was it ever easy?"

The renewed Cold War and my opposition to it led to an invitation to speak from that pro-Soviet Los Angeles organization that I had shocked on my last appearance before it nearly five years earlier. A Soviet delegation was again present at this event, marking the anniversary of Lenin's revolution. I directed my remarks at them:

"During her working lifetime the Soviet woman is distinctly worse off than her husband, because only about one-third of men have by this date advanced to providing a significant degree of help in the home, never mind full sharing....I want to reduce [anti-Soviet] prejudice by calling the attention of the Soviet people present to statements, actions, or inaction in their country that hurt the image of the USSR among American women." I noted that when the top cosmonaut had been asked when there would be a second Soviet woman in space—the very first, twelve years earlier, had been Soviet—he responded: "Women have plenty to do here on earth." I asked whether that meant that Tereshkova, the first, had been merely a token.

Not long before, a top Moscow newspaper had carried an article attacking the retiring U.S. Defense Secretary. In the course of this, the writer lambasted something by a woman in that department. The Soviet article contained such phrases as "the flutterings of the feminist movement," "intellectual Amazon," "learned lady," "ardent lady," "cosmetic tricks," "cherchez la femme," and concluded that she was merely the tool of a man.

"Frankly," I continued, "that article is a veritable textbook of male chauvinist stereotypes and put-downs of women. It is bad enough that a man with the education and qualifications to be a foreign-affairs writer for the official newspaper of the Soviet government—that's what *Izvestia* is—could write such an article. It is much worse that his editor did not understand how insulting it was for him to build his case around the fact that the particular Pentagon thinker was female....In the best of Soviet papers, *Literary Gazette*,...week after week, you find variations on the theme of 'Who was that lady I saw you out with last night? That was no lady, that was my wife.' The explanation is very simple. There are 16 members of the editorial board. Every single one is male, 58 years after the Revolution.

"There is not one female member of the Political Bureau of the Central Committee of the Communist Party. There is not one woman among the 101 members of the Soviet cabinet, the Council of Ministers....No serious pressure is brought by the Soviet Communist Party at home to cause men to share equally the time-burden of caring for the children they are responsible for bringing into the world, and therefore women fall behind in work experience, and in the qualities that bring one to the very top....Yet to change that situation merely requires that the USSR pursue more actively and consistently the policy toward women to which it is already committed."

A member of the Central Committee of the Communist Party of the Soviet Union was in the audience. Dictatorships work fast. My talk was on November 15th. In January a woman's name—one—appeared among the editorial board of the paper I had named, though nothing changed fundamentally. The Soviet government continued to pursue superb policies in terms of women's access to higher education and to professional-level jobs, the provision of childcare facilities on a scale the United States has to this day not remotely approached, the right to terminate a pregnancy, and much else. One woman was later placed in that immense cabinet, and, under Gorbachev, one rose to membership in the Political Bureau. But when the post-Communist government pursued policies leading to greater unemployment among women than men, massive shutdowns of childcare facilities, and gross destruction of the health and education systems by underfunding, women responded by organizing the first female political party in the world to win seats in parliament on its first electoral outing.

It was in the years this chapter discusses that the gay and lesbian movement organized, and so my first letter from an "out" gay did not come until my 14th year on the air, 1971. I replied: "My own convictions are those now embodied in British law: private acts between consenting adults are no crime." I added views with which many will disagree: "The classes (economic and social) among which homosexuality was most widespread in England, by far, would justify defining it as 'bourgeois decadent capitalist imperialist' [the listener's words identifying prevalent attitudes]. And I myself would argue that its large-scale spread in the past decade among the lower middle class and, somewhat, the working class (obviously it was always present in some degree) represents despair, turning inward for personal solutions in a hopeless-seeming society. But I have also come to understand that, in a society repressive of homosexuals, they can be moved to [take] positions of economic and social revolution."

My "have come to understand" was because, until I was thirty-five, I had never met anyone I knew for certain to be gay, except when approached by strangers for sex. At that age, we were invited to dinner by a friend at which a man was present who did not conceal his homosexuality from people he knew. This man, a New York City schoolteacher, was not "out." He'd have been fired at once, and his fellow union members, *perhaps* except for closeted gays, would have turned their backs on him. But he had found a few civilized straight people, and let them know he was gay. Totally contrary to the views to which my generation was raised, he proved to be a perfectly "normal" person in all other respects. And in the second KPFA strike, which occurred in 1974, gay men and women were reliable pickets and activists. And if my standard of judgment seems utterly homophobic, it was: a reflection of the society in which I grew up. Since I was straight, a family man with children, and there was simply no discussion of non-heterosexual relations in the milieus in which I moved, nothing had moved me to give any thought to the question of homosexuality, never mind gay rights.

In the summer of 1970, Tanya had accompanied me on her second trip to the USSR. Her on-air report of that trip brought a letter to us from a friend who remembered Elsa Knight Thompson's interview of her after her first visit there in 1966: "Tanya, I assume you were being 'normally' modest when you gestured to me after I indicated (many years back) how much I enjoyed your KPFA interview. It was one of the finest I have ever heard—your forthrightness and sincerity, as well as your talent for describing things graphically and responsibly....In fact, I heard some of it twice and enjoyed it all so much!" She added something very nice to remember now when we are married sixty-three years: "It appears that you two deserve each other and have an unusually good thing going between you."

In those years Tanya answered all listener mail that did not require specialized knowledge. In the '80s she shared the program with me on air for at least five years. She always critiqued every single broadcast, both the scripts or live interviews and my answers to questions. Very many broadcasts were on subjects she suggested or chose from among alternatives I offered. She visited the USSR five times in all. She also had the knowledge gained by editing all my books and many if not most of my innumerable articles. So this station depending on unpaid broadcasters got two for the price of one.

Yet my single-minded focus wore her down and she finally quit her on-air participation permanently in private protest at my refusal to go along with her on some family matter. On the other hand, the broadcasts also gave occasion for family pride. A New Jersey math teacher and listener of mine heard someone read on the air, over a non-Pacifica station, an article in *Atlantic Monthly* about the trial of a group of Vietnam-War protesters, including our son, Bob. The listener bought the magazine and sent me a paragraph from it, which read:

"Bob Mandel is what is known to the Left as a 'red-diaper' baby. His family all live around Berkeley, and his mother, sister, brother-in-law, and 70-year-old grandfather formed a constant cheering squad during the trial. The Mandel entourage was also the backbone of an Old-Left style Oakland Seven Defense Committee, which raised money, sponsored functions, and otherwise got publicity for the defendants. Mandel's own political history has the mark of his generation. While a student at Reed College, he twice went South for SNCC [the Student Nonviolent Coordinating Committee] and was active in anti-war and anti-draft activities. He has done community organizing in Oakland, and at the time of the indictments, was involved in high school anti-draft organizing around the Bay Area."

Today he is a teacher of English as a second language in the Oakland school system, working with adults. Because the students come from the widest variety of cultural and linguistic backgrounds, to do that work conscientiously requires working with each person individually. By the end of each term he is totally exhausted. There are rewards. Asians particularly have a tradition of honoring teachers with gifts and dinners. But when a Chinese woman too old to gain any benefit in earnings from what she learned put a hundred-dollar bill in a red lucky money New Year's envelope for Bob, I had the right to think my son is a good teacher. To us in the Jewish tradition, there is no higher honor. It goes without saying that Bob is a union activist in that city with the lowest average pay for teachers in the Bay area. Much of his effort goes to maintaining unity in the ranks across racial lines, a permanent problem. In 1999 he created a brief national furor by getting the Oakland teachers' union to sponsor a teach-in during school hours about the death sentence for Mumia Abu-Jamal, Philadelphia radio journalist, author and long-ago Black Panther framed for murder by the notoriously corrupt and racist police of that city. While the authorities ultimately prohibited the formal teach-in, teachers dealt with the subject in their classes that day, and several thousand students were made conscious of the issues.

Bob has no natural children. Years ago he had lived for a period with a woman who had a son, Lael, from a previous relationship. The boy was mentally disabled. She abandoned him. Although her parents raised Lael, Bob essentially adopted him, and he loves Bob. Lael lives in Denver, but Bob would have him brought to Berkeley from time to time. Bob had to work, and our daughter or we would care for Lael, who was totally fascinated with machinery. This had begun, not surprisingly, with fire engines. I still retained my technical library from decades earlier when that was the nature of the translation work available. It soon became routine, when Lael was brought to us, for him to request: "Bill, read me the welding book."

Our eldest, daughter Phyllis, set the pattern for activism among our children, as I described in dealing with the Rosenberg Case and her staunchness in school against futile nuclear-bomb drills and cold war propaganda. I gave the manuscript of *Soviet Women* to her to read in 1973. Since she remains a believer in Marxist socialism today, although I do not, her letter to me after reading it needs no qualification:

"Thank you for having always made socialism come alive for me, so that even in my darkest hours the flame burns and my imagination does not grow dim. And thank you for this book—so perhaps my little sisters will not know the pain of growing old with vast resources of wasted talents because of a society that says NO to women. The book gives me courage to go on fighting even as I am bitter that I shall never be the test pilot, captain of a ship or cosmonaut or surgeon that burned so brightly in my heart as a child, only to learn the bitter lesson that those were not things for little women to dream about....And I shall always tell people that it was not only the living example of socialist society, but thanks to my old man who helped me see it....Love, Phillie."

Phyllis, now sixty and a staunch labor unionist, was a medical secretary in a Kaiser hospital, with the best record in the office for productivity. Like Bob, she was faced day after day with problems of relations with her fellow workers stemming from racial and religious prejudices. The joy of her life (and ours) is her granddaughter, Alana, Irish and Jewish.

Bob and Phyllis were the children in whom I had taken greatest pride in the '60s, because of their activism. But the youngest, hippie Dave, up in Canada because he did not wish to kill or be killed in Vietnam, wrote me a remarkable letter in 1971, when he was twenty-four:

"Somehow this letter is directed towards bringing us closer. You don't have to ever send me carbon copies of people praising your work. I'm your son. I love you and *I know* that you've always worked for and wanted a good life for the human race. I've always resented your *needing* praise, moral and ego support. Especially since you always made me feel inadequate, inferior to you, incapable of being the great scholar. I don't say this to hurt you, it's just time it was said....Don't ever lecture me again. It takes a little love to speak gently-strongly....It's a good fambly we've got, eh?"

I replied: "Agreed, re bringing us closer. One sees one's kids in oneself in various ways. You are like me in frankness....Of course I need moral support. Who doesn't, except an egomaniac or the rare genius— creative artist, extraordinary leader, truly great thinker—who can sit and do his-her thing alone, regardless of what anyone thinks? I'm none of those. Chiefly, I'm a man of principle who, thus far, has had what it takes to stick by them even when very much alone. That's about the only thing about myself about which I'm pretty sure, although it's still nice to get letters indicating that strangers know that. But I'm not a great scholar, just a competent one, plus having the doggedness (really, principle more than anything else), to stick to it....So I'm deeply moved when I find that ordinary people—the people I care about—really have been caused to think, and to change their minds, by my books and my raps, as in the case of those Black students at Merritt College....That's why it's important to me that what I'm doing *now* is valued by people. And I want those I love most to know it. Besides, I've been fucked over a great deal this past year..., and so those term-paper comments were good for my morale. That was a great letter."

Dave responded: "Now, *that* is the kind of letter that means something. Thank you for taking the time (not that I left you an alternative). I *am* sorry if it sounded like I was hitting you when you're down - that wasn't my intention at all, which you seem to realize.

"Getting that carbon copy was like all the other times in my life when you couldn't say to me, 'thing are bad, I'm down.' Instead, you'd talk intellectually, which puts up a hell of a wall of mistrust. So if I've seemed resentful or unappreciative over the years maybe you can understand why, now. *I* was alone. Always."

Subsequently, Dave obtained a graduate degree in landscape architecture, based on twenty years hands-on work as a gardener and contractor in that field. His professors described him as the best teaching-assistant in their experience. One actually said she was honored to have been associated with his thesis, which reflected his background and convictions. It is on public policy in financing urban parks: he wants money to go to those parts of town whose people need parks most, and to be spent in ways that will fit their cultural needs, the decisions to be made with their participation. A paper he wrote in 1999 reflects the same concerns: "Serial Gardens: Landscape architecture for Low Incomes." He has the family love for teaching, and passes on his professional knowledge in the Extension Department of the University of California.

I take the greatest satisfaction in our children's relationship to each other. Immediately before that sharp exchange between Dave and me, Bob had visited him in Canada, and wrote me:

"I got to see Dave....It was great - it was like discovering a whole new person - I haven't really known him for years, and discovered that he's not my 'kid' brother but a flesh & blood human being. He's taken some hard knocks but he's a really good person and his head is in a good place. We listened to each other - it was good. He says he's beginning to find himself. I think he's right - I don't mean that judgmentally - I think and hope he's right....I'm really glad I went."

No matter what one's age, a child regards a parent as impossibly old. In the early 1970s, Dad, born before the turn of the century, still expressed his views with characteristic vigor. The *National Guardian* weekly went Maoist in 1972 as part of the thrashing around to find a magic wand that would keep the '60s actively alive. Dad, now nearly eighty and a founding subscriber, wrote it: "This is a 'Dear John' letter....I considered the *Guardian* as the most valuable organ in the radical movement, because it always acted as a cement for the various groups....I valued chiefly...its even-handedness in dealing with the various factions in the movement, and trying to bring about effective, constructive action....In the international field, your Maoist leaning...has of late become quite dangerous by inculcating anti-Sovietism into your readers' minds." Being Dad, he then documented that for half a page from the paper's articles, and closed: "So, count me out."

More even than his vigor, I admired his open-mindedness with respect to things that had for half a century been sacrosanct to him. He was asked his opinion in 1973, by my Sovietologist friend, Ethel Dunn, of a book she thought him particularly equipped to judge. He replied: "Ivanov's book is definitely fomenting anti-Semitism. For the Soviet Union to publish and circulate this and similar matter is, to say the least, inexcusable."

After my stay in Moscow that summer to gather material for my book on women, I gave him my observations on that visit to read. One sentence read: "Anti-[Angela] Davis feeling is universal among literary intellectuals of any point of view, because they are nearly all critical of govt one way or another (freedom is basis), and anyone their govt officially boosts must automatically be no good." He wrote a comment: "if this is actually the case there is real cause for concern of the future."

But when he and I did disagree, it was hurtful. We had a *very* heated conversation in 1972, ended when I simply walked out on him, because I thought he had fluffed off the significance of Jewish emigration from the USSR. At that point the USSR demanded that emigres reimburse the cost of free higher education. To put things back together again, I wrote him a letter: "It was for this reason that I said your comments about 'a few hundred people' was unworthy of you, as being callous and refusing to reckon with the psychological impact of attempted extermination [by Hitler]....There has never been a free emigration policy...so we simply don't know how many would wish to leave."

He wrote back: "What your walking out on me did to me, you probably wouldn't understand....If you'll re-read my letter you will find that I did not speak of 'a few hundred people.' I stated that 30,000 emigrated in one year, but I guesstimated the number involved in the cost-of-education refund was about a hundred." So I had been unfair to him.

But we were entirely on the same side where this country was concerned. At the end of that year, he wired: "President—Appalled at renewal bombing North Vietnam. Save our honor. Stop genocidal devastation that country." His draft was handwritten, with absolutely no sign of age at seventy-eight. He sent identical handwritten letters to ten senators:

"I don't believe that if the American people were really aware of the cold-blooded, hellish murder and devastation committed by *American* flyers, they would not rise up and stop the Nixon genocide....I can only speak to a few people, but *you* can reach millions by speaking out loud and clear against this criminal, murderous action perpetrated in our name. Don't wait until Congress reconvenes; every minute counts."

Because his spoken language retained a foreign accent, and contained some Lower East Side terms and Jewish phrasings, I did not realize how impeccable was his knowledge of English until I went over such written documents after his death. That was true even in his diary of the year before I was born, which I discovered when moving him to an attended-care residence after his hundredth birthday. When he wrote it, he had only been in this country seven years.

My father was still totally independent in his early eighties. His trip to the Soviet Union at that time resulted in astute observations that were useful to my understanding. He had now found his companion for the rest of his life, Mildred Schoenberger. She was a retired New York City high school math teacher of Communist convictions who had been very active in the Teachers Union in the years when it won superb conditions, including a very generous pension. At her seventieth birthday, in 1976, I found her son decorating the hall that had been hired with a frieze of paper giraffes. I asked her what that signified. It turns out that her nickname was "Giraffe," for she was five foot nine, very tall for a woman of her generation. She still had a lovely figure and exquisite taste in dress. Dad was five foot two, but that didn't bother her at all. Dad, being both a tailor's son and a retired engineer, was a spiffy dresser.

Together they made a most un-Berkeley appearance. They participated in demonstrations as a matter of course. At one, protesting a U.S. invasion—Grenada perhaps?—a young reporter for the *Daily Californian* thought they'd make a good interview. She asked Dad, "Sir, is this your first demonstration?"

He replied, "The first was in 1905."

Stunned, she wondered, "What ever happened in 1905?"

"The first attempt to overthrow the tsar."

He kept that clipping on his wall.

Also that year, when Dad was 101, a film crew from Russia came to Berkeley to interview him, as the last survivor of the American and Dutch radicals who went to Kuzbass in 1925 to start the industrialization of Siberia. I received a copy of the film a few months after his death in 1996. While it uses interviews of a dozen or more people in three countries, it gave me great pleasure that the director chose to open with Dad, setting the tone with his statement that the reason he had gone to Siberia was to build socialism.

It wasn't only Dad with whose Communist ideals I had to deal in the early '70s. The decade had just opened when I received a call from Mary Southard. I had not heard from her in nearly twenty years, when she, as the truest of believers, had informed the Communist Party that I had expressed heretical ideas about Joseph Stalin and what I saw as the tenuous character of McCarthyism here, when the Party saw fascism as a certainty. In consequence, it expelled me. Mary was as brave as they come. One had to be, to have been an open Communist in her native Georgia before World War II.

Mary informed me that she and her husband, Ordway, at least as courageous for daring to be a public Communist in the deep South despite a damyankee accent, had long been living in Kamuela, Hawaii. Would I meet with her and explain why I had understood the failings of the Soviet Union in the Stalin era while others had not? We had a long conversation. My explanation, in a sentence, was that I had always regarded the USSR as a real country of real people, not the abstract embodiment of a theory.

Perhaps, to use her words in a later letter, I was sweet and generous to one who realized she had done me wrong, but never—not to this day—to those who wrote me out of the history of events to which I had contributed. Mike Rossman had been a participant in the demonstration against the HUAC hearing of 1960 where I testified, and was a major figure in the Free Speech Movement at U.C. Berkeley in 1964-5. His *Wedding in the War,* dealing with those years, was published in 1971. I wrote him:

"I've been looking at your book. Fuck you....I would never have written this letter if I were not hurt (of course I'm hurt) by being erased from the event that launched the national movement among white students and made Berkeley a noun, an adjective and a verb as well as a place name. But a writer with some profundity, realizing that the '60s are gone (that you do) would have asked himself about their place in this country's continuing history, and would have been intrigued by the very rare individuals who had the capacity to bridge the gap between the style and experiences of the '30s and those of the '60s....And what it is that enables such individuals to bridge such gaps is of a great deal more importance than a personal anecdote to the future movement....

"How come the editors of the SNCC-affiliated *The Movement*....asked if I would be one of them: again the only person of my generation they would have anything to do with on a day-to-day basis? That was 1966-1968, not ancient history....

"Perhaps I have an inflated notion of how students regarded me? Then why did Michael Lerner [who later became a national figure as editor of *Tikkun* and confidant of first lady Hillary Clinton] ask me if I would debate Clark Kerr, then still president of the university?"

"A couple of days ago a guy of your generation told me of a lecture program at his university that he thought he could fit me into: Forgotten Americans: 'You are a forgotten American, aren't you?' I laughed in recognition and without hurt. But being forgotten means that I was once present in people's consciousness. In no one's more than in Mike Rossman's. From 1960 to 1964, whenever we ran into each other, there was...admiration in your eyes, your smile, your voice, your manner [because of my role in the 1960 HUAC hearing]. After FSM that changed, for the best of reasons. Your generation developed its own heroes and a self-confidence within the very uncertainty. You were no exception....I don't think I should be the central figure in the narration of the HUAC incident....But once the hosing took place, to write of the subsequent events without me is bullshit."

Literally as I wrote these words, the phone rang, and the editor of the first magazine to publish an excerpt from this autobiography said: "I have just listened to the full tape of that hearing for the first time. I simply want to tell you I was deeply moved." Thirty-five years after the event.

CHAPTER 24

Eating Babies

In mid-January 1978 I received a phone call from Hollywood. "This is Haskell Wexler," the caller identified himself.

"I know who you are, Mr. Wexler. Two Oscars," I said.

"Mr. Mandel, I'm one of your listeners on KPFK. There's something I need to know. How do I get into Moscow to make a film?"

"In today's atmosphere of mutual hostility, it'll take a year's negotiation. Or you can do it as a tourist, if you can accomplish what you want with just you and your camera."

"That's out of the question. I must have it done by May."

"The only way I can think of how to help you is if I know who is sponsoring the film," I continued.

"Admiral LaRocque of the Center for Defense Information has engaged me to make a film about the danger of nuclear war, and we want to get the attitudes of ordinary citizens in both countries," said Wexler.

Gene LaRocque had retired at the end of the Vietnam War. As early as 1974 he had founded the organization originally called Soldiers Without Enemies. Limited to those of higher officer rank, the organization sought to wield influence in Washington. I had been at a small lunch for him in San Francisco that year, although there was no reason to believe he would remember me. His grasp of his subject, his sincerity and his determination were unmistakeable. When Wexler called, the U.S. was on the verge of escalating the arms race by making the neutron bomb. Moscow wanted to stop that, because if Washington proceeded with this plan, the Soviets thought they had to match it, further hindering their plans for economic progress.

I told Wexler to have LaRocque speak to Ambassador Dobrynin, the only Soviet diplomat with membership in the Central Committee of the Communist Party, and therefore able to cut red tape. By great luck, a member of its topmost body, the Political Bureau, was on a visit to Washington. Permission came in weeks. Wexler flew up to see me and I gave him *Soviet Women*. He volunteered: "I'd like to film that." He never did. He asked me whether I thought Soviet people would talk with a foreigner about issues of peace as freely as they did to me about their lives. He had been particularly struck by my broadcast interview of a Tajik electrician I had done the previous summer near the border of Afghanistan. I said there was nothing they'd rather talk about than peace. He asked whether I'd come along to do the interviews. I jumped at the chance.

I prepared a page of proposals for the trip such as to avoid wasting time with official types: "Stay at hotels with self-serve meals. Go to non-*restoran* [restaurant] eateries to meet ordinary folks, lobbies of neighborhood movies, apartment-house porches & yards to meet babushki [grandmothers], major war memorials & tombs of unknown soldiers where brides place bouquets...collective-farm memorial honor boards to war victims to talk to veterans & widows. Try to get agreement that we will wander around alone, so people will not stiffen into official stances, or think they have to change into their best clothes, etc. Be ready to shoot & record as soon as I approach someone: I can envisage some of the very best reactions coming the moment I say: 'Good morning. We're Americans, and we're making a film to show why...'"

Naturally I bargained over pay. My letter on that topic, like the one just quoted, provides a notion of how I had gotten the interviews that had brought Wexler to me, and the work involved. A conference interpreter, I wrote: "could not possibly do the job I'm being called upon for, because he would not...know the psychology and history of Soviet people nor have the skills in eliciting replies and life stories I've developed in my four taping trips there since 1966....I'll be working a hell of a lot longer than an 8-hr day, simply because we'll be spending much more than that many hours together in the company of Russians, in meetings and socializing, and I can tell you that bilingual interpreting is a totally exhausting job. The companies that rent out conference interpreters always insist that the customer take at least two, so they can spell each other off."

LaRocque sent me the list of questions he wanted asked of Soviet citizens. I was totally shocked, knowing how they felt about war, and their absolute conviction that their country's policy was one of peace. So I wrote, in the margins, in advance of a day spent in Washington with him and his retired air force and infantry generals and colonels, my anticipation of the answers we would get.

"Q. Would you support your government if it decided to launch a nuclear war to obtain a political objective?"

A. "We prohibit war propaganda."

Q. What would happen to the Soviet Union if it struck first?"

A. "How dare you?"

Q. "Could your country survive and win a nuclear war?"

A. "There mustn't be one."

Q. "In the next 20 years do you think it is likely or not likely a major world power will try to destroy another major power in one blow?"

A. "They must not."

Q. "Which country—the Soviet Union or the United States—do you think is farther ahead in the field of long range missiles and rockets?"

A. "We have enough."

Q. "Do you favor increasing the defense budget?"

A. "We reduced it."

Q. "Looking over the past five years, do you think relations between the Soviet Union and the United States have gotten better, gotten worse, or stayed about the same?"

A. "I don't know, but they *must* get better."

The brass-for-peace were convinced by my air of certainty—it was sincere and I was right —and modified the questions considerably, giving me freedom to ask what I wished provided I elicited Soviet citizens' stands on the issues the film would be about.

Wexler, his female assistant, and I flew to Moscow, with cameras and film stock. There he hired a technical crew and a van. The filming itself was marvelous. I interviewed an elderly woman on line to enter Lenin's tomb, people riding the enormously long escalators down to the subway, musicians recording in the national radio center. One of the best was at the Bolshoi Ballet School. Wexler, a tall and graceful man who had himself studied ballet, wove in and out with hand-held camera during a dress rehearsal. At a break, I approached an unimaginably beautiful seventeen-year-old sweating and panting in the wings, and asked her what she thought of nuclear war. "It would be the end of everything! All I want to do is dance!"

Another fine shoot was of my friend Riurikov, the writer on love, and his wife, at dinner in their typically crowded apartment. Asked what the outcome of nuclear war would be, Yuri replied: "It would be a war without winners!" And that became the name of the film, "War Without Winners." It was shown over the years on some hundred TV stations here. But the Center learned that it might be attacked if my association with the project were known. So I appear only in a single, unidentified head shot at the outset, something like Hitchcock in the mysteries he directed. I am not in the credits; someone was engaged to read my lines in English, off-camera. I had interviewed in Russian, of course. I got a thank-you letter from LaRocque, but he denied my request for use of my original audio materials.

The experience also gave me an unpleasant insight into Soviet society. At the immense USSR-wide radio center I went ahead of the others to find the rehearsal hall we were to film in. On trips to the USSR I deliberately dressed to look like Russians of my station—an unpressed suit, my oldest. When I stepped into the hall, those present apparently were not expecting us as yet, and I was taken for just one more person in that busy place. I heard some stupid lower-rank Party commissar instructing these adult musicians on how to answer us. But the bulk of our interviews were in spontaneous circumstances, and I got marvelous dialogue.

Jimmy Carter, a Democrat, was president at this time. When, after decades of trying, the Soviets finally got the United Nations to hold a special session on disarmament, Carter called a NATO meeting at exactly the same time. There he demanded, and gained agreement, that all members would *increase* their arms spending each year by at least three percent in real value, after inflation. The Republican candidate in the next election could not be expected to be a dove. It turned out to be Reagan, who increased the arms budget to levels previously undreamed of. In any case, a credible peace candidate was needed. I wrote Admiral LaRocque a letter urging that he run:

"As a person, you are the complete opposite of the negative picture some people have of high 'brass.' I remember when we were off-loading the film equipment at the airport, you said to me: 'You're pretty strong for a professor.' I looked at you and thought: why, he's smaller than me, he's had the authority to order people around his whole lifetime, his arm was hurting him badly earlier today, and here he is lugging crates. That's one of the best things there is in the American character, and that's you."

LaRocque did not run.

The atmosphere that had caused me to wind up on the "War Without Winners" cutting room floor manifested itself on the Left as well. At the annual KPFA Christmas Fair of 1977, James Weinstein, editor of a vaguely socialist periodical published in Chicago, *In These Times,* had come to my bookstand and said, "You ought to write for us." Knowing his anti-Soviet politics, I doubted that he would publish me, and therefore pleaded busyness—I was writing my *Soviet But Not Russian.* I sent him six KPFA scripts of unedited transcripts of conversations in ethnic republics the previous summer. One of them was the interview with the Tajik electrician that had caught Wexler's ear. My covering letter said of it:

"No. 4 contrasts with all the first three...by reminding us that traditional, quite literally pre-medieval cultural attitudes do not change *in situ* in one generation or two, and that in some places and respects the USSR is still very much a developing country. This is a marvelous story, genuine literature told by a natural, which I could peddle for a very large figure to *Esquire,* or *Playboy,* or even *Reader's Digest.* There's the rub. They would want only this one, which to the unthinking reader confirms what he thinks he knows. That's why I won't offer it to them, would not accept a proposal from you to use it alone, nor to start a series with it." [It is published in part on pp. 15 and 148-150 of *Soviet But Not Russian.*]

Weinstein replied: "I do want people to get a much more sophisticated view of Soviet life and of the complexity of Soviet society and the dangers of simple-minded rejections or putdowns. I think the series will contribute greatly to such an understanding," but he asked me to rewrite the interviews as articles. He assured me that he would "give it as much play as we can - page 1 head, a press release, and whatever else we can do." I responded: "I wonder if taking them out of interview form will not reduce their credibility, with a very sceptical audience."

I did the rewrites immediately and sent them off. I wrote him a month later: "I'm surprised to find no advance announcement of my series, which you proposed." A week later, en route to speak on International Women's Day at the Catholic College of St. Francis, Joliet, Il., I phoned Weinstein and asked what happened to my articles. He replied: "We can't publish that P[ublic] R[elations] stuff." This bore out my expectation that changing from the unchallengeable verbatim transcript to third person rendition would destroy credibility. I hung up. Months later I wrote requesting the return of my slides. My covering letter described the difference between what opinion-makers wanted the public to think, and had convinced themselves it thought, and reality:

"The response to my lectures on Soviet women at such middle-America places as the College of St. Francis, Kearney State College, Nebraska; and the Missouri Valley History Conference, U. of Nebr. at Omaha, early this month, convince me that my approach is not regarded as 'PR stuff' by student and faculty audiences today. In the fourth year of touring on this subject, this is the first time I have encountered *no* hostile questions from positions either to the right or left of my own. Apparently the failure to pass ERA [the Equal Rights— for women — Amendment], on the one hand, on top of Watergate and Koreagate, and the disappearance of China as a Utopia on the other, have created a willingness to examine what has been accomplished in solving social problems in the USSR with a modesty appropriate to our failure to do so."

My trips to the Soviet Union in 1977, 1978, 1979 gave me insights that were very helpful when that country began to come apart at the seams a decade later. After the first of these, ranging very far into Asia as well as to the western and southern European frontiers, on which Tanya accompanied me, I wrote Prof. John Hazard at Columbia:

"This trip...impressed me so strongly with the objective differences among them [republics] that I am going to refer to them in the future as *countries.*...I refer to immediately manifest cultural differences, psychological attitudes, and pronounced consciousness of ethnic identity. I

found dissatisfactions expressed by individuals in the realm of nationality policy, but within the framework of acceptance as utterly taken for
granted and common sense that they are so much better off as part of
the USSR than they could ever be as independent states in the real
world in which we live that the very notion of separatism is preposterous and not worthy of discussion."

That was true until a decade later, when the unyielding centralism of
the Soviet system caused people in half of the republics to see separatism
as the solution. The other half simply found independence dumped in
their laps by Russian President Yeltsin's dissolution of the Union of
Soviet Socialist Republics in order to oust and succeed the president of
that larger entity, Gorbachev. My letter went on to detail criticisms I
heard in the Baltic states, then part of the Soviet Union. I also remarked
on idealization of the past by Central Asian academics and journalists
following in their wake, and intellectuals there shaping their own
"Quaker" Islam as an ideology for the Turkic-speaking countries of the
USSR.

On the other hand, there was the Turkmen with two Slavic compan-
ions whom I invited to share our table at a restaurant. In response to my
questions he said, in poor Russian, pointing to the men with him:
"They were born here....The Iranians beat us. The Turks beat us. The
English tried to beat us. Soviet power good. [Thumb up]. Lenin good.
[Up again]. The Russians help us," beaming.

My letter to Hazard continued: "I was somewhat surprised by the
complete absence of pan-Turkism [borne out by post-Soviet develop-
ments]....Nationalism is loyalty to their individual ethnic traditions—
which is why the 'country' concept has become so established in my
consciousness."

There had been very little hostility during my four lecture swings the
previous year to promote *Soviet Women,* then just out. Some experiences
were downright inspiring in their confirmation of my belief in the good
sense and openmindedness of Americans. In Milwaukee, the local
American-Soviet Friendship Council had a display table at a pre-
Christmas bazaar in the gym of a Catholic high school with a Polish-
German-Irish workingclass congregation. The sanctuary next door was
used for presentation of "Peace Child." This play was performed
extremely widely across the country, year after year for over a decade.
Two children, one American, one Soviet, both the offspring of diplo-
mats, meet at a reception. Initially they voice the standard suspicions of
each other. They get to know each other better, decide that if the leaders
of their countries would meet there would be a chance for peace, and
they bring that about in highly plausible fashion.

Neighborhood people went into the sanctuary, made the sign of the cross and obeisance as usual, watched the play, and then moved into the bazaar. A local used car dealer, wearing the kind of bright suit one associates with that occupation, stood at the Friendship Council table and called out some catchy slogan to attract attention to me and my book. He told me later that he came from a family that had suffered the ugliest wounds of McCarthyism. An FBI informant had married his mother, had reported on her and her associates, and was found out only because of his sloppiness.

An astounding percentage of the people who came by, including nuns, bought my book. The morning daily ran an interview with me clear across the top of a page under a headline bracketing all eight columns. A radio station that guaranteed a hundred thousand listeners had me answering questions for an hour. The phone lines were lit uninterruptedly, and the callers did not bait but sought real information.

Soviet Women also brought me my first Canadian lecture tour in the thirty years since World War II. Attendance at higher educational institutions averaged four times as high as in the U.S. relative to enrollment. I got a call from a professor in Regina, Peter Smollett. Would I come for a lecture at his university? Peter proved to be an American movie editor blacklisted from Hollywood during Truman's pre-McCarthy Red Scare. He was teaching film. I got in touch with Danny Dorotich—Canadians love the diminutive familiar—a professor in Saskatoon who had looked me up upon hearing my broadcasts in Berkeley while taking summer work there fifteen years earlier. A Yugoslav patriot—in those days Serb or Croat or Bosnian made no difference—he had fought in Tito's partisan forces against the Nazis when a teenager. He was never a Communist but came from a country where the Communist Tito was the national hero. He had found my broadcasts a break from the American atmosphere of wild cold war prejudice at that time.

Peter had lost fingers when working in a Pennsylvania steel mill at the request of the Communist Party in the 1930s. He turned to film only when blacklisted out of his union. He is an extremely nice guy with a wicked sense of humor. I can parry. Our disagreements, and the laughter that came with the sparring, whiled away the hours of high-speed driving over snowy prairie roads between lecture sites. Although the wheatlands are featureless, there was always the attraction of identifying the nationality of the immigrants who had founded each farm town by the architecture of their church steeples or domes: Rumanian, German, Russian.

Peter's wife, Eleanor, an anthropologist, is Canada's pioneer expert on Bulgaria. She also bakes fresh salmon to a taste I'll never forget. As warm a family, with their then teenage daughter, as I have ever met. Peter astounded me by pulling out a copy of the pamphlet of my testimony before the McCarran Committee a quarter-century earlier, and was kind enough to give it to me when I explained that I had only one left and there were requests to borrow it.

Such hospitality provided welcome, needed counterweights to my merciless schedule. I set myself the hopeless task of countering, single-handed, the kind of propaganda in both countries that caused me to snap back at a KPFA listener during a phone-in session: "Does being a Communist disqualify one from membership in the human race?" Or, in the more colorful language of Don Ohlmeyer, who had been appointed NBC executive producer for the 1980 Olympics: "If we show them [the Russians] in any way but eating their babies, we'll be in some trouble." Both those remarks were in 1978, before the Soviet entry into Afghanistan that caused the U.S. boycott of those Olympics. But our press was full of a new fable every month: Moscow's alleged efforts to limit the birthrate of its Asian peoples, for example. In reality, it was then awarding the title "Mother Heroine" to all who raised very large families successfully, and I had broadcast that year's list, consisting, as usual, chiefly of Islamic and Turkic names.

My schedule in Regina opened with an evening lecture on the non-Russian peoples of the USSR. I spent the next day in various professors' classes—"Family Life and Women's Status," "Industrialization in Formerly Feudal Areas," "Soviet Women,"—and a free-for-all question-answer session, with a TV interview squeezed in along the line. The Saskatoon program was virtually the same, plus a national CBC inter-view in which I foolishly predicted that Ted Kennedy would be the Democratic candidate for president.

Perhaps my most exciting contact with Canada came one day in the late '70s when the phone rang at home and a crisp voice said: "This is Geraldine Whitney in Edmonton, and I'm a fan of yours."

"Just a moment, Ms. Whitney. KPFA is an FM station. You can't hear it up there."

"Oh, yes I do."

"How?"

"Dan Glaser in Berkeley and I exchange tapes. He sends me every single one of your broadcasts. My son copies them at the university and I send them to people all over Canada and abroad. New Zealand, for example."

Gerry, a retired high-school teacher, later organized lectures for me in Edmonton and even a Canada-wide tour. Gerry died in 1997, Glaser in 1999.

Grand Rapids, Michigan, is just south of the Canadian border. My lectures at Grand Valley State Colleges were organized by old friend Virginia Jencks, and her new husband, anthopology professor Tom

Chambers, the gentlest of men. Tom really put me to work. I relished the opportunity: 10 a.m. "History of Minority Relations"; 11 a.m., "Social Inequality"; noon, "Sociology of Women" participated in by the Women's Study group; 1 p.m., "Government and Politics of the Soviet Union and Eastern Europe"; 2 p.m., my slide lecture on women. Eight other instructors urged or required their students to attend one of the classes or the lecture. In the evening the local chapter of the Union of Radical Political Economists sponsored a discussion session in town.

Grand Rapids has a large Polish population. An exchange student from Poland attended my lecture, and argued with me over the Jewish issue. I had attacked the Polish Communist Party for its raw anti-Semitism. When I lectured in Chicago the following week he attended, and said to me afterward that I understood the USSR. From East Europeans or Soviet people, such remarks were encouraging to me. He encouraged me very strongly to visit Poland. I said that, as a Jew of Marxist convictions, I would not. It would have hurt too much. For the same reason, I had refused an opportunity to visit the USSR in 1950 when I was a loyal Communist, during Stalin's lifetime, for I knew I would have been lied to whenever I faced them with realities contrary to their official propaganda.

There were types of pain I avoided and, in fact, turned into weapons. A professor at Northern Illinois University informed me that his proposal to have me as a lecturer had been turned down there, and that a prominent colleague "suspects political motives." He wrote that he would reapply for the next fall, and asked me for a vita, "thus taking away their arguments for refusing." I replied:

"To put it very bluntly—and you may quote this if you wish and to whom you wish—one does not request vitas of elder statesmen. One of my sponsors on the April tour...is the retired chairman of the Russian Area Studies Graduate Program at a major university. Thirty years ago he quite literally sat at my feet and asked how to get into that field..." The reference was to Prof. Sam Hendel of CUNY.

Even when lectures were arranged for me, there would be occasional expressions of opposition to my views. When I spoke at Fordham University in New York, a Catholic institution, a priest walked out.

Certain academics whose views of the USSR had areas of similarity to my own, one still quite prominent at the turn of the millenium, avoided and still avoid guilt by association with me. Others voiced very different attitudes. The year before I lectured at his institution, Prof. Lynn Turgeon, a Hofstra University economist, had asked me to read the manuscript of his book, and wrote a very kind note: "I really think you are about the best critic in the business." After my lecture, which he had arranged, he asked me if I could solve the mystery of Western reports that infant mortality was rising in Soviet Central Asia. I could not, and when they were confirmed at the time the Soviet Union collapsed, it became clear that this phenomenon of the mid-1970s was the first statistical evidence of the decay of that society.

Lynn was the first to study the economies of the Communist-governed countries between the USSR and the West. Others stupidly sneered "satellite" and fluffed those countries off. Lynn demonstrated that collective farming, properly conducted, could really work, as in what was then Czechoslovakia.

He was not alone among those who made me feel justified in sticking to my field in the long years of outer darkness after my Stanford appointment.

Very important to me was the reaction of Provost and professor Sheila Tobias at Wesleyan, a total stranger who was the pioneer in insisting that women could really do math, and in developing courses to bring them into the field. She invited me because she liked my book, and wanted me to explain to her class the cultural-historical brakes on women's liberation in the USSR. Subsequently she made *Soviet Women* required reading in her course, "Social Roles of Women in America," and recommended me as speaker to other universities. She asked me to comment on her "Women in Eastern Europe: Some Impressions." I wrote her two single-spaced closely-typed pages, realized that she had stimulated me to think through my views, and asked her to send a copy to a friend in Moscow for a female family sociologist there.

African-American women, Angela Davis and Marylou Patterson, who had gotten her medical degree in Moscow, wrote very positive reviews of *Soviet Women*. Professor Davis made it required reading in her very large class at Stanford.

In the late 1970s, I would still give occasional talks on the Soviet Union for the far Left. The manager of the Communist bookstore in Philadelphia, a remarkable 90-year-old named Jim Dolsen, who had once been put on trial for being a leader of that party in Pennsylvania, invited me. After two hours of talk, questions, and discussion, the audience was asked its reaction. A non-Communist woman present who had participated in U.C. Berkeley's Free Speech Movement said, "I trust this man. He pictures a real place, not a Utopia." Although I supported a goal that proved Utopian, I was free of any illusion that it had been attained. I never ceased encouraging realism. In 1979, the Communist paper in California, the *People's World,* carried an article on Einstein by Conn Hallinan, a generally clear-headed man of my children's generation whom I had known from his teens. He later became a professor of journalism at U.C. Santa Cruz. I wrote the paper a letter criticizing his omission of the stupidities of Soviet treatment of the great scientist. It had for years permitted publication only of references that labeled his views as "reactionary Einsteinism" and called the theory of relativity "obviously unscientific." My letter said:

"For about a decade after Khrushchev's expose of Stalin in 1956, the Soviet popular and scientific press discussed freely the suppressions of scientific truth and discussion in the previous period. But for the past dozen years it has been impossible to find references to that....U.S. advocates of socialism can only make themselves a laughing-stock if they pursue such a policy."

Lecturing was not all work. An invitation from the Women's Studies entity at the University of Hawaii gave us the financial base for a three-week vacation. It was our second visit to the islands and we knew where to go. There is the marvelous aviary and botanical garden uphill from the university's Manoa campus, the temple with its trained carp on the far side of Oahu, and the drive out to Lindbergh's grave beyond the seven sacred pools on Maui. I visit it on each trip because he was a truly modest man, and that quality makes his place of burial a thing of beauty. The monument he designed for himself is a large slab flush with the ground, bearing only his name and dates, and surrounded by smooth football-size natural rocks rather like the border of a rug. It harmonizes totally with the secluded missionary church in whose graveyard he lies. Gazing at it makes me ruminate on human complexity. Lindbergh, like many very highly-focused individuals, was a babe outside his own field. He did a lot of harm before World War II with a naive kind of isolationism, inherited from his much more practical father, a congressman who staunchly opposed U.S. entry into World War I. Hitler was different from the kaiser this country had fought in that war, but Lindy not only didn't realize that, he actually tended to admire Hitler. Anti-Semitism wasn't all there was to Nazism, and besides, forthright anti-Semitism was fairly universal among Americans of that day.

On that drive to Hana, we would swim in the sacred pools, of course, and in the jewel-like mini-lakes beneath waterfalls. On each visit to Hawaii, we drove up to volcano craters live and dead. There were the Filipino fishing villages still using outriggers, and the early morning fish markets. Our eyes relished the pounding waves on the windward side of the Big Island. We visited genuine centers of the revival of Hawaiian culture as well as the Mormons' interesting tourist-oriented water parade of the cultures of the South Pacific. The fine painted churches of early Belgian missionaries humbled us with respect for the devotion and talent of those early priests. On our return home, we told everyone of the decent modern homes of plantation workers thanks to the spectacular jump in their living standards after they were organized by the International Longshoremen's and Warehousemen's Union. It took strikes, jailings and beatings, but they won. Perhaps it is the fragrances of ginger, passion fruit, plumeria, all day, all night, everywhere beyond the reach of exhaust fumes in Honolulu and another city or two, that make the islands a therapy.

My sponsor at the University of Hawaii, teaching a course, "Literature by Women," provided much-needed support for my view that the women's movement should give more attention to workaday life. She wrote me: "I have gotten information about various matri-archists, perhaps most particularly related to women in the arts and music. There is little interest in such matters here, but a tremendous interest in working conditions, advancement opportunities, and fringe benefits for women."

The last full-term course I was ever permitted to teach was in Soviet law at Golden Gate University Law School in 1978. What qualified me to do so was that by that date I had translated sixty quarterly collections of Russian writings in that field, selected by American specialists. Doing that successfully required that I study American standard texts and dictionaries as well as works on the European civil law system on which Russian law had been modeled. Soviet law was a revision of pre-existing law to suit Marxist concepts, favoring human needs over prop-erty. (Unfortunately it also essentially abolished the law of property except for possessions for personal use. Since disputes inevitably arose among the hundred thousand government-owned enterprises, it became necessary to establish a terribly complex system of arbitration that even-tually tripped over its own feet.)

I planned my thirteen lectures as quick overviews of those fields of Soviet law that American lawyers-to-be would find of interest: labor, housing, environment, health, land and agriculture; education, science and culture; property, inheritance, invention, authorship; family law; women's rights; juveniles; consumer protection; social maintenance and security; crime, justice, penology; the legislative process; civil rights and ethnic minorities; civil liberties and public participation. I list these because of the stupid view persisting in the West that law did not exist in the USSR. Law was perverted and distorted when the Party thought reasons of state justified that. This is not exactly unfamiliar to us, although there it was worse. When Soviet socialism was replaced by an early-19th-century kind of capitalism, it became only too clear that daily life had in fact been governed by law. Crime and racketeering exploded. Corruption of government officials became the rule. Police became dependent on bribes to support their families because inflation destroyed the value of their salaries.

My course at Golden Gate had twenty-four enrollees. I asked them to write anonymous statements as to why they were taking the course. I wanted feedback, so I told them that class participation would be reflected in grades. The students did produce some interesting term papers on the basis of translated materials. At the end of the course one student came up to say he had gotten lots of new listeners for my broadcasts. Another asked how long they would continue. An attorney and faculty member who taught international law and law of the sea introduced himself as an "admirer" and asked if he could audit in the future.

Prof. Nancy McDermid of San Francisco State University, who became Dean of the School of Humanities there for decades afterward, invited me to address her courses on civil liberties regularly in the '60s and '70s. She had never been a student of mine. Yet she wrote me: "I just read a footnote in my [National Lawyers']*Guild Practitioner* and am so glad that you'll be teaching at Golden Gate this spring. You are one of the most provocative, challenging teachers with whom I've studied, from whom I've learned."

I had been invited to teach the course at Golden Gate in response to demand organized by a student who had been a 1960s activist. He graduated that year, and I was not asked to return. In an earlier chapter, I wrote that academe had lost a fine professor when it would not hire Dr. Stephen Dunn because of his cerebral palsy. Perhaps the same could be said of me, except that in my case the proscription was due to my views.

KPFA's monthly *Folio* had a letters section. It usually published about two dozen, in full or briefly excerpted. *For over thirty of my years on the air, most issues had letters on my program.* For fully five years after the appearance of *Soviet Women,* many letters dealt with it. In the fifth year of marketing it in person at the annual KPFA Fair, I sold 114 copies. I wrote the Doubleday editor: "There sure as hell is a market for my stuff if one can figure out where to find it." They had budgeted the munificent sum of $700 for advertising. So they informed me they wanted it off their hands after selling a little over twelve thousand copies. I bought the remaining four thousand and sold them without difficulty at lectures, fairs, and by mail.

That book was criticized by some young lesbians for confining itself to saying that no legal problem existed because their sexual behavior was absent from the Soviet statutes while male homosexuality was a crime. From that they extrapolated to view me as homophobic, with respect to lesbians in any case. But older American women who had fought prejudice and discrimination against their same-sex relationships here for a lifetime felt differently. The San Francisco Sunday *Examiner-Chronicle* once celebrated Elsa Gidlow, "the nation's first published lesbian poet," whose lover was Black. Gidlow wrote me in 1979: "Want to say what I have said to you on chance meetings a couple of times: I have listened to your program since its inception on KPFA ....one of the more useful and interesting. Carry on!" Del Martin, co-founder with her part-ner, Phyllis Lyon, of the Sisters of Bilitis, the first lesbian organization in the KPFA listening area, has five references to my *Soviet Women* and none to any other source on the USSR in her *Battered Wives.*

The purist sectarian Left would not touch *Soviet Women* any more than the Establishment press. I acidly wrote Karen Gellen at the Maoist *Guardian* that absence of a review in its pages meant that it "shares that distinction with the *New York Times* and *The New York Review of Books* ." The *Times* had given long reviews to my first two books in better times, and I had been a welcome writer for the *Guardian* in its original New Deal and later general-Marxist incarnations. The *Guardian* actu-ally refused a paid ad for *Soviet Women* on the grounds that "we do not accept advertisements that attack socialist countries." In the ad there was nothing whatever to justify that sentence, but the last chapter of the book did contrast the situation in the USSR to that in other countries under Communist rule, including China, whose female suicide rate is the world's highest.

In any case, my authorship of that book enabled me to reach extreme-ly wide audiences. It led to my engagement as consultant in 1979 for a "Women of Russia" TV series, with the appropriate credit.

The adventures before publication of my next book, *Soviet But Not Russian,* depict the mood of the times. I had initially offered it to Larry Hill, co-founder of Hill & Wang—an imprint that still exists—and sub-sequently a publisher on his own. Hill had asked me to write, and had published, my most successful book, *Russia Re-examined.* He felt—cor-rectly—that *Soviet But Not Russian* would come up against the wall of save-the-poor-Soviet-Jews-and-while-you're-at-it-save-the-Crimean-Tatars-too propaganda that carried through the '70s. Late in 1977 he wrote me: "The climate has become even more unfavorable toward any books that stress positive aspects of Soviet life....I am in a pessimistic frame of mind about progressive publishing altogether." This was extra-ordinarily similar to a letter I had received thirty years earlier from the John Day publishing house. They declined to publish the encylopedia of the USSR I had written on an advance from them and under my Hoover Institution Fellowship. And it resembled only too closely the response by the Leigh Lecture Bureau, my agents in 1945 and 1946, who now responded to an approach by me by saying my proposals were "too aca-demic." In desperation, for I felt a book on Soviet nationalities was essential to combat the Cold War, I now turned to International Publishers, the Communist house. They rejected it because my book included criticisms of Soviet policy. I had written them beforehand: "It must be absolutely understood that my opinions and conclusions are non-negotiable. I went unpublished for 18 years...because of that...and my stand with respect to my own intellectual integrity has not changed one iota."

When I discovered the booth of Ramparts Press, owned by Lawrence Moore, at a national booksellers' convention in San Francisco, I found my publisher. Moore was a listener to my broadcasts. He readily agreed to my idea for that book and gave me an advance on which to write it. When we became better acquainted, he turned out to be another of those American originals I've had the good luck to know. He was an Atlanta native, white, the son of a salesman. By 1936 he had crossed the Mason-Dixon line to Cincinnati, and had become a member of the Young Communist League like myself. He had also enlisted in the National Guard, and when it was called up for duty in the bloody Little Steel Strike, found himself on duty in Youngstown. Gus Hall, later perennial head of the Communist Party, was then the Young Communist League organizer in Youngstown, sensibly recruited as paid union organizer by the founder of the CIO labor federation, John L. Lewis. Hall organized a pro-strike rally, and presented Larry, in uniform, on the platform, saying, "There are even people in the National Guard with us."

When World War II began, Larry enlisted in the Air Force, but washed out in pilot training for reasons of vision. He served as a bombardier, and subsequently went to Stanford under the GI Bill. He had engineering talents, winning patents very early in the computer field. The owner of a manufacturing company, he sold it to found his independent Left publishing house. Moore was long out of the Party. Nineteen seventy was exactly the wrong time to start his venture, from a business point of view, for the rebellion of the '60s had ended. His first couple of books did well, but from then on things faltered.

When I turned in my manuscript, he felt the atmosphere was such that he would be unable to recover his investment, and he was not in a position to throw good money after bad. The book was published only in 1985, thanks to my solid base of support among KPFA listeners and others who responded splendidly to ads asking them to fund publication by paying Moore in advance.

Although I had very good relations with my publishers, it is only Larry who became a personal friend. He was simply admirable all around. He and his wife cultivated a semi-tropical garden that botanists could envy. When his money ran out, he and his son personally built a second superb hand-crafted home on their prime Palo Alto property. He sold both and used the mortgage income to buy a place up in inexpensive Forestville near the Russian River. Within a few years, the roses were blooming and the fruit trees producing as well as at the old place. But he could not break himself of chain-smoking, and it killed him, as it had at least one other close friend.

It is not only publishers with whom I developed interesting relations in the literary field. Linda Ferguson was editor of the *Pacific Sun Literary Quarterly* in the '70s. I wrote for her a review of *Dissent in the USSR,* a symposium edited by Rudolf Tokes. In it I saw a decade ahead: "Connor...suggests: 'Is it possible that, at the Central Committee level or above, the party itself is penetrated by dissenting reformists...?' Since Khrushchev was one such, and many of the present top leaders rose to prominence during his tenure, that makes sense to me. They could succeed to power constitutionally and without violence..." Gorbachev was in power within nine years.

Linda and I became friends. We had some serious discussions. I haven't found the letter from her—or perhaps it was a conversation— that provoked a tirade I wrote in response, in 1976:

"God damn the navel-gazing, shrink-reliant, petty, fundamental-change-fearful, me-me-me-and-don't-anybody-dare-offend-my-ego liter_ats who created the history-on-its-head myth that the Communist Party was destructive of U.S. literature (specifically, in your words, the little magazines) in the 1930s. Damn them twice for having transmitted that idea to a person like yourself, too young to be responsible for not knowing better, but in a position to pass that vicious and currently-harmful crap on to others. I say currently-harmful not because the *U.S.* Communists have any influence on American literature today that I know of, or show any signs of having any in the future.

"It's currently harmful because the reason for that alleged effect in the '30s is axiomatically assumed to be orders from Moscow, whether in the direct sense or in voluntary subservience. From which it is further axiomatically assumed that there is no literature in the Soviet Union.

"An aged literary critic friend of mine in Moscow who is permanently embittered by the 20 years he himself was barred from literary activity is utterly shocked when I write him of the American view that there is a literary vacuum in the Soviet Union, and sends me lists of people writing and being published there right now whose work he holds in the highest esteem."

I then listed a galaxy of the most famous American writers and artists who contributed in the '30s to the Communist *New Masses*, the greatest of the so-called little magazines of that day, with a circulation of some tens of thousands. I pointed to the chain of John Reed Clubs, cultural institutions across the country, to the New Theater League, to an organization for documentary film-making. I noted that Woody Guthrie was a regular columnist for the Party's *Daily Worker*, and continued:

"The amazing thing to me is that this was done not by a party of intellectuals, but of workers. Except for one great cartoonist, Robert Minor (Texas-born, school classmate of Eisenhower), the top leadership of the Communist Party consisted exclusively of workers, manual work-ers but for one former bookkeeper."

The Communist Party of those years deliberately and successfully revived aspects of America's literary heritage that had been suppressed long before Senator Joe McCarthy or even the earlier post-World-War I Red Scare. That Mark Twain was a flaming anti-imperialist [opposed to U.S. seizure of the Phillipines] was utterly unknown to me when I was required to read *Tom Sawyer* in school. By the end of the '30s, every-body knew it.

"In U.S. history, what other political organization has there ever been that gave a damn about literature, that sought to encourage it, that advo-cated and fought, hard and consistently, for programs to enable writers to eat? I'm talking about the W.P.A. Writers' Project, among others."

Culture is not the only field in which I sought to identify the contri-butions of the Communist Party to American life, though it did nothing positive after the McCarthy period except the defense of Angela Davis in 1970. Robert Allen, having asked me to review the manuscript of his *Black Awakening in Capitalist America,* accepted my numerous correc-tions and suggestions with respect to the Communist role in the move-ment against lynching, judicial frame-ups of Blacks in the '30s through '50s, and the fight for equal opportunity in employment, including such fields as baseball and officer status in the merchant marine.

After the suffragist movement gained women the right to vote, it was the Communist Party that for the next thirty years carried on the strug-gle for an understanding of the bases for the inferior status of women and to gain equality. Laura X received a letter from graduate student Kate Weigand saying that she was working on "a dissertation that docu-ments connections between the gender politics of...the American Communist Party of the 1940s and 1950s, and the women's liberation movement in the 1960s.... Some women and men in the Communist movement...after 1945 were making important progress in the area of women's liberation....Their activities were key to keeping ideas about women's oppression and women's liberation alive in the hostile and anti-feminist years between World War II and the 1960s....The terms 'women's oppression,' women's liberation,' 'male supremacy,' and 'male chauvinism,' for example, come straight out of the Old Left.

"Your *Women and World History* is unusual among the early women's liberation documents...because it makes so many direct refer-ences to Old Left traditions, literature and activists and because it does-n't dismiss the Old Left as irrelevant for women's history."

"I am also curious about how you learned about women such as Sadie Van Veen, Margaret Krumbein, Rose Wortis, Betty Millard, Grace Hutchins, Carol King and others like them who are not well-known outside of Old Left circles? Finally, I wonder why your group, unlike most who were compiling information about women's history, decided that these women and their activities and achievements were important and historically significant instead of duped or dangerous?"

I plead guilty. Forwarding a copy to me, Laura wrote: "Actually, this is a thank-you note to Bill Mandel."

There were no more witch-hunt hearings or arrests, trials or draft evasion issues in the family to deal with in the late '70s. Reminders of them were more often pleasant than otherwise. A Trotskyist who I had known in our very first years in Berkeley was now working for a labor research institute at U.C.L.A. We had had no contact for probably fifteen years, but something had moved him to write a letter of reminiscence: "Another point on which you can claim some credit, however, is that on that day twenty years ago when the traumatic fact became clear to me that I would have to 'take the First' and probably serve some time should I be called before Senator Burns' committee, you were an important factor that inspired that decision."

Another reminder was not pleasant, but amusing. A fellow-translator, Dale Cunningham, was removed as president-elect of the American Translators Association (ATA) for being a defendant in the case of the Camden 28, direct-action pacifists who conducted a raid on a draft board. He acquired his FBI file and sent me pages with several entries on me. I was never a direct-action pacifist and had nothing to do with that event, but he and I had corresponded on association business. So the FBI spent taxpayer money on investigating me. Its findings contained ludicrous inaccuracies. They quenched any desire on my part to have it copy whatever it would choose to release from its file on me. The problem is that it interprets the Freedom of Information Act to decide what to release. It withholds information or allegations on the excuse that releasing them would endanger its informants.

Oddly enough a family problem did arise due to conflict on the Left. Son Bob, then a manual worker active in the International Warehousemen's and Longshoremen's Union, took extreme Leftist positions critical of the leadership. I didn't agree with him. I was, and remain, a great admirer of that union's legendary founder and then still president, Harry Bridges, whom I knew. But in 1975 Bob's health and life were threatened at a local meeting. Bob "is a person of exceptional strength of conviction and plain ordinary courage," I wrote Harry. "Any attempt by anybody to frighten him out of activity by sending him to the hospital is just not going to work....If the people who have actually threatened to kill him do so, that's another matter....I would not rest until those ultimately responsible are exposed and brought to justice....If all the foregoing is the result of my being misinformed by a young man with a vivid imagination...file...and forget....No one has accused you of direct involvement."

A year later Bob was beaten up at a meeting of shop stewards of the Warehousemen's Local. A tooth was broken and he needed six stitches. This time my letter to Bridges was tough: "As I wrote you last year, Bob was not intimidated by this, and is back at his usual activities, which do *not* include violence against fellow union members. Also as I wrote you last year, nothing short of a tragedy can silence him. I am, as of now, out to prevent that. For one thing, I am now sending him a copy of the letter I wrote you last year."

This time I had a reply: "Dear Bill:...there is no doubt that the incident took place," but people denied that it happened as I described it. Bridges' main source insisted that there was nothing organized or pre-arranged, as Bob believed. But there were no further incidents of that kind.

By 1978, in accordance with his political principles and his effort to remain part of the working class and in his union, Bob, that one-time accelerated-Ph.D.-program candidate in history at U.C. Berkeley, took a job as toilet-cleaner with a company having an ILWU union contract. The chemicals employed caused him double vision, headaches, breathing difficulties. He was diagnosed with toxicosis. He got out of that job before any then identifiable permanent damage was done. With the health problems he has today though, I wonder.

While Bridges represented the level of union militancy possible in a period of general membership decline—he had told me, accurately, that big business intended to wipe out the labor movement—I had little respect for the unions in general. In 1977 a listener sent a letter upbraiding me for criticizing a TV special on Joe McCarthy in the San Francisco weekly *Bay Guardian*. I had written: "The special did not present a single one of the hearings in which witnesses with faith in the American people cut Joe down to size, for that would destroy the myth of an Establishment that saved democracy".

The listener responded: "It was a shock to read your recent article in the strike-bound scab *Bay Guardian*."

I replied: "The [daily San Francisco] *Chronicle* is a Newsguild union shop. I've been on its shit list for ten years, and can't even get a letter to the editor published, never mind being called by them as an expert regarding news in my field. The Newsguild, as I'm sure you know, cooperated directly with the CIA internationally, as Senator Church' official investigation brought out, and as anyone with his eyes open knew beforehand. On political matters, American unions have stunk for 30 years. The tiny ILWU and UE [Electrical Workers] are the only exceptions....If I had to depend upon American labor to support my right to be heard, specifically with respect to the Soviet Union, which is why I was called before McCarthy, I would have been gagged and handcuffed for 30 years. So the responsibility is upon you in labor, not upon me. Unions are essential for economic reasons, and I hope some day they'll be different politically. But I'm not going to wait until I'm dead. In the specific case of the *Bay Guardian,* I would not have written for them while the strike was a live issue. By the time I did, it was dead. But the fundamental issue for me as a writer is for what I do to see the light. I've no intention of committing suicide because U.S. labor has castrated itself politically."

Bay area union members I knew did not always judge me on labor issues. In 1976 an elderly longshoreman phoned to congratulate me on the 30th anniversary of the publication of my *Guide to the Soviet Union,* which I had autographed for him on a lecture swing in the year it appeared. But the same man subsequently broke relations with me over my refusal to accept the notion that the status of Jews in the USSR was one unbroken horror. He was Jewish. This kind of reaction made me extremely careful in writing the chapter on the Jews in *Soviet But Not Russian.* Here I went beyond my nuclear family, and friends in California, for criticism. It is in New York, with a larger Jewish population than any other city on earth, that attention on the status of Soviet Jews was focused most sharply.

KPFA's fall fund-raising marathon that year had included a Writers' Day. I dug out the two good poems I have written, and read them. Listeners responsed by sending me their verse. When opportunity offered, I tried to raise money for the station without waiting for marathons. A bookstore in Grass Valley asked me to speak. I wrote it: "I'll repeat the offer I made to you off the cuff: to do my slide show on Soviet women in conjunction with an autographing thing for my book, if in some way funds can be raised for KPFA."

As always, the range of listeners fascinated me. A couple describing themselves as "very low income", wrote to ask if I would send reprints of my scripts free of charge. A San Francisco cabbie informed me that his fares had no choice but to listen to KPFA. A professor of Chinese language at Stanford sought my advice on selecting American literature to send to people he had met on a visit to the USSR under the cultural exchange.

The prisoner's rights movement brought listeners at the opposite end of the social spectrum. One was a Latino poet, Pancho Aguila: "My interest is based on my own writing and that of the smashed Folsom prison Writers' Workshop....KPFA has been supportive of our defense. I'm currently in the hole because of such activity, consequently my enthusiasm to learn of others under similar conditions." I wrote a detailed response. We kept in touch. I got Doubleday to send him a copy of a volume of poetry he wanted.

Despite my broad-based and often passionate support among listeners, the political attacks never ceased. The KPFA *Folio* carried a letter of mine in 1977: "I've had my bellyful after 20 years on KPFA of opinions such as that of D.N. in February's *Folio* that I'm 'unabashedly pro-Soviet.'" I re-told the story of KPFK in Los Angeles having me secretly monitored by the RAND Corporation in 1960. That resulted in a clean bill of health both for the representativeness of my materials from the Soviet press and the accuracy of my translations. "Unfortunately, present management of other Pacifica stations seems to share D.N.'s opinions, with the result that their listeners are left to the tender mercies of wire service coverage of the USSR....The real problem is this country's religion—anti-Sovietism. Regrettably, I have no illusion that I can change it."

Race relations within the station were and remained an unending problem. I had broken a roadblock to giving the Third World Department—people of color and Spanish-speakers—prime time. Everyone had agreed that it should get such a slot, but no one proposed a solution until I offered to surrender my coveted time right after the Evening News. When I did, others followed, and that department had 7 p.m. all five weekdays. I wound up broadcasting at 10:15 p.m., too late for people with early jobs, those having to make long commutes, or the elderly. It was not until the close of 1979 that I was put back on my previous spot right after the News.

Friends and family always played a role in my activities associated with the station. When songwriter Malvina Reynolds died early in 1978, I broadcast and the *Folio* published a remembrance of mine about her and her husband Bud. At a memorial for her, I told of giving away copies of her records on a visit to the Soviet Union, and of the publication there of a booklet of her songs with excellent translations into Russian.

I am delighted that the photo of me Matthew Lasar chose to use in his book, *Pacifica Radio ,* (1999) shows me singing over KPFA's air. My closest association with the world of song had come through Malvina, beginning in 1956. We were still living on 164th St. at Amsterdam Avenue in Manhattan, two blocks from Audubon Ballroom, where Malcolm X was later assassinated. The neighbors in the next apartment were a Communist writer, George Marion, a truly top-notch journalist, and his remarkable wife, Betty, paralyzed from the buttocks down. They were visited once by a couple who seemed quite old to us. We were thirty-nine, and these people, superficially very plain, straightforward workingclass types, were in their 50s. They were from Berkeley, he a carpenter, she the West-Coast representative of a radical weekly.

She had a guitar. They sat in our kitchen one evening, and she sang a couple of things she had written, words and music both. First came a very lengthy ballad take-off on the Pied Piper of Hamelin, which our children, particularly younger son Davey, who later made a living for some years as a singer-guitarist, fell in love with. The second was short and wonderful, "Bury Me In My Overalls." It was a pithy, straightforward tribute by a workingclass wife to a workingclass husband—very obviously it was to her own husband. I'd never heard anything on that theme before:

> Bury me in my overalls, don't use my gabardine
> Bury me in my overalls, or use my beat-up jeans.

I turned to Malvina and said: "Mrs. Reynolds, I know when someone is good. I've spotted a lot of winners, and knew they would be winners, when no one knew they existed. You are good. *This* is what you must do." And so when we emigrated to Berkeley a year later, Malvina and Bud and the Mandels became friends. The following year I began my KPFA broadcasts. The Reynolds' home was just a few blocks down: she was later known as "the sage of Parker Street." It became routine that, every Monday evening after my program, I would go there and she would sing and play for me the song she had written that past week. With the exception of her husband and perhaps her daughter, I was the first to hear her classic satire on tract housing, "Little Boxes," which made the Top 40 in 1963:

> Little boxes on the hillside,
> Little boxes made of ticky-tacky—

Her word, "ticky-tacky," is now in major dictionaries.

She asked me to perform with her—until my throat was struck in an auto accident when I was sixty-six I had a voice good enough sometimes to win spontaneous applause when I would just sing for fun in a crowd. I declined, just as I had declined to become a professional dancer when pro modern dancers suggested that to me at age thirty. They had ballet in mind. Or act in a play by a friend who gave Sidney Poitier his first role. And just as I had declined to give a piano concert on the air when KPFA's then music director, Alan Rich, happened upon me doing my exceedingly limited Beethoven-Chopin-Bach repertoire on the studio's concert grand. Despite my admiration for Robeson, Malvina herself, and others, I didn't understand that establishing a reputation as a performer would enhance and not diminish the impact of whatever I wrote and said. I thought being an activist and scholar was a higher calling. Yet I bemoaned Bob North's having abandoned literature for academe. I'm afraid I wasn't consistent in this regard. But the fact that I would have to sacrifice either my family's material well-being or my ongoing study of the Soviet Union in order to hone my performing skills played a major role in these decisions.

Malvina became a national figure when Pete Seeger began to sing her work. Pete believes, as I do, that she deserves to be performed more widely, and remembered more fully than is the case at this writing. So in his autobiography of only 287 pages, he gives nine to Mal's songs. And I'm delighted that he spares a paragraph and photo for her husband Bud, very typically carrying her guitar.

Bud grew up on a Michigan farm, and was an early auto worker. Immediate family members became big executives in the industry, but that was not for him. He worked in the plants, and, during World War I, sailed before the mast to Australia on a square-rigger. During the Great Depression, he organized a stupendous Hunger March of "downsized" Ford workers through that plant's grounds. Four were shot dead by company police. As the demonstrators passed a particular building, Bud pointed to a series of second-floor windows and hollered: "Let 'em have it!" Rocks shattered them. I asked him: "Why those?" He said: "Russians were up there, learning automobile manufacturing. I wanted them to know there's a class struggle in this country." Bud was a Communist, and later an organizer for the Party in Omaha. Mal accompanied him, and their daughter was born there. Later a carpenter, he was expelled from that union when it adopted an anti-Communist clause during the Cold War. But when Mal won fame with her songs, Bud abandoned his own interests totally to further her career. He was entirely self-effacing. Only friends, family, and those who got business mail from him knew he existed at all. I actually was quite angry with Malvina that she never taped his wonderful and meaningful reminiscences. That was her job, not mine. But when she died, it was her permanent contribution to American folk music that counted, and that's what I memorialized on the air.

By the end of the '70s I was expressing my disagreement with the shallowness of KPFA News directly on the air. To me doing this was a perfectly normal thing in a station devoted to arriving at the truth by the expression of diverse opinions. Listeners approved. One wrote wondering if the News Department was "reading the wire services as the dispatches are ripped off the machines. If KPFA is doing the latter, then it is time for some questions."

The station's response was to prohibit on-air discussion of "internal" matters. I violated that, cautiously but at least once a year, as a matter of principle. I also took problems to the press, which worked. For example, in 1977 the *Bay Guardian* ran a letter of mine complaining that three of my last six programs had been pre-empted by music specials and that three of the following six would be pre-empted by a minithon to raise money. My standing with the listeners was too high for management to act against me at that time, as it did after the USSR collapsed.

Even my KPFA broadcasting had its light side, despite constant friction with the production and news departments and, on policy matters, with management. We had a softball team, consciously co-ed from the outset, on which I played every Sunday morning during the season. I wasn't very good, but it certainly helped keep me in shape and to unwind.

And there was always the pleasure of small social gatherings. As Berkeley is an international center of learning, we frequently hosted visitors from abroad, most often from the Soviet Union. Others would invite us to dinner with interesting people from France or Spain or Italy or the Netherlands. When we traveled abroad, we'd look them up and they'd help provide us with a native's view.

At the close of the 70s, relations between African-Americans and Jews were beginning to become tense. Blacks were trying to free themselves of any residue of white tutelage in the civil rights movement. Jews, to their honor, had been a huge proportion of the whites who had gone to Mississippi, where two Jewish young men had been killed. The prominent Black youth leader, Stokely Carmichael [I use his name of that day; subsequently he adopted an African name] had made anti-Zionist speeches that were unquestionably anti-Semitic as well. I wrote a letter to the bi-weekly of the overall "movement" in Berkeley, *Grassroots:*

"Relations between Jews and Blacks have been worsened by the attempt to stop Stokely Carmichael from speaking at Cal. That is tragic. I write in an effort to correct that by showing that one can be aggressively loyal to his human dignity as a Jew (something certain younger progressives seem to run away from) without being a Zionist, and at the same time uphold the human dignity and rights of Blacks."

When the station asked for programming pertinent to Black History Month, the four programs I did were on the Soviet-born daughter of an African-American, Soviet views on Africa, Soviet views on Blacks in the U.S., and the USSR as seen by Blacks: Langston Hughes, the African George Padmore, Dr. DuBois, Paul Robeson, boxing champion Mohammed Ali.

I waged another battle in the late 70s at extreme long distance. I have already made clear that people who would not fight injustice in their own back yards did not have my respect when they undertook to instruct others far away. But as one who fought oppression of women at home I felt I had the right to carry on that battle elsewhere. The foreign editor of a Soviet national-circulation weekly of deservedly high prestige, the *Literary Gazette*, [*Literaturnaia gazeta*] had promised to review my *Soviet Women*. I wrote him, early in 1976, that while the review in *The Working Woman* [*Rabotnitsa*] had been "entirely favorable, I hope the review in your newspaper will be more serious. For example, your country wants its population to increase....You will have no population increase unless husbands are taught to share housework and child upbringing *equally* with their wives....Women...no longer will accept the double burden: a job during the day and another job at night....The only hope is for women to feel that the marriage is truly equal. It will take time to bring about such a change in men's attitudes toward housework. The sooner you start, and the earlier in life, the sooner you will get results. Secondly, your country is troubled by the rising divorce rate. If people know nothing about sex when they get married, there will be incompatibility, trouble, divorce. Without institution of real sex education in the schools, you will have no reduction in the divorce rate. I hope your review will deal with other controversial matters in my book."

No review appeared.

I did most of my fuming on Soviet failings during my working hours. As I translated, I would think about the articles I was rendering from Russian into English. Computers were not yet cheap enough for my employer to require camera-ready copy, so I used a typewriter and knew that my work would be gone over by a subject-specialist editor and then a copy-editor. When the material before me provoked thought, I would skip a line, switch to all capital letters, and write it. Usually what I wrote were acid or creative criticisms, occasionally original ideas. I didn't have to watch my language. I kept carbon copies, and these notes served me in radio broadcasts, books, and lectures. I knew that the editors enjoyed them. The copy-editor wrote me: "Your comments on translations provide the only saving grace in many of those horrors you have to work with (*Soviet Philosophy, S. Literature, S. Law & Govt.*, etc.) and I much resent some of the editors' making them undecipherable before I get a chance to read them!"

Given all the personal and professional frustrations I'd managed during the witch-hunts, my translating job was pretty much ideal. I would send the boss news clippings on the salary scale of academics at the University of California, and he kept mine at the level of full professors in the social sciences, by far higher than any translator on earth except at the United Nations. Yet nothing having to do with my employment was remotely as important to me as dealing with the ever-escalating arms race. Its peak before Reagan came in the last months of 1979, when President Carter was insisting that NATO deploy in Europe intermediate-range missiles that could strike the USSR, thus reducing warning time to zero for all practical purposes. An immense movement against this had arisen in Europe, including retired high-ranking officers, counterparts of Admiral LaRocque and his associates, in the major NATO countries. Europeans previously had conceived of nuclear war as a long-range duel between American and Soviet intercontinental missiles flying overhead. Now they knew that the USSR could strike at the European countries hosting intermediate-range missiles. A smaller anti-arms-race movement came into being at home, and I put maximum energy into it.

In October, 1979 the Soviet leader, Brezhnev, made an offer to stop the missile deployment. He announced withdrawal of a thousand tanks from East Germany, something that could easily be monitored by Western satellites. Further, if the West would drop the missile plan, he would reduce the number of Soviet missiles already aimed at West Europe where a huge American army was permanently stationed.

With a little research, I found that the tanks to be withdrawn were the equivalent of all the armor in twelve U.S. infantry divisions of the day, a stupendous force. I did a broadcast, published in the KPFA *Folio,* pointing out that the U.S. move to deploy intermediate-range nukes in Europe was the equivalent of the Soviet Union's action in 1962 introducing missiles into Cuba capable of striking our entire industrial East as far as Chicago. Another version of this story appeared in the *Women for Peace Newsletter*, which enjoyed much prestige.

I also submitted a proposal for inclusion in the Democratic Party platform for the presidential election: in view of Soviet withdrawal of fourteen percent of Warsaw Pact tanks from East Germany, a) not to install missiles in Europe capable of striking the Soviet homeland, b) to withdraw 14 percent of existing U.S. short-range battlefield missiles from West Germany, and c) to proceed with the stalled talks on mutual force reductions in hope of withdrawing the 250,000 U.S. troops in Europe, thus reducing arms budget, inflation, and taxes.

The intensity of my effort must have shown in my voice as I answered questions on the air, for mail at that time included letters like this one from a senior woman. "Tonight I am worried about you in case the pressures are becoming too great for you to endure. I can't bear to think of the loss it would be to us if you were to break - let alone your suffering."

But the 1980s brought world-shaking developments. They prompted the emergence of totally unexpected forces, citizen diplomacy here and Gorbachev there.

CHAPTER 25

Battle for the Air Waves

Fifteen hundred worried students looked up at me from a green field at the University of California Davis campus in the middle of the Central Valley farmlands. This demonstration, early in 1980, was the largest by students anywhere in this country since the 1960s. I had been invited to speak by a law student who listened to my broadcasts.

"You are being asked to register for military service allegedly because of Soviet action in Central Asia," I said. Moscow had just sent its troops into Afghanistan. "Strange that India, the largest country in the path of what we have been told is Soviet expansionism...has taken no similar step, nor any other comparable to the long list of military, political, economic, and cultural measures [against the U.S.S.R.] instituted by Candidate Carter." President Carter was running for re-election.

I had opposed the Soviet invasions of Hungary in 1956 and that of Czechoslovakia in 1968, and took a plague-on-both-your-houses stand against the 1969 border war between the USSR and China. My view of the Soviet entry into Afghanistan at the end of 1979 was different. I believed it was a response to the entry of U.S. aircraft carriers into the Persian Gulf which had just occurred for the first time ever. Ostensibly they had been placed there because revolutionary Iran, having just overthrown the Shah, had taken the American Embassy staff hostage. To the Soviets, those carriers represented a potential for lightning nuclear attack by their aircraft upon what Winston Churchill had long since called its "soft underbelly." Think of Russian entry into Kosovo in 1999.

Moscow, I believed, now felt itself surrounded by short-range U.S. nuclear capability. The North Atlantic Treaty Alliance had only just succumbed to the American demand for stationing U.S. Pershing and cruise missiles in Europe, after years-long resistance by peoples, parliaments, and even former NATO officers, and despite one Soviet compromise after another. Moscow responded two weeks later, in my view, by entering Afghanistan in an attempt to show that no American action could effectively change the world balance of power.

In addition to these factors, I was very impressed by the top American expert on Afghanistan, who at that point was with the

Carnegie Foundation for International Peace. He wrote that it was the Shah of Iran, in power until very recently, who had stimulated the slaughter of Marxist officers by the government of neighboring Afghanistan. This had caused survivors to engage in a revolt they knew they could not win and to call upon Moscow for aid.

This was the fourth consecutive decade of hysterical trumpeting of the Soviet threat by Washington, echoed by the mass media, and it finally pushed me to the brink of losing hope. On April 24, 1980, the U.S. failed in a desperate attempt to rescue the Iranian-held hostages. America went wild with frustrated patriotism. On my broadcast immediately after this event, I deliberately chose words designed to stimulate the peace movement to a now-or-never effort.

A young man phoned during my KPFA talk-show period, and cried, "We have been humiliated; America has been humiliated." He continued, "My country, right or wrong!" I had thought that the Vietnam War, which ended only seven years earlier, put an end to that attitude. I answered him: "Sir, that's the beginning of a toast offered by one of Lincoln's generals, Carl Schurz. No one ever quotes the rest of that toast, which goes: 'When right, to be kept right; when wrong, to be put right.'"

Listeners responded to that broadcast in such a range of ways that I had to conclude that each heard what he wanted to. One in Berkeley wrote: "I thank you from the bottom of my heart for your program last night, for saying what you said, for hearing the young man out, for your compassion and restraint in replying to him." A man in Sacramento summarized what he believed I had said, and offered his view: "You said you had always been optimistic about the American to have a... progressive outlook on the world and within the country itself. But now for the first time you are pessimistic....I was amazed with your discipline and self control when you allowed that Jingo to speak as long as he did."

The Iranian hostage-taking on top of the Afghan crisis brought the first *ad hominem* attacks upon me by university professors I had ever experienced. I was totally aware of the snide sniping from the Hoover Institution that had preceded my removal from KQED-TV in 1960, and from a cabal at U.C. Berkeley in an effort to accomplish the same at KPFA at that time. However, twenty years had passed since then.

Within days after the failed helicopter caper in Iran, the *Daily Collegian* at the Fresno campus of California State University carried a full page letter by a Prof. David Jones which criticized another professor there for recommending my broadcasts, particularly with respect to Afghanistan. Jones' politically stupid but savage letter also attacked me for allegedly not having spoken to my son Bob for years because he was a Trotskyist. Inasmuch as Bob had snapped lots of pictures of me playing softball at a recent picnic of his organization of Trotskyist young people, and everyone there had witnessed our good relationship, any number of people could testify to the falsity of Jones' charge. I wrote the *Collegian* a raging letter as long as his, which the editor published in full under a fine headline, "Mandel Calls Jones Liar." All this at a university where I had never spoken.

A few weeks later the same thing happened at U.C. Davis, where I had. A professor Brzeski wrote a brief letter in the *Aggie,* the student newspaper. "Bill Mandel blames the Carter administration for the Afghani crisis. Naturally, what else would you expect of Mr. Mandel? You describe him as a 'Soviet affairs specialist'; in truth, he is but a Soviet propagandist conveniently domiciled in Berkeley. Mr. Mandel's life work is to misinform the public about the Soviet Union. He did his bit in Davis," Brzeski wrote.

The student who had invited me to Davis sent this clipping to me, with a note: "While I myself have my differences with some of your presentation, I am appalled by this libelous personal attack on your career, your reputation, and even your domicile."

But Brzeski was unluckier even than Jones. The *Aggie* published my response under the headline: "Used to Tag After Me," lifted from a sentence that continued "like a groupie. Witnesses are available." That had been during the struggle against HUAC, when Brzeski was a graduate student at Berkeley. I wonder how long it was before he was able to show his face again in the Davis faculty dining room.

The letter that affected me most came from Sol Mandelblatt, one of the volunteer Lincoln Battalion I have been in awe of all my life because they fought to defend Spain against Hitler and Mussolini and I did not. He wrote: "Got back from New York to hear your *cri de coeur* and - Stay On - you're the only game in town." In 1984 he wrote a poem about me:

Mandel Again

        this guy:
                when the irises close,
                when the bullets
                armor   uniforms
                commissaries
                bugles blare
                        battle readiness

            mans the advance posts
                issuing sustenance   balance
                        red blood corpuscles.

A fund-raising marathon for the station at this time included a USSR Day consisting of my best programs of recent years. This was to replace my weekly program for the duration the marathon. A "sizeable" contributor wrote the station: "NO Mandel - NO money this year!!" Despite the gag rule against discussing internal affairs on air instituted in the late '70s, I announced: "I will be on as usual, thanks to the flood of letters you have sent the station management." At that time, it still paid some attention to subscriber mail.

For that USSR Day, which occurred before the Iranian helicopter crisis, I selected from my interviews with Soviet workers, farmers, union officers, the vice-mayor of a Lithuanian city, the 'mayor' of a borough, Moslems, Jews, Ukrainians, Belorussians, peoples of the Caucasus, and a Black woman of U.S. parentage raised and resident in the USSR; film-makers, writers, sculptors, a metal-chaser, scientists. There were recordings of music, readings of creative literature, an interview with the head of a women's health center and teenagers and mature women discussing sex.

The upsurge of super-patriotism prompted by the hostage-taking led to an attempt by the American Nazis to speak at San Francisco's City Hall shortly thereafter. Our son Bob was a chief organizer of a demonstration to prevent that, and asked me to speak. Attendance was fairly substantial and, to my surprise, did not consist primarily of people who had been directly touched by Nazism. Rather, it was youthful working-class, interracial, with a number of Vietnam veterans. When a listener wrote asking me to broadcast my words there on KPFA, I did so. Some remain pertinent:

"When Jewish organizations today speak of the Holocaust as simply a Jewish tragedy, they are furthering the kind of anti-Semitism on which those Nazi leaflets played." I had quoted leaflets dropped by the Germans on those Soviet forces in World War II whose commanding generals, under Stalin, happened to be Jewish: "Don't die for the sake of the Jews!" I continued, using a statistic presented by the American prosecutor at the War Crimes Trial, U.S. Supreme Court Justice Jackson. From his figure of 25 million non-military victims of the Nazis, compiled from their own meticulously-kept written records, I concluded, based on the fact that 6 million Jews had been killed: "Over three-quarters of the civilians, children, the aged and sick, women and men, whom they murdered deliberately, were not Jewish."

I opposed allowing the Nazis to speak, on the basis of America's adherence to the U.N. Convention on Genocide, which reads: "the following acts shall be punishable:... (c)...incitement to commit genocide." "The framers of that Convention," I explained, "found...that there was no point at which they could draw the line between the propaganda to put the Germans in a frame of mind to wipe out other peoples by accident of birth and the actual commission of that deed." This is why any public allegation that the Holocaust did not occur is a crime in Germany and some other countries to this day. An American Nazi propagandist was sentenced to years in a German jail in 1996 after being extradited to that country by Denmark, which has a similar law.

Apparently the endless cold war propaganda campaigns—yellow rain in Vietnam was allegedly some kind of mysterious Soviet chemical agent, the escape of anthrax bacilli from a Russian facility was a biological threat to the world, etc.—got to me. A listener wrote: "I'm sorry for your hurt and rage but find it understandable and I'm glad you did so eloquently express your feelings." But there were letters that made me feel like dancing down the street. From a poet, Susu Jeffrey: "I remember telling you that I am late for Monday evening poetry readings so I can catch your show. You grinned.... And I remembered how open and young your face is. Hmmm."

Eight Fresno subscribers, including two of the KFCF staff, jointly wrote: "we would like to suggest that you devote a whole day to U.S.-Soviet relations." That was after Reagan's election as president. The prevalent view among KPFA listeners was that his presidency would mean nuclear war. I looked for signs beneath his rhetoric for what his policy would really be, and had come to a different conclusion than most listeners. One Reagan interview provided the answer. He said that the U.S. would protect Saudi Arabia against foreign aggression or internal overthrow. That was actually a prediction of Bush's Desert Storm against Iraq a decade later. Oil *über alles*. But Reagan continued in that interview to say the U.S. wouldn't do anything about Iran, if Moscow endangered it, because we didn't have the strength, which was "too bad." I concluded that his administration would be based upon acquiring that strength—a prediction which turned out to be exactly right. A speech I gave at a huge 1981 protest in the Santa Rosa Civic Auditorium against the Bohemian Club's annual encampment of Establishment males from all over the country was built around the notion of Caspar Weinberger, Reagan's Secretary of Defense, as the most dangerous man in the world.

In a further attempt to calm the prevalent hysteria among peace-minded people, I had done a broadcast reviving my argument from the earliest cold war years. Its theme was that the U.S. and Russia had been allies in major world crises from the time of the American Revolution through World War II. President Wilson's participation in the armed Intervention against Lenin had been the only exception.

A Fresno listener named Brandon, who the next year brilliantly demonstrated in a letter to me that the Soviet system was failing, nearly a decade before I recognized that development, at this time wrote in the *Folio* a criticism of my view of history. The heat of the time brought equally heated responses from listeners, depending on their points of view. One listener wrote: "Please try not to put emotions under stress by antagonizing callers. The effect on some listeners (not me) is counter-productive." This was spelled out by the son of Latvian parents who were in that country during World War II: "When you receive calls that are in agreement with your position, you carry on a normal mutual con-versation....When the caller brings up points that put the Soviet Communists in a negative light, two changes come over you: One, your tone of voice becomes high pressured; and two, you railroad the caller off the air as soon as possible."

Actually, I had a very specific practice that explains these differences. When listeners were clearly intelligent and rational, as this Latvian-American was, I deliberately sought to shake them into abandoning what I regarded as mental blocks to considering other points of view. When they were not rational or not particularly intelligent, I was gentle and tried to lead them along.

The relative quiescence of social movements in the '80s left a vacuum that fringe groups sought to fill. In the context of the Pacifica stations, these were of two types, extremist Black nationalist elements on the one hand, and ultra-Leftist whites on the other. The former did not affect me directly, the latter did. In mid-1981 KPFK, Los Angeles, removed me from the air. The program director, Clare Spark, told a lis-tener seeking to get me back on the air there that she was "disinclined to use any of your tapes on the grounds that you are a biased observer of the Soviet scene. She said she is looking for an unbiased observer. When I suggested that she was posing an impossible task for herself, her answer was 'so be it'."

I made a one-time announcement of this on KPFA, and asked listen-ers to write KPFK, with copies to me. Sixty-four took the trouble to write to that station in another city. Over three-fourths were people from whom I had never even had mail, much less met. As always, I was fascinated by the kind of people I found to be on my side. A former Air Force Russian language specialist wrote: "His format provides the only direct commentary on news events concerning the Soviet Union that can be considered objective." The founding president of the San Francisco Newspaper Guild was an "ardent listener." A female Japanese-American attorney wrote that my program "serves an impor-tant, crucial function in helping to counter the distortions about the Soviet Union all too prevalent right now." A very different kind of lis-tener: "And to think that I support listener sponsored radio; which is not an easy task from Folsom State Prison, doing life." A professor at

UC San Francisco described me as: "one of the most erudite, thorough and well-prepared men on radio - of any kind at all." Three of the writers were Black.

Despite difficulties on the air, there was still plenty of reason to regard myself as useful. A Chicano writer, Francisco Alarcon, welcomed two long translations of articles on Latin American literature I had sent him from *Soviet Studies in Literature* in consequence of broadcasts. A long-term Latino prisoner, David Martinez, listening in Folsom State Prison, asked for concrete data on the Soviet prison system. He wanted to know about mandated sentences, the death penalty, prison population per capita, approximate length of sentences. "In California for instance the buildings are bulging with 15 and 25-to-life *first* termers," he informed me, "most not even up for parole consideration until 16 years 8 months of that life sentence....I have a lot of fun just listening to the local dummies call you with the U.S. media hysteria and getting their bubbles popped with a little backed up fact. Anyway, I just wanted to let you know that someone here in Folsom is getting a great deal from your program, and I appreciate you being there with it. Adelante! In continued struggle."

My broadcasts were not confined to politics. A woman who identified herself as half-Aztec thanked another programmer and me "for putting together that beautiful Soviet music show....I have also enjoyed hearing your wife's [Tanya's] comments on [the film] 'Moscow Does Not Believe in Tears' and other topics. Your show devoted to science fiction writers was particularly interesting." I appreciated indications that I could see the world beyond my own sphere: "I'd also like to thank you for the time you graciously relinquished your program on the sad occasion of Rasta Bob Marley's death. It was an act of compassion."

I always had a substantial listenership among Third-World students studying in the U.S. A Kenyan asked for a transcription of a broadcast on Namibia. A Sudanese electronics engineer in Silicon Valley was a frequent participant in the phone-in discussions. An Iranian asked to use my broadcast on Secretary of Defense Weinberger in his class at Foothill College.

One advantage to KPFA's powerful 59,000-watt signal is that it provided intellectual contact for people living in physical isolation. "I am not a mainstream American, one listener wrote...I live in a tiny cabin in the woods and listen to KPFA, supporting myself as a carpenter even though I have a degree in philosophy." His address was Cohasset, which is someplace uphill from Chico, at the north end of California's Central Valley.

When KPFA needed a new manager, I wrote in the newsletter of the unpaid staff, *Intercom* , that we needed a person who knew "how and on what principles we handled the events that made us what we now are: the Free Speech Movement, the resistance to the Vietnam War, the civil rights movement in the South and the hot-summer rising, the Huelga [farm labor strike], People's Park, the women's movement, the lesbian-and-gay rights movement, the ecology movement in all its forms." The person must be "of long Northern California residence, with a gut feel for the difference in style and mood this special region requires, as distinct from the slickness and other characteristics needed elsewhere....The new person should be an individual demonstrably more devoted to free radio than to any specific solution to this country's social and economic problems. We don't need sectarianism."

The new manager, David Salniker, did correspond to those requirements, but unfortunately also brought a corporate mentality that marginalized the participation of unpaid staff in policy-making and ended the role of KPFA as an organizing center for popular movements.

But I became more and more alarmed over the fact that KPFA News had gone far beyond what could be dismissed as tearing off and reading the news as presented by wire services. Its morning edition on November 2, 1981, caused me to write a letter to the station manager, program director, and the heads of the public affairs and news departments. I pointed out that the News had dealt, for the third straight day, with Swedish allegations, probably true, of a Soviet spy sub off its coast, unquestionably a violation of international law. I wrote:

"It was news when it happened, and it will be news when the incident is settled. But does anyone seriously contend that it endangered world peace or even local peace?" I then pointed out that there had been two stories that morning not carried at all by KPFA but reported, buried, in the *San Francisco Chronicle,* that did represent such a danger. One was of the sale of an aircraft for controlling warfare from the air to Saudi Arabia. According to the story, this was part of a deal to make Saudi Arabia the storage ground for a six-month supply of everything needed by the U.S. Rapid Deployment Force in a Middle East War. Such a war did, of course, take place when Bush attacked Iraq in 1990. The other *Chronicle* story KPFA didn't think worth reporting was an attack by China's leader, Deng Hsiao-ping, on the European anti-cruise-missile movement as weakening the worldwide alliance (NATO plus China) against the USSR.

My letter continued: "How many dozens of times (daily, for a long period) did it [KPFA] carry speculations on the Soviet 'drive to the sea' from Afghanistan through Pakistan? That was obvious cold war disinformation. The U.S. government knew better, because its own estimate of Soviet troops in Afghanistan has been 85,000, totally inadequate to such a task...."

"In the 500 days of Poland's crisis, there have been at the very least 100 KPFA stories on Soviet invasion. If it occurred, that *would* be news. The real news...is that it has *not* occurred....Has KPFA News ever asked itself, out loud, before the listeners, *why* all sources made 'news' of a non-story?....I could cite examples of disinformation about the USSR endlessly: the 'poison toxins' in Cambodia, at least half a dozen times on KPFA News....The news *featured* about the USSR is consistently that which strengthens cold-war attitudes....It is precisely such 'news' stories, endlessly repeated, that turned the American people around from their very warm feelings toward their Soviet ally in World War II to the attitude that could elect a Reagan.

"The problem, in my view, is acceptance of the wire services and major newspapers as proper judges of what constitutes news. The fact that they are themselves extraordinarily big business, with a fundamental stake in anti-Sovietism, is totally ignored.

"There's a lot of talk about 'balance' at the station nowadays. There can never be 'balance' in foreign news reporting unless TASS [the USSR news service] is added to the services used. And even if it were, its dispatches would be read with the scepticism toward everything Soviet that our newspeople unavoidably were indoctrinated with from the first TV they watched in childhood or the first day in school. Let them learn to regard as equally self-serving whatever Reuters or UPI feeds them with."

In the '60s and early '70s KPFA News had regarded stories from those sources as automatically tainted. Its staffers had first-hand experience with their lying about student and Vietnam demonstrations, the mass shootings and beatings over People's Park in Berkeley, and the civil rights struggles they had been part of. The staff now was different, with a few exceptions. Memories had faded, and those who had gone to journalism school or worked on college papers were in awe of the mechanisms that supplied them.

Having hit a stone wall within the station, I went outside, doing pieces at intervals for the organ of the general Berkeley Left, *Grassroots*. In the first, I wrote that the KPFA News "did not publicize [San Francisco Catholic] Archbishop Quinn's remarkable pastoral letter [on peace] until I xeroxed it, circulated it at a KPFA staff meeting, and pointed out that even Herb Caen [San Francisco *Chronicle* columnist] had stood up on his hind legs and criticized his own paper in print for putting it on an inside page instead of page one."

The hysteria within the station was indicated in a letter to me from a major donor: "When I tell Ralph Steiner," a paid staff member, "that I'm sending Bill Mandel's program to three senators, ten congressmen and to [Pulitzer journalists] Woodward & Bernstein, Ralph is affrighted out of his skin and begs me not to send it to strangers who may use in against Pacifica!"

I lost some and won some. The next fund-raising marathon included a full USSR Day, which I was asked to conduct. I put on my earlier interview with Helen Caldicott. This was the first time the Australian physician, peace worker, environmentalist, and feminist had appeared on KPFA. Gerry Whitney in Edmonton, Alberta, organized a symposium via telephone, the speakers being Admiral Eugene Carroll of the Center for Defense Information and myself. I pleaded with the Canadians to save us from our own folly. Next came a replay of an interview I had done with Soviet movie director Andrei Konchalovsky. At 10 p.m. came the last chance for a big money pitch, so we used the sure thing, my 1960 hearing before the House Committee on Un-American Activites. USSR Day brought letters like this one from a then schoolteacher at Mission High in San Francisco, Steph Lady. He is now a screenwriter and director and a personal friend: "I listened to the entire day with unflagging interest and have already forwarded hours of tape to distant points and respected friends around the country."

A woman in McKinley Park, Alaska, wrote for a copy of the Caldicott interview. Women I never met have often put a light note in my life. Marion Wylie was out of it with Alzheimer's when I drafted this chapter, and has since died. But in 1982 her letters were fun: "I like your style...you are an unusually useful man in a time when it is getting harder and harder to like men, in particular. Not that women are holding up their end of things very well, either....You have gotten better and better as you have talked on air...I hope you realize that! Since you were pretty good to begin with, this is really something....I was terrified of women for years...being one myself."

In mid-year, someone did a survey of the unpaid staff. My response provided a clear picture of my attitude: "Inasmuch as my purpose coincides with a stated principle of the Pacifica charter, I expect conscious cooperation with my efforts....There was a time when I was rebroadcast in the morning....I want minimal pre-emptions, because they destroy audience. I want to go on right on time, because that is what Americans expect of the media."

What I gave the station: "Highly valuable time in $$. Knowledge that is not offered to the American people by any other medium; a program that is unique in the entire world; broadcasts that are sufficiently good radio to bring in 45 minutes of phone-ins every time."

At the end of the year I made an unsuccessful stab at getting back on KPFK in Los Angeles, writing its news director: "What has kept my program on the air for a quarter century, against uninterrupted attack from Right and Left, is that I know my facts, and that, as one Pacifica

National Board member put it, I am 'too honest'. That's a criticism I can live with."

When I think of what kept me doing those unpaid broadcasts so long I am reminded of another Folsom prisoner's letter of 1982: "In the 1930s Joe the Working Man organized himself because he *had* to. All the social benefits that resulted from that labor movement are now being voided by a class of people who are as shrewd as they are cruel....The U.S. strategy is to break up the USSR by preferably engaging them in an arms race the USSR cannot support ....Breakfast is at five, the next and *only* meal is at 5 p.m. That's how 'coddled' we inmates are. Ciao."

I replied: "How the hell did a guy with a mind as clear as yours wind up in that joint? Not that I don't know a couple of others with respect to whom the same question could be asked. And in one case at least, the answer is pretty heavy, unfortunately." Despite the clarity of the sentences I quoted, part of his letter made comparisons between this country and Nazi Germany. This gave me the chance to state a point of view that I find very pertinent when people confuse the appearance of militias, the destruction of the Oklahoma City federal office building by terrorist bombing with hundreds of deaths, the Ruby Ridge shootout, and the government's own military assault and burning out of a religious sect at Waco, Texas, with fascism. I wrote him:

"U.S. 'book-burning, union busting, arming, hysteria...' etc., to quote you, are extremely mild, except for the arming, compared to Nazi Germany. No prisoner of the Nazis would be allowed to write a letter like yours, or receive one like this. Don't oversimplify. Life, and politics, and individual human beings are extremely complicated and internally contradictory. The fact that people with heads like yours listen to my broadcasts is what keeps me going after a quarter of a century on the air. And the fact that I'm able to talk simply enough for people with less than college education to understand, even though my subject is most complex, I take as a compliment."

Who knows where that man, Al Angulo, is today, or *if* he is? Therefore I give him the last word, in his reply: "Your letter...pleased me almost to the point of flattery, even more importantly, it made me reconsider some of my ideas. The latter is *no* easy task. I am from the Mission [Latino district of San Francisco], and all about me were robbers, burglars, hookers, pushers, and just plain tough guys. Yet no one else from my family has so much as been busted; *that* is my guilt. In the end, try as I may, I am confused. Welcome Al, to the world of matter and contradiction, eh?

"Those Indians and Africans who weren't wiped out *outright*, now have the liberty to inhabit either a reservation, a slum, a prison, or a Methadone clinic. Domestically then, the difference is that we have no *actual* Dachaus. Whether a Viet-Namese is napalmed directly or an African starved to death, a San Salvadorean or a Lebanese is beheaded, or one thousand babies die from malnutrition daily, I think this distinction is lost on the victim. I bow to your wisdom and concede that Nazi Germany was a mad dog; this being so, the elite of the U.S. are then cunning and cowardly vultures. *Any* progressive change is good and desirable. Do a people deserve its form of government? Does a patient deserve a greedy physician? Shalom, Mr. Mandel."

For four solid years, while I was researching and writing *Soviet But Not Russian,* my primary social activism was on behalf of prisoners. The credit is due them, for it was initiated by their letters stimulated by my broadcasts and sometimes deeply involving KPFA as a station.

Further conflict between me and the News Department arose out of my efforts for Larry Pinkney, a former Black Panther. His militancy started with his experiences as the only African-American student in a Maryland High School of three thousand, which had Ku Klux Klan agitators. Years later, Pinkney had been appointed by San Francisco Mayor Alioto, under pressure from segments of the Black, white, and Chicano communities, to the Civil Service Commission oral board interviewing candidates for the Fire Department. He had been the only Black member, the only civilian, the youngest. Having lost the key to an apartment available to him, he tried to get in through a window. Police, tailing him, said as they seized him: "We have you now, nigger!" and beat him badly. He was convicted of burglary under the illegal-entry clause of the penal code.

Pinkney wrote me early in 1983, when completing in Vacaville a nine-year term that began in Canada. He is best described in a "To Whom It May Concern" letter about him from a member of the Canadian Parliament from the Conservative Party. Canada had cooperated with the U.S. desire to imprison Larry after he fled this country subsequent to that frame-up in 1973. It was only after the UN Human Rights Committee officially condemned the actions of the Canadian government in his case that he was transferred to imprisonment in the U.S. in his seventh year of incarceration, instead of being released. The Canadian M.P. wrote:

"I am our Party's spokesman on issues relating to Correction and Parole...I became acquainted with Mr. Larry Pinkney....I was quickly impressed with the high level of personal integrity which he displayed. He was not looking for any favours, he was not enumerating an inventory of complaints or alibis. In short, there was no evidence that he had ever become a part of the criminal sub-culture which makes up so much a part of our prison population....I have...found...him...meticulously honorable. My experience with him is that his word is his bond."

I sent him poems I had written in the early '50s, primarily about

Black freedom struggles I had participated in. He wrote: "They made me feel love, but most of all, your poems make me feel *hope*. Your poem, 'For My Children, To Dr. DuBois,' is my favorite. Its strength lies in its combined gentleness and searing truthfulness; so powerful, yet so gentle."

A few months after our correspondence began, the Soviets shot down a Korean 747 that had overflown the most sensitive of Soviet bases and had Americans aboard. The American media frothed at the mouth. Larry wrote in "appreciation for your having demonstrated courage and integrity by addressing the incident....I find it difficult to understand how a cockpit crew of a huge airliner could mistakenly and repeatedly violate the USSR's air space for a period of two and one half hours."

I wrote him: "Korean Airlines Double Oh Seven has been killing me. In addition to my own show, I've been on Traffic Jam, the Morning Show, Bari Scott's Saturday night show, two hours on a talk show in the south Bay, and by phone on WBAI in New York." After the third week of KAL 007 on my show, Larry wrote, regarding a Black caller the previous night: "the caller was speaking more out of frustration and despair....I am pleased that you were gentle with that caller, yet honest in your reply to him. You demonstrated not only your knowledge, which is immense, but also your sensitivity."

With respect to the Korean airliner I wrote Vera Hopkins, Pacifica historian, "People have sent me clippings on that from Toronto, Cleveland, Denver, St. Paul, and of course San Jose, Los Angeles, etc. [I was heard only in the last two of the cities listed. The others were former listeners who had moved but who felt that their information would help me bring clarity to those within range of our stations.] Other KPFA programmers have asked me onto their shows more than in any similar period during my quarter-century with the station. WBAI interviewed me by phone. So did Youth News. A West German magazine correspondent came by the house and did a long interview. Frankly, I find this encouraging. People feel I can be turned to when they are shaken, frightened, puzzled."

After a full month of intense pressures due to the airliner incident, I asked Tanya if we could take a week to unwind, and we drove along the Coast. North of Fort Bragg the driver of an oncoming pick-up truck suddenly decided to go in for coffee on our side of the road. He hit us head-on, and my vocal cords were paralyzed for six days from my throat hitting the shoulder strap. My singing voice was gone forever. Yet that safety device probably saved my life. Tanya was also spared by her safety-belt. I wrote Pinkney that I'd have to postpone a scheduled visit.

A year after we became acquainted, he was framed for allegedly trying to start a riot in prison. None had occurred. In fact—I had been kept informed of the situation as it developed in the previous week—he was trying to stop one from developing. When I told Bari Scott, the African-American woman who headed KPFA's Third World Department, about the situation, she contacted U.S. Senator Cranston's and Congressmember Dellums' offices. I wrote the Vacaville warden and the head of the state prison system essentially identical letters:

"I intend to broadcast on this matter...," of course in my Soviet program time, "and to ask listeners to write you....I visited Mr. Pinkney last Monday. Mr. Pinkney was greatly troubled by events earlier that day. He had taken the lead in calming the situation, which required approximately four group meetings in the course of the day. He was proud of the fact that he enjoyed the confidence of white and Chicano inmates as well as Black, and that this had made it possible to cool the situation....The removal of peacemakers looks to me like a great way to guarantee a riot next time racial friction occurs. Is that what the authorities desire?"

I described the situation to the News Director , who didn't cover it. When I asked why, she replied that it had "slipped her mind." So I went to the African American woman heading the Third World Department, who contacted the (independent) KPFA Saturday News. They phoned me and broadcast a good story, ending with a request for communictions to the authorities. On my own show, on which I gave the case five minutes at the start and two at the end, I got numerous phone calls from people who wanted to write.

Eight days after I informed the News Director of the situation, she could no longer resist the pressure, accepted a call from Larry, and broadcast it on the 6 p.m. news. I wrote him: "Everyone commented on your articulateness."

Representative Dellums wrote the Vacaville warden protesting the violation of state-wide prison rules in the Pinkney case, and saying that U.S. Senator Cranston and a state senator had also had their mail to Pinkney opened. This stimulated a "To Whom It May Concern" letter from the public information department of the prison system saying they got "a large number of similar letters and postcards regarding the situation of Larry Pinkney. Correspondents apparently learned of Mr. Pinkney's situation via a radio broadcast." Pinkney wrote me: "The reason I was found not guilty was *not* due to my firm presentation or even the witnesses in my defense. I was found not guilty due to the strong support from you, your listeners, and the other listeners to KPFA who contacted the Calif. Dept. of Corrections [CDC]." The authorities tried to get even by inferring in his record that he had provided them with information. He was really scared about them "setting me up with an untrue 'snitch jacket.' Nothing has changed since the demise of brother George Jackson!"

On my next show I included three paragraphs of his letter thanking listeners, and his frightened letter about being set up. I asked listeners to write the authorities about this. I wrote the warden and the director of the CDC: "To describe an inmate as an informer is an invitation to kill him. Such documents do not remain secret. Yet Mr. Pinkney wrote in that letter: 'At no time did I ever name the names of anyone.' This is a request that Mr. Pinkney be returned to Unit V [minimum security], that his personal papers be restored to him, that he not be transferred out of Vacaville, and that no 'snitch jacket' be placed in his file or, that if that has already been done, it be removed, expunged from the record, and destroyed. I have asked my listeners to join me in writing you...to this effect."

Jack McLean of Citizen Advocates, Sacramento, who had heard my update, hand-delivered pertinent information to the governor of California, mailed the same to all members of the Board of Corrections, talked to receptionists at the offices of sixteen state senators and assembly members. The governor wrote a letter of inquiry. State Senator Petris sent an aide to talk to Pinkney, who wrote me: "The officials of this prison were in almost total shock that a senator would actually take personal interest in the situation of a prisoner."

Early 1984 saw the wrap-up of my controversy with KPFA News over its handling of Pinkney. At a staff meeting, I said that the News Director's failure to deal for eight days with the story that prison authorities were trying to discipline him for what was actually his role in *preventing* a riot was an act of racism. In a memo written for circulation within Pacifica, I wrote:

"I do not believe that [the News Director] believes in slavery, lynching, segregation, or discrimination. However, in a country in which the latter two are prevalent realities, plus regular police murder of Blacks, including young children, special sensitivity is demanded in any story where Blacks are involved, particularly in a situation in which the victim has a history of political militancy...Failure to act with such sensitivity is racist. I cannot avoid the conclusion that the very bad relationship between [the News Director] and myself over my 4 1/2 years of criticism of the News Department's handling of Soviet matters played a role in her not acting on the story."

For anyone with any doubt about why militant activists like Pinkney wound up in prison, the following excerpt from his FBI file, obtained under the Freedom of Information Act, speaks for itself: "Pinkney is potentially dangerous due to his demonstrated ability to unify black and white. His associates are Negro, White, and Chinese. Special attention is being given to neutralizing him. The areas of sex and drugs appear to be the most effective ones to utilize. His habits in these areas are unknown, but are being monitored with this objective. The FBI is working in conjunction with [blacked out, but a covering note to the U.S. Secret Service, San Francisco, accompanies this]."

Pinkney asked me to pick him up on his release. His parents lived in Washington, D.C., and he had a sister in the Northwest. "There are very few people indeed that I would want to be anywhere near on that day," he wrote me, "as I doubt strongly that they would or could conceive of what it means to me, what I have been through, or my psychological state of mind. With you however, there is no doubt that you know all these things far more poignantly than most people could ever know or hope to know."

Larry 's indomitable spirit had come through most strongly in a letter to me describing a most unusual event behind prison walls:

"When I heard that you were going to play that [HUAC hearing] recording, I did something that I have never done before [in over nine years behind bars]. I rounded up all the prisoners in my dorm and requested that they listen to it, which they did. They were elated hearing you do battle; and afterwards, there were many questions to me from the prisoners (both black and white) about what they had heard. They all clearly got the drift of what you were saying before HUAC, though they asked me to explain some of the words that you used after they heard it....They were cheering you on (something that utterly amazed me)....A couple of the prisoners are adamantly anti-communist; but even they were cheering you on....You got across even to people who have virtually no political astuteness at all."

Another prisoner with whom I developed a relationship was Jon (Mpaka) Meachum, in Folsom, serving double life for the murder of two fellow heroin dealers when in his mid-20s, plus a technical kidnapping charge and a gun enhancement, since he had been a parolee. The spelling in his first letter to me reflected his incomplete high school education, which he had just enrolled in a GED program to correct: "I'm a Black prisoner at Folsom Prison. I've listen to your Monday night show for the past month. I believe I'm asking you to be my mentor; for at this point I want to know all you know about everything you know...I've no outside contact...My goal: to learn all I can about the Social Sciences, particularly Economics, Sociology and Politics. As you can see I've a long long way to go....I'm 28 years of age. I'm now beginning to break the bonds of fatalism and nihilism, in part thanks to Felix Greene's book *The Enemy: What Every American Should Know About Imperialism.*"

I responded with a long letter, in order to tell the story of Johnny Vinnaccia, the youthful Mafioso with three felony terms behind him whom I met when I was seventeen. Johnny had become a hero of Spain and subsequently of the Italian underground in part because I helped him get a political education. "I keep his memory alive by telling and writing this story whenever I get a chance, 35 years after his death," I wrote Meachum. "That's the only real immortality we have: to live the kind of lives that cause others to remember us long, long after we're gone. I'll help all I can. You seem to have that kind of potential."

He answered with a cry from the heart. "Received your letter...Words do not describe the beautiful feeling its content delivered. Most prisoners have no idea of the ramifications of what brought them to prison and what keeps them regulated to the cycle of in and out the revolving prison door. One's limited awareness becomes depleted when surrounded by hundreds of people who suffer profoundly from nihilism, fatalism, fear and ignorance, compounded by not having outside contact with progressive people.

"I originally wrote you on assumption and hope.

"For three years I've been trying to keep my rage and bitterness in check, to keep it from becoming self-destructive. That is very bad when compounded with the fight against self-pity, historically inherent self-hatred, family rejection beginning with my mother rejecting me 22 years ago. No, I don't hate her, for I understand (now a little) the psychological pressures/changes young black women went through in the 1950s."

It is very difficult not to let the correspondence with Meachum, and his life the next seven years, become a book in itself. He was a Jean Valjean of *Les Miserables*. However, instead of being pursued through life out in the "free" world by a single human bloodhound as in that novel, he was ultimately beaten down by the routines of the prison system. After a few more letters and my first visits, it became clear to me that the way to get him out was on educational parole to pursue an advanced degree, which he unquestionably had the capacity for. He didn't know what a Ph.D. was. I explained, but told him that I could approach my professor friends to act on his behalf only if he could show straight A's. First he had to get his high school equivalency diploma and then the junior-college degree, both attainable from behind bars, albeit great external obstacles had to be overcome.

It was common enough for a prisoner to stab another inmate or try to escape from Soledad, the prison to which Meachum had been transfered. Every time that happened, the whole place was locked down, requiring classes to be cancelled. That occured more or less monthly and lasted for days. He did not get straight A's, but was very proud when he made the dean's list after moving on to junior college, conducted at Soledad by Hartnell College in Salinas.

When his cellmate hid a window sash weight in their cell, both were put in solitary. Mpaka (his adopted African name, by which everyone called him) did not look good when I visited him during that period.

The cellmate insisted to the authorities that he alone was guilty and Mpaka knew nothing about it, so it did not go into his "jacket" (record). Later, a nineteen-year-old from East Palo Alto, Mpaka's home turf, was sent to Soledad. The kid wanted to show he was the big man in that town, and needled Mpaka for months to get him into a fight. In a visit during that period, Mpaka visibly shook with rage in his effort to control the desire to strike back. He did not yield to the provocations.

For some reason, the administration decreed that a prisoner could have no more than ten books in his cell. That limited his library almost exclusively to textbooks for his courses. Perhaps that was the reason. I worked hard as a tutor. When he sent me a term paper, I wrote four hundred words of corrections. I pointed out Black English usages the instructor wouldn't accept. I offered suggestions as to how to avoid such mistakes in the future.

Just as I knew Mpaka through KPFA, so the people I rallied to his assistance were fans of my broadcasts: a prominent San Jose lawyer, a psychology professor at San Jose State, a plumber and his wife. I built that support network in part by reading a letter of his on the air in one of my deviations from Soviet subject-matter. My father, then eighty-six, had bought him a subscription to the *African Communist*, which Mpaka had asked for: "Please express to the Elder Mandel my deepest gratitude for his kindliness and contribution. Out of 24 of my 29 years of existence I can count on one hand the times I've been subject to kindness without an ulterior motive.

"I need a better understanding of the women's side of the struggle. Perhaps Mrs. Mandel can give better insight in this. The last type of friend I need is one whom is hesitant about speaking their true thoughts for fear of disturbing my feelings. I'll need criticism sometime, so don't get passive on me. You and Mrs. Mandel have been together over 45 years, that draws forth my deepest respect."

When I had visited him several times, and after reading our correspondence, Tanya agreed to come along. Mpaka wrote: "The visit has had (and still is) a profound effect upon me. Tanya's outspokenness strengthens my belief in mentally independent women. I need more exposure to her type of woman. Tanya, you had such a affect [sic] on me during our visit that I wouldn't write until now. You see I don't like to be led by emotions." In a later letter: " Tanya, I meant no harm when you kissed my cheek after our last visit, I walked off so abruptly. Actions like that, especially from you, have a mother-son effect on me. Motherly affection was a very rare experience for me during my formative years and several things you've done during the short period I've known you have given rise to dormant emotions that I'd equate with a mother-son relationship.

"There once was a time I wouldn't talk to middle class whites. I believe it due to bitterness, fear and ignorance....I have a nine year old daughter living in Milpitas, do you go in that area when you're in San Jose?"

He was extraordinarly perceptive in dealing with this daughter. She had been caught stealing in Safeway for the second time: "Fay [the mother] first question to me was did I want to holler at, chastize, Shelby. My response: no. I think she needs to be talked to. I'm not the Authoritarian type with children, although I can be firm. I don't believe in rigid parental control. Nor am I familiar with pre adolescence's."

I was letter carrier between him and a female prisoner, because inmates were not allowed to correspond with each other. Letters had to be open for reading. She was a beauty he had known, and he tried to show her another way to live: "In the past we were more into the criminal (fast Life) mentality form of rebelling against the system. When we get out we have the tendency to say 'fuck the struggle' and become side tracked by drugs, pretty clothes, big pretty cars, etc. I don't measure people in weight, feet, inches nor by their financial assets, but I do judge them by their actions and deeds toward humanity. I don't believe in male domination of women. If Black women aren't free Black people won't be free! You are a woman, which unlike a Lady have no pretenses: Ladies are bourgeois oriented pseudo excuse for women."

In a later letter to her: "Bill and Tanya are more than mere friends to me, they are also my immediate family. Very very close to a mother/father/son relationship in a sense."

The years went by and the parole board refused to set him even a parole date, while the completion of junior college was pushed farther and farther back. His letters became less and less frequent. He wrote of his "waning sense of hope. If I didn't have a gradual, sometimes rapidly, growing political awareness, I would have given up, like so many others, on my people and the majority of the U.S. population. We [Black people] treat each other with increasing indifference and apathy. And it's so intense here in prison, I don't know how much more I can handle. Psychological torture is the worst and over the long term the most painful & destructive....You see I couldn't fit in like an Andrew Young, Jesse Jackson, Willie Brown nor Nathan Hare, and never like Huey P. Newton or Eldridge Cleaver." The last two references were to drugs.

Ultimately Tanya and I became a taxi service for bringing his daughter on visits, and a woman to whom he became attached by mail. The authorities eventually transferred him to San Luis Obispo. We would have visited him even down there in southern California, although that trip meant an overnight stay, in addition to car expenses, and the fine radio we got him so he could pick up KPFA at the very extreme of its range. But he had the decency to make no such demand, since he grew psychologically no longer able to continue holding up his end of our agreement: regular correspondence and progress toward the degree. Truly a tragedy.

Meachum has the unusual distinction, for an uneducated lifer, of acknowledgment in a volume that had fairly wide use in higher education, my *Soviet But Not Russian:* "Particular thanks are due to Jon 'Paka' Meachum, who made meticulous comments under the difficult circumstances of a prisoner sharing a cell in a state penitentiary." I had asked him for "your most detailed comments: things you don't understand, or want more about, or disagree with. Likewise, I would wish to know what changes you would want to see made, to improve it."

Larry Pinkney had also read the manuscript of many chapters of that book: "I found the Russian equivalent of 'kike' or, for Blacks, 'nigger,' to be extremely interesting. I again emphasize that it was refreshing and important that you draw parallels for the reader between the prerevolutionary struggles in Russia and the peoples, i.e., Black people, Puerto Ricans, Chinese, poor whites in America, etc."

The anti-Soviet panic promoted by government, supposedly impartial organizations, and media during Reagan's second term reached such a peak that it is forgotten by most in a form of denial. My first broadcast of 1983 was with three women who had just visited the USSR as peace activists. They told the audience that some members of their group had been warned by family members not to go "because they'll never leave that place alive."

I quoted that in writing a listener who had sent me a long letter with respect to Soviet dissidents. I commented: "Amnesty International [whose reports the listener had forwarded to me] deserves a *great* deal of the credit for the existence of that state of mind, which I regard as horrible, monstrous." I then quoted the Secretary-General of Amnesty as stating that his organization had not published a report on political prisoners in China: "One of our problems has been we felt the Chinese prisoners would not be helped by pressure from abroad." But it was always okay to hammer the Soviet Union. I defined my own position: "My program has been aggressively critical of Soviet civil liberties practices in three periods *when the war danger receded.... When the danger of war is high, I focus on relieving tensions, not worsening them."*

Later events proved that I did not understand *why* the USSR had developed at variance with its proclaimed ideals. But I never closed my eyes to factual reality. A listener asked my opinion, in 1983, of a book by a Soviet official who had emigrated, called *The Corrupt Society.* I wrote in reply, before having read the book:

"There is a great deal more corruption in the USSR than I would like to see....People try to get what they can and what they need....If Reagan and Weinberger force a diversion of raw materials, power, transportation, machinery, labor, from Soviet production of consumer goods to keeping up with us in arms, the things available for purchase do not keep up with demand. People try to solve that problem by offering to pay under the table, or offering presents, or outright bribes. A few actually engage in setting up secret manufacturing plants using materials, etc., obtained from government enterprises by malfeasance. The penalties are severe, but some will take the chance. Some individuals very high in the Soviet structure have peddled influence....Corruption in the USSR does not change the non-exploitative essence of the society."

The supporter of Amnesty International continued our discussion in a second letter, to which I replied: "There is not *anything* Amn. Int'l. can publish about civil liberties violations in the USSR without adding to Cold War tensions unless it deals with *U.S. human rights* violations to a comparable degree: the three million totally homeless in this country right now. The figure in the USSR is zero. The 20,000,000 wholly or partially unemployed here; the figure there is zero. The elderly, not homeless, who die of hypothermia because the utilities turn off their heat for nonpayment of bills. The figure there is zero. The police who kill Blacks every day of the week (no exaggeration: see Urban League nationwide figures), and lower-class whites as well....Our 'civil libertarian' society won't even give me the status that attaches to a college professor, although it was delighted to use my knowledge when we were wartime allies [with the Soviets] and just thereafter."

A certain public awareness that KPFA had a place in history emerged at this time. The *East Bay Express* had an article on that theme. The following week a letter to the editor appeared: "How can David Lerner purport to have written an historical article about KPFA while not having mentioned Bill Mandel, Elsa Knight Thompson...?"

The station's in-house historian, Vera Hopkins, who was a founding member of Pacifica and thus knew it at least a decade longer than I, interviewed me in 1983 and sent me the transcription of her notes:

"He said in reply to my question that early KPFA was devoted to the ideals of pacificism and civil liberties, to about the mid-1960s. After that the station began to make time for people who were involved rather than people who reported. From the mid 1960s to the mid 1970s participatory democracy was in vogue....Today we are at our best in representing the ethnic minorities and women. In public affairs and news *we have become a radio station rather than a unique institution* [all emphasis added - W.M.]....We don't go as deep as we used to. At KPFA in the past five years, in news and public affairs, we have moved away from the notion of content as the primary concern to the notion that polish on the air is important."

This was widely perceived, and in January 1984 Pacifica President Peter Franck had a private statewide meeting in San Luis Obispo with personalities then entirely outside Pacifica. They alleged that Pacifica had abandoned its principles in favor of commercialism. Ultimately this resulted in the replacement of Franck as president and also of his chief opponent, Executive Director Sharon Maeda. But it naturally created a furor at the station, and I signed a document along with several others, which read in part:

"For a wide variety of reasons, National Public Radio exerts a pull on KPFA and its programming. Sometimes, that pull is strong....American media has been much improved by the presence of Pacifica 'graduates'....Asking the question, 'What issues should I address in my programming?' is different from asking, 'What programming can I find funding for?'" With respect to people trained at NPR, we stated: "These people may bring...a view of how a radio station should function and what a radio station should do that might not be fully consistent with Pacifica's aims and objectives."

Staff in those years took it for granted that the most fundamental matters of policy were its concern. While the perceived issues were very much the same as a decade later, management in the 1980s proceeded from the premise that it must find solutions that would satisfy sentiment down below. The lack of social, economic, and political analysis and of a Left outlook affected me. Pacifica News Service (PSN) inside the Washington Beltway now turned to academics for comment on Soviet developments. In earlier years such people were automatically suspect as trained seals of the Establishment, and I was *the* Pacifica source in that field as a matter of course. I wrote a scathing Open Letter to PNS about this in February 1984. I pointed out that when Soviet leader Brezhnev's successor, Andropov, had recently died, I was interviewed about that on commercial KCBS - the number two station in Northern California, by the *San Jose Mercury-News* and separately by KPFA, KPFK and WBAI. Pacifica News Service, on the other hand, phoned a professor at the University of Edinburgh, another in Georgia (U.S.A.), and a researcher at the Brookings Institution.

I commented: "That is McCarthyism. Here's why. I am one of the tiny handful of most senior professional Soviet-affairs experts in the world, in the field far longer than any of the people you interviewed....The fact that Pacifica has carried me since 1958 is something it should wear like a medal...as the clearest proof that it does not yield. This truly is 1984. I have been unpersoned. Not only am I unknown to the general public outside Northern California, but the youngest generation of U.S. Soviet scholars doesn't know that I exist. But it is shameful when that is the case in a radio network I have been associated with for a quarter century. And it is worse than shameful when McCarthyist standards are applied: to the degree that my conclusions do not fit into the conventional wisdom of...younger radicals who haven't the remotest fraction of my experience...My expertise and competence are shunted aside. I expect that from most commercial publishers and the Sovietology profession—the academic embodiment of the Cold War. It is outrageous when it happens at Pacifica."

To people who had just begun listening, my programs continued to be a discovery. An old acquaintance wrote me about a "new KPFA subscriber [who] heard your program during the marathon, and during the re-play of your appearance before HUAC he drove off the freeway and telephoned his subscription to the station!"

Although KPFA's listeners are thought of as being intellectuals and yuppies, this was far from universal. A letter to me read: "I am now 72 years old. In my working years I was just an uneducated drifting manual construction worker and country worker. In the early '30s I rode freight trains and slept in hobo jungles. I've lived a hard, full life, and I can't die younger. I don't trust the American newspapers or news services. Keep on beating at these fascist bastards and their pimps."

But there were intellectuals whose support I particularly welcomed. The rising role of Latinos in California made me happy about a letter from a retired Chicano college teacher who was proud of the fact that a novel of his, "which presents the case for Chavez' UFW [United Farm Workers] and farmworkers...has been widely used in Chicano studies around the country the past ten years." He wrote me that he was impressed by my "intense honesty....The world badly needs more good Americans like you."

The cold war tension in the first half of the '80s, before Gorbachev came to power, was heightened by Israel's invasion of Lebanon and bombing of Beirut. A listener's reaction to my speech during a protest left me feeling at peace with myself. Alberto Miranda by name, a Puerto Rican, he wrote me:

"I know everyone addresses their letter with Dear whatever, whether they mean it or not, but you are indeed very dear to me. I try to always listen to your show. I always learn something. I am proud that KPFA has you on. During the demonstration at the Federal Building soon after the massacre of hundreds of Palestinians, when your name was announced, I clapped and cheered along." A young mother introduced herself on that occasion, and then wrote me: "My daughter [age nine] was delighted to meet you at the demonstration, and happy (and surprised) to discover that [I was] such a nice, friendly man." There is a wonderful word in Yiddish describing my reaction to that: *kvell*.. It means "rejoice," but that's too cold. "Warms the cockles of my heart" is closer, if clumsy. At bottom, I am an educator, and it is very important to me when something I do influences the youngest generation. And so, when another letter on that same occasion read: "Even my ten-year-old son is becoming a listener," that put me on cloud nine. A dozen years later I broadcast on a tiny station after being dropped by KPFA. A listener called and said: "I was raised on Bill Mandel."

It goes without saying that approval by fellow-Jews was particularly welcome in the aftermath of the bombing of Beirut. Ann Gonick had organized and raised the money for the remarkable ad, "Menachem Begin [the Israeli premier] Does Not Speak For Us," signed by four hundred Bay Area Jews, overwhelmingly not Leftists, in the *San Francisco Chronicle*. It was the first-ever statement of opposition to Israeli policy by Jews outside the Jewish press. In consequence, Ann, a KPFA broadcast volunteer from South Africa, appeared on national TV. She wrote me: "Thank you for your inspirational show tonight. I was falling into a deep depression and hopelessness when you came on the air. Your strength of feeling and devotion bring back life and courage."

This, of course, was one of the many times I stepped outside Soviet affairs in a broadcast. Generally, the more critical the situation, the warmer the letters I received: "There were so few of us at my college in Santa Barbara who would defend Iranian students [when the American Emnbassy staff in Teheran was held prisoner for months]! I remember the hysteria, the attacks on *any* dark-skinned person, the huge and ugly crowds, how we had to escort our friends around campus for fear of attack, the serious discussions about 'safe house' in case things got bad. Thank you again, Mr. Mandel - for your courage, your honesty, your sensitivity, your sense of perspective. Thanks especially for being a voice of reason in these times. Oh - and a link with our past and our history."

On the anniversary of the Russian Revolution, November 7, I invited my father, then eighty-nine, to guest on my show and reminisce about working in the Soviet Union in 1925 and 1931-2. Eve Buckner, then the assistant manager of KPFA, sent me a note:

"I am writing this right after your show tonight which I found very inspiring. Apparently our listeners got turned on, too....Your father was a real joy to hear tonight. You should encourage him to come back to KPFA. I always think that these old folks have so much to tell us and that we too often push them aside."

After the Polish and Afghan crises, I had continued intermittently sending the station manager notes I titled "KPFA Newswatch." One brought my criticisms to a sharpness exceeding anything earlier. The evening News had stated flatly, not as a quote and without attribution or qualification, that the credentials of a local TV newsman had been seized from him by a member of Soviet military intelligence at their consulate. I wrote: "No consulate is permitted to have any military intelligence people. Therefore the only possible ultimate source for such a statement has to be the FBI, CIA, or other U.S. counterintelligence source. Is KPFA News taking their word nowadays?"

The following day the News interviewed a spokesperson for the TV station regarding its ad showing a Soviet missile killing Santa Claus. This was during the shopping weeks before Christmas. The interview ended with the spokesperson repeating the ad's closing paragraph reference to two little children having been among those who died on the Korean airliner. On this, my letter to the manager read: "KPFA News made no comment of any kind on the flat reaffirmation that the Soviets are baby-killers." I pointed out that the *San Francisco Chronicle's* icon columnist, Herb Caen, attacked that ad two days running, and another writer in that paper devoted an entire column to attacking it. A columnist in the competing Hearst *San Francisco Examiner* called the promo "an affront to adult sensibilities."

Whenever our government went to extremes, I tried to prevent people from going over the edge, politically. With respect to the 1984 election, I responded to a young artist in the town of Pacifica: "Elections, however poor the choice, represent one important difference between democracy and fascism....The system we now have does permit you and me some say in our destiny....Fascism has the capacity to exterminate entire categories: Jew, Gypsies, and homosexuals, in the German instance, plus political opponents. That is why one must not confuse it with milder forms of capitalist rule, in which public opinion, at the ballot-box and otherwise, does have some effect, and opponents can physically survive."

Citizen diplomacy sprang into existence after the shooting down of that Korean airliner over strategic Soviet military installations in 1983. Relatively prosperous whites, chiefly New Age, lost faith that either our government or the Soviet would save us from nuclear holocaust. Perhaps the most important organizer of citizen diplomacy was Sharon Tennison, an intensive-care nurse and small manufacturer of nursing supplies. She had been married to an army officer, and has a southern accent one can cut with a knife. Sharon had been taken to see a lynching when a child, at a time when that was regarded as instructional for a little white girl. She is a born humanist, and at one point I had to dissuade her from dropping her efforts to end the Cold War by citizen-to-citizen activity and going to Nicaragua as a nurse. Sharon began her citizen diplimacy simply by organizing perhaps twenty people to take a tour to the Soviet Union and make contact with ordinary Soviet people. She informed the FBI, so that no one could think she was acting behind the back of the government. Her group was so frightened of the KGB that it practiced splitting up to enter Moscow subway cars, two persons to a car, and entering last so they could not be followed. They would then distribute "we want peace" materials, translated into Russian, and were amazed to find plain folk inviting them to their homes. Eventually she organized a massive "Moscow Meets Middle America" homestay exchange in small American cities funded by local governments and professional and business people.

In the first couple of years of her activity, I was the source of basic information and counsellor to her Center for U.S.-U.S.S.R. Initiatives. On one occasion I conducted an all-day seminar for about fifty of its members at a lighthouse-turned-hostel. When the USSR broke up, her Soviet contacts formed the basis of efforts, for which she obtained funding from major foundations and then from Washington's Agency for International Development, to train Russians and Ukrainians to run elementary businesses. Yet when I told her, in the early '90s, that I had given up on socialism, she was most disappointed. To her it was not the rigorous Marxism that had been my only hope of making socialism a reality, but a vague dream of a fair and equitable society. Of course I want that too, but the questions are how does one define it and how do we get there.

Citizen diplomacy spread like wildfire. At the beginning of 1984, a Berkeley private school teacher sought my help for a letter exchange between her 7th-graders and Soviet kids. A deluge of such requests followed. But my decade of isolation from academe—my last teaching was a course in Soviet Law at the Golden Gate University Law School in 1978—pigeonholed me as a radio person rather than a scholar, even in the Bay Area. A teacher wanted me to speak on Soviet education at one of many panels while a Cal doctoral candidate would address the entire school. I replied by picking up on a phrase Berkeley's Black Congressmember Ron Dellums had used often a decade earlier, when he referred to "women as niggers," "the aged as niggers," "the disabled as niggers." I said I was that Ph.D. candidate's academic grandfather, and I would not accept the status of "the blacklisted as niggers."

Such incidents proved to be very minor impediments to the usefulness of my broadcasts to the citizen diplomacy movement. In mid-1984 a listener wrote me that, during the spring, she heard me read a letter from a boy in Baku, Azerbaijan, and talk about my friend there, Ilya Kamenkovich. He was a very Communist Jewish war veteran who spent his time talking to school classes about what the Nazis had done to children. I had given his address on the air. This listener wrote him and received a reply.

"I was so very touched by the letter," she wrote me later, "and by

Ilya's effort, and so moved by my fury at being told whom I should hate and whom I should fear that I...sent a letter to Ilya that I intended also for the entire population of Baku. I wanted him to run through the streets waving my letter (I am only partly joking) and shouting, Mary Anne does not hate you, Mary Anne is not your enemy."

The final eighteen months before Gorbachev began to reverse American attitudes toward the USSR were, in some respects, the worst ever in my relationship to Pacifica until I was fired in 1995. Yet they were the best in my relationship to listeners subsequent to the period of hero-worship following the HUAC hearing. In January 1984 I turned to the listenership for financial support to publish my book on Soviet minority peoples by advance purchase. A female electrician, Gwen Winter, got La Semilla Cultural Center in Sacramento to mail nine hundred xeroxes of my appeal to their list. Linus Pauling's medical librarian obtained copies to distribute at the Physicians for Social Responsibility annual meeting in Washington. [Pauling, a biochemist, was the only person ever to be awarded two Nobel Prizes, one for chemistry in 1954, and, in 1962, the Nobel Peace Prize for his efforts against nuclear weapons.] A Palo Alto student at Columbia University's Russian Institute xeroxed copies and posted them. The San Franciusco *Bay Guardian* phoned, shocked that I'd had trouble being published, and made a news story of my appeal. A Davis listener xeroxed and circulated copies at a Christian Peace-Making Conference. A broadcaster on independent KKUP in Silicon Valley phoned and sent money. A listener to Pacifica's Los Angeles station, KPFK, mailed xeroxes to his acquaintances. A woman with whom I had traveled to the South thirty years earlier to save the Martinsville Seven sent for more copies. A WBAI listener, formerly a New York City official, "deeply moved" by an ad publicizing the information in this paragraph, sent fifty names for me to send my appeal to.

That was my standing with listeners, but not with Pacifica. I foresaw the possibility of my being dumped: "I am an indelible part of its history, no matter when or under what circumstances my broadcasts come to an end....The fact that there are Pacifica people...to whom I am unknown is a reflection of not-so-unconscious *yielding* to McCarthyism in Pacifica." In 1994 the nationally-syndicated conservative columnist George Will wrote that it was time to forget "human rights" as an issue, since its function was anti-Soviet, and the USSR was gone!

A letter from a Fremont listener summed up what I tried to say in my complaints to the Pacifica management over various matters: "you appear to be objective; you admit there are things about the country and its institutions you don't like or don't understand. All this sounds reasonable to me. Further, I think that if we had men and women of your caliber in the State Department today, our relations with the USSR would be as good or better than they are with Communist China, and we could cut our defense budget 90 %."

In addition to my show on the Soviet Union, I was then broadcasting an earlier version of this autobiography in another time slot provided by the Drama and Literature Department. The idea that my American people, the people who had elected Roosevelt, was apparently going to re-elect Ronald Reagan, made me desperate. It was clear to me that the swing to the Right was going to last. I hoped that if I could help people understand how my generation had learned to fight to improve life for ordinary folk, a new generation might be aided by that knowledge. Knowing that human lives are more interesting listening than history as such, and having participated in virtually every movement for social progress since I was ten, I thought that presenting this message in the form of personal experience would win the broadest audience.

The department originally found eighteen half-hour slots for this. Had I tried to fit my life into that amount of time, the result would have been a list or at best a chronology. Fortunately, I let it write itself. But the result was that, at the end of that series, I had only reached age thirty-five, when I had been called before McCarthy.

Listeners asked for more time. An artist in San Francisco wrote: "Even though I am only a low income individual, I sense the importance of your work enough that I will pledge a $40 subscription to KPFA if they will allow you to complete your autobiography." Another wrote: "Hurry up and finish your book. It will make powerful reading," and sent a letter to management asking for additional time for me. The nicest read: "I'll probably buy his book, but there's nothing like hearing it, especially from such a dynamic and possessed individual - he makes the radio bleed and breathe."

I was ultimately given a total of fifty-one half-hours. The story was deliberately carried only through the end of the '60s in the belief that one needs some distance in time in order to have a proper perspective.

Broadcasting and trying to keep Pacifica on track continued to require enormous energy. *Mother Jones'* publisher Adam Hochschild and Saul Landau of the Institute for Policy Studies visited the USSR and broadcast their observations and conclusions. They joined the human rights bandwagon. I wrote the KPFA *Folio:* "The most important human right is the right to live. Hochschild and Landau agreee that the USSR supports that by its foreign policy. It is also the most important civil liberty. Police killings are as rare as in England. Quite recently, a couple of Soviet cops were actually executed for killing when neither self-defense nor protection of others required it. Ever heard of that in the U.S.? Or even England?"

Earlier I quoted a wonderfully warm letter from Alberto Miranda. He wrote me another a year later: "A few weeks ago, you started your program by saying you appreciated those listeners that aren't highly educated, don't consider themselves intellectuals. It put me at a sort of ease, since I only finished high school. Because you have good teaching qualities, it facilitates comprehension to almost anyone. When you answer a question, you expand it, you might take it from a different angle, from our cultural viewpoint, you exude a sense of fairness. When you have guests, you ask questions with the listener in mind....Whenever I hear the hearing with Joe McCarthy, what amazes me is that you never allowed yourself to be subjugated. No: 'oh no, poor me versus them' attitude on your part. Dramatic? yes, but you were the star. You had to be. Joe McCarthy and his sidekick Roy Cohn never would have agreed to the script. I end up thinking, that's him, none other than our own Bill Mandel." Such letters still cause me to choke up and bring tears to my eyes when I re-read them years later in the privacy of my study.

My contacts across the social spectrum continued. Two San Quentin prisoners wanted to subscribe to English-language Soviet newspapers and magazines. One of them wished to work toward a law degree in Soviet jurisprudence. They followed up by sending me their lengthy document on prison civilization, asked me to do a broadcast on the Soviet prison system, and wanted KPFA to increase my program time.

Out in the "free world," just as the letter from the retired Chicano professor three years earlier remained sharp in my memory, so did one that arrived now from a Tomasita Alvarado in San Jose: "I come from a migrant farm-working background and have experienced and still experience intense poverty, discrimination and all the things that come with the latter and the former (segregation, poor education, demoralization, crime)." What impressed me was not only that such a person would listen to me and write, but that the occasion for doing so was to send me a review in the *Mercury-News* of my *Soviet But Not Russian,* which she was reading.

As always, rank-and-file listeners kept me aware of where their interests lay. One in bucolic Marshall on Tomales Bay asked me to do a broadcast on environmental matters such as Russia's Lake Baikal "and other critical issues that have been overshadowed by Arms talk and the socio-political arena." But in that arena, a listener in Happy Camp, up in gold country, asked for evidence of war crimes by CIA-supported mullahs in Afghanistan to support the civil suit he had filed against the CIA in federal court. It asked the Director of that agency whether "operations" which cause the deliberate death of innocent participants are in conflict with Article 6 of the Constitution binding U.S. citizens to its treaties, particularly the Geneva Convention on the Law of War prohibiting violence against persons taking no part in hostilities.

My delightful Puerto Rican fan, Alberto Miranda, sent me a video-tape of my appearance on TV discussing my book: "I ask *no* reimburse-ment. I am pleased just to hear you....By the way, as Billy Crystal would say, 'you look marvelous.' Sorry, I just couldn't help that." Next he sent me a Chanukah card consisting of lines from my McCarthy hearing that remained in his memory. Shortly afterward, an expensive hard-cover book by Noam Chomsky arrived: "Seeing you surrounded by books" in a photo accompanying an article on me in the Sunday *San Francisco Chronicle*, "thought you would care to have this one. Plus, I want to have the feeling that I've given you one. So please, accept."

There was life outside KPFA. Son Bob, a member of the International Longshoremen's and Warehousemen's Union, secured passage of a res-olution to engage in the most militant action against apartheid in South Africa ever taken by any labor organization in this country. It proposed to block the loading or unloading of cargo to or from South Africa. This meant, among other possibilities, loss of at least one day's pay, a good deal more money than most anti-apartheid activists ever contributed. The day one such vessel arrived in San Francisco, he phoned and asked if Tanya and I would join the picket line shortly after dawn the follow-ing morning. We were now sixty-eight.

As always when there was a possibility of arrest or violence, I dressed straight-arrow in a conservative suit and tie, plus a wool overcoat against the chill and fog. A family affair: son Dave was also there. He actually had his body against the hood of an immense tractor-trailer, heading a long line of trucks coming to pick up the freight. A picket line of longshoremen, Black and white, and other opponents of apartheid, many of them former or still Communists, circled and blocked the road-way. An African-American longshoreman, with bullhorn, addressed the line of trucks seeking to enter the pier, calling upon the union Teamsters not to cross their line. They didn't.

CHAPTER 26

"If I Were Gorbachev..."

The year I turned seventy was the first of four, 1987-1990, that equalled or surpassed any that had gone before in terms of sheer demand upon my energy.

By 1986 there had been forty years of a consistent, relentless bipartisan U.S. policy honestly and accurately described by one of its founders, President Eisenhower's Secretary of State John Foster Dulles, as "going to the brink of war" to destroy the Soviet Union. This made possible essentially limitless military budgets to drive the USSR out of business via bankruptcy due to efforts to match us in armament.

From 1982 on, a citizen diplomacy movement gave hope that a groundswell of peace sentiment in the U.S. might have some effect. It was based essentially on an equal mistrust of our government and that of the USSR. A sense of urgency propelled it, brought on by the Reagan budgets and the Soviet invasion of Afghanistan. Then, in 1985 Mikhail Gorbachev, who understood that Americans would only change their attitude toward the arms race if Moscow made the first real moves, came to power.

He initiated steps to eliminate the restrictions on freedom that, aided by lies and exaggerations on the part of the CIA and the media, had alienated people in the West. Gorbachev's measures gave me hope that the socialism I then thought could provide a civilized life would finally be allowed civil liberties and the rule of law. Consequently, both in pursuit of peace and to observe the efforts toward democratic socialism, I participated in the American-Soviet Peace Walks organized chiefly by Allan Affeldt, a man in his 20s from Southern California. They went from Leningrad to Moscow in 1987, Odessa on the Black Sea to Kyiv in the Ukraine in 1988, from the western border with Czechoslovakia to Kyiv in 1989, and in 1990 across Kazakhstan in Central Asia to the nuclear test site.

In retrospect it is fascinating that I lost patience with stagnation in the USSR at exactly the same time as its then leaders, the Political Bureau of the Communist Party. Gorbachev was elected General Secretary on March 11, 1985, upon the death of his predecessor. His first important act gave no inkling of the line he would pursue, rather the opposite. He organized a stupendous commemoration in May of the 40th anniversary of victory over Germany in World War II. There was no way of knowing at the time that this was his way of giving the war-veteran generation the equivalent of a gold watch and sending it into retirement.

In connection with that anniversary, the National Council of American-Soviet Friendship flew me to New York City to speak at its commemorative meeting. I had withdrawn from its list of national sponsors nearly thirty years earlier because of its refusal to condemn the Soviet invasion of Hungary. This invitation indicated that the organization's top figures had deduced, or someone had told them, that times were changing in the USSR. When I learned that the other principal speaker was to be the Soviet Ambassador to the United Nations, I decided that it was time to lay out some home truths. To me, he, not the couple of hundred elders who would attend, was the important audience.

First I sought to get across to the ambassador, whom I had never met or communicated with, that I approached his country with the very greatest sympathy. I detailed the forty-year effort by all in that room, including myself, to combat the Cold War, a phenomenon demonstrated earlier in this book to have been launched by the United States. I described the imprisonment of the postwar head of the American-Soviet Friendship Council, Rev. Richard Morford, and my own blacklisting.

I then quoted an article on the subject of genocide that had appeared only two weeks earlier in *Pravda,* the Communist Party's newspaper, in which the Armenians were described as victims of that crime, but not the Jews. At which point I exploded, but in measured words and voice: "(This) justifies the gravest of doubts on the part of a Jewish person. It re-opens old wounds, awakens old memories. *Why* did it take seven years after Stalin's death for the very first beginnings at restoration of Yiddish-language culture, destroyed by him in 1947, to appear? Why has the fact of that destruction never been made known to the Soviet people as a whole?"

I asked why "I still encounter a collective-farm chairman repeating to me the...lie that Ford and Rockefeller are Jews" while nothing was published in the Soviet Union to combat that lie? "Why is it not possible today to take a course to learn the Yiddish language anywhere in the USSR...? Why is there no course in Jewish history anywhere in the USSR...? Why is there not...a periodical in the Russian language devoted to Jewish interests as there was before World War II?"

At this point the chair interrupted and asked me to stop speaking. I said that if I were permitted to conclude the speech it would not go outside that hall, but if silenced I would make it public. This was the first time in my life that I had been prevented from finishing a speech. Not even McCarthy or the House Un-American Activities Committee had been able to do this, because they considered the impact upon the viewing audience and the media. But the same mentality was at work. The chair insisted I stop. I gave the speech to WBAI, Pacifica's station in New York, and published it in the monthly magazine of KPFA. New York friends of forty-five years' standing, the Communist school teacher and husband with whom we had organized a rent strike in our apartment house in the mid-'40s, broke relations with us over that speech. But when the leader of the American Communist Party called Cleveland police to bar dissenters from its national convention in 1990, they quit the Party, re-thought many things, and we are friends again.

My speech could hardly affect the situation in the USSR. Whether in taking on McCarthy and the House Un-American Activities Committee in their own hearing rooms, or opposing Khrushchev personally on the bomb-testing issue, or in wiring President Kennedy and phoning men with access to him during the Cuba Missile Crisis, I took it for granted that the individual had the right to try to affect events on national and global levels. Laura X, the feminist friend whose sharp questions and criticisms of the manuscript of my *Soviet Women* are largely responsible for what I believe to be its lasting value, was constantly urging me to "go to the Soviet Union and fix it."

I did not share her illusions that that was within my power. True, the efforts of Americans from evangelists to Harvard professors to do just that in the '90s gave me a better understanding of the messianic streak, and the arrogance, in our national character. But I thought that every little bit helps. So I looked for the right opportunity to place that 1985 speech in the hands of Soviet people. It did not come until three years later.

I did not take copies along when Tanya and I left to spend the summer of 1986 in Moscow. That was to be my longest period of residence in the USSR since 1932, and I wanted to give the KGB no excuse to cut the stay short, even though there had never been any indication of rummaging through my belongings or other interference during my ten previous visits.

The highlight of that visit came when a Moscow visionary, Joseph Goldin, put me in touch with one of the earliest grassroots movements to spring up under Gorbachev. These were young people, chiefly in their late 20s, usually married and most of them with one child, who had banded together to build what they called Youth Housing Complexes (MZhK). They were tired of waiting a dozen years or more until an apartment was available, and crowding in with parents. A three-generation urban family of four people generally lived in two rooms plus kitchen and bath.

Under the Soviet system, every large enterprise, institution, or office was responsible for housing its employees, and was issued budgetary appropriations for this. But as the agency's purpose—manufacture, communications, education, or whatever, naturally got first priority, housing construction almost invariably lagged behind schedule, sometimes by years. These young people had gone to their employers and said that, unless they wanted to lose valued employees, they should turn the housing money over to this new organization, which would do the building itself. Its members would contribute sweat equity. Very often they got the money.

If the object were purely housing, I would not have developed the attachment to this movement that caused me to meet with them weekly for three months. But it had a broader vision. They did not like apartment-house living in its usual form, in which one rarely gets to know even neighbors on the same landing. They wanted the new buildings to be youth communities, with cooperatively-operated childcare centers in which they could try innovative approaches instead of the highly-structured schedules of the government's centers. They envisaged, down the line, production activities as well.

Their meetings of twenty to sixty people were as democratic as anything I have participated in, in over half a century of civic activism. Clearly the forms of democracy were present in Soviet life. But in the past they had been used to cloak passage of what the Party wanted. At the end of our stay, the entire leadership of this movement presented me with copies of their major documents, inscribed: "To William Mandel, lifelong participant in all progressive movements."

In 1987 I was back in the USSR again, taking part in the American-Soviet Leningrad-Moscow Peace Walk. I saw my purpose as helping the two hundred American walkers to see the realities of rural and small-city life along our camping route from the perspective of Russian and Soviet history rather than that of Americans. They certainly knew equivalent American realities. Consider some of the places from which they came: Black Mt., NC; Coralville, IA.; Lincolnville, ME.; El Prado, NM;, as well as every major city.

I quickly came to admire these people—an absolute cross-section of middle America. There was a Mennonite hog farmer who wore clean Sunday overalls throughout, a software engineer of Palestinian parentage, students at all levels from graduate to pre-schoolers with their parents, business owners, a Chicano ex-farmworker attorney with his wife and three young children, a Taos Indian, a retired colonel, a former judge, a Hollywood personality who was a household name, a waitress, a Diesel mechanic, housewives, gays and lesbians. This was the most varied group of my fellow countrymen and women I had ever lived with.

The less sophisticated their place of origin, occupation, or education, the more I thought them heroic. The word is carefully chosen. To me, heroism is doing something one believes to be dangerous, whether or not it is. President Reagan's evil-empire-police-state image of the Soviet Union was strong when people made their decision to go. More than one person had been told by family or friends that if they entered Russia, they would never be allowed to leave again. I take satisfaction in the fact that they came to accept and value me. Trepidation in general was present, and uneasiness high.

The walk organizers had invited State Department and FBI representatives to address the orientation encampment before we left the US. Such speakers hardly reduced the tension. Spokepersons for peace organizations and citizen diplomacy were also invited. I secured an invitation to retired Air Force Major General Jack Kidd, a remarkable man of my age, movie star handsome, who had during his career performed acts of high military courage. We had become friends at a bilateral citizen diplomacy conference in Moscow earlier in the year. There he had presented an extraordinarily well-thought-out mutual disarmament proposal, the savings from which, if the plan were adopted, would be used to end hunger and save the environment. The invited Soviet Embassy representative could not attend, because our Quaker camp near Leesburg, Va., was in an area the State Department had proclaimed off limits to the Soviets.

From the first welcoming talk by a female city official at the Leningrad airport to the highly emotional farewells as we boarded our plane in Moscow to leave three weeks later, the walk was a crescendo of stereotype smashing on both sides. Religious Russians would bring large icons from their homes to bless us with as we walked by, in an ancient tradition. Toil-worn, bemedalled Russian veterans (peasant and worker veterans wear their decorations at all times) would spot the overseas caps of the American veterans (or vice versa), and the one-time allies would invariably throw their arms around each other and weep. As the enormity of Soviet losses in World War II sunk in at the mass grave of 900,000 who died in the siege of Leningrad, two American veterans fell to their knees in prayer. The Russians were tremendously affected by the men at prayer, and pictures of the Americans were on the front pages of Soviet national papers as well as on TV. Some people are natural bonders. Pat Herson of Van Nuys, California, a retired music teacher, wore a sweatshirt inscribed "Babushka (Grandma) Pat" in Russian. She didn't know a word of the language, but always approached Russian women in the crowds of the curious who assembled around us when we stopped. Via sign language, she knew in minutes whether they had grandchildren, how many and of what sex, whether their children were married, whether their husbands were alive (rarely, in the case of Russians of the

World War II generation). They would bundle her off to their cottages, stuff her with food, and load her with flowers from their yards.

Dick Sherwood, from Utah, had been the hot-shot Air Force pilot and photographer on the plane accompanying the bomber that nuked Nagasaki in 1945. He has never recovered emotionally from what he saw. He spent the entire walk recruiting Russian war veteran couples and harassing Soviet officials for a residential exchange, in which each would live for some months in the home of the other. By the next February, permission had come through.

Acts of spontaneous goodwill were innumerable. Edward and Adrien Helm are both lawyers and church activists. They came with their three children, of whom the two younger had to be carried at frequent intervals. One or another of them was on Ed's back all the way. In Novgorod, a woman saw this, ran off to her apartment, came back with her baby carriage, and insisted that the Helms take it. Broadcaster Jim Bottini treasures a worn monkey doll given him by a Russian child just old enough to understand the meaning of the word, "mir" (peace). An Englishman resident in the U.S. wore pictures of his three children on his back. Two young Russian women realized they must be his and went home for gifts. The entire next day they waited in the town square till we walked by once again. They then indicated by sign language who the gifts were for.

Two young Russian women, who proved to be electronic engineers, fell in step with me on our entry into Novgorod. They had a number of lacquered painted wooden spoons, which were not cheap even in 1987 prices. When they gave me a very small one, I said unthinkingly, "That's just the right size for my greatgranddaughter," whereupon they asked how many children I have, and gave me three more.

Very few people talked politics with their gifts. One young man gave one of our women a large pin depicting Stalin, his hero. A man had read an interview with me in a local newspaper, tramped ten miles to catch up with us in the next town, and gave me a serious book critical of morality in the West, *The Distraught Society*, in Russian. He was a youthful physician, and said it would teach me more about my country than I knew. We had quite a discussion. The book had copious quotations from Erich Fromm, Toffler, Norbert Wiener, Charles Reich, Betty Friedan, pollster Yankelovich, Vance Packard, David Reisman, Thornton Wilder, Marcuse, Skinner, ecologist Meadows, Freud and others.

What I sought to get the American walkers to think about was this: the United States has had no war on our own soil for a century and a quarter, but the villages and towns along the walk had all been occupied in the 1940s by the Nazis, who had gotten to within binocular range of Moscow. Leningrad was starved and bombed in a nine-hundred-day siege.

One youthful American restaurant owner, son of a state legislator, could not get away from Gulag, Stalin's concentration camps, in discussing the Soviet Union. But the founder and director of a shelter for homeless men in Los Angeles moved from her first impression— that the whole country looked like America in the '50s— to more thoughtful conclusions after her failure to encounter any beggars or see homeless people.

The Americans were struck by the Soviets' warmth and personal honesty. We carried what was for them fabulous wealth in cameras and state-of-the-art camping and backpacking equipment, and were often very careless in leaving it around. Yet there was only one reported case of theft on the entire journey and the police somehow recovered the items. The post-Soviet elimination of economic security has brought a weakening of the morality we encountered.

The Soviets were struck by our mutual helpfulness. They stood amazed as we spontaneously formed chains to get our camping gear on and off the large trailer-trucks provided by the Soviet Peace Committee, which transported whatever we did not choose to carry. The worst of the walk was the weather: endless rain, cold, mud. But the wettest night of all brought a bonding of the two groups as Soviets and Americans helped each other erect tents and carry belongings.

A Russian dissident attached himself to the walk. He carried documents showing he had been in a Gulag camp, and insisted he had been tortured. I talked to him at length, and was convinced he was telling the truth. The Soviet walk leadership banned him. I approached Affeldt, our 29-year-old leader. I urged him to insist to our hosts that the dissident be allowed to be with us, and that for them to refuse would be to reinforce the stereotype of the USSR as the evil empire America must arm against. They caved in.

At general meetings, I was sharply critical of both delegations for the gross underrepresentation of non-whites in our case, and non-Russians in their's. Among two hundred Americans there were only thirteen people of color, of whom only two were Black. Fifty non-whites, including twenty African-Americans, would have been an accurate reflection of our population in proportion to the size of our group. Among the ninety Soviets there was a lopsidedly high presence of Jews in addition to Russians. Total representation from the fourteen non-Russian republics did not nearly match their share in the USSR population. But the Soviet representation of minorities was proportionately far better than ours.

Novgorod, one of the two good-sized cities on our route, welcomed us with open arms. Literally a hundred thousand people, nearly half the population, poured into the streets, many joining us well before we came into sight of buildings.

A Russian walker guided me to a small street-corner rally discussing the country's situation. The chair said to the audience: "Right now, you and I face one major objective: that socialism continue to exist." That remark in 1987 is the earliest indication known to me that any Soviet supporter of the existing system realized that its very survival was in question. Excerpts from my tape of that rally comprise a selection in the 1991 edition of a Houghton-Mifflin reader for Western Civilization courses, *Sources of the Western Tradition.* The editors understood better than I yet did that belief in freedom of discussion demarked the Western tradition from all others.

In Novgorod, local media had informed the people that we were coming. In Kalinin, another large city, the population was caught by surprise, and lined the route in thin numbers. We were guided into a stadium of about ten thousand capacity, half of it blocked off and empty. At each city or town on route —this was the 14th— we had held a rally with Soviet and American walkers speaking. I had refrained from doing so, but felt that the apparatchiks here had to be pushed into an awareness of Gorbachev's "perestroika" policy, and the people needed encouragement to take part. I told Affeldt that I wished to speak.

My tape records what follows: "I will speak in Russian" (applause) "and translate into English. I remember when even in Moscow one saw people in birch-bark sandals, rag leggings, and homespun. I remember my fellow students at Moscow University going out to teach the workers on the pre-war industrialization projects to read and write. During World War II, I did my best, as Russian Expert for UPI, to make sure that the Second Front—Eisenhower's landing in France—took place as early as possible." Applause. "I remember how after the war you rebuilt without any help whatever from outside. And I want to say that my heart ached in the years of stagnation you underwent recently. That is why I personally deeply welcome the changes your country is now undergoing. For us participants in this walk, the most important thing until now has been the participation of the Russian people in our walk. In other places, there would be simply a few speeches in the central square. But the whole population turned out. In Novgorod over 100,000 people. Perhaps 20,000 in Vyshnii Volochek, maybe 10,000 in Torzhok."

Everyone present knew that the latter two were much smaller than Kalinin, where the apparatchiks had limited attendance to five thousand by using a stadium rather than a square and sealing half of it off. "In consequence all of us Americans are convinced that no one among you wants war." Long applause. "The problem now is what you and we can both do from this point on. For us the job is to spread the word, to interpret what we experienced, when we get back home....What is it that you can do further so that there will be peace? In our country there are two major excuses that are used against you. One is your alleged aggression. That is the realm of foreign policy. Your foreign minister deals with that. The second argument used against you is that your country supposedly has no democracy. It is precisely for this reason that the matter of democratization in your country, about which Mikhail Sergeyevich Gorbachev spoke so eloquently recently, is a matter not only of your internal affairs but has to do with the future of the world. The anti-Sovieteers in our country do their work very subtly. There are not many direct lies about you. But they write about every instance of burocracy. This is why I —I as a member of the first generation of American friends of the Soviet Union —want to say that the sooner you put an end to money-grubbing, burocracy, nepotism, bribery, the more you will do for the cause of peace."

The following year I felt the time was ripe to present the Jewish issue to the Soviet walkers. In 1988 Affeldt led us on a walk from the Ukrainian Black Sea port of Odessa hundreds of miles north to its capital, Kyiv. I took along a couple of hundred xeroxes of that 1985 speech, "Re-opening Jewish Wounds." While Jewish organizations in the United States made very sure that the issue of anti-Semitism was prominent in the American mind, the Ukraine had impinged itself upon us via an event that crossed all ethnic or other lines: the Chernobyl nuclear meltdown of 1986.

One evening we erected our pup tents on the grounds of a school in the home village of the Ukrainian national hero, Taras Shevchenko, a 19th-century serf-born poet and painter. As we approached the village, virtually every family living along the road had a table set up to feed us garden-grown fruit, grapes, raw vegetables, home-baked goodies. There was no question of paying. They handed out volumes of Shevchenko's poetry, in Ukrainian. This was obviously spontaneous, because the editions differed in date and elaborateness from giver to giver. In Soviet times, literature regarded as classical was heavily subsidized. These mementos were something people could afford to give, although the peoples of the former Soviet Union simply do not measure hospitality. It is absolute, total.

After dinner that night, a campfire was built and a discussion conducted by the head of the Ukrainian Peace Committee. His purpose was to inform us about the Ukraine. I asked in what languages school was taught. He said Ukrainian, Russian, German, Hungarian, for those minorities. I asked about Yiddish. He replied that Jews could learn Yiddish in their synagogues.

Obviously his answer was a shot in the dark, because the language of the synagogue is Hebrew. It has less relationship to the folk language, Yiddish, than Latin has even to such Latin-derived languages of Catholic countries as Italian, Spanish, French, and Romanian. Synagogues, whether in the United States, Israel, or anywhere else, rarely teach Yiddish, except for congregations of the Hassidic sect. Hebrew is related to Arabic, while Yiddish grew out of medieval German.

Moreover, the speaker was from Kyiv, with a large Jewish population active in all spheres of life. Therefore, he had to know that Soviet Jews were secular. American rabbis learned that to their surprise when they tried to get the hundred thousand recent immigrants from the former USSR to attend synagogue.

I was furious at the man and announced that I would conduct a discussion group on the status of Jews in the Soviet Union. About forty people came, about evenly Soviet and American. Perhaps half a dozen were Jews. A Russian woman from Siberia said that in her area Russians and indigenous people had simply, on their own, organized classes to teach the local language, Altai. Why didn't the Jews do likewise? At least half a dozen other Soviet walkers endorsed that approach. A Ukrainian young man from Lviv, which my parents' generation knew as Lemberg, offered to help such an endeavor in his city. I gave him the addresses of three prominent Jewish intellectuals I knew in Lviv. A year later he sent me a news clipping announcing the establishment of a Jewish cultural society there.

In Kyiv we visited Babi Yar, a ravine where the Nazis slaughtered a hundred thousand human beings, mostly Jews, and then filled it in. When we Jews among the walkers—I had my arms around a Soviet woman three of whose immediate family lay somewhere beneath us— broke into uncontrollable weeping, the Ukrainian walkers sobbed from the bottom of their guts. It was then that I distributed my article, "Reopening Jewish Wounds."

In 1989 I attended a Yiddish-language theater in Kyiv that had been founded during the intervening year, as had Jewish cultural societies in twenty-five cities in what was still the USSR. The founding convention that year of the Ukrainian nationalist movement, RUKH, passed a resolution attacking anti-Semitism. It spoke specifically of "fascist genocide" against the Jews during World War II. It appealed to "all socially-conscious citizens of the Ukraine, members of all nations and peoples living on its territory, to raise their voices against any forms of anti-Semitism whatever, to rise in defense of their own dignity and that of the Jewish people, its culture, learning, religion, right to representation in all elected bodies, and its inalienable right to speak, create, and teach its children in either the Yiddish or Hebrew languages."

I had reason to accept the sincerity of that statement that reached beyond the behavior of the Soviet walk participants at Babi Yar and at my spontaneous seminar. On the 1989 Walk, before reaching Kyiv, we passed through the typical county seat of Medzhibozh, burial site of Bal Shem-Tov, founder of the Jewish sect of Hassidism. Since the Holocaust forty-five years earlier, almost no Jews lived there. Yet the Ukrainian country people living near the overgrown cemetery who came to watch us as we visited it showed very respectful attitudes toward Jews as a people who had long been part of their history.

During the 1988 Walk, two extremely energetic, youthful female reporters for Ukrainian newspapers attached themselves to me. They questioned me so long and vigorously for my opinions on anything and everything, American and Soviet, that I thought perhaps they were KGB. I learned at least as much from them as they did from me, if only from the psychology revealed by the way they put questions and their reactions to what I said.

They showed up again on the 1989 Walk. It became clear that, as on all my previous visits to the USSR, people were drawn to me not only because I could express myself freely in Russian —not terribly uncommon—but because I understood Soviet life and its way of thought. My Communist background and my desire to help their country reject whatever prevented that dream of a good society from coming true—I then still thought it could come true—put us on the same track.

The two reporters repeatedly published extensive interviews with me in newspapers of large circulation among young people in the Ukraine, to the point at which my name in a headline alone served as identification. I said things that were extremely radical in the context of that day, when the Berlin Wall had not yet fallen. For example, that if artificial controlled prices were not replaced by market prices, I said, they would never know what something was really worth and would be unable to solve their economic problems. These ideas were published. I failed to reckon with the fact that the predominance of monopolies in Soviet fuel production, manufacturing, distribution and transport would enable them to drive prices skyward, even after privatization, with no regard for the state of demand. (I still believe an alternative could have been found to the subsequent crazy printing-press approach to the ruble that drove prices up thousands of times. It probably would have required retaining some dictatorial elements in government until a market-based economy had replaced central planning and monopolies had been broken up. Clearly, the Chinese leadership proved wiser than the Russians in this regard.)

In 1988 we walkers had visited a village newly built by the government for evacuees from the vicinity of Chernobyl, sixty miles north of Kiev. One of these reporters took me into homes. I was shocked to find peasant couples, although living in comfortable surroundings and receiving ample financial aid, pining so badly for their native place that they were willing to return. They simply could not grasp the meaning of a danger that could not be seen or felt, by contrast to the battles of World War II and the German occupation of their territory.

In 1989 that same reporter told me she was native to Chernobyl and her parents were buried there —they had died long before the nuclear catastrophe. She arranged for me to visit the plant. As soon as our interview with its executives ended, the top man drove off to Kyiv to attend the founding convention of the Ukrainian Greens. I was asked to address it. I presented them a one-world ecology flag brought by an American walker, a Vietnam-War exile living permanently in Canada. It flew the following day at the Greens' first mass rally, attended by fifteen thousand people. I was elsewhere that day: the reporter had arranged for me to visit a county seat directly bordered by the barbed wire marking the evacuated zone. The people of this town were demanding that it, too, be evacuated, for the sake of their children's health. Again, as at the street meeting in Novgorod where I was the only foreigner present when people said they were speaking freely for the first time in their lives, it was my good fortune to be present at the birth of a leap in consciousness.

A committee of six, including four mothers, sat at a table with the local heads of government and Communist Party, plus a high official sent from Kyiv on this matter. The citizens berated the officials for evacuating their own children while not moving to do so for everyone's, and for arranging food supplies for themselves far superior to those of ordinary citizens. One woman said, "I am defenseless in this society, among people such as these, our Party leaders. Helpless." This was the first time in my visits to the USSR over a span of then 59 years that I heard ordinary citizens criticizing Party officials to their faces. The people were handing down their verdict, not only with respect to the Party. "It looks as though it's our system we have to get angry about."

Yet this event was openness to a degree I cannot conceive of in the United States: officials permitting a total outsider to be present at an informal meeting when they knew they were susceptible to being damned to their faces both for their official and personal conduct.

In 1990, when American entrepreneurs engaged me as consultant to help develop business in the USSR, I was able to get the national leadership of the Youth Housing Complexes to invite me and another person to tour the country under its auspices. We slept not in hotels but in people's apartments—these new developments averaged one more room per apartment than government housing. It was always possible to find couples without parents who could spare a room for one of us for a few days.

I arranged the itinerary. I made sure we'd get to places that not only offered prospects for our purposes but would enable me to pursue my lifetime agenda of puzzling out where the Soviet Union was going. In 1989 organized labor had emerged as a factor in social change, with stupendous strikes of coal miners in the Ukraine, Russia, and Kazakhstan. I included the major coal centers of each of these republics on our route, which took place in the dead of winter.

When I left Moscow on January 26, 1990, I thought I had hit the highest of possible highs. The previous evening, in Moscow's Hall of Columns, where Lenin had lain in state and where, on March 8, 1932, I had heard his widow speak on the occasion of International Women's Day, the Seattle Center for Soviet-American Dialogue had presented me with a sculpted trophy inscribed "BILL MANDEL. For Outstanding Achievement in the Field of Soviet-American Relations." When I was introduced, the audience, which included pioneering American businessmen in Moscow and Gorbachev's foreign-affairs spokesman, welcomed me with substantial applause and then gave my brief acceptance speech a standing ovation. I warned against that insane adulation of anything and everything American which continued for another three years until U.S. failure to provide any significant assistance to the Russians, while giving huge sums to Israel, Mexico, Korea, Brazil, and other countries, caused a backlash of disillusionment.

Three days later, I was even higher, both emotionally and physically. Almaty, then still the capital of Kazakhstan, is like Denver, but even more spectacular. Mountains tower twelve thousand feet above it. My local hosts had hired a huge helicopter with a three-man crew to show me the tourist possibilities in the forty-mile width of the range between Almaty and Lake Issyk-kul, which is at the same altitude as Tahoe in California's Sierra Nevada, and several times larger. When the copter put down on its beach—illegally in fact, for the crew had the right to fly there, but not to put me ashore—I was the first American to reach its shores by air. This was within the frontier security zone of the USSR. Except for several writers brought in by the Kyrgyz playwright Ghenghis Aitmatov a couple of years earlier, no one from the U.S. had ever been to the lake at all.

I gazed at the even higher peaks gleaming between the far side of the lake and the Chinese border 30 miles away. And I waded into the gently lapping water in the cold-weather high shoes which my son Dave had carefully waterproofed. Did I dare ever clean them again? "These boots have walked in Issyk-kul..."

On the way back, the copter again climbed vertical walls just a few feet away, hovered over a very wide frozen river two miles in the sky, skimmed glaciers and moraines, and passed above a cosmic-ray research station of impressive size. Has that station survived the post-socialist slashing of all funds for science and culture? I wonder today.

Kyrgyzstan, which followed American prescriptions more closely than any other former Soviet republic, is in particularly bad shape.

Below the snow line, we picnicked in a pristine meadow, wildflowers up to our hips. Their scents mixed with that of the conifers climbing the steep slopes on all sides. We lifted off, were deposited at the heliport, and then went by car uphill again to the Olympic-class ice rink, Medeo. Soviet-built, it shares the reputation of world's fastest with that at Davos, Switzerland. On weekdays it is reserved for training, but on weekends —this was a Sunday —it is for public enjoyment.

A short drive above the rink brought us to Chembulak, the only lift-served ski hill around Almaty. It provides a two-mile run, with a pitch adequate for Olympic downhill and slalom, but wide enough for recreational skiing. The head of the tourism co-op, a strikingly handsome half-Kazakh half-Russian psychologist, lent me his boots, skis, and ski overalls. They asked a professional instructor to accompany me.

Later I learned that when they informed him that he was to keep an eye on this then 72-year-old American, he did his best to get out of it: "What are you giving me this grandfather for? He'll get hurt, and I'll be in trouble." Seniors didn't do downhill skiing in the USSR.

The lift chairs were singles, so the video and TV cameramen, who were not skiers, followed the instructor and me. At the top, the instructor simply motioned me to follow him, and I did. When the cameramen got off, we were gone. A myth arose that I was some kind of world-class skier and eventually reached Moscow. It was helped along by the instructor, to whom an elder getting down in one piece was a miracle. In fact, although the snow was excellent, I fell three times. That wouldn't have happened on a similar intermediate-level hill at home. Too much food the previous week, too much unrefusable vodka, too little sleep, no exercise in two weeks, too little time to acclimatize, and ski bindings somewhat to the rear of where they should properly have been, all added up.

We bundled into the car again and drove higher to a cozy camp in several feet of snow, where we ate Kazakh *beshbarmak* (boiled sheep everything), *manty* (stuffed dumplings), warmed ourselves at the fireplace, drank of course, and danced.

There was also a night in a marble-lined public bath house built by the former head of the Communist Party of Kazakhstan, whom Gorbachev had fired for corruption. Like Roman emperors, Russian tsars, and his Central Asian predecessors such as Tamerlane, this man will be remembered as much for the magnificent structures erected during his reign —this block-square bath, the gorgeous and excellent Museum of Kazakhstan, and the art museum —as for his alleged misdeeds. Kazakhstan has since rehabilitated him.

I also spent one evening with old friends, Tatars, he a social scientist, she an obstetrician-gynecologist. This couple, by then past sixty, represented what I found to be the typical attitude of Soviets of the World War II generation, regardless of nationality or geography. They liked that they could now speak freely, but did not think things were all that bad in the USSR. The husband, who had personally known Kunayev, the ousted Party leader, insisted that he had been pure as the driven snow but had been used and misled by his entourage. I can say only that this couple, whom I have known since we met in Moscow's Red Square twenty years earlier and have visited repeatedly in Almaty, are honest and decent people who built their home with their own hands, have the closest relations with their multi-ethnic neighbors (Slavs, Germans, settled Gypsies) on the block , and got along fine with Tanya and me although they are practicing Moslems and we are atheist Jews.

They were more than just lavishly hospitable in the tradition of the East. They wanted to be reassured, over and over again, that every member of my family, from my then ninety-six-year-old father to my great-granddaughter, was in good health and otherwise doing well. Was my pillow all right? Was I warm? Eat! Eat! And they reached for whatever was handy to give me as presents.

In Almaty I also visited the Korean mother of a half-Kazakh emigrant then living in San Francisco. This widow, residing in a very comfortable apartment, well-furnished in an old-fashioned way, told me a story to match the worst I've heard from Japanese-American friends who had been in our wartime concentration camps. Although Korea was a colony of Japan before World War II, and hated it, Stalin in his paranoia had deported all Soviet Koreans to Central Asia from their homes near the Pacific Coast. Children were forbidden to speak their native language. Yet, despite the terrible hardships of the wartime transfer, once they arrived in Kazakhstan they enjoyed all the educational and other opportunities anyone else did. Her daughter, a graduate of Moscow University, the finest institution in the USSR, later got her Ph.D. in psychology at UC Santa Cruz. Moscow U. had refused to consider her thesis topic: the self-realization of women. I had reinforced her decision to stick to it.

I asked her mother about the ethnic riots in Almaty in 1987, the first anywhere under Gorbachev. She agreed with me that they would not have occurred if he had replaced the ousted Kunayev with another Kazakh, rather than a Russian. After the riots, he replaced the Russian by Nazarbayev, still president of independent Kazakhstan in 1999.

But things had not stood still in Almaty. My hosts in the Youth Living Complex movement had put up one of their own as a candidate in the upcoming elections, and they were campaigning to have the complex recognized as a territorial entity in the city, which would give them some of the powers that incorporation does in the U.S.

From Almaty in Kazakhstan I went north to Novosibirsk, the Chicago of Siberia. Here I discovered Siberian winter, no worse that mild January than Chicago when the wind blows down from Canada. Snow all over. Modern, monotonous buildings. American correspondents raised in cities of private homes never tire of denouncing the appearance of Soviet housing developments. I, who grew up in New York lower-middle-class apartment houses, feel differently. The truly immense courtyards of Soviet apartment developments, frequently containing staffed childcare centers in buildings of their own, were always planted with trees and grass, and provided with play structures for children and benches for adults. Think of what life in American "project" housing would be like if everyone in them had jobs, childcare, and a gathering place. The land planning of Soviet housing was a quantum leap ahead of the use of space in New York or San Francisco, where real estate values cause apartment buildings to be virtually glued to each other and built right up to the sidewalk easement.

The new subway in Novosibirsk was totally walled in against the elements as it crosses its bridge over an immense river. A young man I met wanted Siberia to be an independent republic. Puzzled, I asked, "You're Russians, just like the people west of the Urals, aren't you?"

"Yes."

"So why a separate republic?"

"We don't want to be a colony any more."

I heard that "colony" phrase all over the USSR. Economically it is nonsense. Russia subsidized the development of every other republic, as the Ukrainians and Balts learned in 1993 when, after independence, they had to pay world market prices to Russia for oil and gas, and found they just didn't have the money. Russia also subsidized the development of Siberia. But "colony" was the word everyone outside Moscow employed to describe their subordination to a supercentralized state in which everything of importance was decided in the capital, including the disposition of virtually all products of industry and agriculture.

Later on this trip, an intellectual whom the miners of Kuzbass in western Siberia accepted as advisor told me that after the various regions of the country —Russian as well as ethnic —have gained economic independence from the dictates of Moscow, they would doubtless have to re-unite the economy on a market basis. At present writing, U.S. policy opposes that with utmost vigor.

I did not encounter support, either in Kuzbass to the west of Novosibirsk or Vladivostok on the east, for the Siberian republic idea. But in the Pacific seaport of Nakhodka there was enthusiasm for making that city a duty-free zone where hard currency would govern and

Pacific Rim relationships would prevail over ties with the Russian interior. It later won that status, but learned the hard economic lesson that its long-standing integration with the rest of Russia was more important than its foreign contacts.

A few hundred miles south of Novosibirsk is a spectacular region called Gorny (Mountainous) Altai, where the first joint American and Soviet whitewater rafting had been done a year earlier. We traveled there by bus. Maintenance was rough and ready. En route, the bus driver found something wrong with the brake line. He crawled beneath the vehicle in his suit jacket to fix it. Done, passengers helped him brush off the snow, he straightened his tie and hair, and off we went.

Our local hosts were late meeting us at Biisk, a county seat. We killed time by eating at a co-op cafe adjacent to the bus stop. Greasy spoons, greasy food, many Asian faces —the local Altai people. Food was plentiful in 1990, including meat. Prices were obviously within the range of plain working people, by the dress and manner of the customers. Nor were there any beggars, except at the very few churches, where that is traditional in Russian Orthodoxy.

When our hosts arrived, they drove us to the local capital through lovely rolling farm country. This is where then President Gorbachev's wife was born. In one village a farm house had a statue behind it. It was of the fine writer, actor, and film director, Shukshin, who died young in the 1970s. He had promised his mother that he would build her a house with the first money he earned from writing, and this was it. Writers in the USSR were paid well.

The Altai illustrated well my objection to the term "colonial" as description of Soviet ethnic areas. Along the road there were very small single-room log cabins reminiscent of housing in California's Indian country east of the Sierra at least as late as the 1970s. I assumed that was where the Altai lived, but my hosts said the residents of those cabins were Russian settlers. That fact was borne out by the Slavic faces of people out walking. In our hotel, Altai went in and out as guests, and were served by Russian personnel as a matter of course.

Along a river road, the driver stopped at a spring so we could have a drink of fresh water. Trees on both sides of it were hung with hundreds of ribbons. There was a handsome road house a few feet away. The Altai come to that spring to be married and to party in the road-house. They are animists, and the ribbons are prayers.

Back to Novosibirsk on a wild drive. It was a lowering gray day, with signs of a Siberian blizzard in the offing. The road, two-lane of course, was intermittently crusted with an inch or two of hard snow. We were in a Japanese four-wheel-drive vehicle that had been bought across the border in Mongolia, probably illegally in that pre-capitalist time. My hosts bragged about the driver. He did his best to prove they were right. The speedometer crept up to 140 km.—eighty-four miles per hour — and he kept it there as far as possible. My seat-belt was fastened—Russians never use their's—but in an accident at that speed it wouldn't have helped much. The industrial city of Barnaul, two hundred miles north, was our first stop. On that stretch we passed one trailer rig and one car that had gone off the road. Both were right side up, and their occupants were standing alongside.

If Biisk had fed us at a greasy spoon, and Gorno-Altaisk with Altai cuisine, Barnaul offered a disco co-op of good Russian food, with American and European dance videos blaring. My hosts made bitter remarks as we drove past the immense and modern KGB building.

From Novosibirsk I flew southwest to a place of special meaning to me, the Kuzbass coal country, about the size of Wisconsin, where Dad had worked in 1925-26 with other American, Dutch, and English radicals. A book about these foreign professionals and skilled workers, published in Kuzbass in 1990, contains a chapter: "Tradition: The Mandels, Father and Son." They put me in it because of my efforts to promote understanding between the two countries.

In Dad's day, the Kuzbass state capital of Kemerovo, where he was stationed, had been an overgrown village on the bank of the Tom River. I had known the coal country of western Pennsylvania in the 1930s, and expected the same: grimy, smoggy, with no zoning. In 1990 Kemerovo was a handsome, well-planned city of more than half a million, with broad boulevards lined with trees that must have been planted in Stalin's day, given their present height in the Siberian climate. Under the Soviet system land had no price, and was at the government's disposal. For city planning purposes, that was a tremendous advantage.

This mining town had three permanent theater companies—drama, musical, and puppet —in buildings erected specifically for them. Kemerovo also had a theater-people's club, wood-paneled in decorative high relief. There I met with candidates running for election to posts at all levels in the Russian Republic. They were youthful, well-dressed, sharp, and fundamentally pessimistic about the capacity of the Communist Party to continue to lead the country.

The Youth Living Complex movement was exceptionally well-developed in the Kuzbass, with at least a dozen massive residential complexes already built. Its two local leaders were both ethnic Germans. Stalin had exiled their grandparents from settlements on the Volga and in the Ukraine which were built by their ancestors who were invited to immigrate by Catherine the Great, herself a German. One of these men was a former Soviet army officer who retired in his 30s to devote himself to this much more constructive activity. He had no thought of emigrating, but volunteered that his ethnic origin had denied him the gold medal that was given to high-school students who get straight A's—an honor that entitled students to university admission without examination. But he had had no problems with discrimination in his military career.

The other, an architect, had his design of a private home hung up on the office wall. It was planned for the three-generation-family-under-a-single-roof model that most people outside the greatest cities of the former USSR regard as desirable. He had every right to be proud of the design, which gave privacy to grandparents, parents, and children in a three-story, modified A-frame building. The anticipated price was close to what it would be in the U.S. I wondered how people could afford it. He replied that the privacy arrangements made it possible to rent out one or two floors, if the income were needed to pay off the house. Chances are, he has become rich. There's been a significant amount of construction in Russia for the small minority of people who became wealthy in the subsequent Yeltsin years.

A woman was third-in-command of the Youth Housing Complex, and the equivalent of its mayor in its capacity as a self-governing subdivision of the city. The organization's business activities in 1990 included operating workshops and housing for the disabled. Efforts to build a better community lifestyle involved bringing retired people into contact with young families whose children needed pre-school or after-school care.

In the smaller coal town of Prokopyevsk, south of Kemerovo, where the unprecedented 1989 strike had begun, I met with the strike committee. These workingmen (and one woman, representing a very large clothing factory that had walked out in support of the strike) were extraordinarily impressive. They reminded me of people I'd known in Cleveland and Akron in the mid-'30s when rubber, auto, and steelworkers won union recognition in similar massive strikes, and I had been actively on their side. My background made it easy for us to talk to each other in a very different way than when correspondents for the Western media came to Kuzbass. I did not regard their apartment-house dwellings as "project housing." I did not look down upon them because they were less educated.

The Siberian miners looked the part but thought like statesmen. In setting forth what they wanted and how they proposed to get it, they were neither arrogant nor shy. They had won the right to run the mines in which they work—impossible under a capitalist system because of property rights—but they were refusing to exercise that right, because Moscow still controlled all supplies and also stipulated to what customer the coal must go, and at what price. That was still true under Yeltsin. The miners argued that to take over management under these conditions was to have responsibility without rights. They wanted the mines to be transferred to state and local government, with which they would then deal. They wanted Kuzbass, as a region, to have economic independence, with the right to sell its output wherever it could to whoever would buy it, inside or outside Russia, at an agreed-upon negotiated price. In consequence, Kuzbass swung back to giving the Communists fifty percent of its vote in a later election.

I spent that evening at the pleasant disco in the basement of the local Youth Living Complex, whose residents are chiefly miners. Teenagers attending the local high school of music gave us a performance. This was an original hour-long act in the tradition of Russian peasant minstrels, *skomorokhi,* using instruments the students had made of local reeds and other gifts of nature. These kids from the Siberian hinterland would wow them on American network TV. Is there a mining town of a quarter million with a high school of music in the United States?

Southward the Kuzbass becomes increasingly beautiful, as woods and meadows rise to peaks that have glaciers at less than six thousand feet. The southernmost mining town, Mezhdurechensk ("Between the Rivers": it's at a fork), doubles as health resort for the entire area. Each mine had built its own vacation facility. There are lakes for swimming, the river for boating and fishing, and forests for mushrooming, hiking, hunting.

Our arrival in Mezhdurechensk, in a driving Siberian snowstorm, was out of a movie. A crowd of people, warmly dressed contrary to the American propaganda image, had gathered in the spacious main square, which was handsomely bordered in granite. They were listening to speakers on a permanent reviewing stand. The public-address system was first rate, again at variance with the Western portrayal of anything non-military in the Soviet Union. Our driver, a local helicopter pilot who had quit because the agency that employed him had no copters (!), said, "The miners must be on strike again." The 1989 coal strike, the first independent labor action in the Soviet Union in nearly seventy years, had begun in the Kuzbass.

The actual reason for the gathering was more interesting. This rally was the first ecology demonstration in the city's history. A map taped to the front of the reviewing stand showed the route of a proposed three-hundred-mile surface conduit for moving liquefied coal (slurry) to Novosibirsk. Doubtless this would be more economical than hauling out by train (the method in use) or by truck. But the liquefaction process requires the use of toxic chemicals, and the demonstration organizers feared the consequences if the conduit were damaged or failed. It would also require enormous amounts of water. A dam was already being built in the hills behind a ski jump. The authorities insisted that it was for water supply and hydropower. Speakers said that was a lie, and that the authorities wanted to present the people with an accomplished fact. Speakers also mentioned the silting that reduces the storage capacity of reservoirs over time, and objected to reduction of water flow into the splendid river. They demanded a national park to protect the hinterland forever.

After the meeting, I met with the protest organizers. The leader was a female mining engineer in a mood of utter outrage. Also present was a male in the same profession bearing the surname, Sixteen-hundredpounder (Sorokopudov), who became fond of me. His bear hug matched his name. Also present was the head of the local Youth Living Complex, who had quit his mining-engineer job to manage this huge development to house 5,000 people. His English was good enough so that he could later correspond with me in it. He, his wife, and child, were still living in two rooms in a dormitory. Another of the organizers was a high-ranking uniformed police officer, running as a liberal candidate in the elections.

The real power in the room was represented by two coal miners, one the head of the local Workers' (ex-Strike) Committee. The other was a Shorian, of an indigenous tribe, numbering fourteen thousand. So the miners, among whom the Asian-looking Shorians are a very small minority, were sufficiently free of prejudice to elect one of them to their leadership.

I asked a question about the Shorians. The Youth Living Complex head began to answer: "The Shorians want..." but was cut off by the Shorian miner: "Don't you speak for the Shorians," he said, and took over. He wanted no paternalism.

The committee wanted me to get them support from American environmentalists. I told them that I live within walking distance of David Brower, founder of the Sierra Club, Friends of the Earth, and Earth Island Institute. Would I talk to him about visiting Kuzbass? I did.

I slept that night in the home of Sixteenhundredpounder. He, his wife, and sixteen-year-old daughter had a nicely-furnished apartment in a standard multi-story building, with a surprisingly large living room. They were very proud of their small collection of paintings by local artists. Most remarkable, he had developed a complete, rounded, and sophisticated American Civil Liberties Union philosophy, although he didn't know of that organization's existence. He was no mere parlor radical. During the strike, he had been fired for supporting the blue-collar miners. Initially they did not support him because of their distrust of any who did not work with their hands in the dark and danger of the mines. Later, they had helped him get his job back.

Our next destination, Vladivostok on the Pacific, is as far from Kuzbass as the distance between our two coasts. En route, the plane put down near the southern end of mile-deep, four-hundred-mile-long Lake Baikal. It contains more than four-fifths of all the fresh water in the entire USSR and one-fifth of all on earth, nearly twice as much as in Lake Superior. The stopover was at Ulan-Ude, capital of the autonomous republic of Buriatia, to which a Mongol people is indigenous. The young woman in charge of the Intourist waiting room at the airport, unmistakeably Mongolian—flat, round face, small nose and mouth, eyefold—spoke excellent English. In a 15-minute conversation, she made very clear her desire for a revival of Mongol traditions, customs, and culture.

In Vladivostok I was arrested—not at the airport, but a couple of days later while eating in a superb new restaurant built by Korea under a joint venture. (Only the waiters were Soviet). My host was an obstetrician who had quit to organize the local Youth Living Complex. We had begun eating when he was called outside, and returned to say that a couple of detectives wanted us to go to the local precinct. I sent word we'd do so when we finished our meal. That was neither foolhardy nor arrogant. I wouldn't dare do that at home, but local Soviet authorities were always courteous to foreigners. I had learned that 20 years earlier in a fuss over taking pictures at the border between Russia and Estonia, when I bawled out a local Russian police chief for exposing film of places I would not be visiting again. He was obviously an admirer of the long-dead Stalin, painstakingly imitating his moustache, hairstyle, and pipe. There had been no consequences.

This time the issue was that we had no visas for Vladivostok. We did have visas for Nakhodka, but it had no civilian airport, so one had to land at Vladivostok. However, we had spent a couple of days there, despite the fact that, as the major Soviet naval base on the Pacific, it was then still closed to foreigners.

I told the police precinct captain that our purpose was to improve relations between our two countries. But the detective who had brought us in after waiting two hours till we finished dining said that, as someone who had visited the USSR seventeen times before, I should know that their laws require a visa for each place one visits. I didn't tell them that I not only knew it, but that I had been the translator of that set of rules for a research quarterly called *Soviet Statutes and Decisions*. We pledged in writing never to commit this offense again, and we left.

During those days in Vladivostok, I was housed in a Youth Living Complex apartment. Their huge cluster of apartment houses crown a hill with views of the Pacific and the city that in San Francisco would command rents in the thousands per month. I was placed with a couple just under thirty years of age who had a school-age son and a kindergarten-age daughter. They had come to the big city —almost the same population as San Francisco —only two years earlier from a very small town about 1 1/2 hours away. He was a blue-collar worker in a concrete-panel plant, and she in a candy factory. They insisted that I take their bedroom. There was a rug on the wall over the head of the bed. That's not unusual in Russia. But they had mounted on the rug a smallish reproduction of an early Renaissance painting —Giotto, perhaps —and a crucifix. The proportions and positioning of these accent pieces created a sense of sheer elegance.

I had brought presents for any children in families I might stay with. To the little girl I gave a set of crayons, and to the boy a protractor set. The evening I arrived, he carried it around carefully by its packaging mount, and took it to school the next morning. A day later, a boy and a girl his age —eight, I would say —came to the house with him. After being introduced, the girl asked, quite politely: "Are you an American?"

"Yes."

"Say something in English." I did. The children were studying English and departed, satisfied.

Their visit was no accident. My hosts' boy had gone to school and told his classmates that there was an American staying in his home. They had hooted him down and all but beaten him up for this preposterous story. When his father learned of this, he went to school and, instead of storming in outrage, asked the teacher if he might talk to the class. He told them that his son had told the truth, and invited them to choose a boy and girl to come to the house and see for themselves.

When I packed to move on, he gave me a color photo of the family. He explained that it would help me convince my fellow Americans that I was telling the truth when I said that I had slept in the home of a Soviet family! To me, for whom it was the fourth consecutive year of spending the night in such homes, that appeared naive. But he was much closer to the truth than I. Our government, media, and churches had done an effective job of convincing Americans that such personal contact was forbidden.

A year later the Vladivostok Youth Living Complex organizer phoned across the Pacific to tell me he had become a ruble millionaire, and could I direct him to a source of used clothing for resale there?

Next stop was Nakhodka, three hours down the Pacific coast by car. I should really have done a *New Yorker*-style article on that, "Cow Hunting in Siberia." The driver was Shakespeare's Falstaff to the life, a three-hundred-pounder of huge appetites. He and our host decided they wanted some raw milk. Se we left the road and wandered through village lanes looking for signs that someone owned a cow. Punitive taxation on the assumption that private cow ownership might make someone rich had long since done away with most such ownership in the region. After a great deal of laughter and much very bumpy and slippery riding on snowed-over dirt roads, we finally spotted a cow. But she was about to calve, and the owner did not want to milk her. No raw milk.

Shortly we reached a Navy residential town where Falstaff, who was boss of an efficient "co-op" of seventy taxis, knew that the stores sold foodstuffs not available in Vladivostok. He stocked up. A measure of the collapse of the economy is that, three years later, several Navy recruits died of starvation in a barracks in that very area. The Russian Far East gets most of its food by rail from areas far to the west.

Much of our time was spent sightseeing on coastal roads, for our hosts were busy pushing the ocean shore as a U.S. tourist destination. It is like the less spectacular portions of our Pacific coast, pine-covered low mountains and fine beaches. This is essentially virgin wilderness, with the cleanest of water, fine fishing, hunting, endless back-packing potential. The numerous stories of ecological damage in Siberia presented to the American public are not lies. They are simply blips in a boundless sea of untouched nature. The one exception is the near-extinction of the Siberian tiger, made virtually complete in post-Soviet times by poaching for their skins—something like the disappearance of the grizzly from our Pacific coast a century earlier.

The trip to Nakhodka occurred just after Gorbachev got the Soviet Communist Party leadership to agree to repeal the constitutional guarantee of its monopoly of power, and to try bringing perestroika into the party itself. Radio programs those two days were an uninterrupted series of panels and talk shows about this. The head of public affairs broadcasting for Radio Vladivostok was a progressive running for the parliament.

We listened to hours of radio as we drove. What we heard on the air was that there were rank-and-file members who had suddenly come alive. They demanded to know the Party's budget, which was secret. They insisted that henceforth its local branches, not Moscow, would decide whether they will have paid officials, if so how many, what their salaries will be, and what they will do. I repeatedly heard the phrase: "The Party is ours."

I wrote immediately upon my return home that the months ahead "will determine whether it [the Party] will reform itself to the point of being acceptable to the populace, or whether it will self-destruct, suddenly or gradually. That is obviously of importance to the outside world."

Today we know that the apparat proved stronger than the rebels, and the mass of the members had long since forgotten how to take initiative. So when Yeltsin dissolved it, it did not resist. But a new Communist party emerged in 1993 as the largest political membership organization in Russia and later won forty-three percent of the vote in the 1996 presidential election. I would imagine that people of the kind I heard on the air those two days were active in it.

Our sponsors in Vladivostok thought of their city as conservative, because it was as much a Navy town as San Diego before the population shift to our sun belt. But the Vladivostok voters behaved in the elections more like those of Berkeley after the '60s. One seat was won by a radical academic over a major fisheries executive with quite a progressive reputation. Much more remarkable, the other seat in this overwhelmingly Russian city of macho occupations —the military and sea-faring —had been won by a female anthropologist of the tiny Nanai tribe, running against a general. Yet in a TV documentary made by a cable station sponsored by the Vladivostok Youth Living Complex, I saw a Nanai teenager say to the reporter: "The Russians think of us as an inferior race." Nevertheless, she herself was an illustration of the positive aspects of Soviet ethnic policy: well-dressed and with perfect mastery of the Russian language.

Perhaps the explanation for the election of the Nanai congresswoman is the same as that for the quarter-century of re-election of Black Congressmember Ron Dellums in California. He was the first in the country to be elected by a white-majority district: Berkeley and Oakland. African-Americans there have no doubt that racism is the bottom line in white attitudes. In both cases, white-majority populations have advanced, recognizing merit in individual members of minority groups, while retaining various levels of prejudice toward those groups as a whole.

Congresswoman Gaier, the Nanai, was in Moscow, but I visited and was impressed by her permanent place of employment, the Institute of the History, Archeology, and Anthropology of the Peoples of the Far East. It had published three hard-bound volumes in 1989 alone, one about the pre-Russian history of the area, one on its ethnic traditions and decorative arts, and one on a single people, the Udegei. Her Russian fellow-scholars there clearly had the highest respect for the people they studied. One of them had an extraordinary collection of netsuke, which he had spent a lifetime studying. He contends that these charming miniature carvings, which all others regard as indigenous to Japan, actually originated with the Scythians in Central Asia, from which trade brought them eastward.

On the flight back to Moscow we sat next to a Navy officer just retired from service on an ICBM sub with enough multiply-targeted warheads to destroy the United States by itself. "You know all about ours, and we know all about yours," he said, drunk, in celebration of his return to civilian life. "So I can show you this souvenir model of my boat, even though I'm sworn to secrecy." Being Russian, he pressed upon us his excellent sausage, canned fish, aromatic fresh black bread, and vodka.

From Moscow I traveled, alone, southeast to the Donbass coal country of the Ukraine. A local newspaper published a very romantic account of this elderly American stoically withstanding hours of waiting for a late plane in the Kiev airport and travelling in midwinter in his "light coat." The airport wait was useful: it gave me a chance to watch virtually a full day of TV fare under glasnost. The "light coat" was a woolen dress winter coat with lapels that could be folded up and buttoned tightly at the neck. It proved entirely adequate, over a wool suit and longjohns, for a dry 20 below zero, the lowest I personally encountered that January even in Siberia.

The Donbass, comparable to a state in the U.S., has twin cities: Donetsk, with over a million people, and Makeyevka; with half a million. The former is extremely proud that the World Health Organization named it, year after year in Soviet times, as the greenest industrial city on earth. City government and the people worked very hard to maintain that status. Like Kemerovo, Donetsk consists chiefly of very wide tree-lined boulevards bordered by fairly monotonous apartment houses.

In addition to coal mines, Donetsk does have one steel mill. That plant, immense though it is, cannot overwhelm so large a city. It once had the very un-Slavic name of Hughesovka, for an Englishman, Hughes, who founded the mill in tsarist times. There still remain a couple of what the locals call "glass houses," which he ordered built for his managers and other foreign staff. They're not of glass at all, but typical urban English dwellings of a century ago, gloomy by today's standards, but with much more window space than the local people could afford. When I was there, preservationists wanted to convert them into a pedestrian shopping mall.

Nearby Makeyevka is the quintessential steel town, with stupendous blast furnaces, coke ovens, smokestacks visually dominant. The region was in mourning because of the death of over a dozen miners in an accident the previous day. A formal entertainment to show me what the city could offer tourists was cancelled on that account. Instead I was asked if I'd mind attending the birthday dinner of the wife of one of my hosts. It was in a standard, externally shabby apartment house in a miners' neighborhood. The party bore out the quip of Soviets who had visited the U.S.: "In America there's everything in the stores and nothing on the table; in our country there's nothing in the stores and everything on the table."

It isn't simply that there was endless bounty at that coal-mining family's birthday party. Cooking as well as what I was offered in home after home all over the country demands practice. And you can't get practice if there isn't any food. Both in my Moscow year before World War II and in early visits from 1959 on, the only way they then knew to prepare meat was as hamburgers cooked to death. That simply wasn't true any more. Salads were now superb and imaginative, cakes too rich.

Makeyevka has a particularly striking war monument. A rough-hewn soldier, perhaps half as tall as the Statue of Liberty, with bayonetted rifle, towers over one lip of a shallow valley. On the other rim, perhaps a mile away, are several barren hills —culm piles of coal-mining waste, rock brought to the surface. The local people know that during the two-year Nazi occupation, Germany murdered literally tens of thousands of people here and dumped their bodies into the mine shafts.

As in Siberia, I met with the leaders of the previous year's coal strike. I asked if RUKH, the Ukrainian nationalist movement representing majority sentiment in the western provinces recovered from Poland in World War II, was strong here. A foreman replied, "Look, one of the guys in my team is German. Another is Tatar. There's even a Jew, although they're usually up in some office somewhere. So how can I make them all speak Ukrainian? We speak Russian." He was Ukrainian, as is fifty-two percent of the local population.

In the later referendum on independence, the Donbass voted over-whelmingly "yes." But in 1993, the miners struck yet again for business independence for the mines. Russian continued to be the working language, and there were no reports of cleavage along ethnic lines. In 1994 the Donbass voted for the Communists and other parties favoring close cooperation with Russia, and then helped elect a new president with a similar platform.

One of my hosts gave me a guided tour of the square where the miners had sat down for days on end during the strike. He said, of the 1989 walkout, "We had no political demands. This was simply a labor strike." But then: "See the building on that side of the square? It was the Communist Party's center for political education. Hardly ever used. Marble. Fine furniture. So one of the strike demands was that it be made into a children's activities center. We won that."

I asked, "You don't think that was political?"

"How was that political?" I pointed out that a very militant coal miners' strike in West Virginia that had gained national attention was then in its 16 month.

"Those miners would never dream of making such a demand," I said. "In our country everyone regards property as sacred. That building did-n't belong to your coal mine management. It didn't belong to the miners' union. It belonged to the Communist Party. Sure, some of you are members, but most aren't. You were able to make that demand, and win it, because you were taught to regard all property as public, and so were those you were negotiating opposite. That's socialism."

Strange, but also significant, that it was I who had to explain to them what socialism is. Since dissidents in the Ukraine believed that independence was a panacea for all problems, they gave no thought to socioeconomic change. In consequence, no significant reform had occurred. The Ukraine, which previously had a higher living standard than Russia—hardly what happens in a colony— fell to a very much lower one. A dictatorial economic system continued, with no government dictatorship to enforce it. The new Ukrainian currency, designed to be equal to the ruble, fell to a tiny fraction of the value of the Russian currency, on top of a spectacular fall in the purchasing power of the ruble itself. In 1998 the government accepted an American demand that it cancel proposed resumption of economic cooperation with Russia in the manufacture of heavy transport aircraft and satellite propellants, both of which the Soviets had sited in Ukraine.

From the Donbass I went west to Kyiv and the loveliest experience of that trip. I should have guessed from the nature of my welcoming "committee": no men, but a tall, beautiful young woman and her four-year-old boy. Moreover, she kissed me on the cheek, which is not at all an east Slavic welcome to a male stranger, even one older than her father.

Irina Horobets had been the female lead in a Hungarian film, "Madonna of the 20th Century," at age eighteen. She had fallen hopelessly in love with the director, "first love, of the kind that never happens again," she told me. They parted, and she abandoned film forever in consequence. Now, at thirty-four, she was something like an accountant, but currently engaged in heading the cultural activities of a Youth Housing Complex. One building was completed, another under construction across the street. Her accomplishments thus far were astounding. The walls of the recreation rooms on the ground floor were covered by murals on Ukrainian themes in ethnic style by superbly-trained artists. Partitions were magnificently carved. When I was asked to lecture on America to future tenants during their lunch break from building their own apartment house, it was in a spacious ballet room, one side mirrored from floor to ceiling, a barre before it. Children in the preschool learned Ukrainian and English simultaneously, in consequence of a three-generation tradition of Ukrainian emigration to Canada. A tourism club showed me slides of its wanderings all over the immensity of the Soviet Union. A member of their photography club took an excellent shot of Irina dancing with me at a memorable party, which I keep on my wall.

One day Irina invited me to go somewhere with her and her son. I asked if I might invite two other Kyivans I knew. One was the reporter who had gotten me to Chernobyl. The other was a most extraordinary woman, Liubov Kovalevskaia, formerly a reporter for the Chernobyl newspaper. She had managed to get an article published predicting the nuclear accident simply on the basis of her observations of sloppy procedures, and was also the author of published books of poetry.

Her personal history is almost a capsule of Soviet and post-Soviet times. Her father, a Polish Communist living in the USSR, was exiled to Siberia by Stalin for the crime of being Polish. He was lucky. Stalin had executed the entire top leadership of that party, living in exile in the USSR before World War II, for what he regarded as nationalism. He had also killed fifteen thousand Polish officers taken prisoners of war after he divided Poland with Hitler in 1939.

So Kovalevskaia was a Siberian of Polish ancestry, native to the Russian language. She was still a member of the Communist Party when I first met her, but already felt the need for spiritual sustenance that it had long since ceased to provide. She had just been baptized into the Russian Orthodox Church, and had a daughter, but no husband. The daughter, in her teens, beautiful, mentally retarded, and extremely affectionate, needed particular care. Liuba herself danced and sang with the abandon of a Russian Gypsy. We corresponded, but letters from her became increasingly infrequent as the Ukraine sank into an amorphous miasma.

My last first-hand memory of the Soviet Union before its dissolution was the 1990 Peace Walk across Kazakhstan to the nuclear test site near Semipalatinsk.

A dozen years before that I had had as guest on my Pacifica radio show the leading poet of Kazakhstan, Olzhas Suleimenov. He was already then famous enough to have had a full-hour reading on USSR network TV. Subsequently he was placed in charge of the movie industry of his native republic. He hosted Tanya and me in Almaty in 1982.

Chernobyl triggered sharp concern for the dangers of nuclear testing, and Kazakh intellectuals were well aware of illnesses caused to downwinders by the explosions. Toward the end of the decade, Suleimenov organized what became the world's only successful anti-testing movement. It was deliberately called Nevada-Semipalatinsk. In 1988 the head of the Soviet Peace Committee, Henry Borovik, a journalist and playwright who had become host of a popular TV show when Gorbachev instituted glasnost, did a sensational broadcast of a mass march onto the test site in Kazakhstan. Pro-test military and anti-test scientists were interviewed. Unlike American protesters in Nevada, the Kazakhs were not arrested, much less beaten by the Soviet authorities. Contrary to the experience of the thirty-years-long anti-testing movement in the United States, Suleimenov's movement gained termination of testing from

Gorbachev in a single year. Our 1990 Walk, sponsored there by Suleimenov, helped. In 1998 the U.S. was dodging the comprehensive nuclear test-ban treaty by computer simulation of explosions, and in 1999 Clinton proposed a narrower version of Reagan's Star Wars project.

During the four years of walks in the USSR in which I took part, I had thought the Soviet participants were more or less typical, at least in terms of the professional stratum to which most of them belonged. But during the 1990 walk, and subsequently via correspondence and visits of a number of the Soviet walkers here, I realized they were not. Many of them proved to be people who wanted to emigrate and thought establishing contacts with Americans might find them sponsors. Others saw us as good prospects for future business ventures. Still others sought spiritual sustenance for anti-Establishment viewpoints, particularly of a nationalist nature. They were most certainly for peace and opponents of testing. None sought personal profit from the walks, except for the possible resale of a few things they bought.

Among the Kazakh walkers, I encountered levels of nationalism never felt in my seven previous visits to that republic. A tall, burly sculptor insisted that the independent Kazakhstan to come would need its own army. I asked against whom: Russia, with ten times the population? Symbolic forces have since been established. He wanted it to have its own currency, which is now the case. It is not a democratic place. President Nazarbayev learned from neighboring China to retain tight controls during the transition away from central planning. But because Kazakhstan had not caught up with Russia in processing and manufacturing, its living standard dropped even more than Russia's.

Already in 1990, a year before independence, the Kazakh Walk leaders refused to have the flag of the USSR at the head of the parade along with the American. They insisted on that of the Soviet republic of Kazakhstan instead. A Russian woman visiting one of our campsites said she was moving to Russia, although born in Kazakhstan, because she was being pushed aside in favor of Kazakhs in her profession, teaching.

This was not comparable to the consequences of affirmative action to provide jobs for minority teachers in the U.S. I knew from my own research that Kazakhs were already more than proportionately represented in that profession and its administration, thanks to deliberate Soviet policy. What I encountered in 1990 was nationalism pure and simple —ethnic cleansing at the occupational level. The most remarkable aspect of this development, which was happening in ethnic republics throughout the USSR, was that the Russians in Kazakhstan offered no organized resistance, despite being equal in numbers to the Kazakhs. The Russians had been educated to understand that ethnic republics were exactly that. They recognized the right of the Kazakhs to rule their own country. That to me explains the very poor Russian military record in failing to suppress the nationalist rebellion in Chechnya in 1995 and 1996. When retired Gen. Lebed, briefly Yeltsin's National Security Advisor, achieved a cease-fire, an officer said to Reuters: "They are on their land here, and we are their guests." It would be a tragic error to think that Russian response to foreign intervention in Russia proper would not equal their resistance to Hitler. Again, think Kosovo.

There were stupid extremist attitudes on both sides during the Peace Walk. A youthful Kazakh shocked an anti-Communist Soviet Jewish mining engineer and me by referring to the Russians as "dirty, low-down people." He was a teacher of Russian literature by profession! A forty-ish Russian nuclear scientist at the test site referred to the general area as "ancient Russian lands." At this a local Kazakh schoolteacher turned away in silent disgust. Russian Cossack freebooters commissioned by the Tsar, somewhat like Sir Francis Drake on the high seas, had seized that territory at about the same time as the first English settlements in North America. But the Kazakhs, a much more numerous people than American Indians, were already there and always remained a plurality.

Kazakh nationalism was internally reactionary in much the same way as Islamic fundamentalism south of the Soviet border. The young men on the walk pretty universally favored a return to polygamy. Women we met kept silent when that topic was broached. Yet upbringing in a society that opened all posts below the very top to women was evident. The Kazakhstan delegation's field leader acting on Suleimenov's behalf was a woman, and Russian at that (married to a Kazakh). No one challenged her status, or even whispered that her having that position was wrong.

The whole walk was a living demonstration of the contradictions pervading Soviet society. On the one hand, there was use of the territory of an indigenous people for bomb testing, exactly as in the U.S. On the other hand, a cattle town, virtually a hundred percent Kazakh, in these dry grazing plains right outside test territory, had six teachers of English in its schools, also one of German. I was particularly struck by the Kazakh and Russian schoolgirls walking arm in arm, and boys of both nationalities playing together.

The coal city of Karaganda in north Kazakhstan, six hundred thousand population, was another of those contradictions. Built by prison-camp labor in the 1930s, today's miners, ethnic German and Russian, Tatar and Kazakh, are largely the grandsons of those prisoners and exiles. The city itself is very well planned: broad boulevards, trees, theaters, higher educational institutions. There is a splendid miners' community center right on the main avenue, and a permanent circus building of spectacular architecture. To anyone who knows coal mines, those in Karaganda were externally the last word, although they have internal problems due to geology. Coal trucks are not filled to the brim, so none spill over into the streets as I have seen happening in this country.

But the far-off nuclear explosions were felt by the miners underground. In Kazakhstan the Demand Number One of the 1989 coal strike was not economic at all, but an end to nuclear testing. And there were other political explosions. When the walk passed through Karaganda, I asked to speak to the workers' leaders. The meeting was actually in the multi-story headquarters building of the Communist Party. Only a disabled Jewish lawyer representing the handicapped was not anti-Party. The miners were teaching themselves archival research, with the help of a Kazakh professor who was their intellectual mentor. They wanted to go through the Communist Party's records, determine which of its properties had been given it by the government, which it had simply appropriated by virtue of its hitherto untouchable authority, and what were its sources of income other than membership dues, which were not contested. The idea was to return everything else to the people. That of course was resolved when the party was dissolved fifteen months later. In Kazakhstan President Nazarbayev did not permit its re-establishment, by contrast to the situation in Russia. He had headed it!

As we traveled eastward for several days from Karaganda to the test site, one night's stop was near a miners' union vacation resort. Government funded, it stands at the loveliest spot in all north Kazakhstan. A hill a few hundred feet high, then clothed in glorious autumnal foliage, rises from the near-barren plain with its thousands of saddle and meat horses herded by these descendants of Genghis Khan, the most splendid cowboys imaginable. At the top of the hill is a lake sacred to the Kazakhs, at the bottom the resort buildings and an artificial lake-reservoir. We spent a couple of nights in the buildings of a children's camp a short distance away. School had begun, so they were available. A drunken watchman kept order, supposedly, at the showers.

Soviet history was evident even in this remote place. A small town nearby was the original home in Kazakhstan of the Jewish mining engineer referred to earlier. The only non-Asian among the Soviet walkers who had bothered to learn Kazakh, a Turkic language, he had found himself there at age twelve, over half a century earlier, when his Trotskyist mother was exiled. His own son, a cardiologist in Karaganda who had never been abroad, speaks and writes the very finest English. He dreamt only of emigration — to the U.S. if possible, to Israel if not. That someone of his ethnic and political background had been able to rise to the top of a respected profession, as had his mother, also a physician, never crossed his mind in evaluating his place in life.

The evening before we broke camp there was a bonfire. Kazakh youth came from the small town, and sang informally for hours on end. The Kazakhs prize themselves on their musicality. At the end of this walk, in Semipalatinsk, a company of perhaps a hundred children put on an extraordinary performance of song and dance. Lambada was interspersed with Kazakh and Russian dances and ballet. Only kids with long schooling in dance could have done that well.

When American-Soviet Peace Walks were held in the U.S., the national media ignored them. That was also the treatment given by American media to our walks in the USSR. The only exception was when Affeldt recruited the late impresario Bill Graham. He got major rock stars — Santana, Bonnie Raitt, James Taylor, the Doobie brothers — to perform at a groundbreaking concert in Moscow in 1987. The Soviet media treated us as the most welcome guests conceivable. In 1990 I co-hosted, with a Kazakh woman, a program broadcast over national Kazakh TV. Everyone in that country must have watched, judging by the number of people who approached later along the walk route to say they'd seen me on the tube.

By the time we left Kazakhstan, it was clear that the very foundations of Soviet society were being questioned, not only at the pragmatic and political levels, but, in the deepest sense, intellectually. One of the Kazakh walkers, a pioneer businesswoman, took me to her home to meet her husband, a man of perhaps forty. He is one of those very rare individuals whose profundity, not mere knowledge, awes one at first meeting. He challenged Marx on philosophical fundamentals, giving me a paper of his arguing that the author of the *Communist Manifesto* had added nothing significant to the work of the German philosopher Hegel.

In 1969 I had published a fifty-five-page essay, "Soviet Marxism and Social Science," in a symposium volume, *Social Thought in the Soviet Union,* edited by Alex Simirenko, subsequently president of the American Sociological Association. I brought reprints of that paper on the walk, and in Semipalatinsk distributed it to a number of young academics at various institutions, who were eager to receive it. In the months that followed correspondence was already totally free. I received a number of letters from Kazakhstan on other subjects, but there was not one comment on my piece. Marxism had become a dead issue.

Another writing of mine was received very differently indeed. In the January 1991 issue of the *KPFA Folio,* I published what had been a fifteen-minute broadcast two months earlier, "If I Were Gorbachev." It had been prompted by the first public demand ever in the Soviet Union to cancel the celebration of the anniversary of the Communist Revolution, the major national holiday, November 7th. I was outraged, because at that time I still believed in socialism, and that holiday was sacred to me.

Socialism to me is Marxist socialism. Any other kind is too vague to pin down: merely an expression of desired ends, with no clear picture of how to achieve them.

I felt that Gorbachev, who still said he advocated socialism, had never made a good case for what it had done for the Soviet people. I deliberately did the broadcast as though I were ghost-writing for him, in his good-schoolteacher style. And while carefully setting forth the negatives —not merely dumping on Stalin—I wrote:

"Did your greatgrandparents know Dostoyevsky...? They did not, because they could not read....Out of every ten of you who are professionals or intellectuals, only one would have been before 1917....Your greatgrandparents died, on the average, at age 45. The Revolution has given you at least twenty more years of life....

"Do you want to return to the thatched roofs typical of rural housing until a generation ago? Do you want to see mass-scale prostitution as described in pre-Revolutionary novels...? Do you want women in Central Asia returned behind the horse-hair veil, confined to family compounds?

"Women: do you want to be driven out of medicine, or teaching, or engineering, or law, and returned to your prerevolutionary status? Half the judges are women. Where else is that the case?...

"There are serious social scholars and Sovietologists, not Communists at all, who believe the social progress made in Scandinavia and Western Europe occurred primarily because those who controlled these countries were afraid that otherwise their workers would have followed the example of the Russian proletariat." I re-read this five years later, current reports of the rollback of social benefits in Germany before me. Employers were saying frankly that they were instituted "after the war, in a different time," a time when it was essential to match the benefits then being instituted in Communist East Germany. That East Germany failed is a small part of the reason for my abandonment of socialism, but that does not change the historic reason for the granting of benefits to labor, women, children, and the aged in Western Europe.

Returning to my article:

"Yes, it is *true* that the most agriculturally productive and most industrially developed portions of the country were destroyed in the war, and that we lost 30 million lives....

"It is also *true* that our opponents in the Cold War launched an arms race at a time when our country could not possibly have launched a war. We had not yet developed the atom bombs, nor the missiles capable of delivering them....

"People talk of the progress made by Germany and Japan. But as the losers in World War II, they were not permitted to build large modern armies, or manufacture nuclear weapons and missiles. They did not have to divert material resources and scientific and engineering brains to this purpose....

"From 1917 to today, thanks to our Revolution, we have moved ahead immensely. If one considers all aspects of life and the conditions of all segments of the people, I do not believe there is any other country that has made as much progress from where it was at that time —particularly when one considers that we alone, among all nations on earth, have faced unremitting hostility for perhaps all but five of the past 73 years."

I mailed that article to all the six hundred Soviet people whose addresses I had acquired on the four peace walks and in earlier years, and to all the Soviet papers of nationwide circulation. Two reprinted it, *Pravda* and the *Teachers' Gazette*, then having a combined circulation of four million. So did local papers in cities in Russia, the Ukraine, Kazakhstan, and Kirgizia, that I know of. They all published my home address.

I received dozens of letters from total strangers in six republics, teachers above all, doctors, scientists, retirees, workers— none of them people of prominence. This resulted in correspondence. An Azerbaijani nationalist who has since become a businessman cussed me out. So did someone in Belarus, and, in more polite language but great detail, the Jewish safety engineer Peace Walk participant in Kazakhstan. But a Jewish school teacher in the Ukraine thought the article was wonderful. A Ukrainian gym teacher wrote a heartbroken letter about how impossible it was to do a good job without decent basketballs. I read that on the air simply as a matter of information, was flooded with contributions, and shipped her dozens of basketballs.

The letters as a whole presented so exceptional a picture of life and opinion at the grassroots level that my friends Ethel and Stephen Dunn, who then published a small learned journal, devoted an entire issue to fifty of the letters and the transcripts of my interviews with the coal miners in Russia, Kazakhstan, and Ukraine, and with the leaders of the RUKH Ukrainian nationalists. The journal was mailed free to every academic Sovietologist in the United States, of whom there are many hundreds. Exactly three acknowledged receiving it, and I am not aware that any has made use of this material as source documents. The interests of the common people in the USSR and its successor states are foreign to all but a handful of them.

CHAPTER 27

Parting With Illusions

In 1994, when Tanya and I were 77, the Committees of Correspondence, primarily people who had been members of the Communist Party, organized a "Tribute of a Lifetime" at Oakland's Masonic Auditorium for us old radicals. There were then still perhaps a hundred in Northern California. About half joined an ad hoc chorus for the occasion, which had a few rehearsals. As they got on the stage to sing, several urged me to participate. I was reluctant, because I knew they would do "The Internationale," with its line I now regarded as silly: "The international working class shall be the human race."

But I loved these people, despite the many arguments I had had with them in the nearly forty years since I had left the Party. Fundamentally they were practical idealists. We all contributed one-page autobiographies to a small book with the same title as the event.

I rarely read books more than once. This one I read twice in two weeks. The people in it were native-born and immigrant, rural and urban, white, Black, and Asian, industrial workers female and male, teachers, Dustbowl farmers, Southern sharecroppers, blacklisted professors, straight people and gay, veterans of the Abraham Lincoln Brigade, of the Mississippi Freedom Summer of 1964, of hearings before witchhunt committees, of internment in World War II concentration camps for Japanese-Americans, and of innumerable strikes, demonstrations of the unemployed during the Great Depression, battles against racist and class-prejudiced court decisions.

Some had had parents murdered by police in strikes and by Hitler in Auschwitz. Even as that tribute was held they were on the cutting edge: one African-American Berkeley woman was an AIDS nurse. One of the men, a founder of the Mattachine Society forty years earlier, was currently a member of Queers for Cuba. As a group, they reminded me of the listing in "Ballad for Americans" which I had heard Paul Robeson sing on network radio in far-off 1939, and which I have spun on my record player innumerable times in the intervening years.

So I joined them on stage, but in the rear row, as I did not want to introduce a note of discord when I did not raise my clenched fist as I knew they would when closing with the Communist anthem by which they had lived most of their lives.

My father turned 100 that February, the mayor issued a proclamation in his honor, and I went to pick it up. The proclamation read:

"WHEREAS, Max Mandel is an example of the finest in the American immigrant tradition, coming from Russia in his early teens and laboring with his hands until he earned his degree in civil engineering...; and

"WHEREAS, MAX worked in his profession for over half a century and returned temporarily for jobs in Siberia and Moscow to apply these skills toward improving the living standards of the country of his birth; and

"WHEREAS, Max and his late wife, Dora, educated their children in the spirit of absolute equality of all people and have had the satisfaction of seeing their children and grandchildren work actively toward this goal; and

"WHEREAS, Max has been a resident of Berkeley for thirty years, and during this time has been active in the movements for civil rights, academic freedom and opposition to unjust wars and invasions;

"NOW, THEREFORE, BE IT RESOLVED" that 26 February 1994 be Max Mandel Day in the city of Berkeley."

A birthday party was held at the residence for ambulatory elders where Dad lived. Even this place, Strawberry Lodge, named for the creek that meanders through the grounds, is part of the history of left progressivism. It was founded under a Lyndon Johnson administration Great Society program by the efforts of Isabel Van Frank, who had been business manager of the *National Guardian.* Strawberry was uniquely interracial when it opened, and retained that character, although fortunately it was no longer one of a kind in that regard. The celebration was wonderful. Dad listened to all the sincere, honest words with the impassive face of the very old, and then announced: "I want to say something." His words were: "The past century has seen more change in human life than any previous one. I am happy to have had the good fortune to have lived in this time." That is all. But it was vintage Max Mandel: thoughtful, contemplative, and with a firm opinion.

Six months later my son Bob took his grandfather for an afternoon's ride. Dad talked for most of two hours, extremely unusual in his last years. He had clearly thought through in advance what he wanted to say. He reviewed his life, expressed satisfaction with it, and said he was tired of fighting advancing feebleness and disability. When Bob asked what he wanted now, Dad responded with one word: "communication." He then explained that although he went downstairs and sat in the public room at Strawberry daily, he just wasn't interested in what those present wanted to talk about.The collapse of the Soviet Union and shift toward capitalism in all Communist-governed countries but Cuba left him with nothing to believe in. He remained as firmly atheist as he had been when he rejected religion before he was ten. In a near-death hemorrhage at eighty-eight, when he still had a tenacious desire to live, I was constantly by his side, and he showed not the slightest sign of death-bed conversion.

The clearest sign of letting go was that he simply hadn't been listening to radio news and analysis, virtually an addiction since declining vision made reading newspapers and magazines impossible. He had even lost interest in manipulating the monitor-type electronic magnifier that did offer a way to read. But his capacity to love remained, in his affection for his children, for my wife, who regarded him as a father since her's died forty years ago, and for his grandchildren. His sense of humor, too, was still very much there.

Later that week I visited him to take care of routine housekeeping needs, as I did every three or four days, and steeled myself to talk about the things he had said to Bob. To my amazement, he opened with: "There was interesting news on the radio yesterday from Ireland and also about Sarajevo." I switched gears, and said, "Reading the capsule Irish history in yesterday's paper, I remembered when de Valera became president. I was four years old, so you must have been talking about that."

He replied: "I've always been interested in Ireland."

"Why?"

"I worked alongside Irishmen in the Brooklyn Navy Yard, and I learned about it from them." At this age, he had some difficulty in keeping his descendants straight, so I asked: "You know who Kevin is?"

"Sure, my greatgrandson, Phyllis' son."

"You know he's named for Kevin Barry, the martyr in the Easter Rebellion."

"Yes." And I sang him the mournful ballad bearing Barry's name. The talk with Bob had apparently caused Dad to snap back.

Tanya and I are surprised when people express wonderment that we go on doing the things that have always made life meaningful to us. Tanya persists in Women for Peace, a small organization whose members are all about her age, but which has won great respect in the years since its founding. Its members, young mothers when they established it, fought atmospheric bomb-testing because strontium-90 found its way into milk—like the people in ghettos and barrios today fighting environmental racism: the siting of polluting plants and dumps in their communities.

I continued my radio broadcasts on the former Soviet Union, partly because the possession of ICBMs and nuclear warheads in the tens of thousands made the situation even more dangerous than before, due to Russia's political instability. That is not hindsight. I broadcast that conclusion early in 1995. The U.S. later worsened this danger by expanding NATO to the border of the former USSR. Moscow retaliated by dropping the permanent Soviet no-first-strike policy and adopting a mirror image of the long-standing American policy: that an attack upon the country or one of its allies with weapons of any kind could be responded to with nuclear weapons.

There was another reason for continuing the radio program. Somebody had to stand up to the unwillingness of our media to abandon the Cold War. Consider a report in the *New York Times*, August 24, 1994, from a former war industry company town northeast of Moscow. It reads: "Employees keep coming to work because factories, even dormant ones, still provide many social services the Government cannot afford to duplicate: subsidized apartments, health care, gardening plots, discount food, day-care centers and sports installations." And what does the *Times* call these things, in the text of what is supposedly an objective *news* story? "A monument to Soviet feudalism." The reader no longer interested in the details of that failed Utopia gets his brain washed just by seeing the four-column headline: "In a Factory Town, Soviet Feudalism Dies Hard."

That paragon of intellectualism, the *New York Review of Books,* published, on July 14, 1994, the sheer idiocies of Robert Conquest and Richard Pipes, in a book review essay by the former. It asserted in all seriousness that the Communists won Russia's Civil War of 1918-20 despite the fact that, supposedly, *no* social class—not peasants, not workers—supported them. How could I *not* write that august journal? I quoted the book written by the commanding general of the U.S. intervention army in Siberia at that time, and another by a colonel on his staff, saying precisely the opposite: "most of the villages through which [the Trans-Siberian Railroad] passed were peasants, who as a class were in sympathy with Bolshevism." Of course my letter was not published.

The *New York Review* carries, each year, the list of authors worldwide given grants by Human Rights Watch from monies left by San Francisco mystery writer Dashiell Hammett and playwright Lillian Hellman to assist writers who have suffered from political persecution. The best-known grantee of 1994 was Taslima Nasrin, a Bangladeshi, attacked by fundamentalist groups for her feminist views. Among the thirty grantees that year, I was the only American. I had been nominated by poet Lawrence Ferlinghetti, who said he'd "regard it as an honor" when asked to do so. The announcement read: "William M. Mandel (United States), author and screenwriter, is still hampered by the effects of his ... refusal to name names to the House Un-American Activities Committee."

I wrote the *New York Review:* "To paraphrase a formula familiar to my generation, I am not now nor have I ever been a screenwriter." I have nothing against professional screenwriters, one of whom tried to interest Hollywood in a film on my life, but it is outrageous that a younger generation of Americans has been raised to believe that it is only members of that profession who were called before HUAC. My letter continued: "I applied to the Hellman/Hammett project for a very specific reason. Because its purpose is to aid writers who have been victims of political persecution, I hoped that, if it made a grant to me, that would begin the process of discovery by Americans that their support for the Cold War was based on denying them access to information that might have led them to a different conclusion."

Early in 1994 an American doctor residing in Israel, Baruch Goldstein, sprayed Arabs at worship with an assault weapon, killing thirty. I went on the air with a broadcast opening: "This is an appeal from an old Jew...urging...a modern version of the Student Nonviolent Coordinating Committee of the '60s, this time to go to Israel, confront the murderous 'settlers' who endorse Baruch Goldstein's Final Solution for Palestinians...and compel the Rabin government to decide *which* Jews it is going to protect: the civilized human beings seeking peace with Palestinians or those utilizing religious extremism for self-delusion." If that had been done, perhaps Prime Minister Rabin would not have been assassinated by a Jewish extremist.

The French writer, de Exupery, wrote: "Happiness is when one is understood." Broadcasts like those brought me mail that kept me going. Some letters spoke directly to the issue: "Thanks for saying what needs to be said about Israel. If we picket anything: my signs are ready: 'DO NOT DO UNTO OTHERS WHAT YOU WOULD NOT HAVE THEM DO UNTO YOU'." Another letter on that occasion, from a business demographer in real estate who had been a student of mine in the '60s, falls into a category that takes my breath away: "You never fail to amaze me with your timely and thoughtful strategic planning. You have always been on the cutting edge of social and political issues and you always will be. You are a national treasure."

Letters in that class are no mere ego-boosters. They make me think about the degree to which they are true and where they are not, if only by omission. One conclusion that particular letter reinforced is that I am not good at abstract thought. If I were, I would have realized decades earlier that a Marxist society could not long endure. But he was right that I do not run away from the need to think through the most sweeping of practical questions. That January of 1994 I had done a broadcast titled "'Fixing' the 'Soviet Union'." It consisted of excerpts from my essay-type response to a questionnaire from the Russian Academy of

Sciences seeking the opinions of foreigners that body regarded as knowledgeable about what Moscow should do in the post-communist era. I had responded in Russian. My translation of excerpts into English that follows reflects a style of writing permissible in Russian but not in an academic communication in English:

"To erase 74 years is impossible. And only fools would undertake that. Unfortunately, you have such....The choice you will have is between wild capitalism such as existed in the U.S. before [Franklin D.] Roosevelt, and social-democratic, under which the elderly and the disabled and even the unemployed can exist in a more or less human fashion. Historically, of course, this is thanks to the Soviet Union. Except for sick-benefit societies in Germany and even prerevolutionary Russia, *all* the social reforms of the 20th century *followed* the Bolshevik Revolution, in response to the demands of the masses of the people in the West that they too have free higher education and health care and pensions for all and even the right of women to participate in elections and the right of ethnic minorities to be equal human beings."

"Russia will not be either the USA or China or Japan or Sweden....You've got to avoid making everything fit a set pattern. Unfortunately Russians love to do that....Today supercentralization is your scourge. You've got to unlearn it....You have to bear in mind that the successes of Japan and Germany were to a very large degree due to the fact that capitalism there is not free at all, but develops specifically under the strong influence of government policy....You've got to give thought to...the results of the recent elections in Greece, Poland, and Lithuania [where Communists self-reformed to social-democracy had won]. In your country, too, the people will not long endure the policy of the International Monetary Fund and the World Bank. Your political powers-that-be have got to reckon with that."

"You've got to protect your products against competition from foreign goods by tariffs and quotas....You today have very little hard currency. It is necessary to prevent that currency from leaving the country....Today your wealth in raw materials and metals is being exported at fire-sale prices. Let Yeltsin use his rapid-response police and internal-security troops against specifically this kind of criminal."

"If a capitalist actually engages in production...all honor to him, and every possible material reward. But if...he simply...buys in order to resell without benefit to the consumer...one has to put the heat on that."

"As to monopolies. They exist in your country and in mine....One should either privatize them, but only in pieces, so as not to leap from the frying pan into the fire, or divide them, as, for example, the Black Sea fisheries were divided into four."

"The uncentralized component of the economy must be considerably larger than the centrally-controlled....The rules governing the decision must be the rules of the market. That is the heart of the matter."

Being Russian intellectuals, the authors of the questionnaire naturally asked for opinions on the future role of their stratum. I replied:

"The intelligentsia played a role in your country in the 19th century, in the 20th both under the undeveloped capitalism of the tsarist period and under the Communists, who gave culture a place of honor, although they did everything possible to control it. But today? Just look at the U.S. We have plenty of genuine intellectuals, but what influence do they have upon the course of the country's politics?"

They wanted advice on social movements. I answered: "The only powerful movements in your country today are the labor unions, both old and new. Attempts by the government to control them are no better than the Communists' behavior in this regard. If you don't allow unions to develop freely, a new cycle of appearance of a Bolshevik underground will begin."

"You need a strong women's movement. The whole world laughs at the antediluvian attitude of Russian men to women. Kuche, Kinder, Kirche [kitchen, children, church] was Hitler's slogan. It is simply unseemly, shameful that so large a number of Russian men think in fascist terms where women are concerned....You have a stupendous number of highly-educated women. Not to make use of that force is like a wrestler who goes into the ring with one arm tied behind his back....You had the largest system of pre-school care in the world. This is what made it possible for women to participate in production, in medicine, in science, in culture. To throw that advantage away is just plain stupid. But as of now that's the path you are following. Too bad."

"With respect to the...question...regarding the desirability of further destruction of bodies of representative government — that is simply awful. Whoever drafted that question literally understands nothing at all about democracy, or opposes it. Direct democracy — referenda, etc. — is useful specifically when representative government is well-developed. Otherwise it becomes the most gross kind of populism, favoring the demagogue or dictator (very often one and the same person) currently in power."

The next question dealt with inter-ethnic conflicts. I responded: "A very major positive is the fact that the local Russians did not resist the declarations of sovereignty in Tatarstan, Bashkortostan, Sakha and elsewhere, especially where the indigenous peoples comprise a minority of the population....The fact that the Russians behaved in civilized fashion...makes incomparably easier the obligatory process of finding the way to new economic and military relationships both among the former republics of the Soviet Union and within Russia itself.

"One warning in that regard...When Russians live in the Baltic or Kazakhstan for 40 years, or are even born there, and do not learn the local language, that is exactly the same as the chauvinism of the English colonialists in India or Americans in Latin America...or of today's American tourist anywhere in the world. A condescending attitude toward members of minority nationalities is the sure road to centrifugal phenomena, peaceful or bloody....Literally everything depends upon the psychological attitude of the Russians toward non-Russians." This was a year before the monstrous war in Chechnya, toward which the Russian people lived up to my high opinion of them in their opposition to it, but Yeltsin and the drunken-and-drugged troops he used did not.

The following group of questions had to do with societal relationships and conflicts. "So long as today's absurdity continues," I replied, "the present trends will also go on. A small handful will get richer and richer without any positive consequences for the economy. The overwhelming majority will fall lower and lower. The internal market will narrow....In answer to the question as to whether it is possible to use social policy to stop the process of lumpenization [creation of an underclass] without interfering with the process of formation of a middle class, I have to offer a counter-question to whoever framed that question: are you a human being or some kind of amoral mechanism? Is the history of primitive capitalism — the England of 1844 as described by Engels — the Bible for you? The Russian people is educated to world standards. Science is developed. Industry exists albeit at the level of your living standard of 1985. A transportation network exists. You mean it is not possible to devise a form of social development on these inherited foundations under which all these advantages will be utilized and not cast into the wastebasket?

"The same holds for the question on general access to higher education. It reflects the viewpoint of a medieval guild. Protect one's own, and to hell with everyone else. For shame! I cannot understand for the life of me why you want to adopt from our experience all that is worst, all that is misanthropic. You hold in reverence the 'technology' of our social sciences but its ethics or, to be more exact, lack of ethics, does not interest you....Of course, if you agree with the objective of the International Monetary Fund to reduce Russia to Third World status... the thing to do is to return to the illiterate [pre-revolutionary] Russia of birchbark sandals and rag leggings, accompanied by export of grain while people starved to death in one or another part of the country every year."

I saw many things in the serious Russian press representing views similar to mine after I sent that questionnaire response. I have no way of knowing whether those were independent conclusions, or whether any of my ideas were regarded as useful and seeped down from people in the

Academy of Sciences who agreed with me. I do know that an internationally renowned Russian crystallographer, who had just been here to work for Livermore Lawrence Laboratory, wrote me that she had circulated my letter to her stating these views in condensed form, "and virtually every one of my colleagues at Moscow University said they would put their names to it."

The fact is that the Primakov government held office Fall 1998 - Spring 1999 pursued more than a few of the policies I had proposed.

In 1994 I received letters from Russia, Kazakhstan, Ukraine, Belarus. They illustrated very clearly the confusion of ideas underlying the confused socio-political situation in the country. In Kurgan, Siberia, lives a Russian, Valerian Sinelnikov, raised in a Soviet orphanage which enabled him to go clear through conservatory. He detested the Communists, however, because of the constraints placed upon his teaching of music in the schools. His complaints in 1994 covered the waterfront: "I am always beside myself over the fact that those who drove all religion out of the minds of the people have suddenly become believers???" He is horrified by the use of force: "I cannot understand to this day how one can justify the violence wreaked against people on Oct. 3 and 4." This reference is to Yeltsin's 1993 shelling of the parliament in Moscow, elected in Gorbachev's day, which drove it out of existence, and the massacre of demonstrators outside TV headquarters. "How can those 'fighters for human rights,' Clinton, Mitterand, Major, Kohl and the rest, statesmen of civilized countries, support Yeltsin's genocide? I regard their actions as having the direct selfish object of converting Russia into their economic appendage."

The U.S. has not won him as a friend: "As I see the implantation of the American way of life into our country, I hate that way of life more and more. We are people, Peo-ple! — animals endowed with reason, who filter everything we do through that capacity to reason....Today we have lost much of what we had and, regrettably have gained nothing in its stead, not even democracy, for even that was beaten down by tank-mounted cannon. Doesn't America know that? And if it does? And supports the bandit behavior of Yeltsin and his followers? If that is the case, I curse America! And neither I, nor the majority of the Russian people — of this I am certain — need the American way of life, not because America knows or doesn't know what has happened, supports or doesn't support the Yeltsin crew, but because America helped drive our people into poverty, tore people away from their friends and relatives [he's referring to the break-up of the Soviet Union: he has friends from his orphanage days living in other republics] and helped in the revival of two classes, the rich crooks and the poor honest people who work."

His hatred for Communists did not mean that he wanted abandonment of the socio-economic system they introduced: "I will never agree that the restoration of capitalism in our country is an objective process. It is the subjective desire of short-sighted people, capable...of seizing power, but having not the slightest notion of how to run the country, where to lead it, and by what route, and compelled to turn for help not to Russian minds but to psychologists and politicians from the other side of the hill who had been waiting for this opportunity for decades."

This letter merits such extensive quotation because of where this reasoning led him at the polls: "I make so bold as to pose a question to you, or, more properly, through you to Clinton! Who is really the fascist in Russia? He who is preparing to give away the keys to the Kremlin, or he who wishes to revive Russia. Of course I am talking about Yeltsin and Zhirinovsky," the wild nationalist demagogue who was then highly popular. I am again reminded of the words Hitler carefully selected as the name of his organization: the *Nationalist* Socialist German WORKERS' Party.

To his letter was appended a rap-style poem of his own, in which he compared Yeltsin to Boris Godunov in the troubled times of Ivan the Terrible, and predicted for him the awful vengeance of the people as in early times. By 1996, however, this same man not only voted for the reformed Communist Party, but personally worked for the election of its presidential candidate. He insisted to me that a majority of Russians could not possibly have voted for Yeltsin, and therefore the presidential election had to have been stolen. I would regard his evolution as a fair example of how the Communists recovered to win nearly as many votes as Yeltsin.

February brought a letter from a Russian newsman in Kazakhstan, Viktor Minin, then holding its own elections: "I took an interest in the campaign promises of the candidates. How smoothly they all talk, but anybody can make a promise. The question is: who will carry it out?" He provides an insight into the thinking of an extremely important group: the 27 million Russians who then lived in the other republics. "People feel insecure as they hear very unflattering epithets regarding their ignorance of the Kazakh language thrown at them," he continued. "You will agreee that it is difficult, at 30, 40, or 50 years of age to learn a language to perfection....It's stupid to introduce Kazakh [a Turkic language] as the language of all paperwork in regions where 75 to 80% or even more of the population consists of Russian-speaking people. Nor are personnel policies entirely comprehensible. This is the origin of people's sense of insecurity, their have-a-suitcase-packed mentality. Yes, I was born and grew up here and have no intention of leaving." But he was just plain depressed: "I'm thinking about changing my profession. It seems to me that journalism is not of any special value to anyone today."

March brought a letter from that Liubov Kovalevskaia who had had the courage to predict the Chernobyl nuclear power plant disaster in print thanks to her observations as a reporter for the local newspaper. She has paid the price.

"Dear Bill of mine, how are you?" she wrote. "Oh, there are always reasons for not writing....Chernobyl has caught up with me, seized hold of me firmly and for a long time, forever, to tell the truth....This year I spent nearly two months in bed in the radiology center....I have long sought solace not in man but in God. You are wise; you will understand....I bear my cross and I hold my head even higher, so that no one will guess that I am already halfway to the end of my sickness. And if someone suddenly shows up from out of somewhere, my smile appears, and I reach for my accordion. Remember our drunken night? Harmony of the spirit is a great blessing. It alone justifies life on earth....I deeply hope that your family is all right and that you yourself are healthy and vigorous as you were, as always kind and inexhaustible in warmth, jokes and the most ready of smiles. I will always remember you and love you."

She had, in fact, been in love with a Colorado newsman I brought to meet her when he and I went to Chernobyl in 1990, the last time I ever saw her. But her soul was big enough for more than one. She had been living for many years in the Ukraine, and her letter reacted to what had happened in that nuclear-armed country of fifty million: "The bitterness of the Ukrainian loaf with the trident baked into it." The trident is the symbol of Ukrainian nationalism. "But after all we are independent! I'll tell you from what: from normal existence, from honor, from conscience, from individual security....God knows that Soviet times tasted like too much horse-radish, but a person had a very firmly-established past, a present, and there really was a future before one.

"Today the past is being rewritten, which means that yet again history is being adapted to the needs of those in power....And if the Ukrainians were actually slaves for centuries, how many years will it take in order—never mind actually becoming free—merely to understand what freedom is, and what to do with it?....In the passion of their inferiority complex they are ready to find justification even for fascism." She was referring to those Ukrainian nationalists who fought for Hitler, served as police, participated in the Holocaust.

"The real present reminds one of a cheap Arab bordello: there are such on the outskirts of Hamburg, near the railway terminal, where a half-mile strip reeks of all that is cheap: cheap paint, cheap smells, cheap relationships, cheap illusions....About the future there is nothing to say, because the future is my daughter," who was left a retarded and beautiful teenage orphan.

May brought a letter from someone who presents the mirror image of the two just excerpted. Gulshara Mukatova is a Kazakh physician, also the mother of a teenage daughter . She was unique among my correspondents of 1994 in that she was politically active, an elected member of local government. But she is not at all unique in that, as a member of the Soviet-educated stratum of intellectual professionals, she expressed her views on events of the day through easy reference to history and culture:

"Things here now are as they were when Omar Khayyam wrote 400 years ago:

> Of what use do you expect your wisdom to be?
> You'd have a better chance of getting milk from a billy-goat.
> Pretend to be a fool and you'll do better.
> In our day wisdom comes cheaper than onions."

Turning to the economic situation, she cited a literary figure as solidly in the Western tradition as Khayyam is in the Eastern: "The writer and humanist Thomas Mann wrote: 'Inflation is a tragedy that causes society to become cynical, cruel, and indifferent.' Inflation has stunned our society in consequence of a mistaken economic policy. Commercial banks, and sometimes even those owned by the government, are constantly extending large loans to particular firms to buy Mercedes and TV and radio equipment abroad. Loans should in fact only be extended to build factories and mills in Kazakhstan to manufacture its own equipment and machines."

She closed with words from the most famous Russian Communist poet: "In consequence of the present policy, the executives of industrial enterprises and of investment funds may in some cases make a profit, but the majority of the people will, as Mayakovsky wrote, get 'the hole in the doughnut'."

Her worldwide horizons did not interfere with her being a Kazakh patriot, and from having differences with the Russian journalist born in Kazakhstan I have cited. Gulshara continued, "You write, further, that we are trying to move our capital northward because there are more Russians there." She lived in the then capital, Almaty, near the southern border. "It isn't Russians of whom there are so many there, but Russian speakers: Mordva, Poles, Belorussians, Ukrainians, etc. The capital should be moved urgently to the center of Kazakhstan....The official language must be Kazakh alone, because it is on the verge of disappearance." Having visited Kazakhstan eight times over a thirty-year span, and done research on the matter in question, I know that is not so; but to a city-dwelling Kazakh it may well appear to be the case. "Nothing will happen to the Russian language in consequence, because we urban people continue to favor it in everyday use," she concluded.

Unlike my correspondents in Russia and the Ukraine, for whom the United States became either a country that did not keep its promises or one actively engaged in dismembering the former Soviet Union, she idealized this country as late as 1996. Possibly that was because the oil wealth of Kazakhstan had attracted substantial American investment.

Since my roots are in the political far left, and will always be well left of center, I am particularly encouraged by mail from Americans who choose to identify themselves as existing solidly within the Establishment. My first piece of fan mail in 1994 was a xeroxed letter to the executive director of the Pacifica network. The listener was reacting to a protest I had made on the air against the fact that its national news service was boycotting me in seeking comment on developments in the former USSR. I had been called upon for such comment ever since we had grown beyond the founding station in Berkeley, in the '60s.

This listener identified himself as a Yale graduate in a year when that institution was still exclusively white, male, and upper crust. He had a graduate degree from Stanford, and was a retired Navy Commander and an architect and engineer by profession. His letter concluded: "KPFA needs people like Bill, so that people like me can continue to need KPFA."

In September of that year, a private financier in Newport Beach, Frank Randall, who had been a fellow peace walker in the Ukraine in 1988, donated $2,500 to publish the dozens of letters I received between 1992 and 1994 from people in six republics of the Commonwealth of Independent States. They appeared at the end of the year under the title, *The Struggle to Survive.* This collection also incorporated my lecture of 1991 renouncing Marxist socialism, and another, at Johns Hopkins University. In the latter I offered my explanation for the rise of the nationalisms that had triumphed in that same Soviet Union which had once legislated and funded advances for the non-Russian republics not paralleled in the former colonies of any other empire.

The letters that move me emotionally and make me feel very, very humble are from people who have chosen never to leave the working class and to fight for its uplift from within. Among those to whom I circulated a first draft of a preface to this book were two people who have worked with their hands all their lives. Norman Roth is a Chicagoan I have known for forty-five years, since the very bottom of the McCarthy era. He has the broken nose of a one-time boxer, used to write poetry, and was elected and re-elected to head the huge International Harvester local of the Auto Workers' Union until retirement. That was not an office job. Strikes, picket lines, police brutality, biased and corrupt judges, employers for whom workers are labor cost and not human beings, have been the pattern of his life. He is gentle, yet tough as wrought iron. He wrote me:

"Flattery, the coin of the sycophant, can only damage your

work....After reading and rereading the material you sent and listening to the tape you sent about your appearance before the witch-hunters, I put it all together with my memories of your books and our long discussions. Putting all this together, I could find no reason for your having any trace of guilt for your not going to Spain with the Brigade. A single fascist bullet could have robbed us of all the wonderful work you have contributed to the struggles for peace, equality, democracy, jobs. There is no reason for even the slightest sense of ambivalence about your efforts to understand and portray the main political and social forces that have dominated our lives....You have helped prepare the material from which the world will create a more humane society and future for all of its inhabitants. I wish we had more Bill Mandels even though I am not always in agreement with all your conclusions."

Readers who think of the lifetime factory worker as a semi-literate appendage to a machine should read that paragraph again.

George Winter was born, raised, and worked on the family farm in the gold country foothills of the Sierra. One grandmother was an Indian, and he identifies ethnically with her, although his bearded face is precisely that of Karl Marx in his middle years. He was a conscientious objector in the late '50s, a factory worker, a civil rights activist in Mississippi with SNCC in 1964, and a union organizer in Sacramento Valley canneries. I had first met him as a result of my broadcasts, and in connection with efforts to save Cuba from American invasion when he was attending U.C. Davis in 1962. I got to know him well only in the '80s, through his then wife, Gwen, a pioneering female union electrician, who was organizing citizen diplomacy trips to the USSR of women in the trades. They lived in Bryte, a poor workingclass suburb of Sacramento. He worked as a one-man construction contractor, was active in Jesse Jackson's Rainbow Coalition and on behalf of the homeless. In an article about him, someone wrote: "He looks as though he was born in a blue work shirt." He has been adopted into the Tlinkit Indian tribe. He wrote me in response to my request for comments on the preface and title:

"Even if there are times we disagree, people who were really looking for solutions, for the truth, respect you as few will ever be respected. Part of this comes from the fact that you were on many firing lines, sometimes...the first or one of the first and almost alone. So to many of us who came along later you are a hero of a very special kind....To me you have been an intellectual mentor, a modern day shaman to far more people than you think, strong and searching enough to be doing the right thing when it was hardest to do....Bill, if our fellow beings survive another thousand years it will be because some of what you've been doing will be alive and well. Not many friends, comrades or brothers leave so many waves for us to ride as they swim through life." He added in pencil: "You know I bet you still have another 20 years to sing."

I wrote back: "Maybe, as you say, I do have another 20 years. But if my autobiography is never published, all the work on it will have been worthwhile for having elicited your letter. I'd like somebody to read it to me again in my last moments of consciousness."

Continuing to write about the former Soviet Union was not exactly singing, but for me a matter of common sense and of honor. Common sense, because it is silly to permit my sixty years of accumulated knowledge to go to waste. Honor, because, as both Roth and Winter know very well, the biggest battle of my life has been to gain and maintain access to the public with my knowledge and views about the societies of the United States and the former Soviet Union, both independently but also, most importantly, in relation to each other. In 1994 I wrote a review of a book, *Eyewitness,* about the attempted coup against Gorbachev in 1991 by the most conservative wing of perestroika Communists, which boomeranged and resulted in Yeltsin's dismemberment of the USSR. I used that occasion to sum up my conclusions from the Gorbachev decade:

"The coup leaders, whose sincerity, ability, and in some cases even selflessness Pozner is at pains to point out, simply had no program to offer other than maintenance of the socio-economic-political status quo....The question is: can there be an *economic* system, as distinct from one of administrative command, where there is no market? If not, can there be socialism, as Marx and Engels understood it throughout their lifetimes?" My own answer was no, which was why I had, three years earlier, abandoned my lifelong belief in Marxist socialism.

CHAPTER 28

Not Yet Sunset

The Congressional elections in November 1994 were won by an ultra-conservative Republican cabal. Many of the candidates had been quietly chosen and trained beforehand by the man they elected Speaker, Newt Gingrich. Once in office, he announced that the victory meant an endorsement of his Contract With America. This was a list of measures repealing or reducing the social gains won initially under Franklin Roosevelt sixty years earlier, and expanded under a succession of presidents, up to and including the moderate rightist Nixon. Polls later showed that most voters had never heard of the so-called contract. Their ballots had been cast on the customary American basis of dissatisfaction with the state of affairs rather than preference for a specific program of change. Most candidates in both parties had, as usual, avoided discussion of real issues.

After the election, affirmative action became the wedge, the issue that would run interference for the rest of the "contract." The reasoning was simple. Allege that minorities, particularly African-Americans and women, are taking the jobs of white males, and distract public attention. The arms budget, an anachronism once the Soviet Union had collapsed, could then be maintained essentially at its cold war level. Aid to families with dependent children could be wiped out, on the vile racist notion that ignorant young women have babies to obtain the pittance provided by the welfare system through its demeaning procedures. Social Security could be converted into market insecurity, by transferring payments not into a federal fund, but into the shell game of the stock exchanges. The argument was subtler than in the past. We should be "color-blind," and think of the poor without regard to color, language, gender. The reasons why the percentage of poor among non-whites, native Spanish-speakers, and women, was vastly higher than among white males, were ignored.

I reacted with amazement and rising anger to this ocean of one-sided propaganda. When a local daily newspaper columnist with an excellent record on civil liberties, civil rights, the Vietnam War, and militarism, denounced affirmative action in terms that were objectively falsehoods, I could take it no longer.

KPFA management had convinced me to give up every second weekly evening broadcast in exchange for a brief morning drive-time spot
with a listenership several times as large, in which I was interviewed.
One morning in March 1995 I came in and handed the interviewers a
sheet with the introduction and questions I wanted asked. What I said
that morning led to my morning spot being cancelled and, indirectly, to
my being taken off the air entirely after thirty-seven years on KPFA. It
quite literally brought part of my life to an end. Therefore it merits
extensive quotation. The show opened with one of the co-hosts saying:

"Bill has decided today we're not going to talk about things formerly
Soviet; we're instead going to talk about Art Hoppe of the *San Francisco
Chronicle*."

On the air, I said: "When the hysteria about affirmative action reaches the point where a man whom I regard as honest tells what are
unquestionably lies, has psyched himself into that situation, then I feel
that this is something that requires discussion. He's got classic sentences
like this: 'Surely it is unfair to give the son of a Black banker preference
over the son of a white sharecropper.' There are actually a couple of
Black bankers in this country....

"Yes, there are white sharecroppers. But the ratio of white sharecroppers to the white farming population is a tiny fraction of the ratio of
Black sharecroppers to the Black farming population. This business of
putting equal signs where equal signs do not exist is in some ways the
mildest of what he has to say. Here is a statement—he's my age: 'As far
as my career goes, I would have had an easier time of it in many respects
had I been Black.' His job is poking barbs into the Establishment. Find
me today, in 1995, a Black man in this country in a general medium
whose job is poking barbs into the white Establishment! His job could
not have been given to a Black man, and I don't believe it can be given to
a Black man today.

"He goes on to say: 'It would have been easier for a Black to be admitted to Lowell' [the academic high school in San Francisco]. That is a lie.
There was no affirmative action [in his youth]. No Black kid squeezed
into the high school I went to, which was the New York equivalent of
Lowell. In a racist society, admissions officers, teachers, take it for granted that if you come in looking Latino, looking Black, and, for many purposes, if you come in looking female, you are not going to be tracked into
the top level of anything, because either it was taken for granted that
genetically you did not have the brains or it was taken for granted that
you had no future in that field...

"He has a sentence: 'The *Chronicle* was eager then as it is now to hire
Black reporters, and a Black columnist would have been a feather in its
journalistic cap.' That last sentence means that [he believes] there was

no Black person who had the brains to be a columnist."

"I think of my daughter, going to a school that was 90 percent Black, because that was our neighborhood school; her boyfriend, going to a school that was overwhelmingly white because that happened to be his neighborhood school. In her school, the classes were 40 to 45 kids, the textbooks came two months into the school year. In his school, the classes were 30 kids, and the textbooks were there right at the very beginning, so—yes, a Paul Robeson is going to make it—but your ordinary kid, who has to fight this and then apply to Lowell High School? And don't tell me things are different today. One of my sons is a school teacher in Oakland, and the only difference between Oakland today and my daughter's day is that they've got the fig leaf of Black administrators. In all other respects, the underfunding...this is typical.

"What white people have to understand is that Black people, and not only Blacks, grow up in neighborhoods which are consistently mistreated in terms of street lights, in terms of paving, in terms of garbage collection, in terms of the presence and the purpose of the police, so that a kid who grows up under those circumstances starts ten yards behind the other in terms of competition, and so the gap can never be closed if we simply leave it to color-blindness to solve it. Here are the actual figures of...Black representation in the major professions...today. Blacks comprise 12.4 percent of the U.S. population but only 1.4 percent of America's lawyers. In short, of every nine [Black] lawyers there would be on a population basis, there is one; 4 percent of physicians: there is one Black physician for every three there would be; 3.7 percent of engineers....I would lay a rather heavy bet that the figures for journalism are pretty much the same. So unless we give [preference to] the kid who grows up under the circumstances we have described, plus the racism that pervades the white mentality in this country, whether it is executives, whether it is government officials, or whether it is journalists, [nothing will change]....

"This is characteristic of the society, and if we don't understand that, not only is there going to be unending injustice to Black people, but there is going to be unending turmoil because, in the world of today, oppressed nations and nationalities just aren't taking it any more, as the area of my specialty, the ex-Soviet Union, will tell you."

In closing my segment, the co-host, Phillip Maldari, also co-Public Affairs Director of KPFA, said, "Bill, I certainly thank you for bringing this column to our attention, and opening the issue."

Top management thought differently. The Program Director sent me an Inter-Office Memo: "I have written to you and spoken to you...about our requirements for the segment you do on the Morning Show...that you stick to issues of the former Soviet Union and Eastern

Europe....Therefore, effective immediately, I am cancelling your appearance as a regular guest on the Morning Show."

Because of KPFA's reputation, this gained national attention. An article in *The Nation* called it "scarcely credible arrogance." But it was also unquestionably a matter of political judgment. The *Examiner,* San Francisco's afternoon daily, quoted me on this as follows: "I believe the station committed suicide in terms of the old KPFA when it did not pre-empt programming to broadcast the U.C. Regents meeting [that cancelled affirmative action]...That decision on the regents personified the switch they have made from a station that sought to be a leader in social movements to one that is looking solely for an increased 'market share,' a term I find wholly inappropriate to a public radio station."

I waited for over a month for management to offer some explanation to listeners of my disappearance from the Morning Show. None was forthcoming, but the station had the unmitigated brass to ask me to appear on its quarterly fund-raising marathon. I declined. A listener in his 20s, in Fresno, where I was carried by an affiliated station, wrote me subsequently that he had thought I had passed on, as he knew that I was quite elderly. Ultimately I used my remaining once-in-two-weeks evening program to explain the situation.

The station used my on-air explanation as excuse to terminate my remaining program because I had violated the gag rule against discussing station affairs on air. There was no such rule during the first quarter-century of KPFA's existence, and I had deliberately violated it at least once each year during the following decade as a matter of democratic principle, with no action ever taken against me previously. Over five hundred listeners now signed petitions demanding my reinstatement. A large number were young people at an anti-Gingrich demonstration of thousands in San Francisco. How many letters were written to the station I have no way of knowing, but senders provided me with copies of more than a hundred. Some of them posed a problem of self-evaluation. I was simply overawed and taken aback by letters like this:

"Bill remains one of the most politically perceptive and morally persuasive intellectuals in our contemporary society. We are fortunate indeed that he lives in the Bay Area."

The letters to management were all the more convincing to me because they did not ignore my faults, and comparisons they made showed the writers to be deeply rooted both in classical and contemporary culture:

From the world of music: "Take an analogy. Say you're Director of the Vienna Philharmonic sometime in the latter half of the eighteenth century. You contract with this kid named Mozart for five new symphonies for the season. But the kid is arrogant and difficult, and he gets his scores in late, and they're full of coffee stains. Worst of all, instead of a symphony, sometimes he tries to hand you a piano concerto, or even a divertimento. It's enough to drive you up the walls. So what do you do? Do you say, 'That's it, Wolfgang. If you can't follow the rules, we won't do your stuff anymore"?

Art: "Like a Picasso it looks [like] we are lucky enough to have found a [sic] asshole that loves us & we have only to look at his scars to appreciate the depth of that life."

Learning: "Playing tapes of Noam Chomsky is not the same as employing a broadcaster of Noam Chomsky's calibre, responsible to, and resident among those whose understanding he has helped to develop."

I look at those last and reflect that KPFA had been quite a radio station in its ability to attract listeners whose searches for parallels would draw upon that range of interests, and who could express themselves with such style.

A galaxy signed the petitions: actor Ed Asner, environmental icon David Brower, journalist Alexander Cockburn, Mime Troupe founder R.G. Davis, novelist Tillie Olsen, folksinger Pete Seeger, stage and screen director Luis Valdez (who had once been a student of mine), clown and ice-cream flavor Wavy Gravy. At least as important to me personally was the signature of Maudelle Shirek, an African-American Berkeley city councilmember re-elected when in her mid-80s.

Lawrence Ferlinghetti, the most widely-published contemporary American poet, and 1950s broadcaster on KPFA, wrote the station that its founders would be "turning over in their graves" over "the recent treatment of one of your oldest and most respected programmers, Bill Mandel."

As a father, I was most moved by a letter son Dave wrote to the manager: "WE [my children] know the price better than you can ever hope to, yet WE applaud Bill and his equally courageous partner, Tanya, and honor them for their incredible courage, unending honesty, selfless lifetime of (unpaid) contributions to world peace, civil rights, common decency, and anti-fascism—hell...you name it and, if it's in the name of humanity, they've fought for it....Tell me that you are not such trash that you would beat up on an old but fearless man who has given his life for his country! Tell me to control the terrible rage I feel towards you, to put it away 'cause it was all a thoughtless accident....Tell me I'm wrong, apologize to Bill like brave humans, and let's get on with the task of rebuilding human decency around the world."

The anger was not limited to my family. A listener my age, referring to the Pacifica Executive Director and the KPFA manager and program director, wrote: "A great many people over the years have sacrificed much to create a unique institution, Pacifica Radio, and you come from nowhere to destroy it. Who invited you to the party in the first place?"

All to no avail.

My supporters were by no means confined to people from one side of the political spectrum. Rush Limbaugh, on the far right, was far and away the most popular national radio talk-show host at this time. A listener in Sacramento wrote me: "Even Rush Limbaugh regulars such as I are willing to put their money where their mouths are when it comes to high-quality, listener-sponsored personalities like William Marx Mandel....Rush Limbaugh would treat you with a lot more respect and deference. He may agree with little that you opine, but he would treat you right."

It was time to crystallize this spontaneous outrage into organized opposition.

In the mid-1990s, Bolinas, California, was still a time-warp. A small community of three or four thousand perhaps, it lies on a coastal plateau peninsula above the Pacific ninety minutes north of San Francisco via twisting, sliding U.S. 1. Until I was fired from KPFA, Bolinas was simply the place where Tanya and I routinely stopped on relaxing drives for lunch in its funky eatery, The Store.

In May a stranger from there phoned to say they were organizing a meeting in its school to hear why I had been removed from the air. I attended. Thirty were present, the equivalent of a thousand in Berkeley in proportion to population. Half were, in dress and manner, typical northern Californians. The other half were hippies who didn't care that they had aged: long hair tied in buns, beards, tie-dyed shirts and sandals. When the discussion turned to what to do, I suggested that a picket line be held at KPFA. All agreed, and some said they would help distribute an announcement of it at a major demonstration to be held in San Francisco that weekend against the rightist legislation being pushed through Congress.

This tiny town of Bolinas had a tinier every-other-daily, the *Hearsay News*. Although the *Hearsay News* was xeroxed, all the original material was ordinary typewriter copy with old-fashioned ragged right margins. The retro appearance of the Bolinas paper was no handicap to the quality of its journalism. Five issues of May 15-24, 1995 serialized a report on the picketing by Peter Axelson, which opened as follows: "When I showed up in Berkeley on Wednesday afternoon I was ready for anything. I had on me: $40.00 in cash for bribes; some loose change; a mini FM stereo walkman; a Canon S-6 camera good to fifty feet underwater (because one never knows); earplugs; a pair of John Lennon purple moonglasses; a 1/4 ounce of pot; a few sticks of Nom Champa incense; and a rubber, unribbed.

"I was ready.

"And this was good because the story of people picketing the studios of KPFA in protest to the firing of Bill Mandel was news of historic proportions. After all, wasn't KPFA supposed to be an oasis of sanity and culture in the dangerously narrow-minded world of media? You don't protest before such an institution lightly because you may be shooting yourself in the foot....

"I ambled over to KPFA and MY GOD! There it was: a hundred-plus people walking in a circle in front of the doors....There was a drum beating and a trumpet tooting. There were people in costumes, and gold toilet seats (toilet seats?)"....

"We were all part of that strange and beautiful phenomenon called a Berkeley demonstration. And right in the middle of all this, wearing a suit and tie, carrying his briefcase and looking distinguished as hell, walked Bill Mandel himself. With his silver hair and his head held high this was his big moment, and the smile on his face showed that he was enjoying it completely....

"In boardrooms, classrooms, and nursery schools across our country these two rules are practically universal: 'color within the lines' and 'don't talk back.' Except that in the case of Bill Mandel talking back is his life and we depended on him to do this. So we came to KPFA with Bill Mandel so we could all talk back."

I asked a man festooned with bandoleers of toilet tissue rolls, who had trucked the bowls— no mere seats—what they meant. He replied: "They treated you like shit, didn't they?"

My dismissal from KPFA was followed by a general housecleaning in which dozens of programs were cancelled, including that of the only broadcaster on its air longer than I, Phil Elwood, jazz critic for the *San Francisco Examiner.* The night before the changes went into effect, a meeting was held in Berkeley, attended by three hundred listener-subscribers, to protest the massive dismissal of community-based broadcasters each with weekly programs, to make room for three national "stars" with daily hour-long programs. An ongoing organization, Take Back KPFA, was established, led by long-time friends like Lester Radke and Hulda Nystrom, former station executives such as Maria Gilardin and Bob Bergstresser, and activists among whom Jeffrey Blankfort was the most devoted, creative, and persistent. Former executive John Whiting helped via brilliantly-written polemics on the Internet and published articles in England, where the similar decline of BBC was an issue among intellectuals.

I parted company with the group, without rancor, when it seemed that we could not win without obtaining, by whatever means necessary, the full list of subscribers without which we had no way of presenting them with our point of view. But the persistence of Take Back KPFA and the efforts of employed staff at other Pacifica stations, particularly WBAI in New York, ultimately won broader and broader support in the progressive community nationwide.

The person presiding over the changes in the Pacifica chain was its Executive Director, Pat Scott, a Black woman. In responding to a question about the self-perpetuating nature of Pacifica's board from Per Fegereng of the *Portland Free Press*, Scott said that if the board were elected it would be all white. Fagereng published a rejoinder by me. I wrote that her statement was totally contrary to the history both of Berkeley, where the chain originated, and of KPFA and Pacifica.

"Berkeley, predominantly a white city, was the first to introduce busing in an attempt to eliminate racially discriminatory education. Berkeley elected Black mayors. Its votes made possible the election of the first African-American member of Congress to come from a white-majority district, Ron Dellums....So there are absolutely no grounds for Scott's fear that an elected Pacifica board would be all white. On the contrary, the reason why it is now largely, perhaps predominantly non-white is because it reflected the culture of Bay Area progressivism regarding affirmative action, and of people in the other Pacifica cities who accepted that....It is a sorry reflection on this country that Scott's belief, expressed in that remark, and probably shared by her fellow non-white Pacifica Board members, is justified by her life experience. But it is not justified by the record of Pacifica..."

Within weeks after being dropped by KPFA, I had two invitations, entirely unsolicited, to do ongoing broadcasts on other stations. One series, on a college radio station in Silicon valley, lasted a year. The other, on "pirate" Free Radio Berkeley, continued for three years until the Federal Communications Commission obtained an injunction against its further broadcasting from a federal judge. The former program took the form of reading an earlier version of this autobiography, followed by phone-ins. One caller described it as "inspirational" while another asked: "Who was this entertainer Robeson?" Yet another: "How does one become an activist?" To me, they all justified my writing and broadcasting it. This station had about a million people living within its signal range, including the Stanford University community. This station also depended largely upon on-air appeals to listeners for funds. I thought my host's requests were too modest, with $20 being asked for. So I pitched. One listener, having heard that Tanya and I were then married sixty years, gave $60, another $100. The total for our three weekly shows during that drive were the highest of any on that station. Earlier, during that fund drive, I had played my 1960 testimony before the House Un-American Activities Committee. The next week a listener, saying he was twenty, informed me that he had duplicated that and my

McCarthy hearing of 1953 and sent them to friends. People asked questions about McCarthyism and the Soviet Union.

Free Radio Berkeley had been founded the previous year. FRB was one of the first micropower stations deliberately broadcasting with such low power that it could not be accused of interfering with any station licensed by the Federal Communications Commission. That government body refused to license broadcasts at under one hundred watts and set other standards placing the air waves beyond the purse of ordinary citizens or neighborhood groups. In early 1996 it was already possible to hold a statewide conference of such stations. That gathering was thrilling, because among the hundred people present there were twenty Latinos from the barrios, speaking either Spanish or bilingually, including several women, and eight African-Americans— well in proportion to their share in the state's population. There was a representative from Haiti and one from the Zapatista rebels in Chiapas, Mexico (the founder of the micropower movement, Stephen Dunifer, personally built transmitters for them). My mere mention that I had been an activist from the 1930s on brought applause from these new radio pioneers. Those present knew they were building on previous history.

When I began those broadcasts, the audience of FRB was very small, but that had the same advantage that small class size provides in teaching. A young ultra-Leftie called one night, and I answered his questions for nearly an hour: why Soviet socialism failed; what I thought of the Black former Chief of Staff of the U.S. Army, Colin Powell, who the Republicans would dearly have loved to have had as presidential candidate; my opinion of former California governor Jerry Brown, now a populist. When the listener finally hung up, he said, "Thank you for the wonderful conversation."

The FRB collective wrote and circulated a lengthy article, "How Free Radio Stations are Giving Communities Their Own Voice." Several hundred words of it were on my program. At that point I was the regular guest of another broadcaster, the "unabashed anarchist" Rad Man:

"The two work quite well together despite their different political philosophies. Mandel's years of experience complements what the Rad Man calls his own 'cynical optimism.' Together they make for very interesting philosophical discussions. Mandel entertains the possibility of a social democratic, labor based party in the U.S. whereas the Rad Man is fiercely anti-capitalist and opposed to statist government of any sort."

Life continued to provide riches other than the satisfactions of broadcasting. The end of the spring semester in 1995 gave Dave the first real breather in a year of graduate work at the University of Washington. We spent a week with him and Traci Eckels, his partner. We drove north along the coast, my most favorite trip in all the world. In Portland it rained, of course. But the roses in its hilltop botanical garden were too numerous for the rain to have ruined them all. On the freeway north of Portland, however, the rain was the heaviest I could recall in half a century. Wipers were useless. We could move only because the headlights of cars on all sides in late-afternoon rush hour provided orientation.

Dave and Traci were renting a ridiculous cottage whose owner had permanently sealed nearly all the windows. However, Seattle weather permits front and rear doors to be kept open most of the time. Seattle, like San Francisco, is perfect for the kind of tourist, like us, to whom a city's outdoor qualities are at least as important as those indoors. The rain let up for the rest of our stay, and we took a fine ferry ride to Bremerton—which was spoiled a bit by the sight of an ugly monstrous submarine capable of exterminating a big fraction of humanity with a single salvo of its intercontinental nuclear missiles. The damn things look as beastly as their mission. While the body wallows heavy in the water, the diving fins rise above the tail in a satanic black cross.

We drove up alone to Vancouver, British Columbia, for a few days, and our fondness for Canadians and their civilized way of life was refreshed. The art museum had a major show which prompted thought about the interconnectedness of the modern world across cultures and social systems. The theme was Canadian-Chinese art. The artists had all received first-class academic training in the socialist-realist tradition in the People's Republic of China. Having emigrated from a country where huge public walls were available for frescoes, their work was too large for anything but a museum. Yet the subject-matter was intimate. One painter, working on an immense scale, used the traditional Chinese scroll form combined with his realist schooling to show the people's recent rediscovery of Buddhism.

The trip home was lovely. The surf was up, way up, from the southernmost Oregon coast all the distance to San Francisco. We spent the night in redwood country where U.S. Highway 101 turns inland to bypass the super-rugged Lost Coast. Garberville, the marijuana capital, is as mixed-up American as can be. We found perhaps the last supermarket in the country that didn't take credit cards. Was this a reflection of the anti-Establishment spirit of this town of ex-hippies, or of the illegal business that was the core of its economy, in which people stayed away from traceable records of expenditures?

The final day, we drove the coast the full length of U.S. 1 to Muir Beach. We walked the Mendocino headlands. In Richardson Redwood Grove we walked again, and watched convicts pulling truss bridges into place on the Eel River in advance of the rainy season.

Back home I found a message inviting me onto a special broadcast by WBAI, the Pacifica station in New York. It turned out to be a discussion of the Rosenberg Case in which the other guest was William Reuben, the journalist who forty-five years earlier had been alone in the country to cast doubt on the government's charges, an act of most extraordinary courage at the height of McCarthy's power. We had had no contact in all the intervening years. During the broadcast he said, with utmost gratitude to those who had treated and nursed him, that he had just recovered from a life-or-death operation. I nearly broke down on the air. Afterward I thought about that and realized that I can retain the very warmest feelings for people yet have no need to connect unless there is a concrete reason to do so.

Another couple of weeks passed and I got a call from a man who thirty years earlier had been the first Black university professor of geography outside the Negro colleges, as far as I know. Bill Brown had seen me the night before in yet another TV documentary on McCarthyism, though the man voicing the defiant words against the senator was not identified.

As always in summer, I swam daily in Lake Anza, a five-minute drive from the house. One day in September, I met Sydney Clemens at the beach. She is the stepdaughter of Morton Sobell, the Rosenbergs' co-defendant who had served fourteen years on Alcatraz although only a first offender. She knew of the CIA's just-released so-called Wynona papers: selected documents of electronic surveillance that claimed to be definitive proof of the Rosenbergs' guilt. Sydney had spent her entire life believing they were innocent, and said, "this is a terrible shock." What did I think? I described my responses to questioning on this subject by Senator McCarthy and Roy Cohn when the Rosenbergs were in the death house. I had carefully avoided any opinion on guilt or innocence, but attacked the outrageously tainted trial, the convictions, and the death sentences. Then I described how Phyllis had been affected as a thirteen-year-old. Sydney's composure cracked (she is Phyllis' age), and I hugged her. Then I broke down. Later, an elderly female friend of her's who had been present told her she regarded our conversation as a "historical event." I realized that what, to Sydney and myself, was simply a discussion of a part of our lives was, to this other person, a page of history come to life.

The following week I wore a different hat entirely.

Wilbur Hot Springs lies at the end of a bumpy, dusty, twisting gravel road high in the dry mountains a hundred miles north of us. The twenty-room hotel at the springs was built in 1865, with no private baths— the toilet down the hall is still called the commodium. In a sense the whole place is a memorial to Yankee enterprise. Mexican government had been swept out only eighteen years earlier, and the gold strike that populated northern California had come the following year. During the

Civil War, mines in the area had provided potash and iron to the Union, hauled out by wagon train. No railroad existed.

Some of the hotel clientele must have been the owners of those mines and haulage lines, and of Spanish land grants in the Central Valley. But most must have been miners who had struck it rich days eastward by horse or stagecoach in the Sierra Nevada, or city folk nearly as far south in the new boomtown, San Francisco.

New Agers discovered Wilbur after its renovation in the 1970s, when a washstand with running water (cold only) was added in each room. Writers found it a quiet retreat. The old concrete hot tubs in the river had been replaced by a charming complex of soaking tubs under a partly-open gabled structure. There is also a kidney-shaped swimming pool at normal temperature sunk in an enclosure of natural boulders. Nudism is permitted in the bathing and swimming area, but the hotel requires that one remove shoes in the lobby.

Brigeda Bank and Jeff Goldsmith had found Wilbur for themselves in the early 1990s, not long after they found each other. Brigeda is a strongly feminist attorney. I met Jeff in 1989 after he had written me into his successful play, "McCarthy," on the basis of my testimony—which was presented before Jeff was born. It ran seven months in Los Angeles and a month in the senator's home state of Wisconsin. Jeff and I had become friends and I was for a period a father figure, because his own father, whom I had known, was long dead. I surprised Jeff once when I told him how much it meant to me that people so very much younger regarded us as good company. He said that thought had never occurred to him.

In the spring of 1995 they decided to marry, and asked me to become a minister of the Universal Life Church in order to perform the ceremony. This church requires adherence to no theology whatever, and does not mention Christ, god, deity, or a higher being. It is like the Quakers in regarding the individual as the sole repository and judge of the spiritual. I also knew that an effort to disqualify its ordination as minister of anyone who so desired had been rejected in the courts—a decision flatly recognizing that judges have no authority to define personal beliefs. I took it for granted that Brigeda, as an attorney in family law, would not have her own marriage solemnized in a manner about which there could be any legal question.

I said I'd be delighted, but I had never done anything of that kind before, and had no idea whether they would be satisfied with what I would say. I said that all I could do would be to pass on to them whatever a long married life had taught me. That was exactly what they wanted.

The wedding was to be on September 10, absolutely the hottest time of year in California. The previous week, there had been days well over

80 degrees even in our very temperate area, where the hills surrounding San Francisco Bay moderate the weather year round. Inland, where we were bound, the papers reported 95 to 100 degrees. But the heat wave broke two days earlier, the cooling fog rolled in from the ocean, and even the cloudless interior came down to temperatures that were tolerable when I stripped to the waist to drive.

The wedding became a terrific weekend. Brigeda and Jeff had scouted around Oakland clubs and hired a really fine small band that could both swing and rock. I found a young partner who responded to jazz as I do and danced my ass off. Tanya even swam in the mildest of the pools, the first time in a couple of years that she had found the air and water both warm enough.

My sermon summed up what Tanya and I had learned from sixty years of married life. Some guest asked for my copy. Jeff wanted one, and I subsequently printed it out for him. Later he told me he consulted it repeatedly in rocky times. Here it is:

Tanya and I have managed to stay together for 60 years. And if we have, then perhaps there is something to be learned from us about how to do that, aside from the miracles of health and medicine that have kept us both alive.

How do people of strong character overcome the disagreements thoughout a lifetime inherent in the fact that none but narcissists marry individuals they cannot distinguish from themselves in the mirror?

If I had to use a single phrase to answer, it would be: respect and shared joys. To marry a person one does not respect is stupid, because such a marriage cannot last, except in the horrible form, however common, of dominance of one partner over the other. That is dishonorable, and genuine honor—which is another way of saying adherence to principle, to ethics—is a major virtue.

Life does not leave the bases for respect undisturbed. It is tested most severely when children are born, and the two parents find themselves facing roles without precedent in their personal experiences, and the pressures of expectations and patterns imposed by society, relatives, friends. But there are few joys in life to compare with watching children grow and learn and become human beings standing on their own two feet, and some day giving one grandchildren and even greatgrandchildren. Perhaps the greatest happiness in that regard is when parents find that their efforts to transmit their values to the children have been successful.

That in turn creates the basis for the most important of all support systems toward the end of life, as inability to work and just plain decline must be made good by those who are near and dear: children first of all.

The joys of marriage include shared pleasures, both intimate and in the spending of leisure time. In the course of this each partner comes to rejoice in and gain by the qualities of the other.

Respect involves recognition of permanent differences in viewpoint over things that are trivial to outsiders, but very important indeed when one lives with them day in and day out. For Tanya floors must be clean; for me it is windows. Extend that to tastes in arrangement of the house, clothing, or, most difficult, explosive, and emotionally exhausting: how to guide and respond to the children as they grow. Consider the worst problem of all: finances. This is exacerbated by the fact that the ups and downs of the economy are beyond our individual control. When the other person's insistence upon a particular choice in any of these areas appears to you to be unbearable, ask yourself whether it overrides the respect you have for your partner and the joy of spending your lives together. If it is truly an equal marriage—and none other is worthy— each finds that there are things which to the other are absolutes, while to you they are not. So you decide that, when push comes to shove, you will yield in those particulars.

Only respect and shared joys, not love? If respect grows, as each sees the other's responses to the vicissitudes of life become more appropriate and courageous, love grows deeper. And nothing can so build respect as adherence to common ideals, and admiration for how one's partner's adherence manifests itself through thick and thin.

In the course of life, a woman inevitably encounters other wonderful and handsome men, a man other wonderful and beautiful women. But, given mutual respect and understanding, and the growing love that a life governed by those principles and shared experience engenders, a marvelous thing happens. One concludes that, after all is said and done, that there is no other individual on earth with whom one would rather have spent one's life.

The photographer got a particularly fine picture of Tanya and me on that occasion, because she is happy when others are happy. When our sixtieth anniversary date arrived a month later, John Whiting, former KPFA executive long resident in London, phoned to congratulate us. Hulda Nystrom drove across town to bring us half-a-dozen E-mail congratulations from others in the movement to take back KPFA. (I was still holding out against getting onto the Internet. I'm an information junkie, and doubted that I would ever get anything done with all that world at my fingertips.)

I stopped following internal Russian affairs after my KPFA program was cancelled because I believed they had no further significance for the future development of human society. But it was good to find that my past work was still of interest to some in that field. Barbara Hazard is an artist friend who had opened the doors to exhibition in America for Leningrad artists whose non-objective styles had kept them barred from the public in Soviet times. She gave an American professor friend in the Soviet studies field a copy of *The Struggle to Survive*, the collection of letters to me from people in several republics I had published nearly a year earlier. Her friend said she had never seen any such material elsewhere.

In April of 1996 Israeli artillery wiped out a large number of children in a UN refugee camp in southern Lebanon. A picket line, with open mike, was held at the Israeli Consulate on Montgomery Street in San Francisco, the equivalent of Wall Street in New York. The line was respectable in size, its composition impressive. Among the Arabs, it cut across all lines. There was a man in a very fine silk suit who looked as though he came from an executive suite. There were young women in head scarves wheeling baby carriages, who I realized may have been risking their right to remain in the U.S. African-Americans, Anglos, and Jews carryied picket signs identifying themselves as such. I spoke, said I was a Jew, and expressed my horror and shame. I felt better when a young Arab thanked me for my remarks.

A few days later I spoke at a similar rally, sinfully small, held on what are now officially the Mario Savio steps of the administration building at the University of California in Berkeley. There was a fine response from the Lebanese present. Professor Laura Nader, anthropologist, sister of the renowned consumer advocate Ralph Nader, was in the audience and phoned a few days later to tell me of UN figures that the ratio of Palestinian to Jewish deaths over all the years of conflict was 1000-to-1. It has hardly narrowed since, despite vigorous resistance in southern Lebanon.

The *San Francisco Chronicle* published a letter of mine reading: "I am an American Jew, soon to be 79. I have seen the pictures of the dead Lebanese children in the UN camps. I will not give one penny to any organization, family, or individual in Israel that does not actively oppose Israeli slaughter of the innocents. I will not give one penny to any American candidate for any political office whatever or to any political party that does not call for an end to sending American taxpayers' money to Israel until that government stops murdering children."

The first reduction ever in American funds going to Israel, both from government and from Jewish organizations, actually did occur in the months immediately following. [Subsequently the Israeli government decided that it did not want the loss of face that would accompany further reductions. With the most extraordinary brass, it announced that it would forego all further American non-military aid if the U.S. increased its military assistance by some hundreds of millions of dollars.]

A response to that letter of mine was published, critical of me, and my daughter called to say she didn't like my letter. How about Hezbollah, the Arab group using terror, in which children were also killed, to protest the occupation? I told her Hezbollah consisted of young people whose entire lives had been spent under Israeli occupation, and who could see no light at the end of the tunnel. A retired WASP physician, whose father had headed a department at the American University in Beirut, phoned to agree with my letter. He informed me that, at the Paris Peace Conference following World War I, the Zionists had asked that the Litani River watershed of Lebanon be included in the Palestine Mandate. They occupied it in 1948, but President Eisenhower told them to get out. Israel wants its water. This is the "security" zone it occupied since 1982, and it is where the camp massacre occurred.

A very fine characteristic of the annual Jewish Film Festival, founded by two Berkeley women of the 1960s rebel generation, is that it always included films by or about Palestinians. In 1998 there was a documentary, "Forbidden Marriages," on a great variety of ethnic and religious mixed marriages in Israel and its occupied territories. The film is one of only three I can remember ever seeing that treated lifelong marriage as something positive, entirely aside from ethnic aspects. And there was the very sad "Voices From Gaza," another documentary, in which a Palestinian truck-driving instructor has problems in teaching a released Palestinian prisoner because of the psychological consequences of torture by Israeli jailers. In all, ninety thousand Palestinians have undergone imprisonment, of whom a majority suffered torture.

Zvi Aharoni, formerly of Mossad, the Israeli secret service, has said of this: "When I was head of the interrogation department, nobody would touch a prisoner. Sure, you could do all kinds of tricks, you could bug them, listen in on their conversations. But beating them? Torturing them? And today, not only is it being done, it's legal. Arabs can be tortured. It's legal in my country. It's not my country anymore."

He now lives in England.

Films at the annual Jewish Film Festival provided more food for thought about the Soviet Union. One from France, "Not Everybody Had the Luck to Have Communist Parents," brought home the sharp difference between European and American attitudes. In this semi-autobiographical film, a Parisian mother had been sent to the Nazi extermination camp at Auschwitz by the French government of collaborators with Hitler. The advancing Soviet Army liberated the camp before her turn to be killed, so upon returning to France she joined its Communist Party and remained in it. The film demonstrated that this was typical of the Jewish population at that time, for that quarter of Paris is shown voting

Communist overwhelmingly in a presidential election.

A documentary, "Cardiogram," from Kazakhstan, shown at the 1996 San Francisco Film Festival, reinforced my conviction that the Soviet era would leave a lasting impress upon the countries that emerged from it. This documentary made clear that in post-Soviet Kazakhstan it was still taken for granted that a poor herdsman's young son from the steppes would be admitted to a sanatorium for children with heart conditions without consideration of ability to pay.

The summer of 1996 was an emotional roller-coaster. We flew to Seattle to be present when Dave got his master's in landscape architecture. Our trip to Victoria, B.C., by ultra-fast and ultra-expensive jet ferry happened to be on one of the very rare days when Mt. Rainier is totally cloud-free. We were able to watch it the whole trip, both ways. The next day Dave drove us up to a pass on the shoulder of the mountain. Deep snow. A frozen lake. Magnificient landforms. On returning home, the first message on the answering machine was that Dad had died a few hours earlier, totally peacefully and without pain. His companion of recent years, Mildred Schoenberger, had visited him the previous day. He had recognized her as she came in the door—remarkable given his near-total blindness. I wondered if that were not the body rallying itself for a last stand.

We held no memorial, feeling that the 100th anniversary celebration two years earlier had said all that needed to be said, all the better because he was present to enjoy it. San Francisco and Oakland dailies, and a Berkeley weekly carried extensive obituaries which I wrote. While Dad did not live to know of the completion of the Siberian documentary, "The Island," I know of no better memorial. My showings of the film as an episode in the history of both countries gave me the personal satisfaction that audiences learned of my father's existence and that he put his body and skills to the service of his ideals.

In June the seat of Tanya's exercise bike loosened, she fell backward, and broke a rib. She also had unpredictable bouts of angina resulting in headlong drives to the emergency room via our twisting hilltop roads at all hours. Add her tremor and frequent digestive upsets, and it is not surprising that she became fearful and unwilling to be alone. Twice during the summer, son Bob stayed with her for a day to give me a chance to relax. Once I went to San Francisco, watched the sea lions that had taken over numerous pleasure-boat docks near Pier 39, had fish soup in a workingclass Salvadorean restaurant in the Mission district, walked around the peak of Mt. Tamalpais in Marin County, then up to the fire lookout at the top, and had a great drive back via Fairfax through the redwoods and past stunning local reservoirs.

Tanya had long hoped for one more trip to London for theater, but she worried whether her body could handle it. When the doctor said that her recovery from the rib injury was progressing satisfactorily, I urged that trip on Tanya. The doctor agreed enthusiastically. We had thought our overseas travelling days were over, but we were wrong. Extraordinary. I saw nine plays, heard six concerts, pushed Tanya around four great museums in the wheelchairs they provided. The weather cooperated: only two days of rain out of thirteen, in London!

Several of the plays simply could not be produced in the United States, because they require a level of social consciousness American audiences do not possess. I had known all my life about Gerhart Hauptmann's *The Weavers*, thanks to the lithograph of the same title by his fellow-German, Käthe Kollwitz. His was the most famous, if not the first, of social realist plays. It told of a rebellion of those who worked at that trade in Germany before real factories were established. They would slave at their looms endless hours on wool provided by a capitalist, whose foreman would then pay them on his judgment of the quantity and quality of their weave. The weavers teetered on the edge of starvation. The rebellion was led by a local boy home on leave from the army, in which he was a corporal, and who was rich by comparison to those he had left behind. The quality of the play derives from the fact that its types are not caricatured. The capitalist in his finery, for example, sincerely pitied himself for the risks he was taking in an unpredictable market. A very modern touch is provided by a weaver wife more courageous and militant than her husband. These "fringe" ("off-Broadway") actors are something else. For them, the play's the thing. *The Weavers* was staged pit style, with the audience looking down from elevated seats in a rectangle around the action. In this case, there was room for thirty-two to watch a show in which the cast numbered twenty.

The second of these nowhere-but-in-London plays described an episode in the city's modern history. In 1938 the leader of Britain's avowed fascists, Sir Oswald Mosley (brother-in-law of left-wing humorist Jessica Mitford, whose memorial I had attended in San Francisco only days before this trip) organized a parade through the East End, then the Jewish workingclass ghetto. The local Communist Party branch—the largest in England—disobeyed their top leadership by deciding to stop the fascists physically. The entire Jewish population, sweatshop clothing workers for the most part, turned out—250,000 in all—plus local Irish and English workers. After a while, the police gave up their attempt to clear a way for Mosley, in an exceedingly rare retreat by the bobbies. The leader, a young clothing worker, was later elected to something equivalent to state assembly here, on the Communist ticket.

The play, not great theater but very interesting, was written by a ninety-year-old who had been a participant in this event. The audience covered the entire age spectrum, including others who had taken part, as we learned while hoisting a pint during intermission in the pub below. One of them later mailed me a volume, *The Story of Unity Theatre,* a history of Left theater in England from the 1920s on. It emerged that many of the plays of social awareness in the United States that I had seen in New York in the '30s had later been staged over there. Some day we should return the favor. Our knowledge of the world would benefit.

Our return home was a nightmare far beyond travellers' complaints. American Airlines sent us via its hub city of Dallas, a nine-hour flight from London. After seven hours, the recycled air and less-than-normal air pressure brought on an episode of Tanya's angina. A physician aboard recommended that we not continue until Tanya could be thoroughly examined.

During our six days in Fort Worth, I learned that the South had changed seriously for the better. Nursing staff was entirely interracial, although the only Black physician was an African. Blacks also worked in the front office. The paramedical team that took Tanya from the airport to the hospital consisted of three properly-trained police officers, of whom the man in charge was an African-American. They clearly respected each other and worked well together. Nearby fast-food places had Black managers over white and Latino staffs. But local TV made clear that Texas was not about to give up its distinctive ethnic hierarchy. African-American newscasters and other on-camera people were omnipresent although second to whites, but Mexicans and Chicanos, a larger proportion of the people, comprising the traditional local exploited population, were totally absent. True, a Chicano was one of the two candidates for governor of Texas in the election that occurred while we were there, but he lost by a margin that clearly indicated that a great many white Texans would not vote for anyone of Mexican origin.

Mario Savio, leader of the Free Speech Movement at the University of California thirty years earlier, died the day after we returned from London. The following day, students protested against the fact that California voters had just passed by referendum misleadingly-worded Proposition 209 which effectively abolished affirmative action. They occupied the Campanile at the University of California and were forcibly ejected and arrested. I went to the campus to see what was happening, listened to a spontaneous mass meeting, stepped to the open mike, and said that they needed to work for overt majority student support and off-campus community support. Having stated that I had been an FSM Executive Committee member, I was asked if its success was due to having older advisers. I said no, that each generation has its own style, and that the situation in 1996 was different than in 1964-5, but that the experience of elders can help. I did not think that there was anything notable about my remarks in content or delivery, but ten months later a stranger, graduate-student age, stopped me on campus, asked me if I were the man from that occasion, and said, "You are a seeker for the truth, aren't you?"

The evening of that spontaneous meeting I skipped ahead in my reading of this autobiography over Free Radio Berkeley to read the chapter on FSM so listeners could learn about Mario. The next night, at a national conference of micropower stations, I was asked to open it by talking about him, and the weekend meeting was then formally dedicated to his memory. Three days later, I attended the large open student meeting to plan to nullify the anti-affirmative-action proposition. As with the Mt. Madonna statewide student meeting thirty-six years earlier, I was the only off-campus intellectual who appreciated the meaningfulness of the event sufficiently to come. Not one faculty member was present. The meeting was extraordinary in that all three people conducting it were female. There was no sign of resentment of this by the males present, who were of five races. That represented a nearly complete turnaround from attitudes during FSM. In the course of the meeting, with four hundred attending, a Chinese-American student who occupied the next seat to mine rose to say that the struggle should be aimed at changing the composition of the highly corporate Board of Regents. I wrote him a note recommending he contact ex-FSMer Prof. Bettina Aptheker at UC Santa Cruz, explaining that I had been associated with that earlier movement. Later, he nominated me on that basis to close the meeting, and I did. Many reached out to shake my hand as I left.

A memorial for Savio was in the planning during these weeks. The *San Francisco Chronicle* published a letter of mine on him. It closed: "This country is a somewhat better place for Mario's having lived. We are all a little diminished by his passing."

The memorial, attended by eight hundred, was a lovely reunion. Art Goldberg, a lifetime poor people's lawyer in Los Angeles, hugged me and expressed delight that I had not yet suffered any serious health setbacks. I exchanged hugs, too, with Burton White, cheerleader against HUAC at the 1960 hearing, subsequently a KPFA staffer for years, and now a nurses' union representative in Portland. Meredith Burke, a genuine conservative and at this point a Hoover Institution scholar, told me she had xeroxed my *Chronicle* letter on Mario and circulated it to friends. Another FSM veteran, Richard Schmorleitz, gave me his long poem to Mario and family, which had some thought-provoking lines: "An arrogant humility, The courage to be afraid, Compassion thoroughly ruthless....His heart's voice...bled truth for mercy." Regrettably, the event as a whole was a wake for the Free Speech Movement. Had the organizers made an attempt to make a connection with the movement against the anti-affirmative-action proposition it could have been otherwise. But no Chicano or Asian student speaker was among the long list invited to the podium.

By this time I thought my association with the Soviet Union was a closed page in my life. But when I received from Kuzbass, Siberia, a print of the film, "The Island," for which Dad had been interviewed the previous year, I found that segments of an interview the film-makers had done of me appeared at three points in it, in my capacity as Sovietologist. The notion that a documentarist in post-Soviet Russia, himself with no nostalgia, regarded my views as deserving presentation to his fellow-countrymen, was the kind of substantiation of my knowledge of the USSR that justified my six decades in the field. The film-maker's standpoint was quite interesting: the "American Industrial Colony" was a success while Lenin lived, because he let its Dutch Communist manager run it on capitalist lines, while it fell apart after Lenin's death when Russian ex-guerrilla apparatchiks incorporated it into the general Soviet bureaucracy. Fundamentally, the director was reflecting the post-Communist view that some form of capitalism is better. [Lenin's New Economic Policy, instituted in 1921, corresponds more closely to the mixed economy that polls in 1999 showed Russians to favor than any other policy, Communist or post-Soviet, pursued in the eight intervening decades.]

I translated the script from the film, and in 1997 found broad-based peace organizations in the Bay Area interested in having me show it. It also led to my making the acquaintance, by mail, of a most remarkable figure.

Nearly fifty years earlier, I had refused a request by the *New York Times* to delete my specific defense of Prof. Dirk Struik and Dr. W.E.B. DuBois from a letter of mine attacking McCarthyism. Struik was a mathematician of national reputation at M.I.T. He was also an avowed Communist and the brother of one of those who had gone from the Netherlands, as Dad had from the U.S., to work in Kuzbass. This brother was interned by the Nazis when they conquered his country, and killed when a British air raid hit his prison. Dirk Struik, born the same year as my father, tells this story and other reminiscences in the Kuzbass film. But unlike Dad, who was clearly an ancient summoning up all his resources to make himself clear, Struik was hardly less vigorous than myself, a generation younger. At one point he pounds his fist in time with each word in a sentence in a letter of seventy years earlier from another Dutchman in Kuzbass: "'Every blow of a hammer brings us closer to a socialist society.' That was the spirit. 'Every hammer blow brings us closer and closer to a socialist society'."

The society failed, but the energy and total alertness of the centenarian Struik overawed me.

There were other reminders at this time of my career in Sovietology
and the hypocrisy of the Establishment both in using and discarding me.
The Center for Slavic and East European Studies at UC Berkeley pub-
lishes a newsletter. Its last issue for 1996 carried an article, "Jerome B.
Landfield and the Beginning of Teaching of Russian History at the
University of California, Berkeley," before the Russian Revolution of
1917. The article said that the university president and the head of the
History Department wired this "young man, who had neither a professional degree nor teaching experience nor *any publications to his name*
[my emphasis] to come to Berkeley as instructor in...Russian history...a
field in which there were virtually no specialists." His qualifications
were "money [enabling him to travel]...his knowledge of the Russian
language...and no less important...his passion for Russia." He had been
there twice. When the Hoover Institution invited me in 1946, I too had
no degree, but had published two books and a string of publications in
learned journals. I never stopped publishing. The one year I had spent
in Moscow expanded into twenty visits over a span of sixty-eight years,
the most recent in 1998, giving me longer first-hand knowledge of
Russia than any foreigner in recorded history. My academic teaching
experience, beginning with a brief stint for the Army Specialized
Training Program at Syracuse University in World War II, included six
higher educational institutions by 1978. But when cold war specialists
had been trained, there was no longer room for someone who opposed it
and did not have the protection of tenure. I had no degree!

Almost simultaneous with the appearance of that newsletter article,
the mail brought a letter that told the same kind of story. The letter was
from Vladimir Pozner, who wrote that the president of CNBC had found
the show he and TV talk-show pioneer Phil Donohue had in 1996 "too
liberal," and demanded editorial control. "I told him I had had enough
censorship at" [the Soviet radio-and-TV monopoly], "Phil told him to go
to hell, so the show was cancelled (this kind of thing is called freedom of
speech)." Pozner returned to a fat TV contract in Yeltsin's Russia,
where it was all right to be what was regarded as too liberal in the U.S.

Somehow early 1997 was a memory-jogger. We who had been active
in Berkeley in the '60s had developed a bit of a tendency to mourn the
passing of the good old days. But something happened that restored, at
least somewhat, my faith in this remarkable city. An activist for People's
Park in that earlier time, David Nadel, had opened a folk-music dance
club, Ashkenaz, and operated it for twenty years. The bands that played
there were from four continents and virtually every American ethnicity. David had fought continually to keep People's Park out of the hands

of the University of California bureaucracy, which brought suit against him in a deliberate effort to cripple him financially. Toward the very end of 1996 David, a totally gentle, non-violent man, was shot dead by a drunken youth turned away from the club for rowdy behavior.

A memorial the following January was an outpouring of love by the dance and folk music community beyond anything in my experience. Homeless men, primarily African-American, for whom David would find some kind of work—if only pulling placard staples out of walls— stood guard and directed traffic on busy San Pablo Avenue outside. A Black woman operating a shelter for battered women in Oakland spoke of his financial assistance to them, of which no one had known. He was not a man of means, but had lived in a single room attached to his club. Newspaper coverage made it clear that he was significant well beyond Berkeley—in part, of course, because Berkeley is significant beyond Berkeley.

The performances at the memorial were interracial and cross-cultural to a degree I had not seen since the Communist-led efforts of the '30s to '50s. An African sang a dirge and a rabbi chanted Kaddish, most beautifully. There was Jewish and Turkish folk-dancing, American clogging, Southern hymns by whites including an Orthodox Jew with temple curls, Anglo-Saxon women doing flamenco, an Asian man in a Jewish immigration playlet, an Asian and a Black woman in an otherwise white female chorus doing Russian songs, non-Slavic dancers doing a Russian sailors' dance in the constructivist style of the early 1920s. Bands represented every conceivable kind of music of folk origin. But not a single group came from a labor union, a shocking change from even the McCarthy period, when I did a study of union cultural activities and found an amazing wealth and variety.

The "wake" went on for two days, fourteen hours each. Perhaps eight thousand people came, over the weekend. Food Not Bombs, whose founder, Keith McHenry, was a descendant of one of the writers of the United States Constitution and had been arrested innumerable times for feeding the homeless in San Francisco, somehow resupplied free food tables throughout that days-long memorial. Many individuals brought food for the tables spontaneously. I left with the feeling that Berkeley retained, although in diminished degree relative to even a decade earlier, the qualities that make it the best place I know. The city issued a proclamation honoring Nadel. I wrote city councilmember Dona Spring urging that public funds be used to keep Ashkenaz going, and noted that eight thousand votes in a place the size of Berkeley are not to be ignored. A foundation was established, and the doors of Ashkenaz re-opened in mid-1997.

Despite the fact that my radio show was axed in 1995, two very different books appearing late in the decade made clear that my role at KPFA had made a permanent impress upon people. *The Radio Red Killer*, by well-established mystery writer Richard Lupoff, a twenty-year KPFA broadcaster, was published in 1997. In the words of a review in the San Francisco *Bay Guardian,* the book is structured around the murder of "an elderly lefty political commentator...at radio station KRED, a Berkeley institution that bears a startling...resemblance to KPFA." The commentator "was engaged in a running battle with the station's new management—the 'capitalist sellout gang'....Although the station is clearly fictional, its internal struggles do indeed echo those at KPFA."

The other volume was Dr. Matthew Lasar's Ph.D. thesis, *Pacifica Radio: The Rise of an Alternative Network,* published in 1999 by Temple University Press. After a description of the head of the network when I came on, he writes: "In retrospect, however, Harold Winkler's main contribution to Pacifica history can be summarized in the recruitment of a single man." This is immediately followed by a section subheaded, "The Dissenting Scholar," which details my contribution to and relationships within the station. He wrote that I had played "a crucial role in the history of the Pacifica Foundation" and, at another point, that I was probably "KPFA's most popular commentator."

Carlton Goodlett, a medical doctor, publisher of San Francisco's Black weekly, the *Sun-Reporter,* died at this time. I had known him for forty-five years, since seeking his assistance, when he headed the local NAACP, to find housing for a traveling theater company whose one Black actor had been denied accomodation in the hotel they had booked. We had both participated in the 1962 Peace Congress in Moscow. He had been a signatory to the call for a demonstration organized by our son Bob in 1981 to prevent a meeting of the American Nazi Party in San Francisco by any means necessary.

I attended the memorial. One of the speakers was Congressmember Ron Dellums. By now he had spent a quarter-century in Congress, and had headed its immensely powerful Armed Services Committee. Yet he spoke with the wonderment of a little boy as he recalled how, immediately after his first election, when he was, in his words, a Black Oakland kid who had never been abroad, Dr. Goodlett had gotten him to attend and speak at a meeting of the World Peace Council in Stockholm during the Vietnam War. He told of the tears that flowed from his eyes and those of an elderly Vietnamese member of the presidium after Dellums denounced the American invasion. After the memorial, I sought Dellums out and told him he was still a wonderful human being.

In closing that event, Rev. Amos Brown, pastor of Goodlett's church and also the one Black member of San Francisco's Board of Supervisors, proposed that the traditional main street of its ghetto, Fillmore, be renamed for Goodlett. The city had torn it down as a slum and yuppi-fied it, with the result that African-Americans, unable to afford sky-rocketing rents and in their majority unable to purchase homes, were the only ethnic group in San Francisco's population to decline in the intervening years. But Goodlett's offices and the major Black churches were still in the immediate vicinity. The dailies set up a howl against Rev. Brown's proposal because of the discomfiture the change would cause to the new businesses on the street. I wrote a letter to the *Sun-Reporter*, which closed:

"Should Fillmore be renamed Goodlett? How can it not be? How can one compare a pro-slavery president"—he signed the Fugitive Slave Law—"with a descendant of slaves who demonstrated, by his Ph.D. at age 23, his exceptional diagnostic skills as a physician, his business acu-men, his very early encouragement of talented young people of his race including Mayor [Willie] Brown and Congressmember Dellums, and his willingness to stand up against the foreign policy of his own country when he believed it wrong, the groundlessness of all claims of white superiority?"

Mayor Brown had no desire for conflict with the downtown big-money interests or the businessmen on the street in question, among whom distaste for Dr. Goodlett's politics was pronounced. The militan-cy of the 1960s in the city's African-American population was gone. The matter was resolved by renaming only the long block fronting city hall, the other side of which is a park. No business had to change his sta-tionery, but all official San Francisco mail originating in City Hall now carries his name as its address.

Another death, that of my former son-in-law, brought the matter of race very much closer to home. He had been a longshoreman and the memorial was held in that union's headquarters. My grandson Danny, now also a longshoreman, presided. As the event opened, Danny, his brother Kevin, and a Black man of their age, Kelvin, the son of Cassandra Lopez, a longtime friend of Phyllis, stood together. Danny referred to both of the others as his brothers. Cassandra and Phyllis had lived together when their first children were born. Danny and Kelvin grew up literally as brothers and, now in their thirties, were as close as ever. When Cassandra spoke she referred to all three as her sons. Phyllis expressed herself similarly. I took it as a marvelous unspoken compli-ment to the late Keith's parents and to Tanya and me that we had raised our children in a way that had made it possible for such a relationship to develop.

When one is past eighty, memorials become an all-too-frequent part of one's social life. But when the lives celebrated have been vivid, these events are not at all morbid. Mama O'Shea, the broadcaster other than myself whose dismissal by KPFA was most resented by listeners, died early in 1998. A woman whose skin color and features were totally Caucasian, her life could have been considerably easier had she concealed the fact that she was part African-American. Neither would she accept the identification, rooted in slavery, of anyone of mixed origin as Black. She referred to herself as bi-racial. The daughter of vaudevillians, she was show business all the way, and her vivacious ad lib commentary, "Shoutin' Out With Mama O'Shea," greatly lightened the often self-righteous tone of KPFA's voice of dissent. She would have totally approved the fact that her memorial was held on the spacious bandstand of the town park in Petaluma without notice to any local authorities. I offered the thought that her joyous rebelliousness was exactly what the station needed when she, already in late middle age, had started her twenty-year stint on KPFA in 1975, a time when the youthful staff was badly demoralized because the '60s had gone down the tubes.

The *San Francisco Chronicle* gave the rare distinction of two full columns to the obituary of our friend of forty years, Emmy Lou Packard, who died within days of O'Shea. Emmy Lou was the most widely-talented artist I have ever met. San Franciscans and enormous numbers of tourists visiting that city daily see her work when they view the murals of Diego Rivera at the Art Institute, at City College, and in the Stock Exchange. He had taken her under his wing as a thirteen-year-old when her father accepted a Mexican invitation to help with irrigation problems in the 1920s. Rivera ultimately made her the physical conservator of his murals, which she helped paint as his assistant. She was also the best user of the linoleum-cut technique I know. Her cuts of the town of Mendocino and of a felled redwood tree sold in large numbers. She did an anti-nuclear-bomb color litho of children, for Women for Peace, that is internationally known. Students, faculty, and visitors to the University of California at Berkeley daily see her own immense carved concrete frieze, 85' by 4', over the lower plaza cafeteria next to the main performance venue, Zellerbach Auditorium. And thereby hangs a pertinent tale.

Emmy Lou believed that art should have meaning to the people. Therefore the only use she ever voluntarily made of abstraction was in predominantly realist pieces, such as a scene of farm laborers tilling artichoke fields beneath the looming peaks of the Coast Range, where she employed swirls of blue and gray to provide the sense of the fog that so frequently crowns them. But the architect in charge of the building on which the frieze appears insisted that it be abstract. When I first saw it in about 1965, I told her I was amazed that she had done something that didn't say anything. So she came over to Berkeley and pointed out to me that it was actually a map of California, with curved streaks representing rivers, dots serving as the trees in forests, diagonal slashes rendering the farmlands of the Central Valley, and so forth. For how many years did we have it dinned into our ears that artists in the Soviet Union were required to be photographic representationalists against their will?

Emmy Lou, a Communist, was the best of good citizens. She organized a successful movement to save the Mendocino headlands from development, and a plaque there honors her for this effort. During the McCarthy years, she led another successful drive, this one to prevent erasure of the history-of-San-Francisco murals in the Rincon Annex Post Office by an acquaintance of mine, Anton Refregier, also a Communist, and a Russian to boot. His sin was that he thought the anti-Chinese riots early in the city's history and the general strike of 1934 were legitimate parts of the city's history. Her most recent civic effort had been teaching young Chicano artists the technique of the mural, resulting in the extraordinary abundance of them all over the Mission district of the city, even in a branch of the Bank of America.

But life, and the course of history, went on. Early in 1998 an accidental encounter resulted in my going to Siberia and made me once again a first-hand observer, reporter, and analyst of Russian affairs.

CHAPTER 29

Siberia, Free Radio, Mumia, and Kosovo

Our daughter Phyllis called one day early in 1999 and asked what my favorite song was. I answered that I'd never thought about it. Tanya had also picked up the phone, and offered: "How about 'This Land is My Land'?"

I said, "I guess Earl Robinson's musical setting of Abraham Lincoln's words in his inaugural address about the people's right to revolution. What brings this up?"

"I was thinking of what to do at your memorial." I roared with laughter, because the idea seemed ludicrous, since there was no indication that that would be soon. Phyllis said she would sing American and Russian songs, "I think of you as a man of two countries."

"I think of myself as an American."

She settled on, "Well, an American who is a world citizen."

Events in the previous year explain her initial response. One evening in the spring of 1998 I was chatting in the lobby of a movie theater. A man I did not recognize introduced himself, and reminded me that, thirty years earlier, as an activist graduate student, he had been instrumental in getting me a teaching appointment at U.C. Berkeley. He was now a professor and also responsible for developing a series of books for a publisher.

That conversation resulted in a contract for a book, *Russia Yesterday, Today, and Tomorrow*, which I will complete after this one has gone to press. I did not dare undertake that project without going there once again. Not doing so would be like someone who knew tsarist Russia well, trying to write about the USSR without visiting it after the revolutions of 1917. I had not been there in the eight years since Marxist socialism imploded.

As always, I wanted contact with the grassroots. Lester Radke, a long-time fan of my radio broadcasts and volunteer promoter of my books, had spent a year teaching in Moscow after the collapse of the Soviet regime and therefore knew his way around under the new circumstances, which

I did not. He wanted to get a sense of the country's interior and gladly accepted my notion of spending time in the Kuzbass: the coal, steel, and chemicals country of Siberia where my father had worked long ago and I had visited after the miners had begun the upheaval against Gorbachev in Soviet times. They were now striking and blocking the railroads to oust Yeltsin because their wages were many months overdue. Radke was able to arrange for us to stay in the standard Soviet-era apartment of Russian friends in Moscow and to be hosted in Kemerovo, center of Kuzbass, where he had established relations with a technical junior college now under American sponsorship. I, in turn, got Sixteen-Hundred Pounder— Valentin Sorokopudov— my mining-engineer civil-libertarian Kuzbass acquaintance of 1990, to tour us around the region. That proved ideal, because he is a native of the area (about the size of Wisconsin), has friends and associates in each of its cities, and had become a private businessman, partner in an operation employing thirty miners. They had brought the cost of production down below the level that demands subsidy in the publicly-owned or formally privatized huge mines. They pay wages daily, on time. No wage is paid for days when, for whatever reason, there is no work.

For all my wariness of Western reporting on the Soviet Union and then Russia, I could not help being influenced by the materials I read in our daily press, heard on radio, watched on TV. When I arrived in Moscow in July I expected, on that basis, a country with visible signs of hunger and poverty relative to the past, and on the verge of massive social upheaval and geographic splintering. I anticipated that Tverskaia, Moscow's Broadway, would be glaring with neon—if not quite Times Square then at least akin to downtown San Francisco.

Nothing of the sort. Advertising was modest, but shocking in that it created the impression of a colonial country. American, European, Japanese, Korean products blanketed the billboards. Beggars had their hands out in subway passages, but not on the streets. They were quiet, not importunate. No signs of hunger were manifest and literally no one was in rags comparable to those of the American homeless.

There were no significant parades or demonstrations, except for the encampment of several hundred coal miners behind the seat of Yeltsin's new government. While everyone knew the miners had been there for weeks, one lived one's life in this city of 9 million untouched by that unless one made a special trip. A constant trickle of people, usually middle-aged or older, did. They brought food and reading matter. I talked to them, and they proved in virtually all cases to be supporters of the minuscule Anpilov movement of orthodox Communists, not of the massive Communist Party of the Russian Federation, led by Gennady Ziuganov, whose mixed-economy politics are not far left of Franklin

Roosevelt's.

Nevertheless, the setting of the miners' encampment was impressive and thought-provoking. In this city built on the grandest of horizontal scales, they had set up their tent town between the parliament building and a soccer field surrounded by a high, decorative iron fence. Along the fence, for the entire length of the field, were folk memorials to the citizen defenders of the previous competitively-elected parliament. They had been killed when Yeltsin shelled it out of existence in 1993. Our media had given the impression that casualties were few, but here were individual photographs of the four hundred, primarily young men, who lost their lives. Each was identified by name. There were flags: of pre-1917 tsarist Russia, of the Soviet Union, and, for some reason, of the Navy. There was no flag of the government under which they now lived. It was a very Russian mix: patriotism, socialism, and religion—the latter expressed in a lovely hand-built wooden Orthodox chapel with bulb cupola, and words from Scripture carved on plaques scattered through the area or painted on the fence.

But the miners simply packed up and went home a few weeks later when Yeltsin fired the last cabinet of shock-therapy capitalism, and named Yevgeny Primakov prime minister.

Moscow's remarkable and immense subway system operated as well as ever, clean and with trains every minute or two. Many fewer people read while riding than in earlier years, and those who did favored novels rather than the newspapers. There was a wider variety of dress, with a noticeable sprinkling of people, usually youthful, who had acquired Western clothing for office jobs: stylish dresses or suits with ties.

Once or twice I saw young men drinking beer in the cars, formerly strictly prohibited. I believe reports that rowdyism occurs, but I never witnessed it, nor patterns of behavior indicating that people were on guard against it. Once I saw a militiaman—the Soviet term replacing a hated word, "police," is still in use—try to hassle a couple of young men with the swarthy faces of people from the Caucasus. An elderly female station official in subway-system uniform told him to lay off, and he did.

The neighborhoods created the same impression of normal existence. The boulevards were rich in green. Permanent private kiosks now sold all kinds of everyday necesssities, forming mini-malls around the subway stations. At many the Orthodox church had built charming small wooden chapels in the broad grass strips between roadway and sidewalk. Buses ran on time and were well-patronized but not jam-packed. There were now private lines, charging slightly higher fares, competing with the city's system and offering somewhat faster and less-crowded service. The established courtesies prevailed everywhere: younger people offering their seats to older, regardless of gender.

A major change for the better was in store service. Previously the number of stores was inadequate as the Soviet living standard rose, supplies were irregular, and clerks simply couldn't care less. Now the stores were totally comparable to European counterparts: immaculate and attractive. Clerks behaved as people do when their jobs depend upon the quality of their work.

There was simply no evidence of crime impinging upon the life of the average citizen, even though one cop with a tommy-gun would be among those hanging around—patrolling doesn't describe it—the mini-malls. Foot traffic at night continued as always. People did not walk faster or cross the street to avoid strangers. This was watermelon season, and truckload-size piles were stacked for sale in the streets every couple of blocks. At night they were surrounded by portable metal fences, and one of the owners, presumably—because these were invariably people visibly of Caucasus origin, would stand guard—unarmed.

The one evident, and very meaningful, difference from the Moscow I had known was that the rich flower plantings with which this recently-rural population had previously decorated its apartment balconies were now entirely gone, and the buildings looked barren in consequence. The time and effort people had given to flowers now went to cultivating garden plots in distant suburbs or on their dachas farther still, which the Soviet government had granted free on request, and which now provided a very large part of the diet: potatoes, cabbage, beets, tomatoes, cucumbers, fruits and berries, some eggs and chickens, plus mushrooms gathered in woods after rain.

In the apartment houses, all services were working: water supply, electricity, plumbing. While TV now had a full complement of western soap operas and films full of violence and soft-core porn, one could still watch shows of solid cultural value. I was approached once by a pimp with a couple of prostitutes on the Arbat, Moscow's equivalent of New York's 42nd St. west of Broadway, but never elsewhere. There, too, I encountered a retired medical specialist, Jewish, who used his excellent command of several foreign languages to supplement his inflation-devalued pension as a volunteer guide with rich knowledge of local history.

With the single exception of that retiree, the Russians I met showed no signs of impaired circumstances. A couple in early middle age were doing exceedingly well, he a computer scientist now running those operations for a bank, she a conference interpreter. For them things got worse after I left, in consequence of the financial crash. A long-time popular figure in local radio was, as before, mildly drunk most of the time, and although very obviously a Georgian by appearance—his mother was English—insisted that he did not suffer from discrimination because his slangy Russian immediately told anyone that he was a native of Moscow. One night, as he took me home by cab, he elicited a conversation with the cabbie, presenting my questions and views as his own. This produced what he knew I wanted: the cabbie's viewpoint. He was poorer but freer than in Soviet times. He had not abandoned hope for the future, and was trying to save the money to send his child to college. The broadcaster's son was very Russian in that he stayed home with his parents to welcome a foreign guest, and very teenage in his outspoken disagreements with mother and father.

Only one person of my acquaintance favored the economic shock therapy of the preceding half-dozen years. That was strange, because he and his wife were living very poorly on their pensions, but in the same apartment as in Soviet times. Nor was there evidence that furnishings had been sold.

Our media insisted that Moscow was an exception, an island of prosperity. The concentration of foreign investments in that city, particularly as headquarters of firms, did give about a million Muscovites a decent income until the financial crash of August 17, 1998, which happened to be the day on which we left for home. But I did not find in Siberia the pattern of desperate poverty I had been led to expect, much less the culture change that goes with it. This was the more striking because Kuzbass is industrial. Industry nationwide had dropped sixty percent—three-fifths!— from the Soviet level. Kuzbass, a locale of heavy basic industry, suffered even more.

The first night in Kemerovo, a city of half a million, was the only one on the entire trip spent in a hotel. Clean, spacious, old-fashioned, it dated from the Soviet era. It overlooked the broad and lovely Tom River. After checking in, we walked to the town center, perhaps half a mile, and found ample and tasty snacks available at an outdoor eatery. The other customers were no different in dress or evident economic status than people walking down the street. We walked back to the river, along the city's main boulevard, tree-lined, with patterned flower beds still maintained as in the past, and watering trucks both serving the gardeners and flushing the very clean streets. Where the road ends, intersected by a paved promenade along the river bluff, an obelisk stands in memory of the dead of World War II, as in every Soviet city. Standing honor guard, precisely as in Communist times, were high-schoolers of both genders, rifles in hand. I do not know what organization now maintains this custom, which in the past was a function of the Young Communist League.

We followed the promenade back to our hotel. Families with strollers, husband and wife often arm in arm. Lovers. Friends. Schoolmates. The pace leisurely, no sense of stress. The mood on the street was precisely as in Soviet times on this weekday evening.

In the wee hours of the morning, I heard a woman screaming outside the hotel. That was the only evidence of violence in our three weeks in Moscow, Siberia, and on the Trans-Siberian Railroad. While traveling by train, I saw one teenager, his arm gripped—not twisted or cuffed—by a policeman, being walked calmly to the police office in the station at Omsk. One, once.

My only encounter with organized crime was when a bulky individual challenged Radke's picture-taking in a huge market in the mining town of Mezhdurechensk. Our host explained that the muscleman was on the lookout for tax police. When he was convinced that we were simply visitors, we were not even asked to leave. Yes, the gangsters take ten percent, as everyone was convinced that Mayor Luzhkov of Moscow did as well. The stall-keepers did not cater to, fawn over, or show fear of the muscleman. He was simply part of the new order of things. You paid your protection money and went about your business. I saw the same thing at a fairly upscale large cafe I visited in Moscow, where a cluster of uniformed police outside were clearly in the service of the owner. To the customers and passers-by they were simply part of the woodwork.

We traveled from city to city in the Kuzbass on a new freeway. Four lanes for a substantial distance outside Kemerovo, it later becomes three and then two, very broad for passing. Traffic was steady, with incomparably more cars than in Soviet times, many of them foreign. However, by western standards, volume was still very light. There were now enough gas stations that the eternal waits of Soviet days no longer occurred. Local people stood by the roadside selling freshly-caught or dried fish, and freshly-picked vegetables and fruits. Shashlyk stands were frequent. At one otherwise empty crossroads, a young woman stood in dressy clothes, without a suitcase to suggest that she was awaiting an anticipated lift. A prostitute?

Signs that a new middle class had arisen were everywhere. Most persuasive were the very numerous freshly-erected private homes, larger and of more varied design than in Soviet times. Some of them had been built as entire developments, which always had a new church. The people who lived in those homes all had cars.

I got to understand the situation of these "new Russians" close up in the case of the principal of a privatized vocational high school. The principal, a youthful though retired Cossack army officer, veteran of the Afghan war, housed us in his comfortable apartment in Kemerovo in a typical late-Soviet-era highrise. He and his wife had just separated. She had the children. I was put in the room of their teen-age daughter, whose work on the walls showed artistic promise. Lester's room was that of their young boy, with the well-designed very compact gymnastics equipment—bar and rings—that I had already seen in Moscow apartments twenty years earlier. There was a third bedroom and quite a spacious living room. By Soviet standards this was very good housing.

The principal also had a dacha a very short distance out of town. He hosted us there one week-end, with the aid of students from his school who worked off part or all of their tuition by doing jobs at his place. This was an aspect of the barter economy that accounts for three-fourths of all transactions in Russia today. I believe that the costs of operation of his school were met in part by barter with business-owner parents of other students. It also rented space to a commercial computer operation.

The principal also had another building—both were newly-erected, and of brick—solid, gabled, two stories high—which he called the academy. The notion was that it would be a branch of his school. I suspect that that device was a means of evading limitations on private home-building carried over from Soviet times, because the size and design of the building would enable it to serve as a spacious dwelling.

The principal also owned a station wagon and one suit, dark, for formal purposes, of excellent cloth and very well cut. He wore it to welcome us and at other meetings. His school taught everything from auto repair to cooking, and we were served truly delicious meals, well-prepared and of excellent ingredients. But at the end of our stay he most apologetically said that the costs for this service were simply not in his budget, and could we make them good? We asked for a figure, he gave it, and we paid. He was clearly surprised that we had not bargained. I conclude that Russians would have.

The same thing occurred with my friend Sixteen-Hundred-Pounder. I failed to understand how he could take time off from his business responsibilities to spend well over a week with us. He probably convinced them that we could provide business contacts, for the first appointment he arranged was with a mining executive and engineer of the highest qualifications who bestowed on us detailed technical data about the coal he wished to export. But at the end of the trip, Sixteen-Hundred-Pounder gave us a tally of his costs, which we reimbursed.

This behavior represented distant ripples of the tight-money policies then being pursued in Moscow and, as events proved, occurred within weeks of total collapse and international default. When we first arrived, I found a major Moscow bank lacking sufficient rubles to exchange $1,200 for me, and I finally got it done at an exchange office in a hotel inhabited by the richest foreign businesspeople.

If the picture I have painted seems idyllic relative to that presented by our media, that is only because they are driven by sensationalism, and bad news sells. The life I saw was not idyllic at all, although it had still not affected the calm and stability of Russian character. Nonetheless, the death rate had risen by genocidal proportions. The population dropped by nearly 5 million in Russia alone in seven years since the end of the Soviet period, and probably by twice that in what had been the USSR as a whole. This reduction did not take the form of people dropping dead of hunger in their apartments or on the streets, as in Leningrad during World War II. It expressed the consequences of greater susceptibility to disease, shortage of and unaffordable prices for imported medicines, poor government control over the quality of alcoholic beverages, earlier death of the vulnerable elderly, and higher infant mortality. Reports of increased alcohol consumption notwithstanding, I saw only one drunk in Siberia, supposedly notorious for drinking. He was being helped home by a couple of buddies. There was also one woman in early middle age, decently-dressed, passed out drunk in downtown Moscow.

In one of the Kuzbass mining towns an elderly woman, not emaciated, was seated at a cafeteria table. She asked for nothing. Sixteen-Hundred-Pounder recognized that she was waiting for food handouts. We gave her our leftovers, and the cafeteria staff took this as a matter of course. On another occasion, in the main square of Kemerovo, another elderly woman sat, begging. So was one at a railroad station. But these were the only three I saw during the entire trip, except for the many in the Moscow subway stations.

The saddest and most troubling encounter with poverty occurred during our meeting with the strike committee of a Kuzbass coal mine and the mine manager. The committee was, by a whole order of magnitude, lower in outlook and objectives than its predecessors in that region whom I had met eight years earlier. The members of the 1990 committee had developed a vision for their country, their region, and their industry. It had not come to fruition, and the members had largely left the industry. The men of 1998 were labor unionists in the American sense, seeking nothing more than a change in the margin of their product that reached them rather than their employers. Since they had not been paid for months, they were now asking for crumbs such as individual cash grants for medicines. The manager was not at all arrogant or hostile. Because the industry was on the rocks, he simply didn't have money.

One of the miners, a huge man of about forty, began to fulminate about Jews. They run everything, he said. Look at how many there are in the government. He even misprounounced Yeltsin's name as Yeltseh to suggest that he was Jewish. It turned out that this man was of a family that had farmed in northern Kazakhstan for generations. After the break-up of the Soviet Union, the economic ethnic cleansing drove his family out of that country, and he had become a miner. He was now physically disabled. His daughter had completed four years of the five required by medical schools and he had no money to pay for the fifth. It was all the fault of the Jews.

Our conversation with the miners before we all went in to meet the manager, and then during that meeting (which had ranged into foreign policy and Russia's domestic course) had made clear to all, including this man, that we were totally on the side of the miners and the suffering Russian people. We also clearly supported Russia in its conflict with current U.S. policy and the International Monetary Fund. (In the six months after my return home, numerous Sovietologists came to take that position and welcomed my signature on a joint statement others had drawn up.)

When I failed totally to shake the anti-Semite—his fellows would not break with him, although they laughed sympathetically at some points I made and clearly did not share his views—I blew up. I had already told them that I was a Jew. I reached into my wallet, took out the ruble equivalent of several hundred dollars, and asked which of them had the authority to accept donations for the strike committee. One of them, who had made a good impression on me, said that he did.

I slapped the cash on the table and said, "All right. Before I left on this trip, a very elderly Jewish woman in Berkeley, Alice Hamburg, daughter of an immigrant from Russia, handed me this money. She said to give it to people in need in Russia, Jewish or not. She supports labor. Here it is."

The anti-Semite said: "She is an exception."

Whatever attitudes such as his may mean for the future, the fact is that Jews play a role in the Russian government today such as had rarely happened in history outside the young state of Israel. It was known to the general public that the prime minister, Primakov, was Jewish on both sides, although his mother had divorced and remarried in his youth, and his name was that of his Slavic stepfather. This situation does not exist in a social vacuum. One of the people we met in Kemerovo was a computer scientist immediately identifiable as Jewish by face, married to a Latvian professor. He insisted that anti-Semitism had never been a problem for him, in Soviet times or now, although of course he had met anti-Semites. That experience and attitude is probably shared by a majority of American-born Jews of post-World-War-II generations.

Russia is a country with virtually no previous record of political tolerance, except for a dozen years after the unsuccessful 1905 Revolution, during which political parties were permitted to exist and elect a parliament as hobbled as that under Yeltsin. But the Kemerovo vocational junior college is run by a remarkable group of four. We already know that the principal is a Cossack. (This is a traditional caste of peasant cavalry who had special privileges under tsarism because every man was permanently on call for military duty with his personal horse and rifle.) The principal's three closest associates are women, all fluent in English, which he does not know. One is Tatar by nationality and an atheist Communist. A second is Russian and a firm adherent of the Old Believer sect of Russian Orthodoxy that suffered severe persecution over the centuries. The third is a delightful woman in her early twenties who is quite objective in her attitudes toward Soviet times and now, is in charge of the computers, and would like to start a tourist business of her own some day. Jealousies resulted in the elimination of the Old Believer after our departure, I have learned.

Openness to the new was visible in other spheres as well. One day we visited the building in which my father had worked, newly converted into a museum of the American Industrial Colony. They found his letter of application of July 22, 1925, and xeroxed it for me: "It has long been my hope to go to the U.S.S.R. and contribute all I possess, i.e., my knowledge and energies, to the upbuilding of the Soviet industries."

We were then shown a nearby park. There we happened upon a group of perhaps twenty, of both genders and a wide age range, practicing Qi Tung. Both Lester and the principal are adepts at that Chinese system of exercise, and joined the group. The leader later invited us to their headquarters, a home of Chinese architecture, belonging to a Russian Chinese. Another group, who looked like street toughs, were practicing in the street in front of that house. Not far away loomed the new Orthodox Cathedral of Kemerovo. Coexistence indeed.

Russia is a country resembling the United States prior to the '60s in its culture of shame and helplessness with respect to the severely disabled. The Soviet Union had established a large system to assist them, but it was limited by the relative poverty of the society and inability to fund costly access provisions and the like. Most severely disabled people continued to live in protected shelters when not hidden in back rooms of the family residence. In Kemerovo I spent hours with an extraordinary woman who was seeking, with tremendous energy and self-confidence, to change that situation. She had been run over by a train at age ten, and did not exist below the hips.

We had traveled eastward by air, but returned to Moscow via the Trans-Siberian, a two-and-a-half day rail trip. I got out at every station stop, many of them lengthy, which gave me a picture of local life that can be appreciated only by Americans who can remember World War II and earlier when passenger trains were our Highway 66 and their platforms were Main Street. In Omsk, central Siberia, I misunderstood the length of the stop, wandered through the station and out into the square in front, and returned just as our train, pulling out, had gathered enough speed so that I could not hop aboard. Lester organized the train to search for me, assuming I had boarded the wrong car. A man in an adjacent compartment denounced me for a fool: "So what if he is 81? I'm 82, and I've never missed a train in my life!"

We had had an air-conditioned coupe for two, in 90 degree weather. With me gone, my space was sold to a man of ethnic Caucasus appearance, who double-locked the doors from within because, he told Lester, cops had beaten him up because of his evident nationality. As African-Americans say of police behavior toward Black motorists: "guilty of driving while Black."

I went to the stationmaster of this very busy junction and found the post to be held by a woman. She looked at the schedules, and found another train some distance away that would join the Trans-Siberian farther on and get me to Moscow some hours after Lester. She also communicated with his train, and he had the foresight to repack my things, putting necessities for the trip into a small bag that would be left with the stationmaster where my train joined the main line.

From this point on I had the good luck of sharing compartments with Russians all the way. Not air-conditioned. A couple of hours ride brought me to a station where I would pick up the Moscow express. My compartment companion on the connecting train was a woman who had taught for a while in a Women's Studies Institute in St. Petersburg that later ran out of money, and was back teaching in a standard higher educational institution. She told me that every political party now realized that it must stand for improving the status of women, and has female affiliates of one kind or another. I was reminded of an interview I had had with the female second-in-command of one of the two miners' unions in Kemerovo and her utter contempt for the men she represented; of the young computer expert at the vocational school who was postponing her marriage because she wanted to get on her feet professionally before having a baby; of the female leader of the disabled; of the totally equal family and professional status of the interpreter whose apartment we used in Moscow. Russian women have suffered considerable losses since Soviet times, but the condescending attitude of Americans toward their status continues to represent the outlook of a professionally successful stratum of feminists with little knowledge of how the majority of women here at home live and work.

When I transferred to the long-distance train, this junction's stationmaster was waiting for me. In her office, she gave me the bag, not locked, that Lester had left. He had written a list of contents, which she asked me to verify. Nothing was missing. He also left a note reading: "A strange way of telling me you don't want to room with me! :—))"

The days and night of the remaining trip were one long series of conversations with people in the corridor and my compartment. No one wanted to talk politics. Neither had people in Kuzbass or in Moscow. No political posters or signs were to be seen anywhere on the route, except for a few crude inscriptions of the initials of Zhirinovsky's ultra-nationalist party. But people eagerly discussed the situation in the country. One phrase echoed over and over again: "Chtob ne bylo krovi"—there must be no bloodshed.

I posted my overall conclusions from the trip on a Web Russian-affairs chat room immediately after my return in August, distributed it at an academic discussion at U.C. Berkeley, and broadcast it in appearances over KPFA, this time as an invited guest. "As of this moment, I do not see a social upheaval," I said. All other observers, from *The Nation* to the far right, were then predicting the opposite. I added that whichever side had recourse to violence—whether the government to disperse protesters, or any protest movement itself— would immediately lose the country to the other side. The government evidently sensed this, for it did not use force to remove those blocking railway tracks or camping outside its offices. Their actions compelled Yeltsin to remove the monetarist prime minister, and the miners camped outside parliament went home.

I drew some other conclusions in addition to the observation that political tolerance had been added to the culture. In Moscow I sought out the editor of *Rabotnitsa,* The Working Woman, one of the only two Soviet-era magazines that had proved capable of retaining a mass circulation. In a long conversation, she agreed totally with my New Dealish interpretation of what the country, and women, needed. I asked her how to bring about these various changes. She said, "The teachers struck, the scientists struck, the miners struck. I don't know." When I responded that what is needed are ongoing movements and organizations to bring uninterrupted pressure on the politicians, it just didn't register. This basic concept of what Europeans call civil society had not yet struck root.

The United States treats the Soviet Union as non-existent. But the Trans-Siberian railroad at one point runs through Kazakhstan, no longer a republic of the USSR. The station stop there, at Petropavlovsk, had no customs formalities, no border guards of either country. The frontier was more open than that between the U.S. and Canada. The station differed from others only in the enormous presence of *chelnoki:* platform shuttle traders of Asian appearance. Their excellent Russian convinced me that they were overwhelmingly Kazakhs and not Chinese. My compartment companion at this point was a Cossack architect from the Russian Far East, on her way to Moldavia, which had been the western frontier of the USSR, for vacation. She couldn't afford air fare, twice as expensive. (She was reading a Hindu guru, translated from English. When I asked her whether such literature made her want to change her country into one resembling the U.S. for its adoption of New Age ideas by professionals such as she, she said not at all, but it was fine to be able to read anything and everything nowadays.) The woman would also have to pass through the Ukraine: four ex-Soviet republics in all. She had done this before, and said it was exactly as in the days of the USSR: no borders for all practical purposes. But in 1999 the Ukraine denied Russia permission for overflights to Kosovo.

Returning to the U.S. thrust me into events that left no time for culture shock. Immediately before the trip to Russia the joint Sunday edition of the *San Francisco Chronicle* and the *Examiner* had done a long article on me, subtitled "Berkeley Radio Legend still fighting for Free Speech," and leading with:

"At age 81, Bill Mandel still has a passion for free speech. And the longtime Berkeley resident says he is willing to go to jail to prove it, to protest a recent injunction closing down Free Radio Berkeley."

The article closed with an opinion, "'He's not a fanatic,' says "Marshall Windmiller, professor emeritus of international relations at S.F. State, who first heard Mandel in a 1947 debate on U.S.-Soviet relations while an undergraduate...His whole life has been a crusade on a number of issues, and free speech is definitely one of them. I think he's a guy who says, 'I have to keep the faith. I have to put my body where my mouth is. I'm not going to end my life as a wimp; I never have been one, and I won't now'."

Right after my return, Free Radio Berkeley did a public pirate broadcast from the steps of the city hall as the council was considering the matter of our use permit. I spoke, and the *Oakland Tribune* wrote "Mandel said he was willing to go to jail 'to jolt the public into understanding that the only freedom supported by (broadcast regulators) is the freedom to sell air time to advertisers'."

I had opened by saying: "This broadcast is a deliberate violation of Judge Wilken's order outlawing Free Radio Berkeley." Although the statute of limitations has not yet run, I'm inclined to think no action will be taken. Free Radio Berkeley stopped broadcasting, to protect its founder, Stephen Dunifer, who suffers a particularly painful and debilitating arthritis.

A month later there was a two-day walkout of three to five thousand U.C. Berkeley students protesting the abolition of affirmative action admissions because the state's voters had passed a referendum on that subject. The walkout substituted discussion panels for scheduled classes. I attended a large one on the future of Ethnic Studies and Asian Studies, which the university was trying to incorporate, course by course, into standard departments, just as KPFA had resorbed its programming in these areas. I was quite surprised to find that three of the four professors on the panel had been listeners of mine: African-American Barbara Christian, Latino Carlos Munoz, and Japanese-American Richard Aoki, who teaches elsewhere. They impressed me deeply and I took the floor to urge the students to "take care of these people" against the kind of retaliation by the university that had occurred in the loyalty-oath years. There was strong general applause.

The following day I attended another walkout teach-in group, and spoke, emphasizing the need to prove to whites that affirmative action is good for them, citing my "Whiteness of the University" analysis thirty years earlier. I said that they must campaign off campus, in their statewide home communities, use talk shows, and listen to and speak ordinary folks' language. A young Black woman nodded approvingly.

Ten days later, the Pennsylvania Supreme Court denied the appeal of an African-American, Mumia Abu-Jamal, sentenced to death for allegedly having killed a Philadelphia police officer eighteen years earlier. Mumia had been in prison all that time. With my background in such cases, going back to the Scottsboro frame-up in 1931, my personal involvement in the successful movement to save Angelo Herndon, and the tragically unsuccessful effort in Virginia to save the Martinsville Seven, I had not the slightest doubt that this was a combination of police racism and political repression.

Mumia had joined the Black Panthers as a teenager in the '60s. He had matured into a radio commentator endowed with a mellifluous voice and presence, of extraordinary intelligence and fearlessness. Photos showed an exceptionally handsome man with kindness writ large in his features and a gentleness that can only be described as Christ-like. I can think of no other public figure, here or abroad, whose appearance made that impression on me.

He had devoted his efforts to exposing the pervasive racism and brutality of the Philadelphia police, unique in that the entire force had been condemned for corruption by federal action. His focus could hardly be expected to produce radio advertising income that would support his family, so he worked as a taxi driver at night. In that work it was quite normal to carry a gun for protection, for which he had a permit. In a fracas at night, a policeman was shot dead, and Mumia lay on the ground severely wounded.

He was convicted by a jury. The leading U.S. authority on race and the court system found that Blacks were 5.2 times as likely to be dismissed as prospective jurors in Philadelphia as whites. In Mumia's case, the figure was sixteen times—higher than in any other instance. Eyewitnesses, fearful to come forward for years, finally did so and said that they had seen either one or two men fleeing from the scene. An internationally renowned ballistics expert found evidence that the alleged deadly bullet was intact, contrary to the testimony given in court. As such, it could not have been fired from Mumia's gun, which was of smaller caliber. A policeman in the same precinct as the one who was killed said that the latter was an extremely violent and racist officer.

The police had claimed that they did not know who Mumia was at the time of his arrest for the killing. It turned out that the highest ranking officer on the scene had been the top officer at Mumia's high school a decade earlier when he led a fight to re-name it for Malcolm X. This same officer led the police action in 1978 including the dropping of a bomb from the air on the residence of the MOVE "family," a Black movement. This destroyed an entire block of homes by fire. That officer had not been called to testify in the trial because he was indicted for massive corruption and plead guilty in federal court.

In response to the Pennsylvania court's appeal denial, five hundred people turned out the next day to protest in downtown San Francisco. There had been no time to get a parade permit, but both the mayor and the board of supervisors were on record against the execution, so the police did not interfere. Dennis Bernstein of KPFA put a mike in front of my face, and asked: "Why are you in this illegal demonstration?" I said that, aside from all the other facts in the case, while there had been assassinations of Black leaders by police—almost certainly with the involvement of federal agencies—there had never been an instance of official execution of an African-American leader, a status that Mumia had achieved through his book and radio interviews from prison, and a documentary film about him.

Our son Bob had been active in the campaign to prevent the execution and win a new trial. A week after that spontaneous parade, he and I were both among the speakers at another rally and march in the city for which a permit had been obtained. He proposed a teach-in at Oakland's schools to familiarize students with the case, and later successfully organized it, winning sponsorship by the teachers' union. This was unprecedented and won attention in the national media, including a solid week of stories in the *San Francisco Chronicle*.

As each speaker had only two minutes, I wrote my remarks beforehand: "Demonstrating the falseness of the evidence against Mumia has not been enough to produce a movement with sufficient strength to prevent the Pennsylvania Supreme Court from re-affirming his conviction. That is because only a small minority of white Americans are convinced that police forces are fundamentally racist and therefore kill people of color under circumstances in which they do not kill whites. This lack of understanding by a majority of whites creates an immediate prejudice against anyone accused of killing a cop....

"Police and other armed officials behave as though the way to deal with a person of color who they think *might* present any problem whatever is to blow him away. The fact that an individual is unarmed and that whatever he is suspected of doing *cannot* bring a death penalty in court makes no difference.

"The massacre in Los Angeles after the Rodney King verdict is proof of that...Of 51 people killed, not one was a cop...They did the killing, in 41 cases. Twenty-six of the dead were Black, 18 Latino, seven other, including white. No authorization of 'shoot to kill' was ever issued. In the American historical context, this was lynch justice against Blacks, and Yankee imperialism against Latinos.

"Most cops...never kill anyone in their entire careers. But try to prove that to the numerous families, right here in the Bay Area, of innocent people of color killed by the cops who do. So long as police maintain the code of silence about fellow-officers who kill without justification, and most often as a consequence of racist discrimination, they are all tarred with the same brush, and deservedly so. In criminal law, they are guilty of conspiracy.

"The movement to free Mumia will become invincible when it contacts every family in which a cop has killed someone, and convinces those families to recruit their neighbors in Mumia's behalf. For the majority of white people, who think they are decent, and want to be, the testimony of such families will be persuasive in getting them to understand that the issue is not cop killers, but killer cops."

I essentially repeated those remarks in a panel discussion on Dennis Bernstein's KPFA show several months later, and had the profound satisfaction of having my hand shaken for those words by inner-city Black supporters of Mumia who had come to the station with Pamela Africa, an extraordinary Philadelphia woman who is his spiritual advisor. For an old white male intellectual to find approval by ghetto African-Americans in today's America is a most moving experience.

What of the future? I guess it is marked out in a letter received when KPFA cancelled my broadcasts. It came from Lodi in California's Central Valley, and was signed Bill Scoville: "I am homeless and poor. I listen in my vehicle. I am 65 and you 78, and I love you for your contribution to humanity and the enormously complex contribution you continue to make. I want your voice loud and clear and strong as long as you are able. Keep going Bill - remain strong and healthy—be your very best all of your life—I am with you."

By all logic, that is where this book should end. But events as it goes into production override logic in many ways. They also illustrate what he wants me to do. They demand that I try.

A war against Yugoslavia was launched in March 1999. The instrumentality employed was NATO. The United Nations was disregarded because it requires unanimity of its permanent members. It was known beforehand that Russia and China would oppose such a war. Washington desired it, and the commander of NATO is an American general.

Humanitarian grounds—saving the Albanians of Yugoslavia's province of Kosovo—were offered as the explanation for the war. They were unquestionably being discriminated against, oppressed, and repressed by Yugoslavia. But over half a million Tutsis had been slaughtered in Rwanda five years earlier, and permission to intervene to avert the catastrophe requested by the Canadian UN general in charge was denied. His force was reduced by nine-tenths. During the war against Iraq, the United States encouraged the oppressed Kurds in the north of that country to rebel against the Iraqi dictator. When Washington ended the war without seeking to remove him, he wreaked vengeance on the Kurds and the U.S. did not seek to save them. The 25 million Kurds in Turkey were being repressed more severely than the Albanians in Kosovo before Washington's "NATO" war on Yugoslavia began. Neither the U.S., nor NATO—of which Turkey is a member—nor the UN moved to aid them. Nor were military means used to aid the Tibetans against China, or the East Timorese against Indonesia, or the Tamils against Sri Lanka.

In light of this consistent ignoring of massive brutalities on ethnic grounds occurring at the very same time, the claim of humanitarianism in the case of Kosovo is hypocrisy. The reason for the war must be sought elsewhere.

On March 24, 1999, hours before the bombing of Yugoslavia began, I posted the following on the worldwide chat room site of Russian-affairs professionals: "[Russian Premier] Primakov has taken the most dramatic possible nonmilitary step to say what a great deal of the world has been waiting for: that the U.S. cannot run the world. When is the last time any prime minister has turned his plane around in mid-ocean to signal total rejection of the policy of the country he was en route to visit?

"Primakov has said [by this action] that if the price of the IMF money is subservience, Washington, which determines IMF policy, can take that money and shove it....

"If the U.S. and its military arm, NATO, which has replaced the UN thanks to Washington's policies, is able to intervene in the internal affairs of a sovereign country, Yugoslavia, the precedent exists for a Desert Storm to isolate Moscow from the rest of Russia, and...prop up whoever Clinton wants. The result would be dismemberment of Russia, as Brzezinski desires. [Russian General] Rokhlin warned against that and he was assassinated.

"All this is not yet the Cuba Missile Crisis, but it is the closest since 1962. It's time for Americans to take a hard look at where present policy is leading us."

In the days immediately following, a Stanford expert reported with alarm that 18-year-olds in Russia, a generation that had been totally apolitical, were turning against the United States. That is the age at which people usually establish their views for a lifetime. Russian nationalists found great popular support for a slogan summing up their view: "Yugoslavia Today, Russia Tomorrow." A dependable polling agency found 92 percent of Russians against the bombing, 2 percent for it, at a time when a poll in the U.S. showed 58 percent of Americans in favor, as well as 54 percent favoring introduction of ground troops. A nonproliferation specialist at the Carnegie Endowment for International Peace Moscow office said a "strong anti-NATO" consensus had emerged. Another poll in Russia showed 43 percent holding the view that the International Monetary Fund had brought harm to Russia, while only 14 percent thought it brought benefits.

The overall consequences were estimated by Sergei Rogov, Director of the Institute for the Study of the U.S. and Canada of the Russian Academy of Sciences. This institute had been strongly pro-American. He said: "It's a full-blown crisis....It covers economic relations, foreign credits, debts, sanctions, arms control, START II, the anti-ballistic-missiles treaty....It's a bad crisis, which could have very long-term implications for Russian-American relations, producing something between...'cold peace' and maybe something more serious."

On April 5th, the Pentagon announced a Cold War Recognition Certificate, for which all 22 million Americans who had served in the armed forces during that period of history would be eligible. This would be of no serious significance but for the fact that it officially specified the U.S. Defense Department's view of two critical dates in history. The first was its identification of when the Cold War started: September 2, 1945, the date of Japan's surrender. In other words, the U.S. began the Cold War on the day the military alliance with the Soviet Union ended, before Moscow had any opportunity to do the things which the American people were told for half a century were the reasons for the hostility. The other date is the last for which a former serviceman can claim the certificate. This is December 26, 1991, the day the Soviet Union was dissolved. So we have official admission that the object of the Cold War was not keeping the peace, but bringing Soviet socialism to an end.

The war against Yugoslavia was begun at a time when there was marked fear in Washington that the late 1999 parliamentary election in

Russia and the presidential election scheduled for 2000 might bring to power Communists or others opposed to unhindered future penetration of American capital into Russia, and might endanger the investments already made in oilfields around the Caspian Sea in former Soviet territory. A ring of bases as close to Russia as possible from which to launch military action, if required to support U.S. objectives, was needed. On the West, NATO expansion into Poland, the Czech Republic, and Hungary had accomplished that. The war in Yugoslavia had the purpose of extending the ring to the southwest.

President Yeltsin opposed that but still wanted International Monetary Fund financing, which the U.S. controlled, in order to roll over existing debt. He installed a pro-Western gas magnate to pressure Yugoslavia and then fired Prime Minister Primakov. The consequence was a deal that required UN Security Council approval for occupation of Kosovo, and the inclusion of some Russian troops. When the U.S. ("NATO") ignored that requirement, Russian forces came in uninvited, in a subtle but dangerous decision forced by the military upon Yeltsin. Europe, which had just initiated the euro currency to enable it to offer united business and financial competition to the U.S., was thoroughly frightened by Washington's determination to manage the whole world. While the Yugoslav War was still on, the fifteen member states of the European Union organized a military force for it. This gave Europe armed might independent of U.S.-dominated NATO and potentially capable of confronting Washington. The Union made friendly advances to Russia. The object was clearly to realize a Europe united from the Atlantic Ocean to the Ural Mountains, an idea put forth nearly half a century earlier by French President de Gaulle. Much later, it had advanced to the stage of an agreement on coordinated economic planning between France and the Soviet Union in 1966, decades before Gorbachev, trumpeted the idea of "our common European home."

So a war that began with the world looking unipolar, Washington making all basic decisions, ended with the beginnings of a new bloc to confront it, and nuclear wild cards such as China and India in a position to throw their weight to one side or the other. Russia was free to side with the Asian giants or Europe or seek to unite both against us.

My response to Scoville's lovely words is that I will be engaged, unfortunately probably as long as my health permits, in trying to spare us all the consequences of the policy that led to this.

INDEX